P9-DUD-758

Contents

Networking Essentials Plus
Third Edition

Microsoft®

PUBLISHED BY
Microsoft Press
A Division of Microsoft Corporation
One Microsoft Way
Redmond, Washington 98052-6399

Library of Congress Cataloging-in-Publication Data
Academic Learning Series Networking Essentials Plus -- 3rd ed.
       p. cm. -- (Academic learning series)
   Includes index.
   ISBN 1-57231-902-X
  . ISBN 0-7356-0912-8 (Academic Learning Series)
   1. Computer networks. I. Series.

  TK5105.5 N4669   2000
  004.6--dc21   99-054166

Printed and bound in the United States of America.

1 2 3 4 5 6 7 8 9   WCWC   5 4 3 2 1 0

Distributed in Canada by Penguin Books Canada Limited.

A CIP catalogue record for this book is available from the British Library.

Microsoft Press books are available through booksellers and distributors worldwide. For further information about international editions, contact your local Microsoft Corporation office or contact Microsoft Press International directly at fax (425) 936-7329. Visit our Web site at mspress.microsoft.com.

Macintosh is a registered trademark of Apple Computer, Inc., used under license. Intel is a registered trademark of Intel Corporation. Microsoft, Microsoft Press, MSN, Windows, and Windows NT are either registered trademarks or trademarks of Microsoft Corporation in the United States and/or other countries. Other product and company names mentioned herein may be the trademarks of their respective owners.

The example companies, organizations, products, people, and events depicted herein are fictitious. No association with any real company, organization, product, person, or event is intended or should be inferred.

Acquisitions Editor: William Setten
Project Editor: Maureen Phillips
Technical Editor: Steve Perry

Part No. 097-0002874

Part II   Implementing a Network

Part III   Appendixes and Glossary

About This Book

Welcome to the MCSE Training Kit *Networking Essentials Plus, Third Edition.*
This training kit will guide you through the fundamentals of current networking
technology. As an interactive self-study kit, this book is designed to meet three
primary goals:

1. To serve as a general introduction to the full range of computer networking,
   from local-area network to wide-area network technology.

2. To prepare Microsoft Certified Professional (MCP) program candidates to
   successfully complete the MCSE *Networking Essentials* examination.

3. To prepare CompTIA certification candidates to successfully complete the
   CompTIA *Network+* examination.

Note For more information on how to become a Microsoft Certified Systems
Engineer (MCSE), refer to the section titled "The Microsoft Certified Professional
Program" later in this chapter. For more information on the CompTIA *Network+*
certification program, see the section entitled "The *Network+* Certification
Program" later in this chapter.

Intended Audience

This book was developed for information system (IS) professionals who need to
design, plan, implement, and support computer networks or who plan to take the
related Microsoft Certified Professional exam 70-058, *Networking Essentials,* or
the CompTIA *Network+* exam. The book is intended to reach a broad audience,
encompassing readers who are relatively new to networking as well as more
experienced computer professionals. For tips on how to customize the course to
meet your needs, see the section "Finding the Best Starting Point for You" later
in this chapter.

Prerequisites

Readers need not have completed any computer courses prior to working through
this self-paced training kit. Anyone who wishes to do so is eligible to take the
Networking Essentials and *Network+* exams. The *Network+* exam is targeted to
computer service technicians with at least 18 to 24 months on-the-job experience,
although no specific requirements are set out.

The "Getting Started" section later in this chapter describes the hardware and software you will need in order to complete the exercises and view the demonstration
files that are a part of this course. Read through that section carefully before you
start the lessons.

About the CD-ROM

The Supplemental Course Material compact disc contains informational aids that can be used throughout this book. These include multimedia presentations and demonstrations designed to supplement some of the key concepts covered here. You should view these presentations when suggested, then use them as review tools while you work through the material. The presentations and demonstrations are stored as .ASF files. If your machine has standard multimedia support, such as Windows Media Player, you can view these demonstrations by double-clicking on them. See the Readme.txt file on the CD for more information about viewing the demonstration videos.

A complete electronic version of this book is also available on the CD. The electronic version features hot links, full search capabilities, and an index. For information about using the electronic book, see the section "About the Electronic Book" later in this introduction, or see the Readme.txt file on the CD.

Features of This Book

- Each chapter opens with a section titled "Before You Begin" that prepares you for completing the chapter.

- At the beginning of each lesson, you will find an estimate of how long it will take to complete that lesson. While actual times will vary with readers, these estimates can give you a general idea of how much time you'll need to set aside for completion of the lesson at hand.

- In each chapter, procedures, exercises, and lesson review questions are included to give you an opportunity to apply the knowledge and skills being presented.

- At the end of each lesson, the "Lesson Summary" section reviews the concepts covered in that lesson. At the end of each chapter, the "Chapter Review" section allows you to test what you have learned in the entire chapter.

- Appendix A, "Questions and Answers," contains each review and exercise question for every chapter, along with corresponding answers.

- The Glossary defines key computer-networking and relevant scientific terms used in the book.

Notes

Notes appear throughout the lessons.

- Notes marked **Tip** contain explanations of possible results or alternative methods.
- Notes marked **Important** contain information that is essential to completing a task.
- Notes marked **Note** contain supplemental information.
- Notes marked **Caution** contain warnings about possible loss of data or other hazards.

Icons

Icons represent specific sections in the book as follows:

Icon	Represents
	A multimedia presentation. You will find the applicable multimedia presentation on the Supplemental Course Material compact disc.
	A hands-on exercise. You should perform the exercise to give yourself an opportunity to use the skills being presented in the lesson.
	Lesson Checkup and Chapter Review questions. These questions appear at the end of many lessons and of each chapter, giving you the opportunity to test what you learned in the lessons. You will find the answers to these questions in Appendix A, "Questions and Answers," at the back of the book.

Chapter and Appendix Overview

This self-paced training course combines notes, hands-on procedures, multimedia presentations, and review questions to teach you the essentials of computer networking. The course is designed to be completed in sequence, from beginning to end, but you can also choose a customized track and complete only the sections that interest you. (See the next section, "Finding the Best Starting Point for You," for more information.) If you choose the customized-track option, check the "Before You Begin" section in each chapter before you begin to read it; these sections describe any prerequisite text that readers are expected to have read before beginning the new chapter.

The book is divided into the following parts and chapters:

- The section you are reading, "About This Book," contains a self-paced training overview and introduces the components of this training. Reading this section thoroughly will help you get the most educational value from this self-paced training and plan which lessons you will complete.

- Part I, "Networking Fundamentals," introduces, in seven chapters, the basic concepts and principles that underlie computer networking. It presents an overview of networking terminology, examines different network topologies and architectures, discusses the physical components of computer networks, and reviews the principles of network connectivity.

- Chapter 1, "Introduction to Networking," acquaints you with some of the fundamental concepts upon which computer networks are built. The chapter discusses advantages and effects of networking computers—whether to create a local area network (LAN), such as a corporate intranet, or a wide area network (WAN), such as the Internet. It also gives an overview of how an organization's information needs help to determine its optimal network configuration.

- Chapter 2, "Basic Network Media," looks deeper into how networks are physically assembled and discusses the cables and circuitry that connect one computer to another. The chapter examines the construction, features, and operation of the primary cable types, citing the advantages and disadvantages of each. It explores the different types of network interface cards (NICs)—the components that provide the interface between cables and computers—as well as the various connectors used to attach the cards to the cables, and looks at how their performance affects a network. It also presents an overview of wireless-network technology.

- Chapter 3, "Understanding Network Architecture," explores the three principal access methods used to convey data onto network cables: contention, token passing, and demand priority. This chapter also advances the discussion of network architecture by examining the data itself and how it is put together before it is sent on its way. Last, this chapter examines the most common network architectures (Ethernet, Token Ring, AppleTalk, and ArcNet).

- Chapter 4, "Survey of Network Operating Systems," outlines various network operating systems (NOSs), focusing primarily on Novell and Microsoft network operating systems, but also including AppleTalk, UNIX, and Banyan Vines. The chapter briefly surveys peer-to-peer LANs, including systems running Microsoft Windows for Workgroups, Windows 95 and 98, and IBM's OS/2.

- Chapter 5, "Introducing Network Standards," describes the Open Systems Interconnection (OSI) reference model standards that provide for how data is packaged and transmitted from a sending application through the physical cables to a receiving application. The text goes on to discuss the 802 project, enhancements to the OSI model specific to NICs and cabling, developed by the Institute of Electrical and Electronics Engineers (IEEE). This chapter also looks at device drivers and how they relate to the OSI model.

- Chapter 6, "Defining Network Protocols," discusses the prominent protocols used with networks and defines the relationship of each protocol to the OSI reference model, including Transmission Control Protocol/Internet Protocol (TCP/IP), an industry-standard suite of protocols that provide communications in a heterogeneous environment. This chapter also explores the protocols used by Novell NetWare, as well as several of the lesser, yet most commonly used, protocols and how they relate to the OSI model.

- Chapter 7, "Elements of Network Connectivity," explores the devices and technologies available to expand networks beyond the scope of LANs. The discussion begins with modems, moves on to repeaters, bridges, routers, brouters, and gateways, and concludes with a look at remote-access computing.

- Part II, "Implementing a Network," chapters 8–13, shifts the focus from general networking principles to implementation. Integrating elements from Part I, the emphasis now is on the nuts and bolts of designing and rolling out a complete network: choosing a network type (peer-to-peer or server-based), selecting hardware and software for installation, and choosing and establishing security through setting up shares and accounts. Part II examines environmental impacts on networks, as well as how to administer, upgrade, and relocate networks, and concludes with tips for troubleshooting problems and where to find helpful resources.

- Chapter 8, "Designing and Installing a Network," expands the reader's knowledge of networking hardware. How to take a detailed inventory of network hardware and software is described. By creating a simple networking plan for a fictitious company and exploring how to install and configure networking hardware for it, readers have the opportunity to design a network. The chapter concludes by taking a look at some related hardware-compatibility issues.

- Chapter 9, "Establishing Network Shares and Accounts," describes the process of establishing sharing on a peer-to-peer network, including how to make directories or printers available to other network users. For server-based networks, readers are shown how accounts are used to establish who can access which files, directories, and printers. This chapter explores the differences between shares and accounts and demonstrates how to use each appropriately.

- Chapter 10, "Ensuring Network Security," revisits some of the ways to enable sharing on a network that were covered in Chapter 9. Here, the focus shifts away from sharing procedures; instead, the chapter discusses sharing from the perspective of how to establish and maintain network and data security. Security is more than preventing unauthorized access to computers and their data; it includes maintaining the proper physical environment to permit the network to function effectively. Special attention is paid to preventive maintenance and how to take steps to prevent data loss and minimize network failures, whether from human or other causes, such as natural disasters.

- Chapter 11, "Printing on a Network," covers one of the fundamental reasons for networking: to be able to share printers among workstations. Network printers are expensive and draw extensively on electrical resources; however, a single user is likely to require a printer only intermittently. By sharing the printer among many users, considerable savings in cost and energy are achieved. This chapter covers the devices and management of network printers and takes a look at fax modems.

- Chapter 12, "Administering Change," discusses how to document a running network and how to develop a baseline by carefully recording network performance and components. This baseline can be referred to later when assessing network performance issues. When and how to upgrade network components and confirm that the upgrading was successful are also discussed. The chapter concludes with a look at how to physically relocate a network installation.

- Chapter 13, "Troubleshooting a Network," surveys the process of troubleshooting a network. It begins by exploring how to get to the bottom of network problems, then looks at the various hardware and software tools that can help in troubleshooting. A point usually comes when outside expertise is needed. What resources are available, what they can do, and how to access them round out this chapter.

- Appendix A, "Questions and Answers," lists each lesson-checkup question, review question, and exercise sequentially for every chapter, referencing the page number where the question appears in the text. In Appendix A, suggested answers are also provided for each question and exercise.

- Appendix B, "Common Network Standards and Specifications," contains a summary of standards, specifications, and a description of standard-setting organizations that preside over aspects of computer networking.

- The Glossary includes definitions of key networking and relevant scientific terms used in the book.

Finding the Best Starting Point for You

Because this book has been designed to be self-paced, you can skip some lessons and revisit them later. Use the following table to determine the best starting point for you:

If...	Follow this learning path
You are preparing to take the Microsoft Certified Professional exam 70-058, *Networking Essentials*...	Read the "Getting Started" section of this chapter. Be sure to focus on the exam objectives as presented in the "Networking Essentials" portion of the "Where to Find Specific Skills in This Book" section. Work through the remaining chapters in any order you prefer.
You are preparing to take the *Network+* exam...	Read the "Getting Started" section of this chapter. Be sure to focus on the exam objectives as presented in the "*Network+*" portion of the "Where to Find Specific Skills in This Book" section. Work through the remaining chapters in any order you prefer.
You'd like to review information about specific topics for either of the exams...	Use the "Where to Find Specific Skills in This Book" section that follows this table.

Where to Find Specific Skills in This Book

The following tables provide a list of the skills measured on the Microsoft certification exam 70-058, *Networking Essentials,* and on the CompTIA *Network+* certification exam. The tables describe each skill and where in this book you will find the lesson relating to that skill.

Note Microsoft Certified Professional exam skills are subject to change without prior notice and at the sole discretion of Microsoft. CompTIA *Network+* exam skills are subject to change without prior notice and at the sole discretion of CompTIA.

Networking Essentials

Standards and Terminology

Skill Being Measured	Location in Book
Define common networking terms for LANs and WANs.	Chapter 1, Lesson 1; Chapter 2, Lesson 1
Compare a file and print server with an application server.	Chapter 1, Lesson 2; Chapter 4, Lesson 1; Chapter 6, Lesson 3
Compare user-level security with access permissions assigned to a shared directory on a server.	Chapter 9, Lesson 1; Chapter 10, Lesson 1
Compare a server-based network to a peer-to-peer network.	Chapter 1, Lesson 2; Chapter 8, Lesson 1; Chapter 9, Lesson 1
Compare connection-based communications with connectionless communications.	Chapter 2, Lesson 3; Chapter 7, Lesson 2
Distinguish whether SLIP or PPP is used as the communications protocol for various situations.	Chapter 7, Lesson 2
Define the communication devices that communicate at each level of the OSI reference model.	Chapter 5, all lessons; Chapter 6, Lesson 2
Describe the characteristics and purpose of the media used in IEEE 802.3 and IEEE 802.5 standards.	Chapter 3, Lesson 1; Chapter 6, Lesson 3; Chapter 7, Lesson 1
Explain the purposes of NDIS and Novell ODI network standards.	Chapter 5, Lesson 3

Planning

Skill Being Measured	Location in Book
Select the appropriate media (including twisted-pair cable, coaxial cable, fiber-optic cable, wireless technology) considering various situational elements including cost, distance limitations, and number of nodes.	Chapter 2, Lesson 1; Chapter 12, Lesson 2
Define the limitations of media.	Chapter 2, Lesson 1
Select the appropriate topology for various token-ring and Ethernet networks.	Chapter 2, Lesson 1; Chapter 3, Lessons 3 and 4; Chapter 7, Lesson 2
Understand network and transport protocols.	Chapter 6, all lessons
Describe connectivity for Token Ring and Ethernet (repeaters, bridges, routers, and so on).	Chapter 3, Lessons 3 and 4; Chapter 7, Lessons 1 and 2
Define characteristics of WAN connections (X.25, ISDN, frame relay, and ATM).	Chapter 7, Lesson 2

Implementation

Skill Being Measured	Location in Book
Create an administrative plan for performance, accounts, and security.	Chapter 9, Lessons 1 and 2; Chapter 10, Lesson 1
Design a disaster recovery plan.	Chapter 10, Lesson 3
Install and configure network hardware.	Chapter 8, Lessons 3 and 4; Chapter 12, Lesson 2
Implement NetBIOS.	Chapter 6, Lesson 4
Describe hardware and software monitoring tools.	Chapter 12, Lesson 1; Chapter 13, Lesson 2

Troubleshooting

Skill Being Measured	Location in Book
Identify common errors associated with communication components.	Chapter 13, Lesson 1
Diagnose and resolve connectivity problems with cards, cables, and related hardware.	Chapter 12, Lesson 2; Chapter 13, all lessons
Resolve broadcast storms.	Chapter 7, Lesson 1
Identify and resolve network performance problems.	Chapter 12, Lesson 2; Chapter 13, all lessons

Network+

The *Network+* exam objectives are divided into two broad categories: Knowledge of Networking Technology and Knowledge of Networking Practices.

Knowledge of Networking Technology
Basic Knowledge

Skill Being Measured	Location in Book
Understand network structure.	Chapter 1, Lesson 3; Chapter 2, Lesson 1
Describe network operating systems, clients, and directory services.	Chapter 1, Lesson 2; Chapter 3, Lesson 3; Chapter 4, Lessons 1, 2, 3, and 4; Chapter 8, Lesson 1
Define IPX, IP, and Net BEUI.	Chapter 5, Lesson 1; Chapter 6, Lessons 1 and 4; Chapter 7, Lesson 2;
Describe fault tolerance and its implementation methods.	Chapter 10, Lesson 3
Describe the OSI reference model and identify the protocols, services, and functions that relate to each layer.	Chapter 5, all lessons
Recognize and describe types and characteristics of network media (coaxial, fiber-optic, UTP, STP, 10BaseT, 100Base, VGAnyLan, RJ24, BNC, and so on).	Chapter 2, Lesson 1; Chapter 3, Lesson 3; Chapter 8, Lesson 1
Describe the basic attributes, purposes, and functions of such network elements as:	
Full and half duplexing.	Chapter 2, Lesson 1
WANs and LANs.	Chapter 1, Lesson 1
Servers, workstations, and hosts.	Chapter 2, Lesson 2
Server-based and peer-to-peer networking.	Chapter 1, Lesson 2; Chapter 8, Lesson 1
Cabling, NICs, and routers.	Chapter 2, Lessons 1 and 2
Broadband and baseband transmission.	Chapter 2, Lesson 1
Use of gateways as default IP routers and the means by which to connect dissimilar systems or protocols.	Chapter 4, Lessons 2 and 5; Chapter 7, Lesson 1

Physical Layer

Skill Being Measured	Location in Book
Configure and troubleshoot network interface cards.	Chapter 2, Lesson 2; Chapter 12, Lesson 2; Chapter 13, Lesson 1
Describe and differentiate the following network components:	
Hubs.	Chapter 1, Lesson 3; Chapter 2, Lesson 1
MAUs.	Chapter 3, Lessons 1 and 4
Transceivers.	Chapter 2, Lesson 2
Repeaters.	Chapter 1, Lesson 3; Chapter 7, Lesson 1

Data-Link Layer

Skill Being Measured	Location in Book
Define bridges and why they are used.	Chapter 2, Lesson 3; Chapter 3, Lesson 3; Chapter 5, Lesson 1; Chapter 7, Lesson 1; Chapter 8, Lesson 3
Explain the IEEE Project 802 specifications, including 802.2, 802.3, and 802.5.	Chapter 5, Lesson 2
Describe the function and characteristics of MAC addresses.	Chapter 5, Lesson 2

Network Layer

Skill Being Measured	Location in Book
Define the following routing and network-layer concepts:	
Routing, including the difference between static and dynamic routing.	Chapter 7, Lesson 1
The difference between a router and a brouter.	Chapter 7, Lesson 1
The difference between routable and nonroutable protocols	Chapter 6, Lesson 4
Default gateways and subnetworks.	Chapter 6, Lesson 2
The reason for employing unique network IDs.	Chapter 2, Lesson 2; Chapter 13, Lesson 3

Transport Layer

Skill Being Measured	Location in Book
Describe the purpose of name resolution.	Chapter 5, Lessons 1 and 3; Chapter 6, Lesson 1
Describe the difference between connection and connectionless transport.	Chapter 2, Lesson 3; Chapter 7, Lesson 2

TCP/IP Fundamentals

Skill Being Measured	Location in Book
Demonstrate knowledge of the following TCP/IP fundamentals:	
IP default gateways.	Chapter 6, Lesson 2
DHCP, DNS, WINS, and host files.	Chapter 13, Lesson 3
Main TCP/IP protocols, including TCP, UDP, POP3, SMTP, SNMP, FTP, HTTP, and IP.	Chapter 6, Lesson 2
Broad acceptance of TCP/IP by operating systems and hosts worldwide.	Chapter 6, Lesson 2
Internet domain-name server hierarchies.	Chapter 13, Lesson 3
TCP/IP addressing, including the A, B, and C classes of IP addresses and the use of port numbers (HTTP, FTP, SMTP) and the port numbers commonly assigned to a given service.	Chapter 5, Lesson 2; Chapter 6, Lesson 1
TCP/IP configuration concepts, including IP proxy and the identity of the normal configuration parameters for a workstation, including IP address, DNS, IP proxy configuration, WINS, DHCP, host name, and Internet domain name.	Chapter 10, Lesson 1; Chapter 13, Lesson 3

TCP/IP Utilities

Skill Being Measured	Location in Book
Explain how and when to use each of the following TCP/IP utilities to test, validate, and troubleshoot IP connectivity:	
ARP	Chapter 6, Lesson 2
Telnet	Chapter 6, Lesson 1; Chapter 13, Lesson 3
NBSTAT	Chapter 12, Lesson 1
Tracert	Chapter 12, Lesson 1
NETSTAT	Chapter 12, Lesson 1
Ipconfig/winipcfg	Chapter 6, Lesson 4
FTP	Chapter 13, Lesson 3
Ping	Chapter 12, Lesson 1

Remote Connectivity

Skill Being Measured	Location in Book
Describe PPP and SLIP.	Chapter 7, Lesson 2
Describe PPTP.	Chapter 7, Lesson 2
Explain the attributes, advantages, and disadvantages of ISDN and PSTN (POTS).	Chapter 7, Lesson 2; Chapter 13, Lesson 3
Describe modem configurations, including serial port IRQ, I/O address, and maximum port speed.	Chapter 7, Lesson 1; Chapter 11, Lesson 3
Specify the requirements for a remote connection.	Chapter 7, Lesson 2

Security

Skill Being Measured	Location in Book
Describe issues to consider when selecting a security model, including user and share level.	Chapter 9, Lessons 1 and 2; Chapter 10, Lesson 1
Describe standard password practices and procedures.	Chapter 10, Lesson 1
Explain the need to employ data encryption to protect network data.	Chapter 10, Lesson 1
Explain the purpose of a firewall.	Chapter 10, Lesson 1

Knowledge of Networking Practices

Implementing and Installing the Network

Skill Being Measured	Location in Book
Describe accounts and their role in a network.	Chapter 9, Lessons 1 and 2; Chapter 10, Lesson 1
Demonstrate awareness that administrative and test accounts, passwords, IP addresses, IP configurations, relevant SOPs, and so on must be obtained prior to network implementation.	Chapter 9, Lesson 2; Chapter 10, Lesson 1
Evaluate environmental factors that affect networks.	Chapter 10, Lesson 2
Recognize common peripheral ports and external SCSI devices (especially DB-25 connectors).	Chapter 2, Lesson 2
Identify common network components, including:	
Print servers.	Chapter 1, Lesson 2; Chapter 11, Lesson 1
Peripherals.	Chapter 1, Lessons 1 and 2; Chapter 4, Lesson 1
Hubs.	Chapter 1, Lesson 3
Routers.	Chapter 1, Lesson 3
Brouters.	Chapter 1, Lesson 3
Bridges.	Chapter 1, Lesson 3
Patch panels.	Chapter 2, Lesson 1; Chapter 3, Lesson 1; Chapter 8, Lesson 1
UPSs.	Chapter 10, Lesson 3
NICs.	Chapter 2, Lesson 2
Token Ring media filters.	Chapter 3, Lesson 4
Demonstrate awareness of such compatibility and cabling issues as trying to install an analog modem in a digital jack, variations in the use of RJ-45 connectors depending on cabling, and implications of using patch cables.	Chapter 2, Lesson 2; Chapter 3, Lesson 1; Chapter 8, Lessons 3 and 4; Chapter 13, Lessons 1 and 2

Maintaining and Supporting the Network

Skill Being Measured	Location in Book
Describe how to document a network.	Chapter 8, Lesson 1; Chapter 12, Lessons 1 and 2
Identify components of a network that need upgrading and describe how to upgrade them.	Chapter 12, Lesson 2; Chapter 13, Lessons 1 and 2
Explain how to restore a network by backing up data.	Chapter 10, Lesson 3
Describe the effects of computer viruses and how to protect against them.	Chapter 10, Lesson 1

Troubleshooting the Network

Skill Being Measured	Location in Book
Identify standard troubleshooting methods.	Chapter 13, Lesson 1
Address network problems by isolating the cause.	Chapter 12, Lesson 1; Chapter 13, Lesson 1
Address problems caused by user errors.	Chapter 10, Lesson 2
Troubleshoot the network by employing the following techniques:	Chapter 13, Lessons 1 and 2
Recognizing abnormal physical conditions.	Chapter 10, Lesson 2
Isolating and correcting problems with physical media.	Chapter 12, Lesson 1; Chapter 13, Lesson 1
Checking the status of servers.	Chapter 13, Lesson 1
Checking for configuration problems with DNS, WINS, and HOST files.	Chapter 13, Lesson 1
Checking for viruses.	Chapter 10, Lesson 1
Checking the validity of the account name and password.	Chapter 9, Lesson 2
Rechecking operator logon procedures.	Chapter 13, Lesson 1
Selecting and running appropriate diagnostics.	Chapter 13, Lesson 2
Describe a variety of tools for troubleshooting a network, including crossover cables, hardware loopbacks, tone generators, and tone locators.	Chapter 13, Lesson 2

Getting Started

This self-paced training course contains demonstration videos that enhance and supplement the text. The following sections discuss the hardware and software required to view the demonstration videos on the companion CD-ROM.

Hardware Requirements

Each computer must have the following minimum configuration. All hardware should be on the Microsoft Windows Hardware Compatibility List.

- Pentium 90 MHz processor (Pentium 120 MHz or better recommended)
- 16 MB RAM (32 MB or more of RAM recommended)
- 16-color display card (256-color display card or better recommended)
- 16-bit sound card
- VGA or better monitor (SVGA monitor or better recommended)
- CD-ROM drive
- Mouse or other pointing device (recommended)

Software Requirements

The following software is required to view the demonstration videos in this course.

- Microsoft Windows 95, or later, or Microsoft Windows NT 4.0, Service Pack 3, or later
- Standard multimedia player, such as Windows Media Player (which is included on the companion CD)
- Microsoft Internet Explorer 4.01 or later (required for Media Player to install correctly; Internet Explorer 5 is included on the companion CD)

About the Electronic Book

The CD-ROM also includes an electronic version of this book that enables you to view and search the contents on-screen. See the Readme.txt file on the CD for system requirements and instructions on how to use the electronic book.

The Microsoft Certified Professional Program

The Microsoft Certified Professional (MCP) program provides the best method to prove your command of current Microsoft products and technologies. Microsoft, an industry leader in certification, is on the forefront of testing methodology. Our exams and corresponding certifications are developed to validate your mastery of critical competencies as you design and develop, or implement and support, solutions with Microsoft products and technologies. Computer professionals who become Microsoft certified are recognized as experts and are sought after industry-wide.

The Microsoft Certified Professional program offers eight certifications, based on specific areas of technical expertise:

- *Microsoft Certified Professional (MCP).* Demonstrated in-depth knowledge of at least one Microsoft operating system. Candidates can pass additional Microsoft certification exams to further qualify their skills with Microsoft BackOffice products, development tools, or desktop programs.

- *Microsoft Certified Professional + Internet (MCP+ Internet).* MCPs with a specialty in the Internet are qualified to plan security, install and configure server products, manage server resources, extend servers to run CGI scripts or ISAPI scripts, monitor and analyze performance, and troubleshoot problems.

- *Microsoft Certified Professional + Site Building (MCP + Site Building).* MCPs with a specialty in site building are qualified to effectively plan, build, maintain, and manage Web sites using Microsoft technologies and products.

- *Microsoft Certified Systems Engineer (MCSE).* Qualified to effectively plan, implement, maintain, and support information systems in a wide range of computing environments with Microsoft Windows NT Server and the Microsoft BackOffice integrated family of server software.

- *Microsoft Certified Systems Engineer + Internet (MCSE+Internet).* MCSEs with an advanced qualification to enhance, deploy, and manage sophisticated intranet and Internet solutions that include a browser, proxy server, host servers, database, and messaging and commerce components. In addition, an MCSE+Internet-certified professional is able to manage and analyze Web sites.

- *Microsoft Certified Solution Developer (MCSD).* Qualified to design and develop custom business solutions with Microsoft development tools, technologies, and platforms, including Microsoft Office and Microsoft BackOffice.

- *The Microsoft Certified Database Administrator (MCDBA).* The premier certification for professionals who implement and administer Microsoft SQL Server databases. This certification is appropriate for individuals who derive physical database designs, develop logical data models, create physical databases, create data services by using Transact-SQL, manage and maintain databases, configure and manage security, monitor and optimize databases, and install and configure Microsoft SQL Server.

- *Microsoft Certified Trainer (MCT).* Instructionally and technically qualified to deliver Microsoft Official Curriculum through a Microsoft Authorized Technical Education Center (ATEC).

Microsoft Certification Benefits

Microsoft certification, one of the most comprehensive certification programs available for assessing and maintaining software-related skills, is a valuable measure of an individual's knowledge and expertise. Microsoft certification is awarded to individuals who have successfully demonstrated their ability to perform specific tasks and implement solutions with Microsoft products. Not only does this provide an objective measure for employers to consider; it also provides guidance for what an individual should know to be proficient. And as with any skills-assessment and benchmarking measure, certification brings a variety of benefits: to the individual, and to employers and organizations. To learn more about how certification can help you or your company, see the backgrounders, white papers, case studies, and other information available on the Microsoft Training & Certification Web site at http://www.microsoft.com/train_cert.

Microsoft Certification Benefits for Individuals

As a Microsoft Certified Professional, you receive many benefits:

- Industry recognition of your knowledge and proficiency with Microsoft products and technologies.
- Access to technical and product information directly from Microsoft through a secured area of the MCP Web Site.
- Logos to enable you to identify your Microsoft Certified Professional status to colleagues or clients.
- Invitations to Microsoft conferences, technical training sessions, and special events.
- A Microsoft Certified Professional certificate.
- Subscription to *Microsoft Certified Professional Magazine* (North America only), a career and professional development magazine.

Additional benefits, depending on your certification and geography, include:

- A complimentary, one-year subscription to the Microsoft TechNet Technical Information Network, providing valuable information on monthly CD-ROMs.
- A one-year subscription to the Microsoft Beta Evaluation program. This benefit provides you with up to 12 free monthly CD-ROMs containing beta software (English only) for many of Microsoft's newest software products.

Microsoft Certification Benefits for Employers and Organizations

Through certification, computer professionals can maximize the return on investment in Microsoft technology. Research shows that Microsoft certification provides organizations with:

- Excellent return on training and certification investments by providing a standard method of determining training needs and measuring results.

- Increased customer satisfaction and decreased support costs through improved service, increased productivity, and greater technical self-sufficiency.

- Reliable benchmarks for hiring, promoting, and career planning.

- Recognition and rewards for productive employees by validating their expertise.

- Retraining options for existing employees so they can work effectively with new technologies.

- Assurance of quality when outsourcing computer services.

Requirements for Becoming a Microsoft Certified Professional

Certified Product Specialists are required to pass one operating system exam. Candidates may pass additional Microsoft certification exams to further qualify their skills with Microsoft BackOffice products, development tools, or desktop applications.

Microsoft Certified Professional + Internet candidates are required to pass the prescribed Microsoft Windows NT Server 4.0, TCP/IP, and Microsoft Internet Information System exam series.

Microsoft Certified Systems Engineers are required to pass a series of core Microsoft Windows operating system and networking exams, and BackOffice technology elective exams.

Microsoft Certified Solution Developers are required to pass two core Microsoft Windows operating system technology exams and two BackOffice technology elective exams.

Microsoft Certified Trainers are required to meet instructional and technical requirements specific to each Microsoft Official Curriculum course they are certified to deliver. In the United States and Canada, call Microsoft at (800) 636-7544 for more information on becoming a Microsoft Certified Trainer. Outside the United States and Canada, contact your local Microsoft subsidiary.

Technical Training for Computer Professionals

Technical training is available in a variety of ways, with instructor-led classes, online instruction, or self-paced training available at thousands of locations worldwide.

Self-paced Training

For motivated learners who are ready for the challenge, self-paced instruction is the most flexible, cost-effective way to increase your knowledge and skills.

A full-line of self-paced print and computer-based training materials is available direct from the source—Microsoft Press. Microsoft Official Curriculum course-ware kits from Microsoft Press are designed for advanced computer system professionals are available from Microsoft Press and the Microsoft Developer Division. Self-paced training kits from Microsoft Press feature print-based instructional materials, along with CD-ROM-based product software, multimedia presentations, lab exercises, and practice files. The Mastering Series provides in-depth, interactive training on CD-ROM for experienced developers. Both are excellent ways to prepare for Microsoft Certified Professional (MCP) exams.

Online Training

For a more flexible alternative to instructor-led classes, online instruction is a good choice, as near as the Internet and ready whenever you are. This approach allows you to learn at your own pace and on your own schedule in a virtual class-room, often with easy access to an online instructor. Online instruction covers a variety of Microsoft products and technologies. It includes options ranging from Microsoft Official Curriculum to choices available nowhere else. Training is on demand, with access to learning resources 24 hours a day.

Online training is available through Microsoft Authorized Technical Education Centers.

Authorized Technical Education Centers

Authorized Technical Education Centers (ATECs) are the best source for instructor-led training that can help you prepare to become a Microsoft Certified Professional. The Microsoft ATEC program is a worldwide network of qualified technical training organizations that provide authorized delivery of Microsoft Official Curriculum courses by Microsoft Certified Trainers to computer professionals.

For a listing of ATEC locations in the United States and Canada, call the Microsoft fax service at (800) 727-3351. Outside the United States and Canada, call the fax service at (206) 635-2233.

The *Network+* Certification Program

Network+ is a testing program sponsored by the Computing Technology Industry Association (CompTIA) that certifies the knowledge of networking technicians who have accumulated 18 to 24 months of experience in the IT industry. This test is administered by Sylvan Prometric and was launched April 30, 1999.

Development of *Network+* certification began in 1995, when a group of technology-industry companies came together to create the IT Skills Project. This committee was formed to direct CompTIA in identifying, classifying, and publishing skills standards for networking professionals employed in three types of organizations: information technology companies, channel partners, and business/government firms. Acting on the committee's recommendations, CompTIA defined these job skills through an industry-wide survey. Results and analyses of this survey were used as a foundation for the *Network+* certification program.

Earning the *Network+* certification means that the successful candidate possesses the knowledge needed to configure and install the TCP/IP client. This exam covers a wide range of vendor and product-neutral networking technologies.

Network+ Exam Objectives

The *Network+* exam objectives are organized into two distinct groups: "Knowledge of Networking Technology" and "Knowledge of Networking Practices." The following table lists objective domains within each of these groups. (This table is included to clarify the test objectives and should not be construed as a comprehensive listing of the content of the exam.)

I. Knowledge of Networking Technology	77%
1. Basic Knowledge	
2. Physical Layer	
3. Data Link Layer	
4. Network Layer	
5. Transport Layer	
6. TCP/IP Fundamentals	
7. TCP/IP Suite: Utilities	
8. Remote Connectivity	
9. Security	
II. Knowledge of Networking Practices	**23%**
1. Implementing the Installation of the Network	
2. Maintaining and Supporting the Network	
3. Troubleshooting the Network	

Note All percentages are approximate and are subject to change.

Registering for the *Network+* Exam

Anyone who wishes to do so can take the *Network+* test; there are no specific requirements or prerequisites, except payment of the fee. However, exam content is targeted to computer technicians with 18 to 24 months of experience in the IT industry. A typical candidate would have CompTIA *A+* certification or equivalent knowledge, but *A+* certification is not required. The *Network+* exam consists of 65 questions that must be answered within a maximum allowable time of 90 minutes.

For more information on *Network+* or to register for the exam, call Sylvan Prometric at 1 (888) 895-6116. Companies that are members of CompTIA can register for the *Network+* test using Internet registration at www.2test.com.

To learn more about *Network+* certification, see the CompTIA Web site at www.comptia.org.

Technical Support

Every effort has been made to ensure the accuracy of this book and the contents of the companion disc. If you have comments, questions, or ideas regarding this book or the companion disc, please send them to Microsoft Press using either of the following methods:

E-mail: TKINPUT@MICROSOFT.COM

Postal Mail: Microsoft Press
Attn: Networking Essentials Plus, Third Edition Editor
One Microsoft Way
Redmond, WA 98052-6399

Microsoft Press provides corrections for books through the World Wide Web at the following address: mspress.microsoft.com/support/.

Please note that product support is not offered through the above mail addresses. For further information regarding Microsoft software support options, please connect to www.microsoft.com/support/ or call Microsoft Support Network Sales at (800) 936-3500.

For information about ordering the full version of any Microsoft software, please call Microsoft Sales at (800) 426-9400 or visit www.microsoft.com. Information about any issues relating to the use of this evaluation edition with this training kit are posted to the Support section of the Microsoft Press Web site (mspress.microsoft.com/support/).

Networking Fundamentals

In Part I, we introduce the basic concepts and principles that underlie computer networking, from the simplest peer-to-peer local area networks to the vastly complex wide area networks that reach across international boundaries and around the world. We present an overview of networking terminology, examine different network topologies and architectures, and focus on the physical components of computer networks, including server and client computers, and cabling and connectors. We also investigate what occurs within computers when they are linked and how they send and receive messages, including the standards and protocols that govern network communication. Part I concludes with an examination of network connectivity beginning with old-fashioned analog telephone lines and extending to the newest forms of digital and remote-access communication.

C H A P T E R   1

Introduction to Networking

About This Chapter

Welcome to the world of computer networking. As you begin your study, it is important that you understand some of the fundamental concepts upon which computer networks are built. This chapter introduces you to these concepts.

Before You Begin

This training kit assumes that you are just beginning your study of computer networking; therefore, there are no prerequisites. A general familiarity with computers and computing is helpful.

Lesson 1: What Is a Network?

This lesson introduces some basic principles of computer-based networking, discusses advantages of networking, and presents the idea of connecting computers together to form a local area network (such as a corporate intranet) and a wide area network (such as the Internet).

After this lesson, you will be able to:

- Define a computer network.
- Discuss advantages of using a network.
- Describe a local area network (LAN) and a wide area network (WAN).
- Identify the primary difference between a LAN and a WAN.

Estimated lesson time: 20 minutes

The Concept of Networking

The idea of networking has been around for a long time and has taken on many meanings. If you were to look up "network" in your dictionary, you might find any of the following definitions:

- An openwork fabric; netting
- A system of interlacing lines, tracks, or channels
- Any interconnected system; for example, a television-broadcasting network
- A system in which a number of independent computers are linked together to share data and peripherals, such as hard disks and printers

Obviously, the last definition is the one we are concerned with in this course. The key word in the definition is "share." Sharing is the purpose of computer networking. The ability to share information efficiently is what gives computer networking its power and its appeal. And when it comes to sharing information, human beings are in many ways similar to computers. Just as computers are little more than collections of the information they have been given, so we are, in large part, collections of our experiences and the information given to us. When we want to expand our knowledge, we broaden our experience and gather more information. For example, to learn more about computers, we might talk informally with friends in the computer industry, go back to school and take a class, or work through a self-paced training course like this one. Whichever options we choose, when we seek to share the knowledge and experiences of others, we are networking.

Another way to think of networking is to envision a network as a team. This might be a sports team, such as a football team, or a project team, such as the one that created this training course. Through the efforts of all involved—the sharing of time, talent, and resources—a goal is accomplished or a project is completed. Similarly, managing a computer network is not unlike managing a team of people. Sharing and communicating can be simple and easy (a quarterback calling a play in the huddle) or complex (a virtual project team located in different time zones around the world that communicates through teleconferencing, e-mail, and multimedia presentations over the Internet to complete a project).

Introducing Computer Networking

At its most elementary level, a computer network consists of two computers connected to each other by a cable that allows them to share data. All computer networking, no matter how sophisticated, stems from that simple system. While the idea of connecting two computers by a cable may not seem extraordinary, in retrospect it has proven to be a major achievement in communications.

Computer networking arose as an answer to the need to share data in a timely fashion. Personal computers are powerful tools that can process and manipulate large amounts of data quickly, but they do not allow users to share that data efficiently. Before networks, users needed either to print out documents or copy document files to a disk for others to edit or use them. If others made changes to the document, there was no easy way to merge the changes. This was, and still is, known as "working in a stand-alone environment." (See Figure 1.1.)

Figure 1.1   Stand-alone environment

Copying files onto floppy disks and giving them to others to copy onto their computers was sometimes referred to as the "sneakernet." This early form of computer networking is one that many of us have used and perhaps still use today. See Figure 1.2; it might bring back some fond memories.

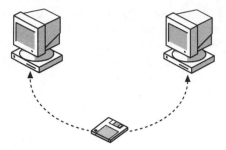

Figure 1.2   The sneakernet

This system works well in certain situations and has its advantages—it allows us to stop for a cup of coffee or socialize with a friend while we exchange and merge data—but it is far too slow and inefficient to meet the needs and expectations of today's computer users. The amount of data available to be shared and the distances we want the data to travel far exceed the capabilities of the sneakernet.

But what if the computer shown in Figure 1.1 were to be connected to other computers? Then, it could share data with the other computers and send documents to the other printers. This connecting together of computers and other devices is called a *network*, and the concept of connected computers sharing resources is called networking. (See Figure 1.3.)

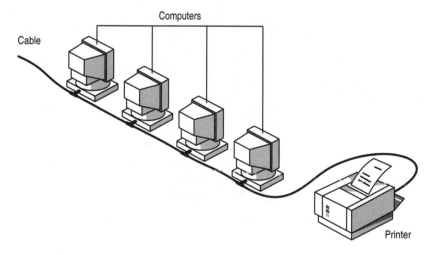

Figure 1.3   A simple computer network

Why Use a Computer Network?

With the availability and power of today's personal computers, you might ask why networks are needed. From the earliest networks to today's high-powered personal computers, the answer has remained the same: networks increase efficiency and reduce costs. Computer networks achieve these goals in three primary ways:

- Sharing information (or data)
- Sharing hardware and software
- Centralizing administration and support

More specifically, computers that are part of a network can share:

- Documents (memos, spreadsheets, invoices, and so on).
- E-mail messages.
- Word-processing software.
- Project-tracking software.
- Illustrations, photographs, videos, and audio files.
- Live audio and video broadcasts.
- Printers.
- Fax machines.
- Modems.
- CD-ROM drives and other removable drives, such as Zip and Jaz drives.
- Hard drives.

And more sharing options exist. The capabilities of networks are constantly expanding as new ways are found to share and communicate by means of computers.

Sharing Information (or Data)

The ability to share information quickly and inexpensively has proven to be one of the most popular uses of networking technology. It has been reported that e-mail is by far the number-one activity of people who use the Internet. Many businesses have invested in networks specifically to take advantage of network-based e-mail and scheduling programs.

By making information available for sharing, networks can reduce the need for paper communication, increase efficiency, and make nearly any type of data available simultaneously to every user who needs it. Managers can use these utilities to communicate quickly and effectively with large numbers of people and to organize and schedule meetings with people drawn from an entire company or business enterprise far more easily than was previously possible. (See Figure 1.4.)

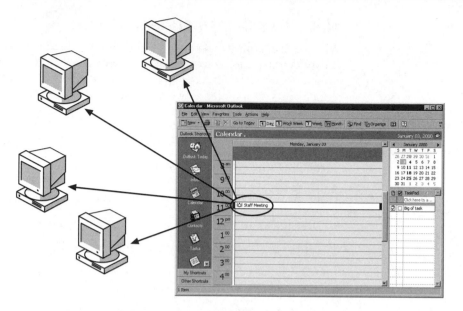

Figure 1.4   Scheduling a meeting with Microsoft Outlook

Sharing Hardware and Software

Before the advent of networks, computer users needed their own printers, plotters, and other peripherals; the only way users could share a printer was to take turns sitting at the computer connected to the printer. Figure 1.5 shows a typical stand-alone workstation with a printer.

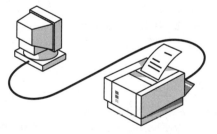

Figure 1.5   A printer in a stand-alone environment

Networks make it possible for several people to share data and peripherals simultaneously. If many people need to use a printer, they can all use the printer available on the network. Figure 1.6 shows a typical network environment in which five workstations share a single printer.

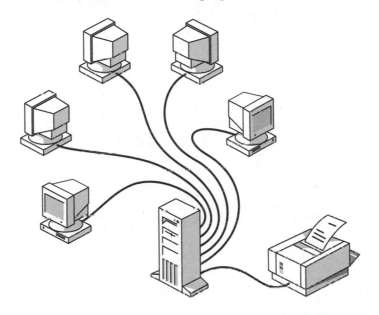

Figure 1.6   Sharing a printer in a networking environment

Networks can be used to share and standardize applications, such as word processors, spreadsheets, inventory databases, and so on, to ensure that everyone on the network is using the same applications and the same versions of those applications. This allows documents to be shared easily and creates training efficiencies: it is easier for people to master one word processing application thoroughly than to try to learn four or five different word processing applications.

Centralizing Administration and Support

Networking computers can simplify support tasks as well. It is far more efficient for technical personnel to support one version of one operating system or application and to set up all computers in the same manner than to support many individual and unique systems and setups.

The Two Major Types of Networks: LANs and WANs

Computer networks are classified into one of two groups, depending on their size and function. A *local area network (LAN)* is the basic building block of any computer network. A LAN can range from simple (two computers connected by a cable) to complex (hundreds of connected computers and peripherals throughout a major corporation). (See Figure 1.7.) The distinguishing feature of a LAN is that it is confined to a limited geographic area.

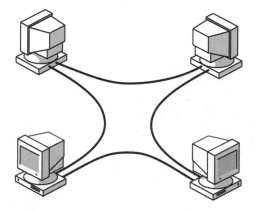

Figure 1.7   A local area network (LAN)

A *wide area network (WAN),* on the other hand, has no geographical limit (see Figure 1.8). It can connect computers and other devices on opposite sides of the world. A WAN is made up of a number of interconnected LANs. Perhaps the ultimate WAN is the Internet.

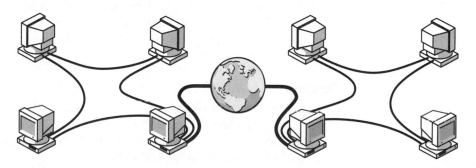

Figure 1.8   A wide area network (WAN)

Lesson Checkup

1. What is a computer network?

2. What are three advantages of using a computer network?

3. Give two examples of a LAN configuration.

4. Give two examples of a WAN configuration.

Lesson Summary

The following points summarize the main elements of this lesson:

- The primary reasons for networking computers are to share information, to share hardware and software, and to centralize administration and support.

- A local area network (LAN) is the smallest form of a network and is the building block for larger networks.

- A wide area network (WAN) is a collection of LANs and has no geographical limitation.

Lesson 2: Network Configuration

In Lesson 1, we discussed LANs and WANs. When we define a network in these terms, we are taking into account the size and geographic area of the network. How the computers in the network are configured and how they share information determine whether the network is peer-to-peer or serverbased—another important network classification. This lesson explores the major features and advantages of these kinds of networks.

After this lesson, you will be able to:

- Identify a peer-to-peer network.
- Identify a server-based network.
- Identify server functions and assign specialized servers as needed.
- Determine which type of network is appropriate for a site.

Estimated lesson time: 45 minutes

Network Configuration Overview

In general, all networks have certain components, functions, and features in common, shown in Figure 1.9. These include:

- Servers—Computers that provide shared resources to network users.
- Clients—Computers that access shared network resources provided by a server.
- Media—The wires that make the physical connections.
- Shared data—Files provided to clients by servers across the network.
- Shared printers and other peripherals—Additional resources provided by servers.
- Resources—Any service or device, such as files, printers, or other items, made available for use by members of the network.

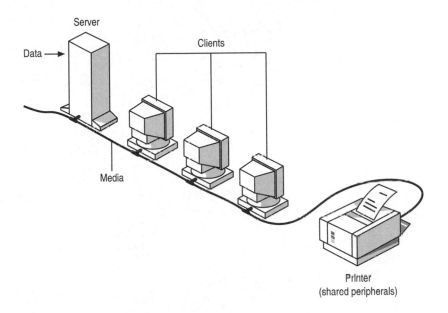

Figure 1.9   Common network elements

Even with these similarities, networks are divided into two broad categories, illustrated in Figure 1.10:

- Peer-to-peer networks
- Server-based networks

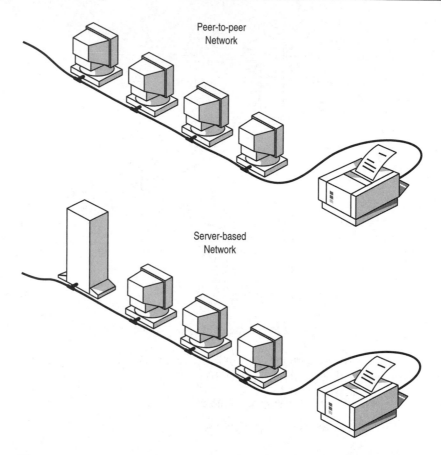

Figure 1.10   Typical peer-to-peer and server-based networks

The distinction between peer-to-peer and server-based networks is important because each type has different capabilities. The type of network you choose to implement will depend on factors such as the:

- Size of the organization.
- Level of security required.
- Type of business.
- Level of administrative support available.
- Amount of network traffic.
- Needs of the network users.
- Network budget.

Peer-to-Peer Networks

In a peer-to-peer network, there are no dedicated servers, and there is no hierarchy among the computers. All the computers are equal and therefore are known as peers. Each computer functions as both a client and a server, and there is no administrator responsible for the entire network. The user at each computer determines what data on that computer is shared on the network. Figure 1.11 shows a peer-to-peer network in which each computer functions as both a client and a server.

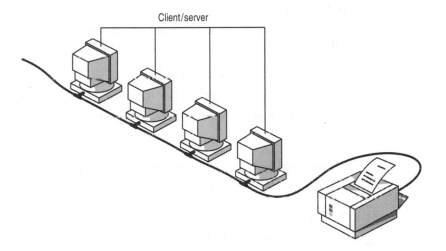

Figure 1.11   Peer-to-peer network computers act as both clients and servers

Size

Peer-to-peer networks are also called *workgroups*. The term "workgroup" implies a small group of people. There are typically 10 or fewer computers in a peer-to-peer network.

Cost

Peer-to-peer networks are relatively simple. Because each computer functions as a client and a server, there is no need for a powerful central server or for the other components required for a high-capacity network. Peer-to-peer networks can be less expensive than server-based networks.

Operating Systems

In a peer-to-peer network, the networking software does not require the same standard of performance and level of security as the networking software designed for dedicated servers. Dedicated servers function only as servers and not as clients or workstations. They are discussed in more detail later in this lesson.

Peer-to-peer networking is built into many operating systems. In those cases, no additional software is required to set up a peer-to-peer network.

Implementation

In typical networking environments, a peer-to-peer implementation offers the following advantages:

- Computers are located at users' desks.
- Users act as their own administrators and plan their own security.
- Computers in the network are connected by a simple, easily visible cabling system.

Where a Peer-to-Peer Network Is Appropriate

Peer-to-peer networks are good choices for environments where:

- There are 10 users or fewer.
- Users share resources, such as files and printers, but no specialized servers exist.
- Security is not an issue.
- The organization and the network will experience only limited growth within the foreseeable future.

Where these factors apply, a peer-to-peer network will probably be a better choice than a server-based network.

Peer-to-Peer Network Considerations

Although a peer-to-peer network might meet the needs of small organizations, it is not appropriate for all environments. The rest of this section describes some of the considerations a network planner needs to address before choosing which type of network to implement.

Administration

Network administration tasks include:

- Managing users and security.
- Making resources available.
- Maintaining applications and data.
- Installing and upgrading application and operating system software.

In a typical peer-to-peer network, no system manager oversees administration for the entire network. Instead, individual users administer their own computers.

Sharing Resources

All users can share any of their resources in any manner they choose. These resources include data in shared directories, printers, fax cards, and so on.

Server Requirements

In a peer-to-peer environment, each computer must:

- Use a large percentage of its resources to support the user at the computer, known as the *local user*.
- Use additional resources such as hard-disk space and memory, to support the user's accessing resources on the network, known as the *remote user*.

While a server-based network relieves the local user of these demands, it requires at least one powerful, dedicated server to meet the demands of all the clients on the network.

Security

On a computer network, *security* (making computers and data stored on them safe from harm or unauthorized access) consists of setting a password on a resource, such as a directory, that is shared on the network. All peer-to-peer network users set their own security, and shared resources can exist on any computer rather than on a centralized server only; consequently, centralized control is very difficult to maintain. This lack of control has a big impact on network security because some users may not implement any security measures at all. If security is an issue, a server-based network might be a better choice.

Training

Because every computer in a peer-to-peer environment can act as both a server and a client, users need training before they are able to function properly as both users and administrators of their computers.

Server-Based Networks

In an environment with more than 10 users, a peer-to-peer network—with computers acting as both servers and clients—will probably not be adequate. Therefore, most networks have dedicated servers. A *dedicated* server is one that functions only as a server and is not used as a client or workstation. Servers are described as "dedicated" because they are not themselves clients, and because they are optimized to service requests from network clients quickly and to ensure the security of files and directories. Server-based networks (see Figure 1.12) have become the standard models for networking.

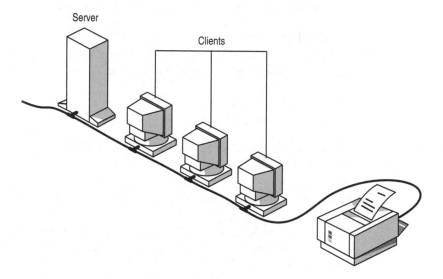

Figure 1.12   Server-based network

As networks increase in size (as the number of connected computers, and the physical distance and traffic between them, grows), more than one server is usually needed. Spreading the networking tasks among several servers ensures that each task will be performed as efficiently as possible.

Specialized Servers

Servers must perform varied and complex tasks. Servers for large networks have become specialized to accommodate the expanding needs of users. Following are examples of different types of servers included on many large networks. (See Figure 1.13.)

File and Print Servers

File and print servers manage user access and use of file and printer resources. For example, when you are running a word-processing application, the word-processing application runs on your computer. The word-processing document stored on the file and print server is loaded into your computer's memory so that you can edit or use it locally. In other words, file and print servers are used for file and data storage.

Application Servers

Application servers make the server side of client/server applications, as well as the data, available to clients. For example, servers store vast amounts of data that is organized to make it easy to retrieve. Thus, an application server differs from a file and print server. With a file and print server, the data or file is downloaded to the computer making the request. With an application server, the database stays on the server and only the results of a request are downloaded to the computer making the request.

A client application running locally accesses the data on the application server. For example, you might search the employee database for all employees who were born in November. Instead of the entire database, only the result of your query is downloaded from the server onto your local computer.

Mail Servers

Mail servers operate like application servers in that there are separate server and client applications, with data selectively downloaded from the server to the client.

Fax Servers

Fax servers manage fax traffic into and out of the network by sharing one or more fax modem boards.

Communications Servers

Communications servers handle data flow and e-mail messages between the servers' own networks and other networks, mainframe computers, or remote users who dial in to the servers over modems and telephone lines.

Directory Services Servers

Directory services servers enable users to locate, store, and secure information on the network. For example, some server software combines computers into logical groupings (called *domains*) that allow any user on the network to be given access to any resource on the network.

Planning for specialized servers becomes important with an expanded network. The planner must take into account any anticipated network growth so that network use will not be disrupted if the role of a specific server needs to be changed.

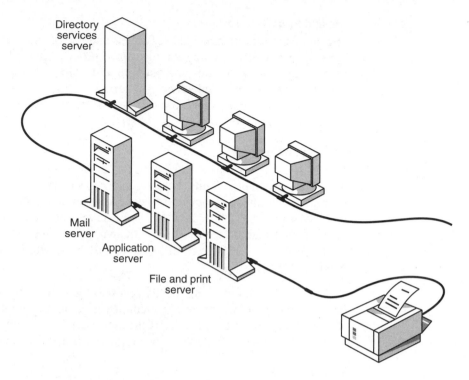

Figure 1.13   Specialized servers

The Role of Software in a Server-Based Environment

A network server and its operating system work together as a unit. No matter how powerful or advanced a server might be, it is useless without an operating system that can take advantage of its physical resources. Advanced server operating systems, such as those from Microsoft and Novell, are designed to take advantage of the most advanced server hardware. Network operating systems are discussed in detail in Chapter 4, "Survey of Network Operating Systems," and Chapter 8, "Designing and Installing a Network."

Server-Based Network Advantages

Although it is more complex to install, configure, and manage, a server-based network has many advantages over a simple peer-to-peer network.

Sharing Resources

A server is designed to provide access to many files and printers while maintaining performance and security for the user.

Server-based data sharing can be centrally administered and controlled. Because these shared resources are centrally located, they are easier to find and support than resources on individual computers.

Security

Security is often the primary reason for choosing a server-based approach to networking. In a server-based environment, one administrator who sets the policy and applies it to every user on the network can manage security. Figure 1.14 depicts security being centrally administered.

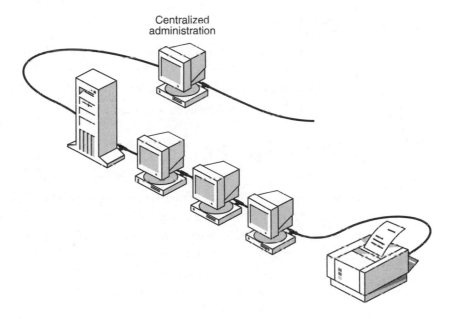

Centralized
administration

Figure 1.14   One administrator handles network security

Backup

Backups can be scheduled several times a day or once a week depending on the importance and value of the data. Server backups can be scheduled to occur automatically, according to a predetermined schedule, even if the servers are located on different parts of the network.

Redundancy

Through the use of backup methods known as *redundancy systems*, the data on any server can be duplicated and kept online. Even if harm comes to the primary data storage area, a backup copy of the data can be used to restore the data.

Number of Users

A server-based network can support thousands of users. This type of network would be impossible to manage as a peer-to-peer network, but current monitoring and network-management utilities make it possible to operate a server-based network for large numbers of users.

Hardware Considerations

Client computer hardware can be limited to the needs of the user because clients do not need the additional random access memory (RAM) and disk storage needed to provide server services. A typical client computer often has no more than a Pentium processor and 32 megabytes (MB) of RAM.

Lesson Checkup

1. List three factors that can influence the choice of whether to implement a peer-to-peer or server-based network configuration.

2. Describe the advantages of a peer-to-peer network.

3. Describe the advantages of a server-based network.

Lesson Summary

The following points summarize the main elements of this lesson:

- Networks are classified into two principal groups based on how they share information: peer-to-peer networks and server-based networks.

- In a peer-to-peer network, all computers are equal. They can either share their resources or use resources on other computers.

- In a server-based network, one or more computers act as servers and provide the resources to the network. The other computers are the clients and use the resources provided by the server.

- Features of the two major network types are summarized in Table 1.1 that follows:

Table 1.1   Comparison of Network Types

Consideration	Peer-to-Peer Network	Server-Based Network
Size	Good for 10 or fewer computers	Limited only by server and network hardware
Security	Security established by the user of each computer	Extensive and consistent resource and user security
Administration	Individual users responsible for their own administration; no full-time administrator necessary	Centrally located for network control; requires at least one knowledgeable administrator

Lesson 3: Network Topology

This lesson describes designs for connecting computers. You will also learn about variations that are often used and what you need to consider when planning your network.

After this lesson, you will be able to:
- Identify the four standard topologies and their variations.
- Describe the advantages and disadvantages of each topology.
- Determine an appropriate topology for a given network plan.

Estimated lesson time: 80 minutes

Designing a Network Topology

The term *topology*, or more specifically, network topology, refers to the arrangement or physical layout of computers, cables, and other components on the network. "Topology" is the standard term that most network professionals use when they refer to the network's basic design. In addition to the term "topology," you will find several other terms that are used to define a network's design:

- Physical layout
- Design
- Diagram
- Map

A network's topology affects its capabilities. The choice of one topology over another will have an impact on the:

- Type of equipment the network needs.
- Capabilities of the equipment.
- Growth of the network.
- Way the network is managed.

Developing a sense of how to use the different topologies is a key to understanding the capabilities of the different types of networks.

Before computers can share resources or perform other communication tasks they must be connected. Most networks use cable to connect one computer to another.

Note Wireless networks connect computers without using cable. This technology is discussed in Chapter 2 in Lesson 3: Wireless Networking.

However, it is not as simple as just plugging a computer into a cable connecting other computers. Different types of cable—combined with different network cards, network operating systems, and other components—require different types of arrangements.

To work well, a network topology takes planning. For example, a particular topology can determine not only the type of cable used but also how the cabling runs through floors, ceilings, and walls.

Topology can also determine how computers communicate on the network. Different topologies require different communication methods, and these methods have a great influence on the network.

Standard Topologies

All network designs stem from four basic topologies:

- Bus
- Star
- Ring
- Mesh

A *bus topology* consists of devices connected to a common, shared cable. Connecting computers to cable segments that branch out from a single point, or hub, is referred to as setting up a *star topology*. Connecting computers to a cable that forms a loop is referred to as setting up a *ring topology*. A *mesh topology* connects all computers in a network to each other with separate cables.

These four topologies can be combined in a variety of more complex hybrid topologies.

Bus

The bus topology is often referred to as a "linear bus" because the computers are connected in a straight line. This is the simplest and most common method of networking computers. Figure 1.15 shows a typical bus topology. It consists of a single cable called a *trunk* (also called a backbone or segment) that connects all of the computers in the network in a single line.

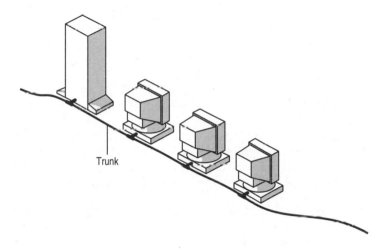

Trunk

Figure 1.15   Bus topology network

 Run the **c01dem01** video located in the **Demos** folder on the compact disc accompanying this book to view a demonstration of a bus-topology connection.

Communication on the Bus

Computers on a bus topology network communicate by addressing data to a particular computer and sending out that data on the cable as electronic signals. To understand how computers communicate on a bus, you need to be familiar with three concepts:

- Sending the signal
- Signal bounce
- Terminator

Sending the Signal   Network data in the form of electronic signals is sent to all the computers on the network. Only the computer whose address matches the address encoded in the original signal accepts the information. All other computers reject the data. Figure 1.16 shows a message being sent from 0020af151d8b to 02608c133456. Only one computer at a time can send messages.

 Run the **c01dem02** video located in the **Demos** folder on the compact disc accompanying this book to view a demonstration of how data is transferred in a bus topology.

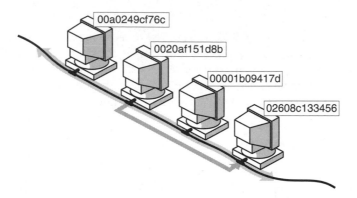

Figure 1.16   Data is sent to all computers, but only the destination computer accepts it

Because only one computer at a time can send data on a bus network, the number of computers attached to the bus will affect network performance. The more computers there are on a bus, the more computers will be waiting to put data on the bus and, consequently, the slower the network will be.

There is no standard way to measure the impact of a given number of computers on the speed of any given network. The effect on performance is not related solely to the number of computers. The following is a list of factors that—in addition to the number of networked computers—will affect the performance of a network:

- Hardware capabilities of computers on the network
- Total number of queued commands waiting to be executed
- Types of applications (client-server or file system sharing, for example) being run on the network
- Types of cable used on the network
- Distances between computers on the network

Computers on a bus either transmit data to other computers on the network or listen for data from other computers on the network. They are not responsible for moving data from one computer to the next. Consequently, if one computer fails, it does not affect the rest of the network.

Run the **c01dem03** video located in the **Demos** folder on the CD accompanying this book to view a demonstration that shows how a failed computer does not affect data transmission in a bus topology.

Signal Bounce   Because the data, or electronic signal, is sent to the entire network, it travels from one end of the cable to the other. If the signal is allowed to continue uninterrupted, it will keep bouncing back and forth along the cable and prevent other computers from sending signals. Therefore, the signal must be stopped after it has had a chance to reach the proper destination address.

Run the **c01dem04** video located in the **Demos** folder on the CD accompanying this book to view a demonstration of signal bounce.

Terminator   To stop the signal from bouncing, a component called a *terminator* is placed at each end of the cable to absorb free signals. Absorbing the signal clears the cable so that other computers can send data.

Both ends of each cable segment on the network must be plugged into something. For example, a cable end can be plugged into a computer or a connector to extend the cable length. Any open cable ends not plugged into something must be terminated to prevent signal bounce. Figure 1.17 shows a properly terminated bus topology network.

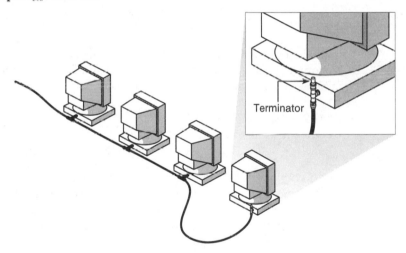

Terminator

Figure 1.17   Terminators absorb free signals

Run the **c01dem05** and **c01dem06** videos located in the **Demos** folder on the CD accompanying this book to view a terminator component and a demonstration of how a terminator eliminates signal bounce.

Disrupting Network Communication
A break in the cable will occur if the cable is physically separated into two pieces or if at least one end of the cable becomes disconnected. In either case, one or both ends of the cable will not have a terminator, the signal will bounce, and all network activity will stop. This is one of several possible reasons why a network will go "down." Figure 1.18 shows a bus topology with a disconnected cable. This network will not work because it now has unterminated cables.

The computers on the network will still be able to function as stand-alone computers; however, as long as the segment is broken, they will not be able to communicate with each other or otherwise access shared resources. The computers on the down segment will attempt to establish a connection; while they do so, workstation performance will be slower.

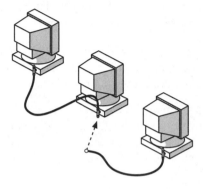

Figure 1.18   An unplugged cable is not terminated and will take down the network

 Run the **c01dem07** and **c01dem08** videos located in the **Demos** folder on the CD accompanying this book to view a demonstration of what happens when there is a break in the cable of a bus-topology network.

Network Expansion
As the physical size of the site grows, the network will need to grow as well. Cable in the bus topology can be extended by one of the two following methods:

- A component called a *barrel connector* can connect two pieces of cable together to make a longer piece of cable (see Figure 1.19). However, connectors weaken the signal and should be used sparingly. One continuous cable is preferable to connecting several smaller ones with connectors. Using too many connectors can prevent the signal from being correctly received.

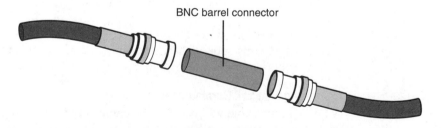

BNC barrel connector

Figure 1.19   Barrel connectors can be used to combine cable segments

- A device called a *repeater* can be used to connect two cables. A repeater actually boosts the signal before it sends the signal on its way. Figure 1.20 shows a repeater boosting a weakened signal. A repeater is better than a connector or a longer piece of cable because it allows a signal to travel farther and still be correctly received.

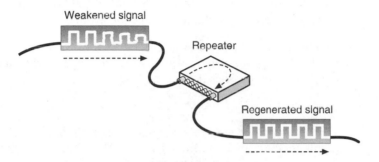

Figure 1.20   Repeaters connect cables and amplify the signal

Star

In the star topology, cable segments from each computer are connected to a centralized component called a *hub*. Figure 1.21 shows four computers and a hub connected in a star topology. Signals are transmitted from the sending computer through the hub to all computers on the network. This topology originated in the early days of computing when computers were connected to a centralized mainframe computer.

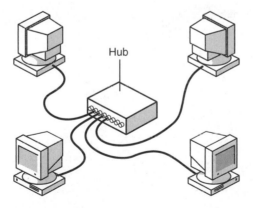

Figure 1.21   Simple star network

 Run the **c01dem09** and **c01dem10** videos located in the **Demos** folder on the CD accompanying this book to view demonstrations of a star topology.

The star network offers the advantage of centralized resources and management. However, because each computer is connected to a central point, this topology requires a great deal of cable in a large network installation. Also, if the central point fails, the entire network goes down.

If one computer—or the cable that connects it to the hub—fails on a star network, only the failed computer will not be able to send or receive network data. The rest of the network continues to function normally.

 Run the **c01dem11** video located in the **Demos** folder on the CD accompanying this book to view a demonstration of what happens when a computer on a star topology network goes down.

Ring

The ring topology connects computers on a single circle of cable. Unlike the bus topology, there are no terminated ends. The signals travel around the loop in one direction and pass through each computer, which can act as a repeater to boost the signal and send it on to the next computer. Figure 1.22 shows a typical ring topology with one server and four workstations. The failure of one computer can have an impact on the entire network.

Note A network's physical topology is the wire itself. A network's logical topology is the way it carries signals on the wire.

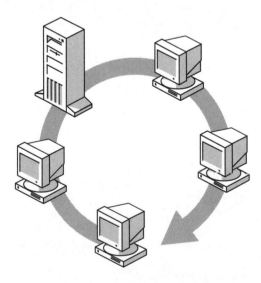

Figure 1.22   Simple ring network showing logical ring

 Run the **c01dem12** and **c01dem13** videos located in the **Demos** folder on the CD accompanying this book to view demonstrations of logical and actual flows of data on a ring-topology network.

Token Passing

One method of transmitting data around a ring is called *token passing*. (A *token* is a special series of bits that travels around a token-ring network. Each network has only one token.) The token is passed from computer to computer until it gets to a computer that has data to send. Figure 1.23 shows a token ring topology with the token. The sending computer modifies the token, puts an electronic address on the data, and sends it around the ring.

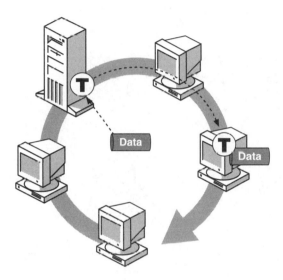

Figure 1.23   A computer grabs the token and passes it around the ring

The data passes by each computer until it finds the one with an address that matches the address on the data.

The receiving computer returns a message to the sending computer indicating that the data has been received. After verification, the sending computer creates a new token and releases it on the network. The token circulates within the ring until a workstation needs it to send data.

 Run the **c01dem14** and **c01dem15** videos located in the **Demos** folder on the CD accompanying this book to view demonstrations of both the logical and actual flows of token passing on a ring topology network.

It might seem that token passing would take a long time, but the token actually travels at roughly the speed of light. A token can circle a ring 200 meters (656 feet) in diamcter about 477,376 times per second.

 Run the **c01dem16** video located in the **Demos** folder on the CD accompanying this book to view a demonstration of what happens when a computer on a token ring–topology network goes down.

Mesh

A mesh topology network offers superior redundancy and reliability. In a mesh topology, each computer is connected to every other computer by separate cabling. This configuration provides redundant paths throughout the network so that if one cable fails, another will take over the traffic. While ease of troubleshooting and increased reliability are definite pluses, these networks are expensive to install because they use a lot of cabling. Often, a mesh topology will be used in conjunction with other topologies to form a hybrid topology.

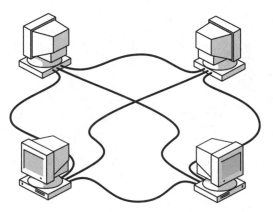

Figure 1.24   In a mesh topology, all computers are connected to each other by separate cables

Hubs

One network component that has become standard equipment in networks is the hub. Figure 1.25 shows a hub as the central component in a star topology.

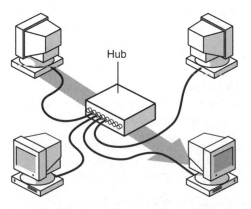

Figure 1.25   A hub is the central point in a star topology

Active Hubs

Most hubs are active; that is, they regenerate and retransmit signals in the same way as a repeater does. Because hubs usually have eight to twelve ports for network computers to connect to, they are sometimes called multiport repeaters. Active hubs require electrical power to run.

Passive Hubs

Some types of hubs are passive; examples include wiring panels or punch-down blocks. They act as connection points and do not amplify or regenerate the signal; the signal passes through the hub. Passive hubs do not require electrical power to run.

Hybrid Hubs

Advanced hubs that will accommodate several different types of cables are called *hybrid hubs*. Figure 1.26 shows a main hub (the hybrid) with three sub-hubs.

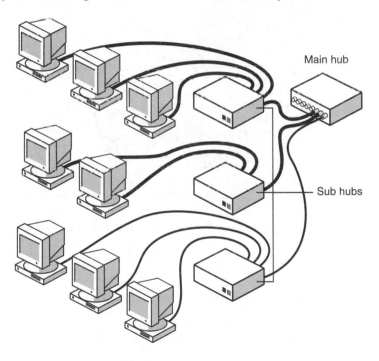

Figure 1.26   Hybrid hub

Hub Considerations

Hub-based systems are versatile and offer several advantages over systems that do not use hubs.

In the standard linear-bus topology, a break in the cable will take the network down. With hubs, however, a break in any of the cables attached to the hub affects only a limited segment of the network. Figure 1.27 shows that a break or disconnected cable affects only one workstation while the rest of the network keeps functioning.

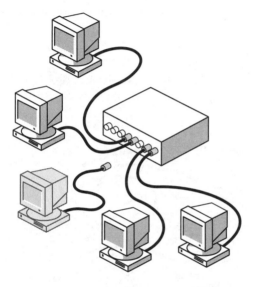

Figure 1.27   A break or unplugged cable takes down only the unplugged computer

Hub-based topologies include the following benefits:

- Wiring systems can be changed or expanded as needed.
- Different ports can be used to accommodate a variety of cabling types.
- Monitoring of network activity and traffic can be centralized.

Note Many active hubs have diagnostic capabilities that can indicate whether or not a connection is working.

Run the **c01dem017** video located in the **Demos** folder on the CD accompanying this book to view a discussion and demonstration of the role of hubs in network topologies.

Variations on the Standard Topologies

Many working topologies are hybrid combinations of the bus, star, ring, and mesh topologies.

Star Bus

The *star bus* is a combination of the bus and star topologies. In a star-bus topology, several star topology networks are linked together with linear bus trunks. Figure 1.28 shows a typical star-bus topology.

If one computer goes down, it will not affect the rest of the network. The other computers can continue to communicate. If a hub goes down, all computers on that hub are unable to communicate. If a hub is linked to other hubs, those connections will be broken as well.

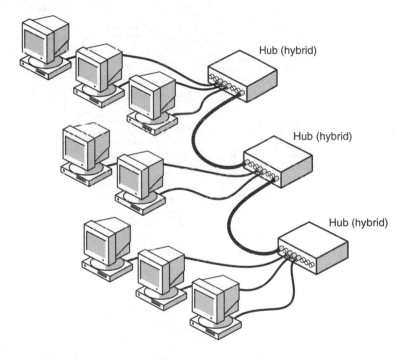

Hub (hybrid)

Hub (hybrid)

Hub (hybrid)

Figure 1.28   Star-bus network

Run the **c01dem018**, **c01dem19**, and **c01dem20** videos located in the **Demos** folder on the CD accompanying this book to view demonstrations of what happens when computers and hubs in a star-bus topology go down.

Star Ring

The *star ring* (sometimes called a star-wired ring) appears similar to the star bus. Both the star ring and the star bus are centered in a hub that contains the actual ring or bus. Figure 1.29 shows a star-ring network. Linear-bus trunks connect the hubs in a star bus, while the hubs in a star ring are connected in a star pattern by the main hub.

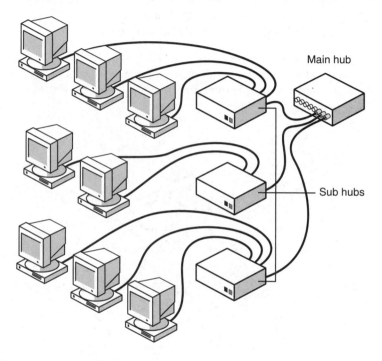

Figure 1.29   Star-ring network

Peer-to-Peer

Many small offices use a peer-to-peer network as described earlier in this chapter in Lesson 2: Network Configuration. Such a network can be configured as either a physical star or a bus topology. However, because all computers on the network are equal (each can be both client and server), the logical topology looks somewhat different. Figure 1.30 shows the logical topology of a peer-to-peer network.

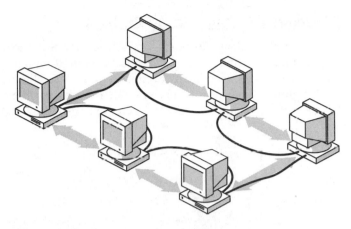

Figure 1.30   Logical peer-to-peer topology

Selecting a Topology

There are many factors to consider when deciding which topology best suits
the needs of an organization. Table 1.2 provides some guidelines for selecting
a topology.

Table 1.2   Topology Advantages and Disadvantages

Topology	Advantages	Disadvantages
Bus	Use of cable is economical.	Network can slow down in heavy traffic.
	Media is inexpensive and easy to work with.	Problems are difficult to isolate.
	System is simple and reliable.	Cable break can affect many users.
	Bus is easy to extend.	
Ring	System provides equal access for all computers.	Failure of one computer can impact the rest of the network.
	Performance is even despite many users.	Problems are hard to isolate.
		Network reconfiguration disrupts operation.
Star	Modifying system and adding new computers is easy.	If the centralized point fails, the network fails.
	Centralized monitoring and management are possible.	
	Failure of one computer does not affect the rest of the network.	
Mesh	System provides increased redundancy and reliability as well as ease of troubleshooting.	System is expensive to install because it uses a lot of cabling.

Exercise 1.1: Case Study Problem

A small, independent, business/home/life insurance company consisting of an owner, a business manager, an administrator, and four agents decides to implement a network. The company occupies half of a small building in an office park. Their volume of business had been stable for the past three years, but recently it has been increasing. To handle the increased business volume, two new agents will be hired.

Figure 1.31 illustrates the current arrangement.

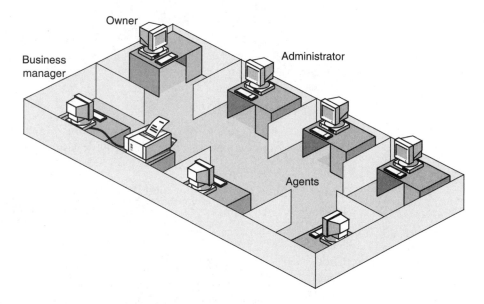

Figure 1.31   Case study model

Everyone in the company has a computer, but the business manager has the only printer. These computers are not connected by any form of networking. When agents need to print a document, they must first copy the file to a floppy disk, then carry it to the business manager's computer, where they are finally able to print it. Similarly, when staff members want to share data, the only means available is to copy the data on one computer to a floppy disk and insert the disk in another computer.

Recently, problems have arisen. The business manager is spending too much time printing other people's documents; and it is frequently unclear which copy of a given document is the current and authoritative version.

Your task is to design a network for this company.

To clarify the task of choosing a solution, you ask some questions.

Circle the most appropriate answers to the following questions:

1. Which type of network would you suggest for this company?
   - Peer-to-peer
   - Server-based
2. Which network topology would be most appropriate in this situation?
   - Bus
   - Ring
   - Star
   - Mesh
   - Star bus
   - Star ring

Exercise 1.2: Troubleshooting Problem

Use the information in the next section to help you solve the troubleshooting problem that follows.

Background Information

Choosing a network that does not meet an organization's needs leads directly to trouble. A common problem arises from choosing a peer-to-peer network when the situation calls for a server-based network.

A peer-to-peer, or workgroup, network might begin to exhibit problems with changes in the network site. These are more likely to be logistical or operational problems than hardware or software problems. The presence of several indicators is a sign that a peer-to-peer network is inadequate. Possible scenarios include the following:

- Lack of centralized security is causing difficulty.
- Users are turning off computers that are providing resources to others on the network.

When a network's design is too limited, it cannot perform satisfactorily in some environments. Problems can vary depending on the type of network topology in effect.

Bus Topology

A few situations will cause a bus network's termination to fail and thereby take the network down. Possible scenarios include the following:

- A cable on the network breaks, causing each end of the cable on either side of the break to lose its termination. Signals will bounce, and this will take the network down.

- A cable becomes loose or is disconnected, thereby separating the computer from the network. It will also create an end that is not terminated, which in turn will cause signals to bounce and the network to go down.

- A terminator becomes loose; thereby creating an end that is not terminated. Signals will start to bounce and the network will go down.

Hub-Based Topology

While problems with hubs are infrequent, they do occur. Possible scenarios include the following:

- A hub drops a connection. When a computer becomes disconnected from the hub, that computer will be off the network, but the rest of the network will continue to function normally.

- An active hub loses power, causing the network to stop functioning.

Ring Topology

A ring network is usually very reliable, but problems can occur. Possible scenarios include the following:

- One of the cables in the ring breaks, causing the network to stop functioning temporarily. In token-ring networks, restoring the cable will immediately restore the network.

- One of the cables in the ring becomes disconnected, causing the network to temporarily stop functioning. In token-ring networks, restoring the cable will immediately restore the network.

The Problem

Use what you have just read to troubleshoot the scenario that follows.

A small company with three departments recently began networking and has installed peer-to-peer networks in each department. The peer-to-peer networks are not connected to each other. A user in one department must make a diskette of the information to be loaded on the next network. Four employees in one department are working on a project. Each person has a different set of responsibilities, and each produces documentation for a different part of the project. Employees have each made the hard drive on their own computers available to everyone else on the project.

As the project grows, each user produces more documents, and questions arise about who has which document and which employee last revised a given document. Also, employees outside the department who have an interest in the project are asking to see some of the completed material.

1. Why are problems arising concerning who has which document? Suggest at least one reason.

2. What one change could you make that would give you centralized control of the access to these documents?

3. Describe one change that your solution will bring to the users' operating environment.

Exercise 1.3: Network Planning Problem

The following exercise will not only help you determine whether a peer-to-peer environment or a centralized, server-based environment is most appropriate for your site, but it will also help you form a general picture of the role that servers should play in your network and help you choose an appropriate topology.

Important This network planning problem assumes there is no network on your site. If your site has an existing network, use these questions as a guide, and apply the information in the text to the network on your site to help familiarize yourself with an actual network environment.

Part 1

Put a check mark on the line next to the choice that applies to your site. To determine which type of network would be most appropriate for your site, add up the number of peer-to-peer selections with check marks next to them, and compare the total with the number of server-based selections that have check marks next to them. The network with the most check marks should be the first option you consider.

1. Approximately how many users will the network at your site serve?

   0–10 _____ Peer-to-peer

   11 + _____ Server-based

2. Will data and resources on your network need to be restricted or regulated?

   Yes _____ Server-based

   No _____ Peer-to-peer

3. Will your computer be used primarily as a:

   Client computer _____ Server-based

   Server   _____ Server-based

   Both   _____ Peer-to-peer

Note If you want your computer to be used as both a client and a server, you might think you need to choose a peer-to-peer environment; however, in many server-based networks today, client computers share in a peer-to-peer fashion. This type of combined network has become the most common kind of network used for new installations, primarily because networking capabilities are now an integral part of most client-computer operating systems.

---

4. Will the users on your network be able to meet their own network administration and management needs?

   Yes _____ Peer-to-peer

   No _____ Server-based

5. Will users be allowed to share their own resources and set other network policies for their own computer?

   Yes _____ Peer-to-peer

   No _____ Server-based

6. Will your network use centralized servers?

   Yes _____ Server-based

   No _____ Peer-to-peer

7. Will your network have one central administrator who sets network policies?

    Yes _____ Server-based

    No _____ Peer-to-peer

8. Will your network have more than one server?

    Yes _____ Peer-to-peer or server-based, depending on other issues

    No _____ Server-based

Part 2

The following questions help you identify and resolve issues that arise in a server-based environment.

1. Check the tasks below that will apply to your servers:

    Communication   _____

    Backup/redundancy   _____

    Application   _____

    Database   _____

    E-mail   _____

    Fax   _____

    Print   _____

    User directories   _____

    General data storage   _____

2. Are some of the servers designated for special tasks?

    Yes _____

    No _____

3. Approximately how many servers does your network have?

    0–5   _____

    6–10   _____

    11–50   _____

    51–100   _____

4. Will your network's servers be centrally located or spread out in different locations?

    Centrally located _____

    Spread out   _____

5. Will some of your network's servers be in a secure location?

    Yes _____

    No _____

    If not, why not? _____

Part 3

The following section helps you to choose an appropriate topology for your network. (The answers to these questions can be used in conjunction with Table 1.2 in Lesson 3: Network Topology earlier in this chapter.)

Put a check mark on the line next to the choice that applies to your site. To determine which type of topology would be most appropriate for your site, add up the number of bus selections with check marks next to them, the number of star-bus selections with check marks next to them, and the number of star-ring selections with check marks next to them. The topology with the most check marks should be the option you consider first.

Note Because the ring is more expensive than the bus, a star bus would be more economical than a star ring. In a case where both star bus and star ring would work, star bus would usually be the preferred choice.

---

1. Approximately how many users will the network at your site serve?

   0–10 _____ All

   11 + _____ Star bus, star ring

2. Is cost a consideration in choosing your network topology?

   Yes _____ Star bus

   No _____ All

3. Does your building have drop ceilings?

   Yes _____ All

   No _____ Star bus, star ring

4. Does your building afford easy access to crawl spaces or wiring conduits?

   Yes _____ All

   No _____ Star bus, star ring

5. Is ease of troubleshooting important?

   Yes _____ Star bus, star ring

   No _____ All

6. Does the physical layout of the computers and office spaces naturally lend itself to a particular topology?

   Yes _____

   No _____

7. If the answer to Question 6 is No, go on to Question 8. If the answer to Question 6 is Yes, which topology does the layout lend itself to using?

   Circle one: bus   star bus

8. Is ease of reconfiguration important?

   Yes _____ Star bus, star ring

   No _____ All

9. Can the existing wiring in the building be used for your new network?

   Yes _____

   No _____

10. If the answer to question 9 is yes, which kind of topology could it be part of?

    Circle one: bus   star bus

Exercise Summary

Based on the information generated in the three parts of this Network Planning Problem, your network components should be:

Type of network:

Type of topology:

Lesson Summary

The following points summarize the main elements of this lesson:

- The physical layout of computers on a network is called a topology.
- There are four primary topologies: star, bus, ring, and mesh.
- Topologies can be physical (actual wiring) or logical (the way they work).
- In a bus topology, the computers are connected in a linear fashion on a single cable.
- Bus topologies require a terminator on each end of the cable.
- In a star topology, the computers are connected to a centralized hub.
- Mesh topologies connect all computers in a network to one another with separate cables.
- In a token-ring topology, the computers are connected physically in a star shape, but logically in a ring or circle. The data is passed from one computer to another around the circle.
- Hubs are used to centralize the data traffic and localize failures. If one cable breaks, it will not shut down the entire network.

Chapter Summary

The following points summarize the key concepts in this chapter:

What Is a Network?

- The primary reasons for networking are to share information, to share hardware and software (reducing cost), and to centralize administration and support.

- A local area network (LAN) is the smallest form of a network and is the building block for larger networks.

- A wide area network (WAN) is a collection of LANs and has no geographical limitation.

Network Configuration

- Networks are classified into two principal groups based on how they share information: peer-to-peer networks and server-based networks.

- In a peer-to-peer network, all computers are equal. They can either share their resources or use resources on other computers.

- In a server-based network, one or more computers act as servers and provide the resources to the network. The other computers are the clients and use the resources provided by the server.

- Features of the two major network types are summarized as follows:

Comparison of Network Types

Consideration	Peer-to-Peer Network	Server-Based Network
Size	Good for 10 or fewer computers	Limited only by server and network hardware
Security	Security established by the user of each computer	Extensive and consistent resource and user security
Administration	Individual users responsible for their own administration; no full-time administrator necessary	Centrally located for network control; requires at least one knowledgeable administrator

Network Topology

- The physical layout of computers on a network is called a topology. Topologies can be physical (actual wiring) or logical (the way they work). There are four primary topologies: star, bus, ring, and mesh.

- In a bus topology, the computers are connected in a linear fashion on a single cable. Bus topologies require a terminator on each end of the cable.

- In a star topology, the computers are connected to a centralized hub.

- In a mesh topology, all computers in the network are connected to one another with separate cables.

- In a token-ring topology, the computers are connected physically in a star shape, but logically in a ring or circle. The data is passed from one computer to another around the circle.

- Hubs are used to centralize the data traffic and localize failures. If one cable breaks, it will not shut down the entire network.

Chapter Review

1. Describe the difference between a LAN and a WAN.

2. What are the two basic network configurations?

3. A primary reason for implementing a network is to _____ resources.

4. Name three key resources often shared on a network.

5. In a peer-to-peer network, each computer can act as a _____ and a _____.

6. What is the function of a server in a server-based network?

7. A peer-to-peer network is adequate if _____ is not an issue.

8. Network professionals use the term _____ to refer to the network's physical layout.

9. The four basic topologies are the _____, _____, _____, and _____ topologies.

10. In a bus topology, all the computers are connected in a series. To stop the signals from bouncing, it is important that a _____ be connected to each end of the cable.

11. In a _____ topology all segments are connected to a centralized component called a _____.

12. In a _____ topology, a break anywhere in the cable will cause the entire network to go down.

13. The most reliable as well as the most expensive topology to install is the _____ topology.

14. A ring topology passes a _____ from one segment to another. In order for a computer to place data on the network, the computer must be in possession of the _____.

C H A P T E R 2

Basic Network Media

About This Chapter

In Chapter 1, "Introduction to Networking," we examined the nature of a network. General terms were introduced that describe what networks are, how they are structured, and how they can benefit us. In this second chapter, we look deeper into the physical aspects of a network to learn about the cables and circuitry that connect one computer to another.

Before You Begin

The information presented in this chapter builds on what you learned in Chapter 1. In particular, you need to understand the differences between local area networks (LANs) and wide area networks (WANs), between peer-to-peer networking and server-based networking, and among the various network topologies.

Lesson 1: Network Cabling

Building on our understanding of the different network topologies that connect computers, we focus next on the cables that connect them. In this lesson, we examine the construction, features, and operation of each type of cable, and the advantages and disadvantages of each.

After this lesson, you will be able to:

- Determine which type of cabling is best for any networking situation.
- Define terms related to cabling, such as shielding, crosstalk, attenuation, and plenum.
- Identify the primary types of network cabling.
- Distinguish between baseband and broadband transmissions and identify appropriate uses for each.

Estimated lesson time: 50 minutes

Primary Cable Types

The vast majority of networks today are connected by some sort of wiring or cabling that acts as a network transmission medium that carries signals between computers. Many cable types are available to meet the varying needs and sizes of networks, from small to large.

Cable types can be confusing. Belden, a leading cable manufacturer, publishes a catalog that lists more than 2200 types of cabling. Fortunately, only three major groups of cabling connect the majority of networks:

- Coaxial cable
- Twisted-pair (unshielded and shielded) cable
- Fiber-optic cable

The next part of this lesson describes the features and components of these three major cable types. Understanding their differences will help you determine which type of cabling is appropriate in a given context.

Coaxial Cable

At one time, coaxial cable was the most widely used network cabling. There were a couple of reasons for coaxial cable's wide usage: it was relatively inexpensive, and it was light, flexible, and easy to work with.

In its simplest form, coaxial cable consists of a core of copper wire surrounded by insulation, a braided metal shielding, and an outer cover. Figure 2.1 shows the various components that make up a coaxial cable.

The term *shielding* refers to the woven or stranded metal mesh (or other material) that surrounds some types of cabling. Shielding protects transmitted data by absorbing stray electronic signals, called *noise*, so that they do not get onto the cable and distort the data. Cable that contains one layer of foil insulation and one layer of braided metal shielding is referred to as dual shielded. For environments that are subject to higher interference, quad shielding is available. Quad shielding consists of two layers of foil insulation and two layers of braided metal shielding.

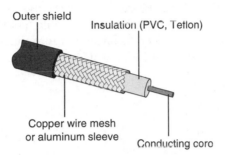

Figure 2.1   Coaxial cable showing various layers

The core of a coaxial cable carries the electronic signals that make up the data. This wire core can be either solid or stranded. If the core is solid, it is usually copper.

Surrounding the core is a dielectric insulating layer that separates it from the wire mesh. The braided wire mesh acts as a ground and protects the core from electrical noise and crosstalk. (*Crosstalk* is signal overflow from an adjacent wire. For a more detailed discussion of crosstalk, see the section Unshielded Twisted-Pair (UTP) Cable, later in this lesson.)

The conducting core and the wire mesh must always be kept separate from each other. If they touch, the cable will experience a short, and noise or stray signals on the mesh will flow onto the copper wire. An electrical short occurs when any two conducting wires or a conducting wire and a ground come into contact with each other. This contact causes a direct flow of current (or data) in an unintended path. In the case of household electrical wiring, a short will cause sparking and the blowing of a fuse or circuit breaker. With electronic devices that use low voltages, the result is not as dramatic and is often undetectable. These low-voltage shorts generally cause the failure of a device; and the short, in turn, destroys the data.

A nonconducting outer shield—usually made of rubber, Teflon, or plastic—surrounds the entire cable.

Coaxial cable is more resistant to interference and attenuation than twisted-pair cabling. As shown in Figure 2.2, *attenuation* is the loss of signal strength that begins to occur as the signal travels farther along a copper cable.

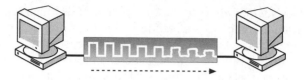

Figure 2.2   Attenuation causes signals to deteriorate

The stranded, protective sleeve absorbs stray electronic signals so that they do not affect data being sent over the inner copper cable. For this reason, coaxial cabling is a good choice for longer distances and for reliably supporting higher data rates with less sophisticated equipment.

Types of Coaxial Cable

There are two types of coaxial cable:

- Thin (thinnet) cable
- Thick (thicknet) cable

Which type of coaxial cable you select depends on the needs of your particular network.

Thinnet Cable   Thinnet cable is a flexible coaxial cable about 0.64 centimeters (0.25 inches) thick. Because this type of coaxial cable is flexible and easy to work with, it can be used in almost any type of network installation. Figure 2.3 shows thinnet cable connected directly to a computer's network interface card (NIC).

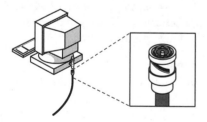

Figure 2.3   Close-up view of thinnet cable showing where it connects to a computer

Thinnet coaxial cable can carry a signal for a distance of up to approximately 185 meters (about 607 feet) before the signal starts to suffer from attenuation.

Cable manufacturers have agreed upon specific designations for different types of cable. (Table 2.1 lists cable types and descriptions.) Thinnet is included in a group referred to as the RG-58 family and has 50-ohm impedance. (*Impedance* is the resistance, measured in ohms, to the alternating current that flows in a wire.)

The principal distinguishing feature of the RG-58 family is the center core of copper. Figure 2.4 shows two examples of RG-58 cable, one with a stranded wire core and one with a solid copper core.

Stranded wire core
(RG-58 A/U)

Solid copper
(RG-58 /U)

Figure 2.4   RG-58 coaxial cable showing stranded wire and solid copper cores

Table 2.1   Cable Types

Cable	Description
RG-58 /U	Solid copper core
RG-58 A/U	Stranded wire core
RG-58 C/U	Military specification of RG-58 A/U
RG-59	Broadband transmission, such as cable television
RG-6	Larger in diameter and rated for higher frequencies than RG-59, but also used for broadband transmissions
RG-62	ArcNet networks

Thicknet Cable   Thicknet cable is a relatively rigid coaxial cable about 1.27 centimeters (0.5 inches) in diameter. Figure 2.5 shows the difference between thinnet and thicknet cable. Thicknet cable is sometimes referred to as Standard Ethernet because it was the first type of cable used with the popular network architecture Ethernet. Thicknet cable's copper core is thicker than a thinnet cable core.

Thicknet core

Thinnet core

Figure 2.5   Thicknet cable has a thicker core than thinnet cable

The thicker the copper core, the farther the cable can carry signals. This means that thicknet can carry signals farther than thinnet cable. Thicknet cable can carry a signal for 500 meters (about 1640 feet). Therefore, because of thicknet's ability to support data transfer over longer distances, it is sometimes used as a backbone to connect several smaller thinnet-based networks.

Figure 2.6 shows a device called a transceiver. A transceiver connects the thinnet coaxial cable to the larger thicknet coaxial cable. A transceiver designed for thicknet Ethernet includes a connector known as a vampire tap, or a piercing tap, to make the actual physical connection to the thicknet core. This connector is pierced through the insulating layer and makes direct contact with the conducting core. Connection from the transceiver to the NIC is made using a transceiver cable (drop cable) to connect to the attachment unit interface (AUI) port connector on the card. An AUI port connector for thicknet is also known as a Digital Intel Xerox (DIX) connector (named for the three companies that developed it and its related standards) or as a DB-15 connector.

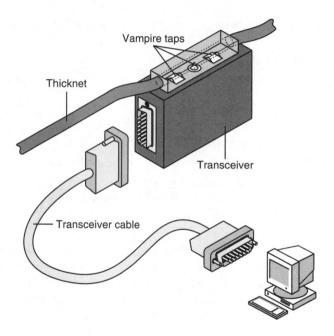

Figure 2.6   Thicknet cable transceiver with detail of a vampire tap piercing the core

Thinnet vs. Thicknet Cable   As a general rule, the thicker the cable, the more difficult it is to work with. Thin cable is flexible, easy to install, and relatively inexpensive. Thick cable does not bend easily and is, therefore, harder to install. This is a consideration when an installation calls for pulling cable through tight spaces such as conduits and troughs. Thick cable is more expensive than thin cable, but will carry a signal farther.

Coaxial-Cable Connection Hardware

Both thinnet and thicknet cable use a connection component, known as a BNC *connector*, to make the connections between the cable and the computers. There are several important components in the BNC family, including the following:

- **The BNC cable connector** Figure 2.7 shows a BNC cable connector. The BNC cable connector is either soldered or crimped to the end of a cable.

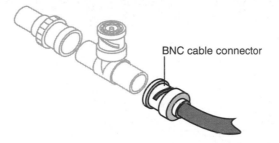

Figure 2.7   BNC cable connector

- **The BNC T connector**   Figure 2.8 shows a BNC T connector. This connector joins the network interface card (NIC) in the computer to the network cable.

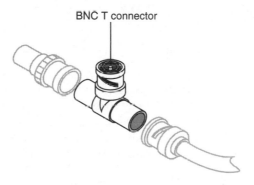

Figure 2.8   BNC T connector

- **The BNC barrel connector**   Figure 2.9 shows a BNC barrel connector. This connector is used to join two lengths of thinnet cable to make one longer length.

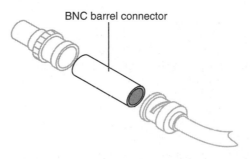

Figure 2.9   BNC barrel connector

- **The BNC terminator**   Figure 2.10 shows a BNC terminator. A BNC terminator closes each end of the bus cable to absorb stray signals. Otherwise, as
we saw in Chapter 1, "Introduction to Networking," the signal will bounce
and all network activity will stop.

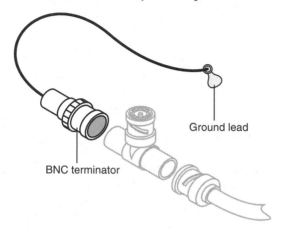

Ground lead

BNC terminator

Figure 2.10   BNC terminator

Note   The origin of the acronym "BNC" is unclear, and there have been many
names ascribed to these letters, from "British Naval Connector" to "Bayonet
Neill-Councelman." Because there is no consensus on the proper name and
because the technology industry universally refers to these simply as BNC-type
connectors, in this book we will refer to this family of hardware simply as BNC.

Coaxial-Cable Grades and Fire Codes

The type of cable grade that you should use depends on where the cables will be
laid in your office. Coaxial cables come in two grades:

- Polyvinyl chloride (PVC) grade
- Plenum grade

Polyvinyl chloride (PVC) is a type of plastic used to construct the insulation and
cable jacket for most types of coaxial cable. PVC coaxial cable is flexible and
can be easily routed through the exposed areas of an office. However, when it
burns, it gives off poisonous gases.

A *plenum* is the shallow space in many buildings between the false ceiling and
the floor above; it is used to circulate warm and cold air through the building.
Figure 2.11 shows a typical office and where to use—or not use—PVC and
plenum-grade cables. Fire codes give very specific instructions about the type
of wiring that can be routed through this area, because any smoke or gas in the
plenum will eventually blend with the air breathed by everyone in the building.

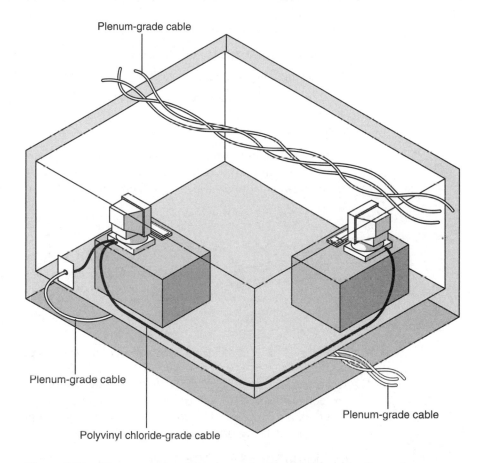

Plenum-grade cable

Plenum-grade cable

Polyvinyl chloride-grade cable

Plenum-grade cable

Figure 2.11   Plenum-grade cabling is required in the plenum by fire codes

Plenum-grade cabling contains special materials in its insulation and cable jacket. These materials are certified to be fire resistant and produce a minimum amount of smoke; this reduces poisonous chemical fumes. Plenum cable can be used in the plenum area and in vertical runs (for example, in a wall) without conduit. However, plenum cabling is more expensive and less flexible than PVC cable.

Note You should consult your local fire and electrical codes for specific regulations and requirements for running networking cable in your office.

Coaxial-Cabling Considerations
Consider the following coaxial capabilities when making a decision about which type of cabling to use.

Use coaxial cable if you need a medium that can:

- Transmit voice, video, and data.
- Transmit data for greater distances than is possible with less expensive cabling.
- Offer a familiar technology with reasonable data security.

Twisted-Pair Cable

In its simplest form, twisted-pair cable consists of two insulated strands of copper wire twisted around each other. Figure 2.12 shows the two types of twisted-pair cable: unshielded twisted-pair (UTP) and shielded twisted-pair (STP) cable.

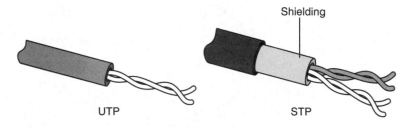

Figure 2.12   Unshielded twisted-pair and shielded twisted-pair cables

A number of twisted-pair wires are often grouped together and enclosed in a protective sheath to form a cable. The total number of pairs in a cable varies. The twisting cancels out electrical noise from adjacent pairs and from other sources such as motors, relays, and transformers.

Unshielded Twisted-Pair (UTP) Cable

UTP, using the 10BaseT specification, is the most popular type of twisted-pair cable and is fast becoming the most popular LAN cabling. The maximum cable length segment is 100 meters, about 328 feet.

Traditional UTP cable, as shown in Figure 2.13, consists of two insulated copper wires. UTP specifications govern how many twists are permitted per foot of cable; the number of twists allowed depends on the purpose to which the cable will be put. In North America, UTP cable is the most commonly used cable for existing telephone systems and is already installed in many office buildings.

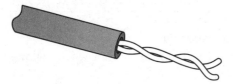

Figure 2.13   UTP cable

The 568A Commercial Building Wiring Standard of the Electronic Industries Association and the Telecommunications Industries Association (EIA/TIA) specifies the type of UTP cable that is to be used in a variety of building and wiring situations. The objective is to ensure consistency of products for customers. These standards include five categories of UTP:

- **Category 1**   This refers to traditional UTP telephone cable that can carry voice but not data transmissions. Most telephone cable prior to 1983 was Category 1 cable.

- **Category 2**   This category certifies UTP cable for data transmissions up to 4 megabits per second (Mbps). It consists of four twisted pairs of copper wire.

- **Category 3**   This category certifies UTP cable for data transmissions up to 16 Mbps. It consists of four twisted pairs of copper wire with three twists per foot.

- **Category 4**   This category certifies UTP cable for data transmissions up to 20 Mbps. It consists of four twisted pairs of copper wire.

- **Category 5**   This category certifies UTP cable for data transmissions up to 100 Mbps. It consists of four twisted pairs of copper wire.

Most telephone systems use a type of UTP. In fact, one reason why UTP is so popular is because many buildings are prewired for twisted-pair telephone systems. As part of the prewiring process, extra UTP is often installed to meet future cabling needs. If preinstalled twisted-pair cable is of sufficient grade to support data transmission, it can be used in a computer network. Caution is required, however, because common telephone wire might not have the twisting and other electrical characteristics required for clean, secure, computer data transmission.

One potential problem with all types of cabling is crosstalk. Figure 2.14 shows crosstalk between two UTP cables. (As discussed earlier in this lesson, crosstalk is defined as signals from one line interfering with signals from another line.) UTP is particularly susceptible to crosstalk, but the greater the number of twists per foot of cable, the more effective the protection against crosstalk.

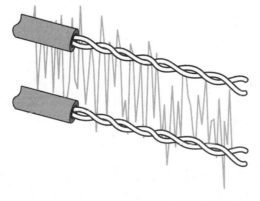

Figure 2.14   Crosstalk occurs when signals from one line bleed into another line

Shielded Twisted-Pair (STP) Cable

STP cable uses a woven copper-braid jacket that is more protective and of a higher quality than the jacket used by UTP. Figure 2.15 shows a two-twisted-pair STP cable. STP also uses a foil wrap around each of the wire pairs. This gives STP excellent shielding to protect the transmitted data from outside interference, which in turn allows it to support higher transmission rates over longer distances than UTP.

Figure 2.15   STP cable

Twisted-Pair Cabling Components

While we have defined twisted-pair cabling by the number of twists and its ability to transmit data, additional components are necessary to complete an installation. As it is with telephone cabling, a twisted-pair cable network requires connectors and other hardware to ensure proper installation.

Connection hardware   Twisted-pair cabling uses RJ-45 telephone connectors to connect to a computer. These are similar to RJ-11 telephone connectors. An RJ-45 connector is shown in Figure 2.16. Although RJ-11 and RJ-45 connectors look alike at first glance, there are crucial differences between them.

The RJ-45 connector is slightly larger and will not fit into the RJ-11 telephone jack. The RJ-45 connector houses eight cable connections, while the RJ-11 houses only four.

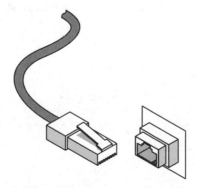

Figure 2.16   RJ-45 connector and jack

Several components are available to help organize large UTP installations and make them easier to work with. Figure 2.17 shows various twisted-pair cabling components.

Distribution racks and rack shelves   Distribution racks and rack shelves can create more room for cables where there isn't much floor space. Using them is a good way to organize a network that has a lot of connections.

Expandable patch panels   These come in various versions that support up to 96 ports and transmission speeds of up to 100 Mbps.

Jack couplers   These single or double RJ-45 jacks snap into patch panels and wall plates and support data rates of up to 100 Mbps.

Wall plates   These support two or more couplers.

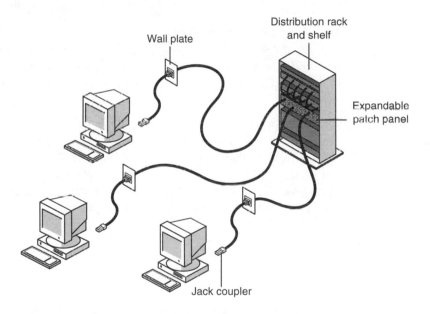

Wall plate

Distribution rack and shelf

Expandable patch panel

Jack coupler

Figure 2.17   Various twisted-pair cabling components

Twisted-Pair Cabling Considerations
Use twisted-pair cable if:

- Your LAN is under budget constraints.
- You want a relatively easy installation in which computer connections are simple.

Do not use twisted-pair cable if:

- Your LAN requires a high level of security and you must be absolutely sure of data integrity.

- You must transmit data over long distances at high speeds.

Fiber-Optic Cable

In fiber-optic cable, optical fibers carry digital data signals in the form of modulated pulses of light. This is a relatively safe way to send data because, unlike copper-based cables that carry data in the form of electronic signals, no electrical impulses are carried over the fiber-optic cable. This means that fiber-optic cable cannot be tapped, and its data cannot be stolen.

Fiber-optic cable is good for very high-speed, high-capacity data transmission because of the purity of the signal and lack of signal attenuation.

Fiber-Optic Cable Composition

An optical fiber consists of an extremely thin cylinder of glass, called the core, surrounded by a concentric layer of glass, known as the cladding. The fibers are sometimes made of plastic. Plastic is easier to install, but cannot carry the light pulses for as long a distance as glass.

Because each glass strand passes signals in only one direction, a cable includes two strands in separate jackets. One strand transmits and one receives. A reinforcing layer of plastic surrounds each glass strand, and Kevlar fibers provide strength. See Figure 2.18 for an illustration of fiber-optic cable. The Kevlar fibers in the fiber-optic connector are placed between the two cables. Just as their counterparts (twisted-pair and coaxial) are, fiber-optic cables are encased in a plastic coating for protection.

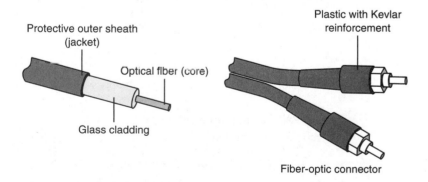

Figure 2.18 Fiber-optic cable

Fiber-optic cable transmissions are not subject to electrical interference and are extremely fast, currently transmitting about 100 Mbps with demonstrated rates of up to 1 gigabit per second (Gbps). They can carry a signal—the light pulse—for many miles.

Fiber-Optic Cabling Considerations

Use fiber-optic cable if you:

- Need to transmit data at very high speeds over long distances in very secure media.

Do not use fiber-optic cable if you:

- Are under a tight budget.
- Do not have the expertise available to properly install it and connect devices to it.

Note Pricing for fiber-optic cable is competitive with high-end copper cabling. Fiber-optic cable has become increasingly easier to work with, and polishing and terminating techniques now require fewer parts and less expertise than just a few years ago.

Signal Transmission

Two techniques can be used to transmit the encoded signals over cable: baseband and broadband transmission.

Baseband Transmission

Baseband systems use digital signaling over a single channel. Signals flow in the form of discrete pulses of electricity or light. Figure 2.19 shows a baseband transmission with a bidirectional digital wave. With baseband transmission, the entire communication channel capacity is used to transmit a single data signal. The digital signal uses the complete bandwidth of the cable, which constitutes a single channel. The term *bandwidth* refers to the data transfer capacity, or speed of transmission, of a digital communications system as measured in bits per second (bps).

Figure 2.19   Baseband transmission showing digital wave

As the signal travels along the network cable, it gradually decreases in strength and can become distorted. If the cable length is too long, the received signal can be unrecognizable or misinterpreted.

As a safeguard, baseband systems sometimes use repeaters to receive incoming signals and retransmit them at their original strength and definition. This increases the practical length of a cable.

Broadband Transmission

Broadband systems, as shown in Figure 2.20, use analog signaling and a range of frequencies. With analog transmission, the signals are continuous and nondiscrete. Signals flow across the physical medium in the form of electromagnetic or optical waves. With broadband transmission, signal flow is unidirectional.

Figure 2.20   Broadband transmission showing unidirectional analog wave

If sufficient total bandwidth is available, multiple analog transmission systems, such as cable television and network transmissions, can be supported simultaneously on the same cable.

Each transmission system is allocated a part of the total bandwidth. All devices associated with a given transmission system, such as all computers using a LAN cable, must then be tuned so that they use only the frequencies that are within the allocated range.

While baseband systems use repeaters, broadband systems use amplifiers to regenerate analog signals at their original strength.

In broadband transmission, signals flow in one direction only, so there must be two paths for data flow in order for a signal to reach all devices. There are two common ways to do this:

- Through mid-split broadband configuration, the bandwidth is divided into two channels, each using a different frequency or range of frequencies. One channel transmits signals; the other receives signals.
- In dual-cable broadband configuration, each device is attached to two cables. One cable is used to send, and the other is used to receive.

Increasing Bandwidth Performance

Increasing the speed of data transmission is a priority as network sizes and data traffic increase. By maximizing the use of the data channel, we can exchange more data in less time. The most basic form of data or information transmission is called *simplex*. This means that data is sent in one direction only, from sender to receiver. A simplex transmission is shown in Figure 2.21. Examples of simplex transmission are radio and television. With simplex transmission, problems encountered during the transmission are not detected and corrected. Senders cannot even be sure that the data is received.

Figure 2.21   A simplex transmission

In the next level of data transmission, called *half-duplex transmission*, data is sent in both directions, but in only one direction at a time. Examples of technology that uses half-duplex communication are shortwave radio and walkie-talkies. Figure 2.22 shows a half-duplex transmission. With half-duplex transmission, you can incorporate error detection and request that any bad data be resent. Surfing the World Wide Web is a form of half-duplex data transmission. You send a request for a Web page and then wait while it is being sent back to you. Most modem connections use half-duplex data transmission.

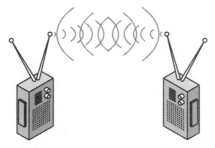

Figure 2.22   A half-duplex transmission

The most efficient method of transmitting data is to use a *full-duplex transmission*, in which data can be transmitted and received at the same time. A good example is a cable connection that not only allows you to receive TV channels, but also supports telephone and Internet connection. A telephone is a full-duplex device because it allows both parties to talk at the same time. Figure 2.23 shows full-duplex communication. Modems, by design, are half-duplex devices. They either send or receive data, switching between transmission mode and receiving mode. You can create a full-duplex modem channel by using two modems and two telephone lines. The only requirement is that both computers be connected and configured to support this type of communication.

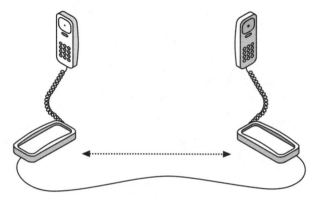

Figure 2.23   Full-duplex communication

The IBM Cabling System

IBM has developed its own cabling system, complete with its own numbers, standards, specifications, and designations. Many of these parameters, however, are similar to non-IBM specifications.

IBM introduced its cabling system in 1984. The purpose of this system was to ensure that the cabling and connectors would meet the specifications of their equipment. The IBM specification includes the following components:

- Cable connectors
- Face plates
- Distribution panels
- Cable types

The one IBM cabling component that is unique is the IBM connector, which is different from standard BNC or other connectors. These are IBM Type A connectors, known elsewhere as universal data connectors. They are neither male nor female; you can connect one to another by flipping either one over. These IBM connectors require special faceplates and distribution panels to accommodate their unique shape.

The IBM cabling system classifies cable into types. For example, in the IBM system, Category 3 cable (voice-grade UTP cable) is referred to as Type 3. (Table 2.2 compares the IBM cabling-system type names with standard cable type names.) The cable definitions specify which cable is appropriate for a given application or environment. The wire indicated in the system conforms to American Wire Gauge (AWG) standards.

AWG: The Standard Cable Measurement

Cable measurements are often expressed as numbers, followed by the initials AWG. (AWG is a measurement system for wire that specifies its thickness.) As the thickness of the wire increases, the AWG number decreases. Telephone wire is often used as a reference point; it has a thickness of 22 AWG. A wire of 14 AWG is thicker than telephone wire, and wire of 26 AWG is thinner than telephone wire.

Table 2.2   IBM Cabling System

IBM type	Standard label	Description
Type 1	Shielded twisted-pair (STP) cable	Two pairs of 22 AWG wires surrounded by an outer braided shield; used for computers and multistation access units (MAUs)
Type 2	Voice and data cable	A voice and data shielded cable with two twisted pairs of 22 AWG wires for data, an outer braided shield, and four twisted pairs of 26 AWG wires for voice
Type 3	Voice-grade cable	Consists of four solid, unshielded twisted-pair, 22 or 24 AWG cables
Type 4	Undefined	
Type 5	Fiber-optic cable	Two 62.5/125-micron multimode optical fibers—the industry standard
Type 6	Data patch cable	Two 26 AWG twisted-pair stranded cables with a dual foil and braided shield
Type 7	Undefined	
Type 8	Carpet cable	Housed in a flat jacket for use under carpets; two shielded twisted-pair 26 AWG cables; limited to one half the distance of Type 1 cable
Type 9	Plenum-grade cable	Fire safe Two shielded twisted-pair cables

Note A Multistation Access Unit (MAU) is a hub device in a token-ring network that connects computers in a physical hub-and-spokes arrangement, but uses the logical ring required in token ring networks.

Selecting Cabling

To determine which cabling is the best for a particular site you need to answer the following questions:

- How heavy will the network traffic be?
- What level of security does the network require?
- What distances must the cable cover?
- What are the cable options?
- What is the budget for cabling?

The better the cable protects against internal and external electrical noise, the farther and faster the cable will carry a clear signal. However, the better the speed, clarity, and security of the cable, the higher the cabling cost.

Cabling Considerations

As with most network components, there are trade-offs with the type of cable you purchase. If you work for a large organization and choose the least expensive cable, the accountants might initially be pleased, but you might soon notice that the LAN is inadequate in both transmission speed and data security.

Which cabling you select will depend on the needs of a particular site. The cabling you purchase to set up a LAN for a small business has different requirements from those of a larger organization, such as a major banking institution.

In the rest of this section, we examine some of the considerations that affect cabling price and performance.

Table 2.3 provides comparative information on cabling types.

Installation Logistics

How easy is the cable to install and work with? In a small installation where distances are short and security isn't a major issue, it does not make sense to choose thick, cumbersome, and expensive cable.

Shielding

The level of shielding required will affect cable cost. Almost every network uses some form of shielded cable. The noisier the area in which the cable is run, the more shielding will be required. The same shielding in a plenum-grade cable will be more expensive as well.

Crosstalk

Crosstalk and noise can cause serious problems in large networks where data integrity is crucial. Inexpensive cabling has low resistance to outside electrical fields generated by power lines, motors, relays, and radio transmitters. This makes it susceptible to both noise and crosstalk.

Table 2.3   Cable Comparison Summary

Characteristics	Thinnet coaxial (10Base2) cable	Thicknet coaxial (10Base5) cable	Twisted-pair (10BaseT) cable[1]	Fiber-optic cable
Cable cost	More than UTP	More than thinnet	UTP: Least expensive STP: More than thinnet	More than thinnet, but less than thicknet
Usable cable length[2]	185 meters (about 607 feet)	500 meters (about 1640 feet)	UTP and STP: 100 meters (about 328 feet)	2 kilometers (6562 feet)
Transmission rates	4–100 Mbps	4–100 Mbps	UTP: 4–100 Mbps STP: 16–500 Mbps	100 Mbps or more (> 1Gbps)
Flexibility	Fairly flexible	Less flexible than thinnet	UTP: Most flexible STP: Less flexible than UTP	Less flexible than thicknet
Ease of installation	Easy to install	Moderately easy to install	UTP: Very easy; often preinstalled STP: Moderately easy	Difficult to install
Susceptibility to interference	Good resistance to interference	Good resistance to interference	UTP: Very susceptible STP: Good resistance	Not susceptible to interference
Special features	Electronic support components are less expensive than twisted-pair cable	Electronic support components are less expensive than twisted-pair cable	UTP: Same as telephone wire; often preinstalled in buildings STP: Supports higher transmission rates than UTP	Supports voice, data, and video
Preferred uses	Medium to large sites with high security needs	Linking thinnet networks	UTP: smaller sites on a budget. STP: Token Ring in any size	Any size installation requiring speed and high data security and integrity

[1] This column provides information for both unshielded twisted-pair (UTP) and twisted-pair (STP) cable.

[2] Usable cable length can vary with specific network installations. As technology improves, usable cable length also increases.

Transmission Rates

Transmission rates are measured in megabits per second. A standard reference point for current LAN transmission over copper cable is 100 Mbps. Fiber-optic cable transmits at more than 1 Gbps.

Cost

Higher grades of cables can carry data securely over long distances, but they are relatively expensive; lower-grade cables, which provide less data security over shorter distances, are relatively inexpensive.

Signal Attenuation

Different cable types have different rates of attenuation; therefore, cable specifications recommend specific length limits for the different types. If a signal suffers too much attenuation, the receiving computer will be unable to interpret it. Most networks have error-checking systems that will generate a retransmission if the signal is too weak to be understood. However, retransmission takes time and slows down the network.

Exercise 2.1: Case Study Problem

You have been asked to review the proposals submitted by a consulting firm to design the cabling scheme for your company's new office building. Table 2.4 and the following diagram illustrate your company's cabling needs.

Table 2.4 Your Company's Cabling Needs

Location	Distance	Location	Distance
A to B	15 meters (50 feet)	Hub to A	152 meters (500 feet)
B to C	15 meters (50 feet)	Hub to B	160 meters (525 feet)
C to D	15 meters (50 feet)	Hub to C	168 meters (550 feet)
D to E	61 meters (200 feet)	Hub to D	184 meters (600 feet)
E to F	23 meters (75 feet)	Hub to E	152 meters (500 feet)
F to G	23 meters (75 feet)	Hub to F	130 meters (425 feet)
G to H	23 meters (75 feet)	Hub to G	107 meters (351feet)
H to I	23 meters (75 feet)	Hub to H	91 meters (300 feet)
I to J	61 meters (200 feet)	Hub to I	84 meters (275 feet)
J to K	15 meters (50 feet)	Hub to J	107 meters (351 feet)
K to L	15 meters (50 feet)	Hub to K	99 meters (325 feet)
L to M	15 meters (50 feet)	Hub to L	84 meters (275 feet)
A to M	221 meters (725 feet)	Hub to M	69 meters (226 feet)
D to M	244 meters (800 feet)	A to J	244 meters (800 feet)

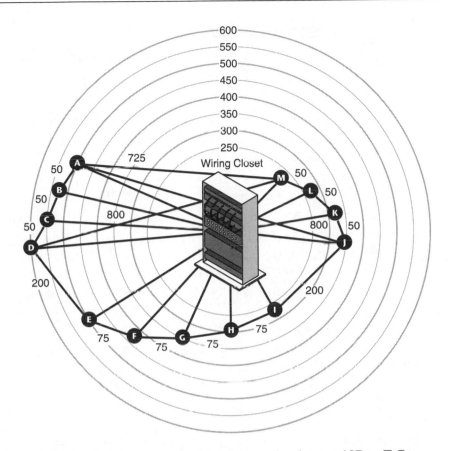

The consulting firm has recommended that you implement 10BaseT Category 5 UTP wire for your company's network. Based on this information, answer the following questions:

1. Where does this recommendation violate the UTP and 10BaseT specifications?
2. What type of cabling might you recommend instead?

Lesson Summary

The following points summarize the main elements of this lesson:

- Three primary types of cables are used with networks: coaxial, twisted-pair, and fiber-optic.

- Coaxial cable comes in two varieties: thinnet and thicknet.

- Thinnet cable is about 0.64 centimeters thick (0.25 inches) and can carry a signal for a distance of up to 185 meters (607 feet).

- Thicknet cable is about 1.27 centimeters (0.5 inches) in diameter and can carry a signal for a distance of up to 500 meters (1640 feet).

- The BNC connector is used with both thinnet and thicknet cables.

- Coaxial cables come in two grades, classified according to how they will be used: PVC-grade cable is used in exposed areas; plenum-grade cable has a fire-safety rating and is used in enclosed areas such as ceilings and walls.

- Twisted-pair cable can be either shielded (STP) or unshielded (UTP).

- The number of twists per unit of length and the protective shielding provide protection from interference.

- Twisted-pair cables conform to five standards, called categories. Each category provides specifications for increasing the speed of data transmission and resistance to interference.

- Twisted-pair cables use RJ-45 telephone connectors to connect to computers and hubs.

- Fiber-optic cables use light to carry digital signals.

- Fiber-optic cables provide the greatest protection from noise and intrusion.

- Data signals can be either baseband or broadband.

- Baseband transmission uses digital signals over a single frequency.

- Broadband transmission uses analog signals over a range of frequencies.

- IBM uses its own system of cabling and standards, but follows the same basic technology as other cables.

Lesson 2: The Network Interface Card

Network interface cards (NICs) provide the interface between cables, discussed in the previous lesson, and computers. This lesson explores the many different types of cards and how their performance affects a network. It also discusses the various connectors used to connect the cards to the cables.

After this lesson, you will be able to:

- Describe the role of the NIC in a network, including preparing, sending, and controlling data.
- Describe the configurable options for NICs.
- List the primary considerations for selecting a NIC.
- Describe at least two enhancements to NICs that will improve network performance.

Estimated lesson time: 85 minutes

The Role of the Network Interface Card

Network interface cards, usually referred to as NICs, act as the physical interface or connection between the computer and the network cable. Figure 2.24 shows a NIC with a coaxial-cable connection. The cards are installed in an expansion slot in each computer and server on the network.

After the NIC has been installed, the network cable is attached to the card's port to make the actual physical connection between the computer and the rest of the network.

 Run the **c02dem01** and **c02dem02** videos located in the **Demos** folder on the CD accompanying this book to view a demonstration of how to install a network interface card (NIC).

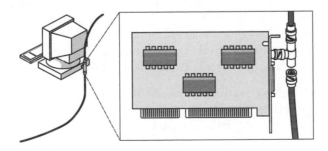

Figure 2.24 A sample NIC

The role of the NIC is to:

- Prepare data from the computer for the network cable.
- Send the data to another computer.
- Control the flow of data between the computer and the cabling system.
- Receive incoming data from the cable and translate it into bytes that can be understood by the computer's central processing unit (CPU).

Stated at a more technical level, the NIC contains the hardware and *firmware* (software routines stored in read-only memory, ROM) programming that implements the Logical Link Control and Media Access Control functions in the data-link layer of the OSI model. (See Chapter 5, Lesson 1: Open Systems Interconnection (OSI) Reference Model, for more information about the OSI model.)

Preparing the Data

Before data can be sent over the network, the NIC must change it from a form the computer can understand to a form that can travel over a network cable.

Data moves through a computer along paths called *buses*. These are actually several data paths placed side by side. Because the paths are side by side (parallel), data can move along them in lateral groups instead of in a single (serial) data stream.

Older buses, such as those used in the original IBM personal computer, were known as 8-bit buses because they could move data 8 bits at a time. The IBM PC/AT computer used a 16-bit bus, which means it could move data 16 bits at a time. Computers manufactured today use 32-bit buses. When data travels on a computer's bus, it is said to be traveling in parallel because the 32 bits are moving along side by side. Think of a 32-bit bus as a 32-lane highway with 32 cars moving side by side (moving in parallel), each carrying one bit of data.

On the network cable, however, data must travel in a single stream of bits. When data travels on a network cable it is said to be traveling as a *serial transmission* because one bit follows another. In other words, the cable is a one-lane highway, and the data always travels in one direction. The computer is either sending or receiving data, but never both at the same time.

The NIC takes data that is traveling in parallel as a group and restructures it so that it will flow through the 1-bit-serial path of the network cable. Figure 2.25 shows a server converting parallel data to serial data on the network. This is accomplished through the translation of the computer's digital signals into electrical or optical signals that can travel on the network's cables. The component responsible for this is the transceiver (transmitter/receiver).

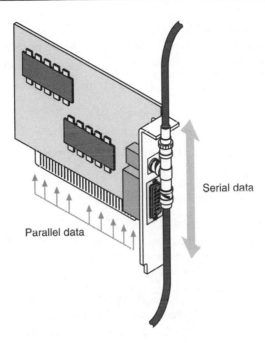

Figure 2.25   Parallel data stream converted to a serial data stream

Network Address

In addition to transforming data, the NIC also has to advertise its own location, or address, to the rest of the network to distinguish it from all the other cards on the network.

A committee of the Institute of Electrical and Electronics Engineers (IEEE) assigns blocks of addresses to each NIC manufacturer. The manufacturers hardwire these addresses into chips on the card by a process known as "burning" the address into the card. With this process, each NIC—and therefore each computer—has a unique address on a network.

The NIC also participates in several other functions in sequence as it takes data from the computer and gets it ready for the network cable:

1. The computer and NIC must communicate in order to move data from the computer to the card. On cards that can utilize direct memory access (DMA, defined later in this lesson), the computer assigns some of its memory space to the NIC.

2. The NIC signals the computer, requesting the computer's data.

3. The computer's bus moves the data from the computer's memory to the NIC.

Because data can often move faster on the bus or the cable than the NIC can handle, the data is sent to the card's buffer, a reserved portion of RAM. Here it is held temporarily during both the transmission and reception of data.

Sending and Controlling Data

Before the sending NIC actually sends data over the network, it carries on an electronic dialog with the receiving NIC so that both cards agree on the following:

- The maximum size of the groups of data to be sent
- The amount of data to be sent before confirmation of receipt is given
- The time intervals between sending data chunks
- The amount of time to wait before confirmation is sent
- How much data each card can hold before it overflows
- The speed of the data transmission

If a newer, faster, more sophisticated NIC needs to communicate with an older, slower NIC, both need to find a common transmission speed that each can accommodate. Some newer NICs incorporate circuitry that allows the faster card to adjust to the rate of the slower card.

Each NIC signals to the other indicating its own parameters and accepting or adjusting to the other card's parameters. After all the communication details have been determined, the two cards begin to send and receive data.

Configuration Options and Settings

Network interface cards often have configurable options that must be set in order for the card to function properly. Some of the older designs use externally mounted dual inline package (DIP) switches as shown in Figure 2.26. The following are examples of configurable options:

- Interrupt (IRQ)
- Base input/output (I/O) port address
- Base memory address
- Transceiver

Note Settings on older NICs are made by means of software, jumpers, or a combination of both; see the NIC product documentation for the appropriate software or jumper settings. Many newer NICs use Plug and Play (PnP) technology; consequently, older cards that require setting options manually are becoming obsolete. (Plug and Play is discussed in more detail later in this lesson.)

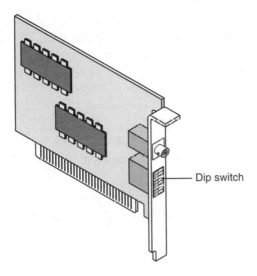

Figure 2.26   Older NIC with DIP switches

Interrupt Request (IRQ) Lines

Interrupt request lines (IRQs) are hardware lines over which devices such as I/O ports, the keyboard, disk drives, and NICs can send interrupts or requests for service to the computer's microprocessor.

Interrupt request lines are built into the computer's internal hardware and are assigned different levels of priority so that the microprocessor can determine the relative importance of incoming service requests.

When the NIC sends a request to the computer, it uses an interrupt—an electronic signal sent to the computer's CPU. Each device in the computer must use a different interrupt request line. The interrupt line is specified when the device is configured. For examples, see Table 2.5 that follows.

In most cases, IRQ3 or IRQ5 can be used for the NIC, as we will see later in this chapter. IRQ5 is the recommended setting if it is available, and it is the default for most systems. Use a system diagnostic tool to determine which IRQs are already being used.

If neither IRQ3 nor IRQ5 is available, refer to the following table for alternative values to use. The IRQs listed here as available usually can be used for a NIC. If the computer does not have the hardware device listed for a specific IRQ, that IRQ should be available for use.

Table 2.5   Standard IRQ Settings

IRQ	Computer with an 80486 processor (or higher)
2 (9)	EGA/VGA (enhanced graphics adapter/video graphics adapter)
3	Available (unless used for second serial port [COM2, COM4] or bus mouse)
4	COM1, COM3
5	Available (unless used for second parallel port [LPT2] or sound card)
6	Floppy-disk controller
7	Parallel port (LPT1)
8	Real-time clock
10	Available
11	Available
12	Mouse (PS/2)
13	Math coprocessor
14	Hard-disk controller
15	Available (unless used for secondary hard-disk controller)

Base I/O Port

The *base I/O port* specifies a channel through which information flows between the computer's hardware (such as the NIC) and its CPU. The port appears to the CPU as an address.

Each hardware device in a system must have a different base I/O port number. The port numbers, in hexadecimal format (the system that uses 16 rather than 10 as the basis for its numbering) in the following table, are usually available to assign to a NIC unless they are already in use. Those with a device listed next to them are addresses commonly used for the devices. Check the computer documentation to determine which addresses are already in use.

Table 2.6   Base I/O Port Settings

Port	Device	Port	Device
200 to 20F	Game port	300 to 30F	NIC
210 to 21F		310 to 31F	NIC
220 to 22F		320 to 32F	Hard-disk controller (for PS/2 Model 30)
230 to 23F	Bus mouse	330 to 33F	
240 to 24F		340 to 34F	
250 to 25F		350 to 35F	
260 to 26F		360 to 36F	
270 to 27F	LPT3	370 to 37F	LPT2
280 to 28F		380 to 38F	
290 to 29F		390 to 39F	
2A0 to 2AF		3A0 to 3AF	
2B0 to 2BF		3B0 to 3BF	LPT1
2C0 to 2CF		3C0 to 3CF	EGA/VGA
2D0 to 2DF		3D0 to 3DF	CGA/MCGA (also EGA/VGA, in color video modes)
2E0 to 2EF		3E0 to 3EF	
2F0 to 2FF	COM2	3F0 to 3FF	Floppy-disk controller; COM1

Base Memory Address

The *base memory address* identifies a location in a computer's memory (RAM).
The NIC uses this location as a buffer area to store the incoming and outgoing
data frames. This setting is sometimes called the RAM start address.

Note A *data frame* is a packet of information transmitted as a unit on a network.
Often, the base memory address for a NIC is D8000. (For some NICs, the final
"0" is dropped from the base memory address—for example, D8000 would
become D800.) When configuring a NIC, you must select a base memory address
that is not already being used by another device.

Note NICs that do not use system RAM do not have a setting for the base
memory address. Some NICs contain a setting that allows you to specify the
amount of memory to be set aside for storing data frames. For example, for some
cards you can specify either 16 KB or 32 KB of memory. Specifying more
memory provides better network performance but leaves less memory available
for other uses.

Selecting the Transceiver

The NIC can have other settings that need to be defined during configuration. For example, some cards come with one external and one on-board transceiver. Figure 2.27 shows a NIC with both on-board and external transceivers. In this case, you would have to decide which transceiver to use and then make the appropriate choice on your card.

Making the choice on the card is usually done with jumpers. *Jumpers* are small connectors that tie two pins together to determine which circuits the card will use.

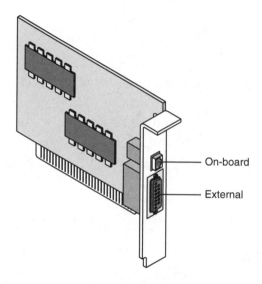

On-board

External

Figure 2.27   Network interface card showing external and on-board transceivers

NIC, Bus, and Cable Compatibility

To ensure compatibility between the computer and the network, the NIC must:

- Fit with the computer's internal structure (data bus architecture).
- Have the right type of cable connector for the cabling.

For example, a card that would work in an Apple computer communicating in a bus network will not work in an IBM computer in a ring environment: The IBM ring requires cards that are physically different from those used in a bus; and Apple uses a different network communication method.

Data Bus Architecture

In the personal computer environment, there are four types of computer bus architectures: ISA, EISA, Micro Channel, and PCI. Each type of bus is physically different from the others. It is essential that the NIC and the bus match. Figure 2.28 shows examples of each type of computer bus.

Industry Standard Architecture (ISA)

ISA is the architecture used in the IBM PC, XT, and AT computers, as well as in all their clones. It allows various adapters to be added to the system by means of plug-in cards that are inserted in expansion slots. ISA was expanded from an 8-bit path to a 16-bit path in 1984 when IBM introduced the IBM PC/AT computer. ISA refers to the expansion slot itself (an 8-bit slot or a 16-bit slot). The 8-bit slots are shorter than the 16-bit slots that actually consist of two slots, one behind the other. An 8-bit card could fit into a 16-bit slot, but a 16-bit card could not fit into an 8-bit slot.

ISA was the standard personal-computer architecture until Compaq and several other companies developed the EISA bus.

Extended Industry Standard Architecture (EISA)

This is the bus standard introduced in 1988 by a consortium of nine computer-industry companies: AST Research, Compaq, Epson, Hewlett-Packard, NEC, Olivetti, Tandy, Wyse Technology, and Zenith.

EISA offers a 32-bit data path and maintains compatibility with ISA, while providing for additional features introduced by IBM in its Micro Channel Architecture bus.

Micro Channel Architecture

IBM introduced this standard in 1988 at the time it released its PS/2 computer. Micro Channel Architecture is electrically and physically incompatible with the ISA bus. Unlike the ISA bus, the Micro Channel functions as either a 16-bit or a 32-bit bus and can be driven independently by multiple bus master processors.

Peripheral Component Interconnect (PCI)

This is a 32-bit local bus used in most Pentium computers and in the Apple Power Macintosh computers. The current PCI bus architecture meets most of the requirements for providing Plug and Play functionality. Plug and Play is both a design philosophy and a set of personal computer architecture specifications. The goal of Plug and Play is to enable changes to be made to a personal-computer configuration without any intervention by the user.

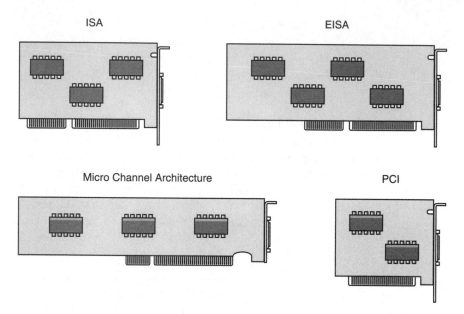

Figure 2.28   ISA, EISA, Micro Channel, and PCI network interface cards

Network Cabling and Connectors

The network interface card performs three important functions in coordinating activities between the computer and the cabling: it

- Makes the physical connection to the cable.
- Generates the electrical signals that travel over the cable.
- Controls access to the cable by following specific rules.

To select the appropriate NIC for your network, you first need to determine the type of cabling and cabling connectors it will have.

As discussed in the previous lesson, each type of cable has different physical characteristics that the NIC must accommodate. Each card is built to accept at least one type of cable. Coaxial, twisted-pair, and fiber-optic are the most common cable types.

Some NICs have more than one interface connector. For example, it is not uncommon for a NIC to have a thinnet, thicknet, and twisted-pair connector.

If a card has more than one interface connector and does not have built-in interface detection, you should make a selection by setting jumpers on the card itself or by using a software-selectable option. Consult the NIC documentation for information on how to properly configure the card. Three examples of typical connectors found on NICs are shown in the following three illustrations.

A thinnet network connection uses a coaxial BNC connector as shown in Figure 2.29.

Figure 2.29   Thinnet network connection for a coaxial BNC connector

A thicknet network connection uses a 15-pin attachment unit interface (AUI) cable to connect the 15-pin (DB-15) connector on the back of the NIC to an external transceiver. As discussed earlier in Lesson 1, the external transceiver uses a vampire tap to connect to the thicknet cable. Figure 2.30 shows a 15-pin AUI connection.

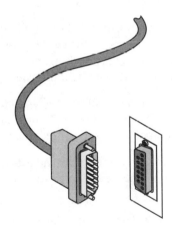

Figure 2.30   Thicknet network connection for a 15-pin AUI

Important Be careful not to confuse a joystick port with an AUI external transceiver port; they look alike, but some joystick pins carry 5 volts DC, which can be harmful to network hardware as well as to the computer. You need to be familiar with the specific hardware configuration in order to determine whether the connector is for a NIC or a joystick. Similarly, be careful not to confuse 25-pin SCSI ports with parallel printer ports. Some older SCSI devices communicated through the same kind of DB-25 connector as these parallel ports, but neither device will function when plugged into the wrong connector.

An unshielded twisted-pair connection uses a RJ-45 connector, as shown in Figure 2.31. The RJ-45 connector is similar to a RJ-11 telephone connector but is larger in size and has eight conductors; a RJ-11 only has 4 conductors.

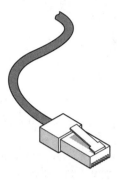

Figure 2.31   RJ-45 connector

Network Performance

Because of the effect it has on data transmission, the NIC has a significant effect on the performance of the entire network. If the card is slow, data will not pass to and from the network quickly. On a bus network, where no one can use the network until the cable is clear, a slow card can increase wait times for all users.

After identifying the physical requirements of the NIC—the computer bus, the type of connector the card needs, and the type of network in which it will operate—it is necessary to consider several other factors that affect the capabilities of the card.

Although all NICs conform to certain minimum standards and specifications, some cards feature enhancements that greatly improve server, client, and overall network performance.

You can speed up the movement of data through the card by adding the following enhancements:

- **Direct memory access (DMA)**   With this method, the computer moves data directly from the NIC's buffer to the computer's memory, without using the computer's microprocessor.

- **Shared adapter memory**   In this method, the NIC contains RAM that it shares with the computer. The computer identifies this RAM as if it is actually installed in the computer.

- **Shared system memory**   In this system, the NIC's processor selects a section of the computer's memory and uses it to process data.

- **Bus mastering**   With bus mastering, the NIC takes temporary control of the computer's bus, bypasses the computer's CPU, and moves data directly to the computer's system memory. This speeds up computer operations by freeing the computer's processor to deal with other tasks. Bus mastering cards can be expensive, but they can improve network performance by 20 to 70 percent. EISA, Micro Channel, and PCI network interface cards offer bus mastering.

- **RAM buffering**   Network traffic often travels too fast for most NICs to handle. RAM chips on the NIC serve as a buffer. When the card receives more data than it can process immediately, the RAM buffer holds some of the data until the NIC can process it. This speeds up the card's performance and helps keep the card from becoming a bottleneck.

- **On-board microprocessor**   With a microprocessor, the NIC does not need the computer to help process data. Most cards feature their own processors that speed network operations.

Servers

Because they handle such high volumes of network traffic, servers should be equipped with the highest-performance cards possible.

Workstations

Workstations can use less expensive NICs if their main network activities are limited to applications, such as word processing, that do not generate high volumes of network traffic. Recall, though, that on a bus network, a slow NIC can increase wait times for all users. Other applications, such as those of databases or engineering, will quickly overwhelm inadequate NICs.

Specialized NICs

So far, this lesson has focused on standard network interface cards. In the majority of situations, you will be using one of these cards to connect each computer to the physical network. In reality, some situations will require the use of specialized network connections and therefore require specialized network cards. The remainder of this lesson introduces you to three varieties of these specialized cards.

Wireless NICs

Some environments require an alternative to cabled computer networking. Wireless NICs are available that support the major network operating systems. Wireless networks are discussed in detail in the next lesson.

Wireless NICs often come with many features. These include:

- Indoor omnidirectional antenna and antenna cable.
- Network software to make the NIC work with a particular network.
- Diagnostic software for troubleshooting.
- Installation software.

These NICs can be used to create an all-wireless LAN or to add wireless stations to a cabled LAN.

Usually, these NICs are used to communicate with a component called a wireless concentrator that acts as a transceiver to send and receive signals.

Note A *concentrator* is a communications device that combines signals from multiple sources, such as terminals on a network, into one or more signals before sending them to their destination.

Fiber-Optic NICs

"Fiber to the desktop" has become a catchphrase for the computing industry. As transmission speeds increase to accommodate the bandwidth-hungry applications and multimedia data streams that are common on today's intranets, fiber-optic network cards allow direct connections to high-speed fiber-optic networks. These cards have recently become cost-competitive, and it's expected that their use will someday be commonplace.

Remote-Boot PROMs

In some environments, security is such an important consideration that workstations do not have individual floppy-disk drives. Without these, users are not able to copy information to floppy or hard disks and, therefore, cannot take any data from the worksite.

However, because computers normally start from either a floppy or a hard disk, there has to be another source for the software that initially starts (boots) the computer and connects it to a network. In these environments, the NIC can be equipped with a special chip called a remote-boot PROM (programmable read-only memory) that contains the hardwired code that starts the computer and connects the user to the network.

With remote-boot PROMs, diskless workstations can join the network when they start.

Lesson Summary

The following points summarize the main elements of this lesson:

- Network interface cards (NICs) are computer expansion cards that provide the interface between the network cabling and the computer.

- The function of the NIC is to prepare, send, receive, and—in a Ring topology—retransmit data on the network.

- A NIC is installed just like any other expansion card. You must properly set the IRQ, the base I/O port address, and the base memory address.

- In order for a NIC to be physically installed in the computer and connected to the network, it must both match the computer's expansion bus type and have the proper connector fittings for the network cabling.

A network's performance is only as good as its weakest link. Many aspects of a NIC can either enhance or restrict the performance of the network. Be careful when selecting an economical card; it just might become the limiting factor in your network's performance.

Exercise 2.2: Troubleshooting Problem

Listed below are questions you need to ask regarding cabling and network interface cards when you are troubleshooting a variety of network problems. Use them to help you troubleshoot the problem that follows.

Background Information

The first troubleshooting question should always be:

- Did the network connection ever function correctly in the past?

The next question should be:

- What has changed since then?

  Most experienced network engineers check cabling first because experience has taught them that the majority of network problems can be found in the cabling.

- Is the cabling connected properly?

- Is the cable broken or frayed?

- Is the cable too long?

- Does the cable conform to the specifications of the NICs?

- Is the cable crimped or bent too sharply?

- Does the network cable run near a source of interference such as an air conditioner, transformer, or large electric motor?

- Is the cabling terminated properly?

  The most common network adapter problems are interrupt conflicts and transceiver settings. The following questions will help you determine if the NIC is the source of your problem.

- Do the settings on the card match the settings in the network software you are using?
- Is there an I/O address conflict between the NIC and another card installed in the computer?
- Is there an interrupt conflict between the NIC and another card installed in the computer?
- Is there a memory conflict between the NIC and another card installed in the computer?
- Is the cable plugged into the correct interface (AUI, BNC, or RJ-45)?
- Is the NIC set to the speed setting that your network is using?
- Are you using the correct type of NIC for your network? (That is, are you trying to use a Token Ring card in an Ethernet network?)
- If you are using more than one NIC in the computer, do their settings conflict?

The Problem

Refer back to the questions to arrive at possible causes of the situation described below. Remember that there can be more than one cause and solution.

You have a 20-user, thinnet, coaxial bus network that has been in use for about a year. Three new client computers are going to be added to the network. Your vendor installed the new computers over the weekend, but when you came in Monday morning, nobody could access the server.

1. List two things that could cause the network not to function.

Note The answers identify some of the potential causes of the problem, but the list is not exhaustive. Even if the answers you have written down are not listed, they might still be correct.

---

2. What could you do to resolve each of the two possible causes you listed above?
3. How would each of your solutions repair the problems you identified (assuming that they are able to repair the problems)?

Lesson 3: Wireless Networking

This lesson presents an overview of wireless-network technology. You are introduced to the characteristics of the various wireless environments as well as the major wireless transmission and reception components.

After this lesson, you will be able to:

- Identify the three types of wireless networks and the uses of each.
- Describe the four transmission techniques used in local area networking.
- Describe the three types of signal transmission used in mobile computing.

Estimated lesson time: 25 minutes

The Wireless Environment

The wireless environment is an often appropriate, and sometimes necessary, networking option. Today, manufacturers are offering more products at attractive prices that, in turn, will mean increased sales and demand in the future. As demand increases, the wireless environment will grow and improve.

The phrase "wireless environment" is misleading because it implies a network completely free of cabling. In most cases, this is not true. Most wireless networks actually consist of wireless components communicating with a network that uses the cabling discussed earlier in this chapter in a mixed-component network called a *hybrid network*.

Wireless Network Capabilities

Wireless networks are attracting attention because wireless components can:

- Provide temporary connections to an existing, cabled network.
- Help provide backup to an existing network.
- Provide some degree of portability.
- Extend networks beyond the limits of physical connectivity.

Uses for Wireless-Network Connectivity

The inherent difficulty of setting up cable networks is a factor that will continue to push wireless environments toward greater acceptance. Wireless connectivity can be especially useful for networking:

- Busy locations, such as lobbies and reception areas.
- Users who are constantly on the move, such as doctors and nurses in hospitals.
- Isolated areas and buildings.
- Departments in which the physical setting changes frequently and unpredictably.
- Structures, such as historic buildings, for which cabling presents challenges.

Types of Wireless Networks

Wireless networks can be divided into three categories based on their technology:

- LANs
- Extended LANs
- Mobile computing

The primary difference between these categories lies in the transmission facilities. Wireless LANs and extended LANs use transmitters and receivers owned by the company in which the network operates. Mobile computing uses public carriers, such as long distance telephone companies, along with local telephone companies and their public services, to transmit and receive signals.

LANs

Except for the media used, a typical wireless network operates almost like a cabled network: a wireless network interface card with a transceiver is installed in each computer, and users communicate with the network just as if they were using cabled computers.

Access Points

The transceiver, sometimes called an access point, broadcasts and receives signals to and from the surrounding computers and passes data back and forth between the wireless computers and the cabled network.

These wireless LANs use small wall-mounted transceivers to connect to the wired network. Figure 2.32 shows a wireless connection between a laptop computer and a LAN. The transceivers establish radio contact with portable networked devices. Note that this is not a true wireless LAN, because it uses a wall-mounted transceiver to connect to a standard, cabled LAN.

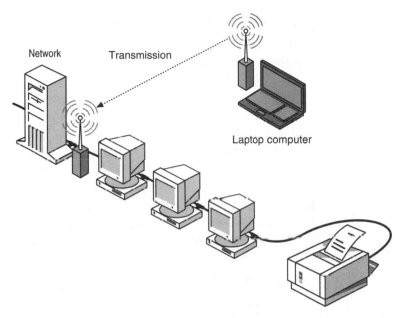

Figure 2.32   Wireless portable computer connecting to a cabled network access point

Transmission Techniques

Wireless LANs use four techniques for transmitting data:

1. Infrared transmission
2. Laser transmission
3. Narrowband (single-frequency) radio transmission
4. Spread-spectrum radio transmission

Infrared Transmission   All infrared wireless networks operate by using an infrared light beam to carry the data between devices. These systems need to generate very strong signals because weak transmission signals are susceptible to interference from light sources such as windows. Many of the high-end printers sold today are preconfigured to accept infrared signals. Figure 2.33 shows a laptop computer using an infrared light beam to send data to a printer.

This method can transmit signals at high rates because of infrared light's high bandwidth. An infrared network can normally broadcast at 10 Mbps.

There are four types of infrared networks:

- **Line-of-sight networks**   As the name implies, this version of infrared networking transmits only if the transmitter and receiver have a clear line of sight between them.

- **Scatter infrared networks**   In this technology, broadcast transmissions are bounced off walls and ceilings and eventually hit the receiver. They are effective within an area limited to about 30.5 meters (100 feet).

- **Reflective networks**   Optical transceivers situated near the computers transmit to a common location that redirects the transmissions to the appropriate computer.

- **Broadband optical telepoint**   This infrared wireless LAN provides broadband services and is capable of handling high-quality multimedia requirements that can match those provided by a cabled network.

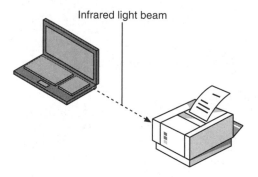

Figure 2.33   Wireless portable computer using an infrared light beam to send data to a printer

While its speed and convenience are generating interest, infrared has difficulty transmitting for distances greater than 30.5 meters (100 feet). It is also subject to interference from the strong ambient light found in most business environments.

Laser Transmission   Laser technology is similar to infrared technology in that it requires a direct line of sight, and any person or thing that breaks the laser beam will block the transmission.

Narrowband (Single-Frequency) Radio Transmission   This approach is similar to broadcasting from a radio station. The user tunes both the transmitter and the receiver to a certain frequency. This does not require line-of-sight focusing because the broadcast range is 3000 meters (9842 feet). However, because the signal is high frequency, it is subject to attenuation from steel and load-bearing walls.

Narrowband radio is a subscription service. The service provider handles all the Federal Communications Commission (FCC) licensing requirements. This method is relatively slow; transmission is in the 4.8 Mbps range.

Spread-Spectrum Radio Transmission   Spread-spectrum radio broadcasts signals over a range of frequencies. This helps it avoid narrowband communication problems.

The available frequencies are divided into channels, known as *hops*, which are comparable to one leg of a journey that includes intervening stops between the starting point and the destination. The spread-spectrum adapters tune in to a specific hop for a predetermined length of time, after which they switch to a different hop. A hopping sequence determines the timing. The computers in the network are all synchronized to the hop timing. This type of signaling provides some built-in security in that the frequency-hopping algorithm of the network would have to be known in order to tap into the data stream.

To further enhance security and to keep unauthorized users from listening in to the broadcast, the sender and the receiver can encrypt the transmission.

Spread-spectrum radio technology provides for a truly wireless network. For example, two or more computers equipped with spread-spectrum network adapters and an operating system with built-in networking capability can act as a peer-to-peer network with no connecting cables. In addition, such a wireless network can be tied into an existing network by adding an appropriate interface to one of the computers on that network.

Although some implementations of spread-spectrum radio can offer transmission speeds of 4 Mbps over distances of about 3.22 kilometers (two miles) outdoors and 244 meters (800 feet) indoors, the typical speed of 250 Kbps (kilobits per second) makes this method much slower than the other wireless networking options discussed.

Point-to-Point Transmission

The *point-to-point* method of data communication does not fall neatly into the present definitions of networking. It uses a point-to-point technology that transfers data from one computer to another instead of communicating among several computers and peripherals. However, additional components such as single and host transceivers are available. These can be implemented in either stand-alone computers or computers already on a network to form a wireless data-transfer network.

This technology involves wireless serial data transfer that:

- Uses a point-to-point radio link for fast, error-free data transmission.
- Penetrates through walls, ceilings, and floors.
- Supports data rates from 1.2 to 38.4 Kbps up to 61 meters (200 feet) indoors or about 0.5 kilometers (0.30 miles) with line-of-sight transmission.

This type of system transfers data between computers, or between computers and other devices such as printers or bar-code readers.

Extended LANs

Other types of wireless components are able to function in the extended LAN environment similarly to their cabled counterparts. A wireless LAN bridge, for example, can connect networks up to 4.8 kilometers (three miles) apart.

Multipoint Wireless Connectivity

A *wireless bridge* is a component that offers an easy way to link buildings without using cable. In the same way that a footbridge provides a path between two points, a wireless bridge provides a data path between two buildings. Figure 2.34 shows a wireless bridge connecting two LANs. The AIRLAN/Bridge Plus, for example, uses spread-spectrum radio technology to create a wireless backbone to tie locations together over distances beyond the reach of LANs. With variations that depend on atmospheric and geographic conditions, this distance can be up to 4.8 kilometers (three miles).

Though costly, such a component might be justified because it eliminates the expense of leased lines.

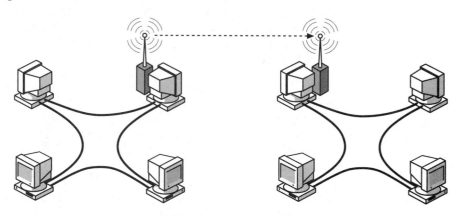

Figure 2.34   Wireless bridge connecting two LANs

The Long-Range Wireless Bridge

If the wireless bridge will not reach far enough, another alternative to consider is a long-range wireless bridge. These also use spread-spectrum radio technology to provide both Ethernet and Token Ring bridging, but for a distance of up to 40 kilometers (about 25 miles).

As with the original wireless bridge, the cost of the long-range bridge might be justified because it eliminates the need for T1 line or microwave connections.

Note A *T1 line* is a high-speed communications line that can handle digital communications and Internet access at the rate of 1.544 Mbps.

Mobile Computing

Wireless mobile networks use telephone carriers and public services to transmit and receive signals using:

- Packet-radio communication.
- Cellular networks.
- Satellite stations.

Traveling employees can use this technology with portable computers or personal digital assistants (PDAs) to exchange e-mail messages, files, or other information.

While this form of communication offers convenience, it is slow. Transmission rates range from 8 Kbps to 19.2 Kbps. The rates slow further when error correction is included.

Mobile computing incorporates wireless adapters that use cellular-telephone technology to connect portable computers with the cabled network. Portable computers use small antennas to communicate with radio towers in the surrounding area. Satellites in near-earth orbit pick up low-powered signals from portable and mobile networked devices.

Packet-Radio Communication

This system breaks a transmission into packets.

Note A *packet* is a unit of information transmitted as a whole from one device to another on a network. Packets are discussed in greater detail in Chapter 3, "Understanding Network Architecture."

These radio packets are similar to other network packets. They include:

- The source address.
- The destination address.
- Error-correction information.

The packets are linked up to a satellite that broadcasts them. Only devices with the correct address can receive the broadcast packets.

Cellular Networks

Cellular Digital Packet Data (CDPD) uses the same technology and some of the same systems that cellular telephones use. It offers computer data transmissions over existing analog voice networks between voice calls when the system is not busy. This is very fast technology that suffers only subsecond delays, making it reliable enough for real-time transmission.

As in other wireless networks, there must be a way to tie the cellular network in to the existing cabled network. An Ethernet interface unit (EIU) can provide this connection.

Satellite Stations

Microwave systems are a good choice for interconnecting buildings in small, short-distance systems such as those on a campus or in an industrial park.

Microwave transmission is currently the most widely used long-distance transmission method in the United States. It is excellent for communicating between two line-of-sight points such as:

- Satellite-to-ground links.
- Between two buildings.
- Across large, flat, open areas, such as bodies of water or deserts.

A microwave system consists of the following:

- Two radio transceivers: one to generate (transmitting station) and one to receive (receiving station) the broadcast.
- Two directional antennas pointed at each other to implement communication of the signals broadcast by the transceivers. These antennas are often installed on towers to give them more range and to raise them above anything that might block their signals.

Lesson Summary

The following points summarize the main elements of this lesson:

- The wireless environment is an often appropriate, and sometimes necessary, networking option.
- Computers operating on a wireless network function like their wire-bound counterparts, except that the network interface card is connected to a transceiver instead of a cable.
- A wireless segment can be either point-to-point (separated by short distances or in view of each other) or long-range.
- Wireless networks use infrared, laser, narrowband radio, or spread-spectrum radio signals for transmitting data.
- A wireless bridge can connect buildings that are situated as much as 40 kilometers (about 25 miles) apart.
- Cellular communication, satellite stations, and packet-radio communications are adding mobility to networks.

Exercise 2.3: Network Planning Problem

This exercise provides you with the experience of planning for two aspects of a network (selecting the right media and selecting the right NIC).

Part 1: Choosing Your Networking Media

Research has shown that about 90 percent of all new network installations are using UTP cable in a star-bus topology. Because most of the cost of cable installation is applied to labor, there is often little cost difference between using Category 3 UTP cable and Category 5 UTP cable. Most new installations use Category 5 because it supports transmission speeds of up to 100 Mbps. Category 5 allows you to install a 10 Mbps solution now and upgrade it to a 100 Mbps solution later. However, UTP cable might not be suitable for all networking situations.

The following questions prompt you to think about your network cable needs. Place a check mark next to the choice that applies to your site. To determine which type of cabling would be most appropriate for your site, simply total the check marks next to each type of cable indicator (UTP, coaxial, STP, fiber-optic). The indicator with the highest number of check marks is the candidate unless there is a specific requirement for a particular cable type such as fiber-optic (distance and security). In cases in which more than one type of cable is indicated, choose UTP where possible.

Note UTP is currently the most popular cabling option. Unless there is a compelling reason to use another type, UTP should be the first choice you consider.

For the purpose of answering the questions that follow, "Any" means that UTP can be a choice, depending on your other site considerations. "Depends on other factors" means that you will need to factor in other considerations apart from those presented in the question you're currently answering.

1. Are ease of troubleshooting and the cost of long-term maintenance important?

    Yes ____ UTP cable

    No ____ Any of the discussed cable types

2. Are most of your computers located within 100 meters (328 feet) of your wiring closet?

    Yes ____ UTP cable

    No ____ Coaxial or fiber-optic cable

3. Is ease of reconfiguration important?

    Yes ____ UTP cable

    No ____ Any of the discussed cable types

4. Does any of your staff have experience with UTP cable?

   Yes _____ UTP cable

   No _____ UTP cable, depending on other factors (See the following Note.)

Note Even if no one on your staff has experience with UTP, someone may have transferable experience with another type of cable such as coaxial, STP, or even fiber-optic cable.

---

5. Does your network have any existing STP cabling?

   Yes _____ STP cable

   No _____ Any of the discussed cable types

6. Does the topology or NIC you want to use require the use of STP cable?

   Yes _____ STP

   No _____ Depends on other factors

7. Do you have a need for cable that is more resistant than UTP to EMI (electromagnetic interference)?

   Yes _____ STP, coaxial, or fiber-optic cable

   No _____ UTP cable, depending on other factors

8. Do you have existing coaxial cabling in your network?

   Yes _____ Coaxial cable

   No _____ Any of the discussed cable types

9. Is your network very small (10 or fewer computers)?

   Yes _____ Coaxial cable (bus), UTP cable

   No _____ Any of the discussed cable types, depending on other factors

10. Will your network be installed in an open area using cubicles to separate work areas?

    Yes _____ Coaxial, or UTP cable

    No _____ Depends on other factors

Note Some situations require fiber-optic cable. This is especially true where other types of cable will not meet specific distance or security requirements. In such cases, fiber-optic cable is the only cable type that can be considered, regardless of what the questions in the other areas indicate.

---

11. Do you have a need for network cabling that is completely immune to electro-magnetic interference (EMI)?

    Yes _____ Fiber-optic cable

    No _____ Any of the discussed cable types, depending on other factors

12. Do you have a need for network cabling that is relatively secure from most eavesdropping or corporate intelligence-gathering equipment?

    Yes _____ Fiber-optic cable

    No _____ Any of the discussed cable types, depending on other factors

13. Do you have a need for network transmission speeds that are higher than those supported by copper media?

    Yes _____ Fiber-optic cable

    No _____ Any of the discussed cable types, depending on other factors

14. Do you have a need for longer cabling distances than those supported by copper media?

    Yes _____ Fiber-optic cable

    No _____ Any of the discussed cable types, depending on other factors

15. Do you have a budget that can absorb the costs of implementing fiber-optic cable?

    Yes _____ Fiber-optic cable or any of the discussed cable types, depending on other factors

    No _____ Any of the discussed cable types, depending on other factors

---

Note In the questions that follow, wireless, like fiber-optic cable, may be the only option in some cases, regardless of what the questions in the other areas indicate. Keep in mind that wireless networking can also be used in combination with a cabled network.

---

16. Do users on your network need to physically move their computers in the course of their workday?

    Yes _____ Wireless network, depends on other factors

    No _____ Any of the discussed cable types, depending on other factors

17. Are there limitations that make it very difficult or impossible to cable computers to the network?

    Yes _____ Wireless network

    No _____ Any of the discussed cable types, depending on other factors

18. Does your network have unique needs that are best fulfilled by one or more of the features of current wireless technology, such as computer mobility, or the ability to have a network in a building in which it is very difficult or impossible to install cable?

    Yes _____ Wireless network

    No _____ Any of the discussed cable types, depending on other factors

Part 2: Choosing Your Network Interface Card

There are dozens of manufacturers making each type of NIC, and each card has slightly different features. Setup is sometimes accomplished with jumpers or switches, sometimes using a software setup program, sometimes by means of a Plug and Play (PnP) bus type, and so on. You should do some research to determine which card is best for you because the industry is constantly changing. The best card this month might be updated or superseded by another manufacturer's card next month.

If you answer yes to each of the following questions, then the card you have chosen will probably work in your environment.

Note These questions are not designed to promote a particular card but, rather, to ensure that the card you choose is compatible with the rest of your network.

---

1. Are drivers available for the card that can work with the operating system you are using?

   Yes _____

   No _____

2. Is the card compatible with the cable type and topology you have chosen?

   Yes _____

   No _____

3. Is the card compatible with the bus type of the computer into which it will be installed?

   Yes _____

   No _____

Chapter Summary

The following points summarize the key concepts in this chapter:

Network Cabling

- Three primary types of cables are used with networks: coaxial, twisted-pair, and fiber-optic.

- Coaxial cable comes in two varieties: thinnet and thicknet.

- Thinnet cable is about 0.64 centimeters (0.25 inches) thick and can carry a signal for a distance of up to 185 meters (607 feet).

- Thicknet cable is about 1.27 centimeters (0.5 inches) in diameter and can carry a signal for a distance of up to 500 meters (1640 feet).

- The BNC connector is used with both thinnet and thicknet cables.

- Coaxial cables come in two grades, classified according to how they will be used: PVC-grade cable is used in exposed areas; plenum-grade cable has a fire-safety rating and is used in enclosed areas such as ceilings and walls.

- Twisted-pair cable can be either shielded (STP) or unshielded (UTP).

- The number of twists per unit of length and the protective shielding provide protection from interference.

- Twisted-pair cables conform to five standards, called categories. Each category provides specifications for increasing the speed of data transmission and resistance to interference.

- Twisted-pair cables use RJ-45 connectors to connect to computers and hubs.

- Fiber-optic cables use light to carry digital signals.

- Fiber-optic cables provide the greatest protection from noise and intrusion.

- Data signals can be either baseband or broadband.

- Baseband transmission uses digital signals over a single frequency.

- Broadband transmission uses analog signals over a range of frequencies.

- IBM uses its own system of cabling and standards, but follows the same basic technology as other cables.

The Network Interface Card

- Network interface cards (NICs) are computer expansion cards that provide the interface between the network cabling and the computer.

- The function of the NIC is to prepare, send, receive, and—in a Ring topology—retransmit data on the network.

- A NIC is installed just like any other expansion card. You must properly set the IRQ, the base I/O port address, and the base memory address.

- In order for a NIC to be physically installed in the computer and connected to the network, it must both match the computer's expansion bus type and have the proper connector fittings for the network cabling.

- A network's performance is only as good as its weakest link. Many aspects of a NIC can either enhance or restrict the performance of the network. Be careful when selecting an economical card; it just might become the limiting factor in your network's performance.

Wireless Networking

- The wireless environment is an often appropriate, and sometimes necessary, networking option.

- Computers operating on a wireless network function like their wire-bound counterparts, except that the NIC is connected to a transceiver instead of a cable.

- A wireless segment can be either point-to-point (separated by short distances or in view of each other) or long-range.

- Wireless networks use infrared, laser, narrowband radio, or spread-spectrum radio signals for transmitting data.

- A wireless bridge can connect buildings that are situated as much as 40 kilometers (about 25 miles) apart.

- Cellular communications, satellite stations, and packet-radio communications are adding mobility to networks.

Chapter Review

1. Coaxial cable consists of a core made of solid or stranded _____ _____.

2. If the coaxial conducting core and wire mesh touch, the cable will experience a _____.

3. The core of coaxial cable is surrounded by an _____ _____ that separates it from the wire mesh.

4. Thicknet cable is sometimes used as a _____ to connect thinnet segments.

5. Thinnet cable can carry a signal for a distance of about 185 meters (607 feet) before the signal starts to suffer from _____.

6. The electronic signals that make up the data are actually carried by the _____ in a coaxial cable.

7. A flexible coaxial cable that is easily routed but that should not go into crawl spaces is _____.

8. Coaxial cable that contains special materials in its insulation and cable jacket is called _____ cabling.

9. The most popular type of twisted-pair cable is _____ (10BaseT).

10. UTP cable for data transmissions up to 10 Mbps is category _____.

11. UTP cable for data transmissions up to 100 Mbps is category _____.

12. STP uses a foil wrap for _____.

13. STP is less susceptible to electrical _____ and supports higher transmission rates over longer distances than does UTP.

14. Twisted-pair cabling uses _____ telephone connectors to connect to a computer.

15. The RJ-45 connection houses _____ cable connections, whereas the RJ-11 houses only ____.

16. Optical fibers carry _____ data signals in the form of light pulses.

17. Fiber-optic cable cannot be _____, and the data cannot be stolen.

18. Fiber-optic cable is better for very high-speed, high-capacity data transmission than _____ cable because of the former's lack of attenuation and the purity of the signal it carries.

19. Fiber-optic cable transmissions are not subject to electrical
    _____.

20. Baseband systems use _____ signaling over a single frequency.

21. Each device on a _____ network can transmit and receive
    at the same time.

22. Broadband systems use _____ signaling and a range of frequencies.

23. With _____ transmission, the signal flow is unidirectional.

24. Wall-mounted _____ connected to the wired LAN maintain
    and manage radio contact between portable devices and the cabled LAN.

25. Broadband optical telepoint transmission is a type of _____ network
    capable of handling high-quality multimedia requirements.

26. A component called a wireless _____ offers an easy way to link
    buildings without using cable.

27. Spread-spectrum radio broadcasts signals over a range of
    _____.

28. Point-to-point transmission involves wireless _____ data transfer.

29. In LANs, a transceiver—sometimes called an _____
    _____ —broadcasts and receives signals to and from the
    surrounding computers.

30. Wireless _____ LANs use telephone carriers and public services to
    transmit and receive signals.

31. CDPD uses the same technology and some of the same systems as
    _____ telephones.

32. Currently, the most widely used long-distance transmission method in the
    United States is _____.

33. The network interface card converts serial data from the computer into parallel
    data for transmission over the network cable.   True   False

34. The 16-bit and 32-bit widths are currently the two most popular bus widths.
    True   False

35. To help move data onto the network cable, the computer assigns all of its
    memory to the NIC.   True   False

36. Data is temporarily held in the NIC's transceiver, which acts as a buffer.
    True   False

37. Both sending and receiving NICs must agree on transmission speeds.
    True   False

38. In an 80386 computer, COM1 typically uses IRQ _____ and LPT1 typically
    uses IRQ _____.

39. IRQ lines are assigned different levels of _____ so that the CPU can
    determine how important the request is.

40. The recommended setting for a NIC is IRQ _____.

41. Every device on the computer must use a _____ IRQ line.

42. Each hardware device needs a default _____ ___/___ _____ number.

43. Choosing the appropriate transceiver on a NIC that can use either an external
    or an on-board transceiver is usually done with _____.

44. ISA was the standard bus until Compaq and other manufacturers developed
    the _____ bus.

45. The _____ _____ bus functions as either a 16-bit or a 32-bit
    bus and can be driven independently by multiple bus master processors.

46. Telephone wire uses an _____ connector.

47. Plug and Play refers to both a design philosophy and a set of personal-
    computer _____ specifications.

C H A P T E R   3

Understanding Network Architecture

About This Chapter

In the first two chapters, we established the foundation for exploring the physical aspects of a network. We learned about cables and the various methods of connecting them so that we can share data. Now that we can physically link computers, we need to learn how to gain access to the wires and cables.

In this chapter, we explore the three principal methods used to access the wires. The first method, called contention, is based on the principle of "first come, first served." The second method, token passing, is based on the principle of waiting to take turns. The third method, demand priority, is relatively new and is based on prioritizing access to the network. Later in the chapter, we continue our discussion of network architecture by examining the data itself and how it is put together before it is sent on its way. Last, we examine the most common network systems (Ethernet, Token Ring, AppleTalk, and ArcNet).

Before You Begin

This chapter continues to build on the lessons presented in chapters 1 and 2. You are expected to be familiar with the concepts of topology, network cabling, and network interface cards discussed in those chapters.

Lesson 1: Access Methods

In networking, to access a resource is to be able to use that resource. This lesson introduces the role of access methods in putting data on a network cable. It focuses on three major access methods: carrier-sense multiple-access methods, token passing, and demand priority.

After this lesson, you will be able to:

- Define the major access methods.
- Describe a primary feature of each of the major access methods:
    - Carrier-sense multiple-access with collision detection (CSMA/CD)
    - Carrier-sense multiple-access with collision avoidance (CSMA/CA)
    - Token passing
    - Demand priority

Estimated lesson time: 55 minutes

The Function of Access Methods

The set of rules that defines how a computer puts data onto the network cable and takes data from the cable is called an *access method*. Once data is moving on the network, access methods help to regulate the flow of network traffic.

Traffic Control on the Cable

To understand traffic on a computer network, it helps to use an analogy. A network is in some ways like a railroad track, along which several trains run. The track is interspersed with occasional railway stations. When a train is on the track, all other trains must abide by a procedure that governs how and when they enter the flow of traffic. Without such a procedure, entering trains would collide with the one already on the track.

There are important differences between a railroad system and a computer network, however. On a network, all traffic appears to move simultaneously, without interruption. Actually, this appearance of simultaneity is an illusion; in reality, the computers take turns accessing the network for brief periods of time. The more significant difference arises from the higher speed at which network traffic moves.

Multiple computers must share access to the cable that connects them. However, if two computers were to put data onto the cable at the same time, the data packets from one computer would collide with the packets from the other computer, and both sets of data packets would be destroyed. Figure 3.1 shows what happens when two computers try to access the network at the same time.

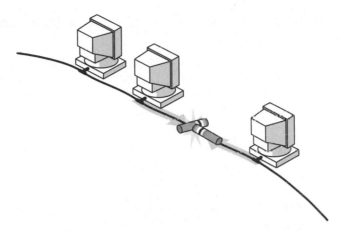

Figure 3.1 Collision occurs if two computers put data on the cable at the same time

If data is to be sent over the network from one user to another, or accessed from a server, there must be some way for the data to access the cable without running into other data. And the receiving computer must have reasonable assurance that the data has not been destroyed in a data collision during transmission.

Access methods need to be consistent in the way they handle data. If different computers were to use different access methods, the network would fail because some methods would dominate the cable.

Access methods prevent computers from gaining simultaneous access to the cable. By making sure that only one computer at a time can put data on the network cable, access methods ensure that the sending and receiving of network data is an orderly process.

 Run the **c03dem01**, **c03dem02**, and **c03dem03** videos located in the **Demos** folder on the CD accompanying this book to view a demonstration of how access methods help ensure orderly transmission of data on a network.

Major Access Methods

The three methods designed to prevent simultaneous use of the network media include:

- Carrier-sense multiple access methods (with collision detection or with collision avoidance).
- Token-passing methods that allow only a single opportunity to send data.
- Demand-priority methods.

Carrier-Sense Multiple Access with Collision Detection (CSMA/CD) Access Method

Using the method known as *carrier-sense multiple access with collision detection (CSMA/CD),* each computer on the network, including clients and servers, checks the cable for network traffic. Figure 3.2 illustrates when a computer can and cannot transmit data.

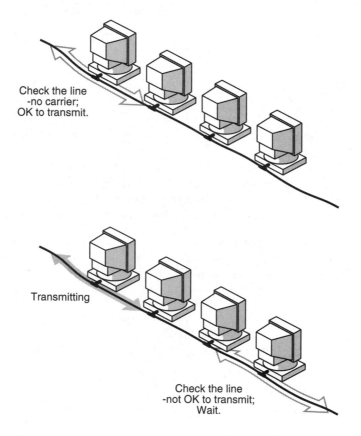

Figure 3.2   Computers can transmit data only if the cable is free

Only when a computer "senses" that the cable is free and that there is no traffic on the cable can it send data. Once the computer has transmitted data on the cable, no other computer can transmit data until the original data has reached its destination and the cable is free again. Remember, if two or more computers happen to send data at exactly the same time, there will be a data collision. When that happens, the two computers involved stop transmitting for a random period of time and then attempt to retransmit. Each computer determines its own waiting period; this reduces the chance that the computers will once again transmit simultaneously.

With these points in mind, the name of the access method—carrier-sense multiple access with collision detection (CSMA/CD)—makes sense. Computers listen to or "sense" the cable (carrier-sense). Commonly, many computers on the network attempt to transmit data (multiple access); each one first listens to detect any possible collisions. If a computer detects a possible collision, it waits for a random period of time before retransmitting (collision detection).

The collision-detection capability is the parameter that imposes a distance limitation on CSMA/CD. Due to attenuation—the weakening of a transmitted signal as it travels farther from its source, discussed in Chapter 2, "Basic Network Media"— the collision detection mechanism is not effective beyond 2500 meters (1.5 miles). Segments cannot sense signals beyond that distance and, therefore, might not be aware that a computer at the far end of a large network is transmitting. If more than one computer transmits data on the network at the same time, a data collision will take place that will corrupt the data.

Run the **c03dem04** and **c03dem05** videos located in the **Demos** folder on the CD accompanying this book to view a demonstration of the CSMA/CD access method.

Contention Method

CSMA/CD is known as a *contention* method because computers on the network contend, or compete, for an opportunity to send data.

This might seem like a cumbersome way to put data on the cable, but current implementations of CSMA/CD are so fast that users are not even aware they are using a contention access method.

Run the **c03dem06** video located in the **Demos** folder on the CD accompanying this book to view a demonstration of why CSMA/CD is considered a contention method.

CSMA/CD Considerations

The more computers there are on the network, the more network traffic there will be. With more traffic, collision avoidance and collisions tend to increase, which slows the network down, so CSMA/CD can be a slow-access method.

After each collision, both computers will have to try to retransmit their data. If the network is very busy, there is a chance that the attempts by both computers will result in collisions with packets from other computers on the network. If this happens, four computers (the two original computers and the two computers whose transmitted packets collided with the original computer's retransmitted packets) will have to attempt to retransmit. These proliferating retransmissions can slow the network to a near standstill.

The occurrence of this problem depends on the number of users attempting to use the network and which applications they are using. Database applications tend to put more traffic on the network than word-processing applications do.

Depending on the hardware components, the cabling, and the networking software, using a CSMA/CD network with many users running several database applications can be very frustrating because of heavy network traffic.

Carrier-Sense Multiple Access with Collision Avoidance (CSMA/CA) Access Method

Carrier-sense multiple access with collision avoidance (CSMA/CA) is the least popular of the three major access methods. In CSMA/CA, each computer signals its intent to transmit before it actually transmits data. In this way, computers sense when a collision might occur; this allows them to avoid transmission collisions. Unfortunately, broadcasting the intent to transmit data increases the amount of traffic on the cable and slows down network performance.

Run the **c03dem07** video located in the **Demos** folder on the CD accompanying this book to view a demonstration of the CSMA/CA access method.

Token-Passing Access Method

In the access method known as *token passing*, a special type of packet, called a token, circulates around a cable ring from computer to computer. When any computer on the ring needs to send data across the network, it must wait for a free token. When a free token is detected, the computer will take control of it if the computer has data to send.

The computer can now transmit data. Data is transmitted in frames, and additional information, such as addressing, is attached to the frame in the form of headers and trailers, discussed later in this chapter.

In Figure 3.3, the server is shown transmitting data. It takes control of the free token on the ring and sends data to the computer with the address 400080865402.

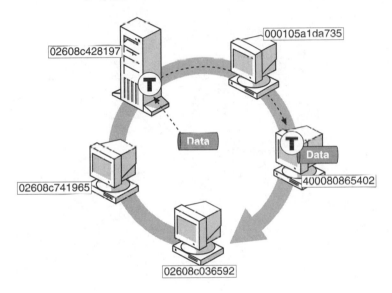

Figure 3.3   Token-passing access method

While the token is in use by one computer, other computers cannot transmit data. Because only one computer at a time can use the token, no contention and no collision take place, and no time is spent waiting for computers to resend tokens due to network traffic on the cable.

Run the **c03dem08**, **c03dem09**, **c03dem10**, **c03dem11**, and **c03dem12** videos located in the **Demos** folder on the CD accompanying this book to view demonstrations of the token-passing access method.

Demand Priority Access Method

Demand priority is a relatively new access method designed for the 100-Mbps Ethernet standard known as 100VG-AnyLAN. It has been sanctioned and standardized by the Institute of Electrical and Electronic Engineers (IEEE) in its 802.12 specification, which is discussed later in this chapter.

This access method is based on the fact that repeaters and end nodes are the two components that make up all 100VG-AnyLAN networks. Figure 3.4 shows a demand-priority network. The repeaters manage network access by doing round-robin searches for requests to send from all nodes on the network. The repeater, or hub, is responsible for noting all addresses, links, and end nodes and verifying that they are all functioning. According to the 100VG-AnyLAN definition, an end node can be a computer, bridge, router, or switch.

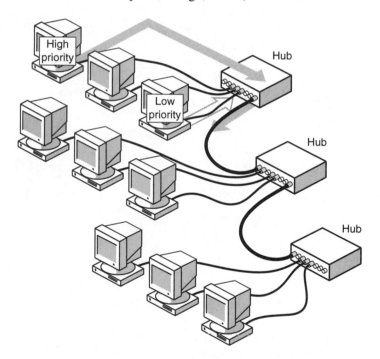

Figure 3.4   Star-bus network access method for 100VG-AnyLAN is demand priority

Run the **c03dem13** and **c03dem14** videos located in the **Demos** folder on the CD accompanying this book to view a demonstration of the demand-priority access method.

Demand-Priority Contention

As in CSMA/CD, two computers using the demand-priority access method can cause contention by transmitting at exactly the same time. However, with demand priority, it is possible to implement a scheme in which certain types of data will be given priority if there is contention. If the hub or repeater receives two requests at the same time, the highest priority request is serviced first. If the two requests are of the same priority, both requests are serviced by alternating between the two.

In a demand-priority network, computers can receive and transmit at the same time because of the cabling scheme defined for this access method. In this method, four pairs of wires are used, which enables quartet signaling, transmitting 25 MHz signals on each of the pairs of wire in the cable.

Demand-Priority Considerations

In a demand-priority network, there is communication only between the sending computer, the hub, and the destination computer. This is more efficient than CSMA/CD, which broadcasts transmissions to the entire network. In demand priority, each hub knows only about the end nodes and repeaters directly connected to it, whereas in a CSMA/CD environment, each hub knows the address of every node in the network.

Demand priority offers several advantages over CSMA/CD including:

- The use of four pairs of wires.

  By using four pairs of wires, computers can transmit and receive at the same time.

- Transmissions through the hub.

  Transmissions are not broadcast to all the other computers on the network. The computers do not contend on their own for access to the cable, but operate under the centralized control of the hub.

Access Methods Summary

Table 3.1 summarizes the major features of each access method.

Table 3.1   Features of Different Access Methods

Feature or function	CSMA/CD	CSMA/CA	Token passing	Demand priority
Type of communication	Broadcast-based	Broadcast-based	Token-based	Hub-based
Type of access method	Contention	Contention	Noncontention	Contention
Type of network	Ethernet	LocalTalk	Token Ring ArcNet	100VG-AnyLAN

Lesson Summary

The following points summarize the main elements of this lesson:

- Managing data on a network is a form of traffic control.

- The set of rules that governs how network traffic is controlled is called the access method.

- When using the CSMA/CD access method, a computer waits until the network is quiet and then transmits its data. If two computers transmit at the same time, the data will collide and have to be re-sent. If two data packets collide, both will be destroyed.

- When using the CSMA/CA access method, a computer transmits its intent to transmit before actually sending the data.

- When using the token-ring access method, each computer must wait to receive the token before it can transmit data. Only one computer at a time can use the token.

- When using the demand-priority access method, each computer communicates only with a hub. The hub then controls the flow of data.

Lesson 2: How Networks Send Data

At first, one might assume that data is sent as a continuous stream of ones and zeros from one computer to another. In fact, data is broken down into small, manageable packets, each wrapped with the essential information needed to get it from its source to the correct destination. This lesson introduces the concept of packets as the basic building blocks of network data communications.

After this lesson, you will be able to:

- Define the term "packet," including its function and components.
- Describe the contents and function of each packet component: header, data, and trailer.

Estimated lesson time: 30 minutes

The Function of Packets in Network Communications

Data usually exists as rather large files. However, networks cannot operate if computers put large amounts of data on the cable at the same time. As you see in Figure 3.5, a computer sending large amounts of data causes other computers to wait (increasing the frustration of the other users) while the data is being moved. This is not called "sharing"; it is called "monopolizing the network." There are two reasons why putting large chunks of data on the cable at one time slows down the network:

- Large amounts of data sent as one large unit tie up the network and make timely interaction and communications impossible because one computer is flooding the cable with data.
- The impact of retransmitting large units of data further multiplies network traffic.

These effects are minimized when the large data units are reformatted into smaller packages for better management of error correction in transmission. This way, only a small section of data is affected, and, therefore, only a small amount of data must be retransmitted, making it relatively easy to recover from the error.

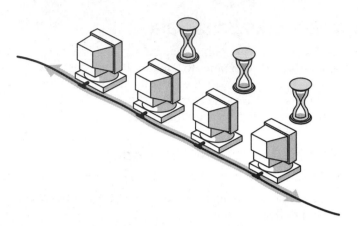

Figure 3.5   Large continuous streams of data slow down the network

In order for many users at once to transmit data quickly and easily across the network, the data must be broken into small, manageable chunks. This way, users each get their share of access to the network. These chunks are called *packets*, or frames. Although the terms "packet" and "frame" are often used interchangeably, there are some differences based on the type of network. This lesson uses the term "packet," meaning "a unit of information transmitted as a whole from one device to another on a network."

Note "Device" is a generic term for a computer subsystem. Printers, serial ports, and disk drives are often referred to as devices; such subsystems frequently require their own controlling software, called *device drivers*. Packets are the basic units of network communication. Figure 3.6 shows data that is being broken into packets. With data divided into packets, individual transmissions are speeded up so that every computer on the network has more opportunities to transmit and receive data. At the target (receiving) computer, the packets are collected and reassembled in the order of the original data.

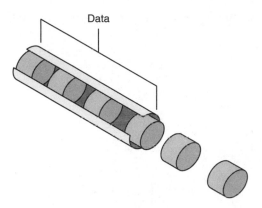

Figure 3.6   Breaking data into packets

When the network operating system at the sending computer breaks the data into packets, it adds special control information to each frame. This makes it possible to:

- Send the original, disassembled data in small chunks.
- Reassemble the data in the proper order when it reaches its destination.
- Check the data for errors after it has been reassembled.

Packet Structure

Packets can contain several types of data including:

- Information, such as messages or files.
- Certain types of computer control data and commands, such as service requests.
- Session control codes, such as error correction, that indicate the need for a retransmission.

Packet Components

All packets have certain components in common. These include:

- A source address that identifies the sending computer.
- The data that is intended for transmission.
- A destination address that identifies the recipient.
- Instructions that tell network components how to pass the data along.
- Information that tells the receiving computer how to connect the packet to other packets in order to reassemble the complete data package.
- Error-checking information to ensure that the data arrives intact.

Figure 3.7 shows these packet components grouped into three sections: header, data, and trailer.

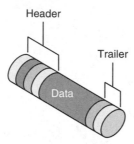

Figure 3.7 Packet components

Header

The header includes:

- An alert signal to indicate that the packet is being transmitted.
- The source address.
- The destination address.
- Clock information to synchronize transmission.

Data

This describes the actual data being sent. This part of the packet varies in size, depending on the network. The data section on most networks varies from 512 bytes—or 0.5 kilobytes (KB)—to 4 KB.

Because most original data strings are much longer than 4k, data must be broken into chunks small enough to be put into packets. It takes many packets to complete the transmission of a large file.

Trailer

The exact content of the trailer varies depending on the communication method, or *protocol*. However, the trailer usually contains an error-checking component called a *cyclical redundancy check (CRC)*. The CRC is a number produced by a mathematical calculation on the packet at its source. When the packet arrives at its destination, the calculation is made again. If the results of both calculations are the same, this indicates that the data in the packet has remained stable. If the calculation at the destination differs from the calculation at the source, this means the data has changed during the transmission. In that case, the CRC routine signals the source computer to retransmit the data.

Note A protocol is a set of rules or standards designed to enable computers to connect with one another and to exchange information with as little error as possible.

Different networks have differing formats for the packets and allow different-sized packets. The packet-size limits determine how many packets the network operating system can create from one large piece of data.

Example: Packets in Printing

The following example illustrates, step-by-step, how packets are used in network communications.

A large print job must be sent from a computer to a print server.

1. In Figure 3.8, the sending computer establishes a connection with the print server.

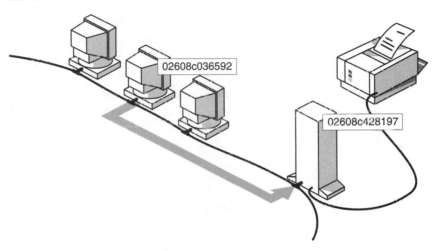

Figure 3.8 Establishing a connection with a print server

2. In Figure 3.9, the computer next breaks the large print job into packets. Each packet contains the destination address, the source address, the data, and control information.

Figure 3.9   Creating packets

3. In Figure 3.10, the network interface card (NIC) in each computer examines the receiver's address on all frames sent on its segment of the network. However, because each NIC has its own address, the card does not interrupt the computer until it detects a frame addressed specifically to it.

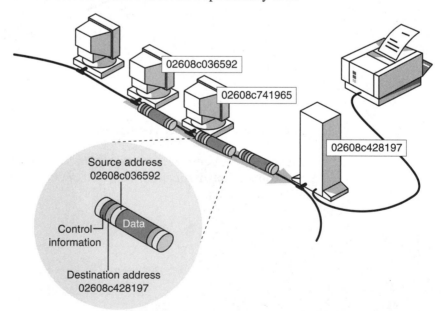

Figure 3.10   Examining the receiver's address

4. In Figure 3.11, the destination computer is the print server. The packets enter through the cable into the NIC.

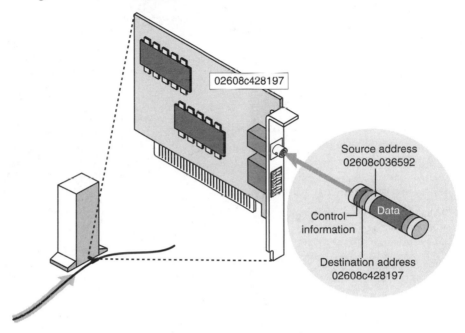

02608c428197

Source address
02608c036592

Control
information

Data

Destination address
02608c428197

Figure 3.11   Network interface card (NIC) accepts packets addressed to the print server

5. The network software processes the frame stored in the NIC's receive buffer. Sufficient processing power to receive and examine each incoming frame is built into the NIC. This means that no computer resources are used until the NIC identifies a frame addressed to itself.

6. In Figure 3.12, the network operating system in the receiving computer reassembles the packets back into the original text file and moves the file into the computer's memory. From there the file is sent to the printer.

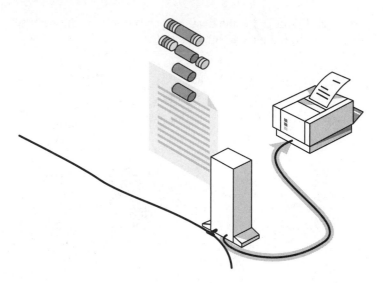

Figure 3.12   Reassembled packets sent to the printer

Lesson Summary

The following points summarize the main elements of this lesson:

- Data on a network is not sent in one continuous stream. It is divided up into smaller, more manageable packets. These packets, or chunks, of data make timely interaction and communications on a network possible.
- All packets have these basic components:
    - Source address
    - Data
    - Destination address
    - Instructions
    - Information with which to reassemble the data package
    - Error-checking information
- Packet components are grouped into three sections:
    - A header that contains clock information
    - The data
    - A trailer that contains the error-checking component

Lesson 3: Ethernet

This lesson introduces the Ethernet network architecture. Over the years, Ethernet has become the most popular media access method to the desktop computer and is used in both small and large network environments. Ethernet is a nonproprietary industry standard that has found wide acceptance by network hardware manufacturers. Problems related to using Ethernet hardware products from different hardware manufacturers in a single network are nearly nonexistent. This lesson presents an overview of the major Ethernet components, features, and functions.

After this lesson, you will be able to:

- Identify the standard Ethernet components.
- Describe the features of each IEEE Ethernet standard topology.
- Identify the cabling for a given IEEE Ethernet standard topology.
- Determine which Ethernet topology would be appropriate for a given site.

Estimated lesson time: 50 minutes

The Origin of Ethernet

In the late 1960s, the University of Hawaii developed a WAN called ALOHA. (A WAN extends LAN technology across a larger geographical area. For more information on WANs, see Chapter 1, "Introduction to Networking.") The university occupied a wide area and sought to connect computers that were spread throughout the campus. One of the key features of the university's network was its use of CSMA/CD as the access method.

This early network was the foundation for today's Ethernet architecture. In 1972, Robert Metcalfe and David Boggs invented a cabling and signaling scheme at the Xerox Palo Alto Research Center (PARC) and in 1975 introduced the first Ethernet product. The original version of Ethernet was designed as a system of 2.94 megabits per second (Mbps) to connect over 100 computers on a 1-kilometer (.62 miles) cable.

Xerox Ethernet was so successful that Xerox, Intel Corporation, and Digital Equipment Corporation drew up a standard for a 10-Mbps Ethernet. Today, the 10-Mbps Ethernet is one of several specifications describing methods for computers and data systems to connect and share cabling.

Ethernet Specifications

Although networking standards are not discussed in detail until Chapter 5, it is important for you to be aware of them at this point. In 1978, the International Organization for Standardization (ISO) released a set of specifications for connecting dissimilar devices. This set of standards is referred to as the *OSI reference model* (OSI stands for Open Systems Interconnection). The Ethernet specification performs the same functions as the OSI physical and data-link layers of this model. As you will see later, these specifications affect how hardware links, or passes information to and from, ISO standards. In the 1980s the IEEE published Project 802. This project generated standards for design and compatibility for hardware components that operated within the OSI physical and data-link layers. The standard that pertains to Ethernet is the IEEE 802.3 specification.

Ethernet Features

Ethernet is currently the most popular network architecture. Figure 3.13 shows a simple Ethernet bus network. Notice that the cable is terminated at both ends. This baseband architecture uses a bus topology, usually transmits at 10 Mbps, and relies on CSMA/CD to regulate traffic on the main cable segment.

The Ethernet media is passive, which means it requires no power source of its own and thus will not fail unless the media is physically cut or improperly terminated.

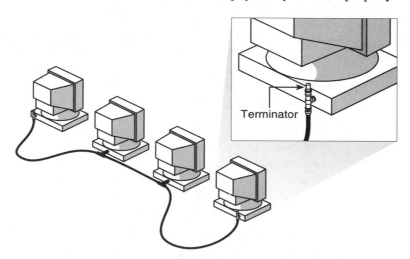

Figure 3.13   Simple Ethernet bus network terminated at both ends

Ethernet Basics

Table 3.2 summarizes Ethernet features:

Table 3.2   Summary of Ethernet

Feature	Description
Traditional topology	Linear bus
Other topologies	Star bus
Type of architecture	Baseband
Access method	CSMA/CD
Specification	IEEE 802.3
Transfer speed	10 Mbps or 100 Mbps
Cable type	Thicknet, thinnet, UTP

The Ethernet Frame Format

Ethernet breaks data down into packages in a format that is different from the packets used in other networks: Ethernet breaks data down into frames. (Remember that the terms "packet" and "frame" can be used interchangeably; in the context of Ethernet, the term "frame" is used.) A *frame* is a package of information transmitted as a single unit. An Ethernet frame can be between 64 and 1518 bytes long, but the Ethernet frame itself uses at least 18 bytes; therefore, the data in an Ethernet frame can be between 46 and 1500 bytes long. Every frame contains control information and follows the same basic organization.

For example, the Ethernet II frame, used for Transmission Control Protocol/ Internet Protocol (TCP/IP), which gets transmitted across the network, consists of the sections listed in Table 3.3 (TCP/IP has become the de facto standard for data transmission over networks, including the Internet):

Table 3.3   Components of an Ethernet II Frame

Frame field	Description
Preamble	Marks the start of the frame
Destination and source	The origin and destination addresses
Type	Used to identify the network layer protocol, usually either IP or IPX (Novell's Internetwork Packet Exchange)
Cyclical redundancy check (CRC)	Error-checking field to determine if the frame arrived without being corrupted

An illustration of an Ethernet frame is shown in Figure 3.14.

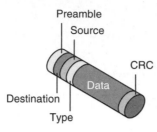

Figure 3.14   Sample Ethernet II frame

Ethernet networks include a variety of cabling and topology alternatives. The remaining sections of this lesson present these alternatives based on their IEEE specification.

The 10-Mbps IEEE Standards

This section looks at four 10 Mbps Ethernet topologies:

- 10BaseT
- 10Base2
- 10Base5
- 10BaseFL

10BaseT Standard

In 1990, the IEEE committee published the 802.3 specification for running Ethernet over twisted-pair wiring. The result, 10BaseT (10 Mbps, baseband, over twisted-pair cable), is an Ethernet network that typically uses unshielded twisted-pair (UTP) cable to connect computers. Usually, 10BaseT employs UTP, but shielded twisted-pair (STP) cabling will also work without changing any of the 10BaseT parameters.

Most networks of this type are configured in a star pattern, but internally they use a bus signaling system like other Ethernet configurations. Figure 3.15 shows a multiport hub used to extend an Ethernet LAN. Typically, the hub of a 10BaseT network serves as a multiport repeater and often is located in a wiring closet of the building. Each computer is located at the endpoint of a cable that is connected to the hub. Each computer has two pairs of wire; one pair is used to receive data, and one pair is used to transmit data.

The maximum length of a 10BaseT segment is 100 meters (328 feet). Repeaters can be used to extend this maximum cable length. The minimum cable length between computers is 2.5 meters (about 8 feet). A 10BaseT LAN will serve 1024 computers.

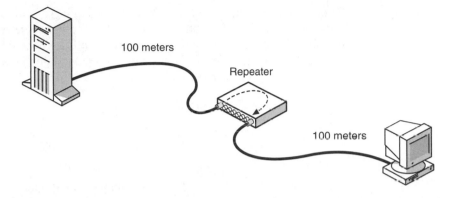

Figure 3.15   A multiport repeater (hub) can be used to extend an Ethernet LAN

Figure 3.16 shows how a 10BaseT solution provides the advantages of a star-wired topology. The UTP cable features data transmission at 10 Mbps. It is easy to make changes by moving a modular patch cord on the patch panel. A change at the patch panel will not affect other devices on the network; this differs from a traditional Ethernet bus network.

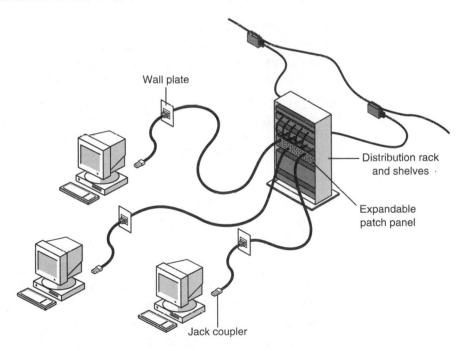

Figure 3.16   A patch panel makes moving computers easy

Patch panels should be tested for rates higher than 10 Mbps. The latest hubs can provide connections for both thick and thin Ethernet cable segments. In this implementation, it is also easy to convert thick Ethernet cable to 10BaseT cable by attaching a mini 10BaseT transceiver to the AUI port of any network interface card. Table 3.4 summarizes 10BaseT specifications:

Table 3.4   10BaseT Specifications Summary

Category	Notes
Cable	Category 3, 4, or 5 UTP.
Connectors	RJ-45 at cable ends.
Transceiver	Each computer needs one; some cards have built in transceivers.
Transceiver to hub distance	100 meters (328 feet) maximum.
Backbones for hubs	Coaxial or fiber-optic cable to join a larger LAN or to carry major traffic between smaller networks.
Total number of computers per LAN without connectivity components	1024 by specification.

10Base2 Standard

Another topology is 10Base2, given this name in the IEEE 802.3 specification because it transmits at 10 Mbps over a baseband wire and can carry a signal about two times 100 meters (the actual distance is 185 meters, or 607 feet).

This type of network uses thin coaxial cable, or thinnet, which has a maximum segment length of 185 meters (607 feet) and a minimum cable length of at least 0.5 meters (20 inches) between workstations. There is also a 30-computer maximum per 185-meter segment.

Thinnet cabling components include:

- BNC barrel connectors.
- BNC T connectors.
- BNC terminators.

Thinnet networks generally use a local bus topology. IEEE standards for thinnet do not allow a transceiver cable to be used from the bus T connector to a computer. Instead, a T connector fits directly on the NIC.

A BNC barrel connector may be used to connect thinnet cable segments together, thus extending a length of cable. For example, if you need a length of cable that is nine meters (30 feet) long, but all you have is a 7.5-meter (25-foot) length and a 1.5-meter (5-foot) length of thinnet cable, you can join the two cable segments together using a BNC barrel connector. However, the use of barrel connectors should be kept to a minimum because each connection in the cable reduces the signal quality and adds to the risk of cable separation and disconnection.

A thinnet network is an economical way to support a small department or workgroup. The cable used for this type of network is:

- Relatively inexpensive.
- Easy to install.
- Easy to configure.

A single thinnet network can support a maximum of 30 nodes (computers and repeaters) per cable segment, as per the IEEE 802.3 specification.

The 5-4-3 Rule

A thinnet network can combine as many as five cable segments connected by four repeaters; but only three segments can have stations attached. Thus, two segments are untapped and are often referred to as "inter-repeater links." This is known as the *5-4-3 rule*.

In Figure 3.17, there are five segments, four repeaters, and trunk segments 1, 2, and 5 are populated (have computers attached to them). Trunk segments 3 and 4 exist only to increase the total length of the network and to allow the computers on trunk segments 1 and 5 to be on the same network.

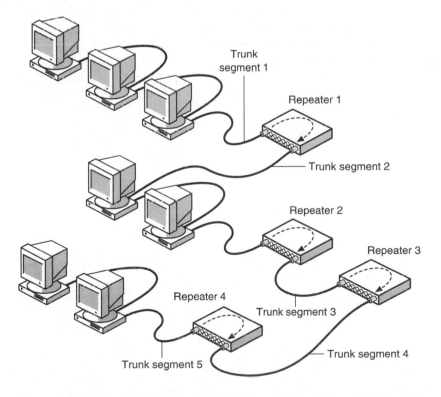

Figure 3.17   The thinnet 5-4-3 rule: 5 segments, 4 repeaters, and 3 populated segments

Because normal Ethernet limits are too confining for a large business, repeaters can be used to join Ethernet segments and extend the network to a total length of 925 meters (3035 feet). The following table summarizes 10Base2 specifications:

Table 3.5   10Base2 Specifications Summary

Category	Notes
Maximum segment length	185 meters (607 feet).
Connection to network interface card	BNC T connector.
Trunk segments and repeaters	Five segments can be joined using four repeaters.
Computers per segment	30 computers per segment by specification.
Segments that can have computers	Three of the five segments can be populated.
Maximum total network length	925 meters (3035 feet).

10Base5 Standard

The IEEE specification for this topology is 10 Mbps, baseband, and 500-meter (five 100-meter) segments. It is also called *standard Ethernet*.

This topology makes use of thick coaxial cable (see Figure 3.18), also known as thicknet. Thicknet generally uses a bus topology and can support as many as 100 nodes (stations, repeaters, and so on) per backbone segment. The backbone, or trunk segment, is the main cable from which transceiver cables are connected to stations and repeaters. The distances and tolerances for thicknet are greater than those for thinnet: a thicknet segment can be 500 meters (1640 feet) long for a total network length of 2500 meters (8200 feet).

Figure 3.18   Thicknet cable composition

The thicknet cabling components include:

- **Transceivers**   These are devices that can both transmit and receive, provide communications between the computer and the main LAN cable, and are located in the vampire taps attached to the cable.
- **Transceiver cables**   The transceiver cable (drop cable) connects the transceiver to the NIC.
- **DIX (or AUI) connectors**   These are the connectors on the transceiver cable.
- **N-series connectors, including N-series barrel connectors, and N-series terminators**   The thicknet components work in the same way as the thinnet components. Figure 3.19 shows a thicknet cable with a transceiver attached and a transceiver cable. It also shows the DIX or AUI connector on the transceiver cable.

Note "AUI," an acronym for attachment unit interface, is a 15-pin (DB-15) connector commonly used to connect a NIC to an Ethernet cable; AUIs and DIXs are discussed in Chapter 2, "Basic Network Media."

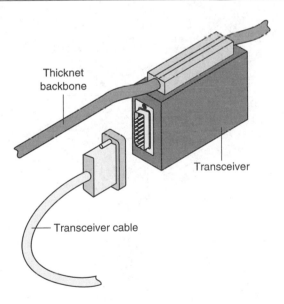

Thicknet backbone

Transceiver

Transceiver cable

Figure 3.19   Thicknet backbone with attached transceiver and cable

The 5-4-3 Rule in Thicknet

One thicknet Ethernet network can have a maximum of five backbone segments connected using repeaters (based on the IEEE 802.3 specification), of which up to three can accommodate computers. Figure 3.20 shows how the 5-4-3 rules are applied to thicknet. The length of the transceiver cables is not used to measure the distance supported on the thicknet cable; only the end-to-end length of the thicknet cable segment itself is used.

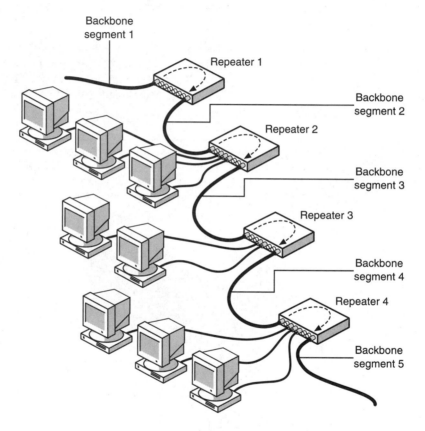

Figure 3.20   Thicknet 5-4-3 rule; 5 backbone segments, 4 repeaters, and 3 segments

Between connections, the minimum thicknet cable segment is 2.5 meters (about 8 feet). This measurement excludes transceiver cables. Thicknet was designed to support a backbone for a large department or an entire building. Table 3.6 summarizes 10Base5 specifications:

Table 3.6   10Base5 Specifications Summary

Category	Notes
Maximum segment length	500 meters (1640 feet).
Transceivers	Connected to the segment (in the tap).
Maximum computer-to-transceiver distance	50 meters (164 feet).
Minimum distance between transceivers	2.5 meters (8 feet).
Trunk segments and repeaters	Five segments can be joined using four repeaters.
Segments that can have computers	Three of the five segments can be populated.
Maximum total length of joined segments	2500 meters (8200 feet).
Maximum number of computers per segment	100 by specification.

Combining Thicknet and Thinnet Cable

It is common for larger networks to combine thick and thin Ethernet cable. Thicknet cable is good for backbones, while thinnet cable is used for branch segments. What this means is that the thicknet cable is the main cable covering the long distances. As described in Chapter 2, "Basic Network Media," thicknet cable has a larger copper core and can, therefore, carry signals for a longer distance than thinnet. The transceiver attaches to the thicknet cable, and the transceiver cable's AUI connector plugs into a repeater. The branching segments of thinnet plug into the repeater and connect the computers to the network.

10BaseFL Standard

The IEEE committee published a specification for running Ethernet over fiber-optic cable. The result, 10BaseFL (10Mbps, baseband, over fiber-optic cable) is an Ethernet network that typically uses fiber-optic cable to connect computers and repeaters.

The primary reason for using 10BaseFL is to accommodate long cable runs between repeaters, such as between buildings. The maximum distance for a 10BaseFL segment is 2000 meters (about 6500 feet).

The 100-Mbps IEEE Standards

New Ethernet standards are pushing the traditional Ethernet limits beyond the original 10 Mbps. These new capabilities are being developed to handle such high-bandwidth applications as:

- Computer-aided design (CAD).
- Computer-aided manufacturing (CAM).
- Video.
- Imaging and document storage.

Two Ethernet standards that can meet the increased demands are:

- 100BaseVG-AnyLAN Ethernet.
- 100BaseX Ethernet (Fast Ethernet).

Both 100BaseVG-AnyLAN and Fast Ethernet are about 5 to 10 times faster than standard Ethernet. They are also compatible with existing 10BaseT cabling systems. This means they allow for Plug and Play upgrades from existing 10BaseT installations.

100VG-AnyLAN Standard

The 100VG (Voice Grade) AnyLAN is an emerging networking technology that combines elements of both Ethernet and Token Ring architectures. Originally developed by Hewlett-Packard, it is currently being refined and ratified by the IEEE 802.12 committee. The 802.12 specification is a standard for transmitting 802.3 Ethernet frames and 802.5 Token Ring packets.

This technology goes by any of the following names, all of which refer to the same type of network:

- 100VG-AnyLAN
- 100BaseVG
- VG
- AnyLAN

Specifications

Some of the current 100VG-AnyLAN specifications include:

- A minimum data rate of 100 Mbps.
- The ability to support a cascaded star topology over Category 3, 4, and 5 twisted-pair and fiber-optic cable.
- The demand-priority access method that allows for two priority levels (low and high).
- The ability to support an option for filtering individually addressed frames at the hub to enhance privacy.
- Support for both Ethernet frames and Token Ring packets.

Topology

A 100VG-AnyLAN network is built on a star topology in which all computers are attached to a hub. Figure 3.21 shows a parent hub with five child hubs. Adding child hubs to the central hub can expand the network. The child hubs act as computers to their parent hubs. The parent hubs control transmission of computers attached to their children.

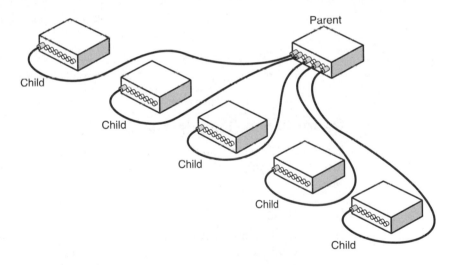

Figure 3.21   Parent hub with five attached child hubs

Considerations

This topology requires its own hubs and cards. Also, the cable distances of 100BaseVG are limited when compared to 10BaseVG and other implementations of Ethernet. The longest cable from the 100BaseVG hub to a computer cannot exceed 250 meters (about 820 feet). Extending this limit requires special equipment used to expand the size of a LAN. These cable-length limits mean that 100BaseVG will require more wiring closets than 10BaseVG.

100BaseX Ethernet Standard

This standard, sometimes called Fast Ethernet, is an extension of the existing Ethernet standard. It runs on UTP Category 5 data-grade cable and uses CSMA/CD in a star-wired bus topology, similar to 10BaseT where all cables are attached to a hub.

Media Specifications

100BaseX incorporates three media specifications:

- 100BaseT4 (4-pair Category 3, 4, or 5 UTP)
- 100BaseTX (2-pair Category 5 UTP or STP)
- 100BaseFX (2-strand fiber-optic cable)

These media are described further in Table 3.7:

Table 3.7   100BaseX Media Specifications

Value	Represents	Actual meaning
100	Transmission speed	100 Mbps
Base	Signal type	Baseband
T4	Cable type	Indicates twisted-pair cable using four telephone-grade pairs
TX	Cable type	Indicates twisted-pair cable using two data-grade pairs
FX	Cable type	Indicates fiber-optic link using two strands of fiber-optic cable

Performance Considerations

Ethernet architecture can use multiple communication protocols and can connect mixed computing environments such as Netware, UNIX, Windows, and Macintosh.

Segmentation

Ethernet performance can be improved by dividing a crowded segment into two less-populated segments and joining them with either a bridge or a router. Bridges and routers are discussed later in more detail in Chapter 7, "Elements of Network Connectivity." Figure 3.22 shows how a bridge is used to extend a network. This reduces traffic on each segment. Because fewer computers are attempting to transmit onto the segment, access time improves.

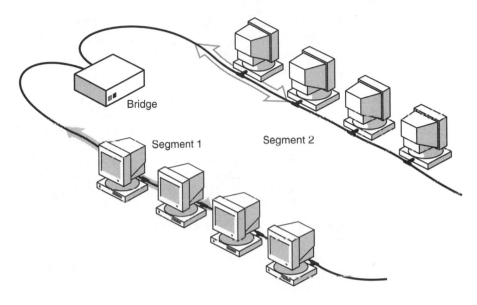

Figure 3.22   Using a bridge to segment a network and reduce network traffic

Consider dividing segments if large numbers of new users are joining the network or if new, high-bandwidth applications, such as database or video programs, are being added to the network.

Network Operating Systems on Ethernet

Ethernet will work with most popular network operating systems including:

- Microsoft Windows 95, Windows 98, and Windows 2000.
- Microsoft Windows NT Workstation and Windows NT Server.
- Microsoft Windows 2000 Professional and Windows 2000 Server.
- Microsoft LAN Manager.
- Microsoft Windows for Workgroups.
- Novell NetWare.
- IBM LAN Server.
- AppleShare.
- UNIX.

Lesson Summary

The following points summarize the main elements of this lesson:

- Ethernet is one of the most popular network architectures.
- Ethernet is governed by the specifications found in the OSI model physical layer and data-link layer, as well as IEEE 802.3.

Table 3.8 summarizes the specifications for Ethernet architecture discussed in this lesson. It outlines the minimum set of standards required to conform to IEEE specifications. A particular implementation of the network architecture may differ from the information in the table.

Table 3.8   Ethernet Specifications (IEEE 802.3)

	10Base2	10Base5	10BaseT
Topology	Bus	Bus	Star bus
Cable type	RG-58 (thinnet coaxial cable)	Thicknet; one-centi-meter (3/8-inch) shielded transceiver cable	Category 3, 4, or 5 unshielded twisted-pair cable
Connection to NIC	BNC T connector	DIX or AUI connector	RJ-45
Terminator resistance, Ω (ohms)	50	50	Not applicable
Impedance, Ω	50 ± 2	50 ± 2	85–115 unshielded twisted-pair; 135–165 shielded twisted-pair
Distance	0.5 meters between computers (23 inches)	2.5 meters (8 feet) between taps and maximum of 50 meters (164 feet) between the tap and the computer	100 meters (328 feet) betweenthe trans-ceiver (the computer) and the hub
Maximum cable segment length	185 meters (607 feet)	500 meters (1640 feet)	100 meters (328 feet)
Maximum connected segments	5 (using 4 repeaters); Only 3 segments can have computers connected.	5 (using 4 repeaters). Only 3 segments can have computers connected.	Not applicable
Maximum total network length	925 meters (3035 feet)	2460 meters (8000 feet)	Not applicable
Maximum computers per segment	30 (There can be a maximum of 1024 computers per network.)	100	1 (Each station has its own cable to the hub. There can be a maximum of 12 com-puters per hub and a maximum of 1024 transceivers per LAN without some type of connectivity.)

Lesson 4: Token Ring

This lesson introduces the Token Ring network architecture. The *Token Ring* architecture was developed in the mid-1980s by IBM. It is the preferred method of networking by IBM and is therefore found primarily in large IBM mini- and mainframe installations. Even though the popularity of Ethernet has decreased the market share for Token Ring, it is still an important player in the network market. Token Ring specifications are governed by the IEEE 802.5 standards, which are covered in more detail in Chapter 5, "Introducing Network Standards." This lesson presents an overview of the major Token Ring components, features, and functions.

After this lesson, you will be able to:

- Describe the features of a Token Ring network.
- Identify the major components of a Token Ring network.
- Determine the components needed to implement a Token Ring network at a given site.

Estimated lesson time: 25 minutes

Overview

IBM's version of Token Ring was introduced in 1984 for the entire range of IBM computers and computing environments including:

- Personal computers.
- Midrange computers.
- Mainframe computers and the Systems Network Architecture (SNA) environment (SNA is IBM's networking architecture).

The goal of IBM's version of Token Ring was to facilitate a simple wiring structure using twisted-pair cable that connects a computer to the network through a wall socket, with the main wiring located in a centralized location.

In 1985, the IBM Token Ring became an American National Standards Institute (ANSI)/IEEE standard. (ANSI is an organization that was formed in 1918 for the development and adoption of trade and communication standards in the United States; ANSI is the American representative of ISO.)

Token Ring Features

A Token Ring network is an implementation of IEEE standard 802.5. Their token-passing ring access method, more than their physical cable layout, distinguishes Token Ring networks from other networks.

Architecture

The architecture of a typical Token Ring network begins with a physical ring. However, in its IBM implementation, a star-wired ring, computers on the network are connected to a central hub. Figure 3.23 shows a logical ring and a physical star topology. The logical ring represents the token's path between computers. The actual physical ring of cable is in the hub. Users are part of a ring, but they connect to it through a hub.

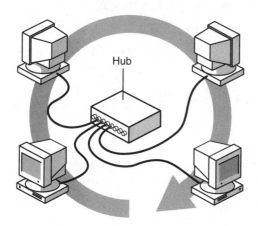

Figure 3.23   Logical ring, in which the physical ring is in the hub

Token Ring Basics

A Token Ring network includes the following features:

- Star-wired ring topology
- Token-passing access method
- Shielded and unshielded twisted-pair (IBM Types 1, 2, and 3) cabling
- Transfer rates of 4 and 16 Mbps
- Baseband transmission
- 802.5 specifications

Frame Formats

The basic format of a Token Ring data frame is shown in Figure 3.24 and described in Table 3.9 that follows. The sizes of the fields in Figure 3.24 are not representative of the sizes of the fields in an actual frame. The data field makes up the vast majority of the frame.

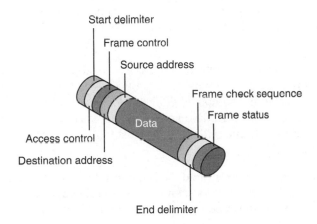

Figure 3.24 Token Ring data frame

Table 3.9   Components of a Token Ring Frame

Frame field	Description
Start delimiter	Indicates start of the frame
Access control	Indicates the frame's priority and whether it is a token or a data frame
Frame control	Contains either Media Access Control information for all computers or "end station" information for only one computer
Destination address	Indicates the address of the computer to receive the frame
Source address	Indicates the computer that sent the frame
Information, or data	Contains the data being sent
Frame check sequence	Contains CRC error-checking information
End delimiter	Indicates the end of the frame
Frame status	Tells whether the frame was recognized, copied, or whether the destination address was available

How Token Ring Networking Works

When the first Token Ring computer comes online, the network generates a token. The token is a predetermined formation of bits (a stream of data) that permits a computer to put data on the cables. The token travels around the ring polling each computer until one of the computers signals that it wants to transmit data and takes control of the token. A computer cannot transmit unless it has possession of the token; while the token is in use by a computer, no other computer can transmit data.

After the computer captures the token, it sends a data frame (such as the one shown in Figure 3.25) out on the network. The frame proceeds around the ring until it reaches the computer with the address that matches the destination address in the frame. The destination computer copies the frame into its receive buffer and marks the frame in the frame status field to indicate that the information was received.

The frame continues around the ring until it arrives at the sending computer, where the transmission is acknowledged as successful. The sending computer then removes the frame from the ring and transmits a new token back on the ring.

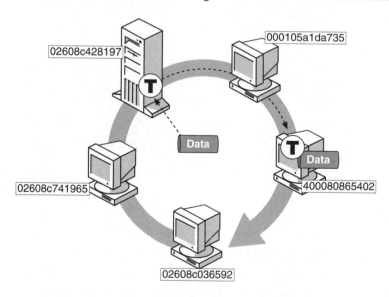

Figure 3.25   Clockwise flow of the token around the logical ring

Only one token at a time can be active on the network, and the token can travel in only one direction around the ring.

Note Does the token flow clockwise or counterclockwise? The answer is that it doesn't really matter. The direction taken depends on hardware connections. Logically, you can make the token travel in any direction or order you wish. The designers of hubs determine the order in which each port is addressed, and you determine the order in which computers are connected to the hub. The IEEE 802.5 standard says clockwise, and the IBM publication SC30-3374, section 3, says counterclockwise.

Token passing is deterministic, which means that a computer cannot force its way on to the network as it can in a CSMA/CD environment. If the token is available, the computer can use it to send data. Each computer acts as a unidirectional repeater, regenerates the token, and passes it along.

Monitoring the System

The first computer to come online is assigned by the Token Ring system to monitor network activity. The monitoring computer makes sure that frames are being delivered and received correctly. It does this by checking for frames that have circulated the ring more than once and ensuring that only one token is on the network at a time.

The process of monitoring is called *beaconing*. The active monitor sends out a beacon announcement every seven seconds. The beacon is passed from computer to computer throughout the entire ring. If a station does not receive an expected announcement from its upstream neighbor, it attempts to notify the network of the lack of contact. It sends a message that includes its address, the address of the neighbor that did not announce, and the type of beacon. From this information, the ring attempts to diagnose the problem and make a repair without disrupting the entire network. If it is unable to complete the reconfiguration automatically, manual intervention is required.

Recognizing a Computer

When a new computer comes online on the network, the Token Ring system initializes it so that it can become part of the ring. This initialization includes:

- Checking for duplicate addresses.

- Notifying other computers on the network of its existence.

Hardware Components

Hardware for Token Ring networks is centered on the hub, which houses the actual ring. A Token Ring network can have multiple hubs, as described later in this lesson. STP or UTP cabling connects the computers to the hubs; patch cables can further extend the connections. Fiber-optic cable, introduced in Chapter 2, "Basic Network Media," is especially well suited to Token Ring networks. Together with repeaters, fiber-optic cable can greatly extend the range of Token Ring networks. Cabling is joined to the components with four kinds of connectors, discussed later in this section. Other Token Ring hardware includes media filters, patch panels, and network interface cards.

The Hub

In a Token Ring network, the hub is known by several names that all mean the same thing. These include:

- MAU (Multistation Access Unit).
- MSAU (MultiStation Access Unit).
- SMAU (stands for Smart Multistation Access Unit).

Cables attach the individual clients and servers to the MSAU, which works like other passive hubs. Figure 3.26 shows a hub in which the internal wiring circulates the token in a clockwise direction. The internal ring automatically converts to an external ring at each connection point when a computer is connected.

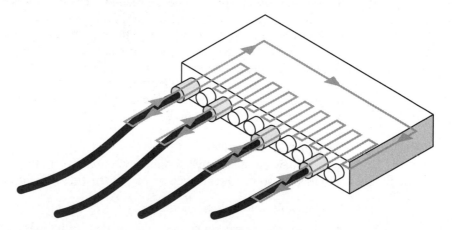

Figure 3.26   Hub showing the internal ring and clockwise token path

Hub Capacity

An IBM MSAU has 10 connection ports. It can connect up to eight computers. However, a Token Ring network is not limited to one ring (hub). Each ring can have up to 33 hubs.

Each MSAU-based network can support as many as 72 computers that use unshielded wire or up to 260 computers that use shielded wire.

Other vendors offer hubs with more capacity; the capacity depends on the vendor and the hub model.

When one Token Ring is full—that is, when every port on an MSAU has a computer connected to it—adding another ring (MSAU) can enlarge the network.

The only rule that must be followed is that each MSAU must be connected in such a way so that it becomes part of the ring. Figure 3.27 shows 1, 2, and 3 MSAU connected and maintaining a logical ring. An MSAU's ring-in and ring-out connection points make use of patch cables to connect many MSAUs on top of each other while still forming a continuous ring inside the MSAUs.

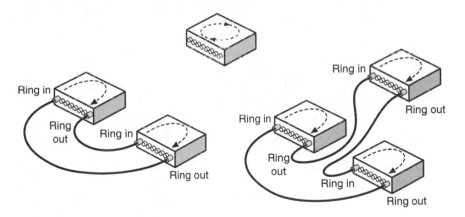

Figure 3.27   Adding hubs while maintaining the logical ring

Built-in Fault Tolerance

In a pure token-passing network, a computer that fails stops the token from continuing. This in turn brings down the network. MSAUs were designed to detect when a NIC fails, and to disconnect from it. This procedure bypasses the failed computer so that the token can continue on.

In IBM's MSAUs, bad MSAU connections or computers are automatically bypassed and disconnected from the ring. Therefore, a faulty computer or connection will not affect the rest of the Token Ring network.

Cabling

The STP or UTP cable to a hub connects computers on a Token Ring network. Figure 3.28 shows cable length limits for three types of cabling. Token Rings use IBM Type 1, 2, and 3 cabling. Most networks use IBM Cabling System Type 3 UTP cabling.

Each computer can be no more than 101 meters (330 feet) from an MSAU when connected with Type 1 cable. Each computer can be up to 100 meters (about 328 feet) from the MSAU when STP cabling is used, or 45 meters (about 148 feet) when UTP cabling is used. The minimum length for shielded or unshielded cable is 2.5 meters (about 8 feet).

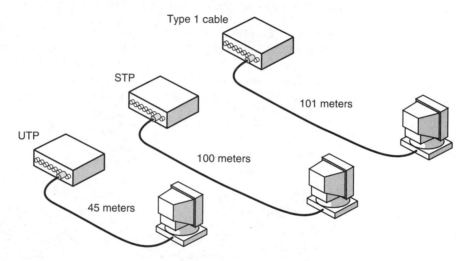

Figure 3.28   Maximum hub to computer distances on Type 1, STP, and UTP cables

According to IBM, the maximum cabling distance from an MSAU to a computer or a file server is 46 meters (150 feet) when Type 3 cabling is used. Some vendors, however, claim that data transmission can be reliable for up to 152 meters (500 feet) between an MSAU and a computer.

The maximum distance from one MSAU to another is limited to 152 meters (500 feet). Each single Token Ring can accommodate only 260 computers with STP cable and 72 computers with UTP cable.

Patch Cables

Patch cables extend the connection between a computer and an MSAU. They can also join two MSAUs together. In the IBM cabling system, these are Type 6 cables and can be any length up to 46 meters (150 feet). Patch cable will allow only 46 meters between a computer and an MSAU.

The IBM cabling system also specifies a Type 6 patch cable for:

- Increasing the length of Type 3 cables.
- Connecting computers to MSAUs directly.

Connectors

Token Ring networks usually join cables to components with the following types of connectors:

- Media interface connectors (MICs) for connecting Types 1 and 2 cable. These are IBM Type A connectors, known elsewhere as universal data connectors. They are neither male nor female; you can connect one to another by flipping either one over.
- RJ-45 telephone connectors (8-pin) for Type 3 cable.
- RJ-11 telephone connectors (4-pin) for Type 3 cable.
- Media filters to make the connection between the Token Ring NIC and a standard RJ-11/RJ-45 telephone jack (outlet).

Media Filters

Media filters are required in computers that use Type 3 telephone twisted-pair cabling, because they convert cable connectors and reduce line noise.

Patch Panels

A patch panel is used to organize cable that runs between a MSAU and a telephone punchdown block. (Patch panels are discussed further later in this chapter. A punchdown block is a kind of hardware that provides terminal connections for bare network cable ends.)

Repeaters

Using repeaters can increase all Token Ring cable distances. A repeater actively regenerates and retimes the Token Ring signal to extend distances between MSAUs on the network. Using one pair of repeaters, MSAUs can be located up to 365 meters (1200 feet) apart using Type 3 cable, or 730 meters (2400 feet) apart using Type 1 or 2 cable.

Network Interface Cards

Token Ring NICs are available in both 4-Mbps and 16-Mbps models. The 16-Mbps cards accommodate an increased frame length that requires fewer transmissions for the same amount of data.

Implementing Token Ring cards requires caution because a Token Ring network will run at only one of two possible speeds: 4 Mbps or 16 Mbps. If the network is a 4-Mbps network, the 16-Mbps cards can be used because they will revert back to 4-Mbps mode. A 16-Mbps network, however, will not accept the slower 4-Mbps cards because they cannot increase speed.

Although several manufacturers make Token Ring NICs and other Token Ring components, IBM currently sells the majority of them.

Fiber-Optic Cable

Because of the mix of data streaming (streaming is an undifferentiated, byte-by-byte flow of data), high speeds, and data traveling in one direction only, Token Ring networks are well suited to fiber-optic cable. Though more expensive, fiber-optic cable can greatly increase the range of a Token Ring network—up to 10 times what copper cabling allows.

The Future of Token Ring Networks

At the beginning of this lesson it was mentioned that Token Ring was losing market share to Ethernet. Even though Ethernet is more popular, token-ring technology is still active and growing. Many large companies are selecting TokenRing to support mission-critical applications. These networks are *bridged networks* (that is, connected by means of bridges) that carry protocols (see Chapter 6, "Defining Network Protocols," for more information) such as Systems Network Architecture (SNA), NetBIOS, Transmission Control Protocol/Internet Protocol (TCP/IP); and IPX. LAN-based applications such as electronic mail, software distribution, and imaging are driving the growth. Meeting the expansion needs of the large company is accomplished by adding new rings using bridges. Typically, each ring accommodates from 50 to 80 users. Token Ring users today face the following challenges:

- Complexities, manageability, cost, and space requirements for many two-port bridges
- Bridge congestion
- Segment congestion
- Upgrading to high-speed technologies

A recent and relatively new concept for Token Ring networks is the use of switches to provide high-performance, low-cost alternatives to using bridges and routers. The idea of switching is to move a device from one Token Ring to another electronically. These switches operate like an electronic patch panel. Hub vendors offer a variety of these new Token Ring switchers.

Lesson Summary

Table 3.10 summarizes the specifications for Token Ring architecture presented in this lesson. It outlines the minimum set of standards required to conform to IEEE specifications. A particular implementation of the network architecture might differ from the information in this table.

Table 3.10   Token Ring Specifications

IEEE specification	Token Ring
Topology	Star ring
Cable type	Shielded or unshielded twisted-pair cable
Terminator resistance, Ω (ohms)	Not applicable
Impedance, Ω	100–120 UTP, 150 STP
Maximum cable segment length	From 45 to 200 meters (about 148 to 656 feet), depends on cable type
Minimum length between computers	2.5 meters (about 8 feet)
Maximum connected segments	33 multistation access units (MSAUs)
Maximum computers per segment	Unshielded: 72 computers per hub; Shielded: 260 computers per hub

Lesson 5: AppleTalk and ArcNet

In lessons 3 and 4, we discussed the two most popular network architectures: Ethernet and Token Ring. Networking professionals also might encounter and be required to support two other architectures: AppleTalk and ArcNet. The AppleTalk architecture is used in the Apple Macintosh environment, while the ArcNet architecture is used in personal computer–based environments. Since the advent of Ethernet, the popularity of ArcNet has decreased.

After this lesson, you will be able to:

- Identify the components and features of AppleTalk.

- Identify the components and features of ArcNet.

Estimated lesson time: 40 minutes

The AppleTalk Environment

Apple Computer, Inc. introduced AppleTalk in 1983 as proprietary network architecture for small groups. Networking functions are built into Macintosh computers, which makes the AppleTalk network very simple to set up compared to other networks.

The primary terms used in the Apple environment can be confusing because they sound similar to terms used in other environments, but relate to different aspects of a network. The following aspects of Apple networking are addressed:

- AppleTalk
- LocalTalk
- AppleShare
- EtherTalk
- TokenTalk

AppleTalk

AppleTalk is the Apple network architecture and is included in the Macintosh operating system software. Figure 3.29 shows a typical AppleTalk network configuration. This means that network capabilities are built into every Macintosh. Appletalk Phase 1 is obsolete. AppleTalk Phase 2 is the current release of AppleTalk. The architecture is a collection of protocols that correspond to the OSI reference model. The OSI model is discussed in detail in Chapter 5, "Introducing Network Standards."

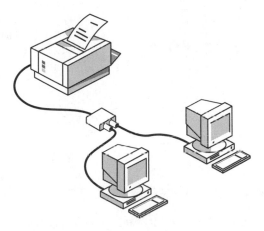

Figure 3.29   AppleTalk network

When a device attached to an AppleTalk network comes online, three things happen in the following order:

1. The device checks to see if it has stored an address from a previous networking session. If not, the device assigns itself an address chosen at random from a range of allowable addresses.

2. The device broadcasts the address to determine if any other device is using it.

3. If no other device is using the address, the device stores the address to use the next time the device comes online.

LocalTalk

AppleTalk networks are commonly referred to as LocalTalk networks. LocalTalk uses CSMA/CA as an access method in a bus or tree topology with shielded, twisted-pair cabling, but will also accept fiber-optic and UTP cable. LocalTalk is inexpensive because it is built into Macintosh hardware. But, because of its comparatively modest performance (the maximum communication data rate for LocalTalk is 230.4 Kbps), and because LocalTalk NICs for PC-compatible computers are obsolete, LocalTalk is not as widely used as Ethernet or Token Ring in large business networks. Figure 3.30 shows the LocalTalk cable and connectors.

LocalTalk also refers to the physical cabling components as well as to the data-link layer protocol. These include:

- Cables.
- Connector modules.
- Cable extenders.

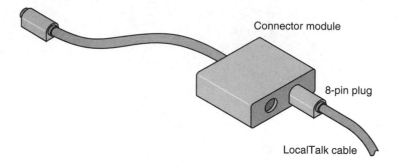

Figure 3.30   LocalTalk connector module with a LocalTalk cable

STP cabling is most often used in a bus or tree topology. A LocalTalk network supports a maximum of 32 devices.

Because of LocalTalk's limitations, manufacturers other than Apple are often preferred for cabling. Farallon PhoneNet, for example, can handle 254 devices. PhoneNet uses telephone cable and connectors and can be implemented as a bus network or plugged into a central wiring hub to form a star topology.

AppleShare

AppleShare is the file server on an AppleTalk network. The client software is included with every copy of the Apple operating system. There is also an AppleShare print server, which is a server-based print spooler.

Zones

Individual LocalTalk networks can be joined together into one larger network through the use of logical groupings called *zones*. Figure 3.31 shows three LocalTalk zones connected. Each connected subnetwork is identified by a zone name. Users in one LocalTalk network can access the services in another network simply by selecting that zone. This is helpful for accessing file servers in a variety of small networks, thereby expanding the size of the network. Networks using other architectures, such as Token Ring, can also be joined to an AppleTalk network in this way.

Conversely, working groups on a single LocalTalk network can be subdivided into zones to relieve congestion on a busy network. Each zone, for example, can have its own print server.

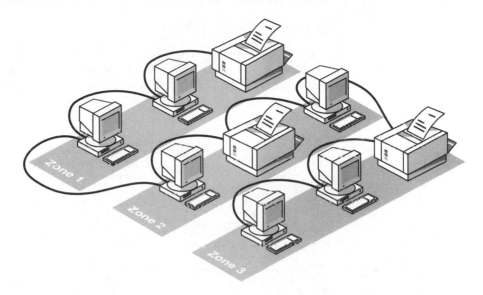

Figure 3.31   Three zones joined together to form a larger network

EtherTalk

EtherTalk allows the AppleTalk network protocols to run on Ethernet coaxial cable. As described in Chapter 2, "Basic Network Media," there are two types of coaxial cable: thinnet and thicknet.

The EtherTalk card allows a Macintosh computer to connect to an 802.3 Ethernet network. EtherTalk software is included with the card and is compatible with AppleTalk Phase 2.

TokenTalk

The TokenTalk card is an expansion card that allows a Macintosh to connect to an 802.5 Token Ring network. TokenTalk software is included with the card and is compatible with AppleTalk Phase 2.

AppleTalk Considerations

Computers from companies other than Apple can also use AppleTalk. These include:

- IBM personal computers and compatibles.
- IBM mainframe computers.
- Digital Equipment Corporation VAX computers.
- Some UNIX computers.

Apple welcomes third-party product development. As a result, the AppleTalk environment is populated by products from a variety of vendors.

The ArcNet Environment

Datapoint Corporation developed the Attached Resource Computer Network (ArcNet) in 1977. Figure 3.32 shows a star-wired ArcNet. It is a simple, inexpensive, flexible network architecture designed for workgroup-size networks. The first ArcNet cards were shipped in 1983.

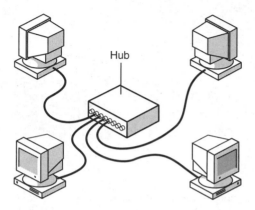

Figure 3.32   Simple star-wired ArcNet network

ArcNet technology predates IEEE Project 802 standards, but loosely maps to the 802.4 document. This specifies the standards for token-passing bus networks using broadband cable. An ArcNet network can have a star-bus or bus topology.

How ArcNet Works

ArcNet uses a token-passing access method in a star-bus topology (shown in Figure 3.33) passing data at 2.5 Mbps. ArcNet Plus, a successor to the original ArcNet, supports data transmission rates of 20 Mbps.

Because ArcNet is a token-passing architecture, a computer in an ArcNet network must have the token in order to transmit data. The token moves from one computer to the next according to the order in which they are connected to the hub, regardless of how they are physically located in the network environment. This means that the token moves from computer 1 to computer 2 (hub connections) in order, even if computer 1 is at one end of the building and computer 2 is at the other end of the building.

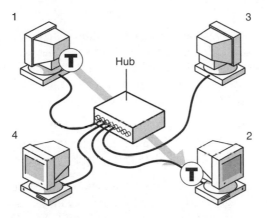

Figure 3.33   Token movement based on numerical order

The standard ArcNet packet (Figure 3.34) contains:

- A destination address.
- A source address.
- Up to 508 bytes of data (or 4096 bytes of data in ArcNet Plus).

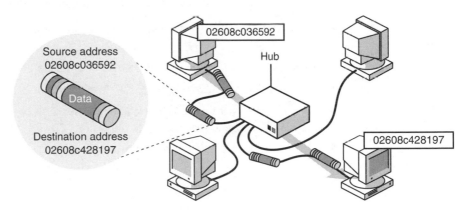

Figure 3.34   An ArcNet packet contains source and destination addresses

Hardware

Each computer is connected by cable to a hub. The hubs can be active, passive, or smart. As discussed in Chapter 1, Lesson 1: What is a Network?, passive hubs merely relay the signal. Active hubs can regenerate and relay signals. Smart hubs have all the features of active hubs and usually add diagnostic features such as reconfiguration detection and operator control-of-port connections.

The standard cabling used for ArcNet is 93-ohm RG-62 A/U, coaxial cable. ArcNet also supports twisted-pair and fiber-optic media. The distances between computers vary, depending on the cabling and the topology.

Using coaxial cable with BNC connectors and active hubs, a maximum cable distance of 610 meters (2000 feet) from a workstation to the hub can be achieved with a star topology. The maximum distance on a linear-bus segment is only 305 meters (1000 feet).

When unshielded twisted-pair cable with either RJ-11 or RJ-45 connectors is used, there is a maximum cable distance of 244 meters (800 feet) between devices on both star and bus topologies.

Lesson Summary

The following points summarize the main elements of this lesson:

- AppleTalk is the network architecture of the Apple (Macintosh) computer environment.
- AppleShare is the network operating system used by AppleTalk.
- CSMA/CA is the access method for AppleTalk.
- To use a Macintosh computer on an Ethernet with coaxial cable, you need an EtherTalk card and the EtherTalk software.
- A TokenTalk card and software allow a Macintosh to connect to a Token Ring.
- ArcNet is designed for workgroup-size networks.
- ArcNet uses a token-passing bus topology.

The following table summarizes ArcNet specifications.

Important The following table includes the minimum set of standards required to conform to IEEE specifications. A particular implementation of the ArcNet network architecture might differ from the information in this table.

Table 3.11   ArcNet Specifications

IEEE specification	ArcNet
Topology	Series of stars
Cable type	RG-62 or RG-59 (coaxial)
Terminator resistance, Ω (ohms)	Not applicable
Impedance, Ω	RG-62: 93 RG-59: 75
Maximum cable distance with coaxial cable, star topology	610 meters (2000 feet)
Maximum cable distance with coaxial cable, bus topology	305 meters (1000 feet)
Maximum cable distance with twisted-pair cable	244 meters (800 feet)
Minimum length between computers	Depends on cable
Maximum connected segments	Does not support connected segments
Maximum computers per segment	Depends on cable used

Exercise 3.1: Case Study Problem

Note Although this case study problem focuses on a particular architecture described in this chapter, you will need to draw on information presented in earlier chapters to formulate a solution.

Also, keep in mind that there is no single right answer to this problem: there are too many variables to take into account. In fact, it is entirely possible that you will find another solution that works better than the one we suggest in Appendix A!

A small public relations firm leases two groups of offices in Building A and Building G of a suburban office park. The business staff, including the human resources and accounting departments, has 12 people and is located in two offices in Building A. The creative staff, including copy writing, graphics, and production departments, with a total of 22 employees, is housed in Building G. Building A and Building G are about 600 meters (about 1970 feet) apart.

The business staff is networked with a four-year-old coaxial bus that ties their PC-compatible computers together in a peer-to-peer workgroup. The creative staff in Building G has a conglomeration of computers including Apple Macintoshes and PC-compatibles; they are not networked.

The owners of the company would like to network all the computers for the creative staff and connect the creative-staff network to the business-staff network. They would also like to standardize the type of network used in both buildings to keep troubleshooting issues to a minimum.

1. What kind of network should they install?

    Server-based _____

    Peer-to-peer _____

Tip This case study can be solved with several different combinations of components and cable.

---

2. What type of network should the company implement within the offices?

    Fiber-optic Ethernet _____

    Fiber-optic Token Ring _____

    Fiber-optic ArcNet _____

    Ethernet 10BaseT _____

    Ethernet 10Base2 _____

    Token Ring _____

    LocalTalk _____

    ArcNet _____

3. What type of network should the company install between the two buildings?

    Fiber-optic Ethernet _____

    Fiber-optic Token Ring _____

    Fiber-optic ArcNet _____

    Ethernet 10BaseT _____

    Ethernet 10Base2 _____

    Token Ring _____

    LocalTalk _____

    ArcNet _____

Exercise 3.2: Troubleshooting Problem

You will need to draw on information presented in chapters 1 and 2 as well as this one to solve this problem. Use your knowledge of network architectures to troubleshoot the situation described below and create a possible solution.

Background Information

You have a 500-node 10BaseT network. It started with 50 nodes five years ago, and you have been expanding it constantly since then. Recently the network has started to suffer from slow response time to the end users, and you have identified the network as the bottleneck. The vendor that you have been working with for the last two years recommends moving to 100BaseX. The vendor says that all you need to do is put the new 100BaseX NICs in your computers, replace your hubs with 100BaseX hubs, and you will be up and running.

The Problem

You and several technicians from your vendor spend an entire weekend installing the new cards and replacing hubs on your network. When the staff arrive at work on Monday morning, most are ecstatic with the performance of the new network, but about 50 staff members report that they cannot connect to the network. When you investigate further, you notice that all 50 are working at stations that had been cabled at least four or five years earlier.

1. List at least two things that could cause those nodes to fail to function.

   Note This list contains the most common errors that could be causing the problem, but these are not the only correct possibilities.

2. What could you do to resolve each of the possible causes you listed above?

Exercise 3.3: Network Planning Problem

Research has shown that about 90 percent of all new network installations use Ethernet 10BaseT with Category 5 UTP. Category 5 allows you to install a 10-Mbps solution now and upgrade it to a 100-Mbps solution later. However, despite its popularity, Ethernet 10BaseT may not be suitable for all situations.

Because the cost of labor accounts for most of the expense of cable installation, there is little difference in cost between using Category 3 UTP and Category 5 UTP cable. Most new installations use Category 5 because it supports transmission speeds of up to 100 Mbps.

The IBM Cabling System is used in a Token Ring environment. The star-wired topology makes moves, changes, and additions simple and easy. Figure 3.35 shows a patch panel with three computers connected. Moving a patch cable on the distribution panel can make changes.

Additionally, a number of minicomputer and mainframe systems have built-in Token Ring connections. Cable manufacturers other than IBM also make Token Ring cabling, of which UTP is the most popular.

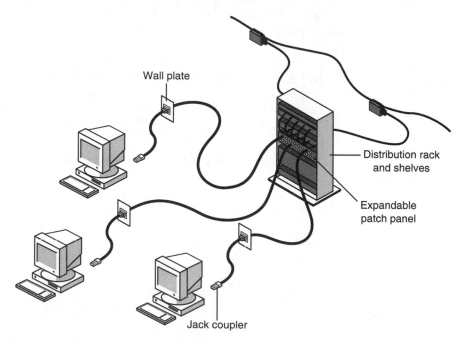

Figure 3.35   A patch panel makes moving computers easy

This UTP star-wired Token Ring network transmits data at 16 Mbps. Changes can be made easily by simply moving a modular patch cord on the patch panel. This network simplifies management by using an intelligent MSAU. Some intelligent MSAUs allow distances of up to 100 meters (330 feet) to each network lobe (the cable distance between the MSAU and a computer). This cabling scheme follows AT&T wiring standards, which make it fully compatible with all 10BaseT applications. It is also compatible with 4-Mbps Token Ring networks.

Because 10BaseT is currently the most popular implementation of the Ethernet architecture, it should be chosen unless there is a compelling reason to choose something else. Therefore, in a case where any architecture will work, 10BaseT should be given first consideration.

Make a check mark on the line next to the choice that applies to your site. To determine which type of architecture would be most appropriate for your site, simply total the number of check marks for each indicator. The indicator with the most check marks should be the first option you consider.

Note In the following questions, **10** indicates 10BaseT; **T** indicates Token Ring; **F** indicates fiber-optic; **C** indicates coaxial; **A** indicates that any will do; and **D** indicates that the appropriate choice depends on other factors.

1. Are ease of troubleshooting and the cost of long-term maintenance important?

   Yes _____ 10

   No _____ A

2. Are most of your computers situated within 100 meters (330 feet) of your wiring closet?

   Yes _____ 10

   No _____ A

3. Is ease of reconfiguration important?

   Yes _____ 10

   No _____ A

4. Do any members of your staff have experience with UTP cable?

   Yes _____ 10

   No _____ A, D

Note Even if no one on staff has experience with UTP cable, someone may have transferable experience with another type of cable such as coaxial, STP, or even fiber-optic cable.

5. Do you have existing coaxial cabling in your network?

   Yes _____ C, if existing cabling is extensive. Otherwise, switch to 10BaseT.

   No _____ A

6. Is your network very small (fewer than ten computers)?

   Yes _____ C

   No _____ A

7. Will your network be installed in an open area using cubicles to separate work areas?

   Yes _____ C, 10, D

   No _____ A

8. Do you need cable that is more resistant to EMI (electromagnetic interference) than UTP is?

   Yes _____ C, F, D

   No _____ A

9. Do you need longer cable runs than are supported by UTP?

   Yes _____ C, F, D

   No _____ A

10. Do you need to cable longer distances than those supported by copper media? For example, do you need to connect two buildings in a campus environment? Or do you need to connect two wiring closets in a single building that are more than 185 meters (607 feet) apart?

    Yes _____ F

    No _____ A, D

11. Do you need network cabling that is relatively secure from most eavesdropping or corporate intelligence-gathering equipment?

    Yes _____ F

    No _____ A

12. Does your network have any existing STP cabling?

    Yes _____ T

    No _____ A

Note While it is possible to use STP cabling with more than one architecture, it is most closely associated with token passing, specifically with IBM's Token Ring implementation. IBM refers to it as Type 1. It is much more expensive than UTP.

---

13. Do you have any equipment that needs Token Ring cards (such as an IBM mainframe, and so on)?

    Yes _____ T

    No _____ A

14. Do you have any equipment already installed that uses Token Ring?

    Yes _____ T

    No _____ A

15. Do you need a network cable system that has built-in redundancy?

    Yes _____ T

    No _____ A

16. Do you need cable that is more resistant to EMI than UTP is?

    Yes _____ T

    No _____ A

17. Do you have existing ArcNet infrastructure you need to connect to?

    Yes _____ Use ArcNet

    No _____ A

18. Do you have an existing LocalTalk network?

    Yes _____ Use LocalTalk or create a multivendor network (see Chapter 4, Lesson 5: Network Operating Systems in Multivendor Environments).

    No _____ A

19. Do you have Macintosh computers that do not have an Ethernet or Token Ring interface?

    Yes _____ Use LocalTalk or create a multivendor network.

    No _____ A

20. Based on the information generated in this exercise, your network architecture should be: _____

Chapter Summary

The following points summarize the key concepts in this chapter:

Access Methods

- Managing data on a network depends on traffic control. The set of rules that governs how network traffic is controlled is called the access method.
- When using the CSMA/CD access method, a computer waits until the network is quiet and then transmits its data. If two computers transmit at the same time, the data will collide and have to be re-sent. If two data packets collide, both will be destroyed.
- When using the CSMA/CA access method, a computer transmits its intent to transmit before actually sending the data.
- When using the token-ring access method, each computer must wait to receive a token before it can transmit data. Only one computer at a time can use the token.
- When using the demand-priority access method, each computer communicates only with a hub. The hub then controls the flow of data.

How Networks Send Data

- Data on a network is not sent in one continuous stream. It is divided up into smaller, more manageable packets.
- All packets include at least the source address, the data, and the destination address.
- Packets are broken into three components:
  - A header—Includes an alert signal, source and destination addresses, and clock information
  - The data—Contains the content being sent
  - A trailer—Contains the error-checking component

Ethernet

- Ethernet is one of the most popular network architectures.
- Ethernet is governed by the specifications found in the OSI model physical and data link layers as well as IEEE 802.3.

The following table summarizes the specifications for Ethernet architecture discussed in Lesson 3 of this chapter. It outlines the minimum set of standards required to conform to IEEE specifications. A particular implementation of the network architecture may differ from the information in this table.

Ethernet Specifications (IEEE 802.3)

	10Base2	10Base5	10BaseT
Topology	Bus	Bus	Star bus
Cable type	RG-58 (thinnet coaxial cable)	Thicknet; one-centimeter (3/8-inch) shielded transceiver cable	Category 3, 4, or 5 unshielded twisted-pair cable
Connection to NIC	BNC T connector	DIX or AUI connector	RJ-45
Terminator resistance, Ω (ohms)	50	50	Not applicable
Impedance, Ω	50 ± 2	50 ± 2	85–115 unshielded twisted-pair; 135–165 shielded twisted-pair
Distance	0.5 meters between computers (23 inches)	2.5 meters (8 feet) between taps and maximum of 50 meters (164 feet) between the tap and the computer	100 meters (328 feet) betweenthe transceiver (the computer) and the hub
Maximum cable segment length	185 meters (607 feet)	500 meters (1640 feet)	100 meters (328 feet)
Maximum connected segments	5 (using 4 repeaters); Only 3 segments can have computers connected.	5 (using 4 repeaters). Only 3 segments can have computers connected.	Not applicable
Maximum total network length	925 meters (3035 feet)	2460 meters (8000 feet)	Not applicable
Maximum computers per segment	30 (There can be a maximum of 1024 computers per network.)	100	1 (Each station has its own cable to the hub. There can be a maximum of 12 computers per hub and a maximum of 1024 transceivers per LAN without some type of connectivity.)

Token Ring

The following table summarizes the specifications for Token Ring architecture presented in Lesson 4 of this chapter. It outlines the minimum set of standards required to conform to IEEE specifications. A particular implementation of the network architecture might differ from the information in this table.

Token Ring Specifications

IEEE specification	Token Ring
Topology	Star ring
Cable type	Shielded or unshielded twisted-pair cable
Terminator resistance, Ω (ohms)	Not applicable
Impedance, Ω	100–120 UTP, 150 STP
Maximum cable segment length	From 45 to 200 meters (about 148 to 656 feet), depends on cable type
Minimum length between computers	2.5 meters (about 8 feet)
Maximum connected segments	33 multistation access units (MSAUs)
Maximum computers per segment	Unshielded: 72 computers per hub; Shielded: 260 computers per hub

AppleTalk and ArcNet

- AppleTalk is the network architecture of the Apple (Macintosh) computer environment.
- AppleShare is the operating system used by AppleTalk.
- CSMA/CA is the access method for AppleTalk.
- To use a Macintosh computer on an Ethernet with coaxial cable, you need an EtherTalk card and the EtherTalk software.
- A TokenTalk card and software allow a Macintosh computer to connect to a Token Ring.
- ArcNet is designed for workgroup-size networks.
- ArcNet uses a token-passing bus topology.

The following table summarizes ArcNet specifications.

Note The following table contains the minimum set of standards required to conform to IEEE specifications. A particular implementation of the ArcNet network architecture might differ from the information in this table.

ArcNet Specifications

IEEE specification	ArcNet
Topology	Series of stars
Cable type	RG-62 or RG-59 (coaxial)
Terminator resistance, Ω (ohms)	Not applicable
Impedance, Ω	RG-62: 93 RG-59: 75
Maximum cable distance with coaxial cable, star topology	610 meters (2000 feet)
Maximum cable distance with coaxial cable, bus topology	305 meters (1000 feet)
Maximum cable distance with twisted-pair cable	244 meters (800 feet)
Minimum length between computers	Depends on cable
Maximum connected segments	Does not support connected segments
Maximum computers per segment	Depends on cable used

Chapter Review

1. Access methods prevent _____ access to the cable.

2. With CSMA/CD, if there is data on the cable, no other computer may _____ until the data has reached its destination and the cable is clear again.

3. CSMA/CD is known as a _____ access method because computers on the network compete for an opportunity to send data.

4. With more traffic on a CSMA/CD network, _____ tend to increase, slowing the network down.

5. With the token-passing access method, only one computer at a time can use the token; therefore, there are no _____ or _____.

6. With the demand-priority access method, the _____ manage network access by doing round-robin searches for requests to send from all nodes.

7. In the demand-priority access method, transmissions are not _____ to all other computers on the network.

8. A token is a special type of _____ that circulates around a cable ring.

9. With data masses divided into _____, individual transmissions occur more frequently so that every computer on the network has more opportunities to transmit and receive data.

10. Packets may contain session-control codes, such as error correction, that indicate the need for a _____.

11. A packet's components are grouped into three sections: _____, data, and trailer.

12. In a packet, the header usually contains an error-checking component called a CRC. True   False

13. The structure of the packets is defined by the communication method, known as a protocol, used by the two computers. True   False

14. Every network interface card sees all packets sent on its segment, but it interrupts the computer only if the packet's address matches its individual address. True   False

15. The trailer of a packet contains the destination address. True   False

16. Typically, Ethernet is a baseband architecture that uses a _____ topology.

17. Ethernet relies on the _____ access method to regulate traffic on the main cable segment.

18. The maximum length of a 10BaseT segment is _____ meters.

19. The 10BaseT topology is an Ethernet network that uses _____ cable to connect stations.

20. Typically, the hub of a 10BaseT network serves as a _____ _____.

21. A thinnet network can combine as many as _____ cable segments connected by four repeaters, but only three segments can have stations attached.

22. Because single-segment 10Base2 Ethernet limits would be too confining for a large business, _____ can be used to join Ethernet segments and extend the network to a total length of 925 meters (about 3035 feet).

23. A 10Base5 topology is also referred to as _____.

24. Fast Ethernet is another name for the _____ topology.

25. Ethernet can use several communication _____ including TCP/IP.

26. The 100BaseTX topology runs on UTP Category _____ data-grade cable.

27. A 100BaseVG network is built on a _____ topology with all computers attached to a hub.

28. A Token Ring network is an implementation of IEEE standard _____.

29. In the IBM implementation of Token Ring, a star-wired ring, the actual physical ring of cable is in the _____.

30. In a Token Ring frame the Access Control field indicates whether the frame is a _____ frame or a _____ frame.

31. When a frame reaches the destination computer, that computer copies the frame into its _____ _____.

32. Token passing is _____ , meaning that a computer cannot force its way onto the network as it can in a CSMA/CD environment.

33. When a frame returns to its sending computer, that computer _____ the frame and puts a new token back on the ring.

34. Cables attach the individual clients and servers to the MSAU that works like other _____ hubs.

35. When an IBM Token Ring network is full, adding another _____ can enlarge the network.

36. MSAUs were designed to sense when a _____
_____ _____ fails and to disconnect from it.

37. Each single Token Ring can accommodate _____ computers using STP
cable.

38. Most Token Ring networks use IBM Cabling System Type _____ UTP cabling.

39. LocalTalk uses _____ as an access method in a bus or tree
topology.

40. When a device attached to an AppleTalk network comes online, the device
broadcasts an _____ to determine if any other device is using it.

41. A single LocalTalk network supports a maximum of _____ devices.

42. Single LocalTalk networks can be joined together into one larger network
through the use of _____.

43. ArcNet uses a token-passing access method in a _____-_____ topology.

44. An ArcNet token moves from one computer to the next according to the order
in which it is connected to the _____, regardless of how they
are placed on the network environment.

45. Each computer in an ArcNet network is connected by cable to a _____.

C H A P T E R 4

Survey of Network Operating Systems

About This Chapter

Chapter 3, "Understanding Network Architecture," introduced us to network architectures and access methods, and described how networks send data. In this chapter, we learn about network operating systems. Although our primary focus is on Novell and Microsoft network operating systems, we also take a look at AppleTalk, UNIX and Banyan Vines, and briefly survey peer-to-peer local area networks (LANs), including systems running Microsoft Windows for Workgroups, Windows 95 and 98, and IBM's OS/2.

Before You Begin

This chapter builds on earlier lessons; a review of Chapter 3 is especially recommended. However, some concepts presented here are more advanced than those in earlier chapters. You might find it helpful to progress more slowly through this chapter than earlier chapters. A good computer dictionary can also be a useful tool.

Lesson 1: Introduction to Network Operating Systems

Just as a computer cannot operate without a computer operating system, a network of computers cannot operate without a network operating system. Without a network operating system of some kind, individual computers cannot share resources, and other users cannot make use of those resources.

This lesson provides a general introduction to network operating systems (sometimes referred to as NOSs). It describes the basic features and functions of an NOS and contrasts these with the capabilities of a stand-alone operating system.

After this lesson, you will be able to:

- Identify essential NOS components.
- Define preemptive and nonpreemptive multitasking.
- Describe the elements of client software.
- Describe the elements of server software.
- Define network services.

Estimated lesson time: 30 minutes

Overview

Depending on a network operating system's manufacturer, a desktop computer's networking software can be either added to the computer's own operating system or integrated with it.

Novell's NetWare is the most familiar and popular example of an NOS in which the client computer's networking software is added on to its existing computer operating system. The desktop computer needs both operating systems in order to handle stand-alone and networking functions together.

Network operating system software is integrated into a number of popular operating systems including Windows 2000 Server/Windows 2000 Professional, Windows NT Server/Windows NT Workstation, Windows 98, Windows 95, and AppleTalk.

Each configuration—separate computer and network operating systems or an operating system combining the functions of both—has benefits and drawbacks. It is your job as a networking technician to determine which configuration best suits the needs of your network.

Coordinating Hardware and Software

A computer's operating system coordinates the interaction between the computer and the programs—or applications—it is running. It controls the allocation and use of hardware resources such as:

- Memory.
- CPU time.
- Disk space.
- Peripheral devices.

In a networking environment, servers provide resources to the network clients, and client network software makes these resources available to the client computer. The network and the client operating systems are coordinated so that all portions of the network function properly.

Multitasking

A *multitasking* operating system, as the name suggests, provides the means for a computer to process more than one task at a time. A true multitasking operating system can run as many tasks as there are processors. If there are more tasks than processors, the computer must arrange for the available processors to devote a certain amount of time to each task, alternating between tasks until all are completed. With this system, the computer appears to be working on several tasks at once.

There are two primary forms of multitasking:

- **Preemptive**   In preemptive multitasking, the operating system can take control of the processor without the task's cooperation.
- **Nonpreemptive (cooperative)**   In nonpreemptive multitasking, the task itself decides when to give up the processor. Programs written for nonpreemptive multitasking systems must include provisions for yielding control of the processor. No other program can run until the nonpreemptive program has given up control of the processor.

Because the interaction between the stand-alone operating system and the NOS is ongoing, a preemptive multitasking system offers certain advantages. For example, when the situation requires it, the preemptive system can shift CPU activity from a local task to a network task.

Software Components

For computer operating systems that do not include networking functions, network client software must be installed on top of the existing operating system. Other operating systems, such as Windows NT, integrate the network and the computer operating systems. While these integrated systems have some advantages, they do not preclude using other NOSs. When setting up multivendor network environments, it is important to consider the issue of *interoperability*. (Elements or components of computer operating systems are said to "interoperate" when they can function in different computer environments.) A NetWare server, for instance, can interoperate with other servers such as Windows NT, and users of Apple computers can interoperate with (that is, access resources on) both NetWare and Windows NT servers.

A network operating system such as the one shown in Figure 4.1:

- Ties together all computers and peripherals.
- Coordinates the functions of all computers and peripherals.
- Provides security by controlling access to data and peripherals.

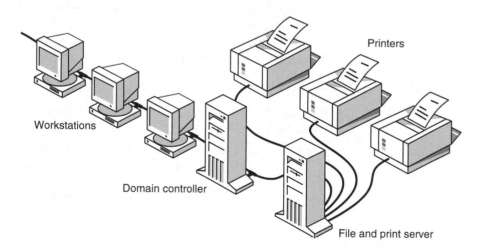

Figure 4.1   A network server ties the network together

Two major components of network software are:

- Network software that is installed on clients.
- Network software that is installed on servers.

Client Software

In a stand-alone system, when the user types a command that requests the computer to perform a task, the request goes over the computer's local bus to the computer's CPU (see Figure 4.2). For example, if you want to see a directory listing on one of the local hard disks, the CPU interprets and executes the request and then displays the results in a directory listing in the window.

Figure 4.2   Directory listing request on a local hard disk

In a network environment, however, when a user initiates a request to use a resource that exists on a server in another part of the network, the request has to be forwarded, or redirected, away from the local bus, out onto the network, and from there to the server with the requested resource. This forwarding is performed by the redirector.

The Redirector

A *redirector* processes forwarding requests. Depending on the networking software, this redirector is sometimes referred to as the "shell" or the "requester." The redirector is a small section of code in the NOS that:

- Intercepts requests in the computer.
- Determines if the requests should continue in the local computer's bus or be redirected over the network to another server.

Redirector activity originates in a client computer when the user issues a request for a network resource or service. Figure 4.3 shows how a redirector forwards requests to the network. The user's computer is referred to as a client because it is making a request of a server. The request is intercepted by the redirector and forwarded out onto the network.

The server processes the connection requested by client redirectors and gives them access to the resources they request. In other words, the server services— or fulfills—the request made by the client.

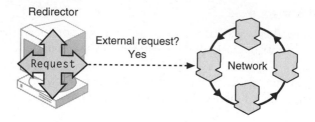

Figure 4.3 The redirector forwards requests for remote resources onto the network

Designators

If you need to access a shared directory, and you have permission to access it, your operating system will usually provide several choices for how to access the directory. For example, with Windows NT you could use Windows Explorer to connect to the network drive using the Network Neighborhood icon. You can also map to the drive. (Drive mapping is the assignment of a letter or name to a disk drive so that the operating system or network server can identify and locate it.) To map to the drive, right-click the directory icon from the Network Neighborhood; a dialog box will prompt you to assign an available letter of the alphabet as a drive designator, such as G:. Thereafter, you can refer to the shared directory on the remote computer as G:, and the redirector will locate it. The redirector also keeps track of which drive designators are associated with which network resources.

Peripherals

Redirectors can send requests to peripherals as well as to shared directories. Figure 4.4 depicts the redirector on a local computer sending a request to a print server. The request is redirected away from the originating computer and sent over the network to the target. In this case, the target is the print server for the requested printer.

With the redirector, LPT1 or COM1 can refer to network printers instead of local printers. The redirector will intercept any print job going to LPT1 and forward it out of the local machine to the specified network printer.

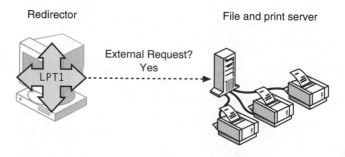

Figure 4.4 Request to print redirected out LPT1 to a printer on the network

Using the redirector, users don't need to be concerned with the actual location of data or peripherals, or with the complexities of making a connection. To access data on a network computer, for example, a user need only type the drive designator assigned to the location of the resource, and the redirector determines the actual routing.

Server Software

With server software, users at other machines, the client computers, can share the server's data and peripherals including printers, plotters, and directories.

In Figure 4.5, a user is requesting a directory listing on a shared remote hard disk. The request is forwarded by the redirector on to the network, where it is passed to the file and print server containing the shared directory. The request is granted, and the directory listing is provided.

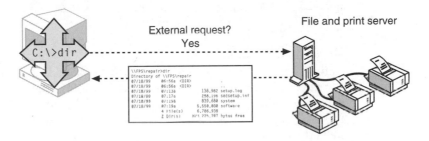

Figure 4.5   Directory-listing request on a remote hard drive

Resource Sharing

Sharing is the term used to describe resources made publicly available for access by anyone on the network. Most NOSs not only allow sharing, but also determine the degree of sharing. Options for sharing include:

- Allowing different users different levels of access to the resources.

- Coordinating access to resources to make sure that two users do not use the same resource at the same time.

For example, an office manager wants everyone on the network to be familiar with a certain document (file), so she shares the document. However, she controls access to the document by sharing it in such a way that:

- Some users will be able only to read it.

- Some users will be able to read it and make changes in it.

Managing Users

Network operating systems also allow a network administrator to determine which people, or groups of people, will be able to access network resources. A network administrator can use the NOS to:

- Create user privileges, tracked by the network operating system, that indicate who gets to use the network.
- Grant or deny user privileges on the network.
- Remove users from the list of users that the network operating system tracks.

To simplify the task of managing users in a large network, NOSs allow for the creation of user groups. By classifying individuals into groups, the administrator can assign privileges to the group. All group members have the same privileges, which have been assigned to the group as a whole. When a new user joins the network, the administrator can assign the new user to the appropriate group, with its accompanying rights and privileges.

Managing the Network

Some advanced NOSs include management tools to help administrators keep track of network behavior. If a problem develops on the network, management tools can detect signs of trouble and present these in a chart, or other, format. With these tools, the network manager can take corrective action before the problem halts the network.

Choosing a Network Operating System

In Chapter 1, Exercise 1.3, we looked at a network planning problem. We saw that network planning decisions must take into account the services and resources expected or required of the network. Those resources, and how they are shared and accessed, are determined by the network operating system.

In planning a network, the choice among network operating systems can be narrowed significantly if you first determine which network architecture—client/server or peer-to-peer—best meets your needs. This choice can often be made by deciding which kinds of security are called for. Server-based networking allows you to include security capabilities well beyond those available to a peer-to-peer network. If security is not an issue, a peer-to-peer networking environment might be appropriate.

After your network security needs have been identified, your next step is to determine the kinds of interoperability necessary for the network as a whole. Each NOS addresses interoperability in different ways, so you should keep your own interoperability needs in mind when evaluating each NOS. If your network choice is peer-to-peer, your options for security and interoperability will be diminished because of the limitations inherent in that architecture. If your network choice is server-based, further assessment is needed to determine whether interoperability will be dealt with as a service on the network server or as a client application on each networked computer. Server-based interoperability is easier to manage because, like other services, it is centrally located; client-based interoperability requires installation and configuration at each computer, making interoperability much more difficult to manage.

It is not uncommon to find both methods—a network service on the server and network client applications at each computer—in a single network. For example, a NetWare server is often implemented with a service for Apple computers, whereas Microsoft Windows network interoperability is achieved with a network client application at each personal computer.

When choosing a network operating system, first determine the networking services that will be required. Standard services include security, file sharing, printing and messaging; additional services include interoperability support for connections to other operating systems. For any given NOS, determine which interoperability services or networking clients are best implemented to suit your needs.

The major server-based network operating systems are Microsoft Windows NT 4 and Windows 2000 Server, and Novell NetWare 3.*x*, 4.*x* and 5.*x*. The principal peer-to-peer network operating systems are AppleTalk, Windows 95 and 98, and UNIX (including Linux and Solaris). The lessons that follow examine the major network operating systems to learn how each of them defines the networking environment.

 Run the **c04dem01** video located in the **Demos** folder on the CD accompanying this book to view an introductory discussion of network operating systems.

Lesson Checkup

1. In a networking environment, _____ provide resources to the network, and client network software makes these resources available to the client computer.

2. In _____ multitasking, the operating system can take control of the processor without the task's cooperation. In _____ multitasking, the task itself decides when to give up the processor.

3. A request to use a remote resource is forwarded out onto the network by the _____.

4. Most NOSs allow different users to gain different levels of access to _____ _____.

5. All group members have the same _____ as have been assigned to the group as a whole.

6. It is not uncommon to find, in a single network, both a network interoperability _____ on the server and network _____ applications at each computer.

Lesson Summary

The following points summarize the main elements of this lesson:

- Without a network operating system of some kind, individual computers cannot share resources, and other users cannot make use of those resources.

- A network operating system can be part of a computer operating system or a separate application that runs on top of the computer operating system.

- Windows NT is an example of an operating system that incorporates both computer and network operating systems in one system.

- By multitasking, computers can perform more than one task at a time.

- Multitasking can be either preemptive or nonpreemptive.

- Server software is the means by which an NOS provides services to other computers on a network.

- A redirector is used to forward client requests to the network.

- Using redirectors, users can access peripheral devices as if the devices were attached directly to the client computer.

- The first step in choosing a network operating system is to decide which network architecture—server-based or peer-to-peer—best meets your needs; this can often be accomplished by determining what level of security your network requires.

Lesson 2: Novell Operating Systems

In this lesson, we take a look at Novell's network operating systems, in particular NetWare, one of the most popular NOSs. Novell also offers client software that is designed to run on top of other computer operating systems.

After this lesson, you will be able to:

- Identify a NetWare operating system.
- Describe some of the features of NetWare.

Estimated lesson time: 20 minutes

Introduction to NetWare

The NetWare NOS consists of server and client applications. The client application is designed to run on a variety of client operating systems. The server application can be accessed by client users from computers running MS-DOS, Microsoft Windows (versions 3.x, 95, and 98, and Windows NT), OS/2, AppleTalk, or UNIX. NetWare is often the NOS of choice in mixed operating-system environments. In small networks, however, NetWare can be expensive and complicated for an inexperienced network technician to install and administer.

Version 3.2 of NetWare is a 32-bit NOS that supports Windows (versions 3.x, 95, and 98 and Windows NT), UNIX, Mac OS, and MS-DOS environments. With NetWare version 4.11, also called IntranetWare, Novell introduced its new NOS, Novell Directory Services (NDS). Version 5, the latest version to be released, addresses the integration of LANs, WANs, network applications, intranets, and the Internet, into a single global network.

Novell Directory Services (NDS) provides name services as well as security, routing, messaging, management, Web publishing, and file and print services. Using X.500 directory architecture, it organizes all network resources, including users, groups, printers, servers, and volumes. NDS also provides a single-point logon for the user; with it, a user can log on to any server on the network and have access to all their usual user rights and privileges.

Other NOSs provide client software for interoperability with NetWare servers. For example, Windows NT provides Gateway Services for NetWare (GSNW). With this service, a Windows NT server can obtain access to NetWare file and print services.

NetWare Services

With NetWare Client installed, any client workstation can take full advantage of the resources provided by a NetWare Server. The following is a summary of some of the more important services provided.

File Services

NetWare file services are part of the NDS database. NDS provides a single-point logon for users and allows users and administrators alike to view network resources in the same way. Depending on the client software installed, you can view the entire network in a format that is native to your workstation operating system. For example, a Microsoft Windows client can map a logical drive to any NetWare file server volume or directory, and the NetWare resources will appear as logical drives on their computer. These logical drives function just like any other drive in their computer.

Security

NetWare provides extensive security, including:

- **Logon security**   Provides authentication verification based on user name, passwords, and time and account restrictions.

- **Trustee rights**   Controls which directories and files a user can access and what the user is able to do with them.

- **Directory and file attributes**   Identifies the kinds of actions that can be carried out on a file (viewed, written to, copied, made shareable or nonshareable, or deleted).

Printing Services

Printing services are transparent (invisible) to the user of a client computer. Any print request from a client is redirected to the file server, where it is handed off to the print server and finally to the printer. (The same computer can serve as both file server and printer server.) You can share printer devices that are attached to the server, to a workstation, or directly to the network by means of the devices' own network interface card (NIC). NetWare print services can support up to 256 printers.

Sending Messages to Others

By using some simple commands, users can send a short message to other users on the network. Messages can be sent to groups as well as to individuals. If all the intended recipients are in the same group, address the message to the group rather than to each individual. Users can also disable or enable this command for their workstations. When a user disables the command, no broadcast messages will be received by that workstation.

Messages can also be handled through the Message Handling Service (MHS). MHS can be installed on any server and configured for a fully interconnected message infrastructure for e-mail distribution. MHS supports most popular e-mail programs.

Interoperability

Full NOS interoperability is not always possible. This is especially true when two dissimilar networks, such as NetWare and Windows NT, are being connected. A NetWare environment, centered on its directory services, and Windows NT, operating on a domain model, are inherently incompatible. To overcome this problem, Windows NT developed NWLink and GSNW, discussed earlier, that allow them to interoperate. These services allow a server on the Windows NT network to act as a gateway to the NetWare network. Any workstations on the Windows NT network can request resources or services available on the NetWare network, but they must make the request through the Windows NT server. The server will then act as a client on the NetWare network, passing requests between the two networks.

Lesson Checkup

1. A NetWare network consists of _____ and _____ applications.

2. NetWare is often the NOS of choice in _____ computer operating system environments.

3. With NetWare client software installed, computers can view NetWare resources as if they were _____ to the client.

4. NetWare _____ _____ can support up to 256 printers.

5. NetWare servers provide services to computers on a Windows NT network through the Windows NT server's _____ service.

Lesson Summary

The following points summarize the main elements of the lesson:

- NetWare client software is designed to be installed over a client computer's operating system.

- The NetWare NOS is designed to work in multivendor network environments.

- NetWare Directory Services (NDS) provide a database that maintains information about every resource on the network.

- NDS provides security, routing, messaging, management, Web publishing, file and print services, and name services.

- A NetWare network requires both NetWare Server software for the server and NetWare Client software for each workstation.

Lesson 3: Microsoft Network Operating Systems

In this lesson, we look at a network operating system that integrates the computer operating system with the NOS. This lesson introduces you to Microsoft Windows NT.

After this lesson, you will be able to:
- Identify a Windows NT operating system.
- Describe some of the features of Windows NT.

Estimated lesson time: 20 minutes

Introduction to Windows NT

Unlike the NetWare operating system, Windows NT combines the computer and network operating system in one. Windows NT Server configures a computer to provide server functions and resources to a network, and Windows NT Workstation provides the client functions of the network.

Windows NT operates on a domain model. A domain is a collection of computers that share a common database and security policy. Each domain has a unique name. Within each domain, one server must be designated as the Primary Domain Controller (PDC). This server maintains the directory services and authenticates any users that log on. The Windows NT directory services can be implemented in various ways by using the account and security database.

There are four different domain models to choose from.

- **Single-domain**   A single server maintains the security and accounts database.
- **Single-master**   A single master network may have several domains, but one is designated as the master and maintains the user-accounts database.
- **Multiple-master**   A multiple master network includes several domains, but the accounts database is maintained on more than one server. This model is designated for very large organizations.
- **Complete-trust**   A "complete trust" means there are several domains, but no single domain is designated as a master. All domains completely trust each other.

 Run the **c04dem02**, **c04dem03**, **c04dem04**, **c04dem05**, and **c04dem06** videos located in the **Demos** folder on the CD accompanying this book to view an illustrated overview of a domain-model NOS.

Windows NT Services

The following services are among the most important services Windows NT Server and Workstation provide to a network:

File Services

There are two approaches to sharing files on a Windows NT network. The first is based on simple file sharing, as on a peer-to-peer network. Any workstation or server can publicly share a directory to the network and set the attributes of the data (No Access, Read, Change, or Full Control). One big difference between Windows NT and Windows 95 and 98 operating systems is that in order to share a Windows NT resource, you must have administrative privileges. The next level of sharing takes full advantage of Windows NT's security features. You can assign directory-level and file-level permissions. This allows you to restrict access to specified individuals or groups. In order to take advantage of the more advanced file sharing, you will need to use the Windows NT file system (NTFS). During installation of Windows NT, you can choose between NTFS or a 16-bit FAT (MS-DOS) file system. You can install both systems on different hard drives or on different partitions of a single hard drive, but when the computer is running in MS-DOS mode, the NTFS directories will be unavailable. Any client not using NTFS can share to the network, but is limited to public sharing and cannot take advantage of the security features of NTFS.

Note Windows 95, version C, and Window 98 use a 32-bit file allocation table (FAT) file system. Windows NT is not compatible with 32-bit FAT. Windows NT cannot be installed on a 32-bit FAT system and will not recognize any files existing on a 32-bit FAT partition.

Security

Like any major NOS, Windows NT provides security for any resource on the network. A Windows NT network domain server maintains all the account records, and manages permissions and user rights. In order to access any resource on the network, a user must have rights to complete a task and the permission to use the resource.

Printing

In a Windows NT network, any client or server can function as a print server. By sharing a printer to the network, it becomes available to anyone on the network (subject to the rules of sharing). When installing a printer, you will first be asked whether or not the printer will be designated as a local printer (My Computer) or a network printer. If you choose the network printer, a dialog box will appear, listing all the available network printers. All you need to do is select the one you want to use. Remember that you can install more than one printer to a machine.

Also, if you are installing a local printer, you will be asked if you want to share the printer to the network for others to use.

Network Services

Windows NT provides several services to help facilitate a smooth-running network. The following list summarizes these services:

- **Messenger Service**   Monitors the network and receives pop-up messages for you.

- **Alerter Service**   Sends notifications that are received by the messenger service.

- **Browser Service**   Provides a list of servers available on domains and workgroups.

- **Workstation Service**   Runs on a workstation and is responsible for connections to servers. This is also referred to as the redirector.

- **Server Service**   Provides network access to the resources on a computer.

Interoperability

The NWLink network protocol is designed to make Windows NT compatible with NetWare. (Protocols are discussed in detail in Chapter 6, "Defining Network Protocols.") The following NetWare services are available:

- **Gateway Services for NetWare (GSNW)**   All Windows NT clients within a domain must contact a NetWare server through a single source. GSNW provides the gateway connection between a Windows NT domain and a NetWare server. This works well for low-volume situations but will cause a decrease in performance as the number of requests increases.

- **Client Services for NetWare (CSNW)**   This service enables a Windows NT Workstation to access file and print services on a NetWare server. It is included as part of GSNW.

- **File and Print Service for NetWare (FPNW)**   This utility allows NetWare clients to access Windows NT file and print services. This is not a part of the Windows NT package and must be purchased separately.

- **Directory Service Manager for NetWare (DSMN)**   This add-on utility integrates NetWare and Windows NT user and group account information. This is not a part of the Windows NT package and must be purchased separately.

- **Migration Tool for NetWare**   This tool is used by administrators who are converting from NetWare to Windows NT. It sends a NetWare server's account information to a Windows NT domain controller.

Lesson Checkup

1. In Windows NT networking, a _____ is a collection of computers that share a common database and security policy.

2. Each Windows NT domain has one _____ _____ _____.

3. Windows NT can provide directory- and file-level sharing on an _____ disk partition, but only directory-level sharing on a 16-bit _____ disk partition.

4. To set sharing on a Windows NT computer you must have _____ privileges.

5. NWLink is a network protocol that helps Windows NT and NetWare _____.

6. On a Windows NT network, any client or server can function as a print _____.

Lesson Summary

The following points summarize the main elements of this lesson:

- Windows NT is Microsoft's network operating system.
- Windows NT incorporates both the computer and the network operating system into one.
- Windows NT Server is the server module of the network.
- Windows NT Workstation is the client module of the network.
- Windows NT networks are designed to take advantage of the domain model in which all computers share a common security database. This information is stored on a server that is designated as the domain controller. Windows Server and Workstation will operate as part of a peer-to-peer network (share model), but you will not be able to take advantage of the additional security features provided in the domain model.
- Windows NT provides several utilities to provide interoperability between NetWare and Windows NT.

Lesson 4: Other Network Operating Systems

Although Windows NT and NetWare are by far the most popular network operating systems in the marketplace, they are by no means the only ones available. This lesson introduces you to some of the lesser-known operating systems, including AppleTalk, Unix, and Banyan Vines. We also take a look at using Windows for Workgroups, Windows 95 and Windows 98 configured in either peer-to-peer networks or as clients in other networks. Other choices exist in addition to those covered in this lesson; many software companies have produced peer-to-peer LAN software. Conducting an Internet search will help you locate these options.

After this lesson, you will be able to:

- Describe the circumstances in which Apple, Unix, or Banyan Vines is a suitable choice for a network operating system.
- Determine when to use a server-based or a peer-to-peer LAN.
- Describe at least two peer-to-peer LAN software packages.

Estimated lesson time: 20 minutes

AppleTalk Network Operating System

The Apple network operating system is seamlessly integrated into the operating system of every computer running the Mac OS. Its first incarnation, called LocalTalk, was slow by today's standards, but it brought networking to computer users who quickly made use of it. (A serial-port form of networking, LocalTalk is still part of the Apple NOS.)

The current implementation of AppleTalk supports high-speed, peer-to-peer networking capabilities among Apple computers as well as providing interoperability with other computer and network operating systems. This interoperability is not obviously part of the Apple operating system, however. Instead, users of computers other than Apple can connect to resources on an Apple NOS most easily by means of Apple IP, Apple's implementation of the TCP/IP networking protocol. (For more information on networking protocols, see Chapter 5, "Introducing Network Standards," and Chapter 6, "Defining Network Protocols.") Apple IP allows non-Apple users to access Apple resources, such as database files.

Computers that are part of the Apple NOS can connect to other networks through services that are supplied by the manufacturers of those other NOSs and that run on their network servers. Windows NT Server, Novell NetWare, and the Linux community all provide Apple interoperability services for their respective platforms; this allows networked Apple users to make use of resources on those network servers.

The AppleTalk form of directory services employs features known as "zones." These are logical groups of networks and resources. (An AppleTalk Phase 1 network consists of no more than one zone, while a Phase 2 network can have up to 255 zones. The two are incompatible, however, and cannot be easily supported on the same network wiring.) These zones provide a means of grouping network resources into functional units.

In the current desktop-computing environment, Apple and Windows users can benefit from a high degree of application software interoperability. Productivity suites—standard applications such as spreadsheets, databases, word processors, and e-mail, for example—are often able to exchange information directly. AppleShare makes it possible for Apple computer users to share those resources with other Apple users who have been given the appropriate permission to access them. With application-level and operating system interoperability, the Apple NOS can provide full networking capabilities to clients and to other NOSs.

UNIX LANs

UNIX is a general purpose, multitasking, multiuser operating system. Two popular versions (called "flavors" by UNIX users) are Linux and Sun Microsystem's Solaris. A UNIX system is usually made up of one central computer and multiple terminals for individual users. It is a self-contained network, designed specifically for large networks, but it does have some applications for personal computers. UNIX works well on a stand-alone computer and, because of its multitasking capabilities, it also performs well in a network environment.

UNIX is highly adaptable to the client/server environment. It can be transformed into a file server by installing file-server software. Then, as a UNIX host, it can respond to requests from workstations. The file-server software becomes just one more application being run by the multitasking computer.

A client of a UNIX host can be another UNIX computer or any other computer running MS-DOS, OS/2, Microsoft Windows, or Macintosh (System 7 or 8). A file redirector will enable the workstation to store and retrieve UNIX files as if they were in its native format.

Banyan Virtual Integrated Network Services (Vines)

Another networking system is the Banyan Virtual Integrated Network Services (Vines). Vines is a client/server-architecture NOS derived from Xerox Corporation's Xerox Network Systems (XNS) protocols.

The current version of Banyan Vines features messaging through integration with Banyan's Intelligent Messaging and BeyondMail software. The creation and management of network services is carried out through Banyan's latest version of StreetTalk Explorer. This interface works with Windows user profiles, allowing users' settings to follow them anywhere on the network. Some other features included in Vines are:

- Client support for Windows NT and Windows 95 and 98.
- Banyan Intranet Connect, which provides remote client access with a standard Web browser.
- Transmission Control Protocol/Internet Protocol (TCP/IP) server-to-server software.
- Banyan Networker, a family of network storage products.
- Multiprocessor support for up to four processors.

Peer-to-Peer LANs

In many offices and small businesses, there is a need for a simple peer-to-peer network. If security is not a concern and where 10 or fewer computers are located within a relatively small area, a peer-to-peer network might be the most economical option. In these networks, all workstations are equal and each can act as either a server or a client. In most cases, these networks will be sharing only files and printers. Most of the popular operating systems include the necessary software to configure a peer-to-peer network.

Windows for Workgroups

Windows for Workgroups (Windows 3.11) functions much like its predecessor, Windows 3.1, but includes a peer-to-peer NOS, an e-mail application, and an appointment-book application. A group of computers connected through workgroups can share printers and disk files. Only items designated as shares can be seen by other members. All other files and printers are hidden from all users except the local computer. When you share a disk directory or printer from a workstation, you give the shared resource a name to which others can refer. During the connection process, a drive letter is assigned to the shared directory and the redirector redirects the LPT port across the LAN to the correct printer.

Although Windows for Workgroups is still in use, it is unlikely that you will be called upon to install a new network based on this operating system. However, you should know how to incorporate an existing Windows for Workgroups network into a larger, more modern networking environment such as NetWare or Windows NT Server.

Windows 95 and 98

Windows 95 and 98 operating systems include software necessary to create a peer-to-peer network and enable sharing of printers and files.

Computers running Windows 95 or 98 will also work well as clients on Windows NT and NetWare LANs. You will have to install the respective client (requester) software. Note that users of Windows 95 and 98 cannot have the full benefit of Windows NT security features; those features require use of the NTFS file format, which is not compatible with Windows 95 or 98.

Warp Connect

Warp Connect combines OS/2 Warp and WIN-OS/2 peer-to-peer networking capabilities. It provides peer-to-peer and client-networking capabilities that are similar to those provided by Windows for Workgroups. With Warp Connect's built-in peer-to-peer capability, you can share applications, printers, modems, and files, without installing any special hardware.

Lesson Checkup

1. AppleTalk zones are _____ _____ of networks and network resources.

2. In a UNIX network, personal computers can be used as _____ terminals.

3. Banyan Vines can communicate with Windows NT using the _____ protocol.

4. Windows for Workgroups, Windows 95 and 98, MacOS, and OS/2 Warp incorporate _____ - _____ - _____ network operating systems.

Lesson Summary

The following points summarize the main elements of this lesson:

- Apple IP allows non-Apple users to access Apple resources such as database files.

- A UNIX computer can be used as a file server by installing file-server software.

- Banyan Vines is a network operating system based on the Xerox proprietary protocol.

- Banyan Vines is a server/client-based network operating system.

- Peer-to-peer LAN networking is popular for small offices in which maintaining network security is not an issue.

- Windows for Workgroups, Windows 95 and 98, and OS/2 Warp NOSs have built-in peer-to-peer LAN software.

Lesson 5: Network Operating Systems in Multivendor Environments

We have taken a look at the principal network operating systems from Novell and Microsoft. We have also briefly surveyed Apple, Banyan Vines, and UNIX systems. Typically, NOSs have to integrate hardware and software products manufactured by different vendors. This lesson presents an overview of the issues and problems involved in implementing a multivendor network.

After this lesson, you will be able to:

- Describe at least one way in which clients and servers can achieve interoperability.
- Describe how manufacturers integrate their products with those of other manufacturers.
- Determine which network operating system and redirector are appropriate for a given site.

Estimated lesson time: 25 minutes

The Multivendor Environment

Most networks today exist in multivendor environments. While such networks can pose challenges, they work well when properly planned and implemented.

The character of a network changes when software components manufactured by different vendors must operate on the same network. Problems can arise when the network is running more than one type of network operating system.

In order for a network to function properly in a heterogeneous computing environment, the server's operating system, the client's operating system, and the redirector must all be compatible. In a multivendor environment, it is necessary to find a common language in which all computers can communicate. For example, in the network shown in Figure 4.6, a Windows NT server is supporting three clients: one computer is running Microsoft Windows 95, another is running UNIX, and a third is running AppleTalk.

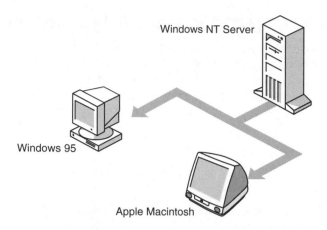

Windows NT Server

Windows 95

Apple Macintosh

Figure 4.6   Windows NT Server supporting clients from multiple vendors

Implementing Multivendor Solutions

Ensuring interoperability in multivendor environments can be carried out at either the server end (also referred to as the "back end") or the client end (also referred to as the "front end"). The choice you make depends on the vendors you are using.

Client Interoperability

In situations involving multiple NOSs, the key to establishing interoperability is the redirector. Just as you can use more than one telephone service provider when you communicate with different people, your computer can have more than one redirector to communicate over a network with different network servers.

Each redirector handles only the packets sent in the language or protocol that it can understand. If you know what your destination is and which resource you want to access, you can implement the appropriate redirector, and the redirector will forward your request to the appropriate destination.

In the example shown in Figure 4.7, a Windows NT client needs to access a Novell server. To accomplish this, the network administrator loads the Microsoft redirector for accessing Novell servers on top of Windows NT, installed in the client.

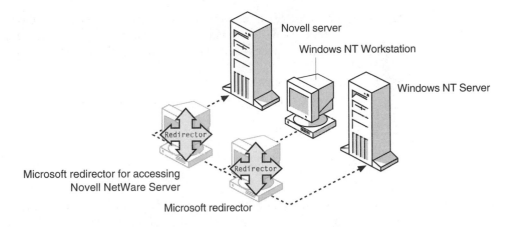

Figure 4.7   Windows NT Workstation using multiple redirectors

Server Interoperability

The second way to implement communication between a client and a server is to install communication services on the server, an approach used to bring an Apple Macintosh into a Windows NT environment. Microsoft supplies Services for Macintosh, software that allows a Windows NT Server–based server to communicate with the Apple client.

The Windows NT Server, shown in Figure 4.8, has had Services for Macintosh installed on it. This allows Macintosh users to access resources on a Windows NT server. The same service also converts files between Macintosh and Windows NT–based computers, which allows Macintosh and Windows NT users to utilize their own interfaces to share the same files.

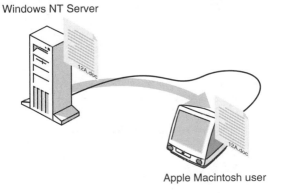

Figure 4.8   Services for Macintosh loaded on Windows NT Server

Thanks to this interoperability, a Macintosh user can follow standard Macintosh procedures and view Macintosh icons, such as the Chooser and Finder, even though that user is accessing resources on a Windows NT server.

Vendor Options

The three major networking product vendors are:

- Microsoft.
- Novell.
- Apple.

Figure 4.9 shows these three operating systems in a multivendor environment. Each of these vendors provides utilities that:

- Make it possible for its operating systems to communicate with servers from the other two vendors.
- Help its servers recognize clients from the other two vendors.

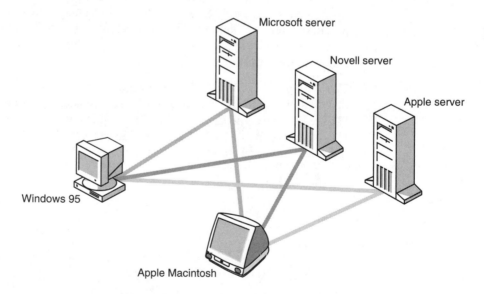

Figure 4.9 Multivendor connectivity

Microsoft

Microsoft has built a redirector that recognizes Microsoft networks into the following Microsoft operating systems:

- Windows NT
- Windows 95 and 98
- Windows for Workgroups

The redirectors are automatically implemented during the operating system installation. A setup utility loads the required drivers and then edits the startup files so the redirector will function when the user turns on the computer.

Microsoft redirector software not only makes it possible for clients to access resources, but also provides each Windows for Workgroups and Windows NT client with the capability to share its own resources.

Microsoft in a Novell Environment   Microsoft and Novell products are interoperable.

- To connect a Windows NT Workstation–based client to a Novell NetWare 3.*x* or 4.*x* network requires either NWLink and Client Service for NetWare (CSNW) or Novell's NetWare Client for Windows NT.

- To connect a Windows NT Server–based server to a NetWare network requires NWLink and Gateway Service for NetWare (GSNW).

  NWLink is the Microsoft implementation of the Internetwork Packet Exchange/Sequenced Packet Exchange (IPX/SPX) protocol. CSNW is the Microsoft implementation of a NetWare *requester* (Novell's term for redirector).

- To connect a Windows 95– or 98–based client to a NetWare network requires IPX/SPX and Microsoft CSNW networks.

Microsoft Service for NetWare Directory Services (NDS) is client software for NetWare that incorporates support for Novell Network 4.*x* and 5.*x* Directory Services. Microsoft NDS provides users with logon and browsing support for NetWare 3.*x*, and 4.*x* bindery services as NetWare 4.*x* and 5.*x* NDS servers.

MS-DOS-Based Clients   Server operating system vendors offer utilities that allow MS-DOS-based clients to access servers from the three vendors. All these utilities can reside on one machine so that one MS-DOS-based client can access servers from all three environments.

Novell

Novell servers recognize the following clients for file and print services. NetWare character-based clients running MS-DOS can connect to:

- Novell NetWare servers.
- Windows NT Server–based computers.

Windows NT clients running Novell's NetWare requester and the Windows NT redirector can connect to:

- Novell NetWare servers.
- Windows NT Workstation–based and Windows NT Server–based computers.

Novell provides requesters for client operating systems including:

- MS-DOS.
- OS/2.
- NetWare Client for Windows NT.

Apple

In the Macintosh environment, the redirector for AppleShare networking is included with the AppleTalk operating system and provides the file-sharing function. The client software is included with every copy of the Apple operating system. There is also an AppleShare print server, which is a server-based print spooler. This means that Macintoshes are equipped to participate in Apple networks.

MS-DOS-Based Client   AppleShare networking software offers MS-DOS-based clients access to AppleShare file and print servers. With LocalTalk personal-computer software and a LocalTalk personal-computer card installed on their personal computers, users can access file-server volumes (file storage) and printers on an AppleTalk network. The LocalTalk personal-computer card contains firmware to control the link between the AppleTalk network and the personal computer. The LocalTalk personal-computer driver software implements many of the AppleTalk protocols and interacts with the card to send and receive packets.

Services for Macintosh   Through Services for Macintosh, a Windows NT server becomes available to Macintosh clients. This product makes it possible for MS-DOS-based and Macintosh-based clients to share files and printers. Services for Macintosh includes AppleTalk Protocol versions 2.0 and 2.1, LocalTalk, EtherTalk, TokenTalk, and FDDITalk. In addition, Services for Macintosh supports version 5.2 or later of the LaserWriter printer.

Lesson Checkup

1. In a multivendor environment, it is necessary to find a _____ _____ in which all computers can communicate.

2. A redirector will _____ your request to the appropriate destination.

3. Each redirector handles only the _____ sent in the language or protocol that it can understand.

4. Apple computers are brought into a Windows NT environment by means of communication _____ that are installed on the server.

Lesson Summary

The following points summarize the main elements of this lesson.

- Interoperability in multivendor environments can be achieved from either the client or server computer.

- Redirectors are used to intercept requests for services and forward them across the network to the appropriate network services.

- A client or a server can have multiple redirectors.

- The three primary manufacturers of products for multivendor environments are Novell, Microsoft, and Apple.

- Apple computers connect to personal computer networks by means of network servers.

Exercise 4.1: Case Study Problem

To carry out this exercise, you will need to draw on information presented in all lessons in this chapter.

A small company in Montana designs and manufactures kits for building log houses. Thanks to a successful product and solid reputation, its prospects are good. The owner of the company wants to connect the office by means of a network that is capable of supporting as many as 10 computers and users. The company employs two salespeople, an office manager, a drafter, a graphic designer, the mill foreman, and a number of employees who do not use computers.

The owner's computer is running Windows 98 with a standard suite of office-application software and a popular project management-software application. The office manager, whose Windows 98 machine runs the same kind of office-application suite as the owner, prints to a letter-size laser printer that is connected directly to the computer. The owner and the office manager have internal modems in their computers that are daisy-chained through the fax machine to the single analog phone line.

The company also employs a computer-aided drafting (CAD) operator, who makes fabrication drawings for the employees in the mill. His computer operating system is Windows NT, and his primary application is a vector CAD program which plots to a roll-feed device that is cabled directly to the computer's printer port.

The two salespeople have portable computers that run Windows 98. Their major applications are included in the same office suite.

The computer graphic artist, who creates catalog art and presentation material, uses an Apple G3 computer running high-end graphics software as well as the same office suite as the owner and office manager. His computer prints to a high-resolution color postscript printer through its standard port.

The owner wants everyone on this network to be able to exchange files, use both printers, and have access to company e-mail through an Internet service provider. She has made it clear that she does not want a network that requires high administrative overhead.

Chapter Summary

The following points summarize the key concepts of this chapter.

Introduction to Network Operating Systems

- Without a network operating system (NOS) of some kind, individual computers cannot share resources, and other users cannot make use of those resources.

- An NOS can be part of a computer operating system or a separate application that runs on top of the computer operating system.

- Windows NT is an example of an operating system that incorporates both computer and network operating systems in one system.

- By multitasking, computers can perform more than one task at a time.

- Multitasking can be either preemptive or nonpreemptive.

- Server software is the means by which an NOS provides services to other computers on a network.

- A redirector is used to forward client requests to the network.

- Using redirectors, users can access peripheral devices as if the devices were attached directly to the client computer.

- The first step in choosing a network operating system is to decide which network architecture—client/server or peer-to-peer—best meets your needs; this can often be accomplished by determining what level of security your network requires.

Novell Operating Systems

- NetWare client software is designed to be installed over a client computer's operating system.

- The NetWare NOS is designed to work in multivendor network environments.

- NetWare Directory Services (NDS) provide a database that maintains information about every resource on the network.

- NDS provides security, routing, messaging, management, Web publishing, file and print services, and name services.

- A NetWare network requires both NetWare Server software for the server and NetWare Client software for each workstation.

Microsoft Network Operating Systems

- Windows NT is Microsoft's network operating system.

- Windows NT incorporates both the computer and the network operating system into one.

- Windows NT Server is the server module of the network.

- Windows NT Workstation is the client module of the network.

- Windows NT networks are designed to take advantage of the domain model in which all computers share a common security database. This information is stored on a server that is designated as the domain controller. Windows Server and Workstation will operate as part of a peer-to-peer network (share model), but you will not be able to take advantage of the additional security features provided in the domain model.

- Windows NT provides several utilities to provide interoperability between NetWare and Windows NT.

Other Network Operating Systems

- Apple IP allows non-Apple users to access Apple resources such as database files.

- A UNIX computer can be used as a file server by installing file-server software.

- Banyan Vines is a network operating system based on the Xerox proprietary protocol.

- Banyan Vines is a server/client-based network operating system.

- Peer-to-peer LAN networking is popular for small offices in which maintaining network security is not an issue.

- Windows for Workgroups, Windows 95 and 98, and OS/2 Warp NOSs have built-in peer-to-peer LAN software.

Network Operating Systems in a Multivendor Environment

- Interoperability in multivendor environments can be achieved from either the client or server computer.

- Redirectors are used to intercept requests for services and forward them across the network to the appropriate network services.

- A client or a server can have multiple redirectors.

- The three primary manufacturers of products for multivendor environments are Novell, Microsoft, and Apple.

- Apple computers connect to personal computer networks by means of network servers.

Chapter Review

1. A multitasking operating system can run as many tasks simultaneously as there are _____.

2. The network operating system can take control of the processor without the task's cooperation in a multitasking operating system that uses _____ multitasking.

3. The process of forwarding requests is carried out by a _____, which is also commonly referred to as a "shell" or a "requester."

4. Redirector activity originates in the _____ computer when the user issues a request for a network resource or service.

5. Redirectors can send requests to either computers or _____.

6. In the past, network operating systems were _____ that were loaded on top of a stand-alone operating system.

7. Novell's NetWare operating system is a _____-based network.

8. An advantage of using NetWare is that it works well in a _____ environment.

9. A Windows NT computer will not communicate with a NetWare network.
   True   False

10. Banyan Vines is an NOS that runs on top of another operating system.
    True   False

11. Your client is a small business, planning to install a small network for the office, which includes five computers, running Windows 95, and two printers. Security is not an issue because all employees work on the same projects. Would you recommend upgrading to Windows NT?

12. Will a Windows 95 or 98 workstation always work on a NetWare network?

C H A P T E R   5

Introducing Network Standards

About This Chapter

As we have seen in the previous chapters, many software and hardware manufacturers supply products for linking computers in a network. Networking is fundamentally a form of communication, so the need for manufacturers to take steps to ensure that their products could interact became apparent early in the development of networking technology. As networks and suppliers of networking products have spread across the world, the need for standardization has only increased. To address the issues surrounding standardization, several independent organizations have created standard design specifications for computer-networking products. When these standards are adhered to, communication is possible between hardware and software products produced by a variety of vendors. This chapter explores these standards in detail.

Before You Begin

Because this chapter builds on material presented in the previous chapters, you might want to review the lesson and chapter summaries of chapters 1 through 4 before you begin this chapter.

 Run the **c05dem01** video located in the **Demos** folder on the CD accompanying this book to view an overview discussion of network standards.

Lesson 1: Open Systems Interconnection (OSI) Reference Model

This lesson describes the Open Systems Interconnection (OSI) reference model. The OSI model represents the seven layers of the process by which data is packaged and transmitted from a sending application through the physical wires to the receiving application.

After this lesson, you will be able to:

- Describe the primary function of each layer of the OSI reference model.
- Identify the OSI layer at which a particular network activity takes place.
- Identify the OSI layer at which a particular network component functions.

Estimated lesson time: 35 minutes

Network Communications

Network activity involves sending data from one computer to another. This complex process can be broken into discrete, sequential tasks. The sending computer must:

1. Recognize the data.
2. Divide the data into manageable chunks.
3. Add information to each chunk of data to determine the location of the data and to identify the receiver.
4. Add timing and error-checking information.
5. Put the data on the network and send it on its way.

Network client software operates at many different levels within the sending and receiving computers. Each of these levels, or tasks, is governed by one or more protocols. (Protocols are introduced in Chapter 3, Lesson 2: How Networks Send Data.) These protocols, or rules of behavior, are standard specifications for formatting and moving the data. When the sending and receiving computers follow the same protocols, communication is assured. Because of this layered structure, this is often referred to as the *protocol stack*.

With the rapid growth of networking hardware and software, a need arose for standard protocols that could allow hardware and software from different vendors to communicate. In response, two primary sets of standards were developed: the OSI model and a modification of that standard called Project 802 (covered in the next lesson).

Acquiring a clear understanding of these models is an important first step in understanding the technical aspects of how a network functions. Throughout this lesson we refer to various protocols. The protocols and how they apply to these models are covered in detail in Chapter 6, "Defining Network Protocols."

The OSI Reference Model

In 1978, the International Standards Organization (ISO) released a set of specifications that described network architecture for connecting dissimilar devices. The original document applied to systems that were open to each other because they could all use the same protocols and standards to exchange information.

Note To set up a network competently, you need to be aware of the major standards organizations and how their work affects network communications. An overview of the most important standards bodies is presented in Appendix B, "Common Network Standards and Specifications."

In 1984, the ISO released a revision of this model and called it the *Open Systems Interconnection (OSI) reference model.* The 1984 revision has become an international standard and serves as a guide for networking.

The OSI model is the best-known and most widely used guide for visualizing networking environments. Manufacturers adhere to the OSI model when they design network products. It provides a description of how network hardware and software work together in a layered fashion to make communications possible. The model also helps to troubleshoot problems by providing a frame of reference that describes how components are supposed to function.

 Run the **c05dem02** video located in the **Demos** folder on the CD accompanying this book to see an overview presentation of the OSI reference model.

A Layered Architecture

The OSI reference model architecture divides network communication into seven layers. Each layer covers different network activities, equipment, or protocols. Figure 5.1 represents the layered architecture of the OSI model. (*Layering* specifies different functions and services as data moves from one computer through the network cabling to another computer.) The OSI model defines how each layer communicates and works with the layers immediately above and below it. For example, the session layer communicates and works with the presentation and transport layers.

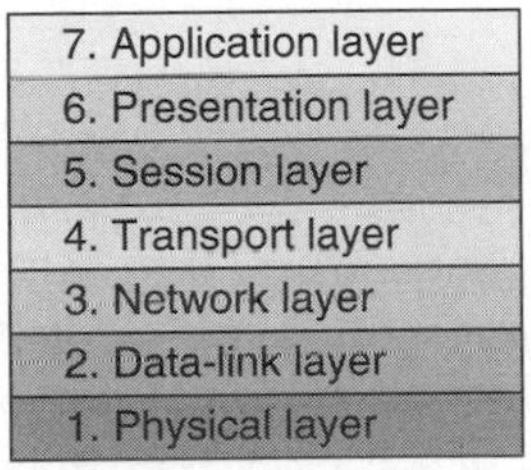

7. Application layer
6. Presentation layer
5. Session layer
4. Transport layer
3. Network layer
2. Data-link layer
1. Physical layer

Figure 5.1   The seven-layer OSI model

Each layer provides some service or action that prepares the data for delivery over the network to another computer. The lowest layers—1 and 2—define the network's physical media and related tasks, such as putting data bits onto the network interface cards (NICs) and cable. The highest layers define how applications access communication services. The higher the layer, the more complex its task.

The layers are separated from each other by boundaries called *interfaces*. All requests are passed from one layer, through the interface, to the next layer. Each layer builds upon the standards and activities of the layer below it.

Relationships Among OSI Model Layers

Each layer provides services to the next-higher layer and shields the upper layer from the details of how the services below it are actually implemented. At the same time, each layer appears to be in direct communication with its associated layer on the other computer. This provides a logical, or virtual, communication between peer layers, as shown in Figure 5.2. In reality, actual communication between adjacent layers takes place on one computer only. At each layer, software implements network functions according to a set of protocols.

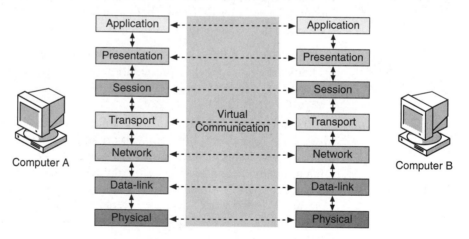

Figure 5.2 Relationships among OSI layers

 Run the **c05dem03** video located in the **Demos** folder on the CD accompanying this book to view a presentation of layer transmission on the OSI reference model.

Before data is passed from one layer to another, it is broken down into packets, or units of information, which are transmitted as a whole from one device to another on a network. (Packets were introduced in Chapter 3, Lesson 2: How Networks Send Data.) The network passes a packet from one software layer to another in the same order as that of the layers. At each layer, the software adds additional formatting or addressing to the packet, which is needed for the packet to be successfully transmitted across the network.

At the receiving end, the packet passes through the layers in reverse order. A software utility at each layer reads the information on the packet, strips it away, and passes the packet up to the next layer. When the packet is finally passed up to the application layer, the addressing information has been stripped away and the packet is in its original form, which is readable by the receiver.

 Run the **c05dem04** and **c05dem05** videos located in the **Demos** folder on the CD accompanying this book to view a presentation of layer transmission between computers using the OSI reference model.

With the exception of the lowest layer in the OSI networking model, no layer can pass information directly to its counterpart on another computer. Instead, information on the sending computer must be passed down through each successive layer until it reaches the physical layer. The information then moves across the networking cable to the receiving computer and up that computer's networking layers until it arrives at the corresponding layer. For example, when the network layer sends information from computer A, the information moves down through the data-link and physical layers on the sending side, over the cable, and up the physical and data-link layers on the receiving side to its final destination at the network layer on computer B.

In a client/server environment, an example of the kind of information sent from the network layer on computer A to the network layer on computer B would be a network address, with perhaps some error-checking information added to the packet.

Interaction between adjacent layers occurs through an interface. The interface defines the services offered by the lower networking layer to the upper one and further defines how those services will be accessed. In addition, each layer on one computer appears to be communicating directly with the same layer on another computer.

The following sections describe the purpose of each of the seven layers of the OSI model, and identify the services that each provides to adjacent layers. Beginning at the top of the stack (layer 7, the application layer), we work down to the bottom (layer 1, the physical layer).

Application Layer

Layer 7, the topmost layer of the OSI model, is the *application layer*. This layer relates to the services that directly support user applications, such as software for file transfers, database access, and e-mail. In other words, it serves as a window through which application processes can access network services. A message to be sent across the network enters the OSI model at this point and exits the OSI model's application layer on the receiving computer. Application-layer protocols can be programs in themselves, such as File Transfer Protocol (FTP), or they can be used by other programs, such as Simple Mail Transfer Protocol (SMTP), used by most e-mail programs, to redirect data to the network. The lower layers support the tasks that are performed at the application layer. These tasks include general network access, flow control, and error recovery.

Presentation Layer

Layer 6, the *presentation layer*, defines the format used to exchange data among networked computers. Think of it as the network's translator. When computers from dissimilar systems—such as IBM, Apple, and Sun—need to communicate, a certain amount of translation and byte reordering must be done. Within the sending computer, the presentation layer translates data from the format sent down from the application layer into a commonly recognized, intermediary format. At the receiving computer, this layer translates the intermediary format into a format that can be useful to that computer's application layer. The presentation layer is responsible for converting protocols, translating the data, encrypting the data, changing or converting the character set, and expanding graphics commands. The presentation layer also manages data compression to reduce the number of bits that need to be transmitted.

The *redirector*, which redirects input/output (I/O) operations to resources on a server, operates at this layer. Redirectors are discussed in Chapter 8, "Designing and Installing a Network."

Session Layer

Layer 5, the *session layer*, allows two applications on different computers to open, use, and close a connection called a *session*. (A session is a highly structured dialog between two workstations.) The session layer is responsible for managing this dialog. It performs name-recognition and other functions, such as security, that are needed to allow two applications to communicate over the network.

The session layer synchronizes user tasks by placing checkpoints in the data stream. The checkpoints break the data into smaller groups for error detection. This way, if the network fails, only the data after the last checkpoint has to be retransmitted. This layer also implements dialog control between communicating processes, such as regulating which side transmits, when, and for how long.

Transport Layer

Layer 4, the *transport layer*, provides an additional connection level beneath the session layer. The transport layer ensures that packets are delivered error free, in sequence, and without losses or duplications. At the sending computer, this layer repackages messages, dividing long messages into several packets and collecting small packets together in one package. This process ensures that packets are transmitted efficiently over the network. At the receiving computer, the transport layer opens the packets, reassembles the original messages, and, typically, sends an acknowledgment that the message was received. If a duplicate packet arrives, this layer will recognize the duplicate and discard it.

The transport layer provides flow control and error handling, and participates in solving problems concerned with the transmission and reception of packets. Transmission Control Protocol (TCP) and Sequenced Packet Exchange (SPX) are examples of transport-layer protocols.

Network Layer

Layer 3, the *network layer*, is responsible for addressing messages and translating logical addresses and names into physical addresses. This layer also determines the route from the source to the destination computer. It determines which path the data should take based on network conditions, priority of service, and other factors. It also manages traffic problems on the network, such as switching and routing of packets and controlling the congestion of data.

If the network adapter on the router cannot transmit a data chunk as large as the source computer sends, the network layer on the router compensates by breaking the data into smaller units. At the destination end, the network layer reassembles the data. Internet Protocol (IP) and Internetwork Packet Exchange (IPX) are examples of network-layer protocols.

Data-Link Layer

Layer 2, the *data-link layer*, sends data frames from the network layer to the physical layer. It controls the electrical impulses that enter and leave the network cable. On the receiving end, the data-link layer packages raw bits from the physical layer into data frames. (A data frame is an organized, logical structure in which data can be placed. Data frames are discussed in more detail in Chapter 3, Lesson 4: Token Ring.) The electrical representation of the data (bit patterns, encoding methods, and tokens) is known to this layer only.

Figure 5.3 shows a simple data frame. In this example, the sender ID represents the address of the computer that is sending the information; the destination ID represents the address of the computer to which the information is being sent. The control information is used for frame type, routing, and segmentation information. The data is the information itself. The cyclical redundancy check (CRC) provides error correction and verification information to ensure that the data frame is received correctly.

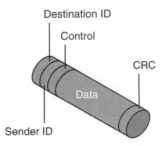

Figure 5.3 A simple data frame

The data-link layer is responsible for providing error-free transfer of these frames from one computer to another through the physical layer. This allows the network layer to anticipate virtually error-free transmission over the network connection.

Usually, when the data-link layer sends a frame, it waits for an acknowledgment from the recipient. The recipient data-link layer detects any problems with the frame that might have occurred during transmission. Frames that were damaged during transmission or were not acknowledged are then re-sent.

Physical Layer

Layer 1, the bottom layer of the OSI model, is the *physical layer.* This layer transmits the unstructured, raw bit stream over a physical medium (such as the network cable). The physical layer is totally hardware-oriented and deals with all aspects of establishing and maintaining a physical link between communicating computers. The physical layer also carries the signals that transmit data generated by each of the higher layers.

This layer defines how the cable is attached to the NIC. For example, it defines how many pins the connector has and the function of each. It also defines which transmission technique will be used to send data over the network cable.

This layer provides data encoding and bit synchronization. The physical layer is responsible for transmitting bits (zeros and ones) from one computer to another, ensuring that when a transmitting host sends a 1 bit, it is received as a 1 bit, not a 0 bit. Because different types of media physically transmit bits (light or electrical signals) differently, the physical layer also defines the duration of each impulse and how each bit is translated into the appropriate electrical or optical impulse for the network cable.

This layer is often referred to as the "hardware layer." Although the rest of the layers can be implemented as firmware (chip-level functions on the NIC), rather than actual software, the other layers are software in relation to this first layer.

Memorizing the OSI Model

Memorizing the layers of the OSI model and their order is very important, especially when preparing to take a computer networking exam. Table 5.1 provides two ways to help you recall the seven layers of the OSI model.

Table 5.1   OSI Model Layers

OSI Layer	Down the Stack ↓	Up the Stack ↑
Application	All	Away
Presentation	People	Pizza
Session	Seem	Sausage
Transport	To	Throw
Network	Need	Not
Data Link	Data	Do
Physical	Processing	Please

Data Packets and the OSI Model

In Chapter 3, Lesson 2: How Networks Send Data, we discussed the data packet in general terms. These data packets are assembled and disassembled according to the OSI model. The packet-creation process begins at the application layer of the OSI model, where the data is generated. Information to be sent across the network starts at the application layer and descends through all seven layers.

At each layer, information relevant to that layer is added to the data. This information is for the use of the corresponding layer in the receiving computer. The data-link layer in the receiving computer, for instance, will read information added at the data-link layer in the sending computer. Figure 5.4 shows the assembly of a packet in the sending workstation and the disassembly of the packet in the receiving workstation.

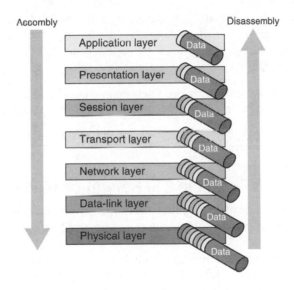

Figure 5.4 Packet assembly and disassembly process

At the transport layer, the original block of data is broken into the actual packets. The protocol defines the structure of the packets used by the two computers.

When the packet reaches the transport layer, sequence information is added that guides the receiving computer in reassembling the data from packets.

When the packets finally pass through the physical layer on their way to the cable, they contain information from each of the other six layers.

Addressing Packets

Most packets on the network are addressed to a specific computer and, as a result, get the attention of only one computer. Each NIC sees all packets sent on its cable segment, but it interrupts the computer only if the packet's address matches the card's individual address. Alternatively, a broadcast-type address can also be used. Packets sent with a broadcast-type address can receive the simultaneous attention of many computers on the network.

In situations involving large networks that cover large regions (or even countries) and offer several possible communication routes, the network's connectivity and switching components use the packet's addressing information to determine the best route for addressing packets.

Directing Packets

Network components use the addressing information in packets to direct the packets to their destinations or to keep them away from network locations where they do not belong. The following two functions play a key role in properly directing packets:

- **Packet forwarding** Computers send a packet on to the next appropriate network component based on the address in the packet's header.
- **Packet filtering** Computers use criteria, such as an address, to select specific packets.

Windows NT and the OSI Reference Model

Network manufacturers use the OSI model when designing their products. When each follows the model, there is a greater likelihood that different systems can communicate. One shortcoming of the model stems from the fact that many manufacturers created their products before the model was accepted; these early products might not follow the model exactly. To demonstrate how the OSI model is adapted to a specific network operating system, we next examine Windows NT and how it fits the model.

OSI Layers and Windows NT

To simplify the model, Windows NT compresses the seven layers into only three layers: file system drivers, transport protocols, and NIC drivers. Figure 5.5 shows how the groups relate to OSI.

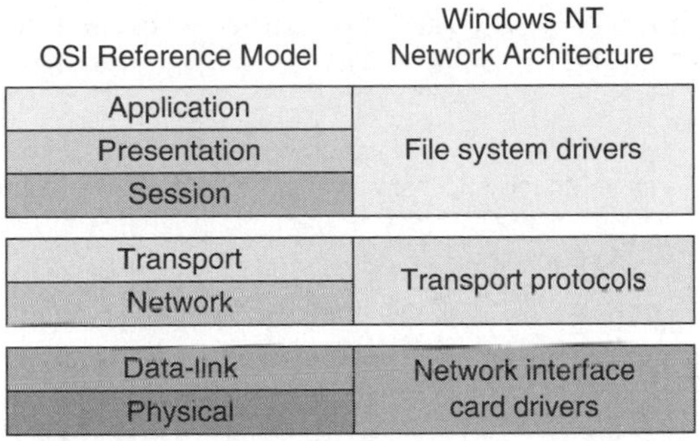

OSI Reference Model
Windows NT Network Architecture

OSI Reference Model	Windows NT Network Architecture
Application	File system drivers
Presentation	
Session	
Transport	Transport protocols
Network	
Data-link	Network interface card drivers
Physical	

Figure 5.5 Windows NT and OSI

Windows NT uses drivers to provide for communication between the operating system and the network. A *driver* is a device-specific control program that enables a computer to work with a particular device, such as a printer or a disk drive. Every time you install a new piece of hardware, such as a printer, sound card, or network card, you need to install the software drivers that operate the card.

File System Drivers

File system drivers work in the application, presentation, and session layers of the OSI model. When these drivers detect that an application is requesting resources on a remote system, they redirect the request to the appropriate system. Examples of these drivers include the Windows NT file system (NTFS) and file allocation table (FAT) drivers, and the services applications installed on Windows NT Server and Windows NT Workstation.

Transport Protocols

Transport protocols operate in the transport and network layers of the OSI model. They are responsible for adding software address information to the data and for ensuring the reliability of the transmission. The transport protocols are bound to or combined with the NIC to provide communication. During installation and configuration of Windows NT, you must always bind these protocols to a specific network card.

Network Interface Card (NIC) Drivers

NIC drivers operate in the data-link and physical layers of the OSI model. They are responsible for adding the hardware address information to the data packet and for formatting the data for transmission through the NIC and cable. NIC drivers are protocol-independent, allowing systems based on Windows NT to transport data to a variety of network systems.

Figure 5.6 shows how software and protocols relate to the OSI model and the Windows NT model.

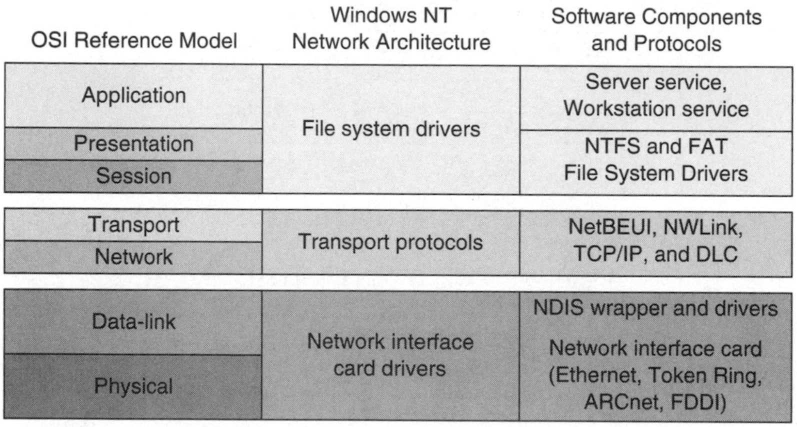

OSI Reference Model	Windows NT Network Architecture	Software Components and Protocols
Application	File system drivers	Server service, Workstation service
Presentation		NTFS and FAT File System Drivers
Session		
Transport	Transport protocols	NetBEUI, NWLink, TCP/IP, and DLC
Network		
Data-link	Network interface card drivers	NDIS wrapper and drivers
Physical		Network interface card (Ethernet, Token Ring, ARCnet, FDDI)

Figure 5.6   Software and protocols

Windows NT Interfaces

Windows NT supports many different network redirectors, transport protocols, and NICs. With so many possible combinations, it was necessary to develop a method of handling the interactions between them. To resolve this problem, Microsoft developed common interfaces—boundary layers—to act as translators between each layer. Thus, as long as any network component was written to communicate with the boundary interfaces, it could be used with the model. Figure 5.7 shows the three boundary interfaces.

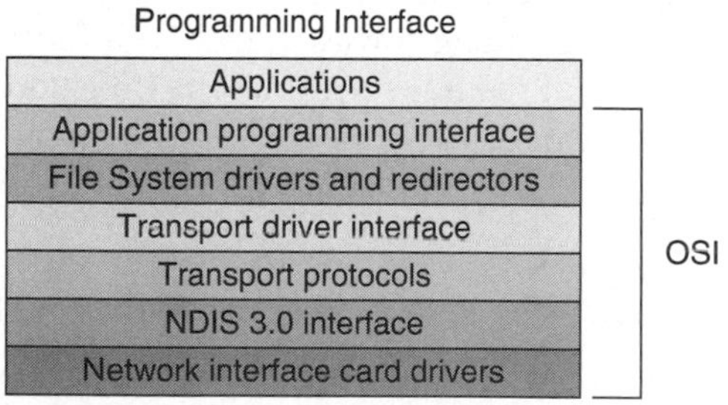

Programming Interface

Applications
Application programming interface
File System drivers and redirectors
Transport driver interface
Transport protocols
NDIS 3.0 interface
Network interface card drivers

OSI

Figure 5.7   Windows NT architecture with boundary interfaces

Application Programming Interfaces (APIs)

The application programming interfaces (APIs) are system routines that give programmers access to the services provided by the operating system. Windows NT networking APIs lie between user applications and the file system drivers and redirectors. These APIs allow an application to control or be controlled by other applications. They are responsible for setting up a session between the sender and the receiver on the network. Windows NT supports a variety of APIs for networking.

Transport Driver Interfaces (TDIs)

The transport driver interfaces (TDIs) work between the file system drives and the transport protocols. These will allow any protocol written to TDI to communicate with the file system drivers.

Network Driver Interface Specifications (NDISs)

The Network Driver Interface Specifications (NDISs) work between the transport protocols and the NIC drivers. As long as a NIC driver is written to NDIS standards, it will communicate with the transport protocols.

Exercise 5.1: Reviewing the OSI Model Layers

This two-part exercise will give you the opportunity to memorize and review the layers of the OSI model.

The left column is a listing of a memorization tool: "All People Seem To Need Data Processing." Next to each word in that column, enter the appropriate name of the applicable OSI layer in the center column and a brief description of that layer's function in the right column.

Memorization Tool	OSI Layer	Function
All		
People		
Seem		
To		
Need		
Data		
Processing		

In the second part of Exercise 1 that follows, a device or standard is listed in the left column. In the space provided in the right column, write in the applicable OSI layer(s) for each device or standard.

Device	OSI layer
Gateway	
NIC	
Hub	
Router	
IEEE 802.x	

Lesson Summary

The following points summarize the main elements of this lesson:

- The OSI model architecture divides network protocols into seven layers: the application, presentation, session, transport, network, data-link, and physical layers.

- Windows NT groups the OSI model into three layers: file system drivers, transport protocols, and NIC drivers.

- The Windows NT network model requires three interfaces to provide communication between groups: APIs, TDIs, and NDISs.

Lesson 2: The IEEE 802.x Standard

The bottom two layers of the OSI model pertain to hardware: the NIC and the network cabling. To further refine the requirements for hardware that operate within these layers, the Institute of Electrical and Electronics Engineers (IEEE) has developed enhancements specific to different NICs and cabling. Collectively, these refinements are known as the 802 project. This lesson describes these enhancements and how they relate to OSI.

After this lesson, you will be able to:

- Describe the 802 enhancements to the OSI model.
- Describe the function of the sublayers to the data-link layer of the OSI model.

Estimated lesson time: 20 minutes

The 802 Project Model

When local area networks (LANs) first began to emerge as potential business tools in the late 1970s, the IEEE realized that there was a need to define certain LAN standards. To accomplish this task, the IEEE launched what became known as Project 802, named for the year and month it began (1980, February).

Although the published IEEE 802 standards actually predated the ISO standards, both were in development at roughly the same time, and both shared information that resulted in the creation of two compatible models.

Project 802 defined network standards for the physical components of a network (the interface card and the cabling) that are accounted for in the physical and data-link layers of the OSI model.

The 802 specifications set standards for:

- Network interface cards (NICs).
- Wide area network (WAN) components.
- Components used to create twisted-pair and coaxial cable networks.

The 802 specifications define the ways NICs access and transfer data over physical media. These include connecting, maintaining, and disconnecting network devices.

Note Choosing which protocol to run at the data-link layer is the single most important decision you make when designing a LAN. This protocol defines the speed of the network, the method used to access the physical network, the types of cables you can use, and the NICs and drivers you install.

IEEE 802 Categories

The LAN standards defined by the 802 committees are classified into 16 categories that can be identified by their 802 number as shown in Table 5.2:

Table 5.2   802 Specification Categories

Specification	Description
802.1	Sets Internetworking standards related to network management.
802.2	Defines the general standard for the data-link layer. The IEEE divides this layer into two sublayers: the LLC and MAC layers (discussed in the previous lesson). The MAC layer varies with different network types and is defined by standard IEEE 802.3.
802.3	Defines the MAC layer for bus networks that use Carrier-Sense Multiple Access with Collision Detection (CSMA/CD). This is the Ethernet Standard.
802.4	Defines the MAC layer for bus networks that use a token-passing mechanism (Token Bus LAN).
802.5	Defines the MAC layer for token ring networks (Token Ring LAN).
802.6	Sets standards for metropolitan area networks (MANs), which are data networks designed for towns or cities. In terms of geographic breadth, MANs are larger than LANs, but smaller than WANs. MANs are usually characterized by very-high-speed connections using fiber-optic cables or other digital media.
802.7	Used by the Broadband Technical Advisory Group.
802.8	Used by the Fiber-Optic Technical Advisory Group.
802.9	Defines integrated voice/data networks.
802.10	Defines network security.
802.11	Defines wireless network standards.
802.12	Defines Demand Priority Access LAN, 100BaseVG-AnyLAN.
802.13	Unused.
802.14	Defines cable modem standards.
802.15	Defines wireless personal area networks (WPAN).
802.16	Defines broadband wireless standards.

Enhancements to the OSI Model

The bottom two OSI layers, the physical layer and the data-link layer, define how multiple computers can use the network simultaneously without interfering with each other.

The IEEE 802 project incorporated the specifications in those two layers to create standards that have defined the dominant LAN environments. Figure 5.8 shows the data-link layer and its two sublayers.

After deciding that more detail was needed at the data-link layer, the 802 standards committee divided the data-link layer into two sublayers:

- **Logical Link Control (LLC)**   Establishing and terminating links, controlling frame traffic, sequencing frames, and acknowledging frames
- **Media Access Control (MAC)**   Managing media access, delimiting frames, checking frame errors, and recognizing frame addresses

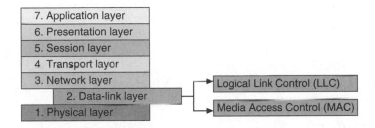

Figure 5.8   Project 802 LLC and MAC sublayers

Logical Link Control (LLC) Sublayer

The LLC sublayer manages data-link communication and defines the use of logical interface points called *service access points* (SAP). Other computers can refer to and use SAPs to transfer information from the LLC sublayer to the upper OSI layers. Category 802.2 defines these standards.

Media Access Control (MAC) Sublayer

As Figure 5.9 indicates, the MAC sublayer is the lower of the two sublayers, providing shared access to the physical layer for the computers' NICs. The MAC layer communicates directly with the NIC and is responsible for delivering error-free data between two computers on the network.

Categories 802.3, 802.4, 802.5, and 802.12 define standards for both this sublayer and OSI layer 1, the physical layer.

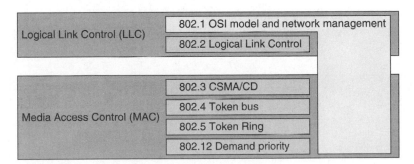

Figure 5.9   Project 802 LLC and MAC standards

Exercise 5.2: Describing IEEE 802.x Standards Categories

In this exercise, IEEE 802 standards categories are listed in the left column. In the right column, enter a description of what each category represents.

802.x Standard	Basis for standard
802.1	
802.2	
802.3	
802.4	
802.5	
802.6	
802.7	
802.8	
802.9	
802.10	
802.11	
802.12	
802.13	
802.14	
802.15	
802.16	

Lesson Summary

The following points summarize the main elements of this lesson:

- IEEE 802 standards define the specifications for NICs, networking components, and media for the data-link and physical layers of the OSI model.

- 802.3 defines the Ethernet specifications.

- 802.5 defines the Token Ring LAN specifications.

- The IEEE 802 standards divide the data-link layer into two subgroups: Logical Link Control (LLC) and Media Access Control (MAC).

Lesson 3: Device Drivers and OSI

NICs play an important role in connecting a computer to the physical part of the network. No discussion of networking standards is complete without including drivers, the small software programs that enable a computer to work with a network card or other device. In this lesson we look at device drivers and how they relate to the OSI model.

After this lesson, you will be able to:
- Describe the function of a driver.
- Describe the role of drivers in the OSI model.
- Describe the function of NDIS and ODI.

Estimated lesson time: 15 minutes

The Role of Drivers

A *driver* (sometimes called a device driver) is software that enables a computer to work with a particular device. Although a device might be installed on a computer, the computer's operating system cannot communicate with the device until the driver for that device has been installed and configured. The software driver tells the computer how to drive or work with the device so that the device performs the job it is assigned in the way it is supposed to.

There are drivers for nearly every type of computer device and peripheral including:

- Input devices, such as mouse and keyboard devices.
- SCSI and IDE disk controllers.
- Hard and floppy-disk drives.
- Multimedia devices such as microphones, cameras, and recorders.
- Network interface cards (NICs).
- Printers, plotters, tape drives, and so on.

Usually, the computer's operating system works with the driver to make the device perform. Printers provide a good illustration of how drivers are used. Printers built by different manufacturers all have different features and functions. It would be impossible for computer makers to equip new computers with all the software necessary to identify and work with every type of printer. Instead, printer manufacturers make drivers available for each printer. Before your computer can send documents to a printer, you must install the driver for that printer on your computer's hard drive.

As a general rule, manufacturers of components, such as peripherals or cards that must be physically installed, are responsible for supplying the drivers for their equipment. For example, NIC manufacturers are responsible for making drivers available for their cards. Drivers generally are included on a disk with the equipment when it is purchased, included with the computer's operating system, or made available for downloading from an Internet service provider such as the Microsoft Network (MSN), CompuServe, or others.

The Network Environment

Network drivers provide communication between a NIC and the network redirector running in the computer. The redirector is the part of networking software that accepts input/output (I/O) requests for remote files and then sends, or redirects, them over the network to another computer. During installation, the driver is stored on the computer's hard disk.

Drivers and the OSI Model

NIC drivers reside in the MAC sublayer of the OSI model's data-link layer. The MAC sublayer is responsible for providing shared access to the physical layer for the computer's NICs. As shown in Figure 5.10, the NIC drivers provide virtual communication between the computer and the NIC. This, in turn, provides a link between the computer and the rest of the network.

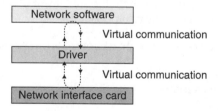

Figure 5.10   Communication between the NIC and network software

Drivers and the Networking Software

It is common for a NIC manufacturer to provide drivers to the networking-software vendor so that the drivers can be included with the network operating software.

Note When purchasing a new hardware device, always make sure that it contains the correct drivers for the specified computer operating system on which it will be installed. If in doubt, or if you are missing the appropriate driver, consult the manufacturer before you install the device. Updated drivers or drivers for various operating systems often are available over the Internet for downloading.

The hardware compatibility list (HCL) supplied by operating-system manufacturers describes the drivers they have tested and included with their operating system. The HCL for a network operating system might list more than 100 NIC drivers. This does not mean that an unlisted driver won't work with that operating system; it means only that the operating-system manufacturer has not tested it.

Even if the driver for a particular card has not been included with the network operating system, it is usual for the manufacturer of the NIC to include drivers for most popular network operating systems on a disk that is shipped with the card. Before buying a card, however, make sure that the card has a driver that will work with a particular network operating system. Installation and configuration of drivers is discussed in detail in Chapter 8, "Designing and Installing a Network."

Network Driver Interface Specification (NDIS)

Network Driver Interface Specification (NDIS) is a standard that defines an interface for communication between the MAC sublayer and the protocol drivers. By permitting the simultaneous use of multiple protocols and drivers, NDIS allows for a flexible environment of data exchange. It defines the software interface, known as the NDIS interface. Protocol drivers use this interface to communicate with the NICs. The advantage of NDIS is that it offers protocol multiplexing, so that multiple protocol stacks can be used at the same time. Three types of network software have interfaces described by NDIS:

- **Protocol stack** Provides network communications. A stack generates and disassembles frames (control information and data) that are sent to and received from the network.

- **Adapter driver** Controls the network interface hardware. Works in the MAC sublayer and moves frames between the protocol stack and the interface hardware.

- **Protocol Manager** Controls the activity between the protocol stack and the MAC.

Microsoft and 3Com jointly developed the NDIS specification for use with Warp Server and Windows NT Server. All NIC manufacturers make their boards work with these operating systems by supplying NDIS-compliant software drivers.

Open Data-Link Interface (ODI)

Open Data-Link Interface (ODI) is a specification adopted by Novell and Apple to simplify driver development for their network operating systems. ODI provides support for multiple protocols on a single NIC. Similar to NDIS, ODI allows Novell NetWare drivers to be written without reference to the protocol that will be used on top of them. All NIC manufacturers can make their boards work with these operating systems by supplying ODI-compliant software drivers.

Bridging NDIS and ODI

ODI and NDIS are incompatible. They present different programming interfaces to the upper layers of the network software. Novell, IBM, and Microsoft offer ODI-to-NDIS translation software to bridge the two interfaces. Two examples are ODI2NDI.SYS and ODINSUP.SYS.

Note Most network card manufacturers supply both NDIS- and ODI-compliant drivers with their boards.

Lesson Checkup

1. Define ODI and describe the role it plays in Novell and Apple NOSs.

2. Printer manufacturers are responsible for writing _____ for their printer products.

3. Drivers described in an operating system manufacturer's _____ have been tested and included with their operating system.

4. NIC drivers reside on the computer's _____ _____.

5. Protocol drivers use an _____ interface to communicate with the NICs.

6. Translation software is required to _____ _____ NDIS and ODI.

Lesson Summary

The following points summarize the main elements of this lesson:

- A driver is a device-specific control program that enables a computer to work with a particular device, such as a printer or a disk drive.

- In networking, drivers are needed to provide the connection between the computer and the NIC.

- NIC drivers reside in the MAC sublayer of the data-link layer of the OSI model.

- NDIS is a standard that defines the interface for Windows NT Server and Warp Server.

- ODI is a standard that defines the interface for Apple and Novell systems.

Chapter Summary

The following points summarize the key concepts of this chapter:

OSI Reference Model

- The OSI model architecture divides network protocols into seven layers: the application, presentation, session, transport, network, data-link, and physical layers.

- Microsoft Windows NT groups the OSI model into three layers: file system drivers, transport protocols, and NIC drivers.

- The Windows NT network model requires three interfaces to provide communication between groups: APIs, TDIs, and NDISs.

IEEE 802.x

- IEEE 802 standards define the specifications for NICs, WAN components, and media for the data-link and physical layers of the OSI model.

- 802.3 defines Ethernet specifications.

- 802.5 defines Token Ring LAN specifications.

- The IEEE 802 standards divide the data-link layer into two subgroups: Logical Link Control (LLC) and Media Access Control (MAC).

Device Drivers and OSI

- A driver is a program that gives directions to the computer for how to operate a device.

- In networking, drivers are needed to provide the software connection between the computer and the NIC.

- NIC drivers reside in the MAC sublayer of the data-link layer of the OSI model.

- NDIS is a standard that defines the interface for Windows NT Server and Warp Server.

- ODI is a standard that defines the interface for Apple and Novell systems.

Chapter Review

1. The OSI model divides network activity into _____ layers.

2. The purpose of each layer is to provide services to the next _____ layer and shield the upper layer from the details of how the services are actually implemented.

3. At each layer, the software adds some additional formatting or _____ to the packet.

4. Each layer on one computer appears to communicate directly with the _____ layer on another computer.

5. The top, or _____, layer handles general network access, flow control, and error recovery.

6. At the sending computer, the _____ layer translates data from a format sent down from the application layer.

7. The _____ layer determines the route from the source to the destination computer.

8. The data-link layer is responsible for sending _____ _____ from the network layer to the physical layer.

9. The _____ information in a data frame is used for frame type, routing, and segmentation information.

10. The _____ layer defines how the cable is attached to the NIC.

11. Windows NT groups the seven OSI layers into three. The three NT layers are _____ _____ _____, _____ _____, and _____ _____.

12. An _____ provides the interface between the Windows NT applications and file system drivers layer.

13. A _____ provides the interface between the Windows NT file system drivers layer and the transport protocols.

14. An _____ provides the interface between the Windows NT, the transport protocols layer, and the NIC drivers.

15. The Project 802 specifications define the way _____ access and transfer data over physical media.

16. The 802 project divided the _____ - _____ layer of the OSI model into two sublayers, the Logical Link Control (LLC) layer and the Media Access Control (MAC) layer.

17. The _____ sublayer communicates directly with the NIC and is responsible for delivering error-free data between two computers on the network.

18. The IEEE category _____ covers LAN standards for Ethernet.

19. The IEEE category _____ covers LAN standards for Token Ring.

20. A driver is _____ that enables a computer to work with a device.

21. NICs work in the _____ sublayer of the _____ - _____ layer of the OSI model.

22. NDIS defines an interface for communication between the _____ sublayer and the protocol drivers.

23. NDIS was jointly developed by _____ and _____ .

24. ODI works just like NDIS but was developed by _____ and _____ for interfacing hardware to their protocols.

C H A P T E R 6

Defining Network Protocols

About This Chapter

Protocols were introduced in Chapter 3, "Understanding Network Architecture," and discussed in Chapter 5, "Introducing Network Standards." Protocols are the system of rules and procedures that govern communication between two or more devices. Many varieties of protocols exist. Not all protocols are compatible, but as long as two devices are using the same protocol, they can exchange data. In this chapter, we discuss the prominent protocols used with networks and define the relationship of each protocol to the OSI model covered in Chapter 5.

Before You Begin

Before starting this chapter, you will find it helpful to review Lesson 1: Open Systems Interconnection (OSI) Reference Model in Chapter 5.

Lesson 1: Introduction to Protocols

This lesson offers an introduction to protocols and their function in a networking environment. It explains the roles of protocols in network communications and describes how different protocols work at different OSI levels.

After this lesson, you will be able to:

- Identify the functions of protocols and protocol stacks.
- Describe the network processes that use protocols and how they utilize them.
- Map specific protocols to the appropriate OSI level.

Estimated lesson time: 45 minutes

The Function of Protocols

Protocols are rules and procedures for communicating. The term "protocol" is used in a variety of contexts. For example, diplomats from one country adhere to rules of protocol designed to help them interact smoothly with diplomats from other countries. Rules of protocol apply in the same way in the computer environment. When several computers are networked, the rules and technical procedures governing their communication and interaction are called protocols.

Keep three points in mind when you think about protocols in a network environment:

- There are many protocols. While each protocol facilitates basic communications, each has different purposes and accomplishes different tasks. Each protocol has its own advantages and restrictions.
- Some protocols work only at particular OSI layers. The layer at which a protocol works describes its function. For example, a protocol that works at the physical layer ensures that the data packet passes through the network interface card (NIC) and out onto the network cable.
- Protocols can also work together in a protocol stack, or suite. Just as a network incorporates functions at every layer of the OSI model, different protocols also work together at different levels in a single protocol stack. The levels in the protocol stack "map," or correspond, to the layers of the OSI model. For instance, the TCP/IP protocol's application layer maps to the OSI model's presentation layer. Taken together, the protocols describe the entire stack's functions and capabilities.

How Protocols Work

The entire technical operation by which data is transmitted over the network has to be broken down into discrete, systematic steps. At each step, certain actions take place that cannot take place at any other step. Each step includes its own rules and procedures, or protocol.

The protocol steps must be carried out in a consistent order that is the same on every computer in the network. In the sending computer, these steps must be executed from the top down. In the receiving computer, these steps must be carried out from the bottom up.

The Sending Computer

Protocols at the sending computer:

1. Break the data into smaller sections, called packets, that the protocol can handle.
2. Add addressing information to the packets so that the destination computer on the network can determine that the data belongs to it.
3. Prepare the data for transmission through the NIC and out onto the network cable.

The Receiving Computer

Protocols at the receiving computer carry out the same series of steps in reverse order. They:

1. Take the data packets off the cable.
2. Bring the data packets into the computer through the NIC.
3. Strip the data packets of all the transmitting information that was added by the sending computer.
4. Copy the data from the packets to a buffer for reassembly.
5. Pass the reassembled data to the application in a usable form.

Both sending and receiving computers need to perform each step in the same way so that the data will have the same structure when it is received as it did when it was sent.

For example, two different protocols might each break data into packets and add on various sequencing, timing, and error-checking information, but each will do it differently. Therefore, a computer using one of these protocols will not be able to communicate successfully with a computer that is using the other protocol.

Routable Protocols

Until the mid-1980s, most local area networks (LANs) were isolated. A LAN served a single department or company and was rarely connected to any larger environments. As LAN technology matured, however, and the data communication needs of businesses expanded, LANs evolved, becoming components in larger data communication networks in which LANs talked to each other.

Data that is sent from one LAN to another along any of several available paths is said to be *routed*. The protocols that support multipath LAN-to-LAN communications are known as *routable protocols*. Because routable protocols can be used to tie several LANs together and create new wide-area environments, they are becoming increasingly important.

Protocols in a Layered Architecture

In a network, several protocols have to work together. By working together, they ensure that the data is properly prepared, transferred to the right destination, received, and acted upon.

The work of the various protocols must be coordinated so that no conflicts or incomplete operations take place. The results of this coordination effort are known as *layering*.

Protocol Stacks

A protocol stack is a combination of protocols. Each layer of the stack specifies a different protocol for handling a function or subsystem of the communication process. Each layer has its own set of rules. In Chapter 5, "Introducing Network Standards," we discussed the OSI reference model. Figure 6.1 shows the OSI model and the rules associated with each layer. The protocols define the rules for each layer in the OSI model.

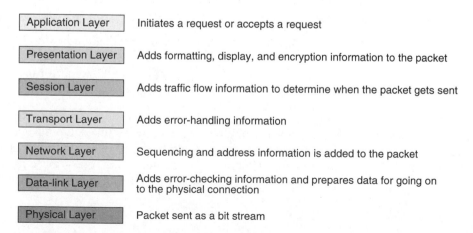

Figure 6.1   The OSI reference model showing the layers of protocols

The lower layers in the OSI model specify how manufacturers can make their equipment connect to equipment from other manufacturers, for example, by using NICs from several manufacturers on the same LAN. As long as they operate with the same protocols, they are able to send and receive data from each other. The upper layers specify rules for conducting communications sessions (the time during which two computers maintain a connection) and the interpretation of applications. The higher they are in the stack, the more sophisticated the tasks and their associated protocols become.

The Binding Process

The *binding process*—the process by which protocols become connected to each other and the NIC—allows a great deal of flexibility in setting up a network. Protocols and NICs can be mixed and matched on an as-needed basis. For example, two protocol stacks, such as Internetwork Packet Exchange and Sequenced Packet Exchange (IPX/SPX), discussed in Lesson 3: NetWare Protocols, and Transmission Control Protocol/Internet Protocol (TCP/IP), discussed in Lesson 2: TCP/IP, can be bound to one NIC. If there is more than one NIC in the computer, one protocol stack can be bound to either or both NICs.

The binding order determines the sequence in which the operating system runs the protocol. When multiple protocols are bound to a single NIC, the binding order is the sequence in which the protocols will be utilized to attempt a successful connection. Typically, the binding process is initiated when either the operating system or the protocol is installed or initialized. For example, if TCP/IP is the first protocol to be bound, the network operating system will attempt a network connection via TCP/IP before attempting to use another protocol. If this network connection fails, the computer will attempt to make a connection by using the next protocol in the binding order.

The binding process consists of more than just binding the protocol stack to the NIC. Protocol stacks need to be bound or associated with the components above and below them so that data can proceed smoothly through the stack during execution. For example, TCP/IP may be bound to the Network Basic Input/Output System (NetBIOS) session layer above as well as to the NIC driver below it. The NIC driver is also bound to the NIC.

Standard Stacks

The computer industry has designated several kinds of stacks as standard protocol models. Hardware and software manufacturers can develop their products to meet any one or a combination of these protocols. The most important models include:

- The ISO/OSI protocol suite.
- The IBM Systems Network Architecture (SNA).
- Digital DECnet.
- Novell NetWare.
- Apple's AppleTalk.
- The Internet protocol suite, TCP/IP.

Protocols exist at each layer of these stacks, performing the tasks specified by that layer. However, the communication tasks that networks need to perform are grouped into one of three protocol types. Each type is comprised of one or more layers of the OSI. As shown in Figure 6.2, these three protocol types map roughly to layers of the OSI model (application, transport, and network).

Note Many protocols were written long before the OSI reference model came into common use. Thus, it is not uncommon to find protocol stacks that do not map directly to the OSI model.

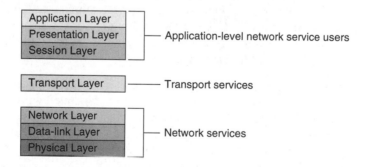

Figure 6.2 Communication tasks within the OSI reference model

Application Protocols

Application protocols work at the uppermost layer of the OSI reference model. They provide application-to-application interaction and data exchange. Popular application protocols are shown in Table 6.1.

Table 6.1   Popular Application Protocols

Protocol	Description
APPC (Advanced Program-to-Program Communication)	IBM's peer-to-peer SNA protocol, mostly used on AS/400 computers. APPC is defined as an application protocol, because it works in the presentation layer of the OSI model. However, it is also considered a transport protocol because APPC uses the LU 6.2 protocol that works in both the transport and session layers of the OSI model.
FTAM (File Transfer Access and Management)	An OSI file access protocol.
X.400	A CCITT protocol for international e-mail transmissions.
X.500	A CCITT protocol for file and directory services across several systems.
SMTP (Simple Mail Transfer Protocol)	An Internet protocol for transferring e-mail.
FTP (File Transfer Protocol)	An Internet file transfer protocol.
SNMP (Simple Network Management Protocol)	An Internet protocol for monitoring networks and network components.
Telnet	An Internet protocol for logging on to remote hosts and processing data locally.
Microsoft SMBs (Server Message Blocks) and client shells or redirectors	A client/server, request response protocol.
NCP (Novell NetWare Core Protocol) and Novell client shells or redirectors	A set of service protocols.
AppleTalk and AppleShare	Apple's networking protocol suite.
AFP (AppleTalk filing Protocol)	Apple's protocol for remote file access.
DAP (Data Access Protocol)	A DECnet file access protocol.

Transport Protocols

Transport protocols facilitate communication sessions between computers and ensure that data is able to move reliably between computers. Popular transport protocols are shown in Table 6.2.

Table 6.2   Popular Transport Protocols

Protocol	Description
TCP	The TCP/IP protocol for guaranteed delivery of sequenced data.
SPX	Part of Novell's IPX/SPX protocol suite for sequenced data.
NWLink	The Microsoft implementation of the IPX/SPX protocol.
NetBEUI (NetBIOS extended user interface)	Establishes communication sessions between computers (NetBIOS) and provides the underlying data transport services (NetBEUI).
ATP (AppleTalk Transaction Protocol) and NBP (Name Binding Protocol)	Apple's communication-session and data-transport protocols.

Network Protocols

Network protocols provide what are called "link services." These protocols handle addressing and routing information, error checking, and retransmission requests. Network protocols also define rules for communicating in a particular networking environment such as Ethernet or Token Ring. Popular network protocols are shown in Table 6.3.

Table 6.3   Popular Network Protocols

Protocol	Description
IP	The TCP/IP protocol for packet-forwarding routing.
IPX	NetWare's protocol for packet forwarding and routing.
NWLink	The Microsoft implementation of the IPX/SPX protocol.
NetBEUI	A transport protocol that provides data-transport services for NetBIOS sessions and applications.
DDP (Datagram Delivery Protocol)	An AppleTalk data-transport protocol.

Protocol Standards

The OSI model is used to define which protocols should be used at each layer. Figure 6.3 shows the OSI model and how several popular network manufacturers apply their protocols. Products from different manufacturers that subscribe to this model can communicate with each other.

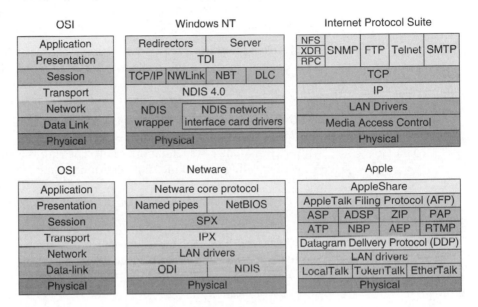

Figure 6.3   Manufacturer compatibility

The ISO, the Institute of Electrical and Electronic Engineers (IEEE), ANSI (American National Standards Institute), CCITT (Comité Consultatif Internationale de Télégraphie et Téléphonie), now called the ITU (International Telecommunications Union), and other standards bodies have developed protocols that map to some of the layers in the OSI model.

The IEEE protocols at the physical layer are:

- **802.3 (Ethernet)**   This is a logical bus network that can transmit data at 10 Mbps. Data is transmitted on the network to every computer. Only computers meant to receive the data acknowledge the transmission. The carrier-sense multiple access with collision detection (CSMA/CD) protocol regulates network traffic by allowing a transmission only when the network is clear and no other computer is transmitting.

- **802.4 (token passing)**   This is a bus layout that uses a token-passing scheme. Each computer receives all the data, but only the computers that are addressed respond. A token that travels the network determines which computer is able to broadcast.

- **802.5 (Token Ring)**   This is a logical ring network that transmits at either 4 Mbps or 16 Mbps. Although this is called a ring, it more resembles a star with each computer branching off a hub. The ring is actually inside the hub. A token traveling around the ring determines which computer can send data.

As described in Chapter 5, Lesson 1: Open Systems Interconnection (OSI) Reference Model, the data-link layer is divided into two sublayers (see Figure 6.4).

The IEEE has further defined these protocols to facilitate communications activity at the Media Access Control (MAC) sublayer.

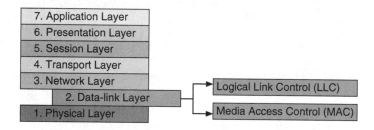

Figure 6.4   MAC driver or NIC driver

A MAC driver is located at the Media Access Control sublayer; this device driver is also known as the NIC driver. It provides low-level access to network adapters by providing data-transmission support and some basic adapter management functions.

A MAC protocol determines which computer can use the network cable when several computers try to use it simultaneously. CSMA/CD, the 802.3 protocol, allows computers to transmit data when no other computer is transmitting. If two hosts transmit simultaneously, a collision occurs. The protocol detects the collision and halts all transmission until the wire is clear. Then, each computer can begin to transmit again after waiting a random period of time.

Implementing and Removing Protocols

Protocols are implemented and removed in much the same way that drivers are added and removed. Essential protocols are installed automatically at the same time the initial operating system is installed on the computer. To install protocols such as NWLink after the initial installation, the network operating system usually includes a utility that leads the administrator through the process. For example, a network operating system setup program might provide a series of graphical windows that lead the administrator through the process of:

- Installing a new protocol.
- Changing the order in which the installed protocols have been linked.
- Removing a protocol.

Exercise 6.1 (a): Matching the OSI Model Rules to Layers

This exercise is designed to help you reinforce your understanding of network protocol stacks. The following table contains two columns. In the left column are listed the seven layers of the OSI reference model. In the right column, enter the rule that applies to the layer on the left.

OSI Reference Model Rules

OSI Layers	Rules
Application layer	
Presentation layer	
Session layer	
Transport layer	
Network layer	
Data-link layer	
Physical layer	

Exercise 6.1 (b): Matching the OSI Model Layers with Communication Tasks

Because many protocols were written before the OSI reference model was developed, some protocol stacks developed earlier don't match the OSI model; in those stacks, tasks are often grouped together.

Communication tasks can be classified into three groups. In this part of the exercise, the seven layers of the OSI model are again listed in the left column. In the right column, write in the name of one of the three groups in the following list.

Your task is to identify which of these three groups maps to each of the OSI layers in the left column.

The three groups are:

- Transport services.
- Network services.
- Application-level network service users.

Matching OSI Reference Model with Communication Tasks

OSI Layers	Communication Task
Application layer	
Presentation layer	
Session layer	
Transport layer	
Network layer	
Data-link layer	
Physical layer	

Lesson Summary

The following points summarize the main elements of this lesson:

- Protocols in a networking environment define the rules and procedures for transmitting data.
- To send data over a network successfully requires a series of separate steps that must be carried out in a prescribed order.
- The sending and receiving computers use protocols to:
  - Break data into packets.
  - Add addressing information to the packets.
  - Prepare the packets for transmission.
  - Take the packets off the cable.
  - Copy the data from the packets for reassembly.
  - Pass the reassembled data to the computer.
- Several stacks are used as standard protocols; the most prominent standard protocols are based on the OSI model layers.
- Protocols are implemented and removed in the same manner as drivers.

Lesson 2: TCP/IP

Transmission Control Protocol/Internet Protocol (TCP/IP) is an industry-standard suite of protocols that provide communications in a heterogeneous (made up of dissimilar elements) environment. In addition, TCP/IP provides a routable, enterprise networking protocol and access to the Internet and its resources. Because of its popularity, TCP/IP has become the de facto standard for what's known as *internetworking*, the intercommunication in a network that's composed of smaller networks. This lesson examines the TCP/IP protocol and its relationship to the OSI model.

After this lesson, you will be able to:
- Define the TCP/IP protocol.
- Describe the four layers of the TCP/IP protocol and how they relate to the OSI model.

Estimated lesson time: 15 minutes

Introduction to TCP/IP

TCP/IP has become the standard protocol used for interoperability among many different types of computers. This interoperability is a primary advantage of TCP/IP. Most networks support TCP/IP as a protocol. TCP/IP also supports routing and is commonly used as an internetworking protocol.

Other protocols written specifically for the TCP/IP suite include:

- **SMTP (Simple Mail Transfer Protocol)**   E-mail.
- **FTP (File Transfer Protocol)**   For exchanging files among computers running TCP/IP.
- **SNMP (Simple Network Management Protocol)**   For network management.

Designed to be routable, robust, and functionally efficient, TCP/IP was developed by the United States Department of Defense as a set of wide area network (WAN) protocols. Its purpose was to maintain communication links between sites in the event of nuclear war. The responsibility for TCP/IP development now resides with the Internet community as a whole. TCP/IP requires significant knowledge and experience on the user's part to install and configure. Using TCP/IP offers several advantages; it:

- **Is an industry standard**   As an industry standard, it is an open protocol. This means it is not controlled by a single company, and is less subject to compatibility issues. It is the de facto protocol of the Internet.

- **Contains a set of utilities for connecting dissimilar operating systems**
Connectivity from one computer to another does not depend on the network
operating system used on either computer.

- **Uses scalable, cross-platform client-server architecture**   TCP/IP can
expand (or shrink) to meet future needs and circumstances. It uses sockets
to make the computer operating systems transparent to one another.

Note A *socket* is an identifier for a particular service on a particular node
on a network. The socket consists of a node address and a port number that
identifies the service.

Historically, TCP/IP has had two primary disadvantages: its size and speed. TCP/IP
is a relatively large protocol stack that can cause problems in MS-DOS-based
clients. However, due to the system requirements (processor speeds and memory)
on graphical user interface (GUI)-based operating systems, such as Windows NT
or Windows 95 and 98, size is not an issue.

TCP/IP Standards

TCP/IP standards are published in a series of documents called Requests for
Comment (RFC). Their primary purpose is to provide information or to describe
work in progress. Although not originally intended to serve as standards, many
RFCs are accepted as true standards.

Internet development is based on the concept of open standards. That is, anyone
who wishes to do so can use or participate in developing standards for the
Internet. The Internet Architecture Board (IAB) is the committee responsible
for managing and publishing RFCs for the Internet. The IAB allows anyone or
any company to submit or evaluate an RFC. This includes any proposed idea
for changes or new standards. After a reasonable amount of time is allowed for
discussion, a newly proposed draft will or will not become a standard.

The InterNIC Directory and Database provided by AT&T is a service that fur-
nishes sources of information about the Internet to the public. The Directory and
Database includes the RFCs. This service can be found at www.internic.net on
the World Wide Web. Furthermore, RFCs can be downloaded from the following
FTP sites:

nis.nsf.net	ftp.ncren.net
nisc.jvnc.net	ftp.sesqui.net
ftp.isi.edu	ftp.nic.it
wuarchive.wustl.edu	ftp.imag.fr

TCP/IP and OSI

The TCP/IP protocol does not exactly match the OSI model. Instead of seven layers, it uses only four. Commonly referred to as the Internet Protocol Suite, TCP/IP is broken into the following four layers:

- Network interface layer
- Internet layer
- Transport layer
- Application layer

Each of these layers corresponds to one or more layers of the OSI model.

Network Interface Layer

The *network interface layer,* corresponding to the physical and data-link layers of the OSI model, communicates directly with the network. It provides the interface between the network architecture (such as token ring, Ethernet) and the Internet layer.

Internet Layer

The *internet layer,* corresponding to the network layer of the OSI model, uses several protocols for routing and delivering packets. Routers, which are discussed in Chapter 7, "Elements of Network Connectivity," are protocol dependent. They function at this layer of the model and are used to forward packets from one network or segment to another. Several protocols work within the Internet layer.

Internet Protocol (IP)

Internet Protocol (IP) is a packet-switched protocol that performs addressing and route selection. As a packet is transmitted, this protocol appends a header to the packet so that it can be routed through the network using dynamic routing tables. IP is a connectionless protocol and sends packets without expecting the receiving host to acknowledge receipt. In addition, IP is responsible for packet assembly and disassembly as required by the physical and data-link layers of the OSI model. Each IP packet is made up of a source and a destination address, protocol identifier, checksum (a calculated value), and a TTL (which stands for "time to live"). The TTL tells each router on the network between the source and the destination how long the packet has to remain on the network. It works like a countdown counter or clock. As the packet passes through the router, the router deducts the larger of one unit (one second) or the time that the packet was queued for delivery. For example, if a packet has a TTL of 128, it can stay on the network for 128 seconds or 128 hops (each stop, or router, along the way), or any combination of the two. The purpose of the TTL is to prevent lost or damaged data packets (such as missing e-mail messages) from endlessly wandering the network. When the TTL counts down to zero, the packet is eliminated from the network.

Another method used by the IP to increase the speed of transmission is known as "ANDing." The purpose of ANDing is to determine whether the address is a local or a remote site. If the address is local, IP will ask the Address Resolution Protocol (ARP), discussed in the next section, for the hardware address of the destination machine. If the address is remote, the IP checks its local routing table for a route to the destination. If a route exists, the packet is sent on its way. If no route exists, the packet is sent to the local default gateway and then on its way.

Note An AND is a logical operation that combines the values of two bits (0, 1) or two Boolean values (false, true) that returns a value of 1 (true) if both input values are 1 (true) and returns a 0 (false) otherwise.

Address Resolution Protocol (ARP)

Before an IP packet can be forwarded to another host, the hardware address of the receiving machine must be known. The ARP determines hardware address (MAC addresses) that correspond to an IP address. If ARP does not contain the address in its own cache, it broadcasts a request for the address. All hosts on the network process the request and, if they contain a map to that address, pass the address back to the requestor. The packet is then sent on its way, and the new information address is stored in the router's cache.

Reverse Address Resolution Protocol (RARP)

A RARP server maintains a database of machine numbers in the form of an ARP table (or cache) which is created by the system administrator. In contrast to ARP, the RARP protocol provides an IP number to a requesting hardware address. When the RARP server receives a request for an IP number from a node on the network, it responds by checking its routing table for the machine number of the requesting node and sending the appropriate IP number back to the requesting node.

Internet Control Message Protocol (ICMP)

The ICMP is used by IP and higher-level protocols to send and receive status reports about information being transmitted. Routers commonly use ICMP to control the flow, or speed, of data between themselves. If the flow of data is too fast for a router, it requests that other routers slow down.

The two basic categories of ICMP messages are reporting errors and sending queries.

Transport Layer

The *transport layer*, corresponding to the transport layer of the OSI model, is responsible for establishing and maintaining end-to-end communication between two hosts. The transport layer provides acknowledgment of receipt, flow control, and sequencing of packets. It also handles retransmissions of packets. The transport layer can use either TCP or User Datagram Protocol (UDP) protocols depending on the requirements of the transmission.

Transmission Control Protocol (TCP)

The TCP is responsible for the reliable transmission of data from one node to another. It is a connection-based protocol and establishes a connection (also known as a session, virtual circuit, or link), between two machines before any data is transferred. To establish a reliable connection, TCP uses what is known as a "three-way handshake." This establishes the port number and beginning sequence numbers from both sides of the transmission. The handshake contains three steps:

1. The requestor sends a packet specifying the port number it plans to use and its initial sequence number (ISN) to the server.

2. The server acknowledges with its ISN, which consists of the requestor's ISN, plus 1.

3. The requestor acknowledges the acknowledgement with the server's ISN, plus 1.

In order to maintain a reliable connection, each packet must contain:

- A source and destination TCP port number.

- A sequence number for messages that must be broken into smaller pieces.

- A checksum to ensure that information is sent without error.

- An acknowledgement number that tells the sending machine which pieces of the message have arrived.

- TCP Sliding Windows.

Ports, Sockets, and Sliding Windows

Protocol port numbers are used to reference the location of a particular application or process on each machine (in the application layer). Just as an IP address identifies the address of a host on the network, the port address identifies the application to the transport layer, thus providing a complete connection for one application on one host to an application on another host. Applications and services (such as file and print services or telnet) can configure up to 65,536 ports. TCP/IP applications and services typically use the first 1023 ports. The Internet Assigned Numbers Authority (IANA) has assigned these as standard, or default, ports. Any client applications dynamically assign port numbers as needed. A port and a node address together make up a socket.

Services and applications use sockets to establish connections with another host. If applications need to guarantee the delivery of data, the socket chooses the connection-oriented service (TCP). If the applications do not need to guarantee data delivery, the socket chooses the connectionless service (UDP).

A sliding window is used by TCP for transferring data between hosts. It regulates how much information can be passed over a TCP connection before the receiving host must send an acknowledgement. Each computer has both a send and a receive window that it utilizes to buffer data and make the communication process more efficient. A sliding window allows the sending computer to transmit data in a stream without having to wait for each packet to be acknowledged. This allows the receiving machine to receive packets out of order and reorganize them while it waits for more packets. The sending window keeps track of data that has been sent, and if an acknowledgement is not received within a given amount of time, the packets are re-sent.

User Datagram Protocol (UDP)

A connectionless protocol, the UDP, is responsible for end-to-end transmission of data. Unlike TCP, however, UDP does not establish a connection. It attempts to send the data and to verify that the destination host actually receives the data. UDP is best used to send small amounts of data for which guaranteed delivery is not required. While UDP uses ports, they are different from TCP ports; therefore, they can use the same numbers without interference.

Application Layer

Corresponding to the session, presentation, and application layers of the OSI model, the *application layer* connects applications to the network. Two application programming interfaces (APIs) provide access to the TCP/IP transport protocols—Windows Sockets and NetBIOS.

Windows Sockets Interface

Windows Sockets (WinSock) is a networking API designed to facilitate communication among different TCP/IP applications and protocol stacks. It was established so that applications using TCP/IP could write to a standard interface. WinSock is derived from the original sockets that API created for the BSD Unix operating system. WinSock provides a common interface for the applications and protocols that exist near the top of the TCP/IP reference model. Any program or application written using the WinSock API can communicate with any TCP/IP protocol and vice versa.

Exercise 6.2: Comparing OSI and TCP/IP Layers

Exercise 6.2 is designed to help you understand the relationship between the OSI model and Transmission Control Protocol/Internet Protocol (TCP/IP). Because TCP/IP was developed before the OSI reference model was developed, it does not exactly match the seven OSI model layers. In this exercise, you will be mapping the four layers of TCP/IP to the seven layers of the OSI model.

The four layers of TCP/IP are the:

- Network interface layer.
- Internet layer.
- Transport layer.
- Application layer.

The left column lists the seven layers of the OSI model. In the right column, fill in the name of the corresponding TCP/IP layer.

Comparison of OSI and TCP/IP Layers

OSI Layers	TCP/IP Layers
Application layer	
Presentation layer	
Session layer	
Transport layer	
Network layer	
Data-link layer	
Physical layer	

Lesson Summary

The following points summarize the main elements of this lesson:

- TCP/IP is an industry-standard suite of protocols providing communication in a heterogeneous environment.
- The four layers of TCP/IP are the network-interface layer, Internet layer, transport layer, and application layer.
- The TCP protocol works in the transport layer and provides connection-oriented communication between two computers.
- The UDP protocol works in the transport layer and provides connectionless communication between two computers.
- The network interface layer of TCP/IP maps to the physical and data-link layers of OSI.
- The Internet layer of TCP/IP maps to the network layer of OSI.
- The transport layer of TCP/IP maps to the transport layer of OSI.
- The application layer of TCP/IP maps to the session, presentation, and application layers of OSI.

Lesson 3: NetWare Protocols

In Chapter 4, we learned that Novell's NetWare is one of the leading network architectures. In this lesson, we explore the protocols used by NetWare and how they relate to the OSI reference model.

After this lesson, you will be able to:

- Define the protocols that make up the NetWare protocol suite.
- Relate the NetWare protocols to the OSI reference model.

Estimated lesson time: 15 minutes

Introduction to NetWare Protocols

Like TCP/IP, Novell provides a suite of protocols developed specifically for NetWare. The five main protocols used by NetWare are:

- Media Access Protocol.
- Internetwork Packet Exchange/Sequenced Packet Exchange (IPX/SPX).
- Routing Information Protocol (RIP).
- Service Advertising Protocol (SAP).
- NetWare Core Protocol (NCP).

Because these protocols were defined well before the finalization of the OSI model, they do not exactly match OSI. Figure 6.5 provides mapping of the NetWare protocols to the OSI model. In actuality, no direct correlation to the layer boundaries of the two architectures exists. These protocols follow an enveloping pattern. More specifically, the upper-lever protocols (NCP, SAP, and RIP) are enveloped by IPX/SPX. A Media Access Protocol header and trailer then envelop IPX/SPX.

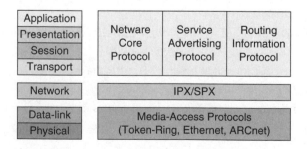

Figure 6.5   Comparing NetWare and OSI reference models

Media Access Protocols

Media Access Protocols define the addressing that distinguishes each node on a NetWare network. The addressing is implemented on the hardware or NIC. The most common implementations are:

- 802.5 Token Ring.
- 802.3 Ethernet.
- Ethernet 2.0.

This protocol is responsible for placing the header on the packet. Each header includes the source and destination code. After the packet has been transmitted and is on the media, each network card checks the address; if their address matches the destination address on the packet, or, if the packet is a broadcast message, the NIC copies the packet and sends it up the protocol stack.

In addition to addressing, this protocol provides bit-level error checking in the form of a cyclical redundancy check (CRC). With the CRC appended to the packet, it is virtually certain that all the packets will be free of corruption.

Note CRC error checking uses a complex calculation to generate a number based on the data transmitted. The sending device performs the calculation before transmission and includes it in the packet that it sends to the receiving device. The receiving device repeats the same calculation after transmission. If both devices obtain the same result, it is assumed that the transmission was error-free. The procedure is known as a redundancy check because each transmission includes not only data but extra (redundant) error-checking values.

Internetwork Packet Exchange and Sequenced Packet Exchange (IPX/SPX)

Internetwork Packet Exchange (IPX) defines the addressing schemes used on a NetWare network, and Sequenced Packet Exchange (SPX) provides security and reliability to the IPX protocol. IPX is a datagram-based, connectionless, unreliable, network-layer protocol that is equivalent to the IP. It does not require an acknowledgement for each packet sent. Any acknowledgement control or connection control must be provided by the protocols above IPX. SPX provides connection-oriented, reliable servers at the transport layer.

Using the Xerox Network System (XNS) Internet Datagram Protocol, Novell adopted IPX protocol. IPX defines two kinds of addressing:

- **Internetwork addressing**   The address of a segment on the network, identified by the network number assigned during installation.
- **Intranode addressing**   The address of a process within a node that is identified by a socket number.

IPX protocols are used only on networks with NetWare servers and are often installed along with another protocol suite such as TCP/IP. Even NetWare is moving toward using TCP/IP as a standard.

Routing Information Protocol (RIP)

Facilitating the exchange of routing information on a NetWare network, RIP, like IPX, was developed from XNS. However, in RIP, an extra field of data was added to the packet to improve the decision criteria for selecting the fastest route to a destination. The broadcast of an RIP packet allows several things to occur:

- Workstations can locate the fastest route to a network number.

- Routers can request routing information from other routers to update their own internal tables. (Routers are discussed in detail in Chapter 7, "Elements of Network Connectivity.")

- Routers can respond to route requests from workstations and other routers.

- Routers can make sure that all other routers are aware of the internetwork configuration.

- Routers can detect a change in the internetwork configuration.

Service Advertising Protocol (SAP)

The Service Advertising Protocol (SAP) allows service-providing nodes (including file servers, printer servers, gateway servers, and application servers) to advertise their services and addresses. Clients on the network are able to obtain the internetwork address of any servers they can access. With SAP, the adding and removing of services on the network becomes dynamic. By default, a SAP server broadcasts its presence every 60 seconds. A SAP packet contains:

- **Operating Information**   Specifies the operation that the packet is performing.
- **Service type**   Specifies the type of service offered by the server.
- **Server name**   Specifies the name of the broadcasting server.
- **Network address**   Specifies the network number of the broadcasting server.
- **Node address**   Specifies the node number of the broadcasting server.
- **Socket address**   Specifies the socket number of the broadcasting server.
- **Total hops to server**   Specifies the number of hops to the broadcasting server.
- **Operation field**   Specifies the type of request.
- **Additional information**   One or more sets of fields can follow the operation field which contain more information about one or more servers.

NetWare Core Protocol (NCP)

The NetWare Core Protocol (NCP) defines the connection control and service request encoding that make it possible for clients and servers to interact. This is the protocol that provides transport and session services. NetWare security is also provided within this protocol.

Exercise 6.3: Comparing the OSI Model with NetWare Protocols

This exercise is designed to help you understand the relationship between the OSI reference model and NetWare protocols. NetWare was developed earlier than the OSI model and, therefore, does not precisely match the seven layers. In this exercise, you will be mapping the various components of NetWare protocols to the seven layers of the OSI reference model.

In the table that follows, the column on the left lists the seven layers of the OSI model. The blank columns on the right represent various components of the NetWare protocol. In the blank columns, map the following NetWare protocol components to the OSI model.

- IPX/SPX
- Media Access Protocol
- NetWare Core Protocol
- Routing Information Protocol
- Service Advertising Protocol

Comparison of OSI Model with NetWare Protocols

OSI Layers	NetWare Protocols
Application layer	
Presentation layer	
Session layer	
Transport layer	
Network layer	
Data-link layer	
Physical layer	

Lesson Summary

The following points summarize the main elements of this lesson:

- NetWare protocols were developed before the OSI reference model and therefore do not match the OSI model.

- The five protocols used with NetWare are Media Access Protocol, Internetwork Packet Exchange/Sequenced Packet Exchange (IPX/SPX), Routing Information Protocol (RIP), Service Advertising Protocol (SAP), and NetWare Core Protocol (NCP).

- The Media Access Protocol defines the addressing on each node of a NetWare network. It is responsible for placing the header with both the destination and source addresses on the packet.

- IPX defines the addressing schemes used on a NetWare network.

- SPX provides connection-oriented, reliable servers at the transport layer.

- SAP allows file servers, printer servers, gateways, and applications to broadcast or advertise their services to the network.

- NetWare security is provided in the NetWare Core Protocol.

Lesson 4: Other Common Protocols

This lesson provides a summary of several of the lesser, yet most commonly used, protocols.

After this lesson, you will be able to:
- Identify several of the more common protocols.
- Determine which protocol is best suited for the network scenario.

Estimated lesson time: 15 minutes

Network Basic Input/Output System (NetBIOS)

Most of the services and applications that run within the Windows operating system use the NetBIOS interface or *interprocess communication (IPC)*. NetBIOS was developed on LANs and has evolved into a standard interface for applications to use to access networking protocols in the transport layer for both connection-oriented and nonconnection-oriented communications. NetBIOS interfaces exist for NetBEUI, NWLink, and TCP/IP. NetBIOS requires an IP address and a NetBIOS name to uniquely identify a computer.

NetBIOS performs four primary functions:

- **NetBIOS name resolution**   Each workstation on a network has one or more names. NetBIOS maintains a table of the names and any aliases. The first name in the table is the unique name of the NIC. Optional user names can be added to provide a user-friendly identification system. NetBIOS then cross-references the names as required.

- **NetBIOS Datagram service**   This function allows a message to be sent to any name, group of names, or to all users on the network. However, because this does not use point-to-point connections, there is no guarantee that the message will arrive at its destination.

- **NetBIOS Session service**   This service opens a point-to-point connection between two workstations on the network. One workstation initiates a call to another and opens the connection. Because both workstations are peers, they both can send and receive data concurrently.

- **NetBIOS NIC/session status**   This function makes information about the local NIC, other NICs, and any currently active sessions available to any application software using NetBIOS.

Originally, IBM offered NetBIOS as a separate product, implemented as a terminate-and-stay-resident (TSR) program. This TSR program is now obsolete; if you should encounter one of these systems, you should replace it with the Windows NetBIOS interface.

NetBEUI

NetBEUI is the acronym for NetBIOS Extended User Interface. Originally, NetBIOS and NetBEUI were tightly tied together and considered one protocol. However, several network manufacturers separated out NetBIOS, the session-layer protocol, so that it could be used with other routable transport protocols. NetBIOS (network basic input/output system) is an IBM session-layer LAN interface that acts as an application interface to the network. NetBIOS provides the tools for a program to establish a session with another program over the network and, because so many application programs support it, it is very popular.

NetBEUI is a small, fast, and efficient transport-layer protocol that is supplied with all Microsoft network products. It has been available since the mid-1980s and was supplied with the first networking product from Microsoft: MS-NET.

Advantages of NetBEUI include its small stack size (important for computers running MS-DOS), its speed of data transfer on the network medium, and its compatibility with all Microsoft-based networks.

The major disadvantage of NetBEUI is that it does not support routing. It is also limited to Microsoft-based networks. NetBEUI is a good and economical solution for a small peer-to-peer network where all workstations use Microsoft operating systems.

X.25 Packet Switching

A set of WAN protocols, X.25 is incorporated in a packet-switching network made up of switching services. The switching services were originally established to connect remote terminals to mainframe host systems. The network breaks up each transmission into multiple packets and places them on the network. The pathway between nodes is a virtual circuit that looks like a single, continuous, logical connection to the upper layers. Each packet can take different routes from the source to the destination. After the packets arrive, they are reassembled into their original data message.

A typical packet includes 128 bytes of data; however, the source and destination can negotiate a different packet size after making the virtual connection. The X.25 protocol can support a theoretical maximum of 4095 concurrent virtual circuits across a physical link between a node and the X.25 network. Typical data-transmission speed for X.25 is 64 Kbps.

The X.25 protocol works in the physical, data-link and network layers of the OSI model. It has been around since the mid-1970s and has been well debugged; therefore, it is a stable network environment. It does, however, have two shortcomings:

- The store-and-forward mechanism causes delays. Typically, the delay is about .06 second and has no effect on large blocks of data. However, in a flip-flop type of transmission, the delay might be noticeable.

> **Note** A "flip-flop" is a circuit that alternates between two possible states when a pulse is received at the input. For example, if the output of a flip-flop is high and a pulse is received at the input, the output "flips" to low; a second input pulse "flops" the output back to high, and so on.

- A large amount of buffering is required to support the store-and-forward data transfer.

X.25 and TCP/IP are similar in that they both use packet-switched protocols. However, there are several differences between the two:

- TCP/IP has only end-to-end error checking and flow control; X.25 has error checking from node to node.
- To compensate for the fact that a TCP/IP network is completely passive, TCP/IP has a more complicated flow control and window mechanism than X.25 has.
- X.25 has tightly specified the electrical and link levels; TCP/IP is designed to travel over many different kinds of media, with many different types of link service.

Xerox Network System (XNS)

Xerox developed Xerox Network System (XNS) for its Ethernet LANs. XNS became widely used in the 1980s, but has been slowly replaced by TCP/IP. It is a large, slow protocol, but produces more broadcasts, causing more network traffic.

Advanced Program-to-Program Communication (APPC)

Advanced Program-to-Program Communication (APPC) is IBM's transport protocol developed as part of its Systems Network Architecture (SNA). It was designed to enable application programs running on different computers to communicate and exchange data directly.

AppleTalk

AppleTalk is Apple Computer's proprietary protocol stack designed to enable Apple Macintosh computers to share files and printers in a networked environment. It was introduced in 1984 as a self-configuring LAN technology. AppleTalk is also available on many UNIX systems that use third-party freeware and commercial packages. The AppleTalk protocol suite encompasses high-level file sharing using AppleShare, LaserWriter printing services and print spoolers, along with lower-level data streams and simple datagram delivery. Table 6.4 illustrates AppleTalk features.

Table 6.4   AppleTalk Protocols

AppleTalk Type	Description
AppleTalk	A collection of protocols that correspond to the OSI model. It supports LocalTalk, EtherTalk, and TokenTalk.
LocalTalk	Describes the simple, shielded, twisted-pair cable used to connect Macintoshes to other Macintoshes or printers. A LocalTalk segment supports a maximum of 32 devices and operates at a speed of 230 Kbps.
EtherTalk	AppleTalk over Ethernet. It operates at a speed of 10 Mbps. Fast EtherTalk operates at a speed of 100 Mbps.
TokenTalk	AppleTalk over Token-Ring. Depending on its hardware, TokenTalk operates at either 4 Mbps or 16 Mbps.

Figure 6.6 shows a typical AppleTalk network including an Ethernet connection.

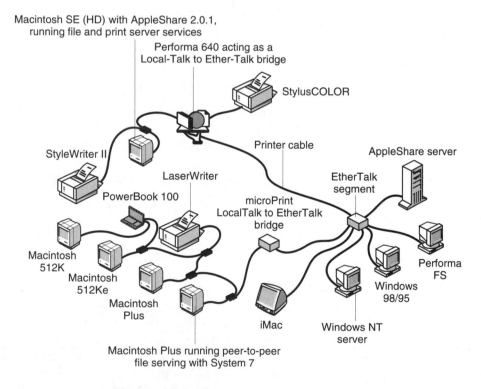

Figure 6.6   AppleTalk network

OSI Protocol Suite

The OSI protocol suite is a complete protocol stack. Each protocol maps directly to a single layer of the OSI model. The OSI protocol suite includes routing and transport protocols, IEEE 802 series protocols, a session-layer protocol, a presentation-layer protocol, and several application-layer protocols designed to provide full networking functionality, including file access, printing, and terminal emulation.

DECnet

DECnet is Digital Equipment Corporation's proprietary protocol stack. It is a set of hardware and software products that implement the Digital Network Architecture (DNA). It defines communication networks over Ethernet LANs, Fiber Distributed Data Interface metropolitan area networks (FDDI MANs), and WANs that use private or public data-transmission facilities. DECnet can also use TCP/IP and OSI protocols as well as its own protocols. It is a routable protocol.

DECnet has been updated several times; each update is called a "phase." The current revision is DECnet Phase V, and the protocols used are both proprietary to Digital and offer a fairly complete implementation of the OSI protocol suite.

Exercise 6.4: Protocol Matching Problem

Along with the better-known protocols, many other lesser, but still common, protocols exist. Five such protocols are listed below. In this exercise, you will be matching each of the protocols in the list that follows with the feature that describes what it does.

Five common protocols

A. AppleTalk

B. DECnet

C. NetBEUI

D. NetBIOS

E. X.25

In each blank space on the left, fill in the letter of the protocol that uses the feature listed on the right. Note that more than one protocol can be matched to a particular feature.

_____ A protocol that is commonly used for Microsoft-based, peer-to-peer networks

_____ A protocol used for packet switching

_____ A protocol that is commonly used for Macintosh networks

_____ A protocol designed by Digital Equipment Corporation (DEC)

_____ A protocol originally offered by IBM

_____ A small, fast, transport-layer protocol

_____ A protocol that is nonroutable

Lesson Summary

The following points summarize the main elements of this lesson:

- Many protocols are used for networking; each has unique advantages and disadvantages.
- NetBIOS and NetBEUI are commonly used for Microsoft-based, peer-to-peer networks.
- NetBIOS and NetBEUI are nonroutable protocols.
- X.25 is a protocol for packet switching.
- AppleTalk is the protocol developed for Macintosh networks.
- DECnet is Digital Equipment Corporation's proprietary protocol stack.

Chapter Summary

The following points summarize the key concepts of this chapter:

Introduction to Protocols

- Protocols in a networking environment define the rules and procedures for transmitting data.

- To send data over a network successfully requires a series of separate steps that must be carried out in a prescribed order.

- The sending and receiving computers use protocols to:

    - Break data into packets.

    - Add addressing information to the packets.

    - Prepare the packets for transmission.

    - Take the packets off the cable.

    - Copy the data from the packets for reassembly.

    - Pass the reassembled data to the computer.

- Several stacks are used as standard protocols; the most prominent standard protocols are based on the OSI model layers.

- Protocols are implemented and removed in the same manner as drivers.

TCP/IP

- TCP/IP is an industry-standard suite of protocols providing communication in a heterogeneous environment.

- The four layers of TCP/IP are the network interface layer, Internet layer, transport layer, and application layer.

- The TCP protocol works in the transport layer and provides connection-oriented communication between two computers.

- The UDP protocol works in the transport layer and provides connectionless communication between two computers.

- The network interface layer of TCP/IP maps to the physical and data-link layers of OSI.

- The Internet layer of TCP/IP maps to the network layer of OSI.

- The transport layer of TCP/IP maps to the transport layer of OSI.

- The application layer of TCP/IP maps to the session, presentation, and application layers of OSI.

NetWare Protocols

- NetWare protocols were developed before the OSI reference model and therefore do not match the OSI model.

- The five protocols used with NetWare are Media Access Protocol, Internetwork Packet Exchange/Sequenced Packet Exchange Protocol (IPX/SPX), Routing Information Protocol (RIP), Service Advertising Protocol (SAP), and NetWare Core Protocol (NCP).

Other Common Protocols

- Many protocols are used for networking; each has unique advantages and disadvantages.

- NetBIOS and NetBEUI are commonly used for Microsoft-based, peer-to-peer networks.

- NetBIOS and NetBEUI are nonroutable protocols.

- X.25 is a protocol for packet switching.

- AppleTalk is the protocol developed for Macintosh networks.

- DECnet is Digital Equipment Corporation's proprietary protocol stack.

Chapter Review

1. A sending computer breaks the data into smaller sections, called _____, that the protocol can handle.

2. Several protocols can work together in what is known as a protocol _____.

3. A receiving computer copies the data from the packets to a _____ for reassembly.

4. Protocols that support multipath LAN-to-LAN communications are known as _____ protocols.

5. The receiving computer passes the reassembled data to the _____ in a usable form.

6. To avoid conflicts or incomplete operations, protocols are _____ in an orderly manner.

7. The _____ order indicates where the protocol sits in the protocol stack.

8. Three protocol types that map roughly to the OSI model are application, _____, and network.

9. Application protocols work at the upper layer of the OSI model and provide _____ _____ between applications.

10. A NIC-driver protocol resides in the _____ _____ _____ (_____) sublayer of the OSI model.

11. Rules for communicating in a particular LAN environment such as Ethernet or Token Ring are called _____ protocols.

12. To help the network administrator install a protocol after the initial system installation, a _____ is included with the operating system.

13. TCP/IP supports routing and is commonly used as an _____ protocol.

14. NetBIOS is an IBM session-layer LAN interface that acts as an _____ interface to the network.

15. APPC (advanced program-to-program communication) is IBM's _____ protocol.

16. NetBEUI is not a good choice for large networks because it is not _____.

17. X.25 is a protocol used for a _____ - _____ network.

18. X.25 works in the _____, _____ - _____, and
    _____ layers of the OSI model.

19. AppleTalk is a proprietary protocol stack designed for _____
    computers.

20. EtherTalk allows a Macintosh computer to communicate on an
    _____ network.

C H A P T E R   7

Elements of Network Connectivity

About This Chapter

The explosive expansion of the Internet and the geographical diversification of corporations have generated a need for large, worldwide networks. While previous chapters discussed networking basics, with a focus on smaller networks, this chapter explores the devices and technologies available to expand networks beyond the scope of simple local area networks (LANs). The discussion begins with modems, moves on to repeaters, bridges, routers, brouters, and gateways, and concludes with a look at remote access computing. You will learn how a network can be expanded across the street or around the world.

Before You Begin

This chapter is an expansion of Chapter 2, "Basic Network Media." You should review the sections on topology and network cabling before starting this chapter. Many of the terms discussed in Chapter 2 are used or expanded in this chapter. Also, references are made to Ethernet and Token Ring architectures. You can review these topics in Chapter 3, "Understanding Network Architecture."

Lesson 1: Connectivity Devices

This lesson is devoted to the hardware that is used to expand networks. We begin with the most basic communication device: the modem. Modems have become so common that they are standard equipment on most computers sold today. Indeed, anyone who has ever used the Internet or a fax machine has used a modem. In addition to modems, several devices are used to connect small LANs into larger wide area networks (WANs). Each of these devices has its own function along with some limitations. They can be used simply to extend the length of network media or to provide access to a worldwide network over the Internet. Devices used to expand LANs include repeaters, bridges, routers, brouters, and gateways.

After this lesson, you will be able to:

- Describe the basic functions of a modem.
- Identify modem standards.
- Describe the function of repeaters, bridges, routers, brouters, and gateways.

Estimated lesson time: 65 minutes

Modem Technology

A modem is a device that makes it possible for computers to communicate over a telephone line.

When computers are too far apart to be joined by a standard computer cable, a *modem* can enable communication between them. Remember from Chapter 2, "Basic Network Media," that network cables are limited in length. In a network environment, modems serve as a means of communication between networks and as a way to connect to the world beyond the local network.

Run the **c07dem01** video located in the **Demos** folder on the CD accompanying this book to view a presentation of how a modem makes it possible for computers to communicate over a telephone line.

Basic Modem Functions

Computers cannot simply be connected to each other over a telephone line, because computers communicate by sending digital electronic pulses (electronic signals), and a telephone line can send only analog waves (sound). Figure 7.1 shows the difference between digital computer communication and analog telephone communication.

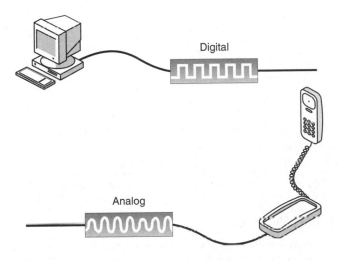

Figure 7.1 Digital signals versus analog waves

A digital signal has a binary form. The signal can have a value of either 0 or 1. An analog signal can be pictured as a smooth curve that can represent an infinite range of values.

 Run the **c07dem02**, **c07dem03**, and **c07dem04** videos located in the **Demos** folder on the CD accompanying this book for an illustrated overview of modem functions.

As shown in Figure 7.2, the modem at the sending end converts the computer's digital signals into analog waves and transmits the analog waves onto the telephone line. A modem at the receiving end converts the incoming analog signals back into digital signals for the receiving computer.

In other words, a sending modem *MO*dulates digital signals into analog signals, and a receiving modem *DEM*odulates analog signals back into digital signals.

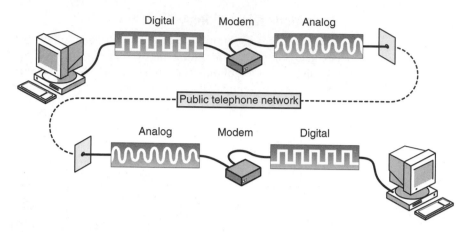

Figure 7.2 Modems convert digital signals to analog waves, and convert analog waves to digital signals

Note To use digital lines, you must install a special digital card in the computer.

Modem Hardware

Modems are known as data communications equipment (DCE) and share the following characteristics:

- A serial (RS-232) communications interface
- An RJ-11 telephone-line interface (a four-wire telephone plug)

Run the **c07dem05** video located in the **Demos** folder on the CD accompanying this book to view a presentation of modem cable interfaces.

Modems are available in both internal and external models. An internal modem, as shown in Figure 7.3, is installed in a computer's expansion slot like any other circuit board.

Run the **c07dem06** video located in the **Demos** folder on the CD accompanying this book to view a presentation of internal modems.

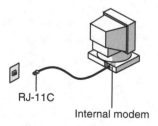

RJ-11C

Internal modem

Figure 7.3 Internal modem installed in an expansion slot

An external modem, as shown in Figure 7.4, is a small box that is connected to the computer by a serial (RS-232) cable running from the computer's serial port to the modem's computer cable connection. The modem uses a cable with an RJ-11C connector to connect to the wall.

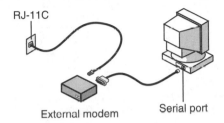

RJ-11C

External modem   Serial port

Figure 7.4   External modem connects through the RS-232 cable to the computer serial port

 Run the **c07dcm07** video located in the **Demos** folder on the CD accompanying this book to view a presentation of external modems.

Modem Standards

Standards are necessary so that modems from one manufacturer can communicate with modems from another manufacturer. This section explains some of the common industry standards for modems.

Hayes-Compatible

In the early 1980s, a company called Hayes Microcomputer Products developed a modem called the Hayes Smartmodem. The Smartmodem became the standard against which other modems were measured, and generated the phrase "Hayes-compatible," just as IBM's personal computer generated the term "IBM-compatible." Because most vendors conformed to the Hayes standards, nearly all LAN modems could communicate with each other.

The early Hayes-compatible modems sent and received data at 300 bits per second (bps). Modem manufacturers currently offer modems with speeds of 56,600 bps or more.

International Standards

Since the late 1980s, the International Telecommunications Union (ITU) has developed standards for modems. These specifications, known as the V series, include a number that indicates the standard. As a reference point, the V.22bis modem at 2400 bps would take 18 seconds to send a 1000-word letter. The V.34 modem at 9600 bps would take only four seconds to send the same letter, and the V.42bis compression standard in a 14,400 bps modem can send the same letter in only three seconds.

The chart in Table 7.1 presents the compression standards and their parameters since 1984. The compression standard and the bps are not necessarily related. The standard could be used with any speed of modem.

Table 7.1   Modem Compression Standards from 1984 to the Present

Standard	bps	Introduced	Notes
V.22bis	2400	1984	
V.32	9600	1984	
V.32bis	14,400	1991	
V.32terbo	19,200	1993	Will communicate only with another V.32terbo
V.FastClass (V.FC)	28,800	1993	
V.34	28,800	1994	Improved V.FastClass. Backward-compatible with earlier V. modems
V.42	57,600	1995	Backward-compatible with earlier V. modems—error-correction standard
V.90	56,600	1998	56K modem standard; resolved competition for standard between U.S. Robotic X2 and Rockwell K56 Flex standards.

Modem Performance

Initially, a modem's speed was measured in either bps or something called the "baud rate," and most people mistakenly assumed the two were identical.

"Baud" refers to the speed at which the sound wave that carries a bit of data over the telephone lines oscillates. The term derives from the name of French telegrapher and engineer Jean-Maurice-Emile Baudot. In the early 1980s, the baud rate did equal the transmission speed of modems. At that time, 300 baud equaled 300 bits per second.

Eventually, communications engineers learned to compress and encode data so that each modulation of sound could carry more than one bit of data. This development means that the rate of bps can be greater than the baud rate. For example, a modem that modulates at 28,800 baud can actually send at 115,200 bps. Therefore, the current parameter to look for in modem speed is bps.

Several of the newer modems feature industry standards, such as V.42bis/MNP5 data compression, and have transmission speeds of 57,600 bps; and some modems go up to 76,800 bps.

Types of Modems

There are different types of modems because different types of communication environments require different methods of sending data. These environments can be divided roughly into two areas related to the timing of communications:

- Asynchronous
- Synchronous

The type of modem a network uses depends on whether the environment is asynchronous or synchronous.

Asynchronous Communication (Async)

Asynchronous communication, known as "async," is possibly the most widespread form of connectivity in the world. This is because async was developed in order to make use of common telephone lines.

Figure 7.5 shows an asynchronous environment, in which data is transmitted in a serial stream.

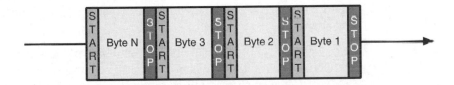

Figure 7.5 Asynchronous serial data stream

Each character—letter, number, or symbol—is turned into a string of bits. Each of these strings is separated from the other strings by a start-of-character bit and a stop bit. Both the sending and receiving devices must agree on the start and stop bit sequence. The receiving computer uses the start and stop bit markers to schedule its timing functions so it is ready to receive the next byte of data.

Communication is not synchronized. There is no clocking device or method to coordinate transmission between the sender and the receiver. The sending computer just sends data, and the receiving computer just receives data. The receiving computer then checks to make sure that the received data matches what was sent. Between 20 and 27 percent of the data traffic in async communication consists of data traffic control and coordination. The actual amount depends on the type of the transmission—for example, whether parity (a form of error checking, discussed in the section that follows) is being used.

Asynchronous transmission over telephone lines can happen at up to 28,800 bps. However, the latest data compression methods can boost the 28,800 bps rate to 115,200 bps over directly connected systems.

Run the **c07dem08** and **c07dem09** videos located in the **Demos** folder on the CD accompanying this book for an overview of asynchronous communication.

Error Control Because of the potential for error, async can include a special bit, called a *parity bit*, which is used in an error-checking and correction scheme called *parity checking*. In parity checking, the number of bits sent must match exactly the number of bits received.

Run the **c07dem10** video located in the **Demos** folder on the CD accompanying this book to view a presentation of parity bits in asynchronous communication.

The original V.32 modem standard did not provide error control. To help avoid generating errors during data transmission, a company called Microcom developed its own standard for asynchronous data-error control, the Microcom Networking Protocol (MNP). The method worked so well that other companies adopted not only the initial version of the protocol but later versions, called classes, as well. Currently, several modem manufacturers incorporate MNP Classes 2, 3, and 4 standards.

In 1989, the Comité Consultatif Internationale de Télégraphie et Téléphonie (CCITT) published an asynchronous error-control scheme called V.42. This hardware-implemented standard featured two error-control protocols. The primary error-control scheme is link access procedure for modems (LAPM), but the scheme also uses MNP Class 4. The LAPM protocol is used in communications between two modems that are V.42-compliant. If only one, but not both, of the modems is MNP 4-compliant, the correct protocol to use would be MNP 4.

Improving Transmission Performance Communication performance depends on two elements:

- Signaling or channel speed describes how fast the bits are encoded onto the communications channel.

- Throughput measures the amount of useful information going across the channel.

Run the **c07dem11** video located in the **Demos** folder on the CD accompanying this book to view a presentation of channel speed and throughput.

By removing redundant elements or empty sections, compression improves the time required to send data. Microcom's MNP Class 5 Data Compression Protocol is an example of one current data compression standard. You can improve performance, often doubling the throughput, by using data compression. When both ends of a communication link use the MNP Class 5 protocol, data transmission time can be cut in half.

Run the **c07dem12** video located in the **Demos** folder on the CD accompanying this book to view a presentation of data compression.

The V.42bis standard, because it describes how to implement impressive data compression in hardware, makes even greater performance possible. For example, a 56.6Kbps modem using V.90 can achieve a throughput of 100 Kbps.

Note Although compressing data can improve performance, it is not an exact science. Many factors affect the actual compression ratio of a document or file. A text file, for example, can be compressed more effectively than a complex graphic file. It is even possible to have a compressed file that is actually larger than the original. Remember, compression numbers cited by vendors are usually based on a best-case scenario.

Coordinating the Standards   Asynchronous, or serial, modems are less expensive than synchronous modems because the asynchronous modem does not need the circuitry and the components to handle the timing involved in synchronous transmission that synchronous modems require.

Synchronous Communication

Synchronous communication relies on a timing scheme coordinated between two devices to separate groups of bits and transmit them in blocks known as "frames." Special characters are used to begin the synchronization and check its accuracy periodically.

Run the **c07dem13** and **c07dem14** videos located in the **Demos** folder on the CD accompanying this book for an overview of synchronous communication.

Because the bits are sent and received in a timed, controlled (synchronized) process, start and stop bits are not required. Transmission stops at the end of one frame and starts again with a new one. This start-and-stop approach is much more efficient than asynchronous transmission, especially when large packets of data are being transferred. When small packets are sent, this increase in efficiency is less noticeable. Figure 7.6 shows a comparison of asynchronous and synchronous data streams.

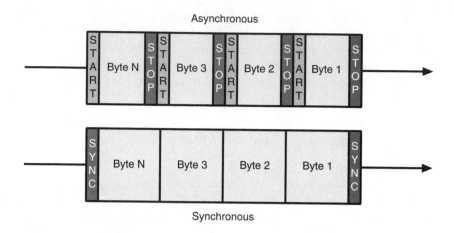

Figure 7.6   Asynchronous data stream versus synchronous data stream

If there is an error, the synchronous error-detection and correction scheme implements a retransmission.

Run the **c07dem15** video located in the **Demos** folder on the CD accompanying this book to view a presentation of a synchronous communication error-correction scheme.

Synchronous protocols perform a number of jobs that asynchronous protocols do not. Principally, they:

- Format data into blocks.
- Add control information.
- Check the information to provide error control.

The primary protocols in synchronous communication are:

- Synchronous Data Link Control (SDLC).
- High-level Data Link Control (HDLC).
- Binary Synchronous Communications Protocol (bisync).

Synchronous communication is used in almost all digital and network communications. For example, if you were using digital lines to connect remote computers, you would use synchronous modems rather than asynchronous modems to connect the computer to the digital line. Generally, their higher cost and complexity have kept synchronous modems out of the home market.

Asymmetric Digital Subscriber Line (ADSL)

The latest modem technology to become available is asymmetric digital subscriber line (ADSL). This technology converts existing twisted-pair telephone lines into access paths for multimedia and high-speed data communications. These new connections can transmit more than 8 Mbps to the subscriber and up to 1 Mbps from the subscriber.

ADSL is not without drawbacks. The technology requires special hardware, including an ADSL modem on each end of the connection. It also requires broadband cabling, which is currently only available in a few locations, and there is a limit to the connection length.

ADSL is recognized as a physical layer transmission protocol for unshielded twisted-pair media.

Expanding a Network Using Components

As companies grow, so do their networks. LANs tend to outgrow their original designs. You know your LAN is too small when:

- The cable begins to get crowded with network traffic.
- Print jobs include longer wait times.
- Traffic-generating applications, such as databases, experience increased response times.

The time usually comes when administrators need to expand the size or improve the performance of their networks. But networks cannot be made larger merely by adding new computers and more cable. Each topology or architecture has limits. There are, however, components that can be installed to increase the size of the network within its existing environment. These components can:

- Segment existing LANs so that each segment becomes its own LAN.
- Join two separate LANs.
- Connect to other LANs and computing environments to join them into a larger comprehensive WAN.

The components that enable engineers to accomplish these goals are:

- Hubs.
- Repeaters.
- Bridges.
- Routers.
- Brouters.
- Gateways.

Hubs

Chapter 2, "Basic Network Media," discusses how a hub is used as the central hardware component in a star topology. Chapter 3, "Understanding Network Architecture," discusses how a hub works with a token-ring topology. Hubs can also be used to expand the size of a LAN. Although using hubs won't convert a LAN into a WAN, connecting or adding hubs to a LAN can effectively increase the number of workstations. This method of growing a LAN is popular, but does come with many design limitations. Figure 7.7 shows how several 10BaseT hubs can be connected to expand a network.

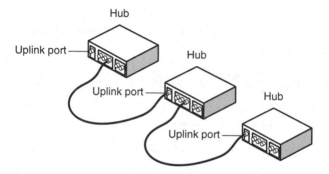

Figure 7.7   Ethernet hubs connected in a series

Figure 7.8 shows how several token-ring hubs can be connected to expand a network.

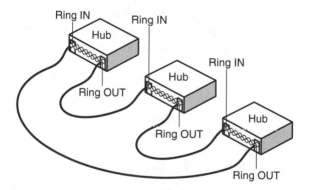

Figure 7.8   Token-ring hubs connected into one large ring

Note It is important to be careful when connecting hubs. Crossover cables are wired differently than standard patch cables, and one will not work correctly in place of the other. Check with the manufacturers to determine whether you need a standard patch cable or a crossover cable.

Repeaters

As signals travel along a cable, they degrade and become distorted in a process called "attenuation." (Attenuation is discussed in Chapter 2, "Basic Network Media.") If a cable is long enough, attenuation will finally make a signal unrecognizable. Installing a repeater enables signals to travel farther.

How Repeaters Work

A repeater works at the physical layer of the OSI reference model to regenerate the network's signals and resend them out on other segments. Figure 7.9 shows how repeaters regenerate weak signals.

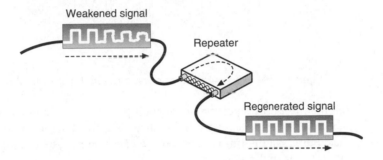

Figure 7.9 Repeaters regenerate weakened signals

The repeater takes a weak signal from one segment, regenerates it, and passes it to the next segment. To pass data through the repeater from one segment to the next, the packets and the Logical Link Control (LLC) protocols must be identical on each segment. A repeater will not enable communication, for example, between an 802.3 LAN (Ethernet) and an 802.5 LAN (Token Ring).

Repeaters do not translate or filter signals. For a repeater to work, both segments that the repeater joins must use the same access method. The two most common access methods are carrier-sense multiple-access with collision detection (CSMA/CD) and token passing (discussed in Chapter 3, "Understanding Network Architecture"). A repeater cannot connect a segment using CSMA/CD to a segment using the token-passing access method. That is, a repeater cannot translate an Ethernet packet into a Token Ring packet.

As shown in Figure 7.10, repeaters can move packets from one kind of physical media to another. They can take an Ethernet packet coming from a thinnet coaxial-cable segment and pass it on to a fiber-optic segment, provided the repeater is capable of accepting the physical connections.

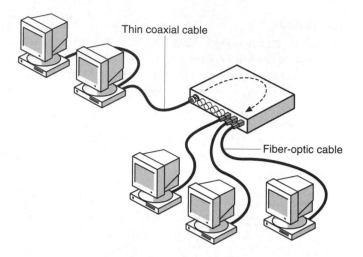

Figure 7.10   Repeaters can connect different types of media

Some multiport repeaters act as multiport hubs and connect different types of media. The same segment limits discussed in Chapter 3 apply to networks that use hubs, but the limits now refer to each segment extending from a hub rather than to the entire network.

Repeater Considerations

Repeaters afford the least expensive way to expand a network. When the need arises to extend the physical network beyond its distance or node limitations, consider using a repeater to link segments if neither segment is generating much traffic or limiting costs is a major consideration.

No Isolation or Filtering   Repeaters send every bit of data from one cable segment to another, even if the data consists of malformed packets or packets not destined for use on the network. This means that a problem with one segment can disrupt every other segment. Repeaters do not act as filters to restrict the flow of problem traffic.

Repeaters will also pass a broadcast storm along from one segment to the next, back and forth along the network. A broadcast storm occurs when so many broadcast messages are on the network that the number is approaching the network bandwidth limit. If a device is responding to a packet that is continuously circulating on the network, or a packet is continuously attempting to contact a system that never replies, network performance will be degraded.

Implementing a repeater   This section summarizes what you need to consider when deciding whether to implement repeaters in your network.

Use a repeater to:

- Connect two segments of similar or dissimilar media.
- Regenerate the signal to increase the distance transmitted.
- Pass all traffic in both directions.
- Connect two segments in the most cost-effective manner.

Note Repeaters improve performance by dividing the network into segments, thus reducing the number of computers per segment. When using repeaters to expand a network, don't forget about the 5-4-3 rule (introduced in Chapter 3, "Understanding Network Architecture").

Do not use a repeater when:

- There is heavy network traffic.
- Segments are using different access methods.
- Data filtering is needed.

Bridges

Like a repeater, a bridge can join segments or workgroup LANs. Figure 7.11 shows a bridge connecting two network segments. However, a bridge can also divide a network to isolate traffic or problems. For example, if the volume of traffic from one or two computers or a single department is flooding the network with data and slowing down the entire operation, a bridge could isolate those computers or that department.

Bridges can be used to:

- Expand the length of a segment.
- Provide for an increased number of computers on the network.
- Reduce traffic bottlenecks resulting from an excessive number of attached computers.
- Split an overloaded network into two separate networks, reducing the amount of traffic on each segment and making each network more efficient.
- Link unlike physical media such as twisted-pair and coaxial Ethernet.

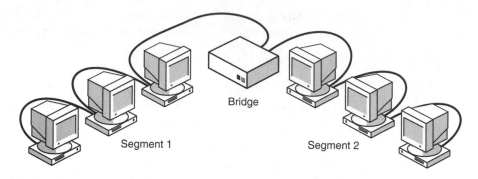

Figure 7.11 A bridge connecting two networks

How Bridges Work

Because bridges work at the data-link layer of the OSI model, all information contained in the higher levels of the OSI model is unavailable to them. Rather than distinguish between one protocol and another, bridges simply pass all protocols along the network. All protocols pass across bridges, so it is up to the individual computers to determine which protocols they can recognize.

As discussed in Chapter 5, "Introducing Network Standards," the data-link layer has two sublayers: the Logical Link Control (LLC) sublayer and the Media Access Control (MAC) sublayer. Bridges work at the MAC sublayer and are sometimes referred to as MAC-layer bridges.

A MAC-layer bridge:

- Listens to all traffic.
- Checks the source and destination addresses of each packet.
- Builds a routing table, as information becomes available.
- Forwards packets in the following manner:
    - If the destination is not listed in the routing table, the bridge forwards the packets to all segments.
    - If the destination is listed in the routing table, the bridge forwards the packets to that segment (unless it is the same segment as the source).

A bridge works on the principle that each network node has its own address. A bridge forwards packets based on the address of the destination node.

Bridges actually have some degree of intelligence in that they learn where to forward data. As traffic passes through the bridge, information about the computer addresses is stored in the bridge's RAM. The bridge uses this RAM to build a routing table based on source addresses.

Initially, the bridge's routing table is empty. As nodes transmit packets, the source address is copied to the routing table. With this address information (See Figure 7.12), the bridge learns which computers are on which segment of the network.

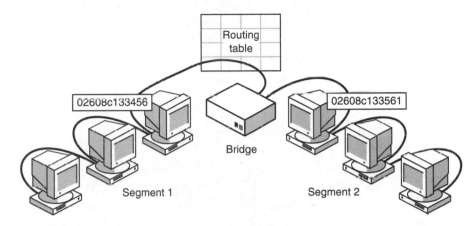

Figure 7.12   The routing table keeps track of addresses

Creating the Routing Table   Bridges build their routing tables based on the addresses of computers that have transmitted data on the network. Specifically, bridges use source addresses—the address of the device that initiates the transmission—to create a routing table.

When the bridge receives a packet, the source address is compared to the routing table. If the source address is not there, it is added to the table. The bridge then compares the destination address with the routing-table database.

- If the destination address is in the routing table and is on the same segment as the source address, the packet is discarded. This filtering helps to reduce network traffic and isolate segments of the network.

- If the destination address is in the routing table and not in the same segment as the source address, the bridge forwards the packet out of the appropriate port to reach the destination address.

- If the destination address is not in the routing table, the bridge forwards the packet to all its ports except the one on which it originated.

In summary, if a bridge knows the location of the destination node, it forwards the packet to it. If it does not know the destination, it forwards the packet to all segments.

Segmenting Network Traffic   A bridge can segment traffic because of its routing table. As shown in Figure 7.13, a computer on segment 1 (the source), sends data to another computer (the destination) also located in segment 1. If the destination address is in the routing table, the bridge can determine that the destination computer is also on segment 1. Because the source and destination computers are both on segment 1, the packet does not get forwarded across the bridge to segment 2.

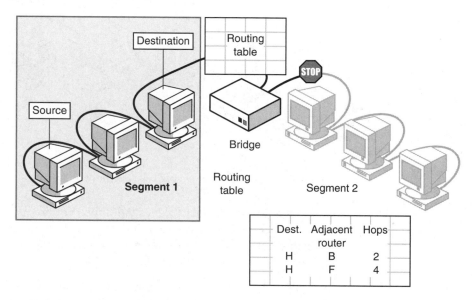

	Dest.	Adjacent router	Hops
	H	B	2
	H	F	4

Figure 7.13   The routing table allows bridges to segment networks

Therefore, bridges can use routing tables to reduce the traffic on the network by controlling which packets get forwarded to other segments. This controlling (or restricting) of the flow of network traffic is known as "segmenting network traffic."

A large network is not limited to one bridge. Multiple bridges can be used to combine several small networks into one large network.

Remote Bridges

Because bridges can be such powerful tools in expanding and segmenting net-works, they are often used in large networks that have widely dispersed segments joined by telephone lines.

Only one bridge is necessary to link two cable segments. However, where two separate LANs are located at a great distance from each other (See Figure 7.14), they can be joined into a single network. Implementing two remote bridges connected with synchronous modems to a dedicated, data-grade telephone line can do this.

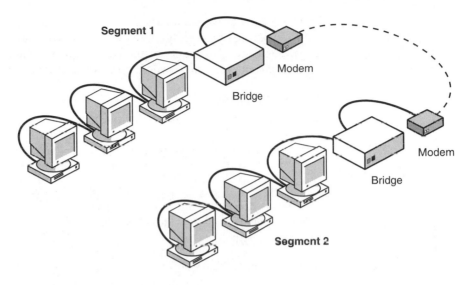

Figure 7.14   Remote bridges can be used to connect remote segments

Because remote LAN segments can be joined over telephone lines, it is possible
for multiple LANs to be joined by more than one path. In this situation, it is
possible that data might get into a continuous loop. To handle this possibility,
the 802.1 Network Management Committee of the Institute of Electrical and
Electronic Engineers (IEEE) has implemented the spanning tree algorithm (STA).
Under STA, software can sense the existence of more than one route, determine
which would be the most efficient, and then configure the bridge to use that one.
Other paths are disconnected using software, although the disconnected routes
can be reactivated if the primary route becomes unavailable.

Differentiating Between Bridges and Repeaters

Bridges work at a higher OSI layer than repeaters. This means that bridges have
more intelligence than repeaters and can take more data features into account.

While bridges resemble repeaters in that they can regenerate data, bridges do this
at the packet level. This means that bridges can send packets over long distances
using a variety of long-distance media.

Bridge Considerations

Bridges have all of the features of repeaters, but also accommodate more nodes.
They provide better network performance than repeaters. Because bridged networks have been divided, fewer computers compete for available resources on
each segment.

To look at it another way, if a large Ethernet network were divided into two segments connected by a bridge, each new network would carry fewer packets, have fewer collisions, and operate more efficiently. Although each network would be separate, the bridge would pass appropriate traffic between them.

Implementing a Bridge

A bridge can be either a separate, stand-alone piece of equipment (an external bridge) or it can be installed in a server. If the network operating system (NOS) supports it, one or more network interface cards (NICs), making an internal bridge, can be installed.

Network administrators like to use bridges because they are:

- Simple to install and transparent to users.
- Flexible and adaptable.
- Relatively inexpensive.

Routers

In an environment that consists of several network segments with differing protocols and architectures, a bridge might be inadequate for ensuring fast communication among all segments. A network this complex needs a device that not only knows the address of each segment, but can also determine the best path for sending data and filtering broadcast traffic to the local segment. Such a device is called a "router."

Routers work at the network layer of the OSI model. This means they can switch and route packets across multiple networks. They do this by exchanging protocol-specific information between separate networks. Routers read complex network addressing information in the packet and, because they function at a higher layer in the OSI model than bridges, they have access to additional information.

Routers can provide the following functions of a bridge:

- Filtering and isolating traffic
- Connecting network segments

Routers have access to more of the information in packets than bridges have and use this information to improve packet deliveries. Routers are used in complex networks because they provide better traffic management. Routers can share status and routing information with one another and use this information to bypass slow or malfunctioning connections.

How Routers Work

Routers maintain their own routing tables, usually consisting of network addresses; host addresses can also be kept if the network architecture calls for it. To determine the destination address for incoming data, the routing table includes:

- All known network addresses.

- Instructions for connection to other networks.

- The possible paths between routers.

- The costs of sending data over those paths.

As shown in Figure 7.15, a router uses its data-routing table to select the best route for the data based on costs and available paths.

Note Remember that routing tables were also discussed in the context of bridges. The routing table maintained by a bridge contains MAC-sublayer addresses for each node, whereas the routing table maintained by a router contains network numbers. Although manufacturers of both types of equipment have chosen to use the term "routing table," it has a different meaning for bridges than it does for routers.

Routers require specific addresses. They understand only the network numbers that allow them to communicate with other routers and local NIC addresses. Routers do not talk to remote computers.

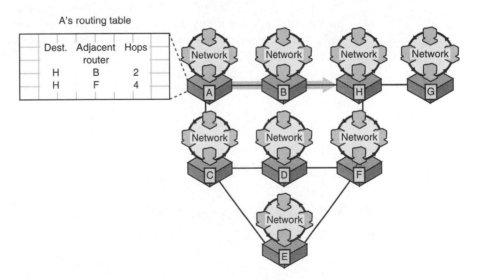

Figure 7.15   Routers talk to other routers, but not to remote computers

When routers receive packets destined for a remote network, they send them to the router that manages the destination network. In some ways this is an advantage because it means routers can:

- Segment large networks into smaller ones.
- Act as safety barriers between segments.
- Prohibit broadcast storms, because broadcasts are not forwarded.

Because routers must perform complex functions on each packet, routers are slower than most bridges. As packets are passed from router to router, data-link layer source and destination addresses are stripped off and then re-created. This enables a router to route a packet from a TCP/IP Ethernet network to a server on a TCP/IP Token Ring network.

Because routers read only addressed network packets, they do not allow corrupted data to get passed onto the network. Because they do not pass corrupted data or broadcast data storms, routers put little stress on networks.

Routers do not look at the destination node address; they look only at the network address. Routers will pass information only if the network address is known. This ability to control the data passing through the router reduces the amount of traffic between networks and allows routers to use these links more efficiently than bridges.

Using the router-addressing scheme, administrators can break one large network into many separate networks, and because routers do not pass or even handle every packet, they act as a safety barrier between network segments. This can greatly reduce the amount of traffic on the network and the wait time experienced by users.

Routable Protocols   Not all protocols are routable. Protocols that are routable include:

- DECnet.
- Internet Protocol (IP).
- Internetwork Packet Exchange (IPX).
- OSI.
- Xerox Network System (XNS).
- DDP (AppleTalk).

Protocols that are not routable include:

- Local Area Transport Protocol (LAT), a protocol from Digital Equipment Corporation.
- NetBEUI (NetBIOS Extended User Interface).

Routers are available that can accommodate multiple protocols such as IP and DECnet in the same network.

Choosing Paths   Unlike bridges, routers can accommodate multiple active paths between LAN segments and choose among redundant paths. Because routers can link segments that use completely different data packaging and media-access schemes, there are often several paths available for the router to use. This means that if one router does not function, the data can still be passed over alternate routes.

A router can listen to a network and identify which parts are busiest. It uses this information to determine which path to send data over. If one path is very busy, the router identifies an alternative path and sends data over that one.

A router decides the path the data packet will follow by determining the number of hops between internetwork segments. Like bridges, routers build routing tables and use these in routing algorithms such as the following:

- OSPF ("open shortest path first") is a link-state routing algorithm. Link-state algorithms control the routing process and allow routers to respond quickly to changes in the network.
- RIP (Routing Information Protocol) uses distance-vector algorithms to determine routes. Transmission Control Protocol/Internet Protocol (TCP/IP) and IPX support RIP.
- NetWare Link Services Protocol (NLSP) is a link-state algorithm to be used with IPX.

Types of Routers

The two major types of routers are:

- Static.

  Static routers require an administrator to manually set up and configure the routing table and to specify each route.

- Dynamic.

  Dynamic routers are designed to discover routes automatically and therefore require a minimal amount of setup and configuration. More sophisticated than static routers, they examine information from other routers and make packet-by-packet decisions about how to send data across the network.

Table 7.2 compares and contrasts the characteristics of static and dynamic routers.

Table 7.2   Characteristics of the Two Types of Routers

Static routers	Dynamic routers
Manually set up and configure all routes.	Manually configure the first route. Automatically detect additional networks and routes.
Always use the same route, determined by a routing table entry.	Can choose a route based on factors such as cost and amount of link traffic.
Use a hard-coded route (designed to handle only a specific situation), not necessarily the shortest route.	Can decide to send packets over alternate routes.
Are considered more secure because the administrator specifies each route.	Can improve security by manually configuring the router to filter out specific network addresses and prevent traffic from going there.

Distinguishing Between Bridges and Routers

Bridges and routers can be confusing even for engineers with LAN and WAN experience because they appear to do the same things: both forward packets between networks and send data across WAN links.

A question often asked is how to decide when to use a bridge and when to use a router.

The bridge, which works at the MAC sublayer of the OSI data-link layer, sees only a node address. To be more specific, a bridge looks for a node's MAC-sublayer address in each packet. If the bridge recognizes the address, it keeps the packet local or forwards it to the appropriate segment. If the bridge does not recognize the address, it forwards the packet to all segments except the one through which the packet arrived.

The bridge first either recognizes the packet's MAC-sublayer address, or it does not, and then it forwards the packet appropriately. Figure 7.16 shows a bridge and a router and how they relate to the OSI model.

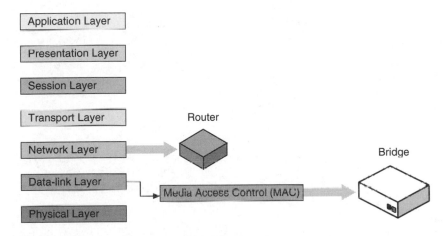

Figure 7.16   Bridges work at the data-link layer MAC sublayer, and routers work at the network layer

Broadcasting   Forwarding the packet is the key to understanding bridges and distinguishing them from routers. With bridges, forwarded broadcast data goes out to every computer from all ports of the bridge except the one through which the packet arrived. That is, each computer on all networks (except the local network from which the broadcast originated) receives a broadcast packet. In small networks this might not have much of an impact, but a large network can generate enough broadcast traffic to slow down a network even though it is filtering for network addresses.

The router, which works at the network layer, takes more information into account than the bridge does, determining not only what to forward but where to forward it. The router recognizes not only an address, as the bridge does, but a type of protocol as well. Additionally, the router can identify the addresses of other routers and determine which packets to forward to which routers.

Multiple Paths   A bridge can recognize only one path between networks. A router can search among multiple active paths and determine which is the best path at that particular moment.

As illustrated in Figure 7.17, if router A has a transmission that needs to be sent to router D, it can send the message to router C or to router B, and the message will be forwarded to router D. Routers have the ability to evaluate both paths and determine which would be the best route for that transmission.

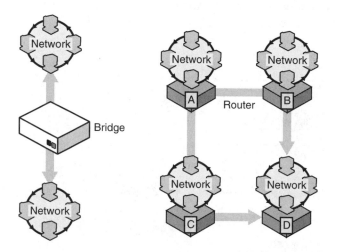

Figure 7.17   Routers recognize and use multiple paths between destinations

Conclusion   Four key pieces of information can help you distinguish between a bridge and a router and determine which would be appropriate in a given situation:

- The bridge recognizes only local MAC-sublayer addresses (the addresses of NICs in its own segment). Routers recognize network addresses.
- The bridge broadcasts (forwards) everything it does not recognize and forwards all addresses it knows, but only from the appropriate port.
- The router works only with routable protocols.
- The router filters addresses. It forwards particular protocols to particular addresses (other routers).

Brouters

A brouter, as the name implies, combines the qualities of both a bridge and a router. A brouter can act as a router for one protocol and as a bridge for all the others.

Brouters can:

- Route selected routable protocols.
- Bridge nonroutable protocols.
- Deliver more cost-effective and more manageable internetworking than separate bridges and routers.

Gateways

Gateways enable communication between different architectures and environments. They repackage and convert data going from one environment to another so that each environment can understand the other environment's data. A gateway repackages information to match the requirements of the destination system. Gateways can change the format of a message so that it conforms to the application program at the receiving end of the transfer. For example, electronic-mail gateways, such as the X.400 gateway, receive messages in one format, translate it, and forward it in X.400 format used by the receiver, and vice versa.

A gateway links two systems that do not use the same:

- Communication protocols.
- Data-formatting structures.
- Languages.
- Architecture.

Gateways interconnect heterogeneous networks; for example, they can connect Microsoft Windows NT Server to IBM's Systems Network Architecture (SNA). Gateways change the format of the data to make it conform to the application program at the receiving end.

How Gateways Work

Gateways are task-specific, which means that they are dedicated to a particular type of transfer. They are often referred to by their task name (Windows NT Server to SNA gateway).

As shown in Figure 7.18, a gateway takes the data from one environment, strips off its old protocol stack, and repackages it in the protocol stack from the destination network.

To process the data, the gateway:

- Disassembles incoming data through the network's complete protocol stack.

- Encapsulates the outgoing data in the complete protocol stack of the other network to allow transmission.

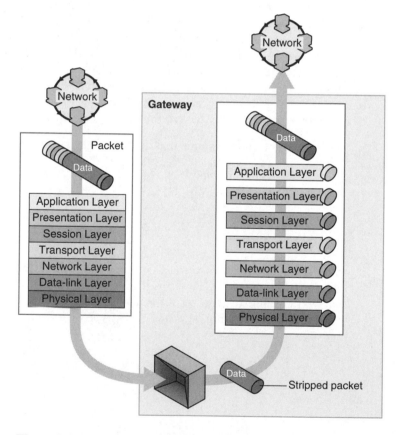

Figure 7.18   Gateways strip off an old protocol stack and add a new protocol stack

Some gateways use all seven layers of the OSI model, but gateways typically perform protocol conversion at the application layer. However, the level of functionality varies widely between types of gateways.

Mainframe Gateways

One common use for gateways is to act as translators between personal computers and minicomputer or mainframe environments. A host gateway connects LAN computers with mainframe and minicomputer systems that do not recognize intelligent computers attached to LANs.

In a LAN environment, as shown in Figure 7.19, one computer is usually designated as the gateway computer. Special application programs in the desktop computers access the mainframe by communicating with the mainframe environment through the gateway computer. Users can access resources on the mainframe just as if these resources were on their own desktop computers.

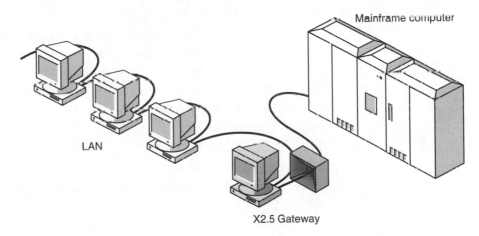

Figure 7.19   Mainframe gateways connect personal computers to mainframes

Gateway Considerations

Typically, gateways are dedicated servers on a network. They can use a significant percentage of a server's available bandwidth because they are carrying out resource-intensive tasks such as protocol conversion. If a gateway server is used for multiple tasks, adequate RAM and CPU bandwidth needs to be allocated or performance of the server functions will be degraded.

Gateways are considered as choices for implementation because they do not put a heavy load on internetwork communication circuits, and they perform specific tasks efficiently.

Lesson Summary

The following points summarize the main elements of this lesson:

- Modems make it possible to communicate over telephone lines.

- There are two types of modems: synchronous and asynchronous.

- It is important to choose the right cable when connecting hubs; crossover cables will not work in place of standard patch cables.

- Asymmetric digital subscriber line (ADSL) is a technology for increasing the speed of transmission on telephone lines.

- Repeaters are used to connect two segments of similar or dissimilar media and to regenerate a signal to increase the distance transmitted.

- Repeaters should not be used where network traffic is heavy, segments are using different access methods, or filtering is needed.

- Bridges have all the features of repeaters.

- Bridges are used to connect two segments to expand the length or number of nodes on the network, to reduce traffic by segmenting the network, or to connect dissimilar networks.

- Routers are used to connect two networks, limit unnecessary traffic, and to separate administrative networks.

- Brouters combine the features of bridges and routers; a brouter can act as a router for one protocol and as a bridge for all the others.

- Gateways perform protocol and data conversion.

- Gateways are limited in several ways: they are task-specific, expensive, and can be slow.

Lesson 2: Connection Services

In Lesson 1, we examined devices that allow us to extend a LAN. As our networks grow, they quickly exceed the capacity of standard network media, and it is no longer practical to run our own cabling, especially if one of the nodes is located across the street or in another state. In this lesson, we explore the various connection services that we can employ with the hardware discussed in Lesson 1 to extend a network.

This lesson examines connection service options. Many network connection choices are available, and each has advantages and disadvantages. We begin with simple telephone lines and move on to cover high-speed digital services.

After this lesson, you will be able to:

- Describe the principles behind moving data quickly and economically across long distances.
- Describe the difference between analog and digital communication.
- Describe how packet switching works.
- Identify the primary features of each of the following: X.25, frame relay, ATM, ISDN, FDDI, SONET, and SMDS.

Estimated lesson time: 45 minutes

Carriers

A modem is useless unless it can communicate with another component. All modem communication takes place over some kind of communication line or cable. Which type of cable it is, as well as who provides it and its related services, makes a difference in network performance and cost.

The issue is simple: it is difficult and expensive to move data quickly over long distances. The three factors an administrator must take into account when considering how to implement modem communications are:

- Throughput.
- Distance.
- Cost.

You need to apply these factors when deciding which type of telephone lines to install for your network.

Telephone Lines

Two types of telephone lines are available for modem communications:

Dial-Up Lines

Dial-up lines are common telephone lines. They are slow, require users to make a connection for each communication session manually, and can be unreliable for transmitting data. However, for some companies it may be practical to temporarily use a dial-up communication link between sites for a certain amount of time each day to transfer files and update databases.

 Run the **c07dem16** video located in the **Demos** folder on the CD accompanying this book to view a presentation of a dial-up communication link.

Carriers are continually improving their dial-up line service. Some digital lines support data transmission speeds of up to 56 Kbps using error correction, data compression, and synchronous modems.

Leased (Dedicated) Lines

Leased, or dedicated, lines provide full-time, dedicated connections that do not use a series of switches to complete the connection. The quality of the line is often higher than the quality of a telephone line designed for voice transmission only. They typically range in speed from 56 Kbps to 45 Mbps or more.

 Run the **c07dem17** video located in the **Demos** folder on the CD accompanying this book to view a presentation of leased (dedicated) lines.

Most long-distance carriers use switched circuits to provide what appears to be a dedicated line. These are called "virtual private networks" (VPNs).

Remote Access Service (RAS)

Frequently, businesses need to be able to communicate beyond the bounds of a single network. Most server-based network operating systems provide a service, called Remote Access Service (RAS), to meet that need. To establish a remote connection requires two services: RAS and a client service known as dial-up networking (DUN). The server or workstation uses RAS to link remote computers to the network by means of a dial-in connection over a modem. DUN, the other side of the service, is used by remote computers to connect to the RAS server. Together, these two services provide the ability to extend a network and can, in effect, convert a LAN into a WAN. Because many Internet service providers use telephone-line access, a RAS server often serves as an Internet interface for its network.

Note The key difference between RAS service on a server computer and on a client computer lies in the number of simultaneous connections allowed. For example, a Windows NT Server allows 256 inbound connections, whereas a Windows NT Workstation client allows only one.

Separate computers and LANs can be connected to each other over the Public Switched Telephone Network, packet-switched networks, or Integrated Services Digital Network; (these services are discussed later in this lesson).

Once a user has made a connection, the telephone lines become transparent (invisible to—not perceived by—the user), and users at the remote client can access all network resources just as they would if they were sitting at their computers at the network site. Figure 7.20 shows a remote client connected to a network server using RAS.

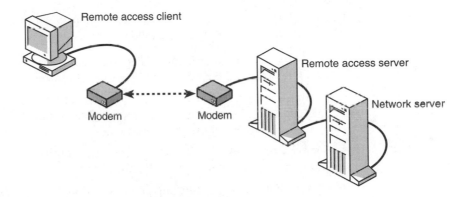

Figure 7.20   RAS allows remote users to access the network

RAS Connections

The physical connection to a RAS server can be made using several different media. These include the following:

- **Public Switched Telephone Network (PSTN)**   This service is otherwise known as the public telephone system.

- **X.25**   This packet-switched network service can be used to make dial-up or direct connections.

- **Integrated Services Digital Network (ISDN)**   This service provides high-speed remote access, but at greater cost than a dial-up connection. An ISDN connection requires an ISDN card in place of a modem.

RAS Protocols

RAS supports three connection protocols. The oldest, dating from 1984, is the Serial Line Interface protocol (SLIP). It has a number of shortcomings. SLIP does not support dynamic IP addressing or the NetBEUI or IPX protocols, it cannot encrypt logon information, and it is supported only by RAS clients.

Point-to-Point Protocol (PPP) overcomes many of the limitations of SLIP. In addition to TCP/IP, it supports the IPX, NetBEUI, AppleTalk, and DECnet protocols. It also supports encrypted passwords.

Point-to-Point Tunneling Protocol (PPTP) is an essential part of VPN technology. Like PPP, it does not discriminate among protocols. PPTP provides secure transmission over TCP/IP networks because its connections are encrypted. This enables highly private network links over the public Internet.

RAS and Security

The actual methods by which RAS ensures security can vary with the operating system. RAS security functions include:

- **Auditing**   An audit trail can be kept that identifies users and the times during which they logged on.
- **Callback**   RAS can be configured to call back to the host that is requesting a connection, and the list of those host telephone numbers can be restricted to prevent unauthorized use of the system.
- **Security host**   A security host can require additional authentication steps in addition to those that exist on the host's network.
- **PPTP filtering**   This filtering process can prevent processing of any packets except PPTP. This provides a secure transfer of data over a VPN, preventing intruders from accessing the server.

Installing RAS

To plan for a RAS installation, begin by gathering appropriate documentation about the network and its users. Information you will need includes:

- Modem specifications, drivers, and settings (you will need a RAS-capable modem).
- Type of communication port to be configured.
- Whether this connection will be dial-in, dial-out, or both.
- Client protocols.
- Security requirements.

Configuring RAS

After RAS is installed, it has to be configured. Be prepared to provide settings for the communication ports, network protocols, and RAS encryption.

Configuring Dial-Up Networks If the server will be used to dial other networks, the Internet, or other computers, these connections must be configured. The method of configuration depends on the computer and network operating systems in use.

Limitations of RAS

Using a RAS connection is not always the best choice to achieve network expansion. But it does provide many features and opportunities that might not be otherwise available. It is important to know when to choose RAS and when to select a different option.

Use RAS if you determine that your bandwidth requirements are not greater than 128 Kbps, if you do not require a full-time connection, or if you must keep system costs down. Do not use RAS if you need a higher bandwidth than that provided by an asynchronous modem or if you need a dedicated full-time connection.

Point-to-Point Tunneling Protocol (PPTP)

This protocol supports multiprotocol VPNs. This support allows remote clients to connect and access the organizations network securely via the Internet. Using PPTP, the remote client establishes a connection to the RAS server on the Internet using PPTP.

PPTP provides a way to route IP, IPX, or NetBEUI point-to-point protocol packets over a TCP/IP network. By encapsulating these dissimilar protocol packets, any of these packets can be sent over the TCP/IP network. This virtual WAN is supported through the public networks such as the Internet.

WAN Overview

While LANs work well, they have physical and distance limitations. Because LANs are not adequate for all business communication, they must be able to connect between LANs and other types of environments to ensure access to full communication services.

Using components such as bridges and routers, along with communications service providers, a LAN can be expanded from an operation that serves a local area to encompass a wide area network that can support data communications statewide, countrywide, or even worldwide. To the user, the WAN appears to function like a local area network. When a WAN has been properly implemented, it appears indistinguishable from a LAN.

Most WANs are combinations of LANs and other types of communications components connected by communication links called "WAN links." WAN links can include:

- Packet-switching networks.
- Fiber-optic cable.
- Microwave transmitters.
- Satellite links.
- Cable television coaxial systems.

Because WAN links, such as wide-area telephone connections, are too expensive and complex for most private companies to purchase, implement, and maintain on their own, they are usually leased from service providers.

Communication between LANs will involve one of the following transmission technologies:

- Analog
- Digital
- Packet switching

Each of these technologies is described in detail in this lesson.

Analog Connectivity

The same network that your telephone uses is available to computers. One name for this worldwide network is the Public Switched Telephone Network (PSTN). In the context of computing, the PSTN, offering voice-grade dial-up telephone lines, can be thought of as one large WAN link.

Dial-Up Lines

The fact that the PSTN was designed primarily for voice-grade communication makes it slow; dial-up analog lines require modems that can make them even slower. Figure 7.21 shows a typical dial-up connection. Because the PSTN is a circuit-switched network, the connection quality is inconsistent. Any single communication session will be only as good as the circuits linked for that particular session. Over long distances—country to country, for example—there can be considerable inconsistency in the circuits from one session to the next. With ADSL technology becoming more available, improvements are likely to be made to dial-up lines in the future.

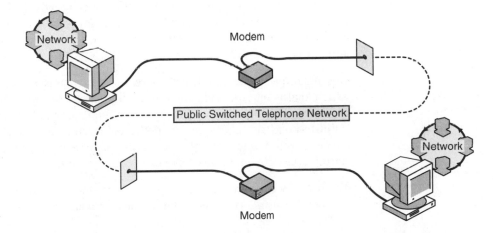

Figure 7.21   An analog telephone line can connect two computers using modems

Dedicated Analog Lines

Unlike dial-up lines that must be reopened each time they are used, dedicated (or leased) analog lines remain open at all times. A leased analog line is faster and more reliable than a dial-up connection. However, it is also relatively expensive, because the carrier is dedicating resources to the leased connection whether or not the line is being used.

Dial-Up or Dedicated?

No type of service is best for all users. The best choice will depend on a number of factors including:

- The amount of time the connection will be used.
- The cost of the service.
- The importance of having higher or more reliable data rates from a conditioned line.
- The need for a 24-hour-a-day connection.

If the need for connectivity is infrequent, dial-up lines can work well. If the connection needs a high level of reliability and usage will be fairly continuous over the month, then the service quality provided by a dial-up line might not be adequate.

Digital Connectivity

In some cases, analog lines provide sufficient connectivity. However, when an organization generates so much WAN traffic that the transmission time makes an analog connection inefficient and expensive, it might be time to consider alternatives.

Organizations requiring a faster, more secure transmission environment than that which analog lines provide can turn to digital data service (DDS) lines. DDS provides point-to-point synchronous communication at 2.4, 4.8, 9.6, or 56 Kbps. Point-to-point digital circuits are dedicated circuits that are provided by several telecommunications carriers. The carrier guarantees full-duplex bandwidth by setting up a permanent link from each endpoint to the LAN.

The primary advantage of digital lines is that they provide transmission that is nearly 99 percent error free. Digital lines are available in several forms, including DDS, T1, T3, T4, and switched 56.

Because DDS uses digital communication, it does not require modems (See Figure 7.22). Instead, DDS sends data from a bridge or router through a device called a Channel Service Unit/Data Service Unit (CSU/DSU). This device converts the standard digital signals that the computer generates into the type of digital signals (bipolar) that are part of the synchronous communication environment. It also contains electronics to protect the DDS service provider's network.

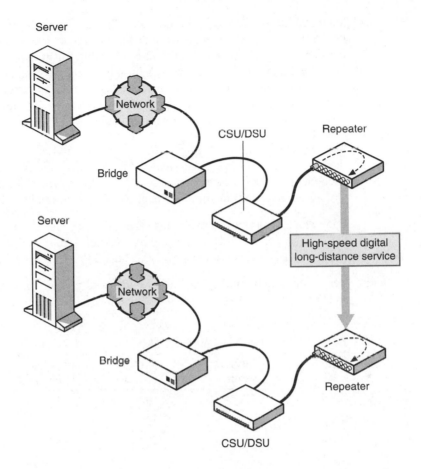

Figure 7.22   Digital data service line connecting two remote networks

T1 Service

For higher data speeds, T1 service is perhaps the most widely used type of digital line. It is a point-to-point transmission technology that uses two-wire pairs (one pair to send and the other to receive) to transmit a full-duplex signal at a rate of 1.544 Mbps. T1 is used to transmit digital voice, data, and video signals.

T1 lines are among the most costly of all WAN links. Subscribers who do not need or cannot afford the bandwidth of an entire T1 line can subscribe to one or more T1 channels in 64 Kbps increments, known as Fractional T-1 (FT-1).

Outside the United States, T1 service might not be available, but a similar service, called E1, often is. E1 is very similar to T1, but has a signaling rate of 2.048 Mbps.

Multiplexing   Developed by Bell Labs, T1 uses technology called *multiplexing*, or "muxing." Several signals from different sources are collected into a component called a multiplexer and fed into one cable for transmission. At the receiving end, the data is demultiplexed back into its original form. This approach emerged when telephone cables, which carried only one conversation per cable, became overcrowded. The solution to the problem, called a T-Carrier network, enabled Bell Labs to carry many calls over one cable.

Dividing the Channel   A T1 channel can carry 1.544 megabits of data per second, the basic unit of T-Carrier service. T1 divides this into 24 channels and samples each channel 8000 times per second. Using this method, T1 can accommodate 24 simultaneous data transmissions over each two-wire pair.

Each channel sample incorporates eight bits. Because each channel is sampled 8000 times per second, each of the 24 channels can transmit at 64 Kbps. This data rate standard is known as DS-0. The 1.544 Mbps rate is known as DS-1.

DS-1 rates can be multiplexed to provide even greater transmission rates, known as DS-1C, DS-2, DS-3, and DS-4. These have the transmission rates listed in Table 7.3 that follows:

Table 7.3   Digital Transmission Rates

Signal level	Carrier system	T-1 channels	Voice channels	Data rate (Mbps)
DS-0	N/A	N/A	1	0.064
DS-1	T1	1	24	1.544
DS-1C	T-1C	2	48	3.152
DS-2	T2	4	96	6.312
DS-3	T3	28	672	44.736
DS-4	T4	168	4032	274.760

Copper wire will accommodate T1 and T2. However, T3 and T4 require a high-frequency medium such as microwave or fiber-optic cable.

T3 Service

T3 and Fractional T-3 leased line service provides voice and data-grade service from 6 Mbps to 45 Mbps. These offer the highest-capacity leased-line service commonly available today. T3 and FT-3 are designed for transporting large volumes of data at high speed between two fixed points. A T3 line can be used to replace several T1 lines.

Switched 56 Service

Both local and long-distance telephone companies offer Switched 56 Service, a LAN-to-LAN digital dial-up service that transmits data at 56 Kbps. Switched 56 is merely a circuit-switched version of a 56-Kbps DDS line. The advantage of Switched 56 is that it is used on demand, thereby eliminating the expense of a dedicated line. Each computer using this service must be equipped with a CSU/DSU that can dial up another Switched 56 site.

Packet-Switching Networks

Because packet technology is fast, convenient, and reliable, it is used to transmit data over extensive areas such as across cities, states, or countries. Networks that send packets from many different users along many different possible paths are called "packet-switching networks" because of the way they package and route data.

How Packet Switching Works

The original data package is broken into packets, and each packet is tagged with a destination address and other information. This makes it possible to send each packet separately over the network.

In packet switching, as shown in Figure 7.23, packets are relayed through stations in a computer network along the best route currently available between the source and the destination.

Each packet is switched separately. Two packets from the same original data package can follow completely different paths to reach the same destination. The data paths selected for individual packets are based on the best route open at any given instant.

Even when each packet travels along a different path and the packets composing a message arrive at different times or out of sequence, the receiving computer is still able to reassemble the original message.

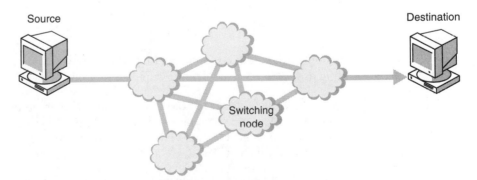

Figure 7.23   Simple packet-switching network

Switches direct the packets over the possible connections and pathways. These networks are sometimes called any-to-any connections. Exchanges in the network read each packet and forward them along the best route available at that moment.

Packet size is kept small. If there is an error in transmission, retransmitting a small packet is easier than retransmitting a large packet. Also, small packets tie up switches for only short periods of time.

Using packet-switching networks to send data is similar to shipping vast quantities of merchandise by truck instead of loading it all onto one train. If a problem should arise with the merchandise on one truck, it is easier to fix or reload than it would be to clean up the mess after a train runs off the track. Also, single trucks do not tie up crossings and intersections (switches) as trains do.

Packet-switching networks are fast and efficient. To manage the tasks of routing traffic and assembling and disassembling packets, such networks require some intelligence from the computers and software that control delivery. Packet-switching networks are economical because they offer high-speed lines on a per-transaction basis instead of for a flat-fee rate.

Virtual Circuits

Many packet-switching networks use *virtual circuits*. These are circuits composed of a series of logical connections between the sending computer and the receiving computer. The circuit is bandwidth allocated on demand, not an actual cable or permanent, physical link between two stations. The connection is made after both computers exchange information and agree on communication parameters that establish and maintain the connection. These parameters include the maximum message size and the path the data will take.

Virtual circuits incorporate the following communication parameters to ensure reliability:

- Acknowledgments
- Flow control
- Error control

Virtual circuits can last either as long as the conversation lasts (temporary) or as long as the two communicating computers are up and running (permanent).

Switched Virtual Circuits (SVCs)   In switched virtual circuits (SVCs), the connection between end computers uses a specific route across the network. Network resources are dedicated to the circuit, and the route is maintained until the connection is terminated. These are also known as point-to-many-point connections.

Permanent Virtual Circuits (PVCs)   Permanent virtual circuits (PVCs) are similar to leased lines that are permanent and virtual, except that the customer pays only for the time the line is used.

Sending Data Across a WAN

If the technologies discussed in previous lessons do not deliver the speed or bandwidth an organization needs, the network administrator should consider several advanced WAN environments that are becoming more popular as their technology matures. These include:

- X.25.
- Frame relay.
- Asynchronous Transfer Mode (ATM).
- Integrated Services Digital Network (ISDN).
- Fiber Distributed Data Interface (FDDI).
- Synchronous Optical Network (SONET).
- Switched Multimegabit Data Service (SMDS).

X.25

X.25 is a set of protocols incorporated in a packet-switching network. The packet-switching network is made up of switching services that were originally established to connect remote terminals to mainframe host systems.

An X.25 packet-switching network, as shown in Figure 7.24, uses switches, circuits, and routes, as available, to provide the best routing at any particular time. Because these components (switches, circuits, and routes) change rapidly depending on the need and what is available, they are sometimes depicted as clouds. The clouds are intended to convey the idea that this is an ever-changing situation, or that there is no standard set of circuits.

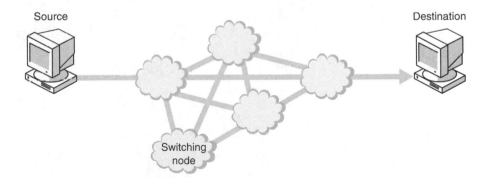

Figure 7.24   X.25 packet switching uses the best routing for each transmission

The early X.25 networks used telephone lines to transmit data. This was an unreliable medium that resulted in frequent errors, so X.25 incorporated extensive error checking. As a consequence of all of the error checking and retransmission, X.25 can appear to be slow.

Today's X.25 protocol suite defines the interface between a synchronous packet-mode host or other device and the public data network (PDN) over a dedicated or leased-line circuit. This interface is a data terminal equipment/data communications equipment (DTE/DCE) interface.

Examples of DTEs include:

- A host computer with an X.25 interface.
- A packet assembler/disassembler (PAD) that receives asynchronous characters, entered from a low-speed terminal, and assembles them into packets to be transmitted over the network. The PAD also disassembles packets received from the network so that the data can be delivered as characters to the terminals.
- A gateway between the PDN and a LAN or WAN.

For all three of these DTE examples, the DCE half of the DTE/DCE is the PDN. See Figure 7.25 for examples of DTEs.

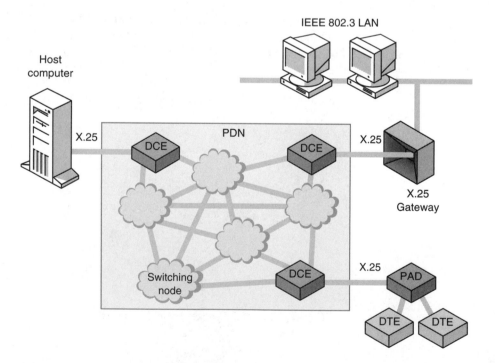

Figure 7.25   Examples of DTEs

Frame Relay

As network communications move toward digital and fiber-optic environments, new technologies are appearing that require less error checking than earlier analog packet-switching methods.

Frame relay is an advanced fast-packet variable-length, digital, packet-switching technology. With this technology, designers have stripped away many X.25 accounting and checking functions that are not necessary in a reliable, secure, fiber-optic circuit environment.

Frame relay, as shown in Figure 7.26, is a point-to-point system that uses a PVC to transmit variable length frames at the data-link layer. The data travels from a network over a digital leased line to a data switch and into the frame-relay network. It passes through the frame-relay network and arrives at the destination network.

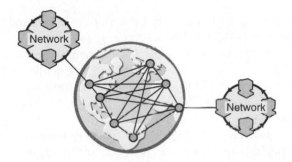

Figure 7.26   Frame relay uses a point-to-point system

Frame-relay networks are popular because they are much faster than other switching systems at performing basic packet-switching operations. This is because frame relay uses PVC so the entire path from end-to-end is known. There is no need for frame-relay devices to perform packet disassembly and reassembly, or to provide best-path routing.

Frame-relay networks can also provide subscribers with bandwidth as needed, which lets the customer make nearly any type of transmission.

Frame-relay technology requires a frame-relay-capable router or bridge to success-fully transmit data over the network. A frame-relay router needs at least one WAN port for a connection to the frame-relay network and another port for the LAN.

Asynchronous Transfer Mode (ATM)

Asynchronous transfer mode (ATM) is an advanced implementation of packet switching that provides high-speed data transmission rates to send fixed-size packets over broadband and baseband LANs or WANs. ATM can accommodate:

- Voice.
- Data.
- Fax.
- Real-time video.
- CD-quality audio.
- Imaging.
- Multimegabit data transmission.

The CCITT defined ATM in 1988 as part of the broadband Integrated Services Digital Network (BISDN), discussed later in this lesson. Because of ATM's power and versatility, it is influencing the development of network communications. It is equally adaptable to LAN and WAN environments, and it can transmit data at very high speeds (155 Mbps to 622 Mbps or more).

ATM Technology

ATM is a broadband cell relay method that transmits data in 53-byte cells rather than in variable-length frames. Figure 7.27 illustrates an ATM cell. These cells consist of 48 bytes of application information with five additional bytes of ATM header data. For example, ATM would divide a 1000-byte packet into 21 data frames and put each data frame into a cell. The result is a technology that transmits a consistent, uniform packet.

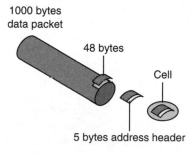

1000 bytes
data packet

48 bytes

Cell

5 bytes address header

Figure 7.27   ATM cells have 48 bytes of data and a 5-byte header

Network equipment can switch, route, and move uniform-sized frames much more quickly than it can move random-sized frames. The consistent, standard-sized cell uses buffers efficiently and reduces the work required to process incoming data. The uniform cell size also helps in planning application bandwidth.

Theoretically, ATM can offer throughput rates of up to 1.2 gigabits per second. Currently, however, ATM measures its speed against fiber-optic speeds that can reach as high as 622 Mbps. Most commercial ATM boards will transmit data at about 155 Mbps.

As a reference point, at 622 Mbps ATM could transmit the entire contents of the latest edition of the *Encyclopedia Britannica*, including graphics, in less than one second. If the same transfer were tried using a 2400-baud modem, the operation would take more than two days.

ATM can be used in LANs and WANs at approximately the same speed in each. ATM relies on carriers such as AT&T and Sprint for implementation over a wide area. This creates a consistent environment that does away with the concept of the slow WAN and the differing technologies used in the LAN and WAN environments.

ATM Components

ATM components are currently available through only a limited number of vendors. All hardware in an ATM network must be ATM-compatible. Implementing ATM in an existing facility will require extensive equipment replacement. This is one reason why ATM has not been adopted more quickly.

However, as the ATM market matures, various vendors will be able to provide:

- Routers and switches to connect carrier services on a global basis.

- Backbone devices to connect all the LANs within a large organization.

- Switches and adapters that link desktop computers to high-speed ATM connections for running multimedia applications.

ATM Media   ATM does not restrict itself to any particular media type. It can be used with existing media designed for other communications systems including:

- Coaxial cable.

- Twisted-pair cable.

- Fiber-optic cable.

However, these traditional network media in their present forms do not support all of ATM's capabilities. An organization called the ATM Forum recommends the following physical interfaces for ATM:

- FDDI (100 Mbps)
- Fiber Channel (155 Mbps)
- OC3 SONET (155 Mbps)
- T3 (45 Mbps)

Other interfaces include frame relay and X.25, discussed earlier in this lesson.

ATM Switches   ATM switches are multiport devices that can act as either of the following:

- Hubs to forward data from one computer to another within a network
- Router-like devices to forward data at high speeds to remote networks

In some network architectures, such as Ethernet and Token Ring, only one computer at a time can transmit. In Figure 7.28, three routers are feeding data into the ATM switch and onto the ATM network at the same time.

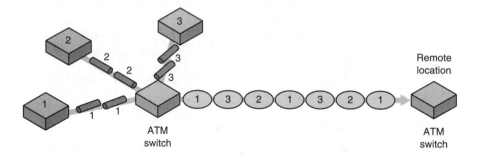

Figure 7.28   ATM switches act as multiplexers allowing multiple data input

ATM Considerations

ATM technology requires special hardware and exceptional bandwidth to reach its potential. Applications that support video or voice would overwhelm most older network environments and frustrate users trying to use the network for normal business. Also, implementing and supporting ATM requires expertise that is not widely available.

Integrated Services Digital Network (ISDN)

Integrated Services Digital Network (ISDN) is an inter-LAN digital connectivity specification that accommodates voice, data, and imaging. One of the original goals of ISDN developers was to link homes and businesses over copper telephone wires. The early ISDN implementation plan called for converting existing telephone circuits from analog to digital. This plan is being implemented worldwide.

Basic Rate ISDN divides its available bandwidth into three data channels. Two of these move data at 64 Kbps, while the third transmits at 16 Kbps.

The 64 Kbps channels are known as B channels. These can carry voice, data, or images. The slower 16 Kbps channel is called the D channel. The D channel carries signaling and link management data. ISDN Basic Rate desktop service is called 2B+D.

A computer connected to an ISDN service can use both B channels together for a combined 128 Kbps data stream. If both end stations also support compression, much higher throughput can be achieved.

Primary Rate ISDN uses the entire bandwidth of a T1 link by providing 23 B channels at 64 Kbps and one D channel at 64 Kbps. The D channel is used only for signaling and link management.

Networks that plan to use ISDN services should consider whether to use Basic Rate or Primary Rate, based on their need for data throughput. ISDN is the digital replacement for PSTN and, as such, is a dial-up service only. It is not designed to be a 24-hour (like T1) or bandwidth-on-demand (like frame relay) service.

Fiber Distributed Data Interface (FDDI)

Fiber Distributed Data Interface (FDDI) is a specification that describes a high-speed (100 Mbps) token-ring network that uses fiber-optic media. It was produced by the X3T9.5 committee of the American National Standards Institute (ANSI) and released in 1986. FDDI was designed for use with high-end computers that required greater bandwidth than the 10 Mbps Ethernet or 4 Mbps of existing Token Ring architectures.

FDDI is used to provide high-speed connections for various types of networks. FDDI can be used for metropolitan area networks (MANs) to connect networks in the same city with a high-speed fiber-optic cable connection. It is limited to a maximum ring length of 100 kilometers (62 miles), so FDDI is not really designed to be used as a WAN technology.

Networks in high-end environments use FDDI to connect components, such as large and small minicomputers, in a traditional computer room. These are sometimes called "back-end networks." These networks typically handle file transfer far more than interactive communication. When communicating with a mainframe, minicomputers or personal computers often require constant, real-time use of the media. They might even need exclusive use of the media for extended periods of time.

FDDI works with backbone networks to which other low-capacity LANs can connect. It is not wise to connect all the data-processing equipment in a company to a single LAN because the traffic can overload the network, and a failure can halt the company's entire data-processing operation.

LANs that require high data rates and fairly extensive bandwidth can use FDDI connections. These are networks composed of engineering computers or other computers that must support high-bandwidth applications such as video, computer-aided design (CAD), and computer-aided manufacturing (CAM).

Any office requiring high-speed network operations might consider using FDDI. Even in business offices, the need to produce graphics for presentations and other documentation can saturate and slow a network.

Token Passing

While FDDI uses a standard token-passing system, there are differences between FDDI and 802.5. A computer on an FDDI network can transmit as many frames as it can produce within a predetermined time before letting the token go. As soon as a computer has finished transmitting, it releases the token.

Because a computer releases the token when it has finished transmitting, there can be several frames circulating on the ring at once. This explains why FDDI offers higher throughput than a Token Ring network, which allows only one frame at a time to circulate.

Topology

FDDI operates at 100 Mbps over a dual-ring topology that supports 500 computers over a distance of up to 100 kilometers (62 miles).

FDDI uses shared network technology. This means that more than one computer at a time can transmit. Although FDDI can provide 100 Mbps service, the shared network approach can still become saturated. For example, if 10 computers all transmit at 10 Mbps, the total transmission will equal 100 Mbps. In transmitting video or multimedia, even the 100 Mbps transmit rate can become a bottleneck.

As shown in Figure 7.29, FDDI uses the token-passing system in a dual-ring setting. Traffic in an FDDI network consists of two similar streams flowing in opposite directions around two counter-rotating rings. One ring is called the "primary ring" and the other is called the "secondary ring."

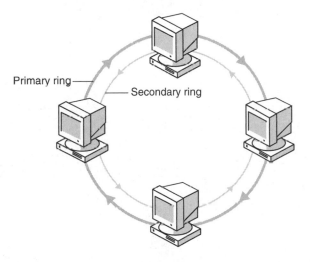

Figure 7.29 FDDI uses a dual-ring topology

Traffic usually flows only on the primary ring. If the primary ring fails, FDDI automatically reconfigures the network so that the data flows onto the secondary ring in the opposite direction.

One of the advantages of the dual-ring topology is redundancy. One of the rings is used for transmission, and the other is used for backup. If there is a problem, such as a ring failure or a cable break, the ring reconfigures itself and continues transmitting.

The total cable length of both rings combined must not exceed 200 kilometers (124 miles), and it cannot hold more than 1000 computers. However, because the second, redundant ring protects against ring failure, the total capacities should be divided in half. Therefore, each FDDI network should be limited to 500 computers and 100 kilometers (62 miles) of cable. Also, there must be a repeater every two kilometers (1.24 miles) or less.

Computers may connect to one or both FDDI cables in a ring. As shown in Figure 7.30, those that connect with both cables are known as Class A stations, and those that connect to only one ring are called Class B stations.

If there is a network failure, Class A stations can help reconfigure the network; Class B stations cannot.

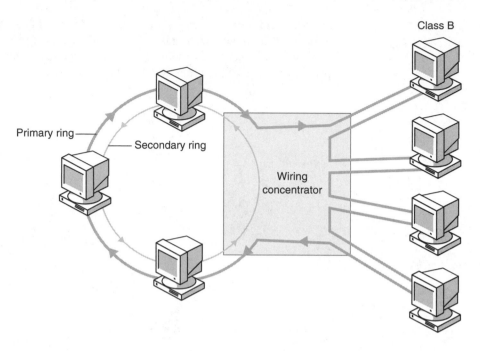

Figure 7.30   Class A computers connect to both rings; Class B computers connect to only one

FDDI in a Star   FDDI computers can accommodate point-to-point links to a hub. This means that FDDI can be implemented using the star-ring topology. This is an advantage in that it can:

- Help in troubleshooting.
- Take advantage of the management and troubleshooting capabilities of advanced hubs.

Beaconing

All computers in an FDDI network are responsible for monitoring the token-passing process. To isolate serious failures in the ring, FDDI uses a system called *beaconing*. With beaconing, the computer that detects a fault sends a signal, called a "beacon," onto the network. The computer continues to send the beacon until it notices a beacon from its upstream neighbor, and then it stops sending. This process continues until the only computer sending a beacon is the one directly downstream of the failure.

As illustrated in Figure 7.31, Computer 1 faults. Computer 3 detects the fault, starts to beacon, and continues to do so until it receives a beacon from Computer 2. Computer 2 continues to beacon until it receives a beacon from Computer 1. Because Computer 1 is the one with the fault, Computer 2 will continue to beacon and pinpoint the fault's location on Computer 1.

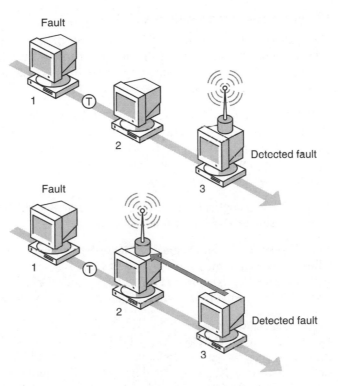

Figure 7.31   FDDI uses beaconing to isolate problems

When the beaconing computer finally receives its own beacon, it assumes the problem has been fixed and regenerates a token; then the network returns to normal operation.

Media
FDDI's primary medium is fiber-optic cable. This means that FDDI is:

- Immune to electromagnetic interference or noise.

- Secure, because fiber-optic cable does not emit a signal that can be monitored, and it cannot be tapped.

- Able to transmit long distances before needing a repeater.

FDDI can also be used on copper wire, known as copper-distributed data interface (CDDI), but this will seriously limit its distance capabilities.

Synchronous Optical Network (SONET)

Synchronous optical network (SONET) is one of several emerging systems that take advantage of fiber-optic technology. It can transmit data at more than one gigabit per second (Gbps). Networks based on this technology are capable of delivering voice, data, and video communication.

SONET is a standard for optical transport that was formulated by the Exchange Carriers Standards Association (ECSA) for ANSI. SONET has also been incorporated into the Synchronous Digital Hierarchy recommendations of the CCITT, also known as the International Telecommunications Union (ITU), which sets the standards for international telecommunications.

SONET defines optical-carrier (OC) levels and electrical-equivalent synchronous transport signals (STSs) for the fiber optic-based transmission hierarchy.

SONET uses a basic transmission rate of STS-1, which is equivalent to 51.84 Mbps. However, higher-level signals are achievable and are integer multiples of the base rate. For example, STS-3 is three times the rate of STS-1 (3 X 51.84 = 155.52 Mbps). An STS-12 would be a rate of 12 x 51.84 = 622.08 Mbps.

SONET provides sufficient payload flexibility that it can be used as the underlying transport layer for BISDN ATM cells. BISDN is a single ISDN network that can handle voice, data, and video services. ATM is the CCITT standard that supports cell-based voice, data, video, and multimedia communication in a public network under BISDN. The ATM Forum is aligning with SONET as the transport layer for cell-based traffic.

Switched Multimegabit Data Service (SMDS)

Switched Multimegabit Data Service (SMDS) is a switching service provided by some local exchange carrier services. Transmission speeds range from 1 Mbps to 34 Mbps with many-to-many connectivity. Unlike a dedicated mesh network (a network with multiple active paths), this connectionless service offers high bandwidth at reduced network costs.

SMDS uses the same fixed-length cell relay technology as ATM. One SMDS line with the appropriate bandwidth connects into the local carrier and can provide connections between all sites without a call setup or teardown procedure. SMDS does not perform error checking or flow control; that is left up to the sites being connected.

SMDS is compatible with the IEEE 802.6 MAN standard as well as with BISDN, but SMDS provides management and billing services not specified in the IEEE 802.6 specification.

SMDS uses the distributed queue dual bus (DQDB) as the interface and access method for the network. SMDS is a dual-bus topology that forms a ring that is not closed.

Lesson Summary

The following points summarize the main elements of this lesson:

- Two types of telephone lines are available for modem communications: public telephone lines (dial-up lines) and leased lines (dedicated lines).

- Most long-distance carriers use switched circuits to provide what appear to be dedicated lines, also called virtual private networks (VPNs).

- To make a Remote Access Service (RAS) connection, the server on the network must be configured with RAS, and the computer connecting to the network must be configured as a client or with dial-up networking (DUN).

- RAS connections can use any one of three protocols: Serial Line Interface Protocol (SLIP), Point-to-Point Protocol (PPP), or Point-to-Point Tunneling Protocol (PPTP).

- RAS provides four levels of security: auditing, callback, security host, and PPTP filters.

- The Point-to-Point Tunneling Protocol (PPTP) allows a remote client to make a secure connection to a network over the Internet.

- Organizations that need a more secure and faster connection than can be provided by an analog line will convert to DDS (digital data service).

- T1 service is the most widely used kind of digital line.

- Packet-switching networks offer a fast and efficient way to transit data over wide areas.

- Frame relay is an advanced fast-packet variable-length, digital, packet-switching technology.

- Asynchronous Transfer Mode (ATM) is an advanced implementation of packet switching that provides high-speed transmission rates to send fixed-size packets over broadband and baseband LANs and WANs.

- Integrated Services Digital Network (ISDN) is an inter-LAN digital connectivity specification that accommodates voice, data, and imaging.

- Fiber Distributed Data Interface (FDDI) is a specification that describes a high-speed token-passing network that uses fiber-optic media.

- Synchronous Optical Network (SONET) is an emerging technology based on fiber optics.

- Switched Multimegabit Data Service (SMDS) is a connectionless switching service provided by local exchange carrier services that offers high bandwidth at reduced network costs.

Exercise 7.1: Troubleshooting Problem

Use the information below to help you solve the troubleshooting problem that follows.

Background Information

One of the key resources for troubleshooting communications problems is the vendor who manufactured the product. Most system administrators do not have extensive knowledge of telecommunications technology, while telecommunications vendors typically have staff members who have this type of expertise. Often, however, actual problems are not nearly as difficult to resolve as they first appear to be. Consider the following example:

A medium-sized computer firm lost its telephone service every Monday morning for nearly six months. Each Monday, employees would arrive at work to find that the telephone system was not working. Because no one in the company had the expertise to solve the problem, they contacted their telephone vendor, who sent someone out to repair the system. The telephone company sent a different technician each time, and each time it took the technician only about 15 minutes to fix the system.

One Monday, one of the computer firm's own technicians went to watch the telephone vendor's technician bring the system back up. The technician simply located the telephone system's surge suppressor and hit the reset switch. That was the total fix, and anyone who knew how to reset the surge suppressor (simply by pressing a reset button) could now repair the telephone system.

The point of this story is that even in a complex environment, problems and their solutions do not necessarily have to be complex.

While the answer was ultimately simple, the telephone company's technician was the only person who had the initial expertise necessary to locate and eliminate the problem. If you have WAN communication problems and you have eliminated the LAN's local components as a source of trouble, do not hesitate to call the service provider to ask for help. While this can result in an initial expense, time and money will be saved in the long run.

With that story in mind, forge ahead and work through the following troubleshooting problem.

The Problem

You are the multitalented network administrator and technician for this computer firm. Your LAN is connected to another LAN in a city 806 kilometers (500 miles) away. The communication link is a digital T1 with a multiplexer that allows you to send telephone conversations and data simultaneously on the same link.

When you came into work on Monday morning, you immediately began to hear complaints from employees who could not use the WAN to access resources at the other site. After some checking, you discovered that you can use the T1 for telephone conversations, but you cannot send or receive data over the link. You now examine all the equipment and connectors but cannot see any obvious loose or frayed connections, and all of the equipment appears to be plugged in and turned on.

What can you do to start the troubleshooting process?

Exercise 7.2: Case Study Problem

A magazine publisher based in Seattle has two branch offices: one in Fort Lauderdale, Florida, and one in New York City. Each office is internally and separately networked. The networks were implemented five years ago, and each has a coaxial linear-bus topology supporting Ethernet 10 Mbps traffic. The branch offices stay in touch with each other by telephone and Federal Express.

Recently, the company has begun to develop projects that involve team members from more than one office. Each office has resources that the other two do not; the current projects require all of these resources. The internal networks have had frequent cable problems, and each time they have a problem, the entire office network goes down until the problem is resolved.

The management team would like a network design that offers easier troubleshooting, less down time, and provides WAN communication between sites. They would like the WAN connection to be able to support about 256 Kbps of data and several analog telephone conversations between sites (the long-distance bills have been unacceptably high). The combination of long-distance and Federal Express charges should be eliminated by the WAN. Management would like the WAN to be able to continue operating even if one of the WAN links should fail.

1. Identify at least two network items in each branch-office network site that need upgrading.

2. The separate branch offices need to maintain voice and data communications with each other. Which type of WAN connection (link) might you use to connect the three sites to each other?

3. Which type of device could be used to collect the multiple signals from voice and data and put them on the same WAN link?

4. Which type of connectivity device should be used to connect the LAN to the multiple paths in the WAN illustrated in the diagram above?

Exercise 7.3: Network Planning Problem

Answering the following questions will help you determine which, if any, WAN or advanced transmission components you should consider for your network needs.

Modems

1. Do you need to communicate with bulletin board services (BBSs) and information service providers such as the Microsoft Network, America Online, or CompuServe?

    Yes _____

    No _____

2. Do you need individual connectivity to the Internet?

    Yes _____

    No _____

3. Do you need to transfer files periodically with another user at a different location?

    Yes _____

    No _____

    If the answers to any of the first three questions was yes, you need a modem. Your next step is to research which vendor's modem best fits your needs.

4. Will several users at once need to communicate occasionally with an online service or any remote resource?

    Yes _____

    No _____

    If the answer is yes, you should consider a modem pool.

5. Do your users periodically need to access the network from home or on the road?

    Yes _____

    No _____

    If the answer is yes, you might need remote access service. To implement this, you will also need a remote access server.

Creating Larger Networks

You should consider adding WAN connectivity devices to your network if it is getting too large and difficult to manage. Difficulties could result from the addition of an unanticipated number of users, or where existing users have acquired new applications that generate greater network traffic than the original network was designed to accommodate. You might also need to connect multiple sites or multiple networks.

The determining factors in choosing a WAN connection service include:

- Which services are available in your area.
- What kinds of services you need.

The following questions will help you identify which connectivity devices would be appropriate for your system.

Repeaters

1. Do you need to extend the cable length of your network to accommodate new users located farther from the server?

   Yes ____

   No ____

2. If you extend the length of your network cable, will the newly extended cable length exceed the specifications for that type of cable?

   Yes ____

   No ____

3. Do you need to transmit signals on different media than that which you are already using for your network? (For example, do you need to connect a thinnet segment to an Ethernet 10BaseT network?)

   Yes ____

   No ____

If the answer to any of the above questions is yes, you should consider using a repeater to expand your network.

Bridges

Note A rule of thumb among many experienced network professionals is to use a bridge when dealing with nonroutable protocols. Otherwise, use a router.

1. Do you need to connect two or more network segments?

   Yes _____

   No _____

2. Do you need to connect two networks with different network architectures (such as Ethernet to Token Ring)?

   Yes _____

   No _____

3. Is your network performance slower than you would like it to be?

   Yes _____

   No _____

   If the answer is yes, keep that in mind while you answer the next question.

4. Does your network serve different departments that usually transmit network traffic only within their own department?

   Yes _____

   No _____

If you answered yes to any of the questions, consider using bridges either to segment a single network or to join two different networks.

Routers

Note Many network professionals prefer to use routers when it is possible to use either a bridge or a router to solve the problem. Their general rule is to use a bridge only with nonroutable protocols. In other cases, they use a router. The cost difference between a bridge and a router is small when weighed against the additional capabilities of a router.

1. Do you need to join several LAN segments into a single network?

   Yes _____

   No _____

2. Do you need to connect different network architectures (such as Ethernet to Token Ring)?

   Yes _____

   No _____

3. Do you need to isolate or filter traffic between multiple segments?

   Yes ____

   No ____

4. Are network performance and data integrity important enough to maintain redundant paths between multiple segments simultaneously?

   Yes ____

   No ____

5. If you have multiple paths available, do you want to route packets on a "best path" algorithm?

   Yes ____

   No ____

If the answer to any of these questions is yes, you should consider implementing routers between the different segments.

Gateways

1. Do you need to allow communication between unlike systems? (For example, do any users need to access a mainframe computer? Do users of Microsoft network software need to access servers running network software from Novell? Do users of network software from Novell need to access files on a computer running UNIX?)

   Yes ____

   No ____

If your answer is yes, you should consider a gateway.

Choosing Advanced WAN Transmission Technologies

Choosing a WAN connection service varies from location to location based on available services and your network needs. You will need to do some market research to determine which service provider can best meet your system needs. The following questions can help you identify some of the services you will need.

1. Do you have only two sites to link?

   Yes ____

   No ____

   If the answer is yes, you probably need point-to-point service.

2. Does your system need to link multiple sites to a central location?

   Yes ____

   No ____

   If the answer is yes, you probably need a point-to-multipoint service.

3. Does your system need to link many sites simultaneously?

   Yes ＿＿

   No ＿＿

   If the answer is yes, you probably need a multipoint-to-multipoint service.

4. Is the data that you transmit so critical to protect that you require multiple links between sites to provide redundancy in case of link failure?

   Yes ＿＿

   No ＿＿

   If the answer is yes, you might need multiple links.

Note Frame relay and other switching technologies provide redundancy, but not at the transmitting or receiving site. Also, because service providers bill for packet switching by the packet, switching technology can be either more or less expensive than T1, depending on the type of data and frequency of transmission. The service provider is the best source of information about costs.

---

5. Which kind of network traffic will be on the link? (Check all that apply.)

   - Voice ＿＿
   - E-mail ＿＿
   - Light file transfer ＿＿
   - Heavy file transfer ＿＿
   - Client/server database activity (likely to be fairly light network traffic) ＿＿
   - Client-computer database activity with the data files stored on a remote server (can be very heavy traffic) ＿＿

6. Based on the amount of network traffic identified in the previous question, approximately how much network bandwidth do you need? (Your WAN vendor might be able to help you determine this.)

   - Less than 56 Kbps ＿＿
   - 56 to 64 Kbps ＿＿
   - 128 Kbps ＿＿
   - 256 Kbps ＿＿
   - 1 Mbps ＿＿
   - More than 1 Mbps ＿＿

7. Which types and speeds of WAN connection services (service providers) are available in your area?

Note You will need to do some homework and research service providers to answer this.

8. Which of the above services can meet your requirements as determined by your answers to questions 1 to 3?

9. Which service that can meet your requirements provides the best price and performance for your WAN needs?

Exercise Summary

Put a check mark next to the component you will need, indicate how many components you will need, and note the parameters. To do this, it can help to draw a map of the network and place the components on the map.

Note Before filling out this chart, you will need to research different vendors and products to identify those that best fit your system's needs.

Components

Component	Number	Notes and parameters
Modem		
Repeater		
Bridge		
Router		
Gateway		

Service Providers

Service	Provider	Cost/notes
1. Point-to-point		
2. Point-to-multipoint		
3. Multipoint-to-multipoint		
4. T1		
5. Multiple T1		

Chapter Summary

Connectivity Devices

- Modems make it possible to communicate over telephone lines.

- There are two types of modems: synchronous and asynchronous.

- It is important to choose the right cable when connecting hubs; crossover cables will not work in place of standard patch cables.

- Asymmetric digital subscriber line (ADSL) is a technology for increasing the speed of transmission on telephone lines.

- Repeaters are used to connect two segments of similar or dissimilar media and to regenerate a signal to increase the distance transmitted.

- Repeaters should not be used where network traffic is heavy, segments are using different access methods, or filtering is needed.

- Bridges have all the features of repeaters.

- Bridges are used to connect two segments to expand the length or number of nodes on the network, to reduce traffic by segmenting the network, or to connect dissimilar networks.

- Routers are used to connect two networks, limit unnecessary traffic, and to separate administrative networks.

- Brouters combine the features of bridges and routers; a brouter can act as a router for one protocol and as a bridge for all the others.

- Gateways perform protocol and data conversion.

- Gateways are limited in several ways: they are task-specific, expensive, and can be slow.

Connection Services

- Two types of telephone lines are available for modem communications: public telephone lines (dial-up lines) and leased lines (dedicated lines).

- Most long-distance carriers use switched circuits to provide what appear to be dedicated lines, also called virtual private networks (VPNs).

- To make a Remote Access Service (RAS) connection, the server on the network must be configured with RAS, and the computer connecting to the network must be configured as a client or with dial-up networking (DUN).

- RAS connections can use any one of three protocols: Serial Line Interface Protocol (SLIP), Point-to-Point Protocol (PPP), or Point-to-Point Tunneling Protocol (PPTP).

- RAS provides four levels of security: auditing, callback, security host, and PPTP filters.

- The Point-to-Point Tunneling Protocol (PPTP) allows a remote client to make a secure connection to a network over the Internet.

- Organizations that need a more secure and faster connection than can be provided by an analog line can convert to DDS (digital data service).

- T1 service is the most widely used kind of digital line.

- Packet-switching networks offer a fast and efficient way to transit data over wide areas.

- Frame relay is an advanced fast-packet variable-length, digital, packet-switching technology.

- Asynchronous Transfer Mode (ATM) is an advanced implementation of packet switching that provides high-speed transmission rates to send fixed-size packets over broadband and baseband LANs and WANs.

- Integrated Services Digital Network (ISDN) is an inter-LAN digital connectivity specification that accommodates voice, data, and imaging.

- Fiber Distributed Data Interface (FDDI) is a specification that describes a high-speed token-passing network that uses fiber-optic media.

- Synchronous Optical Network (SONET) is an emerging technology based on fiber optics.

- Switched Multimegabit Data Service (SMDS) is a connectionless switching service provided by local exchange carrier services that offers high bandwidth at reduced network costs.

Remote Access Computing

- Remote Access Service (RAS) is used to provide remote access to a network.

- A RAS connection requires that the server on the network be configured with RAS service and the computer connecting to the network be configured as a client or dial-up networking (DUN) computer.

- RAS connections can use any one of three protocols: Serial Line Interface Protocol (SLIP), Point-to-Point Protocol (PPP), or Point-to-Point Tunneling Protocol (PPTP).

- RAS provides four levels of security: auditing, callback, security host, and PPTP filters.

- Use RAS if the bandwidth is less than 128 Kps, you do not require a full-time connection, or you need to keep the system cost down.

- Don't use RAS if you need a higher bandwidth than provided by a synchronous-modem, you need a dedicated full-time connection, or if leased lines are already available.

Chapter Review

1. An external modem is a small box that is connected to the computer by a _____ cable running from the computer's port to the modem's computer-cable connection.

2. The modem at the _____ end converts digital signals into analog signals.

3. Baud rate refers to the speed of oscillation of the _____ _____ on which a bit of data is carried.

4. The bps can be greater than the _____ rate.

5. Asynchronous transmission occurs over _____ _____.

6. The Microcom Network Protocol (MNP) is a standard for asynchronous _____ - _____ control.

7. In asynchronous communication, it is possible to double throughput by using _____ without having to pay for a faster channel speed.

8. Synchronous communication relies on a _____ scheme coordinated between two devices.

9. More advanced, complex repeaters can act as multiport _____ to connect different types of media.

10. Repeaters do not have a _____ function and so will pass along all data from one segment to the next.

11. A repeater takes a weak signal and _____ it.

12. A repeater functions at the _____ layer of the OSI model.

13. If the volume of traffic from one or two computers or a single department is flooding the network with data and slowing down the entire operation, a _____ could isolate those computers or that department.

14. The bridge builds a routing table based on the _____ addresses of computers that have sent traffic through the bridge.

15. Bridges work at the OSI _____ - _____ layer and, specifically, the _____ _____ _____ sublayer.

16. Bridges are often used in large networks that have widely dispersed segments joined by _____ _____.

17. Under spanning tree algorithm (STA), software can sense the existence of more than one _____, determine which would be the most efficient, and then configure the bridge to use that one.

18. Bridges connect two segments and regenerate the signal at the _____ level.

19. Routers work at the _____ layer of the OSI model.

20. Because they must perform complex functions on each packet, routers are _____ than most bridges.

21. Routers do not look at the destination node address; they look only at the _____ address.

22. Unlike bridges, routers can accommodate multiple active _____ between LAN segments and choose among them.

23. The two major types of routers are _____ and _____.

24. A brouter will _____ nonroutable protocols.

25. Most often, gateways are dedicated _____ on a network.

26. The gateway takes the data from one environment, strips it, and repackages it in the _____ _____ from the destination system.

27. Gateways are _____ specific, which means that they are dedicated to a particular type of transfer.

28. With the exception of ADSL, public telephone lines require users to _____ make a connection for each communication session.

29. The three factors an administrator must take into account when considering how best to implement communication between two modems are _____, _____, and _____.

30. Leased lines provide _____ connections that do not use a series of switches to complete the connection.

31. A good remote-access option that offers stable lines for companies that are constantly communicating between networks is to use _____ lines.

32. The _____ - _____ - _____ _____
    _____ allows a remote client to establish a secure connection
    to the corporate LAN over the Internet and RAS.

33. Because the PSTN was designed primarily for voice, _____ - _____
    lines do not have the consistent quality required for secure data communi-
    cations.

34. A dedicated line is _____ and more _____ than a
    dial-up connection.

35. One advantage that dedicated lines offer over dial-up lines is that the service
    company implements _____ _____ to improve
    communication, thereby ensuring line quality.

36. Digital lines provide _____ - ___ - _____ synchronous
    communication.

37. Because DDS uses _____ communication, it does not require
    modems.

38. T1 uses a technology called _____ in which several signals
    from different sources are collected into a component and fed into one cable
    for transmission.

39. T1 can accommodate 24 _____ data transmissions over
    each two-wire pair.

40. Subscribers who do not need or cannot afford the bandwidth of an entire T1
    line can subscribe to one or more T1 _____.

41. With packet switching, the data is broken down into packets, and each packet
    is tagged with a _____ _____ and other
    information.

42. At the destination, the packets are _____ into the original
    message.

43. Two packets from the original data package can arrive out of sequence because
    they followed different _____ to reach the same destination.

44. Virtual circuits are composed of a series of _____ connections
    between the sending computer and the receiving computer.

45. Because of its extensive _____ _____, X.25 can appear
    to be slow.

46. X.25 was originally developed for the _____ environment.

47. Frame-relay data travels from a network over a _____ _____ line to a data switch and into the frame-relay network.

48. Frame-relay networks can also provide subscribers with _____ as needed, which lets the customer make nearly any type of transmission.

49. Frame-relay networks are faster at performing basic _____ - _____ operations than are X.25 networks.

50. ATM is an advanced implementation of _____ _____ that provides high-speed data transmission rates.

51. ATM transmits data in 53-byte _____ rather than variable-length frames.

52. ATM switches are multiport devices that can act as either _____ to forward data from one computer to another within a network or _____ to forward data at high speeds to remote networks.

53. ATM uses switches as _____ to permit several computers to put data on a network simultaneously.

54. ATM can be used with existing _____ designed for other communications systems.

55. Basic Rate ISDN divides its available _____ into three data channels.

56. FDDI is a specification that describes a high-speed (100 Mbps) token-ring LAN that uses _____ - _____ media.

57. FDDI can be used for _____ networks to which other, low-capacity LANs can connect.

58. A computer on an FDDI network can transmit as many frames as it can produce within a predetermined time before letting the _____ go.

59. Traffic in an FDDI network consists of two similar streams flowing in opposite directions around two counter-rotating _____.

60. An advantage of the dual-ring topology is _____.

61. To isolate serious failures in the ring, FDDI uses a system called _____ in which a computer that detects a fault sends a signal onto the network.

P A R T   I I

Implementing a Network

In Part II, our focus shifts from overview to implementation, and we begin the process of putting together the elements from Part I. Here, our emphasis is on the nuts and bolts of designing and rolling out a complete network: choosing a network type (peer-to-peer or server-based), selecting hardware and software for installation, and choosing and establishing security through shares and accounts. We also take a look at environmental factors that affect networks, as well as administering, upgrading, troubleshooting, and relocating networks.

C H A P T E R   8

Designing and Installing a Network

About This Chapter

In this chapter, we expand our knowledge of networking hardware. To help us put our knowledge to work in a realistic context, we will create a simple networking plan for a fictitious company and explore how to install and configure networking hardware for it. We conclude by taking a look at some related hardware compatibility issues. Throughout the chapter, we touch on the subjects of upgrading computers and networks. For a more in-depth look at these issues, see Chapter 12, "Administering Change."

Before You Begin

Because this chapter concerns network hardware, you will find it helpful to review chapters 1–3 in Part I of this book.

Lesson 1: Choosing a Network Design

This lesson focuses on the first step in creating a computer network: laying the foundation upon which your network will be built. The decisions that you make now can make life easier for you or come back to haunt you. In this lesson, we explore the decisions and steps that you need to take to design a functional network.

After this lesson, you will be able to:

- Determine the type of network that best fits a company's needs.
- Choose the appropriate media and hardware with which to construct a successful network.

Estimated lesson time: 35 minutes

Peer-to-Peer or Server-Based?

A company that manufactures custom-made bicycles has asked you to install an economical computer network that will bring it up-to-date in communication technology and be flexible enough to allow for future expansion.

The company's network goals are to:

- Network the existing computers so that they can share information and printers.
- Add two additional computers to the network: one for the Product Design Group and one for the Manufacturing Department.
- Allow for the possible addition of three computers at a later date.
- Provide an Internet connection for the Product Design Group.

Table 8.1 provides background information about the bicycle company.

Table 8.1 Background Information on Bicycle Company

Location	Ozona, Florida
Number of employees	23
Product	Custom bicycles
Facility	Single-story building: 245 square meters (2625 square feet)
Current number of computers	Five personal computers, distributed as follows: Managing Director: Pentium III 400 MHz Accounting Dept.: 486/200 MHz Sales Dept.: 486/200 Shipping Dept.: 286/25 Product Design Group: Pentium II 300
Operating systems	Managing Director and Product Design Group: Windows 98 Accounting and Sales Depts.: Windows 95 Shipping Dept.. MS-DOS 5.0
Peripheral equipment	The Managing Director has a modem, Internet connection, and a color ink jet printer.
	The Design Dept. has an old laser printer. The Accounting and Sales Depts. share a second old laser printer on a switch box.
	The Shipping Dept. has a dot matrix printer.

Figure 8.1 illustrates the layout of the bicycle company, including public areas, department offices, and manufacturing facilities.

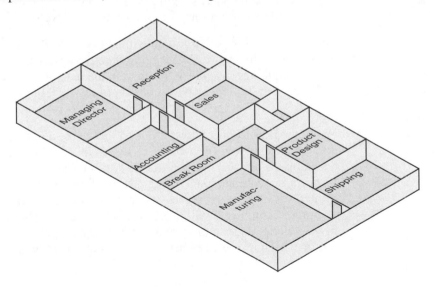

Figure 8.1 Facility layout of bicycle company

Note Throughout the lessons in this chapter, we will build, maintain, and expand this hypothetical computer network. As we work through the lessons, we will discuss various applications and choose those best suited for the needs of our fictional bicycle company. Keep in mind that the choices we make are based on the requirements of this hypothetical company and will not address every company's networking situation and needs.

The first decision we need to make for this new network is whether it should be a peer-to-peer or a server-based network. The factors we need to examine include the:

- Size of the network.
- Level of security.
- Type of business.
- Level of administrative support available.
- Amount of network traffic.
- Needs of the network users.
- Network budget.

In a peer-to-peer network, all users on the network are equal. Each will have equal access to all other computers on the network, provided the owner of the computer has shared that resource with the network. In a small network or business, this "one for all and all for one" system often works well.

Often, in a small business, no individual is able to devote full-time attention to administering the network. This brings another advantage of peer-to-peer networks to light. Here, responsibility for running the network is distributed to everyone, and users determine which information or resources on their computers will be shared.

While the peer-to-peer network option looks like a good choice for our bicycle company, it has some drawbacks that must be considered. For example, imagine a user on the network who has the laser printer attached to her computer. If she turns off her computer and leaves the office, no one else will be able to use the printer. If Computer A freezes or is rebooted while Computer B is trying to use a resource, Computer B will be disconnected. To summarize, usually, in a peer-to-peer scenario, no system administrator is designated, security precautions are few, and each user is responsible for his or her own data.

Another down side of the peer-to-peer network is its limited performance. If another user is accessing the resources on your computer, that user will also be using processor time on your computer. Therefore, regardless of how fast your computer's processor is or how much memory you have, the performance of your computer will slow down when someone else is drawing on its resources.

Even with these drawbacks, a peer-to-peer network might still appear to be a good choice for our network. However, we should also consider the advantages of using a server-based network before we make our decision. On a server-based network, resources are usually centralized. For example, one server manages all the printers, and another server manages all the files. Because servers are rarely turned off, resources will always be available. Server-based networks are also *scalable*. This means that their size can be easily adjusted to respond to changes in the load on the network.

Server-based networks are also more secure than peer-to-peer networks. With a peer-to-peer network, all resources are shared equally across the network. If the Accounting Department shares the directory that contains the salary files so that the Managing Director can access them, everyone else on the network can also access these files. On the other hand, server-based networks allow for the creation of accounts and permissions that provide for further security. For example, a server-based network can share individual files within a directory without making the directory itself available to everyone on the network.

As it grows, a server-based network can be segregated according to organizational needs. For example, one server might be designated for the Accounting Department and another server designated for the Sales Department. Should our bicycle company's network requirements reach this level, we will need to consider using a network that supports file-level sharing and user groups with shared rights to network resources.

At present, the better choice for our company is to use a peer-to-peer network. But in order to provide more flexibility and to prepare it for further expansion, another option exists: create a hybrid network. Thus, while our basic network will be peer-to-peer, we will install one computer as a file server. With this approach, access to the file server requires an account and permissions, while access to other computers on the network is shared equally.

So, after weighing these factors, we arrive at our network-design selection for this bicycle company: a hybrid peer-to-peer network, with one new computer to be installed and configured as a file server and used to centralize company information.

Taking Inventory

After deciding on the overall network design, our next step in creating a network is to take inventory to determine what hardware and software is already available and what needs to be acquired. As an illustration, we turn again to our bicycle company. It has a mixture of computers, ranging from a legacy 286 to a new Pentium III, as well as some older printers. Thus, some obvious updating will be required to get this network up and running. Taking inventory is an important step, because it sets the stage for future network expansion. For example, if all your computers run Microsoft Windows 95 or Windows 98, you will be limited to using a peer-to-peer network. To upgrade to a server-based network in the future, you will have to upgrade one of the computers to run NetWare or Windows NT or add a new server with one of those network operating systems installed.

To take inventory, you'll need to survey four categories:

- Hardware
- Software
- Telecommunications equipment
- Network requirements

Hardware Survey

This is actually a simple process, but one that should not be taken lightly. Begin by recording the specifications of each computer; the details you gather at this stage can save time in the long run. As we will see later, in order to function effectively, networks often require that hardware and software meet certain minimum standards. If you know the specification details of the available equipment in advance, you can prevent many problems later on.

For each computer, you will need to gather information, including:

- Make and model.
- Processor manufacturer and speed.
- Amount of memory (RAM) installed.
- The size and manufacturer of each hard drive.
- Details of any other installed drives, such as compact-disc and removable disk drives.
- Monitor—make, model, and size.
- Video card—make, model, and amount of memory.
- Any installed peripherals.
- Type of bus—EISA, Micro Channel, ISA, or PCI—the computer uses and whether there are any free slots; you will need free slots to install network interface cards. (For more information on bus architecture, refer to Lesson 2: The Network Interface Card, in Chapter 2.)

Make a list of the manufacturer and model number for any peripheral devices, such as printers, plotters, and scanners, whether they are installed or simply sitting on a shelf. For each of these, note whether you have the original disk with drivers.

Software Survey

Be aware of all the software currently in use throughout the potential network. For example, if you were to convert all the computers to Windows NT while you were installing the new network, you might find that some of the old standby programs, once used on a daily basis, now no longer run. Be especially careful when evaluating custom-designed and proprietary programs, such as accounting databases, that have been written especially for the company. You might need to contact the manufacturer for information about running proprietary programs on the network. Not all of these will run in a network environment; the product-licensing arrangement might not allow network operations.

For each software program, gather the following information:

- Program name
- Program version number
- Availability of the original installation floppy disks or compact discs
- Any licensing information

As you carry out your survey of our bicycle company, also note any potential software incompatibilities within and among company departments. For example, the Accounting Department might be using WordPerfect, whereas the Sales Department is using Microsoft Office. If you are planning to upgrade some day, now is the time to make any changes needed to ensure that the same system is used company wide.

Telecommunications Equipment Survey

It might seem strange to review the existing telecommunications equipment when you are installing a LAN, but this is actually a very important element of your survey, especially if you intend to use Internet connections or some form of remote access server. (Known as RAS, this is a host on a LAN that includes modems and enables users to connect to the network over telephone lines; RAS is discussed in Chapter 7, Lesson 2: Connection Services.) Overlooking something as simple as the number of phone lines wired into each office can have a major impact later if you need modem and telephone connections at the same time. For example, if the company has an automated telephone system, while telephone outlets might be located in every office, they might not be capable of a modem connection. In that case, a separate telephone outlet might be required for voice and data communication. Also, if the company is using a high-speed digital telephone service, you might not be able to connect with standard modems. Don't assume a standard RJ-11 telephone jack is going to be sufficient for you to connect a modem and start surfing the Web.

Requirements of the Network

After you have examined the existing facility and equipment, you need to define the requirements of your network. You'll then match these requirements to the existing hardware, software, and telecommunications features available and determine what steps need to be taken to develop the network. At a minimum, you should consider the following:

- The size of the facility (located on a single floor vs. multiple floors)
- The number of users
- Whether the LAN will be extended to several buildings
- The environment (office, manufacturing, out-of-doors)
- The current network media, if any
- The technical competence of users
- The amount of network traffic (initially, and anticipated for the future)
- The level of security

Building a Map

Now it's time to lay out the network. But before you begin to recommend a network plan for our bicycle company, you will first need to make a map of all the elements involved. During this step, you should consider two aspects of the network: the physical layout, including the location of each piece of hardware and how it relates to the others, and the physical and logical topology of the proposed network.

Use a drawing or map of the facility—or make one if it doesn't exist already—and mark the location of the existing equipment. Figure 8.2 shows the facility drawing for the bicycle company, with the location of the existing equipment.

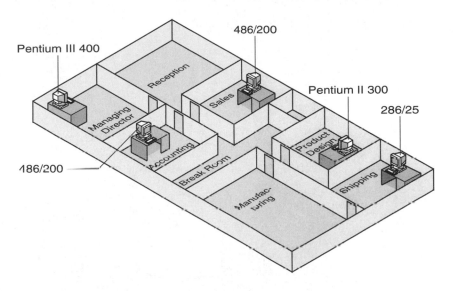

Figure 8.2   Existing equipment for the bicycle company

The second step is to create a layout of the network topology. Don't forget to include printers and other peripherals, such as scanners and modems. Figure 8.3 shows the company network as a physical bus.

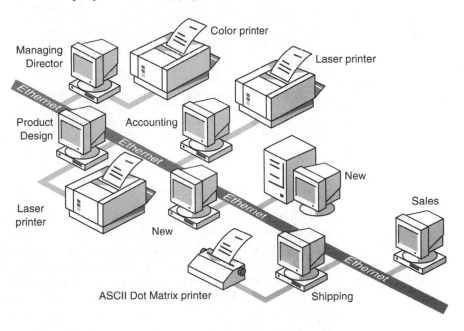

Figure 8.3   Bicycle company network as a physical bus

Figure 8.4 Shows the network as a physical star.

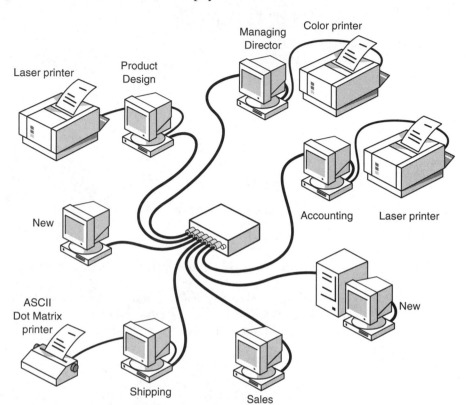

Figure 8.4   Bicycle company network as a physical star

Note Adequately documenting a network is the key to successful troubleshooting in the future. Start with the facility map and equipment survey.

Choosing Network Media

The choice of which media to select should not be taken lightly. The cost of installation can be quite high, especially if you have to do it twice. The media you choose will usually be related to the geographic requirements of the site. For example, if several of the workstations are located in a manufacturing environment in which a large amount of electrical noise is generated, fiber-optic cable might be required because it is unaffected by electrical signals. On the other hand, in a small office, simple twisted-pair cable will usually be appropriate. The most important thing to keep in mind is not the cost today, but the cost in the future. Being overly cost-conscious now can limit the scalability, and thus the life span, of the network.

At our bicycle company, we might decide to install our network using CAT 3 UTP cable. This would give us a functional network with our seven workstations, but limit our network speed to 10 Mbps. Five years from now, when we might have as many as 30 to 50 workstations, a 10 Mbps network would be slow. However, by installing CAT 5 UTP now, we can upgrade our network to 100 Mbps at any time in the future without needing to rewire the building. And CAT 5 UTP cable costs only a few cents more per foot than CAT 3 UTP cable.

Installing Network Media

Installing network media requires special skills and is best left to a professional cable installer if the topology is complex. With a simple topology, however, the necessary skills are well within our reach. Still using our bicycle company as an example, we will next tackle the basics of installing a CAT 5 Ethernet cabling system. (Bear in mind that at this point we are focusing on the cables and are not yet ready to connect any of the devices.)

The simplest way to lay out a network in our small-office environment is to use a physical star. The focal point of the star will be a patch panel. (A *patch panel* is an array of RJ-45 female connectors that have terminals for connecting the wires.) Figure 8.5 shows a typical 12-connection CAT 5 568B patch panel.

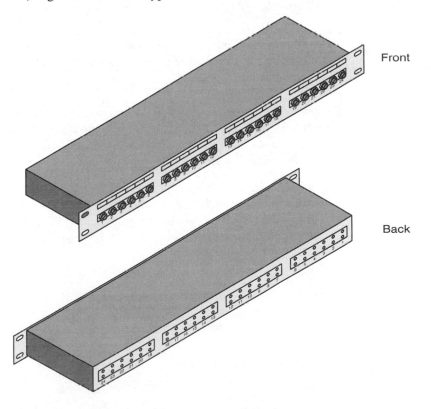

Figure 8.5   12-connection CAT 5 568B Patch Panel

Notice that the front of the panel has 12 RJ-45 connectors. On the back is a terminal for each of the 12 cables. Looking closely, you will notice that each terminal has eight connection points, one for each of the eight wires. The wires are color-coded for easy installation. By mounting the patch panel near the hub (usually next to the server), you can easily make connections to the network.

On the other end of the cable, you will need to install a CAT 5 outlet. This is similar to a standard telephone outlet (see Figure 8.6), but uses an RJ-45 connection, just as the patch panel does. Notice that this connector also has color-coded terminals.

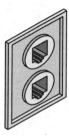

Figure 8.6   CAT 5 outlet

Note Some CAT 5 outlets have two sets of color coding, one for 568A and one for 568B cable termination. Be sure to match the color code of the outlet and the patch panel.

Remember that when installing the cable, as discussed in Chapter 2, "Basic Network Media," any cables that are to be run above the ceiling or below the floor must meet local construction and fire codes. Be sure to use plenum-grade cable where it is required.

If you plan to install a lot of cable and connections (patch panels or CAT 5 outlets), you might want to purchase a punchdown tool. (This is a small hand tool that will ensure that the wires are properly connected to the terminal.) Figure 8.7 shows a typical punchdown tool.

Figure 8.7   Punch down tool

Connecting Media to Computers

After the media has been installed, connecting the computers is a straightforward process. All of the connections are made through CAT 5 patch cables (prewired cables and connectors, manufactured in a variety of solid colors). One end of the cable is secured to the computer's NIC and the other to the RJ-45 outlet. If you are using a hub, you will find that short patch cables connect the patch panel and an outlet on the hub. Don't worry if you find that there is no computer connected to an outlet and the cabling is connected all the way to the hub. The hub will sense that the segment is unoccupied and ignore it.

Figure 8.8 shows a hub connected to a patch panel and a workstation.

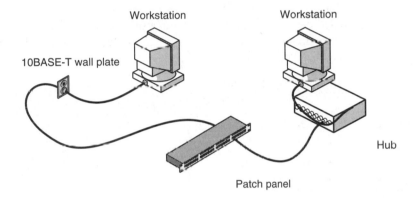

Figure 8.8   Installed media

Exercise 8.1: Creating a Peer-to-Peer Network

In this exercise, your task is to prepare a design of the network for our bicycle company. All the information you need to refer to is provided in this lesson.

This exercise is presented in two parts. First define the topology to use, and second, make a list of materials required.

Part 1: Design a Topology

Because peer-to-peer Ethernet can be implemented in the form of either a physical bus or a physical star, you will need to look at these two different topologies in planning for this network. On separate paper, draw:

1. A logical bus with a physical bus.
2. A logical bus with a physical star.

Check your drawings against the answer figures for this exercise in Appendix A.

Part 2: Select Your Materials

Make a materials list for each of the topologies. Using the facility drawing provided earlier in Figure 8.1, identify the location of each workstation and estimate all the materials you will need to complete the job. Use the following table to help determine which materials are required.

Material Requirements

	Logical bus; physical bus	Logical bus; physical star
Type of cable		
Length of cable		
Connectors (type and count)		
Terminators		
Patch cables		
Patch panel		
Hub		

Save your work to use later in Exercise 2, that follows Lesson 2: Establishing a Client/Server Environment, in which we will build on the physical star logical bus design you have begun to build in this exercise.

Lesson Summary

The following points summarize the main elements of this lesson:

- The first step in network design is to decide whether the network will be peer-to-peer or server-based.

- Take a detailed inventory of all the available networking hardware, software, and telecommunications equipment on hand, before recommending any equipment purchases for a new LAN.

- Create a map of the facility layout and the network (logical and physical) as the beginning of your network-documentation package.

- Installing network media is difficult, and complex configurations require a professional installer. Basic installations can be accomplished without professional assistance.

- By knowing the specifics of each piece of hardware that will be on the network, you can map a network design and foresee potential problems.

- Addressing potential problems before implementing the network can save time and expense.

Lesson 2: Establishing a Client/Server Environment

Large networks are based on the client/server model. This lesson describes how to set up and work on a network that has servers and client workstations.

After this lesson, you will be able to:

- Describe the differences between client/server and centralized computing.
- List the six steps by which server-based networks process data.
- Identify server functions.
- Identify client-workstation functions.
- Determine if a client/server approach is appropriate for a given networking environment.

Estimated lesson time: 30 minutes

Centralized vs. Client/Server Computing

Early networks were based on the centralized-computing model. Usually, in these networks, one large server (a mainframe computer) handled all aspects of the network, while each user accessed the main server from a terminal. Because the centralized computer handled all the high-level computing chores, the terminals were typically inexpensive, low-performance computers. Today, thanks to improvements stemming from the rapid evolution of the personal computer, the old centralized model is being replaced with the client/server model. Today's users have the full power of a mainframe computer at their fingertips, with the added advantage of an interconnected network.

Centralized Computing

In the traditional mainframe environment, an application such as a database runs on a large and powerful centralized mainframe computer and is accessed by terminals. The terminal sends a request for information to the mainframe computer; the mainframe retrieves the information and then displays it on the terminal.

The entire database travels from the server across the network and is downloaded to the client that made the request. The file access takes place through the network operating system (NOS) and the cable. There is very little coordination between the terminal and the mainframe. The data is processed on the mainframe and then delivered to the terminal. The data transfer between the terminal and the mainframe increases network traffic and slows down requests from other terminals.

Client/Server Computing

The term "client/server computing" refers to the process by which data processing chores are shared between the client computer and the more powerful server computer. Figure 8.9 shows a simple client/server network with one server, three clients, and a printer.

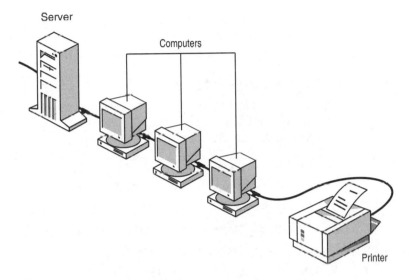

Figure 8.9 A simple client/server network

The client/server approach can benefit any organization in which many people need continual access to large amounts of data.

The client/server network is the most efficient way to provide:

- Database access and management for applications such as spreadsheets, accounting, communications, and document management.
- Network management.
- Centralized file storage.

Client/Server-Model Overview

Most networks operate in the client/server model, also referred to as "server-based networking." A client workstation makes a request for data that is stored on a server. The client workstation processes the data using its own CPU. Data-processing results can then be stored on the server for future use. The data can also be stored on the client workstation and accessed by other client workstations on the network. In peer-to-peer networks, where there is no central server, each client workstation acts as both client and server. Differences between the two kinds of networks are discussed more fully in earlier chapters, especially Chapter 1, "Introduction to Networking."

For an example of how the client/server model operates, let's take a look at a database-management application. In the client/server model, the client software uses Structured Query Language (SQL) to translate what the user sees into a request that the database can understand. SQL is an English-like database query language originally developed by IBM to provide a relatively simple way to manipulate data. (Manipulating data includes entering it, retrieving it, or editing it.)

Other database vendors realized that it would be easier to develop database applications using a common database language. Therefore, they supported SQL and it became an industry standard. Most database management systems today use SQL.

The Client/Server Process

The database query is sent from the client, but processed on the server. Only the results are sent across the network back to the client. The process of requesting and receiving information consists of six steps:

1. The client requests data.
2. The request is translated into SQL.
3. The SQL request is sent over the network to the server.
4. The database server carries out a search on the computer where the data exists.
5. The requested records are returned to the client.
6. The data is presented to the user.

As shown in Figure 8.10, the client/server environment has two principal components:

- The application, often referred to as the "client" or the "front end"
- The database server, often referred to as the "server" or the "back end"

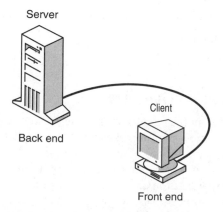

Figure 8.10   The client is the front end and the server is the back end

The Client

The user generates a request at the front end. The client runs an application that:

- Presents an interface to the user.
- Formats requests for data.
- Displays data it receives from the server.

In a client/server environment, the server does not contain the user-interface software. The client is responsible for presenting the data in a usable form.

The user enters instructions from the client computer. The client computer prepares the input for the server. The client computer sends a request for specific information across the network to the server. The server processes the request, locates the appropriate information, and sends it back across the network to the client. The client computer then feeds the information to the interface, which presents the information to the user. The client computer can also process the information further, using its own CPU and software.

Using the Front End

Front ends can present the same information to users in different ways, depending on the request. For example, data that states Columbus first crossed the Atlantic Ocean in 1492 can be organized and presented in several contexts, including:

- Ocean crossings.
- Columbus's achievements.
- Landmark events of 1492.
- Bodies of water crossed by Columbus.

As another example, let's consider our custom-bicycle manufacturer. The company keeps all customer and product information in one database. But this information can be retrieved, organized, and presented through the front end in a variety of ways:

- Marketers can send promotional mailings to customers who are located in a certain zip code.
- Distributors can find out which parts are in stock.
- Service departments can identify which customers are due for service.
- Ordering departments can view each customer's buying history.
- Accounts receivable departments can prevent a client who is in arrears from ordering new products.

Each department needs a front end designed to access the common database and retrieve information for a particular need.

Front-End Tools

A number of tools, applications, and utilities are available for the front end to make the client/server process more efficient. These tools include:

- **Query tools**   These tools use predefined queries and built-in reporting capabilities to help users access back-end data.

- **User applications**   Many common applications programs, such as Microsoft Excel, can provide front-end access to back-end databases. Others, such as Microsoft Access, include their own SQL to provide an interface to multivendor database-management systems.

- **Program development tools**   Many client/server installations need special, customized front-end applications for their data-retrieval tasks. Program development tools, such as Microsoft Visual Basic, are available to help programmers develop front-end tools to access back-end data.

The Server

The server in a client/server environment is usually dedicated to storing and managing data. This is where most of the actual database activity occurs. The server is also referred to as the back end of the client/server model because it fulfills the requests of the client. The server receives the structured requests from the clients, processes them, and sends the requested information back over the network to the client.

The database software on the file server reacts to client queries by running searches. As part of a client/server system, it returns only the results of the searches.

Back-end processing includes sorting data, extracting the requested data, and sending that data back to the user.

Additionally, database server software manages the data in a database including:

- Updates.
- Deletions.
- Additions.
- Security.

Stored Procedures

Stored procedures are short, prewritten data-processing routines that help with data-processing details. The procedures are stored in the server and can be used by any client.

Stored procedures help process data. One stored procedure can be used by any number of clients, thus avoiding the need to incorporate the same routine into the code of each program.

These stored procedures:

- Perform some of the processing usually performed by the client.
- Reduce network traffic, because a single call from the client to the server can begin a series of stored procedures that otherwise would require several requests.
- Can include security controls to prevent unauthorized users from running some of the procedures.

Server Hardware

The server computers in a typical client/server environment should be more powerful and faster than the client computers. In addition to a high-speed processor, these computers need lots of RAM and plenty of hard-drive space. These computers must be able to handle:

- Multiple requests.
- Security.
- Network management tasks.

Any organization that implements a client/server network should use dedicated servers to handle the back-end functions.

Client/Server Architecture

There are several possible client/server arrangements. In the two primary arrangements, illustrated in Figure 8.11:

- The data can be placed on a single server.
- The data can be distributed across several database servers. The locations of the servers depend on the locations of the users and the nature of the data.

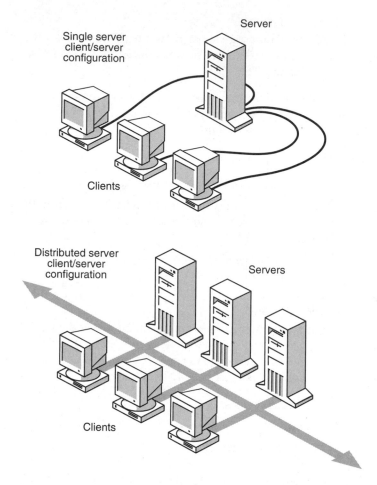

Figure 8.11   Data can be localized on one server or distributed over several servers

Figure 8.12 shows two variations on the distributed server arrangement:

- Servers over a WAN periodically synchronize their databases to ensure that they all have the same data.

- A data warehouse stores large volumes of data and forwards the most sought-after data to an intermediate system that is able to format the data into its most requested form. This offloads some of the data processing from the main server to other servers.

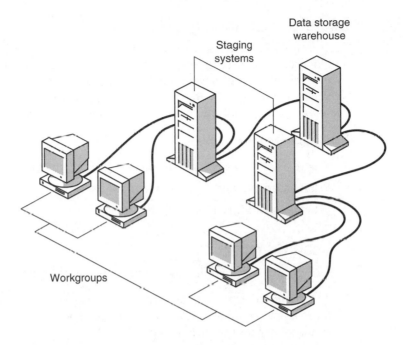

Figure 8.12   Data storage warehouse server offloads data to other servers

Advantages of Working in a Client/Server Environment

Client/server technology creates a powerful environment that offers many real benefits to organizations. A well-planned client/server system provides relatively inexpensive networks. These systems provide mainframe-computing capacity while allowing easy customization for specific applications. Because client/server processing sends only the results of a query across the network, it cuts down on network traffic.

Client/server computing uses a powerful server to store data. The client workstation can process some or all of the requested data. On a busy network, this means that the processing will be distributed more efficiently than in a traditional mainframe-based system.

Because the file services and the data are on the back-end server, the servers are easier to secure and maintain in one location. Data is more secure in a client/server environment because it can be placed in a secure area away from users. The data is also more secure when Windows NT Server–based security is used to prevent unauthorized access to files. When the data is stored in a limited number of locations and managed by one authority, backups are simplified.

Exercise 8.2: Adding a Network Server

In Exercise 8.1, we designed a peer-to-peer network and looked at two different topologies. While these designs meet the immediate needs of our client, the custom bicycle manufacturer, they are likely to fall short if this manufacturer decides to expand the business in the future. In this exercise, you will be modifying the design you carried out in Exercise 1 to include a network server.

In planning your new design, consider the following issues:

- Where should the server be located?
- What additional materials are required?
- What compatibility issues might arise?

Lesson Summary

The following points summarize the main elements of this lesson:

- The client/server model has several advantages over a centralized network; for example, in this model, tasks are divided between client and server, resulting in a more efficient network.
- Client/server networks can be arranged in two ways: data can be stored on a single server or distributed across several servers.
- Client/server networks commonly use structured query language (SQL) for database management.
- In a client/server network, the client, or front end, is responsible for presenting data in a useful form and for writing reports; the server, or back end, is responsible for storing and managing the data.
- Client/server networks can be arranged in two ways: data can be stored on a single server or distributed across several servers.

Lesson 3: Working with Device Drivers and NICs

In this lesson, we examine the role of network interface cards (NICs) and how they are installed. Without a properly configured NIC, our computers will be unable to talk to the physical media that we installed in Lesson 1. NICs were introduced and discussed in detail in Chapter 2 in Lesson 2: The Network Interface Card. It will help to review that lesson and refamiliarize yourself with the concept of interrupts and the types of NICs. Here, we carry that lesson a step farther, covering NIC installation and connection.

After this lesson, you will be able to:

- Describe the role of drivers in a network environment, including their place in the OSI reference model.
- Identify sources for different drivers.
- Describe how to select and implement drivers in a given networking situation.
- Install, update, and remove drivers.
- Choose the correct NIC for your network.

Estimated lesson time: 30 minutes

The Role of Drivers

A driver (sometimes called a device driver) is software that enables a computer to work with a particular device. Drivers are also discussed in the context of the OSI reference model in Chapter 5, "Introducing Network Standards."Although a device might be installed on a computer, the computer's operating system cannot communicate with the device until the driver for that device has been installed and configured. It is the software driver that tells the computer how to work with the device so that the device can perform its job.

There are drivers for nearly every type of computer device and peripheral including:

- Input devices, such as mouse devices.
- Hard and floppy disk drives and controllers.
- Multimedia devices, such as microphones, cameras, and recorders.
- NICs.
- Printers, plotters, and tape drives.

Usually, the computer's operating system works with the driver to make the device perform. Printers provide a good illustration of how drivers are used. Printers built by different manufacturers have different features and functions. It is impossible for computer and operating-system manufacturers to equip new computers with all the software required to identify and work with every type of printer. Instead, printer manufacturers make drivers available for each of their printers. Before your computer can send documents to a printer, you must install, or load, the drivers for that printer so that your computer will be able to communicate with it.

As a general rule, manufacturers of components, such as peripherals or cards that must be physically installed, are responsible for supplying the drivers for their equipment. For example, NIC manufacturers are responsible for making drivers available for their cards. Drivers are usually included on a disk that accompanies computer equipment when it is purchased. Drivers can also be downloaded from a service such as The Microsoft Network (MSN), CompuServe, or the manufacturer's Internet site or bulletin board.

The Network Environment

Network drivers provide communication between a NIC and the network redirector running in the computer. (The redirector is part of the networking software that accepts input/output (I/O) requests for remote files and then sends, or redirects, them over the network to another computer. Redirectors are introduced in Chapter 4, "Survey of Network Operating Systems.") The network administrator uses a utility program to install the driver. During installation, the driver is placed on the computer's hard disk.

Drivers and the OSI Model

NIC drivers reside in the Media Access Control sublayer of the data-link layer of the OSI Reference Model. The Media Access Control sublayer is responsible for providing shared access for the computer's NICs to the physical layer. In other words, the NIC drivers ensure direct communication between the computer and the NIC. This, in turn, establishes a link between the computer and the rest of the network. Figure 8.13 shows the relationship of a NIC to the network software.

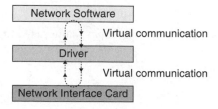

Figure 8.13 Communication between the NIC and network software

Drivers and Networking Software

It is common for the NIC manufacturer to provide drivers to the networking software vendor so that the drivers can be included with the network operating software.

The operating system manufacturer's hardware compatibility list (HCL) lists the drivers they have tested and included with the operating system. Even if the driver for a particular card has not been included with the network operating system, it is common for the NIC manufacturer to include drivers for most popular network operating systems on a disk that is shipped with the card. Before buying a card, however, you should make sure that the card has a driver that will work with your particular network operating system.

Note If you are upgrading from one operating system to another (from Microsoft Windows 95 to Windows NT, for example) you might need to contact your NIC supplier and download a new driver. It is a good idea to do this before you start the upgrade.

Working with Drivers

Working with drivers encompasses a variety of tasks, including installation, configuring, updating, and removal.

Installing Drivers

Each network operating system has its own method for installing drivers. Most popular network operating systems use interactive graphical interfaces, or dialog boxes, that guide the installer through the process.

Microsoft Windows NT Server, for example, features a utility called the Control Panel. This employs dialog boxes that lead the user through the process of installing a NIC driver. Figure 8.14 shows several of the dialog boxes that appear during the installation of a NIC network driver on Windows NT.

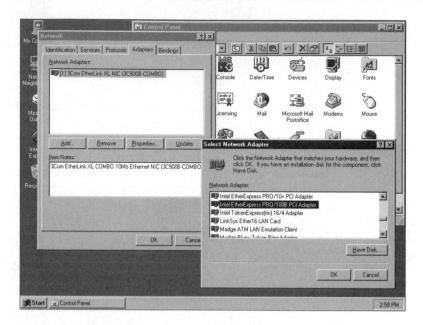

Figure 8.14   Installing a NIC on Windows NT Server

Configuring Drivers

Network interface cards usually have configurable options that must be set correctly for the NIC to function properly. As discussed in Chapter 2, Lesson 2: The Network Interface Card, this can be accomplished with jumpers or switches.

Most of the newer NICs are software-configurable or Plug and Play (PnP) compliant. There are no DIP switches or jumpers to configure. The configuration is accomplished through the software during or after the installation of the drivers, or—as with a PnP-compliant system, such as Microsoft Windows 95 or Windows 98—the operating system attempts to configure the hardware device automatically. While Windows NT 4.0 is currently not PnP-compliant, it will attempt to recognize your devices. If the attempt is not successful, you will be required to supply the drivers from a disk provided by the manufacturer. If you already have that disk with the correct drivers, it is often easier simply to tell Windows NT where to find them.

Updating Drivers

Occasionally, a manufacturer will write additions or changes to a driver to improve a component's performance. Manufacturers can send these driver changes by mail to registered users, post them on an Internet bulletin board, or make them available through a service such as The Microsoft Network (MSN), CompuServe, or the manufacturer's Internet site. The user can download and then install the updated driver.

The process of updating drivers is similar to installing them, although you might need to remove the old driver first. Be sure to look for any readme files that come with the software. The readme files will inform you of the correct procedure for installation. Some drivers, especially those that have been downloaded from the Internet or a bulletin board, are in the form of executable files. For these, double-click on the file name, and the executable file will perform the installation.

Removing Drivers

It is sometimes necessary to remove drivers, such as when the original driver conflicts with newer drivers. If a piece of equipment is being removed, remove its drivers at the same time, too, to ensure that no conflicts arise between the old drivers and any new drivers that are installed.

The process of removing a driver is similar to that of installing a driver. Figure 8.15 shows the Adapters tab of the Network Window in a Windows NT work session. In this window, you need only select the driver and then click on the Remove button.

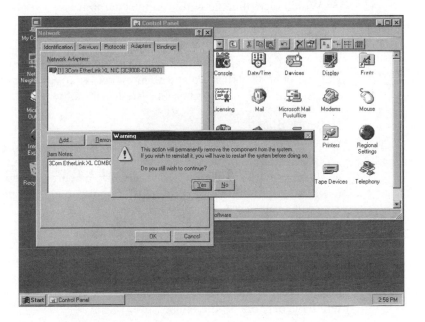

Figure 8.15   Removing a driver

Installing NICs

Tackling a NIC installation can range from a routine, predictable chore to a frustrating failure. The best way to minimize problems is to do a little planning first. Expansion cards were covered in Chapter 2, in Lesson 2: The Network Interface Card. Before purchasing NICs, it's helpful to keep several important points in mind.

Type of Expansion Slot

A NIC is one of several kinds of expansion card for a personal computer. As we learned earlier, a computer can contain a variety of expansion bus types. You might encounter ISA, EISA, Micro Channel, and/or PCI buses. Whether you are purchasing a card for a single computer or cards for an entire network, you need to know the answers to three questions for each computer you plan to link:

1. What type of expansion bus does it have?

2. Does it have a slot available for the card?

3. Which type of cable will be connected to it?

Type of Card

Not all NICs are equal. In addition to being designed for installation on different expansion buses, NICs are specified by network type. For example, a card designed to work on an Ethernet system will not work on a Token Ring system.

Network Speed

Ethernet can be configured in two speeds: 10BaseT (10 Mbps) or 100BaseTX (100 Mbps). Many newer NICs can run at either speed, but older cards run only at 10 Mbps. When designing your network, be sure to keep future networking needs in mind. It might be more cost-effective to obtain dual-speed NICs now than to have to purchase new cards later.

Media Connection

As we have seen, there is a variety of media from which to choose. Be sure to look carefully at the cards you purchase to ensure that they will fit the cabling of the network. Some cards have a selection of BNCs or RJ-45 connectors; some will have only one or the other.

Adding Extras

Purchasing network cards with diagnostic lights built in can be a good investment that will pay off later. The purpose of these lights is to indicate the status of the card and the network. They can tell you if the card is properly connected (it detects the presence of a network) and when data is being processed through the card. As shown in Figure 8.16, some NICs feature one, two, or three light-emitting diodes (LEDs) that are visible on the outside of the computer. Typically, a green light indicates that a proper connection exists between the card and the media. A flashing yellow light usually indicates that the card is processing data.

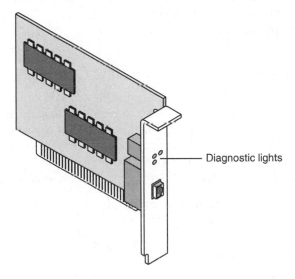
Diagnostic lights

Figure 8.16   Diagnostic lights

Installing a NIC

Installing a NIC is like installing any other expansion card. The following is a summary of the procedure, step-by-step:

1. Read the documentation that comes with the card. Take note of any special requirements or limitations before you begin the installation.

2. Determine which interrupt request numbers (IRQs) and I/O addresses are available on the computer. This is especially true if you are installing in an operating system that is not equipped with PnP technology. This can usually be done with the system information software that accompanies the computer's operating system.

3. Configure any jumpers or switches, if required. If no switches or jumpers are on the card, use the installation software to make any changes after you have installed the NIC. Check the documentation.

4. Turn off the computer and unplug the power cord.

5. Follow the appropriate electrostatic discharge procedures.

6. Remove the cover of the computer.

7. Install the card in a free slot.

8. Reconnect the computer's cables and turn on the computer before replacing the cover. This way, if any conflicts require hardware adjustment, you won't have to remove the cover again.

9. After the new hardware appears to be operating properly (you have resolved any conflicts), replace the cover.

10. Install the appropriate software drivers.

Exercise 8.3: Connecting a New Computer

When you designed the network for the bicycle company, you took into account the possibility that it would eventually be necessary to add additional computers. That time has now arrived. The business manager has acquired one additional computer and brought it to you unannounced. He expects you to have it connected to the network as soon as possible so that a new employee can begin working in two days. The computer does not have a network interface card installed.

What steps do you need to take in order to successfully connect the new computer to the existing company network?

Lesson Summary

The following points summarize the main elements of this lesson:

- Methods for installing drivers in a computer operating system vary with the operating system used.

- Manufacturers release updated drivers for their devices. These drivers can be downloaded from the Internet or a bulletin board and installed to provide improved performance.

- Old and unused drivers should be removed to prevent conflicts.

- When choosing a NIC, be sure to weigh factors such as the type of bus, the speed of the card, and the media connection before making your decision.

- Network interface card (NIC) drivers reside in the Media Access Control sublayer of the data-link layer of the OSI model.

Lesson 4: Ensuring Hardware Compatibility

Networking is hardware-dependent, and not all hardware products are compatible. In Chapter 6, "Defining Network Protocols," we learned that in order for two computers to communicate, they must use the same protocol. Computer hardware raises similar issues. In some instances, two pieces of hardware simply can't communicate with each other. For example, consider an analogy to automobile parts: two parts might look alike and be able to perform the same function, but each is designed to work in a different car. This lesson examines the issue of ensuring hardware compatibility and what you can do to resolve incompatibilities.

After this lesson, you will be able to:
- Determine hardware compatibility issues.
- Take steps to avoid unnecessary hardware problems.

Estimated lesson time: 30 minutes

When Hardware Is a Problem

Hardware incompatibilities are a fact of life. In today's computer industry, hundreds of manufacturers develop hardware and software. Each developer has a unique perspective on the best way to accomplish the same task, and each will provide a unique solution. Copyright and patent issues further complicate the matter.

Evaluating and selecting hardware is a major part of planning for network implementation. If you have the luxury of designing a network from the ground up, you can choose vendors and place the burden of compatibility on them. Before you make a purchase, give them a list of the hardware you plan to use and ask them to certify that those items are compatible with the vendor's products. Also, don't be too quick to accept one vendor's opinion. For example, if you are considering the purchase of two devices—X and Y—ask the vendors of X if their product is compatible with Y, and ask the vendors of Y if their product is compatible with X. Then compare the responses you get; they may help you to find an incompatibility you would otherwise fail to detect.

It is likely that you will have to create a network out of an existing collection of hardware. In such cases, the likelihood that problems stemming from incompatible hardware will arise is very high. It is sometimes more cost-effective to discard the old hardware and start over.

The most common incompatibilities occur between hardware and software. Changing or upgrading a computer or network operating system can lead to major problems. As discussed in the previous lesson, you might need to update hardware drivers at the same time you upgrade the software. Be sure to address this issue before you start.

Reading the Documentation

Read all the documentation about the products involved. Your hardware or software might have a recurring problem or might conflict with another product. Frequently, the manufacturer will document these conflicts and provide a fix. If you do not find the solution in the supplied documentation, you might contact the manufacturer of the product and ask for undocumented conflicts. Search the manufacturer's Web site for additional information.

Detection During Installation

When you install a new computer or network operating system, your computer will usually attempt to detect the hardware in the system during the installation process and load the appropriate drivers for it. Check the list of detected hardware and ensure that it matches what is already in the machine. If you are installing Novell's IntranetWare, for example, the install utility will automatically scan your computer for hardware such as hard disks, CD-ROM drives, and NICs. If the devices are recognized, the appropriate drivers will then be loaded for the recognized devices.

Checking Minimum Requirements

As a first step before you install, make sure that you exceed the minimum requirements for the resources in the computer. These resources include processor speed, memory, and disk space. Table 8.2 lists some minimum hardware requirements for common network software.

Table 8.2   Minimum Hardware Requirements for Network Software

	NetWare 5	Windows NT Server 4.0	Windows 98
Processor	Pentium processor	486 33 MHz or higher	486 66 MHz or higher
Memory	64 MB	16 MB	16 MB
Disk space	200 MB	125 MB	225 MB
Disk	CD-ROM	CD-ROM	3.5 high density
Monitor	VGA	VGA	VGA
NIC	YES	YES	YES

Remember that these are published minimum requirements. Treat these minimum requirements as you would, for example, treat a statement that a bicycle is the minimum requirement for riding up Pikes Peak. It can be done, but it would be much easier and a lot more fun in a powerful car. Windows NT Server with 16 MB of RAM will run and function in a 33MHz processor, but not quickly.

Network Hardware

Network hardware is not as susceptible as software to conflicts and compatibility problems. Chapter 7, Lesson 1: Connectivity Devices, covers the basics of how these devices (repeaters, bridges, routers, brouters, and gateways) work. These devices operate at the two lower layers of the OSI reference model (the physical and data-link layers). Since these devices are common to many different types of networks and work mainly with data packets, they are less likely to present conflicts. The manufacturers of these products maintain strict adherence to the IEEE 802.x standards. Therefore, any device that meets an IEEE standard can communicate with another device that meets the same standard. The only situation in which you can expect incompatibility issues to arise is when two devices meet different standards. For example, Ethernet and Token Ring networks use different methods of accessing the network. Therefore, a device designed to meet the 802.3 Ethernet standard will not communicate with a device designed to operate with the 802.5 Token Ring standard.

Exercise 8.4: Upgrading a Network

Knowing what we now know about network and computer compatibility issues, let's take a look at our bicycle company and see what, if any, problems we might encounter.

Assume that you and the Managing Director have decided that the best long-term solution is to install a server-based network. The director has also decided that she wants to base the network on Windows NT. Provide the answers to the following questions:

1. Which resources do you anticipate are likely to present problems in the future and, therefore, should be upgraded or replaced?

2. What do you suggest as the minimum operational requirements for equipment to be acquired in the future?

Lesson Summary

The following points summarize the main elements of this lesson:

- Many manufacturers produce computer networking hardware, each with unique designs and specifications. Not all hardware products are compatible.

- To minimize hardware conflicts, read the documentation that comes with the hardware product.

- Minimum hardware requirements represent values that are sufficient only to allow the system to start.

- Decisions made before installation will either limit or open up future expansion and performance of a network.

Chapter Summary

The following points summarize the key concepts of this chapter:

Choosing a Network Design

- The first step in network design is to decide whether the network will be peer-to-peer or server-based.

- Take a detailed inventory of all the available networking hardware, software, and telecommunications equipment on hand before recommending any equipment purchases for a new LAN.

- Create a map of the facility layout and the network (logical and physical) as the beginning of your network-documentation package.

- Installing network media is difficult, and complex configurations require a professional installer. Basic installations can be accomplished without professional assistance.

- By knowing the specifics of each piece of hardware that will be on the network, you can map a network design and foresee potential problems.

- Addressing potential problems before implementing the network can save time and expense.

Establishing a Client/Server Environment

- The client/server model has several advantages over a centralized network; in this model, tasks are divided between client and server, resulting in a more efficient network.

- Client/server networks can be arranged in two ways: the data can be on a single server or distributed across many servers.

- Client/server networks commonly use structured query language (SQL) for database management.

- In a client/server network, the client, or front end, is responsible for presenting data in a useful form and for writing reports; the server, or back end, is responsible for storing and managing the data.

- Client/server networks can be arranged in two ways: data can be stored on a single server or distributed across several servers.

Working with Device Drivers and Network Interface Cards (NICS)

- Computer operating systems use software drivers to control devices.

- Network interface card (NIC) drivers reside in the Media Access Control sublayer of the data-link layer of the OSI model.

- Methods for installing drivers vary with the operating system used.

- Manufacturers release updated drivers for their devices. These drivers can be downloaded from the Internet or a bulletin board and installed to provide improved performance.

- Old and unused drivers should be removed to prevent conflicts.

- When choosing a NIC, be sure to weigh factors such as the type of bus, the speed of the card, and the media connection before making your decision.

Ensuring Hardware Compatibility

- Hardware compatibility is important because each piece of hardware on the network must be able to communicate with other hardware on the network.

- Decisions made before installation will either limit or open up future expansion and performance of a network.

- To minimize hardware conflicts, read the documentation that comes with the hardware product.

- Minimum hardware requirements represent values that are sufficient only to allow the system to start.

Chapter Review

1. Using a peer-to-peer network implies that all computers on the network are
   _____.

2. One drawback to using a peer-to-peer network is _____
   _____.

3. On a server-based network, resources are _____.

4. Before beginning to design a new network, you must take an inventory to
   determine what _____ and _____ you already have,
   as well as what you need to acquire.

5. Working with a drawing of the _____ is the place to start when
   creating a map of the new network.

Circle the letter of the best answer for each of the following sentences:

1. A driver is:

   a. hardware.

   b. a peripheral device.

   c. a NIC.

   d. software.

2. In the networking environment, a NIC driver is needed to:

   a. communicate with other NICs on a network.

   b. communicate between the NIC and the computer's operating system.

   c. communicate between the file server and the other computers on the
      network.

   d. communicate between different types of computers on a network.

3. Select the correct statement about printer drivers.

   a. There is no universal printer driver that will ensure full functionality of
      all printers.

   b. Printers made by a specific printer manufacturer can always use the same
      printer driver and have full functionality.

   c. There is a specific printer driver designed for every model of printer that
      can ensure the full functionality of that model of printer on all operating
      systems.

   d. A laser-printer driver from one manufacturer will provide full functionality
      for all laser printers, regardless of the manufacturer.

C H A P T E R   9

Establishing Network Shares and Accounts

About This Chapter

In a peer-to-peer network we share, or make available to the network, any directories or printers to which we want others to have access. In networks that have client/server configurations, we use accounts to establish who can access which files, directories, and printers. This chapter explores the differences between shares and accounts and demonstrates how to use each appropriately. The focus in this chapter is on sharing and account procedures. Using these features to secure the network from harm, intentional or accidental, is covered in Chapter 10, "Ensuring Network Security."

Before You Begin

The concepts presented in this chapter are all new. Because the subject matter is complex, you should be familiar with the network terms presented in previous chapters.

Lesson 1: Creating Network Shares

In this lesson we define network shares, examine which resources can be shared on a network, and look at who is able to set network shares.

After this lesson, you will be able to:

- Describe how to share files and directories with anyone on a network.
- Share a printer on a network.

Estimated lesson time: 20 minutes

Sharing Resources on a Network

Before you can share resources with another computer, your workstation must have client software installed and be configured as a network client. You will have to establish the computer's network identity, enable sharing, and set access privileges for the resources the computer will share. The procedure for installing and configuring client software depends on the operating system you are using and the operating system of the network on which you intend to share resources.

Sharing Disks and Files

At its simplest, resource sharing between computers consists of nothing more than passing files from one computer to another on floppy disks. This method places severe limits on the volume of data, as well as the speed and distance in which it can be shared, but even this method is occasionally useful.

Another technique for resource sharing is to directly connect two computers together by means of a cable link between the serial communications (COM) ports of each computer. Figure 9.1 shows two computers connected through their COM ports. To connect computers in this way requires a null modem cable and serial communication software. (A null modem cable connects the output pins in one computer's serial port to the input pins in the other.)

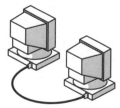

Figure 9.1   Direct connection between two computers

Communication software is required for each computer in order to make use of the physical connection between the computers. You must configure one computer as a host, or server, and one as a client. The client computer will then have access to data on the host. While this is not a true local area network (LAN), it is a practical method for providing a temporary connection between computers for the transfer of files. Direct cable connections are most often used to share files between a desktop computer and a laptop computer.

Sharing information efficiently is not as simple as connecting computers together with cables. In a network environment, with many users and job requirements, access rights, or permissions, need to be established. These allow specific network users to access information according to the needs of their jobs, while blocking unwelcome access to confidential or valuable data.

Sharing in a Peer-to-Peer Environment

The simplest and most convenient method of networking is peer-to-peer. In this networking environment, data sharing occurs at the drive or folder level. Any drive or any folder on a drive can be shared. Each computer shares its drive or folder resources to the network, and each user is responsible for setting the shares. The user can also choose to share printer resources.

Software

In order to share on a peer-to-peer network, no matter which operating system is being used, file and print sharing must first be enabled on the computer. Each operating system has its own methods for enabling sharing.

Sharing Printers, Drives, and Folders

After sharing has been enabled, you can decide which drives, folders, and printers to make available to the network. Sharing options include hard drives, CD-ROM drives, floppy-disk drives, and folders. To set up any of these printer or file-related devices for sharing, you will have to designate each one as a shared resource and identify the level of sharing available. (Devices such as scanners and modems cannot be shared.) Remember that after a resource is shared on a peer-to-peer network, it is available to the entire network.

The rest of this lesson discusses how networks share resources on specific operating systems.

Microsoft Windows 95 and 98 Networking

Software

Microsoft Windows 95 and 98 include several choices of client software. The most common is Microsoft's Client for Microsoft Networks. To install Client for Microsoft Networks, open the Control Panel and double-click the **Network** icon. Click **Add** to display the **Select Network Component Type** dialog box. Because you will be adding a Microsoft network client, select **Client** and then click **Add.** The dialog box shown in Figure 9.2 will be displayed.

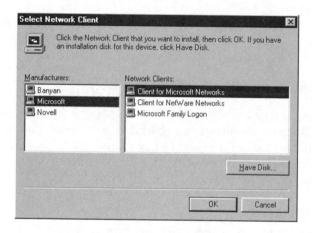

Figure 9.2   Select Network Client dialog box

In the **Manufacturers** list, select **Microsoft** and in the **Network Client** list, select **Client for Microsoft Networks**. Select **OK** to add the client service to the system.

At this point, you will need to add a networking protocol. Client for Microsoft Networks can be used with the IPX/SPX, NetBEUI, and TCP/IP protocols. Select the protocol appropriate to your networking environment.

After you have installed Client for Microsoft Networks software, you will be able to share resources with any network that uses the SMB (Server Message Block) file-sharing protocol. This includes any computer using Windows 95 and 98, Windows NT Workstation, Windows for Workgroups, or LAN Manager.

Sharing Printers, Drives, and Folders

After networking has been enabled on the computer, directorys, folders, and printers can be shared on the network. To share these resources you must enable **File and Print Sharing**.

Right-click the **Network Neighborhood** icon and click **Properties** from the menu to open the **Network Properties** dialog box. Then click the **File and Print Sharing** button. See Figure 9.3.

Figure 9.3   Network Properties dialog box

The **File and Print Sharing** dialog box contains two check boxes:

- **I want to be able to give others access to my files**.
- **I want to be able to allow others to print to my printer(s)**.

You can select either one or both check boxes. After you have enabled either or both check boxes, you can start sharing your computer's resources.

Although you have enabled sharing on the computer, your resources won't be available on the network until you have designated which resources you want to share. To share a device or folder, open Windows Explorer, right-click the device or folder icon, and click **Sharing** from the menu. This displays the **Sharing** tab, as shown in Figure 9.4, in the **Properties** dialog box for the device or folder.

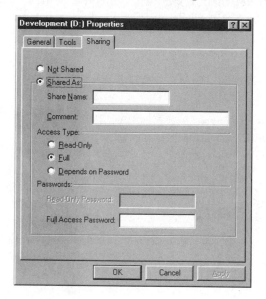

Figure 9.4   Sharing tab

Selecting the **Shared As** radio button allows you to set the share name and add a brief description of the shared resource. (The radio button is a circle appearing next to each of several options in a dialog box; when selected, it has a smaller black circle inside it.) In the **Access Type** area of the dialog box, you can select the radio button corresponding to any one of three access types. Selecting **Read Only** restricts access to the shared folder so that its contents can be read and copied, but not edited in any way. Selecting **Full** gives complete access to the contents of the folder; and selecting **Depends on Password** forces users to provide a password in order to access the shared resource.

Note When a folder or device is shared, you will see a hand as part of the icon displayed in My Computer or Windows Explorer.

In the Windows NT environment, you can apply the added security features provided by the NTFS file system. This file system is a relational database in which everything is seen as a file.

Software

To install networking software, several protocols are available:

- Client service for NetWare
- Client for Microsoft Networks
- NWLink NetBIOS
- NWLink IPX/SPX/NetBIOS Compatible Transport Protocol
- Internet Protocol (TCP/IP)

You must have administrative rights in order to enable sharing on a Windows NT Server.

Sharing Directories and Files

To share a folder locally (you are logged onto the workstation), right-click the folder's icon and select the **Sharing** option. This will open the **Properties** dialog box for the directory, as shown in Figure 9.5. The **Share** tab will be selected.

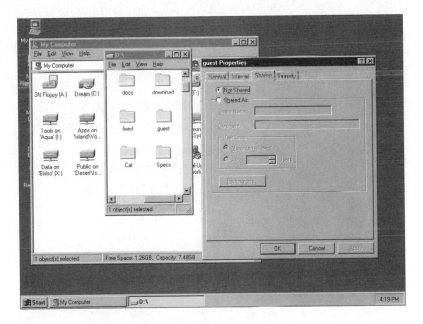

Figure 9.5   Folder Properties dialog box

The maximum number of connections that can be set for Windows NT Workstation is 10, regardless of the setting. This setting is optional.

Assign permissions to the shared folder. By following the dialog boxes, you can limit who has permission to access this folder or give permission to everyone. By using the **New Share** button, you can configure multiple shares using different names and assign different levels of permissions.

To share folders and drives in Windows 2000, you must be logged on as a member of the Administrators, Server Operators, or Power Users group.

To share a Windows 2000 folder or drive with other users, open Windows Explorer, and then locate the folder or drive you want to share. (To open Windows Explorer, click **Start**, point to **Programs**, point to **Accessories**, and then click **Windows Explorer**.) Right-click the folder or drive, and then click **Sharing**. On the **Sharing** tab, click **Share this folder**.

To change the name of the shared folder or drive, type a new name in **Share Name**. The new name is what users will see when they connect to this shared folder or drive; the actual name of the folder or drive does not change.

To add a comment about the shared folder or drive, type the text in **Comment**. To limit the number of users who can connect to the shared folder or drive at one time, under **User limit**, click **Allow**, then enter a number of users.

Sharing Printers

To share a Windows NT/Windows 2000 printer on a Windows NT network, click **Start**, select **Settings**, and click **Printers**. Right-click the printer to be shared, and click **Sharing** from the menu. Select the **Share as** button and enter a name that will clearly identify the printer to the network. After the printer has been shared and identified on the network, security for the printer can be set.

Figure 9.6   Sharing a printer

AppleShare Networking

Software

Apple's file-server software is called AppleTalk. Sharing resources with AppleTalk requires the following steps:

- **To select a network port**   Select the Control Panels' AppleTalk submenu to open the **AppleTalk** dialog box. There you can select the appropriate network connection port.

- **To turn on AppleTalk**   In order to activate AppleTalk on a computer, the computer must be connected to an AppleTalk network. To do so, open the **Apple Chooser** and set the **AppleTalk** radio button to **Active**.

- **To enable sharing**   Establish a network identity by assigning a name to the computer. Then turn on sharing in the Apple Control Panel's **File Sharing** dialog box.

Sharing Drives and Folders

Like all peer-to-peer networks, AppleShare provides sharing at the folder level, but not at the file level. If the owner of the server computer has designated any files or folders for sharing, these will be available to anyone who logs on.

A folder's owner sets the folder's sharing by opening the folder's sharing window. From the **Choose File** menu, select **Get Info**, and click **Sharing**. For each user or group listed, the owner sets one of the following privileges for working within the folder:

- Read & Write
- Read Only
- Write Only (Drop Box)
- None

Restrictions can also be placed on the shared folders themselves so that they cannot be altered by anyone other than the folder's owner. To set such a restriction, open the **Sharing Info** dialog box and click the **Can't move, rename, or delete this item (locked)** check box.

Sharing Printers

To share a directly connected printer from an Apple computer, open the **Apple Chooser** dialog box and select the printer you want to share. Then click the **Setup** button to open the printer **Sharing Setup** dialog box. In this dialog box, you can click the **Share this Printer** check box and enter a name for the printer and a password (optional). You can also click the **Keep Log of Printer Usage** check box if you want to record information about printer usage.

UNIX

The UNIX operating system exists in a number of configurations and is available from a variety of manufacturers or, in the case of Linux, from no corporate entity at all. UNIX support for interoperability with other network operating systems varies with the manufacturer. Sun's Solaris Easy Access Server, for example, includes native support for many Windows NT network services including authentication, file and print services, and directory services. Linux distributions include Apple access modules for AppleTalk access, third-party software such as Samba, which makes UNIX file systems available to any networked computer using the SMB file-sharing protocol, and modules for NTFS and MS-DOS file-system accessibility.

Sharing in a Client/Server Environment

Overview

Sharing folders on a server-based network is similar to sharing on a peer-to-peer network. The primary difference is in the level of security available, which is achieved through the server's directory services. Microsoft NT Server and Novell NetWare provide file-level permissions in addition to printer, drive, and directory permissions.

Novell

Unlike other network operating systems, NetWare does not require that sharing be enabled prior to actually making the server's resources available. Enabled sharing is the default setting for a NetWare network.

A second difference is that access to shared resources is set entirely through user and group account rights. In other words, printers, directories, and files are not themselves restricted. This subject is discussed in the next lesson of this chapter.

Exercise 9.1: Case Study Problem

Your task in this exercise is to designate shares in a peer-to-peer network configuration.

For this configuration, assume that the company to be networked is small, numbering 20 employees, only 10 of which have computers. These computers are running compatible operating systems. Employees include the managing director, three people in the Sales Department, two in the Accounting Department, two in the Product Design Department, and two in the Shipping Department. There are two laser printers available; one is connected directly to the managing director's computer, and the other is connected directly to the lead accountant's computer.

In this exercise you will:

- Designate which resources will be shared.
- Enable sharing on the appropriate computers.
- Share printers, disks, folders, and, if appropriate, files.

Lesson Summary

The following points summarize the main elements of this lesson:

- When files are transferred using a direct cable connection, one computer is configured as a host and the other as a client. The client can then access files and directories on the host computer.
- Client software must be enabled before a computer can access any resources shared on a network.
- Microsoft Network client software enables users to share resources with any network that uses the SMB (Server Message Block) file-sharing protocol.
- Before a computer can act as a server and share resources to a network, it must first have the client software enabled, and then have File and Print Sharing enabled.
- AppleShare provides folder-level sharing on Macintosh machines.
- Linux file systems can be accessed by computers using AppleTalk and by computers using the SMB file sharing protocol.
- The maximum number of connections that can be set for Windows NT Workstation is 10.

Lesson 2: Establishing and Managing Network Accounts

As the size of a network increases, the concept of sharing to the entire network can begin to present some problems. Peer-to-peer networks, for example, sacrifice a degree of security in order to offer simplicity. But imagine the consequences of sharing the directory of your employer's accounting department (or personnel department) to the entire network and perhaps the world over an Internet connection. For these reasons, among others, large networks employ server-based networking. In a client/server environment, sharing is managed through accounts. By creating accounts and then grouping the individual accounts, a network manager has the tools necessary to provide a higher level of security.

After this lesson, you will be able to:

- Describe user and group accounts.
- Describe the process for creating user and group accounts.
- Determine the appropriate types of accounts for a given network environment.
- Create a user account and a group account.

Estimated lesson time: 45 minutes

Network Accounts

Accounts are the means by which users are given access to printer, file, and directory shares. These accounts are created and managed by the network administrator.

An account is composed of a user name and logon parameters established for that user. These parameters can include which computers can be used for access, days and times during which access is allowed, passwords, and so on. This information is entered by the administrator and stored on the network by the operating system. The network uses this account name to verify the account when the user attempts to log on.

Planning for Groups

By default, user accounts have no rights. All user accounts obtain rights through group membership. All user accounts within a group will have certain access rights and activities in common, according to the group in which they reside. By assigning permissions and rights to a group, the administrator can treat the group as a single account.

Access rights that apply to the system as a whole authorize a user to perform certain actions on the system. For example, a user, as a member of a group, might have the right to back up the system.

Groups are used to:

- Grant access to resources such as files, directories, and printers. The permissions granted to a group are automatically granted to its members.

- Give rights to perform system tasks, such as to back up and restore files or change the system time.

- Simplify communications by reducing the number of messages that need to be created and sent.

Creating Group Accounts

Networks can support hundreds of accounts. There will be occasions when the administrator needs to conduct network business with some or all of the accounts. For example, the administrator often needs to send messages to large numbers of users notifying them about an event or network policy. Or the administrator might need to identify every account that has a particular access. If 100 users need a change in their access, the administrator will need to change 100 accounts.

However, if the 100 accounts were to be placed in one group, the administrator could simply send one message to the group account, and each member of the group would automatically get the message. Permissions could be set for the group, and all the members of the group would automatically receive the permissions. Networks offer a way to gather many separate user accounts into one type of account called a *group*. A group is nothing more than an account that contains other accounts. The primary reason for implementing groups is the ease of administration. Groups make it possible for an administrator to manage large numbers of users as one account.

The easiest way to grant a large number of users similar permissions is to assign these permissions to a group. The users are then added to the group. The same process applies to adding users to an existing group. For example, if the administrator wanted a certain user to have administrative capabilities on the network, the administrator would make that user a member of the Administrators group.

Creating User Accounts

All networks have a utility that the administrator can use to enter new account names into the network security database. This process is sometimes referred to as "creating a user."

There are some conventions in naming both users and groups. Unless otherwise stated, a user name cannot be identical to any other user or group name in the computer (and, in the case of Windows NT, of the domain) being administered. Each network operating system has its own set of characters that can be used, but generally, the user name can contain any uppercase or lowercase alphanumeric characters. There are some standard exceptions " / \ : ; | = , + * ? < > that cannot be used in user names.

Network operating systems can also contain information such as the account user's full name, a description of the account or user, and the account password.

Entering User Information

The new user account contains information that defines a user to the network security system. This includes:

- The user name and password.
- Rights the user has for accessing the system and its resources.
- The groups to which the account belongs.

Setting User Parameters

Administrators can set a number of parameters for users. Among these are:

- **Logon times**   To restrict hours during which users can log on.
- **The home directory**   To give the user an area in which to store private files.
- **The expiration date**   To limit a temporary user's access to the network.

Key User Accounts

Network operating systems are designed with certain categories of user accounts already created and that are automatically activated during installation.

The Initial Account

When a network operating system is installed, the installation program automatically creates an account with complete network authority. Some designated individual has to be able to:

- Start the network.
- Set the initial security parameters.
- Create other user accounts.

In the Microsoft networking environment, this account is called *administrator*. In the Novell environment, this account is known as a *supervisor*. And in the Linux environment, it is known as *root*.

The first person to log on to the network is usually the person installing the network operating system. After logging on as administrator, that person has full control over all network functions.

The Guest Account

This default account is intended for people who do not have a valid user account, but who need temporary access to the network.

Passwords

Passwords are not necessarily required by a network operating system. In situations where security is not an issue, it is possible to modify an account so that it no longer needs a password.

In most circumstances, however, passwords are required because they help ensure the security of a network environment. The first thing the administrator should do when setting up an account is to enter an initial password. This will prevent unauthorized users from logging on as administrator and creating accounts. Users should create their own unique password and should change it periodically. The account administrator can require users to do this automatically by setting a password-change time interval for the user.

Traditional guidelines exist that govern the use of passwords. All users, including the administrator, should:

- Avoid obvious passwords such as birthdates, social security numbers, or the names of spouses, children, pets, and so on.
- Memorize the password, rather than write it down and tape it to the monitor.
- Remember the password expiration date—if there is one—so that the password can be changed before it expires and the user is locked out of the system.

The administrator must be informed when a user is no longer employed by the organization or for any reason no longer entitled to be a member of the group. In this case, the administrator should disable the account.

Disabling and Deleting Accounts

Occasionally, an administrator will need to prevent an account from being active on the network. Either disabling the account or deleting the account will deactivate it.

Disabling an Account

If an account has been disabled only, it still exists in the network's account database, but no one can use that account to log on to the network. A disabled account will appear not to exist.

It is best if the administrator disables an account as soon as it has been established that the user will no longer be using that account. If it has been determined that the account will never be needed again, it can be deleted.

Deleting an Account

Deleting an account erases the user's information from the network's user-account database; the user no longer has access to the network. A user account should be deleted when:

- The user has left the organization and will no longer have an occupational reason to use the network.

- The user's employment has been terminated.

- The user has moved within the organization and no longer needs access to that network.

Administering Accounts in a Windows NT Environment

Windows NT Group Accounts

Microsoft Windows NT uses four types of group accounts, as described in the following section.

Types of Groups

Local, Global, System, and Built-In groups are used in the Windows NT network environment.

- **Local Groups**   Implemented in each local computer's account database, local groups contain user accounts and other global groups that need to have access, rights, and permissions assigned to a resource on a local computer. Local groups cannot contain other local groups.

- **Global Groups**   Used across an entire domain, global groups are created on a primary domain controller (PDC) in the domain in which the user accounts reside. Global groups can contain only user accounts from the domain in which the global group is created. Global groups cannot contain local groups or other global groups. Although permissions to resources can be assigned to a global group, global groups should be used only to gather domain user accounts. Members of global groups obtain resource permissions when the global group is added to a local group.

- **System Groups**   These groups automatically organize users for system use. Administrators do not assign users to them; rather, users are either members by default or become members during network activity. Membership cannot be changed.

- **Built-In Groups**   Offered as a feature by many network vendors, built-in groups, as the name implies, are included with the network operating system. Administrators can create accounts and groups with the appropriate permissions to perform standard tasks common to all networks, such as most administration and maintenance chores; however, vendors have saved them the trouble of creating those groups and accounts by offering built-in local or global groups that can be created during the initial installation.

Built-in groups are divided into three categories:

- Members of the administrator group have full capabilities on a computer.
- Members of the operator group have limited administrative capabilities to perform specific tasks.
- Members of other groups have capabilities to perform limited tasks.

Microsoft Windows NT Server offers the following built-in groups:

The Administrator group initially contains local and domain administrators. Members of this group can create, delete, and manage user accounts, global groups, and local groups. They can share directories and printers, grant resource permissions and rights, and install operating system files and programs.

The User and Guest groups, which are global, contain domain users who can perform tasks for which they have been given rights. They can also access resources to which they have been given permissions. User groups can be modified by administrators and account operators.

The Server Operator group, which can be modified by administrators only, can share and stop sharing resources, lock or override the lock of a server, format the server's disks, log on at servers, back up and restore servers, and shut down servers.

The Print Operator group, which can be modified by administrators only, can share, stop sharing, and manage printers. This group can also log on locally at servers and shut servers down.

Backup operators can log on locally, back up and restore servers, and shut down servers.

The Account Operator group can create, delete, and modify users, global groups, and local groups, but cannot modify administrator or server operator groups.

The Replicator group, which can be modified by Administrators, Account Operators, and Server Operators, is used in conjunction with the Directory Replicator Service.

Creating Groups in Window NT

In Microsoft Windows NT Server, the group management interface is called User Manager for Domains and is located in the **Start** menu. Click **Programs** and select the **Administrative Tools (Common)** area.

In User Manager, click **New Local Group** on the **User** menu. This selection presents you with a dialog box for entering the information to create a new local group, as shown in Figure 9.7.

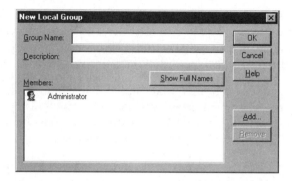

Figure 9.7   New Local Group dialog box

The Group Name field identifies the local group. A group name cannot be identical to any other group or user name of the domain or computer being administered. It can contain any uppercase or lowercase characters apart from these exceptions " / \ : ; | = + * ? < > that cannot be used in group names.

The Description field contains text describing the group or the users in the group.

The Members field displays the user names of the group members.

A newly created group account will have no members until the administrator assigns one or more existing users to the group. The administrator does this from the **New Local Group** dialog box by clicking **Add** and selecting the user account to be added.

Windows NT User Accounts

All the network management tools are consolidated in the **Start** menu, **Programs**, **Administrative Tools (Common)** area. As shown in Figure 9.8, the Microsoft Windows NT Server network utility for creating accounts is called the User Manager for Domains. To manage user accounts, click **Start,** select **Programs**, and click **Administrative Tools (Common)**.

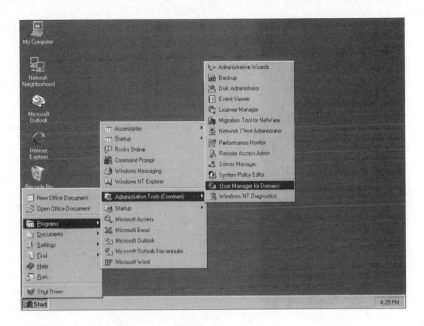

Figure 9.8 Windows NT Administrative Tools area

After you open User Manager, on the **User** menu, select the menu option **New User** as shown in Figure 9.9. A window appears for entering the information to create a new user.

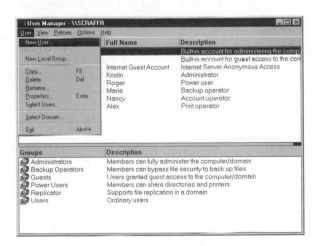

Figure 9.9 Menu showing the New User selection

Figure 9.10 shows all the essential information that the administrator needs in order to create the account.

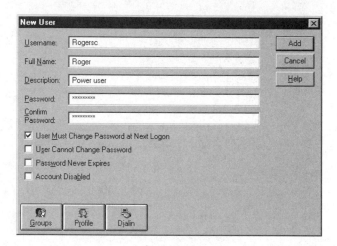

Figure 9.10   New User dialog box

Windows NT Server offers an account-copying feature. An administrator can create a template that has characteristics and parameters that are common among multiple users. To create a new account with the template characteristics, the administrator highlights the template account, selects **User**, Copy (F8), then enters the new user name and other identifying information (full name, description, and so on).

Profiles

An administrator will find it helpful to structure a network environment for certain users. This might be necessary, for example, to maintain a specific level of security, or to guide users who are not sufficiently familiar with computers and networks to have full access to the system.

Profiles used to configure and maintain a user's logon environment, including network connections and the appearance of the desktop, include:

- Printer connections.
- Regional settings.
- Sound settings.
- Mouse settings.
- Display settings.
- Other user-definable settings.

Profile parameters can also include special logon conditions and information about where the user can store personal files.

Microsoft Windows NT Server disables the Guest account by default after installation. The network administrator must enable the account if it will be used.

Windows NT Server uses the User Properties window in User Manager to disable users. To disable a user, double-click the name of the account, select the **Account Disabled** check box, and then click **OK**. The account is now disabled, as shown in Figure 9.11.

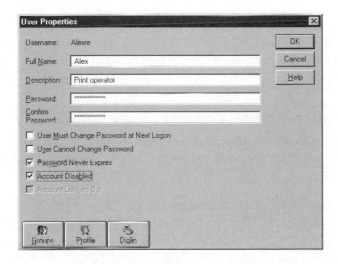

Figure 9.11 Disabling an account

Figure 9.12 shows deleting an account with User Manager.

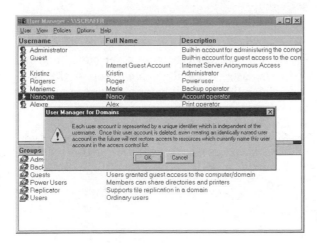

Figure 9.12 Deleting an account

To delete an account, in User Manager, select the account to be deleted, and then press the DELETE key. A dialog box is displayed (see figure 9.12). If **OK** is clicked, another dialog box will be displayed asking for confirmation that the specified user account will be deleted. Clicking **Yes** will delete the account; clicking **No** will cancel the operation.

Note Deleting an account permanently removes the account, along with the permissions and rights associated with it. Recreating the user account with the same name will not restore the user's rights or permissions. Each user account has a unique security identifier (SID); deleting and recreating a user will generate a new SID, not reuse the previous one. Internal processes in Windows NT refer to the account's SID rather than to the account's user or group name.

Administering Accounts in an Apple Environment

The default Apple networking environment includes two users: the person who installed the operating system and a guest. Managing a network of more than a few users is made easier by creating users and groups.

Creating Users and Groups

From the Apple Chooser select **Users & Groups** to open the **Users & Groups** Control Panel. This dialog box lists all the computer's users and groups, and allows you to create, edit, duplicate, and delete users and groups as necessary. In AppleShare, there are three categories of users:

- Owner
- User/Group
- Everyone

To create a new user, click the **New User** button and enter the appropriate information for this user. You will be able to supply the user's name, password, the groups to which the user will belong, and whether or not the user will be allowed to change the assigned password.

To create a new group, click the **New Group** button and enter the appropriate information for this group. You will be able to supply the group's name and the names of users who are to be members of the group.

Administering Accounts in a NetWare Environment

The basis of NetWare security and accounts is NetWare Directory Services (NDS). NDS is a hierarchically organized database.

Security is provided at three levels.

- **Accounts** This level includes user names, passwords, workstation time, and other restrictions.

- **Trustee rights** This level control directories and files a user can access. These rights include creating, reading, erasing, or writing to the files.

- **Directory and file attributes** This level determines what actions users can perform in the file or directory. These actions include sharing, deleting, copying, viewing, or editing.

NetWare uses several naming conventions. Names used must be unique, must include no spaces, and must be made up of fewer than 64 case-insensitive alpha-numeric characters. (Case-insensitive characters are characters, such as numbers, that cannot appear in both lower- and uppercase forms.)

Setting up and Managing Users and Groups

Before you can create, delete, or manage users and groups, you must log on to the network at a workstation or server with administrative privileges. Once logged on, you can launch the Novell Easy Administration Tool (NEAT) to begin managing users and groups. To do so, double-click the **NEAT** icon. A view of the directory tree in the left frame of the user interface shows all the network objects and their relationships to each other. In the right frame are the properties of any object selected.

To create a network account for a new user from the NEAT **New** menu, select **User** or click **Add a New User** on the toolbar. This will open a dialog box in which you can enter the required information, including the user's full name, the login name, and the home directory.

Click the next button to go to the next page and add this user to a group. After the user is added, click the next button to go to the next page to enter the password information. If this is left blank, no password will be required by the user to log on. To create additional users, check the **Create another user** check box before selecting the **Finish** button.

To delete a user, from the directory view in the **NEAT** menu, select the **User** object. Then, from the **Edit** menu, select **Delete selected item** and click **Yes**.

Warning If you delete a user who has relationships with another object, and that object relies on the user who is being deleted, you might encounter problems.

Managing Groups is similar to managing users. From the **NEAT** menu, select **Add a New Group**. This will launch the New Group wizard. Be sure to follow the naming conventions when assigning a group name. After the group is created, you can select the group and add users.

Note You can add only users that appear in the directory.

Editing User or Group Properties

Viewing or editing the properties of any object is easy. Open the **NEAT** administration tool and select the object's icon from the directory in the frame on the left. In the frame on the right are the property sheets for the object. The properties for the object are organized into tabs. User properties are in five tabs (**General, Groups, Applications, Security**, and **Login Script**). Groups properties are organized into three tabs (**Users, Security**, and **Applications**).

Administering Accounts in a UNIX Environment

Most UNIX configuration information is stored in text files that are read as needed. These text files can be edited manually to add users and groups and to set their permissions. Because the different versions of UNIX vary in the details of how they are managed, the names and locations of these files are not consistent from one manufacturer to another. The same holds true for Linux distributions, in which system directory and file locations can be quite different. A graphic interface often spares the administrator from having to know these differences, because user and group parameters can be set from interactive dialog boxes.

UNIX Users and Groups

The initial account, the administrative user, is usually named *root*. The other name to remember is *nobody*. Default UNIX groups can include *root*, *bin*, *daemon*, *tty*, *disk*, *lp*, *mail*, *news*, *dialout*, *trusted*, *modem*, *users*, and so on.

The open-source UNIX incarnation known as Linux creates a number of accounts. Which accounts are created depends on the base operating system and the software installed. The administrative user, *root*, is always created. Additional default accounts are used for tasks not otherwise thought of as meriting accounts at all. These include processes such as file transfer protocol (*ftp*) and *lp* (printers).

Exercise 9.2: Case Study Problem

For this exercise we will return to the same 20-employee company that was the subject of Exercise 9.1 in Lesson 1. Your job is to design user and group accounts for the 10-computer server-based network. To do this, you should determine what kinds of groups are appropriate to the company and its work. You will also need to establish a password policy and a personnel policy that takes into account what will happen when an employee departs from the company.

After you have established the account policies, create the appropriate user and group accounts and set whatever restrictions will be necessary for each of the groups. These should include the days and hours during which groups can log on to the network. Assign printing rights to the groups as needed and, finally, add the users to the appropriate groups.

Lesson Summary

The following points summarize the main elements of this lesson.

- Using a server-based network provides additional security by assigning each user an account with the appropriate rights and permissions.

- User accounts are composed of a user name, logon password, and any logon parameters established for that user.

- User accounts can be created or changed only by someone with administrative rights.

- An administrator can use profiles to configure and maintain a user's logon environment.

- Profiles include printer connections, regional settings, sound settings, mouse settings, display settings, and any other user-definable settings.

- In networks with large numbers of users, it is simplest for an administrator to create groups and assign users to groups. Because users receive the rights and permissions of the group rather than as individuals, the administrator is not required to create them on an individual basis.

- The four types of groups designated by Microsoft Windows NT are local groups, global groups, system groups, and built-in groups.

- Built-in groups include administrators, operator groups, and others.

- NetWare provides security and accounts through NDS (NetWare Directory Services).

- In NetWare, all resources, including users, are objects. An administrator can assign rights and permission to objects.

Chapter Summary

The following points summarize the key concepts of this chapter:

Creating Network Shares

- When files are transferred using a direct cable connection, one computer is configured as a host and the other as a client. The client can then access files and directories on the host computer.

- Client software must be enabled before a computer can access any resources shared on a network.

- The most common client used in a Windows environment is Client for Microsoft Networks.

- Microsoft Network client software enables users to share resources with any network that uses the SMB (Server Message Block) file-sharing protocol.

- Before a computer can act as a server and share resources to a network, it must have the client software enabled and then have File and Print Sharing enabled.

- Devices such as scanners and modems cannot be shared on a peer-to-peer network.

- AppleShare provides folder-level sharing on Macintosh machines.

- Linux file systems can be accessed by computers using AppleTalk and by computers using the SMB file sharing protocol.

- The maximum number of connections that can be set for Windows NT Workstation is 10.

Establishing and Managing Network Accounts

- Using a server-based network provides additional security by assigning each user an account with the appropriate rights and permissions.

- User accounts are composed of a user name, logon password, and any logon parameters established for that user.

- User accounts can be created or changed only by someone with administrative rights.

- An administrator can use profiles to configure and maintain a user's logon environment.

- Profiles include printer connections, regional settings, sound settings, mouse settings, display settings, and any other user-definable settings.

- In networks with large numbers of users, it is simplest for an administrator to create groups and assign users to groups. Because users receive the rights and permissions of the group rather than as individuals, the administrator is not required to create them on an individual basis.

- The four types of groups designated by Microsoft Windows NT are local groups, global groups, system groups, and built-in groups.

- Built-in groups include administrators, operator groups, and others.

- NetWare provides security and accounts through NDS (NetWare Directory Services).

- In NetWare, all resources, including users, are objects. An administrator can assign rights and permission to objects.

Chapter Review

1. Two computers running the MS-DOS operating system can be connected and information can be shared. (Yes or No).

2. Connecting two computers with a communications cable is called
_____ - _____ _____.

3. Sharing on a peer-to-peer network takes place at the _____ level.

4. The first person to log on to a Windows NT network uses the _____ account.

5. The user account contains information that defines a user to the network's _____ system.

6. Most network account-management utilities offer an account _____ feature with which an administrator can create a template user with certain characteristics and parameters that are common among multiple users.

7. A Windows NT administrator can use a _____ to configure and maintain a user's logon environment.

8. Two key pieces of information that should be entered when creating a user account are account name and _____.

9. The _____ account is for people who do not have a valid user account but need temporary access to the network.

10. An administrator can create a _____ account in order to simplify administrative tasks when dealing with a large numbers of users.

11. A global group is used across an entire _____.

12. Groups are used to give users _____ to perform system tasks such as backing up and restoring files.

13. The network administrator assigns _____ to groups to access resources, such as files, directories, and printers.

14. After being deleted, a user can no longer use the network, because the network _____ database will contain record or description of the user.

C H A P T E R   1 0

Ensuring Network Security

About This Chapter

Up to this point, our emphasis has been on sharing as the principal reason for creating a network. However, security—protecting the networked computers and the data they store and share—is also an important factor in networking. The larger the enterprise, the greater the need for security. In this chapter, we revisit some of the ways to enable sharing on a network that were covered in Chapter 9, "Establishing Network Shares and Accounts." Here, however, our focus shifts away from sharing procedures; instead we look at sharing from the perspective of how to establish and maintain network and data security.

Security is more than preventing unauthorized access to computers and their data; it includes maintaining the proper physical environment to permit the network to function effectively. We take a look at preventive maintenance and how to take steps to prevent data loss and minimize network failures, whether from human or other causes, such as natural disasters.

Before You Begin

Because this chapter is a continuation of the lessons presented in Chapter 9, you should be familiar with the concepts and procedures introduced in that chapter.

Lesson 1: Making Networks Secure

Planning for security is an important element in designing a network. It is far easier to implement a secure network from a plan than it is to recover from data loss. This lesson presents an overview of network security. We examine two primary models for ensuring data security and take a look at how to secure the physical components of a network.

After this lesson, you will be able to:

- List the basic security requirements for a network.
- Describe ways to restrict access to the network by unauthorized users.
- Describe the features of password-protected shares and access permissions.
- Identify the common types of computer viruses and describe ways to protect against them.

Estimated lesson time: 35 minutes

Planning for Network Security

In a networking environment there must be assurance that sensitive data will remain private. Not only is it important to secure sensitive information, it is equally important to protect network operations from deliberate or unintentional damage.

Maintaining network security requires a balance between facilitating easy access to data by authorized users and restricting access to data by unauthorized users. It's the job of the network administrator to create this balance.

Even in networks that handle sensitive and valuable business data, security is sometimes an afterthought. Four major threats to the security of data on a network are:

- Unauthorized access.
- Electronic tampering.
- Theft.
- Intentional or unintentional damage.

Despite the seriousness of these threats, data security is not always implemented or supported properly. The administrator's task is to ensure that the network remains reliable and secure, free from those threats.

Level of Security

The extent and level of the network security system required depends on the type of environment in which the network is running. A network that stores data for a major bank, for example, requires more extensive security than a LAN that links the computers in a small community volunteer organization.

Setting Policies

Making a network secure requires establishing a set of rules, regulations, and policies so that nothing is left to chance. The first step toward ensuring data security is to implement policies that set the tone and help to guide the administrator and users through changes, both expected and unplanned, in their network's development.

Prevention

The best way to design data security policies is to take a proactive, preventive approach. When unauthorized access is prevented, the data remains secure. A prevention-based system requires that the administrator understand the tools and methods available with which to keep data safe.

Authentication

To access a network, a user must enter a valid user name and password. Because passwords are linked to user accounts, a password authentication system is the first line of defense against unauthorized users.

It is important not to let overreliance on this authentication process fool you into a false sense of security. For example, in a peer-to-peer network, almost anyone can log on with a unique name and password. This alone can provide a user with complete access to the network, so that anything that is shared becomes available to that user. Authentication works only in a server-based network in which the user name and password must be authenticated from the security database.

Training

Unintentional errors can lead to security failures. A well-trained network user is less likely than an inexperienced novice to accidentally cause an error and ruin a resource by permanently corrupting or deleting data. Figure 10.1 illustrates such a problem.

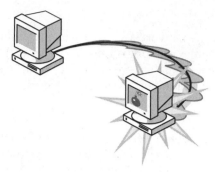

Figure 10.1   Training helps reduce costly user errors

The administrator should ensure that everyone who uses the network is familiar with its operating and security procedures. To accomplish this, the administrator can develop a short, clear guide to what users need to know, and require that new users attend appropriate training classes.

Securing Equipment

The first step in keeping data safe is to provide for the physical security of the network hardware. (Establishing and maintaining an optimal environment for the physical network is discussed in detail in Lesson 2.) The extent of security required depends on:

- The size of the company.
- The sensitivity of the data.
- The available resources.

In a peer-to-peer network, there is sometimes no organized hardware-security policy, and users are responsible for the security of their own computers and data. In a server-based network, security is the responsibility of the network administrator.

Securing the Servers

In a larger, centralized system, in which much individual user and organization data is sensitive, it is important to secure the servers from accidental or deliberate tampering.

It is not uncommon for some individuals to want to demonstrate their technical abilities when the servers have problems. They may or may not know what they are doing. It is best to tactfully prevent these people from "fixing" the server. The simplest solution is to lock the servers in a dedicated computer room with limited access; depending on the size of the company, this might not be workable. Locking the servers in an office or even a large storage closet is often practicable and goes some way toward securing the servers.

Securing the Cables

Copper media, such as coaxial cable, much like a radio emits electronic signals that mimic the information it carries. Information carried in these signals can be monitored with electronic listening equipment. Copper cable can also be tapped into so that information can be stolen directly from the original cable.

Cable runs that handle sensitive data should be accessible only to authorized people. Proper planning can make cable runs inaccessible to unauthorized people. For example, cable can be run inside the building structure, through ceilings, walls, and floors.

Security Models

After implementing security for the network's physical components, the administrator needs to ensure that the network resources will be safe from both unauthorized access and accidental or deliberate damage. Policies for assigning permissions and rights to network resources are at the heart of securing the network.

Two security models have evolved for keeping data and hardware resources safe:

- Password-protected shares
- Access permissions

These models are also called "share-level security" (for password-protected shares) and "user-level security" (for access permissions).

Password-Protected Shares

Implementing password-protected shares requires assigning a password to each shared resource. Access to the shared resource is granted when a user enters the correct password.

In many systems, resources can be shared with different types of permissions. To illustrate, we use Windows 95 and 98 as examples. For these operating systems, as described in Chapter 9, "Establishing Network Shares and Accounts," directories can be shared as Read Only, Full, or Depends On Password.

- **Read Only**   If a share is set up as Read Only, users who know the password have Read access to the files in that directory. They can view the documents, copy them to their machines, and print them, but they cannot change the original documents.

- **Full**   With Full access, users who know the password have complete access to the files in that directory. In other words, they can view, modify, add, and delete the shared directory's files.

- **Depends On Password**   Depends On Password involves setting up a share that uses two levels of passwords: Read access and Full access. Users who know the Read access password have Read access, and users who know the Full access password have Full access.

The password-protected share system is a simple security method that allows anyone who knows the password to obtain access to that particular resource.

Access Permissions

Access-permission security involves assigning certain rights on a user-by-user basis. A user types a password when logging on to the network. The server validates this user name and password combination and uses it to grant or deny access to shared resources by checking access to the resource against a user-access database on the server.

Access-permission security provides a higher level of control over access rights. It is much easier for one person to give another person a printer password, as in share-level security. It is less likely for that person to give away a personal password.

Because user-level security is more extensive and can determine various levels of security, it is usually the preferred model in larger organizations.

Resource Security

After the user has been authenticated and allowed on the network, the security system gives the user access to the appropriate resources.

Users have passwords, but resources have permissions. In a sense, a security fence guards each resource. The fence has several gates through which users can pass to access the resource. Certain gates allow users to do more to the resource than other gates. Certain gates, in other words, allow the user more privileges with the resource.

The administrator determines which users should be allowed through which gates. One gate grants the user full access to or full control of a resource. Another gate grants the user read-only access.

As shown in Figure 10.2, each shared resource or file is stored with a list of users or groups and their associated permissions (gates).

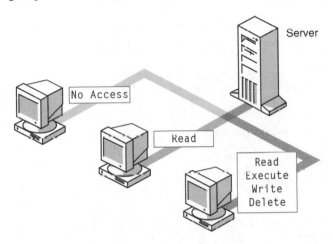

Figure 10.2   Permissions control the type of access to a resource

Table 10.1 contains common access permissions assigned to shared directories or files.

Note Different network operating systems (NOSs) give different names to these permissions. The following table shows some of the typical permissions that can be set on Windows NT Server directories.

Table 10.1   Windows NT Server Permissions

Permission	Functionality
Read	Reads and copies files in the shared directory.
Execute	Runs (executes) the files in the directory.
Write	Creates new files in the directory.
Delete	Deletes files in the directory.
No Access	Prevents the user from gaining access to directories, files, or resources.

Group Permissions

The administrator's job includes assigning each user the appropriate permissions to each resource. The most efficient way to accomplish this is through groups, especially in a large organization with many users and resources. As shown in Figure 10.3, Windows NT Server allows users to select the file or folder for which they want to set group permissions.

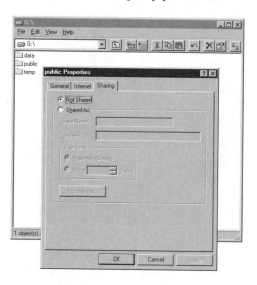

Figure 10.3   Windows NT Explorer is used to set permissions

Permissions for groups work in the same way as they work for individuals. The administrator reviews which permissions are required by each account and assigns the accounts to the proper groups. This is the preferred method of assigning permissions, rather than assigning each account's permissions individually.

Assigning users to appropriate groups is more convenient than having to assign separate permissions to every user individually. For example, giving the group *Everyone* full control of the public directory might not be the best choice. Full access would allow anyone to delete or modify the contents of the files in the public directory.

In Figure 10.4, the group *Everyone* has been granted Read access to the directory public. This allows members of the group *Everyone* to read, but not delete or modify, the files in the public directory.

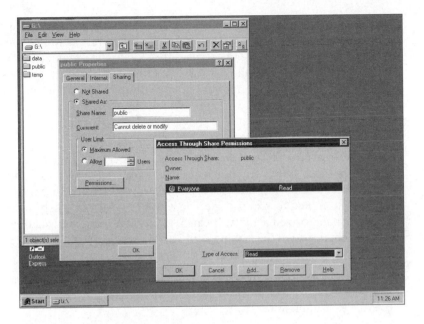

Figure 10.4   Modifying group permissions

The administrator could create a group called *Reviewers*, grant complete access permissions to the student files to that group, and assign staff to the *Reviewers* group. Another group, called *Faculty*, would have only Read permissions in the student files. Faculty members assigned to the *Faculty* group would be able to read the student files, but not change them.

Run the **c10dem01** video located in the **Demos** folder on the CD accompanying this book to view a presentation of share-based and server-based network security.

Security Enhancements

The network administrator can increase the level of security on a network in several ways. This section explores some of the options.

Firewalls

A *firewall* is a security system, usually a combination of hardware and software, that is intended to protect an organization's network against external threats coming from another network, including the Internet.

Firewalls prevent an organization's networked computers from communicating directly with computers that are external to the network, and vice versa. Instead, all incoming and outgoing communication is routed through a proxy server outside the organization's network. Firewalls also audit network activity, recording the volume of traffic and providing information about unauthorized attempts to gain access.

A proxy server is a firewall component that manages Internet traffic to and from a local area network (LAN). The proxy server decides whether it is safe to let a particular message or file pass through to the organization's network. It provides access control to the network, filtering and discarding requests that the owner does not consider appropriate, including requests for unauthorized access to proprietary data.

Auditing

Reviewing records of events in the security log of a server is called *auditing*. This process tracks network activities by user accounts. Auditing should be a routine element of network security. Audit records list the users that have accessed—or attempted to access—specific resources. Auditing helps administrators identify unauthorized activity. It can also provide usage information for departments that charge a fee for making certain network resources available and need some way to determine the cost of those resources.

Auditing can track functions such as:

- Logon attempts.
- Connection and disconnection from designated resources.
- Connection termination.
- Disabling of accounts.
- Opening and closing of files.
- Changes made to files.
- Creation or deletion of directories.
- Directory modification.
- Server events and modifications.
- Password changes.
- Logon parameter changes.

Audit records can indicate how the network is being used. The administrator can use the audit records to produce reports that show activities and their date and time ranges. For example, repeated failed logon attempts or efforts to log on at odd hours can indicate that an unauthorized user is attempting to gain access to the network.

Diskless Computers

Diskless computers, as the name implies, have no floppy-disk drives or hard disks. They can do everything a computer with disk drives can do except store data on a local floppy disk or hard disk. Diskless computers are an ideal choice for maintaining security because users cannot download data and take it away.

Diskless computers do not require boot disks. They communicate with the server and log on by means of a special ROM boot chip installed on the computer's network interface card (NIC). When the diskless computer is turned on, the ROM boot chip signals the server that it is ready to start. The server responds by downloading boot software into the diskless computer's RAM and automatically presents the user with a logon screen as part of the boot process. After the user logs on, the computer is connected to the network.

Although a diskless computer can provide a high level of security, it has shortcomings. Without a local disk available on which to store applications and data, all computer activity must be conducted over the network. Network traffic will increase accordingly, and the network will have to be capable of handling increased demands.

Data Encryption

A data-encryption utility scrambles data before it goes onto the network. This makes the data unreadable even by someone who taps the cable and attempts to read the data as it passes over the network. When the data arrives at the proper computer, the code for deciphering encrypted data decodes the bits, translating them into understandable information. Advanced data-encryption schemes automate both encryption and decryption. The best encryption systems are hardware-based and can be expensive.

The traditional standard for encryption is the Data Encryption Standard (DES). Developed by IBM and adopted in 1975 as a specification for encryption by the government of the United States, this system describes how data should be encrypted and provides the specifications for the key to decryption. The U.S. Government continues to use DES. Both the sender and the receiver need to have access to the decryption key. However, the only way to get the key from one location to another is to physically or electronically transmit it, which makes DES vulnerable to unauthorized interception.

Today, the U. S. Government is also using a newer standard, called the Commercial COMSEC Endorsement Program (CCEP), which may eventually replace DES. The National Security Agency (NSA) introduced CCEP and allows vendors with the proper security clearance to join CCEP. Approved vendors are authorized to incorporate classified algorithms into communications systems.

Computer Viruses

Computer viruses are becoming an all-too-familiar fact of life. It is not uncommon to see a report on a local news channel describing the latest virus and warning about its destructive impact. Computer viruses are bits of computer programming, or code, that hide in computer programs or on the boot sector of storage devices, such as hard-disk drives and floppy-disk drives. The primary purpose of a virus is to reproduce itself as often as possible and thereby disrupt the operation of the infected computer or the program. Once activated, a virus can be a simple annoyance or completely catastrophic in its effect. Viruses are written by people with an intent to do harm.

Viruses are classified into two categories, based on how they propagate themselves. The first type, called a "boot-sector virus," resides in the first sector of a floppy-disk or hard-disk drive. When the computer is booted, the virus executes. This is a common method of transmitting viruses from one floppy disk to another. Each time a new disk is inserted and accessed, the virus replicates itself onto the new drive. The second type of virus is known as a "file infector." Such a virus attaches itself to a file or program and activates any time the file is used. Many subcategories of file infectors exist.

The following list describes a few of the more common file infectors:

- **Companion Virus** A companion virus is so named because it uses the name of a real program—its companion. A companion virus activates by using a different file extension from its companion. For example, suppose we decide to start a program called "wordprocessor.exe." When the command is given to execute the application, a virus named "wordprocessor.com" will execute in its place. It is able to do so because a .com file takes priority over an .exe file.

- **Macro Virus** A macro virus is difficult to detect and is becoming more common. It is so named because it is written as a macro for a specific application. Popular applications, such as Microsoft Word, are targets for these viruses. When the user opens a file that contains the virus, the virus attaches itself to the application and then infects any other files accessed by that application.

- **Polymorphic Virus** A polymorphic virus is so named because it changes its appearance every time it is replicated. This renders it more difficult to detect because no two are exactly the same.

- **Stealth Virus** A stealth virus is so named because it attempts to hide from detection. When an antivirus program attempts to find it, the stealth virus tries to intercept the probe and return false information indicating that it does not exist.

Virus Propagation

Just as computer viruses do not create themselves, neither do they spread through the air unaided. Some kind of exchange between the two computers must take place before transmission can occur. In the early days of computing and viruses, the principal source of infection was through the exchange of data on floppy disks. One infected computer in an organization could easily infect all the computers in the organization, merely by a single user passing around a copy of the latest screensaver program.

The proliferation of LANs and the growth of the Internet have opened many new pathways to rapidly spreading viruses. Now, virtually any computer in the world can be connected to any other computer in the world. As a consequence, the creation of viruses is also on the rise. In fact, some virus creators provide easy-to-use software containing directions for how to create a virus.

A recently emerging method of spreading a virus is through e-mail services. After an e-mail message containing the virus is opened, it attaches itself to the computer and can even send itself to names in the computer's e-mail address book. Usually, the virus is located in an inviting attachment to an e-mail message.

Convincing unsuspecting victims to activate a virus is a goal for virus writers. This is often accomplished by packaging the virus in an enticing cover. Such a virus is known as a "Trojan horse." To attract users, it is presented in the guise of something familiar, safe, or intriguing.

Remember that any means by which computers exchange information provides a potential path for a virus. Methods in common use include:

- CD-ROMs.
- Cabling directly connecting two computers.
- Floppy-disk drives.
- Hard-disk drives.
- Internet connections.
- LAN connections.
- Modem connections.
- Portable or removable drives.
- Tape.

Consequences of a Virus

A virus can cause many kinds of harm to a computer; the creativity of its creator is the only limitation. The following list describes common symptoms of computer virus infection:

- The computer won't boot.
- The data is scrambled or corrupted.
- The computer operates erratically.
- A partition is lost.
- The hard drive is reformatted.

The most common symptom of virus infection in a network is one or more misbehaving workstations. A peer-to-peer network is the most vulnerable. As described in Chapter 1, "Introduction to Networking," in a peer-to-peer network all things are shared equally; therefore, any infected computer has direct access to any computer or resource that is shared to the network. Server-based networks have some built-in protection because permission is required to obtain access to some portions of the server and, therefore, the network. In these networks, it is more likely that workstations will be infected than a server, although servers are not immune. The server, as the conduit from one computer to another, participates in the transmission of the virus, even though it might not be affected.

Virus Prevention

Disastrous viruses are becoming more commonplace and should be taken into account when network security procedures are developed. An effective antivirus strategy is an essential part of a network plan. Good antivirus software is essential. Although no virus protection software can prevent all viruses, it can do some of the following:

- Warn of a potential virus
- Keep a virus from activating
- Remove a virus
- Repair some of the damage that a virus has caused
- Keep a virus in check after it activates

Preventing unauthorized access to the network is one of the best ways to avoid a virus. For example, the best way to prevent a virus from infecting a floppy disk is to use write protection. If you cannot write to the floppy disk, you cannot infect it. Because prevention is the key, the network administrator needs to make sure that all standard preventive measures are in place.

These include:

- Passwords to reduce the chance of unauthorized access.
- Well-planned access and privilege assignments for all users.
- User profiles to structure the user's network environment, including network connections and program items that appear when the user logs on.
- A policy that sets out which software can be loaded.
- A policy that specifies rules for implementing virus protection on client workstations and network servers.
- Ensuring that all users are well-trained and informed about computer viruses and how to prevent their activation.

 ## Lesson Checkup

1. Describe two common ways by which unauthorized users can gain access to a network; for each, describe how unauthorized access can be prevented.
2. Describe the differences between password-protected shares and access permissions.
3. Define data encryption and DES.
4. Identify four common types of computer viruses and describe how they are transmitted; describe three ways to help protect computers in a network against viruses.

Lesson Summary

The following points summarize the main elements of this lesson:

- Network planning must include plans for security.
- The level of security needed depends on the size of the organization and the sensitivity of the data.
- The two security models that keep data and hardware resources safe are password-protected shares and access permissions.
- Merely requiring users to log on does not, in itself, ensure the security of the network.
- The best way to assign permissions is through setting up groups. Administrators can then assign permissions to the group rather than to individuals.
- Ways to enhance security include use of auditing, diskless computers, data encryption, and virus protection.
- Building in virus prevention and recovery policies should be part of a network strategy.

Lesson 2: Maintaining a Healthy Network Environment

The physical environment in which a network resides is an important factor to consider in keeping a computer network physically secure. This lesson explores this frequently overlooked aspect of network management: ensuring a safe environment for computers, peripherals, and the associated network, and looks at what you can do to maintain the health of your network environment.

After this lesson, you will be able to:

- Describe the impact of environmental conditions on a network.
- Describe the environmental conditions required for proper network operation.
- Describe several methods for protecting network equipment in a harsh environment.

Estimated lesson time: 15 minutes

Computers and the Environment

Most kinds of electronic equipment, such as computers, are rugged and reliable, operating for years with little maintenance. Computers have even been to the moon and back. However, negative environmental impacts on electronic equipment, while not always dramatic, do exist. A slow and steady deterioration process can lead to intermittent but ever-more-frequent problems until a catastrophic system failure occurs. By recognizing these problems before they occur and taking appropriate steps, you can prevent or minimize such failures.

Like humans, computers and electronic equipment are affected by environmental conditions. Although more tolerant and less likely to complain, computers and network equipment require specific environments in order to function properly. Most computers are installed in environmentally controlled areas; but even with such controls in place, computers are not immune from the effects of their surroundings. When assessing how environmental conditions will affect a computer network, your first step is to consider the climatic conditions of the region. As shown in Figure 10.5, a network installation in an Arctic or Antarctic location will be subjected to very different conditions than a network located in a tropical jungle.

Figure 10.5   Environmental extremes affect computers

A network installed in an arctic climate will undergo extreme changes in temperature, whereas a network installed in a tropical environment will experience high humidity. Different climatic circumstances require that different steps be taken to ensure that the environment does not negatively affect the network.

Environmental conditions for computers are assumed to be the same as prevailing office conditions. For a single personal computer or workstation, this assumption is usually accurate. However, an individual workstation comprises only part of the network. Remember that network wiring, discussed in Chapter 2, "Basic Network Media," runs through walls and in ceilings, basements, and sometimes outside. Many environmental factors can affect these components and ultimately lead to a network deterioration or breakdown.

When planning or maintaining a network, it is important to think in terms of the global (entire) network, visible or out of sight, and not just the local components that you see every day, as illustrated in Figure 10.6.

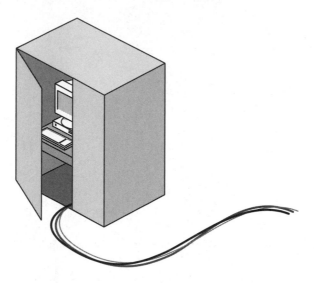

Figure 10.6   Include hidden network components in environmental assessment

Environmentally triggered disasters are usually the result of a long period of slow deterioration, rather than a sudden catastrophe. As an example, consider an iron nail. Left outside and exposed to the elements, it will gradually rust, becoming useless for its original purpose and, eventually, disintegrate. Similarly, networks implemented in poor environments might work well for years; however, eventually intermittent problems will start to occur and the number and frequency of the problems increase until eventually the network goes down.

Creating the Right Environment

In most large organizations, management or the personnel department is respon-sible for providing a safe and comfortable environment for employees. Govern-mental organizations regulate the human work environment. There are no such regulations or guidance for networks. It is the responsibility of the network admin-istrator to create policies governing safe practices around network equipment and to implement and manage an appropriate working environment for the network.

A healthy environment for network equipment is much like a healthy human environment; electronic equipment is designed to operate within the same range of temperature and humidity that feels comfortable to human beings.

Temperature

The basic environmental parameter that we control is temperature. Homes, offices, and work places usually have some means of controlling the temperature. Because electronic equipment generates heat during normal operation, it usually has a cooling fan designed to maintain the temperature within the specified limits. If, however, the room temperature in which the equipment is located is too high, the cooling fan and ventilation slots will be unable to maintain the correct operating temperature and components will begin to overheat and fail. Alternatively, if the temperature outdoors is too cold, the components might not function at all. Figure 10.7 shows the back and side of a computer with its cooling fan and ventilation slots.

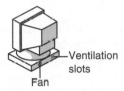

Figure 10.7   Keeping the computer cool

An environment in which the temperature is constantly cycling between hot and cold presents the worst scenario for electronic equipment. These extreme changes cause metal components to expand and contract, which eventually can lead to equipment failure.

Humidity

Factors related to humidity (moisture in the air) can have two negative effects on electronic equipment. High humidity promotes corrosion. Usually occuring first on electrical contacts, corroded contacts on cable connections and expansion cards will cause intermittent failures. Corrosion can also increase the resistance of electrical components, leading to a temperature increase that can be followed by component failure or fire.

In heated buildings, low humidity is common. Static electrical discharge is more common in low-humidity environments and can damage electronic components.

Because we have less control over humidity, network administrators need to be aware of the consequences of very high or low humidity and implement appropriate safeguards where such conditions exist. Most equipment will function adequately between 50 and 70 percent relative humidity.

When implementing a large network that includes a dedicated server room, you should consider controlling temperature and humidity in that room.

Dust and Smoke

Computers and electronic equipment do not function well with dust or smoke. Dust is electrostatically attracted to electronic equipment. An accumulation of dust causes two negative effects: dust acts as an insulator that affects the cooling of components, causing them to overheat, and dust can hold electrical charges, making them conductive. Excessive dust on electronic equipment can cause electrical shorts and catastrophic equipment failure.

Smoke causes a kind of contamination that is similar to the effects of dust. It coats the surfaces of electronic components, acting as both insulator and conductor. Smoke residue also enhances the accumulation of dust.

Human Factors

In designing a network, we can control many environmental factors, such as temperature, humidity, and ventilation. Although it is theoretically possible to create a perfect physical environment for computers, the arrival of human beings on the scene will bring changes that are bound to have an impact on the network. Picture a new, environmentally correct, equipment-friendly office with an up-to-date computer, printer, and desk. Into this pristine space, employees bring plants, pictures, radios, coffee cups, books, papers, and space heaters for cold days. Soon the office is filled up with employees, furniture, storage units, and office supplies. More changes occur; the tops of computers and monitors serve as end tables, and empty boxes are stored under desks next to computers. Because few employees have any awareness of the ventilation requirements for computer equipment, they impede the natural flow of air in and around the equipment. Once this happens, maintaining the proper temperature is impossible and failures begin.

The spilling of liquid refreshment takes a toll on keyboards and computers. When it gets cold outside, space heaters are used in under-heated offices and are usually placed under the desk, often in close proximity to computers. This can present two problems: the computer becomes overheated, and the space heaters can overload power outlets, tripping circuit breakers or even causing fires.

Hidden Factors

As stated earlier, much of a network is out of sight and, therefore, often out of mind. Because we don't see these hidden elements on a daily basis, we assume that all is well until something goes wrong.

Wiring is one network component that can cause problems, especially wires lying on the floor. Wires that run through an attic can easily be damaged by accident during repairs to other objects in the attic.

 Run the **c10dem02** video located in the **Demos** folder on the CD accompanying this book to view a presentation of how environmental factors affect computers, servers, and networks.

Bugs and rodents of all kinds are another hidden factor; these unwanted guests are likely to dine on the network materials or use them for construction purposes of their own.

Industrial Factors

Computers are not limited to the office setting; they are vital to the manufacturing sector as well. At first, computers were used to manage the flow of work through manufacturing operations. In modern plants, computers also run the equipment. By integrating network technology into this environment, the entire manufacturing process can be monitored and controlled from a central location. The equipment can even telephone maintenance personnel at home when there is a problem.

These improvements in manufacturing have led to an increase in productivity, while presenting unique issues for the network administrator. The operation of network equipment in a production environment presents many challenges. Issues that need to be addressed when networks are implemented in a manufacturing setting include the presence of:

- Noise.
- Electromagnetic interference (EMI).
- Vibration.
- Corrosive and explosive environments.
- Untrained and unskilled workers.

Manufacturing environments often have little or no control over temperature and humidity, and the atmosphere can be contaminated with corrosive chemicals. A corrosive atmosphere with high humidity can destroy computer and network equipment within months and even, in some cases, days. Manufacturing environments that utilize heavy equipment with large electrical motors can wreak havoc on the stability of computer-operated systems and networks. To minimize problems that stem from operating a computer network in an industrial environment:

- Install the networking equipment in separate enclosures with outside ventilation.
- Use fiber-optic cabling. This will reduce electrical interference and corrosion problems with the cable.
- Make sure that all equipment is properly grounded.
- Provide proper training to all employees that need to use the equipment. This will help ensure the integrity of the system.

Lesson Checkup

1. Describe the ways in which heat, humidity, dust, and smoke can each have an adverse effect on computer health. For each, describe preventive measures that can be taken to protect computers in such environments.

2. Identify at least three of the human factors that can unintentionally alter a computer's operating environment. Describe how each of these factors can affect the computer and suggest some preventive measures for each.

3. Identify the principal hidden and industrial factors that can affect a network's health. Include out-of-view network equipment in both an office, and a manufacturing environment. Discuss what precautions can be taken, or what changes might need to be made, for each of these hidden and industrial factors.

Lesson Summary

The following points summarize the main elements of this lesson:

- When assessing network environmental conditions and requirements, it is important to consider components that are out of sight, such as wiring, as well as visible components, such as computers.

- Controlling temperature and humidity are key factors in maintaining a user-friendly environment.

- The accumulation of material on and around computers can lead to network failures.

- It is important to be aware of the environmental stresses placed on hidden network components, as well as components in plain view.

Lesson 3: Avoiding Data Loss

Thus far in this chapter, we have covered maintaining network hardware and data security and keeping computer components safe from harm. However, making networks secure also includes protecting the data from corruption or loss. This lesson presents an overview of the possible causes of data loss and how to protect the network against them. You will learn about systems and processes for preventing data loss.

After this lesson, you will be able to:

- Identify the reasons for implementing a backup system.
- Select a backup approach that is appropriate for a given site, including the method and schedule.
- List the considerations for implementing an uninterruptible power supply.
- Describe each of the following types of fault-tolerant systems: disk striping, disk mirroring, sector sparing, clustering.

Estimated lesson time: 45 minutes

Data Protection

A site disaster is defined as anything that causes you to lose your data. Many large organizations have extensive disaster-recovery plans to maintain operations and rebuild after a natural disaster such as an earthquake or a hurricane. Many, but not all, include a plan to recover the network. However, a network can incur a disastrous failure from many more sources than natural disasters. Disaster recovery for a network goes beyond the replacing of the physical hardware; the data must be protected as well. The causes of a network disaster, ranging from human acts to natural causes, include:

- Component failure.
- Computer viruses.
- Data deletion and corruption.
- Fire caused by arson or electrical mishaps.
- Natural disasters, such as lightning, floods, tornadoes, and earthquakes.
- Power-supply failure and power surges.
- Theft and vandalism.

In the event of a site disaster, the downtime spent recovering data from backup storage (if you have backups) could result in a serious loss of productivity. And without backups, the consequences are even more severe, possibly resulting in significant financial losses. There are several ways to prevent or recover from data loss, including:

- Tape backup systems.
- An uninterruptible power supply (UPS).
- Fault-tolerant systems.
- Optical drives and discs.

Any or all of these approaches can be used, depending on how valuable the data is to the organization and on the organization's budget constraints.

Tape Backup

The simplest, most inexpensive way to avoid disastrous loss of data is to implement a schedule of periodic backups with storage offsite. Using a tape backup is still one of the few simple and economical ways to ensure that data remains safe and usable.

Experienced network engineers advise that a backup system should be the first line of defense against data loss. A secure backup strategy minimizes the risk of losing data by maintaining a current backup—copies of existing files—so that files can be recovered if harm comes to the original data. To back up data requires:

- Appropriate equipment.
- A regular schedule for periodic backups.
- Ensuring that backup files are current.
- Personnel assigned to make sure this schedule is carried out.

The equipment usually consists of one or more tape drives and tapes or other mass storage media. Any expense incurred in this area is likely to be minimal compared to the value of what will be saved in the event of data loss.

Implementing a Backup System

The rule is simple: if you cannot get along without it, back it up. Whether you back up entire disks, selected directories, or files depends on how fast you will need to be operational after losing important data. Complete backups make restoring disk configurations much easier, but can require multiple tapes if there are large amounts of data. Backing up individual files and directories might require fewer tapes, but could require the administrator to manually restore disk configurations.

Critical data should be backed up according to daily, weekly, or monthly schedules, depending on how critical the data is and how frequently it is updated. It is best to schedule backup operations during periods of low system use. Users should be notified when the backup will be performed so that they will not be using the servers during server backup.

Selecting a Tape Drive

Because the majority of backing up is done with tape drives, the first step is to select a tape drive, weighing the importance of a variety of factors, such as:

- How much data needs to be backed up.
- The network's requirements for backup reliability, capacity, and speed.
- The cost of the tape drive and related media.
- The tape drive's compatibility with the operating system.

Ideally, a tape drive should have more than enough capacity to back up a network's largest server. It should also provide error detection and correction during backup and restore operations.

Backup Methods

As listed in Table 10.2, an efficient backup policy uses a combination of methods:

Table 10.2   Backup Methods

Method	Description
Full backup	Backs up and marks selected files, whether or not they have changed since the last backup.
Copy	Backs up all selected files without marking them as being backed up.
Incremental backup	Backs up and marks selected files only if they have changed since the last time they were backed up.
Daily copy	Backs up only those files that have been modified that day, without marking them as being backed up.
Differential backup	Backs up selected files only if they have changed since the last time they were backed up, without marking them as being backed up.

Tapes can be backed up based on a multiple-week cycle, depending on how many tapes are available. No rigid rules govern the length of the cycle. On the first day of the cycle, the administrator performs a full backup and follows with an incremental backup on succeeding days. When the entire cycle has finished, the process begins again. Another method is to schedule streaming backups throughout the day.

Testing and Storage

Experienced administrators test the backup system before committing to it. They perform a backup, delete the information, restore the data, and attempt to use the data.

The administrator should test the backup procedures regularly to verify that what is expected to be backed up is actually being backed up. Additionally, the restore procedure should be tested to ensure that important files can be restored quickly.

Ideally, an administrator should make two copies of each tape: one to be kept onsite, and the other stored offsite in a safe place. Remember that although storing tapes in a fireproof safe can keep them from actually burning, the heat from a fire will ruin the data stored on them. After repeated usage, tapes lose the ability to store data. Replace tapes regularly to ensure a good backup.

Maintaining a Backup Log

Maintaining a log of all backups is critical for later file recovery. A copy of the log should be kept with the backup tapes, as well as at the computer site. The log should record the following information:

- Date of backup
- Tape-set number
- Type of backup performed
- Which computer was backed up
- Which files were backed up
- Who performed the backup
- Location of the backup tapes

Installing the Backup System

Tape drives can be connected to a server or a computer, and backups can be initiated from the computer to which the tape drive is attached. If you run backups from a server, backup and restore operations can occur very quickly because the data does not have to travel across the network.

Backing up across the network is the most efficient way to back up multiple systems; however, it creates a great deal of network traffic and slows the network down considerably. Network traffic can also cause performance degradation. This is one reason why it is important to perform backups during periods of low server use.

If multiple servers reside in one location, placing a backup computer on an isolated segment can reduce backup traffic. As shown in Figure 10.8, the backup computer is then connected to a separate NIC on each server.

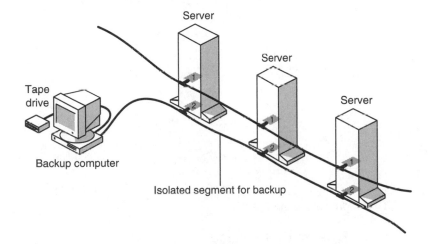

Figure 10.8   Network traffic is reduced by backing up to a separate segment

Uninterruptible Power Supply (UPS)

An uninterruptible power supply (UPS) is an automated external power supply designed to keep a server or other device running in the event of a power failure. The UPS system takes advantage of uninterruptible power supplies that can interface with an operating system such as Microsoft Windows NT. The standard UPS provides a network with two crucial components:

- A power source to run the server for a short time
- A safe shutdown management service

The power source is usually a battery, but the UPS can also be a gasoline engine running an AC power supply.

If the power fails, users are notified of the failure and warned by the UPS to finish their tasks. The UPS then waits a predetermined amount of time and performs an orderly system shutdown.

A good UPS system will:

- Prevent any more users from accessing the server.
- Send an alert message to the network administrator through the server.

As shown in Figure 10.9, the UPS is usually located between the server and a power source.

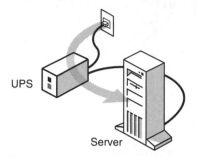

Figure 10.9   Uninterruptible power supply as a backup power source

If power is restored while the UPS is active, the UPS will notify the users that the power has returned.

Types of UPS Systems

The best UPS systems perform online. When the power source fails, the UPS batteries automatically take over. The process is invisible to users.

There are also stand-by UPS systems that start when power fails. These are less expensive than online systems, but are not as reliable.

Implementing UPS

Answering the following questions will help the network administrator determine which UPS system best fits the needs of the network:

- Will the UPS meet the basic power requirements of this network? How many components can it support?
- Does the UPS communicate with the server to notify it when a power failure has occurred and the server is running on batteries?
- Does the UPS feature surge protection to guard against power spikes and surges?
- What is the life span of the UPS battery? How long can it be inactive before it starts to degrade?
- Will the UPS warn the administrator and users that it is running out of power?

Fault-Tolerant Systems

Fault-tolerant systems protect data by duplicating data or placing data in different physical sources, such as different partitions or different disks. Data redundancy allows access to data even if part of the data system fails. Redundancy is a prominent feature common to most fault-tolerant systems.

Fault-tolerant systems should never be used as replacements for regular backup of servers and local hard disks. A carefully planned backup strategy is the best insurance policy for recovering lost or damaged data.

Fault-tolerant systems offer these alternatives for data redundancy:

- Disk striping
- Disk mirroring
- Sector sparing
- Mirrored drive arrays
- Clustering

Redundant Array of Independent Disks (RAID)

Fault-tolerance options are standardized and categorized into levels. These levels are known as redundant array of independent disks (RAID), formerly known as redundant array of inexpensive disks. The levels offer various combinations of performance, reliability, and cost.

Level 0—Disk Striping

Disk striping divides data into 64K blocks and spreads it equally in a fixed rate and order among all disks in an array. However, disk striping does not provide any fault tolerance because there is no data redundancy. If any partition in the disk array fails, all data is lost.

A stripe set combines multiple areas of unformatted free space into one large logical drive, distributing data storage across all drives simultaneously. In Windows NT, a stripe set requires at least two physical drives and can use up to 32 physical drives. Stripe sets can combine areas on different types of drives, such as small computer system interface (SCSI), enhanced small device interface (ESDI), and integrated device electronics (IDE) drives.

Figure 10.10 shows three hard disks being used to create a stripe set. In this case, the data consists of 192 K of data. The first 64 K of data is written to a stripe on disk 1, the second 64 K is written to a stripe on disk 2, and the third 64 K is written to the stripe on disk 3.

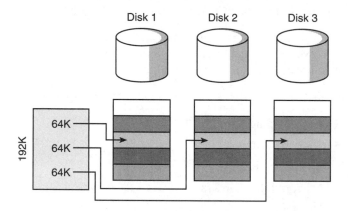

Figure 10.10   Disk striping combines areas on multiple drives

Disk striping has several advantages: it makes one large partition out of several small partitions, which offers better use of disk space; and multiple disk controllers will result in better performance.

Level 1—Disk Mirroring

Disk mirroring actually duplicates a partition and moves the duplication onto another physical disk. There are always two copies of the data, with each copy on a separate disk. Any partition can be mirrored. This strategy is the simplest way to protect a single disk against failure. Disk mirroring can be considered a form of continual backup because it maintains a fully redundant copy of a partition on another disk.

Duplexing   Disk duplexing, as shown in Figure 10.11, consists of a mirrored pair of disks with an additional disk controller on the second drive. This reduces channel traffic and potentially improves performance. Duplexing is intended to protect against disk controller failures as well as media failures.

Disk I/O

Disk mirroring software

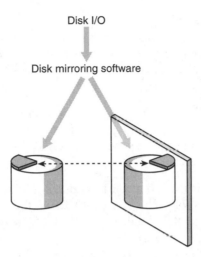

Figure 10.11   Disk mirroring duplicates a partition on another physical disk

Level 2—Disk Striping with ECC

When a block of data is written, the block is broken up and distributed (inter-leaved) across all data drives. Error-correction code (ECC) requires a larger amount of disk space than parity-checking methods, discussed under Level 3. Although this method offers marginal improvement in disk utilization, it compares poorly with level 5, discussed later.

Level 3—ECC Stored As Parity

Disk striping with ECC stored as parity is similar to level 2. The term *parity* refers to an error-checking procedure in which the number of 1s must always be the same—either odd or even—for each group of bits transmitted without error. In this strategy, the ECC method is replaced with a parity-checking scheme that requires only one disk to store parity data.

Level 4—Disk Striping with Large Blocks

This strategy moves away from data interleaving by writing complete blocks of data to each disk in the array. The process is still known as disk striping, but is done with large blocks. A separate check disk is used to store parity information. Each time a write operation occurs, the associated parity information must be read from the check disk and modified. Because of this overhead, the block-inter-leaving method works better for large block operations than for transaction-based processing.

Level 5—Striping with Parity

Striping with parity is currently the most popular approach to fault-tolerant design. It supports from a minimum of three to a maximum of 32 drives and writes the parity information across all the disks in the array (the entire stripe set). The data and parity information are arranged so that the two are always on different disks.

A parity stripe block exists for each stripe (row) across the disk. The parity stripe block is used to reconstruct data for a failed physical disk. If a single drive fails, enough information is spread across the remaining disks to allow the data to be completely reconstructed.

The parity stripe block is used to reconstruct data for a failed physical disk. A parity stripe block exists for each stripe (row) across the disk. RAID 4 stores the parity stripe block on one physical disk, and RAID 5 distributes parity evenly across all disks.

Level 10—Mirrored Drive Arrays

RAID level 10 mirrors data across two identical RAID 0 drive arrays.

Sector Sparing

The Windows NT Server operating system offers an additional fault-tolerant feature called "sector sparing," also known as "hot fixing." The three steps of sector sparing are shown in Figure 10.12. This feature automatically adds sector-recovery capabilities to the file system while the computer is running.

Detects   Moves data   Maps out
bad sector   to good sector   bad sector

Figure 10.12   Sector sparing or hot-fixing steps

If bad sectors are found during disk I/O (input/output), the fault-tolerant driver will attempt to move the data to a good sector and map out the bad sector. If the mapping is successful, the file system is not alerted. It is possible for SCSI devices to perform sector sparing, but ESDI and IDE devices cannot. Some network operating systems, such as Windows NT Server, have a utility that notifies the administrator of all sector failures and of the potential for data loss if the redundant copy also fails.

Microsoft Clustering

Microsoft Clustering is Microsoft's implementation of server clustering. The term "clustering" refers to a group of independent systems that work together as a single system. Fault tolerance is built into the clustering technology. Should a system within the cluster fail, the cluster software will disperse the work from the failed system to the remaining systems in the cluster. Clustering is not intended to replace current implementations of fault-tolerant systems, although it does provide an excellent enhancement.

Implementing Fault Tolerance

Most advanced network operating systems offer a utility for implementing fault tolerance. In Windows NT Server, for example, the Disk Administrator program is used to configure Windows NT Server fault tolerance. The graphical interface of Disk Administrator makes it easy to configure and manage disk partitioning and fault tolerant options. If you move the disk to a different controller or change its ID, Windows NT will still recognize it as the original disk. Disk Administrator is used to create various disk configurations, including:

- Stripe sets with parity, which accumulate multiple disk areas into one large partition, distributing data storage across all drives simultaneously, adding fault tolerant parity information.

- Mirror sets, which make a duplicate of one partition and place it onto a separate physical disk.

- Volume sets, which accumulate multiple disk areas into one large partition, filling the areas in sequence.

- Stripe sets, which accumulate multiple disk areas into one large partition, distributing data storage across all drives simultaneously.

Optical Drives and Disks

The term "optical drive" is a generic term that is applied to several devices. In optical technology, data is stored on a rigid disk by altering the disk's surface with a laser beam.

The use of optical drives and disks is becoming increasingly popular. As the technology evolves from the original read-only and read-write CD-ROMs to the new DVD technologies, these devices are being used more and more to store large amounts of retrievable data. Optical-drive manufacturers provide a large array of storage configurations that are either network-ready or can be used with a network server. They are an excellent choice for permanent backup. Several variations of this technology exist.

CD-ROM Technology

Compact discs (CD-ROMs) are the most common form of optical data storage. CD-ROMs, for the most part, only allow information to be read. The advantages of using CDs for storage are many. The ISO 9660 specification defines an international format standard for CD-ROM. Their storage capacity is high—up to 650 MB of data on a 4.72-inch disc. They are portable and replaceable, and because data on a CD-ROM cannot be changed (it is read-only), files cannot be accidentally erased. Standard recording formats and inexpensive readers make CDs ideal for data storage. CD-ROMs are also available in a multisession format called "CD-recordable" (CD-R). This media can now be used for incremental updates and inexpensive duplication. CD-ROMs are also offered in a rewritable format called CD-rewritable.

Digital Video Disc (DVD) Technology

The digital video disc (DVD) family of formats is replacing the CD-ROM family of formats. Digital video disc technology, also known as "digital versatile disc," is newer and, hence, relatively immature. DVD has five formats: DVD-ROM, DVD-Video, DVD-Audio, DVD-R (the "R" stands for "recordable"), and DVD-RAM. DVD-R is the format for write-once (incremental updates). It specifies 3.95 GB for single-sided discs and 7.9 GB for double-sided discs. DVD-RAM is the format for rewritable discs. It specifies 2.6 GB for single-sided discs and 5.2 GB for double-sided discs, with a disc cartridge as an option. DVD-ROMs (read-only discs) are similar to CD-ROMs and have a storage capacity of 4.7 GB (single-sided, single-layer), 9.4 GB (double-sided, single-layer), 8.5 GB (double-layer, single-sided), 17 GB (dual-layer, double-sided). These are backward-compatible with CD-audio and CD-ROM. DVD-ROM drives can play DVD-R and all the DVD formats. UDF is the file system for DVD-R.

WORM (Write Once, Read Many) Technology

Write once, read many (WORM) technology has helped initiate the document-imaging revolution. WORM uses laser technology to permanently alter sectors of the disc, thereby permanently writing files onto the media. Since this alteration is permanent, the device can write only once to each disc. WORM is typically employed in imaging systems in which the images are static and permanent.

Rewritable Optical Technology

Two new technologies are being employed that utilize rewritable optical technology. These technologies include magneto-optical (MO) and phase change rewritable (PCR) discs. MO drives are more widely accepted because the media and drive manufacturers use the same standards and their products are cross-compatible. PCR devices, however, come from one manufacturer (Matsushita/Panasonic), and the media comes from two manufacturers (Panasonic and Plasmon).

Multifunction Drives

There are two versions of multifunction optical drives. One uses firmware in the drive that first determines whether a disc has been formatted for write-once or rewritable recording and then acts on that disc accordingly. In the other MO version, two entirely different media are used. The rewritable discs are conventional MO discs, but write-once media are traditional WORM media.

Disaster Recovery

Trying to recover from a disaster, regardless of how it was caused, can be a terrifying experience. How successful the recovery is depends on the extent to which the network administrator has implemented disaster prevention and preparedness.

Disaster Prevention

The best way to recover from a disaster is to prevent it from happening in the first place. When implementing disaster prevention:

- Focus on factors over which you have control.
- Determine the best method of prevention.
- Implement and enforce the preventive measures you select.
- Check continually for new and better methods of prevention.
- Perform regular and routine maintenance on all network hardware and software components.
- Remember that training is the key to preventing network disasters of the human kind.

Disaster Preparation

Not all disasters can be prevented. Every jurisdiction has a disaster-preparedness plan, and many hours are spent every year in practicing for such an event. Because each community is different, recovery plans will have to take different factors into account. If, for example, you live in a flood zone, you should have a plan to protect your network from high water.

When considering disaster protection, you will need a plan for hardware, software, and data. Hardware and software applications and operating systems can be replaced. But to do this, it's necessary first to know exactly what assets you have. Take inventory of all hardware and software, including date of purchase, model, and serial number. (For tips on how to make such an inventory, refer to Chapter 8, Lesson 1: Choosing a Network Design.)

Physical components of a network can be easily replaced and are usually covered by some form of insurance, but data is highly vulnerable to disaster. In the case of a fire, you can replace all the computers and hardware, but not the files, drawings, and specifications for the multimillion dollar project that your organization has been preparing for the last year.

The only protection from a data-loss disaster is to implement one or more of the methods described earlier to back up data. Store your backups in a secure place, such as a bank safe deposit box, away from the network site.

To fully recover from any disaster you will need to:

- Make a disaster-recovery plan.
- Implement the plan.
- Test the plan.

Lesson Summary

The following points summarize the main elements of this lesson.

- Planning for a disaster is an essential part of implementing a successful network.
- A network disaster plan should encompass the loss of hardware and data.
- Tape backup is the most common method of preventing data loss.
- Loss of electrical power can causes files to become corrupted, and any data being held in RAM to be lost.
- An uninterruptible power supply provides temporary power so that critical data can be properly stored before the network or computer goes down.
- Fault tolerance is the automatic duplication of data to prevent loss.
- Fault tolerant strategies are called redundant arrays of independent disks (RAID) and include disk striping and disk mirroring.
- Sector sparing is an advanced method of fault tolerance.

Exercise 10.1: Case Study Problem

A small organization recently suffered security breaches in its peer-to-peer network. The intruder stole valuable business data. The organization's need for security became apparent, and now a modest-sized, but more secure, server-based network is in place.

The organization is located in a small California community that experiences frequent earthquakes and power outages. Your job is to plan how to avoid breaches of security and plan for disaster recovery at the same time. In this exercise, examine preventive measures the organization can take to avoid data loss due to human activities and natural disasters such as earthquakes.

List the categories of things that can put the organization's data at risk. Discuss the preventive measures and recovery plans appropriate for each kind of data loss.

Chapter Summary

The following points summarize the key concepts of this chapter:

Making Networks Secure

- Network planning must include plans for security.

- The level of security needed depends on the size of the organization and the sensitivity of the data.

- The two security models that keep data and hardware resources safe are password-protected shares and access permissions.

- Merely requiring users to log on does not, in itself, ensure the security of the network.

- The best way to assign permissions is through setting up groups. Administrators can then assign permissions to the group rather than to individuals.

- Ways to enhance security include use of auditing, diskless computers, data encryption, and virus protection.

- Building in virus prevention and recovery policies should be part of a network strategy.

Maintaining a Healthy Network Environment

- When assessing network environmental conditions and requirements, it is important to consider components that are out of sight, such as wiring, as well as visible components, such as computers.

- Controlling temperature and humidity are key factors in maintaining a user-friendly environment.

- The accumulation of material on and around computers can lead to network failures.

- It is important to be aware of the environmental stresses placed on hidden network components, as well as components in plain view.

Avoiding Data Loss

- Planning for a disaster is an essential part of implementing a successful network.

- A network disaster plan should encompass the loss of hardware and data.

- Tape backup is the most common method of preventing data loss.

- Loss of electrical power can causes files to become corrupted, and any data being held in RAM to be lost.

- An uninterruptible power supply provides temporary power so that critical data can be properly stored before the network or computer goes down.

- Fault tolerance is the automatic duplication of data to prevent loss.

- Fault tolerant strategies are called redundant arrays of independent disks (RAID) and include disk striping and disk mirroring.

- Sector sparing is an advanced method of fault tolerance.

Chapter Review

1. The first consideration in keeping data safe is to ensure the security of the network _____.

2. Another term for access permissions is _____ - _____ _____.

3. Implementing password-protected shares involves assigning a password to each shared _____.

4. If a share is set up as _____ - _____, users can look at the documents or copy them to their machines, but they cannot change the original documents.

5. Access permission security involves assigning certain _____ on a user-by-user basis.

6. The most efficient way to assign permissions is through the use of _____.

7. Through auditing, selected types of events are recorded in the _____ _____ of a server in order to track network activities by user accounts.

8. A data- _____ utility scrambles data before it goes out onto the network.

9. The Commercial COMSEC Endorsement Program (CCEP) authorizes manufacturers to incorporate classified _____ into the communication systems they sell.

10. Diskless computers communicate with the server and log on through the use of a special ROM boot chip installed on the computer _____ _____ _____.

11. The two most important environmental conditions to monitor are _____ and _____.

12. Proper _____ is required to prevent a computer from overheating.

13. The potential for ESD increases as the humidity _____.

14. True or False: If network cables are installed in the walls and in the ceilings, they will be safe from all damage.

15. A _____ atmosphere with high _____ will most certainly destroy any computer equipment in a matter of days or months.

16. The first line of defense against loss of data is usually a _____ _____ system.

17. It is important to have a regular _____ for backing up data.

18. Maintaining a _____ of all backups is important for later file recovery.

19. When backing up across a network, network traffic can be reduced by placing the backup computer on an isolated _____.

20. Fault-tolerant systems protect data by duplicating data or placing data in different _____ sources.

21. RAID level 0, called _____ _____, divides data into 64K blocks and spreads it equally in a fixed rate and order among all disks in an array.

22. Level 0 disk striping does not offer data _____.

23. Disk _____ duplicates a partition and moves the duplication onto another physical disk so that there are always two copies of the data.

24. Duplexing is intended to protect against disk _____ failures, as well as media failures.

25. Writing complete blocks of data to each disk in the array is known as disk _____.

26. In Windows NT Server, the _____ _____ program is used to configure Windows NT Server fault tolerance.

27. In RAID level 10, data that is contained on a physical drive in one array is _____ on a drive in the second array.

28. "Clustering" is the term applied to a group of _____ systems working together as a single system.

C H A P T E R   1 1

Printing on a Network

About This Chapter

One of the fundamental reasons for networking is to be able to share printers among workstations. Network printers are expensive and draw extensively on electrical resources; however, a single user is likely to require a printer only intermittently. By sharing the printer among many users, considerable savings in cost and energy are achieved. In this chapter, we cover the devices and management of network printers and take a look at fax modems.

Before You Begin

Before starting this chapter, you might find it helpful to review Lesson 1: Introduction to Network Operating Systems, in Chapter 4.

Lesson 1: Network Printing

This lesson presents an overview of the network printing process and describes how a shared printer works within a network operating system.

After this lesson, you will be able to:

- Give an overview of the network printing process.
- Describe the role of print spoolers and queues in network printing.
- Describe the steps required to make a printer available for sharing to the network.

Estimated lesson time: 15 minutes

The Network Printing Process

As shown in Figure 11.1, when network users want to print data on a shared network printer, they send their data to a print server. The server then feeds that data to a shared printer.

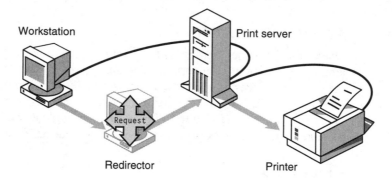

Figure 11.1   Data to be printed goes first to the print server

A *print spooler* is software that intercepts a print job on its way from the application (a word processor, for example) to the printer, and sends it to a print queue. A *print queue* is a buffer where the print job is held until the printer is ready for it.

Network printing occurs in the following four steps.

1. An application formats its document data into a form the printer can use, and sends it out.

2. The computer's redirector sends the data onto the network, where it travels to the print server computer.

3. The print-spooler software on the print server computer places the data in a print queue on the server.

4. The print queue stores the data until the printer is free to print it.

Print queues generally use RAM for storage because it can move data faster than a hard disk can. However, if numerous documents are sent to the printer at once and the queue overflows, the overflow documents will be sent to the print server's hard disk to wait their turn in the queue.

Sharing a Printer

Connecting a printer to a network print server will not, in itself, make the printer available to network users. The printer is a resource on the server, and—like any other resource—it must be shared to the network before anyone can access it. In a server-based network, access to the printer can be controlled in the same way as access to any other resource on the server.

To send print jobs to a printer, users have to be able to identify or see the printer from their computers. In other words, the network operating system (NOS) must provide a way for the printer to contact network computers to identify itself and signal that it is available.

Essential Printer Information

Every NOS has its own version of printer sharing, but each requires the administrator to provide printer drivers and supply the NOS with information about the printer.

These procedures include:

- Loading printer drivers so that the printer can work with the print server.

- Creating a share name for the printer so that other network users are able to recognize and access it.

- Identifying the destination of the output so that the redirector knows where to send the print job.

- Setting information and output format parameters so that the NOS will know how to handle and format the print job.

The Print-Sharing Utility

This process can seem complex, but most network operating systems have utilities to help administrators enter the information. In Windows NT Server, for example, a utility called the Print Manager presents the printer setup screen shown in Figure 11.2.

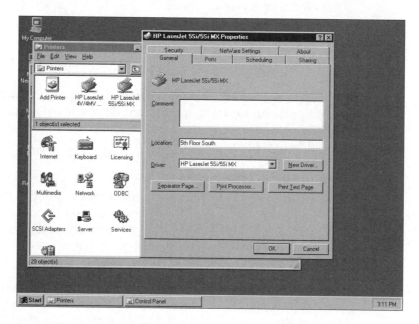

Figure 11.2   Windows NT Print Manager printer setup

Connecting to a Printer

After a printer has been shared, users must use the NOS to connect to it. To do this, users need to know two things:

- The name of the server to which the printer has been connected
- The name of the printer

This explains why the administrator needs to supply a name for the printer during the sharing process. Current computer operating systems, such as Windows, provide a graphical user interface to help users connect to a printer.

To use Windows NT as an example, you can double-click on the server name and select the printer. To connect to the printer on the server, double-click the server icon, and then select the required printer from the list.

Exercise 11.1: Term Definition Review

In this exercise, a list of terms is given in the left column. For each term listed, fill in the definition in the space given in the column to the right.

Term	Definition
Redirection	
Print spooler	
Print queue	
Print-sharing utility	
Share name	
Printer driver	
Print Manager	

Lesson Summary

The following points summarize the main elements of this lesson:

- The redirector is used to direct the print job from the local computer's printer port out to the network.

- A print spooler is software that intercepts a print job and sends it to a print queue.

- A print queue is a buffer in which the print job is held until the printer is ready for it.

- A printer, like files and directories, must be shared on the network before any user can access it.

- Most network operating systems have a utility to help administer the printing process.

Lesson 2: Managing a Shared Printer

Using network printers is a cost-effective strategy. However, a level of management attention is required in order to obtain those benefits. This lesson focuses on how to manage a shared printer.

After this lesson, you will be able to:

- Describe the tasks required to maintain a network printer.
- Manage printer users.

Estimated lesson time: 15 minutes

Printer Management

After a printer has been shared to the network, it needs to be managed and maintained. Printer management tasks encompass two areas of responsibility:

- Maintenance of the printer itself
- Management of the users who access the printer

Printer Setup

Printers connect either directly to a computer's printer port or to the network through a network port device. A network port is much like a stand-alone network interface card. One interface connects to the network, and the other interface connects to the printer. Internal models plug directly into a slot in the printer; external models operate in a compact box slightly larger than a NIC. These require a small, low-voltage power supply to operate. When properly configured, the network port becomes another shared resource on the network. Configuring such devices is the administrator's responsibility.

Printer Maintenance

Maintenance tasks include:

- Supplying the printer with paper and toner.
- Clearing the printer if there is a paper jam.
- Monitoring the printer's output to ensure that print jobs do not back up and overflow the printer's output bin.
- Monitoring the printer's performance and notifying a technician if a serious problem develops.
- Routinely cleaning the printer in accordance with the manufacturer's instructions.

Most of these are routine tasks that can be learned easily. Users generally do not mind doing jobs such as reloading an empty paper tray or even changing the toner if there are clear, systematic instructions for such tasks located near the printer.

However, problems can develop when no single individual is responsible for the printer. It is not unusual for everyone who uses the printer to assume that someone else is taking care of any problems that arise. As a result, simple problems sometimes remain unresolved until a frustrated volunteer decides to take on the responsibility of remedying the situation.

Managing Users

The printer is like any other shared resource. Users must not only be given permission to use it, they must also be assigned a level of permission. (For more information on assigning permissions to network users, see Lesson 1: Making Networks Secure in Chapter 10.)

Users can manipulate print jobs on shared printers. With the appropriate privileges, users can move their print jobs ahead of other users' print jobs in the print queue or delete another user's print job entirely. To avoid user conflicts, it is best to limit the number of users who have these privileges.

The administrator determines which users will have which privileges. Network operating systems provide utilities that the administrator can use to implement appropriate printing permissions. The Windows NT Server Print Manager, for example, features a series of windows, as shown in Figure 11.3, that guide the administrator through the user-management process.

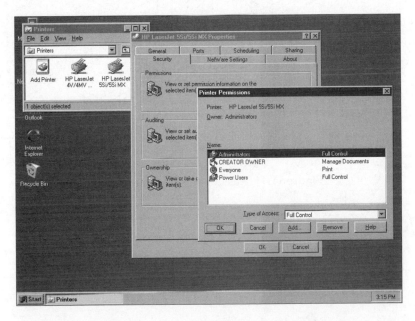

Figure 11.3 Setting user privileges with Windows NT Printer properties

Page-Description Languages (PDLs)

In addition to understanding network printer implementation and maintenance, network administrators should also be aware of any components that affect printer performance or behavior. One of these is called a page-description language (PDL).

PDLs tell a printer how printed output should look. The printer uses the PDL to construct text and graphics to create the page image. PDLs are like blueprints in that they set specifications for parameters and features such as type sizes and fonts, but they leave the drawing to the printer. The Hewlett-Packard Printer Control Language (PCL) is another dominant form of print file formatting.

PDLs and PCLs can have an overall negative effect on network activity because of the large size of files that pass from the application to the printer, even in vector applications. PDL and PCL files are always significantly larger than the equivalent data file—sometimes as much as five times larger. The resulting high volume of network traffic can consume valuable resources.

Managing the Printer Remotely

As shown in Figure 11.4, the administrator does not have to be seated at the print server in order to manage a network printer. Most current NOSs offer utilities that an administrator can use to manage a printer from any computer on the network.

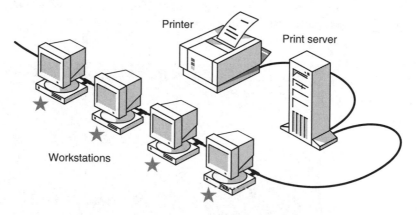

Figure 11.4 An administrator can manage the printer from any network computer

For example, from a remote computer, an administrator can:

- Pause the printer to stop it from printing.
- Delete jobs from the print queue.
- Reorder the jobs in the print queue.

In a small network—one in which all the servers and computers are relatively close together—the ability to direct the printer from a remote location might not seem like an important feature. However, in a large network in which the printer is in one part of a building and the administrator's computer is in another, this feature can be very helpful.

The same utilities used for local printer management are used for remote printer management. The administrator simply chooses the printer to be managed, and the network operating system presents the screens which prompt the administrator through the process.

Lesson Checkup

1. Identify and describe four tasks required for routine printer maintenance.
2. Describe how a network administrator can allocate a single printer's resources among several workstations.
3. Define PDLs and describe their function in printing.

Lesson Summary

The following points summarize the main elements of this lesson:

- Managing a network printer includes maintaining the printer and managing the users who access the printer.
- Managing printer users is similar to managing any other resource on the network; each user must have the appropriate rights and permissions before using the printer.
- Most NOSs offer utilities that allow a printer to be managed from remote computers.

Lesson 3: Sharing Fax Modems

Just like printers, fax modems can be shared to a network. This lesson focuses on sharing a fax modem.

After this lesson, you will be able to:
- Share a fax modem.
- Configure a fax modem for optimum performance.

Estimated lesson time: 10 minutes

Fax Modem Overview

The shared fax server does for fax communication what a shared printer does for printing: it makes fax capabilities available to all users on the network, so that they do not have to leave their desks in order to send a fax. The ability to send a fax from the network can save time and frustration, because users do not have to contend with the uncertainties of a stand-alone fax machine.

A good fax-server service allows an administrator to monitor incoming faxes and route them to the intended recipient, while discarding others, such as advertisements.

Some network fax utilities allow users to link their e-mail addresses to a fax number. This will automatically route faxes to the intended recipient.

Routing Faxes

Faxes arrive at a fax machine with no electronic addressing information; therefore, some thought needs to be given to how they will be routed. Several methods for routing faxes exist. The following list describes some of the available options:

- Faxes can be routed manually—that is, hand-carried to the intended recipient.
- Optical character recognition (OCR) software converts the cover sheet to text and searches for the name of the recipient of the fax.
- Intelligent character recognition (ICR) software converts the cover sheet to text and searches for the name of the recipient of the fax. ICR is slower, but more powerful than OCR.
- T.30 subaddressing is a modified version of the T.30 fax protocol that allows the fax sender to use an extension number that is used to route the fax.
- Novell Embedded Systems Technology (NEST) is similar to T.30 sub-addressing. The fax sender adds an extension phone number when dialing the fax. The extension can be used to route the fax.
- Bar-code routing allows the fax sender to put a bar code on the cover sheet identifying the recipient of the fax.

- Transmission station identification (TSI) routing uses the number of the sender's fax machine to route the fax. The drawback is that all faxes from a certain machine go to the same person.

- Received fax-line routing uses multiple fax lines and modems. All faxes that are received on a given fax line are routed to a particular user or group.

- Direct Inward Dialing (DID) uses a special telephone line (trunk line), provided by the telephone company, which is associated with multiple telephone numbers. When any of these numbers is dialed, the call comes in on the same DID trunk. Before the ring signal is sent, the telephone company sends a special signal down the line, identifying which of the numbers was dialed. In this way, calls can be routed to different numbers, and incoming calls can be routed to the correct person.

Fax-Server Enhancements

The administrator can also purchase software to maximize the fax server. For example, Optus Software's FACSys product provides a fax gateway for Windows NT. This software allows users to send faxes from word-processing packages, databases, spreadsheets, e-mail, and almost any other application. It also provides a dedicated fax server that gives all network users access to the fax server.

FACSys provides both Windows-based and MS-DOS-based interfaces for client computers. It supports HP PCL (Hewlett-Packard Printer Control Language), PCL5, and PostScript with full text, fonts, and graphics. It also provides fully automatic routing of incoming faxes and provides comprehensive activity and status reports. It is compatible with GammaFax, Intel SatisFAXtion, Hayes, JTFax, and other leading fax cards.

FACSys provides complete diagnostics, detailed error reporting, and sophisticated accounting features to make fax servers easy to administer.

Lesson Checkup

1. How does a fax server compare with a shared printer? What are the roles of each?

2. Define the function of a fax server.

3. Describe three enhancements that can be added to a fax server.

Lesson Summary

- A fax server can provide all users on a network with the capability of sending and receiving faxes.

- With a centralized fax service, an administrator can monitor all incoming faxes and route them appropriately.

- Several manufacturers offer software that can be used to enhance the operation of a fax server.

Chapter Summary

The following points summarize the key concepts of this chapter:

Network Printing

- The redirector is used to direct the print job from the local computer's printer port out to the network.

- A print spooler is software that intercepts a print job and sends it to a print queue.

- A print queue is a buffer where the print job is held until the printer is ready for it.

- A printer, like files and directories, must be shared to the network before any user can access it.

- Most network operating systems have a utility to help administer the printing process.

Managing a Network Printer

- Managing a network printer includes maintaining the printer and managing the users who access the printer.

- Managing printer users is similar to managing any other resource on the network; each user must have the appropriate rights and permissions before using the printer.

- Most NOSs offer utilities that allow a printer to be managed from remote computers.

Sharing Fax Modems

- A fax server can provide all users on a network with the capability of sending and receiving faxes.

- With a centralized fax service, an administrator can monitor all incoming faxes and route them appropriately.

- Several manufacturers offer software that can be used to enhance the operation of a fax server.

Chapter Review

1. When network users want to print data on a shared network printer, the data is sent to a _____ that feeds the data to the printer.

2. Each network print job must be _____ away from a computer's local printer port and onto the network cable.

3. The memory buffer in the print server's RAM that holds the print job until the printer is ready is called a _____.

4. In order for users to access a shared printer, they must have a way to _____ the printer.

5. The printer uses the _____ to construct text and graphics to create the page image.

6. Managing users who access printing over a computer network includes assigning _____, as with any other shared network resource.

7. One task an administrator can accomplish from a remote location is to _____ print jobs in the queue.

8. Most current network operating systems allow an administrator to manage a network printer with a _____ - _____ _____.

9. A good fax server service allows an administrator to _____ incoming faxes and to _____ the appropriate one to the proper person.

10. Fax-server enhancements that allow users to send faxes from _____, _____, and _____ are available.

C H A P T E R   1 2

Administering Change

About This Chapter

The chapter begins with a discussion of how to document information about a running network. We look at how, by carefully recording the performance of the network and its components, you can develop a baseline to refer to when assessing problems. Next, following a summary of the upgrading process, we discuss how to evaluate the need for a network upgrade. After examining which components can be upgraded, we offer guidelines for confirming that the network upgrade was successful. The chapter concludes with tips on how to move a network installation.

Before You Begin

A review of Chapter 2, "Basic Network Media," is recommended. It can also help to revisit the earlier chapters of Part II, "Implementing a Network," especially Chapter 8, "Designing and Installing a Network," which covers how to take a network inventory.

Lesson 1: Documenting a Running Network

The principal challenge in implementing a change on any network is to define the existing network and any limitations imposed by its hardware and software configurations. Comprehensive documentation is the key to conducting an effective and economical upgrade for any network. This lesson focuses on how to lay a foundation for making later network changes by documenting the network and looks at some useful tools that can help facilitate the process.

After this lesson, you will be able to:

- Document network components in order to establish a baseline for network performance.
- Identify tools that can help to document a network.

Estimated lesson time: 40 minutes

Documentation

Preparing and maintaining network records are essential tasks that will pay off when you need to implement changes to a network. Up-to-date documentation provides information about how the network should look and perform, as well as where to seek help if there are problems. Documentation developed for maintenance, upgrading, and troubleshooting should contain:

- A map of the entire network, including the locations of all hardware and details of the cabling.
- Server information, including the data on each server and the schedule and locations of backups.
- Software information, such as licensing and support details.
- Essential names and telephone numbers for vendors, suppliers, contractors, and other helpful contacts.
- Copies of all service agreements.
- A record of all problems, their symptoms and solutions, including dates, contacts, procedures, and results.

Documentation should be thorough, well-organized, and stored where it is readily available. While this might seem obvious, it is easy for documentation to be lost or the individual responsible for maintaining these records to leave the organization without training a successor.

Establishing a Baseline

As soon as the network is operational, it is time to establish a *baseline,* which is simply a documentation of the network's normal operating values. The baseline needs to be updated whenever users, hardware, or software are added to or subtracted from the system.

Creating a good inventory and establishing baseline performance values form the basis upon which you can identify future needs for network modification.

The list that follows includes the steps you need to take to document the network:

- Record the model, serial number, and location of the servers, workstations, and routers. Record the warranty information for each device.

- Make a note of where all warranty information is stored. This will be helpful when a product needs servicing or replacement.

- Make a copy of important computer files such as AUTOEXEC.BAT and CONFIG.SYS. Make a complete set of system backup tapes. Copies of important tapes should be kept offsite in a safe deposit box or commercial offsite data storage facility. (See Chapter 10, "Ensuring Network Security," for a discussion of network backup systems.)

- Create a map of your network, noting the approximate distance between the workstations and the server. Make a note of areas where a cable goes through a wall or is placed in the plenum area between the ceiling and the floor above. This will be helpful to network and building architects in planning for future network modifications. Your documentation of cable runs can facilitate building inspections and help to demonstrate compliance with regulations such as fire codes that prescribe rules for cables placed in the plenum area of a building, as depicted in Figure 12.1. (Fire codes are discussed in Chapter 2, Lesson 1: Network Cabling.)

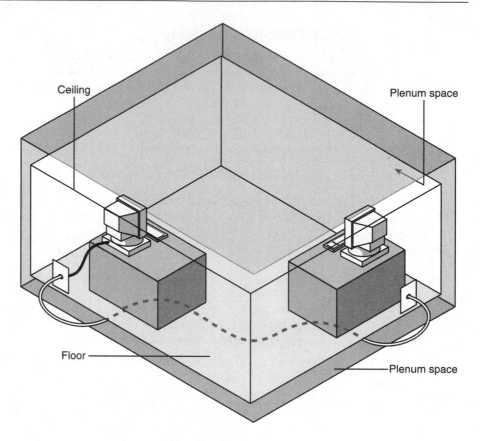

Figure 12.1   The plenum space

Understanding how a healthy network functions is as important as knowing how to solve problems after the network has failed. Monitoring and documenting the network when it is performing well provide baseline measurements against which unusual performance can be compared.

The baseline must be established over time before anything goes wrong. After a baseline exists, all network behaviors can be compared to it as part of the ongoing monitoring process.

The baseline is especially helpful in establishing and identifying:

- Daily network-utilization patterns.
- Bottlenecks.
- Heavy-usage patterns.
- Different protocol traffic patterns.

Documenting Network Performance

After the hardware has been documented and your network is in operation, it is almost time to record the network performance baseline. However, it is best to wait to do this until you have verified that all network connections are correct, all hardware is operational, and any necessary system fine-tuning has been accomplished. When the network's performance has been determined to be acceptable, it is time to record the baseline.

The concept of network performance is a broad one that encompasses the entire network, including:

- Servers.
- Network interface cards (NICs).
- Cable connections to the NICs.
- Hubs.
- Cable runs.
- Routers.
- RJ-45 wall plates.
- Workstation NICs.

A selection of tools is available to help administrators document network performance, including network monitors, protocol analyzers, and other utilities.

Network Monitors

A network monitor is a useful tool that captures and filters data packets and analyzes network activity. It is easy to document the network performance indicators with a network monitor, but it takes extra practice to quickly analyze the network performance statistics. Some network operating systems include network monitoring software among their resources, and a number of other software manufacturers also offer network monitors.

Protocol Analyzers

A protocol analyzer is a tool that keeps track of network statistics. It can capture bad frames and isolate their source. (Data frames are packets of information transmitted as a unit on a network. They are defined by the network's data-link layer and exist only on the wire between network nodes.) A protocol analyzer can be helpful for a company that has a large network with a highly trained staff.

Various protocol analyzers exist. Protocol analyzers can be inexpensive software programs that run on existing networked computers. More advanced and more expensive protocol analyzers are special-purpose portable computers that can be connected to any physical portion of the network to better isolate data-transmission problems.

Packet Internet Groper (Ping)

To test if your network connection is complete from the server to the workstation, you can use a simple utility, the Packet Internet Groper, better known as "ping." The ping utility works by sending a message to a remote computer. If the remote computer receives the message, it responds with a reply message. The reply consists of the remote workstation's IP address, the number of bytes in the message, how long it took to reply—given in milliseconds (ms)—and the length of time-to-live (TTL) in seconds. If you receive back the message "Request timed out," this means that the remote workstation did not respond before the TTL time expired. This might be the result of heavy network traffic or it might indicate a physical disconnection in the path to the remote workstation.

The following is an example of the ping utility:

C:\>Ping 125.55.222.1
Reply from 125.55.222.1: bytes=32 time=100 ms TTL=50
Reply from 125.55.222.1: bytes=32 time=100 ms TTL=50
Reply from 125.55.222.1: bytes=32 time=100 ms TTL=50
Reply from 125.55.222.1: bytes=32 time=100 ms TTL=50

Figure 12.2 shows an example of a ping utility.

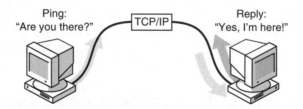

Figure 12.2   Ping utility

Tracert

Another utility that documents network performance is called "tracert." The UNIX equivalent is called "traceroute." While the ping utility merely lets us know that the connection from A to B is complete, tracert informs us of the route and number of hops the packet of data took to arrive at its destination.

Here is a simplified example of a tracert response:

"Tracing route to 100.50.200.10 over a maximum of 30 hops from Widgets in Ozona Fl to Widgets in Seattle WA."

1	125 ms	150 ms	155 ms	Widgets.Ozona.Fl .gte.net
2	160 ms	165 ms	170 ms	BZNet.Memphis.TN
3	175 ms	180 ms	185 ms	Mtnnet Denver. CO
4	190 ms	200 ms	210 ms	Widgets, Seattle.WA mci.net

Run the **c12dem01** video located in the **Demos** folder on the CD accompanying this book to view a presentation of the ping and tracert utilities.

Other Software Tools

There are a variety of utilities available that work with the TCP/IP protocol to document network performance.

Ipconfig

This diagnostic command displays all current TCP/IP network-configuration values. This command is of use on systems running DHCP, allowing users to determine which TCP/IP configuration values have been configured by DHCP.

Winipcfg

A Windows 95 and 98 troubleshooting utility that enables users to access information about TCP/IP and network interface card settings. Winipcfg displays the physical address, IP address, subnet mask, and default gateway settings of the primary TCP/IP NIC (or settings of multiple NICs if more than one is installed).

Netstat

This command is available only if the TCP/IP protocol has been installed. Netstat displays all connections and listening ports, Ethernet statistics, addresses and port numbers, protocol connections and statistics, and the contents of the routing table.

Nbtstat

Nbtstat is available only if the TCP/IP protocol has been installed. It displays protocol statistics and current TCP/IP connections using NetBIOS over TCP/IP. This utility can list:

- A remote computer's name table.
- The remote computer's name table using its IP address.
- The contents of the NetBIOS name cache, giving the IP address of each name.
- Local NetBIOS names.
- Name resolution statistics for Windows networking name resolution.

Nbtstat can also:

- Display both client and server sessions, listing the remote computers by IP address only.
- Display both client and server sessions. It attempts to convert the remote computer IP address to a name using the HOSTS file.

Bottlenecks

Most network activities involve the coordinated actions of several devices. Each device takes a certain amount of time to perform its part of the transaction. Poor performance results when one of these devices uses noticeably more CPU time than the others. The problem device is referred to as a *bottleneck*. Performance monitoring can help identify and eliminate bottlenecks.

Finding bottlenecks is usually an indication that upgrading a portion of the network is necessary. To resolve bottleneck problems, an administrator must be able to identify the devices that are taking more time than they should to perform their tasks. Administrators can use performance monitors, included with the major network operating systems, to identify bottlenecks.

These devices tend to become bottlenecks:

- CPUs
- Memory
- Network cards
- Disk controllers
- Network media

A device becomes a bottleneck for one of the following reasons:

- It is not being used efficiently.
- It is using other resources or CPU time more than it should.
- It is too slow.
- It does not have the capacity to handle the load placed on it.

Proper monitoring will uncover these situations and provide information to help identify the problem component or components.

Documenting Server Performance

Server performance is usually affected by an increase in the number of users who are on the system. Comparing current server performance statistics with your initial baseline information can help you confirm a suspicion that the server is not running as well as it once did. However, your first hint that the server is not performing well is just as likely to come from the end users. Their daily use and familiarity with system response is a good indicator of server performance. (Chapter 13, "Troubleshooting a Network," discusses how to interview users when troubleshooting network problems.)

Performance monitors—software that is included on most operating systems—track server performance on a network and can monitor several system functions, displaying the results in tabular or graphical format. Certain indicators can help locate and isolate problems with server performance, including:

- Demand for server resources.
- Areas of data congestion.
- The activity of an individual process.

A performance monitor can observe the performance of a remote system and alert the system administrator to server conditions that need attention. It can also transfer data from the performance monitor to other performance tools.

Total System Management

As networks have grown in size and complexity, keeping track of an entire system has become more challenging. Because of this, vendors have developed utilities that do for system management what performance monitors have done for system monitoring. These system-wide management applications provide centralized management for distributed systems programs.

System-management software provides centralized administration of computers in a WAN. This service includes:

- Collecting hardware and software inventory information.
- Distributing and installing software.
- Sharing network applications.
- Troubleshooting hardware and software problems.

The system-management software complements other system management utilities found in the network operating system. The examples that follow use Microsoft's Systems Management Server to illustrate these utilities.

Inventory Management   This software collects and maintains an inventory of hardware and software for each computer and stores the inventory in a database. Typical inventory items include the type of CPU, amount of RAM, hard-disk size, operating system, and application software for each component installed.

Software Distribution   After a computer's inventory has become part of the database, a software distribution utility can install and configure new software or upgrade previously installed software directly on a client. This distribution mechanism can also be used to run commands, such as virus scans, on clients. Figure 12.3 shows Microsoft NT Server's Systems Management Server distributing software.

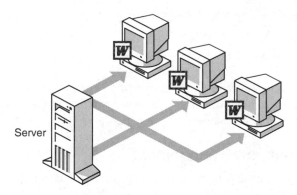

Figure 12.3   Systems Management Server distributes software

Shared Application Management   Shared applications can also be distributed to a server for clients to access. When a user logs on to the network, the management software builds a program folder on each client. See Figure 12.4 for an example. These program folders in turn contain more folders that include the program icons representing the shared applications available to the user. To start the shared application, the user selects an icon from the program folder displayed on the local workstation. (The application is actually stored on the server's hard disk.)

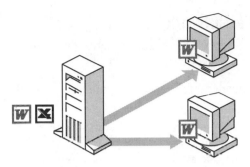

Figure 12.4 Systems Management Server simplifies application sharing

Remote Control and Network Monitor Systems Management Server, shown
in Figure 12.5, provides Help Desk and diagnostic utilities that allow you to
control and monitor remote clients directly. The diagnostic utilities let you view
the client's current configuration. The Help Desk utilities provide direct access
to a remote client.

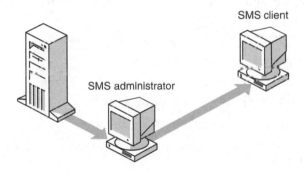

Figure 12.5 Systems Management Server simplifies remote client maintenance

Table 12.1 illustrates the environments supported by Systems Management
Server:

Table 12.1 Environments Supported by Systems Management Server

Environment	Supported
Network operating systems	Windows NT Server 3.51 and later; Windows 2000 Server; LAN Manager 2.1 and later; Novell NetWare 3.1x and 4.*x*; IBM LAN Server 3.0 and 4.0; any network protocol supported by Windows NT Server, including TCP/IP and IPX
Client computers	Windows 3.1 and Windows for Workgroups 3.11; Windows 95 and 98; Windows NT Workstation 3.5 and later; Windows 2000 professional; MS-DOS 5.0 and later; IBM OS/2 2.*x*, and OS/2 WARP; Apple Macintosh (System 7 and later)

Maintaining a Network History

Documenting a network's history is as important as monitoring its real-time performance. A network's written record can:

- Indicate significant performance or equipment issues that real-time monitoring might miss.
- Provide a background against which current information can be compared.

If there is more than one administrator, it is important that they all record in only one shared logbook. This log can become an invaluable guide to future administrators who might need to trace a performance problem or resolve network issues related to system growth as well as equipment, maintenance, and system configuration changes.

This document should record:

- Purchase and installation dates and descriptions.
- Complete descriptive information about key individuals, such as contractors responsible for installation.
- Vendor, model, and warranty information, including serial numbers.
- The installation process and its results.
- The initial and subsequent network configurations.
- Network usage policies and procedures.
- Network resources and drive assignments.
- Copies of crucial network configuration files, such as CONFIG.SYS and .BAT files.
- Any unusual application program configurations.
- Any particular computer, board, or peripheral settings.
- Any problems and their solutions.
- Hardware or software changes.
- Any activities that affect the topology or architecture.

It is important that all network historical documentation be easy to access and easy to read. Graphics or even hand-drawn sketches can be very helpful.

A network's history can be either logged online or in a notebook. Keeping the log in a computer file can cause difficulties, however, especially if the file is stored on a hard disk and the computer or disk crashes. Should such an event occur, this is exactly the type of behavior the log should record.

Lesson Checkup

1. What is a baseline of network performance? Why should you have one? How can you use it to determine if changes should be made to the network?

2. What are network monitors and protocol analyzers? What part do they play in documenting network performance? In what ways can they alert you to degradation of network performance?

3. Should the documentation that makes up a network history include specific information about the network's hardware and software? If so, why?

Lesson Summary

The following points summarize the main elements of this lesson:

- By creating a good inventory and a baseline of performance values, you can establish a benchmark against which to compare network performance in the future and identify any needed modifications.

- A network monitor is used to capture and filter data packets and analyze network activity.

- A protocol analyzer is a tool that is used to track network statistics.

- Ping and tracert utilities are used to confirm network connections.

- The ipconfig utility that displays current TCP/IP network configuration values is useful on systems running DHCP because it allows users to determine which TCP/IP configuration values have been configured by DHCP.

- Identifying network bottlenecks will help to determine what network components need to be upgraded.

- Performance monitors are tools that can be used to track server performance.

- Network operating system manufacturers have created system-management software to aid with monitoring and managing the total system.

- After establishing a baseline, the administrator needs to maintain a history of the network by documenting any subsequent changes and their impact on the system.

Lesson 2: Upgrading a Network

This lesson surveys the process of upgrading a network. Looking first at the network as a whole, then taking different network components in turn, we focus on identifying which components can be upgraded and the benefits to be expected from upgrading each component. We move on to a general discussion of how to upgrade network equipment, and conclude by offering guidelines for confirming that the network-component upgrade was successful.

After this lesson, you will be able to:

- Determine if a network needs to be upgraded.
- Identify which components of a network can be upgraded.
- List the benefits of upgrading given components.
- Distinguish between components that can be upgraded by someone who is not a network professional and those that require installation by a trained technician.
- Identify tools available to confirm the successful upgrade of network components.

Estimated lesson time: 45 minutes

Overview

After you have documented your network, recorded the performance baseline, and identified the need for an upgrade, the next step is to determine which network elements can be upgraded and assess the costs and benefits of doing so.

Note Upgrading a network can be technically challenging. Although this lesson focuses on steps you can take to accomplish and confirm an upgrade, it is important to recognize when to seek outside help. Which kinds of upgrades require professional expertise are identified in this lesson. However, if you experience problems with any components, you should consider contacting the product's manufacturer for help and seek the advice of trained installers, as needed.

Deciding to Upgrade a Network

The addition of new programs and devices to a network is usually a slow process. Therefore, the need to upgrade might not be immediately apparent, but will evolve slowly over time. Documenting network performance and listening to end users will help to determine when the time has come to upgrade the network.

Various factors offer clues that an upgrade might be needed. If your network was configured several years ago, it is possible that the response time of the CPU and network devices are too slow to adequately handle increased user demand and the requirements of new software. In an organization that is using increasingly more powerful software programs, growing demands for resources might necessitate an upgrade. In such a case, the network administrator should refer back to the original network plan to review the types of applications that were initially intended to run on the network. If large multimedia files are being transmitted over a network that was originally designed for simple data entry, a performance problem might develop. Slow data transfer speeds, as shown in Figure 12.6, are usually signs that it is time to upgrade.

Slow
Round trip time = 180ms

Fast
Round trip time = 30ms

Figure 12.6   Slow data and fast data

Upgrading Network Architecture and Media

Many scenarios can lead to the conclusion that an architectural or media upgrade is needed. If a network has been designed as a bus topology and its users are complaining of frequent network crashes, it might be necessary to upgrade to a star or ring topology.

If the original network was strung with copper-based media and devices have been added that create large amounts of electrical interference, it might be necessary to upgrade to fiber-optic media. If the size and number of networked buildings is expanding, again, upgrading to fiber-optic media for the backbone of the network could be a worthwhile investment. Fiber-optic media can also be used for cable runs between remote buildings. If online conferencing or advanced Web-based applications at the desktop are being introduced, the network could also benefit from an upgrade to fiber-optic cable.

There are other factors, such as cost, to consider before making a decision. The price of fiber-optic media is dropping, but the installation of fiber-optic cable requires a trained technician, which is an added expense. Other cost considerations apply during and after installation. The network interface cards, hubs, and other network hardware will need to be upgraded at the same time. New network maintenance expenses are likely to arise that were not incurred with simple, copper-based media.

If the network is to be expanded into a building several blocks away in the inner city, it might be difficult and expensive to install a new cable run. One option is to upgrade to a microwave send-and-receive station between the two buildings. The use of microwave components in a network requires either line-of-sight between the two stations or access to repeaters.

As with all important decisions, you need to consider the negative aspects of any potential upgrade at the same time you look at the benefits. In the case of microwave networking, meteorological conditions merit consideration. Because microwave networking signals pass through the atmosphere, fog, rain, and snow can weaken and distort a microwave signal to the extent that the data becomes unusable.

Upgrading from a Peer-to-Peer to a Server-Based Network

Answering the following preliminary list of questions can help to determine if you should start to plan for a network upgrade to a peer-to-peer network:

- Are you currently in a peer-to-peer network and experiencing problems arising from the fact that everyone has access to secure information?
- Is your organization planning to expand soon?
- Are the users having difficulty administering their own workstations?
- Would you like to add a dedicated file server?
- Does only one person understand how the network operates?

If the answer to any of these questions is "yes," consider upgrading to a server-based network. There is some expense involved, but the network will experience better performance.

An upgrade to a server-based network will provide these benefits:

- The network will be able to handle more users.
- Sensitive data will be secure from unauthorized users.
- A knowledgeable network administrator can assist users.
- Data backups will be easier to schedule and perform.

- The workload of multiple servers can be balanced for better efficiency.
- Servers can be physically isolated for additional security.
- Servers that handle complex tasks can be upgraded for top performance.
- More advanced users can have their network components upgraded for top performance.

As you see, the decision to upgrade is not always easy and straightforward. But by compiling supporting documentation that identifies areas in which system performance needs to improve, network administrators can build the case for appropriate change.

The Server

While server upgrades can be costly and difficult, the advantages will frequently outweigh the disadvantages. If a server is several years old, it might have outlived its usefulness. A new server can be a good information-technology investment. Benefits of upgrading a server include faster processing of requests and the ability to handle more users and run more sophisticated software applications. A server upgrade can consist of a single device or several servers that have been interconnected for increased processing power.

Deciding to Upgrade a Server

The presence of various symptoms can point to the need for a server upgrade. The rest of this section discusses these signs, what they mean, and how to upgrade the server to address them.

To identify and locate causes of reduced system performance, the first step is to compare the initial baseline values with the current values. The place to start is with the component of the server that is taking more time to complete the task than it should. Figure 12.7 shows a server in need of upgrading.

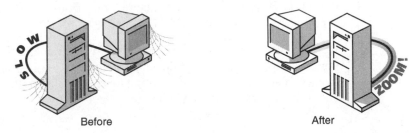

Before   After

Figure 12.7 A server before and after an upgrade

If the server's CPU requires extra time to exchange data between memory and the disks, there might not be enough memory available for the CPU to function efficiently. If the CPU is busy over 80 percent of the time, the CPU or the amount of memory might need to be upgraded. Until recently, the cost of computer memory was very high; consequently, servers were sometimes underconfigured, unable to handle increased user volumes or an increase in the processing power needed for new programs.

The server input/output (I/O) devices can fail gradually. The result is that requests for processor time from the device to the CPU increase. A rise in the frequency of requests might indicate a failing controller, for example. In such a case, what has occurred is that the failing device—unable to have its request fulfilled successfully by the CPU—has interrupted the processor and made another request for processing time. This kind of equipment failure is difficult to diagnose if a graphical history of CPU interrupts has not been recorded. Even if the controller and network cards are not failing, there could be a benefit from upgrading to faster components.

If end users are complaining of slow system response and server components are operating well, the problem might lie in an increase of data received by the server. As new employees are added and the amount of work per employee increases, the maximum capacity of the network throughput might soon be reached. Because network usage can increase slowly, this measurement is important to monitor. Performance-monitoring tools can even check individual disks for excessive activity. When a disk has a slow response due to excess activity, you can balance disk access by moving data to another disk.

Because the cost of servers is falling, and processing power continues to rise, this can present a justification for proposing a general server upgrade. The next step is to look at the tools available to help determine if a network needs to be upgraded. Servers should have enough RAM, disk space, and processing power to allow end users to use their software applications efficiently without having to wait for the server to retrieve, process, or store their information. Time spent waiting for a server to respond quickly adds up.

Despite falling costs, upgrading the server can be one of the most expensive purchases in a network upgrade, so it is important to research the options carefully. A good place to start is by consulting the server's manufacturer for information about the latest products and choices for your network.

How to Upgrade a Server

As computer technology has evolved, so has its ease of use. Until recently, an engineer was needed to set up a medium-sized computer. Today, computers are assembled at the factory and often shipped with an operating system installed on the hard drive. However, setting up any piece of electronic equipment requires an understanding of how to work around electrical components. Hazards still exist, such as the risk of electric shock and accidental damage to the sensitive electronic components in a server.

If you have had experience in setting up and installing personal computers, you will probably be able to install a server. However, while detailed instructions about how to unpack, set up, and connect a server to a network are provided with the new server, you will need a good understanding of how to work with electrical components and the basics of network administration to follow them.

It is also important to avoid damaging sensitive components such as memory modules, CPUs, controllers, and disk drives. Static electric charges can damage these devices. Using a wrist-grounding device or other antistatic equipment will reduce the possibility that a static electric discharge will damage your equipment.

If you are not experienced with staging equipment, it will be best to have a trained technician install the equipment. Some vendors require that one of their employees be present to confirm that the server is operational before they will activate the warranty.

The final step is to use the computer's on-board diagnostic utilities to confirm that the memory and disk drives are operational. Install and configure the server's network operating system, then connect the network interface card (NIC) cable to the network and try to contact a remote host.

Confirming a Server Upgrade

The following sequence of steps will confirm that the server was successfully installed:

- When the server is turned on, the boot sequence diagnostics utility confirms that the memory amount is correct and that the system can recognize all the attached disk drives and devices.

- The server operating system is booted and displays correctly.

- The control panel displays the correct information for internal and external devices.

- It is possible to "ping" a remote host by name and IP address.

The Workstation

Easier to accomplish and less expensive than upgrading the server, workstation upgrades can be a sound investment as user demands on the network increase.

Deciding to Upgrade a Workstation

In a server-based network, the client workstation processes information that has been retrieved from the server. Upgrading a workstation's processor and adding to its RAM and disk capacity can increase the workstation's performance. These upgrades are not usually difficult or expensive.

How to Upgrade a Workstation

A client workstation upgrade is an easy procedure to carry out. Manufacturers include basic information about how to install the component, and device vendors usually have additional information about upgrading, or they offer onsite support.

If the workstation is a recent model, you might want to consider upgrading only the internal components instead of purchasing a new computer. If you are installing a complete replacement workstation, be sure to verify that the new workstation contains the correct version of the client operating system. If you are not upgrading the NIC at this time, you can install the NIC from the old workstation. The steps that apply to a server upgrade also apply to a workstation upgrade:

- Use caution during the staging process.
- Avoid static electric discharge.
- Configure the client version of the network operating system.
- Test for a successful network connection.

Confirming a Workstation Upgrade

Confirming a successful workstation upgrade is similar to confirming a server upgrade. The following sequence of events occurs when you start up a workstation:

- When the workstation is turned on, the boot sequence diagnostic utility displays the correct amount of RAM, and the workstation recognizes all drives and devices.
- The client workstation's operating system boots up correctly.
- The networking operating system diagnostic utilities confirm that the memory and disk drives are operational. Configure the workstation version of the network operating system. The control panel displays the correct information for internal and external devices.

To conclude the workstation upgrade, try to ping a remote host, and log on to the server.

The Network Interface Card (NIC)

Network interface cards are usually upgraded at the time a server is replaced. However, there can be reasons to upgrade NICs at other times as well. This section looks at why and how to upgrade a NIC.

Deciding to Upgrade a NIC

A situation can arise in which, while the server is functioning adequately, the network interface cards are slow, causing a bottleneck of data leaving the server. When the NIC is upgraded, data can move faster from the server to the network media and ultimately to the workstation. Along with the server, the workstation should also have an updated NIC. Upgrading a NIC is not expensive, and the upgrade will result in improved network performance.

How to Upgrade a NIC

Upgrading a NIC is a simple procedure:

- Confirm that the card you are about to install is the correct version for your workstation.
- Read the manufacturer's installation instructions.
- Use antistatic procedures.
- Handle the NIC carefully.
- Line up the pins carefully and connect.
- Check for a successful network connection.

Confirming a NIC Upgrade

If you have either a new workstation or server, you will have to check the network interface card. The procedure for both is the same.

- The NIC should have installed without difficulty.
- The network properties control panel should display the correct information about the NICs.
- You should be able to ping a remote host.

Network Media

While this section offers an overview of how to conduct a network-media (cable runs) upgrade, doing so requires considerable technical expertise and experience. It is strongly recommended that you seek advice from a network professional before undertaking such an upgrade.

Deciding to Upgrade Network Media

If environmental factors, such as electrical interference, are degrading a network's performance, an upgrade is probably needed. The cost for both the media and the installation can be high. Factors can exist that will require different types of media on the same network—for example, a fiber-optic backbone on a 10baseT network.

The network administrator needs to research and identify the various types of media that are available, make a preliminary decision, then consult network professionals before making a final choice for the type and installation of the upgraded network media. The benefit of upgraded network media is faster data transfer and reduction in the number of bottlenecks of data from device to device.

How to Upgrade Network Media

Network media can be upgraded by someone without special training if the media to be used is simple, copper-based cable. If the media is fiber-optic cable, however, a trained installer is required to plan and connect workstations, server, and routers. Wireless networks for a small network can be installed by following the manufacturer's instructions. A trained installer will be needed for more advanced wireless networks or microwave networks.

How to Confirm a Network Media Upgrade

Installation of new media is a big job, but if done properly it should give many years of reliable service. To be sure the installation is correct, check the following:

- The media should be installed without sharp bends or near sources of electromagnetic interference.
- The media should meet or exceed the fire code, especially in the plenum area.
- Connections from the workstation to the routers to the server should be complete.
- The network performance monitor should have normal readings.
- It should be possible to ping a remote host.

Upgrading the Routers, Brouters, Bridges, and Repeaters

Network routers, brouters, bridges, and repeaters can be upgraded to route traffic more efficiently and expand a network. It would be wise to consult a network professional or a router vendor during your research. The efficient use of routers can expand your network and provide increased network traffic throughput.

Planning, installing, and confirming these devices require the services of a trained technician. Although these devices can be very expensive, the placement of a router can add a great deal of throughput for a network. The best way to confirm this upgrade is to have a trained installer perform any diagnostics needed to confirm the complete connection from server to router to workstation. One of the tools the installer will use is ping.

Exercise 12.1: Case Study Problem

You have been assigned to upgrade a network for a small manufacturer. Its network has been in place since 1989. Only minor upgrades or same-model equipment replacements have occurred. The network is configured as peer-to-peer, and there is no file server. The media is coaxial thicknet cable (Standard Ethernet). The network computers are 386-33 PCs. The operating system is Windows for Workgroups 3.11. The company uses shareware word-processing applications and spreadsheets as its office software.

The company would like to upgrade to a server-based network. It is adding office space to the building and would like to rewire the network with flexible, inexpensive media. The company is about to begin using new, powerful design software in its manufacturing process.

What do you recommend for the upgrade?

Lesson Summary

The following points summarize the main elements of this lesson:

- If a network server's CPU is busy over 80 percent of the time, the CPU or the amount of memory in the server might need to be upgraded.

- Performance-monitoring tools can check individual disks for excessive activity. When a disk has a slow response due to excess activity, disk access can be balanced by moving data to another disk.

- If a network has been designed as a bus topology and its users are experiencing frequent network crashes, it might be necessary to upgrade to a star or ring topology.

- The three elements of a server that need to be considered for upgrading are memory (RAM), disk space, and processing power.

- The benefits of upgrading a server are faster processing and the ability to handle more users and run more sophisticated software.

- Upgrading a NIC can increase the speed at which a server or workstation can access a network, thus improving performance.

- Upgrading network media can be expensive, but can improve the speed and performance of an older network.

- To install a new NIC card, you need to follow the same procedures as installing any other expansion card.

- Installing new media for a network can require the expertise of a professional installer. This is especially true if you need to upgrade to fiber optics or wireless systems.

- Upgrading routers, brouters, repeaters, and bridges requires a trained technician.

- When an upgrade is complete, it is necessary to confirm the changes.

- The best way to confirm a working NIC is to use the ping utility to ping the host or another workstation.

Lesson 3: Moving a Network

Moving a network is a challenging task and a major one, requiring careful and systematic planning. This lesson discusses how to plan, conduct, and test a network move.

After this lesson, you will be able to:

- Plan a network move.
- Identify the factors required to successfully move a network.
- Describe how to confirm a network move.

Estimated lesson time: 20 minutes

Planning the Move

Moving a network uses your skills in network planning, installation, maintenance, and troubleshooting. While this lesson offers a general outline of how to plan and move a network, depending on the complexity of the network and the length of the move, it might be best to use professional movers.

Planning is the key to moving a network successfully. However, that plan has to be communicated to the users in advance so that they know what to expect, especially if the network will be down for several days. How long the network can afford to be down is an important factor in planning and timing the move. If the network cannot afford any downtime, it will be necessary for the new network to be operational before the old one is disconnected. In such a scenario, there will need to be duplication of equipment at the old and new sites. The new network components will need to be set up and tested before the network goes live.

It can help to prepare a checklist of questions to identify tasks and establish an orderly and sequential timetable for the move. The person responsible for carrying out each task should be identified.

Questions to ask during the planning phase include:

- When will the new site be available?
- When is the target move date?
- When will the data be backed up before the move?
- Who will back up the data?
- Is the existing equipment attached to the floor or a wall?
- At what time will all users be disconnected from the old network?
- Who will be responsible for turning off the old system?
- How much cable is needed?
- Who will install the new cable? Are professional computer uninstallers/installers needed?
- Who will confirm that the cable runs meet local building codes?
- Will lifting equipment be needed to move the server?
- Are vehicles available to transport the equipment?
- Is the power supply adequate in the new building?
- Are the appropriate power outlets installed?
- Will there be someone on call to troubleshoot if the network fails to start?
- Is there a source from which equipment replacements can be purchased if anything is damaged?
- Who will turn on the new network?
- Who will test the workstations?
- How will the network be tested after the move?

Making the Move

To move a network as efficiently as possible requires coordination of people and equipment. If the network can afford to be down for two or three days, it will not be necessary to have an identical system running at the new location during the move.

The following tasks outline the steps that need to be taken to move a network. An assumption has been made that the new facility has the new network media in place.

- Notify users in advance of when the system will not be available.
- Encourage end users to make backups of their hard drives. The backups should be made to removable media or to a server that will not be involved with the initial relocation.
- Ask end users to label the peripheral device cables connected to the back of their workstations with the type of devices to which they are attached—for example, the printer, scanner, modem, and network cable.
- Ask end users to disconnect their workstations from the power source and to disconnect peripheral device cables from the backs of their workstations.
- Ask end users to leave the peripheral device cables attached to devices and place the cables on top of the devices.
- Arrange for the equipment movers to supply a table on wheels on which to place the workstations and devices during the move from the desktop to the truck.
- Secure the equipment to be moved with plenty of shipping blankets and cushioning between devices. Do not stack more than a couple of devices high, especially if the original shipping containers are not available.
- Place the devices and backup media in an area away from magnetic fields and motors.
- Upon arrival at the new facility, use the table on wheels to transport the devices from the truck to the desktop.
- Install the peripheral device cables to the workstation.
- Turn on the peripheral devices and network connection.
- Turn on the workstations.
- Install the server.
- Inform the end users when the system will be available.

When moving a network for which down time is not possible, the new facility must be fully operational before the old network is turned off.

Verifying the Network After the Move

Computers and peripheral devices operate well for years when they are left in place. When devices are moved, however, the danger that internal and external components will be damaged increases.

After the network has been moved and the devices have been installed, the next step is to confirm that the network and all the devices are communicating.

Where Downtime Is Acceptable

For a network that can afford to be nonoperational for several days, the following guidelines apply for verifying the move:

Servers

The server can be backed up, turned off, disconnected, packed, shipped, unpacked, connected, turned on, restored and tested in a few hours. The boot sequence diagnostics and the control-panel settings should be used to confirm that the server has the same configuration as before the move. A remote host should be pinged to confirm the network is operational, and a network monitor should be used to confirm that the throughput of data is adequate.

Workstations

The workstation should be connected to all peripherals and to the network. Another computer on the network and a different subnet of the network, if there is one, should be pinged. Workstation control-panel settings should be confirmed as correct.

NICs

The NICs can be checked during installation of the server and workstation. Check the network-interface settings within the network operating system software. Ping a remote host. Check the network monitor for data throughput problems.

Network Media

It is likely that the new network media will be in place before the hardware is relocated. Therefore, you have an opportunity to test the media by installing two workstations and pinging them from various locations within the new network. Use the network monitor before and after the relocation to confirm that the network is operating correctly.

Where Downtime Is Unacceptable

The procedures described in the following section should be followed for a network that cannot afford downtime.

Servers

The server on the new network must be staged, installed, configured, and tested before the old network is turned off. The old and new networks will run in tandem for a brief period. When the performance of the new servers and network is satisfactory, the old server can be turned off and migrated to the new network as needed.

Workstations

All workstation components in the new network must be set up and tested before the old network is turned off. The old network workstations should be migrated to the new network as needed.

NICs

The new network must be set up and tested before the old network can be turned off. The NIC for the workstation and the server should be tested before the old and new networks run in tandem.

Network Media

The network media should be installed and tested before the relocation date. The network monitor should be used before, during, and after the move to confirm that the network is operating correctly.

Exercise 12.2: Case Study Problem

You have been assigned to move your company's file server, 10 workstations, and two printers to a new office 500 miles away. The new office has been wired for the new network. Management has told you that the new network must be operational before the old one is turned off, because the business cannot afford any downtime. However, there will be no additional equipment purchased for the new office.

Can this network be moved without any downtime? If so, how? If not, what is your plan for relocating this network?

Lesson Summary

The following points summarize the main elements of this lesson:

- Planning is the key to successfully moving a network.

- For a long or complicated move, it can be best to use professional movers.

- When a network will be down for several days, it is important to communicate to the users the plans for the move and what they can expect and when.

- If the network cannot afford any downtime, the new network will have to be fully operational before the old network is turned off.

- All hardware and software must be verified before the network is turned over to the users.

Chapter Summary

The following points summarize the key concepts of this chapter:

Documenting a Running Network

- By creating a good inventory and a baseline of performance values, you can establish a benchmark against which to compare network performance in the future and identify any needed modifications.

- A network monitor is used to capture and filter data packets and analyze network activity.

- A protocol analyzer is a tool that is used to track network statistics.

- Identifying network bottlenecks will help to determine what network components need to be upgraded.

- Ping and tracert utilities are used to confirm network connections.

- Performance monitors are tools that can be used to track server performance.

- Network operating system manufacturers have created system-management software to aid with monitoring and managing the total system.

- After establishing a baseline, the administrator needs to maintain a history of the network by documenting any subsequent changes and their impact on the system.

Upgrading a Network

- If a network server's CPU is busy over 80 percent of the time, the CPU or the amount of memory in the server might need to be upgraded.

- Performance-monitoring tools can check individual disks for excessive activity. When a disk has a slow response due to excess activity, disk access can be balanced by moving data to another disk.

- If a network has been designed as a bus topology and its users are experiencing frequent network crashes, it might be necessary to upgrade to a star or ring topology.

- The three elements of a server that need to be considered for upgrading are memory (RAM), disk space, and processing power.

- The benefits of upgrading a server are faster processing, the ability to handle more users, and the ability to run more sophisticated software.

- Upgrading a NIC can increase the speed at which a server or workstation can access a network, thus improving performance.

- Upgrading the network media can be expensive, but can improve the speed and performance of an older network.

- To install a new NIC card, you need to follow the same procedures as installing any other expansion card.

- Installing new media for a network can require the expertise of a professional installer. This is especially true if you need to upgrade to fiber optics or wireless systems.

- Upgrading routers, brouters, repeaters, and bridges requires a trained technician.

- When an upgrade is complete, it is necessary to confirm the changes.

- The best way to confirm a working NIC is to use the ping utility to ping the host or another workstation.

Moving a Network

- Planning is the key to successfully moving a network.

- For a long or complicated move, it can be best to use professional movers.

- When a network will be down for several days, it is important to communicate to the users the plans for the move and what they can expect.

- If the network cannot afford any down time, the new network will have to be fully operational before the old network is turned off.

- All hardware and software must be verified before the network is turned over to the users.

Chapter Review

1. Monitoring and documenting the network when it is in good working order provide a _____ against which unusual network performance can be compared.

2. A network _____ is a tool that captures and filters data packets and analyzes network activity.

3. _____ and _____ are utilities that are used to test the network connections by sending a packet to a remote host and monitoring its return.

4. During monitoring of network performance, _____ can indicate areas of poor performance that can benefit from upgrading.

5. Many network vendors provide a _____ _____ _____ software to aid in the monitoring and improvement of network performance.

6. After creating a baseline for a network's performance, you will need to maintain a performance _____ to aid with future troubleshooting.

7. To improve the performance of a network, an administrator can upgrade _____, _____, _____ and _____.

8. When working on electronic components, be careful to prevent _____ _____ _____ that will do damage to the components.

9. Installing a new NIC is the same as installing any _____ card.

10. Upgrading routers, brouters, repeaters, and bridges is best carried out by a _____ _____.

11. The final step in any network upgrade is to _____ the upgrade.

12. The best tool to use to confirm hardware changes to a network is the _____ utility.

13. How long the network can afford to be _____ is an important factor in organizing and timing a move.

C H A P T E R   1 3

Troubleshooting a Network

About This Chapter

This chapter surveys the basics of network troubleshooting and teaches strategies for how to isolate, identify, prioritize, and resolve problems. After problems have been diagnosed, the next step is to locate the tools you need to solve them. In Lesson 2 we review the tools used to monitor networks for obvious and potential problems.

Network problems can be complex and sometimes require outside help to resolve. We conclude by surveying sources that offer expert assistance for network troubleshooting.

Before You Begin

It will be helpful to review Chapter 7, "Elements of Network Connectivity," and Chapter 12, "Administering Change," before starting this chapter.

Lesson 1: Understanding the Problem

This lesson aims to give you the tools you need to become a skilled network problem solver. If you approach a network problem with a plan of action, the cause and resolution will be easier to find. Here, you will learn to apply a structured approach to divide a network into functional units and then identify the problem.

After this lesson, you will be able to:

- Prepare a plan of action to research a network problem.
- Conduct the research needed to isolate the problem.
- Use a structured approach to identify a network problem.
- Identify the severity of a network problem based on its initial symptoms.

Estimated lesson time: 30 minutes

Troubleshooting

Troubleshooting is perhaps the most difficult task that computer professionals face. Added to the need to get to the bottom of a problem afflicting the network is the pressure to do so as quickly as possible. Computers never seem to fail at a convenient time. Failures occur in the middle of a job or when there are deadlines, and pressures to fix the problem immediately are intense.

After a problem has been diagnosed, locating resources and following the procedures required to correct the problem are straightforward. But before that diagnosis occurs, it is essential to isolate the true cause of the problem from irrelevant factors.

Troubleshooting is more of an art form than an exact science. However, to be efficient and effective as a troubleshooter, you must approach the problem in an organized and methodical manner. Remember that you are looking for the cause, not its symptoms; yet frequently, problems as originally reported are just symptoms and not the true cause. As a troubleshooter you need to learn to quickly and confidently eliminate as many alternative causes as possible. This will allow you to focus on the things that might be the cause of the problem. To do this, you must take a systematic approach.

The process of troubleshooting a computer network problem can be divided into five steps.

Step 1: Defining the Problem

The first phase is the most critical, yet most often ignored. Without a complete understanding of the entire problem, you can spend a great deal of time working on the symptoms, without getting to the cause. The only tools required for this phase are a pad of paper, a pen (or pencil), and good listening skills.

Listening to the client or network user is your best source of information. Remember that while you might know how the network functions and be able to find the technical cause of the failure, those operating the network on a daily basis were there before and after the problem started and probably recall the events that led up to the failure. By drawing on their experience with the problem, you can get a head start on narrowing down the possible causes. To help identify the problem, list the sequence of events, as they occurred, before the failure. You might want to create a form with these questions (and others specific to the situation) to help organize your notes.

Some general questions to ask might include:

- When did you first notice the problem or error?
- Has the computer recently been moved?
- Have there been any recent software or hardware changes?
- Has anything happened to the workstation? Was it dropped or was something dropped on it? Were coffee or soda spilled on the keyboard?
- When exactly does the problem or error occur? During the startup process? After lunch? Only on Monday mornings? After sending an e-mail message?
- Can you reproduce the problem or error? If so, how do you reproduce the problem?
- What does the problem or error look like?
- Describe any changes in the computer (such as noises, screen changes, disk activity lights).

Users—even those with little or no technical background—can be helpful in collecting information if they are questioned effectively. Ask users what the network is doing or not doing that makes them think it's not functioning correctly. User observations that can be clues to the underlying cause of a network problem include the following:

- "The network is really slow."
- "I cannot connect to the server."
- "I was connected to the server but I lost the connection."
- "One of my applications will not run."
- "I cannot print."

As you continue to ask questions, you can begin to narrow your focus, as the following list illustrates:

- Are all users affected or only one?

  If only one user has a problem, the user's workstation is probably the cause.

- Are the symptoms constant or intermittent?

  Intermittent symptoms are a sign of failing hardware.

- Did the problem exist before an operating system upgrade?

  Any change in operating system software can cause new problems.

- Does the problem appear with all applications or only one?

  If only one application causes problems, focus on the application.

- Is this problem similar to a previous problem?

  If a similar problem occurred in the past, there might be a documented solution.

- Are there new users on the network?

  Increased traffic can cause logon and processing delays.

- Is there new equipment on the network?

  Check to verify that new network equipment has been correctly configured.

- Was a new application installed before the problem occurred?

  Installation and training issues can cause application problems.

- Has any of the equipment been moved recently?

  The moved equipment might not be connected to the network.

- Which manufacturers' products are involved?

  Some vendors offer telephone, online, or onsite support.

- Is there a history of incompatibility among certain vendors and certain components such as cards, hubs, disk drives, software, or network operating software?

  There might be a documented solution on the vendor's Web site.

- Has anyone else attempted to solve this problem?

  Check for documented repairs and ask coworkers about attempted repairs.

Step 2: Isolating the Cause

The next step is to isolate the problem. Begin by eliminating the most obvious problems and work toward the more complex and obscure. Your purpose is to narrow your search down to one or two general categories.

Be sure to observe the failure yourself. If possible, have someone demonstrate the failure to you. If it is an operator-induced problem, it is important to observe *how* it is created, as well as the results.

The most difficult problems to isolate are those which are intermittent and that never seem to occur when you are present. The only way to resolve these is to re-create the set of circumstances that cause the failure. Sometimes, eliminating causes that are not the problem is the best you can do. This process takes time and patience. The user also needs to keep detailed records of what is being done before and when the failure occurs. It can help to tell the user to refrain from doing *anything* with the computer when the problem recurs, except to call you. That way, the "evidence" won't be disturbed.

While the information collected provides the foundation for isolating the problem, the administrator should also refer to documented baseline information to compare with current network behavior. In Chapter 12, "Administering Change," we learned how to document a network by creating a baseline. Now it is time to put that knowledge to work. Rerun tests under the same set of conditions as prevailed when you created the baseline, then compare the two results. Any changes between the two can indicate the source of the problem.

Information gathering involves scanning the network and looking for an obvious cause of the problem. A quick scan should include a review of the documented history of the network to determine if the problem has occurred before and, if so, whether there is a recorded solution.

Step 3: Planning the Repair

After you have narrowed your search down to a few categories, the final process of elimination begins.

Create a planned approach to isolating the problem based on your knowledge at this point. Start by trying out the most obvious or easiest solution to eliminate and continue toward the more difficult and complex. It is important to record each step of the process; document every action and its results.

After you have created your plan, it is important to follow it through as designed. Jumping ahead and randomly trying things out of order can often lead to problems. If the first plan is not successful (always a possibility), create a new plan based on what you discovered with the previous plan. Be sure to refer to, reexamine, and reassess any assumptions you might have made in the previous plan.

After you have located the problem, either repair the defect or replace the defective component. If the problem is software-based, be sure to record the "before" and "after" changes.

Step 4: Confirming the Results

No repair is complete without confirmation that the job has been successfully concluded. You need to make sure that the problem no longer exists. Ask the user to test the solution and confirm the results. You should also make sure that the fix did not generate new problems. Be sure to confirm not only the problem you fixed, but also that what you have done has not had a negative impact on any other aspect of the network.

Step 5: Documenting the Outcome

Finally, document the problem and the repair. Recording what you've learned will provide you with invaluable information. There is no substitute for experience in troubleshooting, and each new problem presents you with an opportunity to expand that experience. Keeping a copy of the repair procedure in your technical library can be useful when the problem (or one like it) occurs again. Documenting the troubleshooting process is one way to build, retain, and share experience.

Remember that any changes you have made might have affected the baseline. You might need to update the network baseline in anticipation of future problems and needs.

Segmenting the Problem

If the initial review of network statistics and symptoms does not expose an obvious problem, dividing the network into smaller parts to isolate the cause is the next step in the troubleshooting process. The first question to ask is whether the problem stems from the hardware or the software. If the problem appears to be hardware-based, start by looking at only one segment of the network, then looking at only one type of hardware.

Check the hardware and network components including:

- NICs.
- Cabling and connectors.
- Clients/workstations.
- Connectivity components such as repeaters, bridges, routers, brouters, and gateways.
- Hubs.
- Protocols.
- Servers.
- Users.

Often, isolating or removing a portion of the network will help to get the rest of the network up and operational again. If removing a portion solved the problem for the rest of the network, the search for the problem can be focused on the part that was removed.

Network protocols require special attention because they are designed to bypass network problems and attempt to overcome network faults. Most protocols use what's known as "retry logic," in which the software attempts an automatic recovery from a problem. This becomes noticeable through slow network performance as the network makes new and repeated attempts to perform correctly. Failing hardware devices, such as hard drives and controllers, will use retry logic by repeatedly interrupting the CPU for more processing time to complete their task.

When you are assessing hardware performance problems, use the information obtained from the hardware baselines to compare against the current symptoms and performance.

Isolating the Problem

After you have gathered the information, rank the list of possible causes in order, beginning with the most likely and moving to the least likely cause of the problem. Then select the most likely candidate from the list of possible causes, test it and see if that is the problem. Start from the most obvious and work to the most difficult. For example, if you suspect that a faulty network interface card (NIC) in one of the computers is the cause of the trouble, replace it with a NIC that is known to be in good working order.

Setting Priorities

A fundamental element in network problem solving is setting priorities. Everyone wants his or her computer fixed first, so setting priorities is not an easy job. While the simplest approach is to prioritize on a "first come, first served" basis, this does not always work, as some failures are more critical to resolve than others. Therefore, the initial step is to assess the problem's impact on the ability to maintain operations. For example, a monitor that is gradually getting fuzzy over several days would have a lower priority to address than the inability to access the payroll file server prior to a check run.

Exercise 13.1: Troubleshooting Problem

Given the following scenario, describe how you would research, identify, prioritize, and resolve this network problem:

The network has been running well at the site of a small manufacturer. However, a user in the quality control division now calls to report that she is unable to get the daily status reports printed by the printer in the department. Meanwhile, the shipping department reports that a rerouted print job did not print in the quality control department. What is your strategy for solving this network problem?

Lesson Summary

The following points summarize the main elements of this lesson:

- It is essential to take a structured approach to troubleshooting in order to resolve network problems.

- Collecting information lays the foundation for isolating a problem.

- Asking users the right questions will provide the most information. Use open-ended questions.

- The troubleshooting process includes five steps: defining the problem, isolating the cause, making the repair, confirming the solution, and documenting the outcome.

- If the cause of a problem is not obvious, divide the network into logical groups such as clients, NICs, hubs, cabling and connectors, servers, connectivity components, and protocols, and check each separately.

- Repairing network problems sometimes requires working on several problems at once. Because it is not possible to repair everything at the same time, you will need to establish priorities.

- The network administrator should establish the priorities that affect the integrity of the network.

Lesson 2: Troubleshooting Tools

Troubleshooting network problems is often accomplished with the help of hardware and software. To troubleshoot effectively, you need to know how these tools can be used to solve network problems.

After this lesson, you will be able to:

- Name the principal hardware tools used to troubleshoot network problems and identify which hardware tool to use on a particular part of the network.
- Identify software-based monitoring tools.
- Identify the components that each monitor tool checks.
- Describe the methods for monitoring a network.
- Describe the tools used for troubleshooting a network problem.

Estimated lesson time: 30 minutes

Hardware Tools

Hardware tools were once very expensive and difficult devices to use. They are now less expensive and easier to operate. They are helpful to identify performance trends and problems. This section describes the most common of these tools.

Digital Voltmeters

The digital voltmeter (volt-ohm meter) is the primary all-purpose electronic measuring tool. It is considered standard equipment for any computer or electronic technician and can reveal far more than just the amount of voltage passing through resistance. Voltmeters can determine if:

- The cable is continuous (has no breaks).
- The cable can carry network traffic.
- Two parts of the same cable are exposed and touching (thereby causing shorts).
- An exposed part of the cable is touching another conductor, such as a metal surface.

One of the network administrator's most important functions is to confirm source voltage for the network equipment. Most electronic equipment operates on 120 volts AC. But not all outlets will meet these requirements. In older installations, especially in large industrial areas, the system load can drop voltages to as low as 102 volts. Operating for long periods at low voltages can cause electronic equipment problems. Low voltages often cause intermittent faults. At the other end, voltage that is too high can cause immediate damage to the equipment. In new construction, it is possible for circuits to be wired incorrectly and actually put out 220 volts AC.

Note With any new location or new construction, it is important to check the outlet voltages before connecting any electronic equipment in order to verify that they are within an acceptable range.

Time-Domain Reflectometers (TDRs)

Time-domain reflectometers (TDRs), as shown in Figure 13.1, send sonar-like pulses along cables to locate breaks, shorts, or imperfections. Network performance suffers when the cable is not intact. If the TDR locates a problem, the problem is analyzed and the results are displayed. A TDR can locate a break within a few feet of the actual separation in the cable. Used heavily during the installation of a new network, TDRs are also invaluable in troubleshooting and maintaining existing networks.

Figure 13.1   Time-domain reflectometer

Using a TDR requires special training, and not every maintenance department will have this equipment. However, administrators need to know the capabilities of TDRs in case the network is experiencing media failure and it is necessary to locate a break.

Advanced Cable Testers

Advanced cable testers work beyond the physical layer of the OSI reference model (described in Chapter 5, "Introducing Network Standards") in the data-link layer, network layer, and even the transport layer. They can also display information about the condition of the physical cable.

Other Hardware Tools

Several other versatile hardware tools can serve as useful aids to network troubleshooting.

Crossover Cables

Crossover cables are used to connect two computers directly with a single patch cable. Because the send and receive wires are reversed on one end, the send wire from one computer is connected to the receive port on the other computer. Crossover cables are useful in troubleshooting network connection problems. Two computers can be directly connected, bypassing the network and making it possible to isolate and test the communication capabilities of one computer, rather than the whole network.

Hardware Loopback

A hardware loopback device is a serial port connector that enables you to test the communication capabilities of a computer's serial port without having to connect to another computer or peripheral device. Instead, using the loopback, data is transmitted to a line, then returned as received data. If the transmitted data does not return, the hardware loopback detects a hardware malfunction.

Tone Generator and Tone Locator

Tone generators are standard tools for wiring technicians in all fields. A tone generator is used to apply an alternating or continuous tone signal to a cable or a conductor. The tone generator is attached to one end of the cable in question. A matching tone locator is used to detect the correct cable at the other end of the run.

These tools are also able to test for wiring continuity and line polarity. They can be used to trace twisted-pair wiring, single conductors, and coaxial cables, among others. This pair of equipment is sometimes referred to as "fox and hound."

Oscilloscopes

Oscilloscopes are electronic instruments that measure the amount of signal voltage per unit of time and display the result on a monitor. When used with TDRs, an oscilloscope can display:

- Shorts.
- Sharp bends or crimps in the cable.
- Opens (breaks in the cable).
- Attenuation (loss of signal power).

Software Tools

Software tools are needed to monitor trends and identify network performance problems. This section describes some of the more useful of these tools.

Network Monitors

Network monitors are software tools that track all or a selected part of network traffic. They examine data packets and gather information about packet types, errors, and packet traffic to and from each computer.

Network monitors are very useful for establishing part of the network baseline. After the baseline has been established, you will be able to troubleshoot traffic problems and monitor network usage to determine when it is time to upgrade. As an example, let's assume that after installing a new network, you determine that network traffic is utilized at 40 percent of its intended capacity. When you check traffic, one year later, you notice that it is now being utilized at 80 percent capacity. If you had been monitoring it all along, you would have been able to predict the rate of increased traffic and predict when to upgrade before failure occurs.

Protocol Analyzers

Protocol analyzers, also called "network analyzers," perform real-time network traffic analysis using packet capture, decoding, and transmission data. Network administrators who work with large networks rely heavily on the protocol analyzer. These are the tools used most often to monitor network interactivity.

Protocol analyzers look inside the packet to identify a problem. They can also generate statistics based on network traffic to help create a picture of the network, including the:

- Cabling.
- Software.
- File servers.
- Workstations.
- Network interface cards.

Protocol analyzers have built-in TDRs, discussed in the previous section.

The protocol analyzer can provide insights and detect network problems including:

- Faulty network components.
- Configuration or connection errors.
- LAN bottlenecks.
- Traffic fluctuations.
- Protocol problems.
- Applications that might conflict.
- Unusual server traffic.

Protocol analyzers can identify a wide range of network behavior. They can:

- Identify the most active computers.
- Identify computers that are sending error-filled packets. If one computer's heavy traffic is slowing down the network, the computer should be moved to another network segment. If a computer is generating bad packets, it should be removed and repaired.
- View and filter certain types of packets. This is helpful for routing traffic. Protocol analyzers can determine what type of traffic is passing across a given network segment.
- Track network performance to identify trends. Recognizing trends can help an administrator better plan and configure the network.
- Check components, connections, and cabling by generating test packets and tracking the results.
- Identify problem conditions by setting parameters to generate alerts.

Network General Sniffer

Sniffer, which is part of a family of analyzers from Network General, can decode and interpret frames from 14 protocols including AppleTalk, Windows NT, NetWare, SNA, TCP/IP, VINES, and X.25. Sniffer measures network traffic in kilobytes per second, frames per second, or as a percentage of available bandwidth. It will gather LAN traffic statistics, detect faults such as beaconing, and present this information in a profile of the LAN. Sniffer can also identify bottlenecks by capturing frames between computers and displaying the results.

Novell's LANalyzer

The LANalyzer software performs much the same function as Sniffer but is available only on a NetWare LAN.

 Run the **c13dem01** video located in the **Demos** folder on the CD accompanying this book to view a demonstration of network troubleshooting tools.

Monitoring and Troubleshooting Tools

After a network has been installed and is operational, the administrator needs to make sure it performs effectively. To do this, the administrator will need to manage and keep track of every aspect of the network's performance.

Network Management Overview

The scope of a network management program depends on:

- The size of the network.
- The size and capabilities of the network support staff.
- The organization's network operating budget.
- The organization's expectations of the network.

Small peer-to-peer networks consisting of 10 or fewer computers can be monitored visually by one support person. However, a large network or WAN might need a dedicated staff and sophisticated equipment to perform proper network monitoring.

One way to ensure that the network does not fail is to observe certain aspects of its day-to-day behavior. By consistently monitoring the network, you will notice if any areas begin to show a decline in performance.

Performance Monitors

Most current network operating systems include a monitoring utility that will help a network administrator keep track of a network's server performance. These monitors can view operations in both real time and recorded time for:

- Processors.
- Hard disks.
- Memory.
- Network utilization.
- The network as a whole.

These monitors can:

- Record the performance data.
- Send an alert to the network manager.
- Start another program that can adjust the system back into acceptable ranges.

When monitoring a network, it is important to establish a baseline, as discussed in Chapter 12, "Administering Change." This documentation of the network's normal operating values should be periodically updated as changes are made to the network. The baseline information can help you identify and monitor dramatic and subtle changes in your network's performance.

Network Monitors

Some servers include network monitoring software. Windows NT Server, for example, includes a diagnostic tool called Network Monitor, shown in Figure 13.2. This tool gives the administrator the ability to capture and analyze network data streams to and from the server. This data is used to troubleshoot potential network problems.

The packets of data in the data stream consist of the following information:

- The source address of the computer that sent the message.

- The destination address of the computer that received the frame.

- Headers from each protocol used to send the frame.

- The data or a portion of the information being sent.

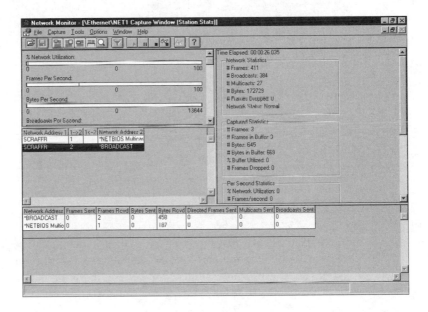

Figure 13.2   Windows NT Network Monitor

Simple Network Management Protocol (SNMP)

Network management software follows standards created by network equipment vendors. One of these standards is the simple network management protocol (SNMP).

In an SNMP environment, illustrated in Figure 13.3, programs called "agents" are loaded onto each managed device. The agents monitor network traffic in order to gather statistical data. This data is stored in a management information base (MIB).

SNMP components include:

- Hubs.
- Servers.
- NICs.
- Routers and bridges.
- Other specialized network equipment.

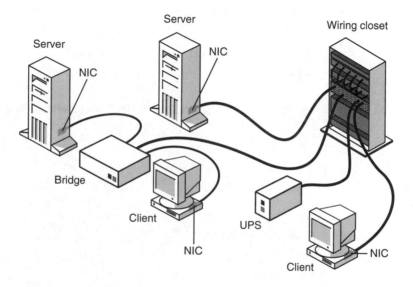

Figure 13.3   SNMP environment showing components

To collect the information in a usable form, a management program console regularly polls these agents and downloads the information from their MIBs. After the raw information has been collected, the management program can perform two more tasks:

- Present the information in the form of graphs, maps, and charts
- Send the information to designated database programs to be analyzed

If any of the data falls above or below thresholds set by the manager, the management program can notify the administrator by means of alerts on the computer or by automatically dialing a pager number. The support staff can then use the management console program to implement changes in the network.

Lesson Checkup

1. The _____ _____ is the primary all-purpose electronic measuring tool used by computer and electronic technicians.

2. _____ - _____ _____ send sonar-like pulses along cables to locate breaks, shorts, or imperfections.

3. _____ are electronic instruments that measure the amount of signal voltage per unit of time and display the results on a monitor.

4. In a crossover cable, the send wire from one computer is connected to the _____ port on the other computer.

5. Protocol analyzers, also called "network analyzers," perform _____ - _____ network traffic analysis using packet capture, decoding, and transmission data.

6. A _____ _____ can help to establish a network's information baseline.

7. A network monitor allows the administrator to capture and analyze network _____ _____ to and from the server.

Lesson Summary

The following points summarize the main elements of this lesson:

- Hardware tools are used to identify network problems, network-performance trends, and to help isolate network malfunctions.

- The most common tool for troubleshooting hardware is the digital voltmeter.

- A time-domain reflectometer (TDR) can be used to find breaks, shorts, or imperfections in network cabling.

- Oscilloscopes are used with TDRs to display precise measurements of voltage and time.

- Network monitors track all or a selected part of network traffic, while protocol analyzers perform real-time network traffic analysis.

- Network General Sniffer can decode and interpret frames from 14 protocols.

- Novell's LANAnalyzer works like Sniffer, but is limited to NetWare.

- The scope of a network management program depends on the size of the network, the capability of the staff, the organizational budget, and the expectations of the users.

- Several monitoring utilities are available to manage network performance. Among these are performance monitors, network monitors, and network management protocols.

Lesson 3: Where to Find Help

If a network problem is beyond the scope of the administrator's knowledge, it is time to seek outside help. Assistance can be sought from coworkers, from sources providing CD-based information, or online. Knowing where to locate the best information resources will help speed up the problem-solving process.

After this lesson, you will be able to:

- Describe sources for network troubleshooting information.
- Identify the best source to help solve a given problem.
- Identify Internet services that offer network-troubleshooting support.

Estimated lesson time: 30 minutes

Network Support Resources

It is as important to know when and where to get support in resolving network problems as it is to give support to others. With the proliferation of hardware, software, protocols, and standards, it is impossible for any network administrator to know everything. This is especially true with the constant product changes being made by network manufacturers and suppliers. Network support resources can be found in a wide range of locations—from coworkers, manufacturer and vendor help desks to CD-based technical references. Software products, online support services, print materials, and telephone-based support services offer additional resources. Obtaining access to several resources is the key to successful network troubleshooting.

TechNet

Microsoft Technical Information Network (TechNet) provides information to support all aspects of networking with an emphasis on Microsoft products. Figure 13.4 shows a sample of a TechNet screen. With Microsoft KnowledgeBase you can find up-do-date articles on many topics and learn about the latest software releases, updates, and revisions.

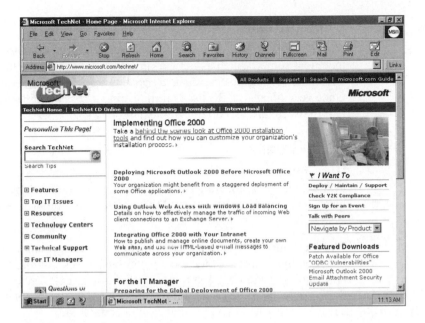

Figure 13.4 Sample TechNet content screen

Installing TechNet

TechNet's compact disc installs just like any other program. When installed, it adds icons to the appropriate program group for easy access.

There are several methods of locating the information you need on TechNet. The TechNet Find tool is an efficient choice. Refer to the Help menu on the CD for more information on using the various features of TechNet.

Subscribing to TechNet

On-line information about Microsoft TechNet can be found at: www.microsoft.com/technet/subscription/about.htm.

The on-line version of TechNet can be found at: www.microsoft.com/technet/

You can subscribe to TechNet by calling: (800) 344-2121

Bulletin Board System (BBS)

Numerous electronic bulletin board systems (BBSs) exist that are devoted to technical subjects such as networking. You can access the knowledge of experienced networking professionals by posting troubleshooting questions to them. Once very popular, BBS use is diminishing and is being replaced by the Internet and the Web, discussed later in this lesson.

User Groups

User groups are a good source of information. There is a wealth of knowledge available at group meetings. Some meetings are held online; at others, groups meet in person. User groups tend to be organized around a particular operating system or hardware platform.

The local addresses or Internet addresses for user groups can be found online or listed on the premises of local computer businesses. Joining a local user group can be beneficial, allowing you to establish a link to colleagues in your area. Through these contacts, you can learn how others have solved problems resembling yours, as well as problems you have not yet encountered.

Periodicals

Networking technology is in a constant state of evolution. There are many books available on networking, but they quickly become outdated. Network industry periodicals are often a better resource because they provide you with the most current information available. Many periodicals and related resources are also available through the Internet.

LAN Magazine, published monthly, features a regular section called "Tutorial." Each tutorial focuses on an important network topic and presents it as an instructional guide to the subject rather than as a news story.

It can be helpful to maintain a catalog of articles from various periodicals. Cut out or copy articles from the periodical, assign them an identification number, and store them in a notebook. Then, using a simple database program, create an index of identification numbers, subjects, and key words. The next time you encounter a problem, you can search the database and then retrieve the article.

The Internet: A Worldwide Resource

The Internet is a source of a wide selection of information that can help those responsible for network—network administrators or support engineers—to perform their jobs. The Internet gives users access to information ranging from the latest technologies to product information to troubleshooting help.

Internet Overview

The Internet is a worldwide collection of networks, gateways, servers, and computers linked together using a common set of telecommunications protocols. The Internet provides worldwide access to vast stores of information resources that are easily accessible from universities, government organizations, the military, libraries, and other private and public organizations.

The Internet evolved from a U.S. Department of Defense project, the Advanced Research Projects Agency Network (ARPANET), which was designed as a test for packet-switching networks. The protocol used for ARPANET was TCP/IP, which continues to be used on the Internet today.

Internet Services

Today the Internet is growing tremendously along with the services it provides. Some of the best-known services available on the Internet today include:

- The World Wide Web.
- File Transfer Protocol (FTP) servers.
- Electronic mail.
- News.
- Telnet.

The World Wide Web

The World Wide Web (the Web) contains a vast storehouse of hypertext documents written using the Hypertext Markup Language (HTML), Extensible Markup Language (XML), and Standard Generalized Markup Language (SGML), among others. Hypertext is a method for presenting text, images, sound, and videos that are linked together in a nonsequential web of associations. The hypertext format allows the user to browse through topics in any order. Internet tools and protocols help to locate and transport resources between computers.

Most of today's network and electronics manufacturers maintain Web sites. While the primary function of these sites is to promote sales, most also offer connections to various levels of technical support. At the very least, a good corporate Web site will have:

- FAQs (Frequently asked questions and answers).
- Updated technical information about their products.
- Updated software drivers (if their products use them).
- E-mail addresses to which users can write to get answers to questions.

Some of the better sites will contain a complete, searchable knowledge base. Within this database is technical information collected about present and past products.

Becoming familiar with the Web sites of network manufacturers can greatly expand your resources for network maintenance, upgrading, and troubleshooting.

Domain Name System (DNS)

Every computer on the Internet has a unique IP address. The IP address is four sets of digits separated by dots (such as 198.46.8.34).

Because these strings of numbers are hard to remember and difficult to accurately type, the domain name system (DNS) was created. Domain names enable short, alphabetical names to be assigned to IP addresses to describe where a computer is located. In the example, http://www.microsoft.com, the domain name is www.microsoft.com. A Web site with a recognizable or memorable name will receive more hits than a site with an unimaginative name. Domain names can represent the corporate identity, as is the case with Amazon.com, or become part of it, as is the case with cnn.com.

In Microsoft Windows NT Server the HOSTS and LMHOSTS files are configuration files that are responsible for name resolution. The HOSTS file resolves host names to IP addresses, and the LMHOSTS file resolves NetBIOS names to IP addresses. Both are ASCII files that can be edited with Microsoft Notepad or any other plain-text editor.

The last three characters of the DNS or UNC address indicate the type of domain.

Examples of domain types common in the United States include the following:

- Commercial organizations: .com
- Educational institutions: .edu
- Governmental organizations (except the military): .gov
- Military organizations: .mil
- Network service providers: .net
- Organizations (such as nonprofit groups): .org

Examples of international domain designations include the following:

- Australia: .au
- France: .fr
- United Kingdom: .uk
- United States: .us

Internet Names

Every resource on the Internet has its own location identifier or Uniform Resource Locator (URL). The URLs specify the server to access as well as the access method and the location.

A URL consists of several parts. The simplest version contains:

- The protocol to be used.
- A colon.
- The address of the resource.

The address begins with two forward slashes. Aside from using forward slashes rather than backslashes, this is very similar to the universal naming convention (UNC) format. The address below is the entry for accessing the Microsoft World Wide Web server. The "http:" indicates the protocol you use. The rest of the entry, //www.microsoft.com, is the address of the computer.

http://www.microsoft.com

The entry below shows how to access the Microsoft FTP server. In this case, you are using the FTP protocol.

ftp://ftp.microsoft.com

File Transfer Protocol (FTP)

The most common protocol used for sending files between computers is the File Transfer Protocol (FTP). FTP support is one method of supporting remote networks. FTP servers can provide vast amounts of information stored as files. The data in these files cannot be accessed directly; instead, the entire file must be transferred from the FTP server to the local computer. This file-transfer program is for TCP/IP environments and is implemented at the Application layer of the OSI model.

FTP allows for transferring both text and binary files. Figure 13.5 shows a client screen for FTP.

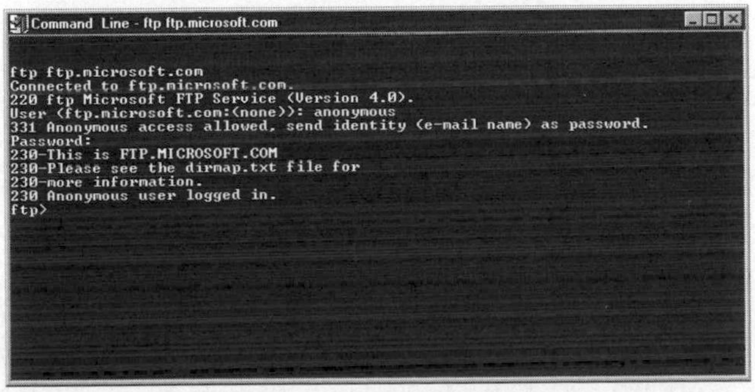

Figure 13.5   Character-based FTP client screen

Microsoft Windows NT, Windows 95 and 98, and Windows 2000 include the traditional character-based FTP client. This is one of the utilities that is copied onto the system when the TCP/IP protocol suite is installed. In addition, most Internet browsers such as Opera, Netscape, and Microsoft Internet Explorer support FTP and use it to transfer files.

When you seek to download files from manufacturers' Web sites, they will often refer you to their FTP sites. The reason for this is that FTP is much faster and better for file transfers and it keeps their Web site open for other users.

Electronic Mail (E-mail)

Electronic mail (e-mail), the sending and receiving of electronic messages, is currently one of the most popular activities on the Internet. E-mail is a staple on most commercial online services and—for many people—is the primary reason for getting onto the Internet or subscribing to an online service.

To send e-mail, you must know the recipient's e-mail address. These addresses are composed of the user's identification, followed by the @ sign, followed by the location of the recipient's computer. For example, the e-mail address of the President of the United States is president@whitehouse.gov. The last three letters indicate this location is a government-sponsored domain on the Internet.

When you access the Internet through a local service provider or one of the large commercial online services, you can exchange e-mail without incurring the expense of a long-distance telephone call. E-mail has the added advantage of allowing you to access messages at your convenience. You can also send an identical message to multiple recipients at one time.

News

Network News Transfer Protocol (NNTP) is an Internet standard protocol defined for distribution, inquiry, retrieval, and posting of news articles. Network News (USENET) is a popular use of NNTP. It offers bulletin boards, chat rooms, and Network News. Network News is a massive system with over 5000 ongoing conferences, called newsgroups, conducted 24 hours a day, 365 days a year. To access these newsgroups, download a special program from the Internet that allows you to participate in any newsgroup you want. Most commercial browsers, including the Microsoft Internet Explorer, have this capability built in. You then "subscribe" to the newsgroups that interest you and communicate through a message system similar to e-mail. The difference between Network News and e-mail is that with Network News, conversations take place in a public forum called a newsgroup.

You can simply view an ongoing dialog without participating; this is called "lurking" and is encouraged for newcomers. To enter a conversation, you post an article in the newsgroup and become part of the forum. As with e-mail, Network News is usually informal communication with little distillation of content. Network News operates at a very high speed, with postings appearing quickly and continuously.

Group administrators set the length of time that messages can remain posted before being deleted from the system. Most do not keep postings longer than a week.

Discussion groups and chat rooms can be excellent sources of information and assistance on technical issues.

Telnet

Telnet was one of the first Internet protocols developed and can be used to act as a remote terminal to an Internet host. When you connect to an Internet host, your computer acts as if your keyboard is attached to the remote computer. Figure 13.6 shows a typical Telnet screen. You can run programs on a computer on the other side of the world, just as if you were sitting in front of it.

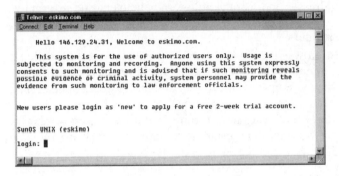

Figure 13.6   Telnet screen

This terminal/host system evolved from UNIX character-based systems in the early days of the Internet. Microsoft Windows 95 and 98, Windows NT, and Windows 2000 install a Telnet program as part of the TCP/IP utilities. This program allows you to act as either a VT-52 or VT-100 terminal to a system accessible by means of TCP/IP, including computers reached by means of the Internet.

Internet Sites

Many companies offer various types of support through Internet sites. For example, Microsoft maintains an Internet server that recognizes FTP. The FTP server contains product information, drivers, and other features for the network administrator or technician.

An administrator can turn to these sites for help with network problems. These include services that often provide information that will help you solve your particular network problem. These subscription support services are available through companies such as Microsoft.

Locating Resources

Today, network vendors have Web sites that serve as important resources for network troubleshooters. If you do not know the URL for your vendor, try typing in *vendorname*.com. If that does not work, use a search engine to look for the company name. Be sure to look through all the results; the information you seek might not be on the first page of the results. If your search yields hundreds or thousands of results, try refining the search. Most sites have instructions on how to narrow your search to the item you want. And finally, if you do not get the results you are seeking, try a different search engine.

Locating resources on the Internet is possible because each resource on the Internet has an address. The programs known as browsers use these resource addresses and search engines to help users find information on a specific topic.

Browsers

To browse the Web you need a graphical interface called a Web browser. Some common Web browsers are Mosaic, Netscape, and Microsoft Internet Explorer. Once you have your browser and an Internet connection, accessing the Internet is fairly straightforward. Because so much information is provided on so many sites, search sites have proliferated to help users access the wealth of information that continues to appear on the Internet. To access them, all you need is their URL. Some of the more common search sites are:

- AltaVista   http://www.altavista.com
- Deja   http://www.deja.com
- Google   http://www.google.com
- GoTo   http://www.goto.com
- HotBot   http://www.hotbot.com
- InfoSeek   http://infoseek.go.com
- Lycos   http://www.lycos.com
- Netscape Search http://home.netscape.com
- Yahoo!   http://www.yahoo.com

Making an Internet Connection

In order to access servers on the Internet, your computer needs to be connected to the Internet WAN. Figure 13. 7 illustrates making an Internet connection.

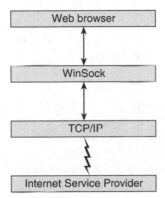

Figure 13.7   Making an Internet connection

There are currently two basic ways to physically connect to the Internet. The first is through dial-up lines, which you learned about in Chapter 7, Lesson 2: Connection Services. This is the most widely used method. The second method for connecting to the Internet is an ISDN connection, also discussed in Chapter 7, Lesson 2.

Dial-Up

There are several variations on the dial-up account, that provide different capabilities, depending on the protocols used. All these connections require the Internet Protocol, and are, therefore, called IP accounts. The three types of IP accounts are: Point-to-Point Protocol (PPP), Serial Line Internet Protocol (SLIP), and CSLIP, which is a compressed version of SLIP. PPP is the emerging connection of choice because it is faster and more reliable than other IP account types. But PPP is also more complex, so many computer platforms still only have built-in support for SLIP. Supplemental programs are being developed to enable most platforms to support PPP accounts. In addition to the increased flexibility of PPP, it also offers a dynamic allocation of IP addresses similar to Dynamic Host Configuration Protocol (DHCP), which makes logging on to the service simpler than having you provide a valid IP address. With a SLIP account, an automated script is generally used to make logging on more automatic.

With both SLIP and PPP, the provider gives you a temporary IP address on the Internet and you can run any WinSock program (a program written to follow the Windows sockets specifications) on it. This includes graphical Web browsers such as Mosaic, Netscape, or Microsoft Internet Explorer.

Commercial online services, such as the Microsoft Network and America Online, often make a WinSock/PPP access method available either as part of their service or as an additional service for a supplemental fee.

ISDN

Integrated Services Digital Network (ISDN), covered in Chapter 7, "Elements of Network Connectivity," is a telecommunications service that connects networks through digital lines using a terminal adapter. ISDN provides a faster connection and can be more economical than dial-up service, if it is offered in your local area code. In the future, ISDN boards designed to support ISDN connections through the personal computer will be commonplace.

Considerations

Theoretically, both the dial-up and the ISDN methods can connect single-user accounts or multiple-user accounts to the Internet. Dial-up accounts are probably most affordable for individual users, but ISDN provides a more economical solution (where available) for LANs, which connect multiple users at a specific location to the Internet.

If you connect directly to the Internet or are directly connected to a service provider, the computers on the Internet are essentially a part of your WAN, which means that you can access them directly. One issue to be aware of with this is that you are also accessible to them, which can lead to potential security concerns. For this reason, it is common for organizations using a direct connection to set up a special machine, called a proxy agent, to act as a gateway between their local network and the Internet. The proxy agent filters requests over the gateway and makes it more difficult for unauthorized requests to reach the local network.

Lesson Checkup

1. Microsoft _____ provides information to support all aspects of networking with an emphasis on Microsoft products.

2. The Web, FTP, e-mail, news, and telnet are all services that are available on the _____.

3. An IP address consists of _____ sets of digits separated by dots.

4. The domain types for commercial organizations, educational institutions, government organizations, military organizations, network service providers, and organizations are _____, _____, _____, _____, _____, _____.

5. Every Uniform Resource Locator (URL) consists of the _____, a colon (:), and the _____ of the resource.

6. The most common protocol used for sending files between computers is the

   _____ _____ _____.

7. An e-mail address is composed of the user's _____, followed by the ____ sign, followed by the _____ of the recipient's computer.

8. The difference between Network News and e-mail is that with Network News, conversations take place in a _____ _____ called a newsgroup.

9. The telnet protocol allows your computer to act as a _____ _____ to an Internet host.

Lesson Summary

The following points summarize the main elements of this lesson:

- Network technology is constantly evolving. Knowing when and where to get help is an important part of being an effective network administrator.

- Useful sources of help include bulletin board services, user groups, and periodicals.

- Joining a local user group can provide the contacts needed to solve problems.

- Internet services include WWW, FTP, e-mail, news, and Telnet.

- Dial-up lines and ISDN connections are two methods by which to physically connect to the Internet.

Chapter Summary

The following points summarize the key concepts of this chapter:

Understanding the Problem

- It is essential to take a structured approach to troubleshooting in order to resolve network problems.

- Collecting information lays the foundation for isolating a problem.

- Asking the users the right questions will provide the most information. Use open-ended questions.

- The troubleshooting process includes five steps: defining the problem, isolating the cause, making the repair, confirming the solution, and documenting the outcome.

- If a problem is not obvious, it will be necessary to divide the network into logical groups such as clients, adapters, hubs, cabling and connectors, servers, connectivity components, and protocols.

- Repairing network problems sometimes requires working on several problems at once. Because it is not possible to repair everything at the same time, you will need to establish priorities.

- The network administrator should establish the priorities that affect the integrity of the network.

Troubleshooting Tools

- Hardware tools are used to identify network problems, network-performance trends, and to help isolate network malfunctions.

- The most common tool for troubleshooting hardware is the digital voltmeter.

- A time-domain reflectometer (TDR) can be used to find breaks, shorts, or imperfections in network cabling.

- Some advanced cable test equipment can display message-frame counts, excess collisions, late collisions, error-frame counts, congestion errors, and beaconing.

- Oscilloscopes are used with TDRs to display precise measurements of voltage and time.

- Network monitors track all or a selected part of network traffic, while protocol analyzers perform real-time network traffic analysis.

- Network General Sniffer can decode and interpret frames from 14 protocols.

- Novell's LANalyzer works like Sniffer, but is limited to NetWare.

- The scope of a network management program depends on the size of the network, the capability of the staff, the organizational budget, and the expectations of the users.

- Several monitoring utilities are available to manage network performance. Among these are performance monitors, network monitors, and network management protocols.

Where to Find Help

- Network technology is constantly evolving. Knowing when and where to get help is an important part of being an effective network administrator.

- Useful sources of help include bulletin board services, user groups, and periodicals.

- Joining a local users group can provide the contacts needed to solve problems.

- Internet services include WWW, FTP, e-mail, news and Telnet.

- Dial-up lines and ISDN connections are two methods by which to physically connect to the Internet.

Chapter Review

1. To isolate a network problem, the engineer can divide the network into
   _____.

2. A TDR sends _____ -like pulses along a cable looking for any kind
   of a break, short, or imperfection that might affect network performance.

3. Protocol analyzers look inside the _____ to determine the cause of
   a problem.

4. Advanced cable testers will tell you if a particular cable or _____ is causing
   problems.

5. One reason it is important to monitor network performance is to provide
   essential information for _____ detection.

6. Windows NT Server Performance Monitor helps a network administrator
   view operations in both _____ time and _____ time.

7. In an SNMP environment, programs called _____ monitor network
   traffic.

8. A _____ monitor is a tool that is used to track network
   performance.

9. Windows NT Performance Monitor has the ability to send an _____
   to the network manager when there is a problem.

10. Windows NT Server Network Monitor gives the administrator the ability to
    _____ and _____ network data streams to and from
    the server.

11. The best source of information for Microsoft products is
    _____.

12. Other useful sources of information for network troubleshooting include
    _____, _____ _____, and _____.

13. _____ is used to perform simple file transfers on the Internet.

14. _____ _____ _____ _____
    is an Internet standard protocol defined for distribution, inquiry, retrieval, and
    posting of news articles.

15. You can use _____ to act as a remote terminal to an Internet host.

16. In addition to URLs, every computer on the Internet has a unique _____
    address.

Appendixes and Glossary

Appendix A contains the questions and answers from the Lesson Checkups, Exercises, and Chapter Reviews from the book. Many of these answers are suggestions. Remember that often there can be more than one workable solution to a problem.

Appendix B, "Common Network Standards and Specifications," contains a summary of standards, specifications, and standard-setting organizations that preside over aspects of computer networking.

The glossary includes definitions of key networking terms used in the book.

A P P E N D I X   A

Questions and Answers

Chapter 1: Introduction to Networking

Lesson 1: What Is a Network

Lesson Checkup

Page 11

1. What is a computer network?

   A computer network is a system in which a number of independent computers are linked together to share data and peripherals, such as hard disks and printers.

2. What are three advantages of using a computer network?

   Three advantages of using a computer network are the ability to share information (or data), to share hardware and software, and to centralize administration and support.

3. Give two examples of a LAN configuration.

   The most basic version of a LAN is two computers that are connected by a cable. An example of a more complex LAN is hundreds of connected computers and peripherals scattered throughout a large organization, such as a municipality. In both cases, the LAN is confined to a limited geographic area.

4. Give two examples of a WAN configuration.

   Because a WAN has no geographical limitations, it can connect computers and other devices in separate cities or on opposite sides of the world. A multinational corporation with linked computers in different countries is using a WAN. Probably the ultimate WAN is the Internet.

Lesson 2: Network Configuration

Lesson Checkup

Page 22

1. List three factors that can influence the choice of whether to implement a peer-to-peer or server-based network configuration.

   Three factors that can influence the choice of whether to implement a peer-to-peer or server-based network configuration are the size of the organization, the level of security required, and the type of business being conducted.

   Other factors include the level of administrative support available, the amount of network traffic, the needs of the network users, and the network budget.

2. Describe the advantages of a peer-to-peer network.

   Peer-to-peer networks are relatively simple and inexpensive. They require no dedicated servers and no administrators, and are connected by a simple, easily visible cabling system.

3. Describe the advantages of a server-based network.

   Server-based networks have a number of advantages over peer-to-peer networks. They can accommodate a larger number of users; they have servers which can be specialized to accommodate the expanding needs of users; and they offer greater security. Server-based networks also support e-mail systems along with application and fax servers.

Exercise 1.1: Case Study Problem

Page 39

1. Which type of network would you suggest for this company?

   - Peer-to-peer
   - Server-based

   There is no completely right or wrong answer to this problem, but a server-based network is suggested. Although there are only seven people in the entire company at present, and thus a peer-to-peer network seems adequate, the company is experiencing growth. Additionally, some of the information that will be sent over the network is confidential. It is better to invest in a server-based network that can accommodate growth and provide centralized security than to choose a peer-to-peer network that growth will render obsolete in a year or two.

2. Which network topology would be most appropriate in this situation?
   - Bus
   - Ring
   - Star
   - Mesh
   - Star bus
   - Star ring

   There is no single correct answer. The most commonly installed networks currently are the star bus and the bus. A hub-centered star bus seems to be the best choice because of the ease of troubleshooting and reconfiguration. Although a bus network might be chosen for its low cost or ease of installation, it does not offer the centralized troubleshooting or administrative advantages of a hub. A ring is probably more complex than is necessary for this network.

Exercise 1.2: Troubleshooting Problem

Page 41

1. Why are problems arising concerning who has which document? Suggest at least one reason.

   The network has clearly outgrown the friendly, trusting, give-and-take style of the workgroup. The number of new users, the undefined nature of their responsibilities on the network, and the increased traffic of network-intensive applications make the peer-to-peer approach inadequate.

2. What one change could you make that would give you centralized control of the access to these documents?

   Add a dedicated server and administrator, and implement a network operating system that can provide extensive, centralized security.

3. Describe one change that your solution will bring to the users' operating environment.

   Changing from peer-to-peer to server-based networking will disrupt the organization's routine, present everyone with the challenge of adjusting to a new communications milieu, and change the entire personality of the work environment. However, the change is required in order for the organization to network successfully. This is why planning is so important in implementing a network. Network planners need to stay current with evolving networking technologies, anticipate future changes in the number of devices, and make purchasing decisions that are cost-effective.

Exercise 1.3: Network Planning Problem/Part 1

Page 42

The following answer pertains to Questions 1 through 8:

An appropriate choice between peer-to-peer and server-based networking can be made only after careful consideration of:

- **The projected number of users**
- **The users' need for access to data**
- **Network management**
- **The number of computers acting as servers**

A server-based network imposes a greater cost than a peer-to-peer network because at least one of the computers on the network is dedicated to serving data, applications, or both. But a server-based network also makes the best use of a centralized, coherent administration of resources. This centralized administration can regulate access to data, making it secure.

Exercise 1.3: Network Planning Problem/Part 2

Page 43

The following answer pertains to Questions 1 through 5:

If some of your servers are going to support more than one of these applications and the number of users is large (25 users or more), you should consider adding more servers and dedicating them to specialized tasks.

Some of these tasks, such as database, e-mail, or application serving, can be resource-intensive. Each of these often requires its own server in order to provide acceptable performance. Other server tasks, such as user directories and general data storage, are not usually so demanding of resources and may be combined on a single computer. And some tasks, such as backup, are usually scheduled in such a way that their impact on network performance occurs during periods of low network activity.

Exercise 1.3: Network Planning Problem/Part 3

Page 44

The following answer pertains to Questions 1 through 10:

Choosing an appropriate topology for your network is often difficult. The most common network being installed today is the star bus, but that might not meet your needs. There are several criteria you can use—based on the information you generated in Part 3 of the Network Planning Problem— to help you make this decision. Again, there is no *one* completely correct choice.

- **If you need an extremely reliable network with redundancy built in, you might want to consider either a ring or a star-wired ring network.**
- **There are at least three considerations involved in estimating the cost of implementing a certain topology:**
  - **Installation**
  - **Troubleshooting**
  - **Maintenance**
- **Eventually, topology translates into cabling, and the installation phase is where theoretical topology meets the real world of the actual network. If cost is an overriding factor, then perhaps you should choose the topology that you can install at the lowest cost.**
- **Ninety percent of the cost of wiring is applied to labor. Anytime cabling has to be permanently installed in any kind of structure, the initial cost multiplies rapidly because of the high cost of labor and expertise.**
- **When a network requires installing cable in a structure, a star bus is usually less expensive to install than a bus. To illustrate this, imagine the task of wiring a large building for a bus network. Then, imagine what it would take to reconfigure that network six months later to add eight new computers. Finally, imagine how much more economically and efficiently those same operations could be performed if the installation were a star bus.**
- **For a small network (5–10 users), a bus is usually economical to install initially but may be expensive to maintain because troubleshooting and reconfiguring take time. However, on a larger network (20 or more users), installing a star bus may cost more initially than installing a bus, owing to the cost of the equipment (a hub); but a star bus will be significantly less expensive to maintain in the long run.**
- **Finally, if there is installed network cabling that you can reuse, you might choose the existing topology if it meets your needs.**

Exercise Summary

Page 45

Based on the information generated in the three parts of this Network Planning Problem, your network components should be:

Type of network:

server-based

Type of topology:

Star

Chapter Review

Page 48

1. Describe the difference between a LAN and a WAN.

   A LAN, or local area network, is the basic building block of any computer network. It can consist of a simple network (two computers connected by a cable and sharing information) or up to several hundred computers connected and sharing information and resources. A LAN has geographical limits, but a WAN has no geographical limits. A WAN can connect several departments within the same building or buildings on opposite sides of the world. Today, the ultimate WAN is the World Wide Web.

2. What are the two basic network configurations?

   The two basic network configurations are peer-to-peer and server-based.

3. A primary reason for implementing a network is to _____ resources.

   share

4. Name three key resources often shared on a network.

   There are many resources to be shared on a network; among them are printers, scanners, applications, files, and network access to the World Wide Web.

5. In a peer-to-peer network, each computer can act as a _____ and a _____.

   server, client

6. What is the function of a server in a server-based network?

   A server provides services and resources to the network.

7. A peer-to-peer network is adequate if _____ is not an issue.

   security

8. Network professionals use the term _____ to refer to the network's physical layout.

   topology

9. The four basic topologies are the _____, _____, _____, and _____ topologies.

   bus, star, ring, and mesh

10. In a bus topology, all the computers are connected in a series. To stop the signals from bouncing, it is important that a _____ be connected to each end of the cable.

    terminator

11. In a _____ topology all segments are connected to a centralized component called a _____.

    star, hub

12. In a _____ topology, a break anywhere in the cable will cause the entire network to go down.

    bus

13. The most reliable as well as the most expensive topology to install is the _____ topology.

    mesh

14. A ring topology passes a _____ from one segment to another. In order for a computer to place data on the network, the computer must be in possession of the _____.

    token, token

Chapter 2: Basic Network Media

Lesson 1: Network Cabling

Exercise 2.1: Case Study Problem

Page 71

1. Where does this recommendation violate the UTP and 10BaseT specifications?

   The distances for A, B, C, D, E, F, and G to the hub all exceed the maximum cable length of 100 meters (328 feet) specified by 10BaseT. Therefore, this solution will not work.

2. What type of cabling might you recommend instead?

   You could use thinnet with a multiport repeater where the hub is in the diagram. All the cable lengths from the hub to individual computers are less than 185 meters (607 feet). You could also use a star-wired, fiber-optic network for this situation; the cost would compare favorably with that of a coaxial-cabling solution.

Lesson 2: The Network Interface Card

Exercise 2.2: Troubleshooting Problem

Page 88

1. List two things that could cause the network not to function.

   Note The answers identify some of the potential causes of the problem, but the list is not exhaustive. Even if the answers you have written down are not listed, they might still be correct.

   The network cable might not be correctly connected; that is, there might be a break in it caused by adding the new computers.

   The new cable added to service the new computers might not be the correct type for your network.

   The new cable added to your network might have a short in it.

   Rough handling during the installation of the new computers might have damaged the existing network cabling.

   The addition of the new cable required to network the new computers might have made your total network cable length exceed the maximum length specified for the type of network you have.

   The bus network might be missing a terminator. It might have been removed or fallen off during the installation of the new computers.

2. What could you do to resolve each of the two possible causes you listed above?

Find and repair the break or disconnection in the cable.

Check the cable type of the existing cable and make sure the new cables are of the same type. If they are of different types, replace the new cables with cables of the correct type. For example, the original cable might be RG-58A/U and the new cables might be RG-62 /U. These two cable types are not compatible. Replace the new cable with RG-58A/U cable.

3. How would each of your solutions repair the problems you identified (assuming that they are able to repair the problems)?

Restoring cable connections will reestablish the continuity of the network cable and allow transmissions to reach all connected network devices.

With all segments of the same cable type, network transmissions will be able to pass uninterrupted from one cable segment to the next.

Replacing a shorted segment of the new cable with a new, tested segment will allow network transmissions to flow correctly.

Chapter Review

Page 103

1. Coaxial cable consists of a core made of solid or stranded _____ _____.

wire conductor

2. If the coaxial conducting core and wire mesh touch, the cable will experience a _____.

short

3. The core of coaxial cable is surrounded by an _____ _____ that separates it from the wire mesh.

insulating layer

4. Thicknet cable is sometimes used as a _____ to connect thinnet segments.

Backbone

5. Thinnet cable can carry a signal for a distance of about 185 meters (607 feet) before the signal starts to suffer from _____.

attenuation

6. The electronic signals that make up the data are actually carried by the _____ in a coaxial cable.

   core

7. A flexible coaxial cable that is easily routed but that should not go into crawl spaces is _____.

   PVC

8. Coaxial cable that contains special materials in its insulation and cable jacket is called _____ cabling.

   plenum

9. The most popular type of twisted-pair cable is _____ (10BaseT).

   UTP

10. UTP cable for data transmissions up to 10 Mbps is category _____.

    3

11. UTP cable for data transmissions up to 100 Mbps is category _____.

    5

12. STP uses a foil wrap for _____.

    shielding

13. STP is less susceptible to electrical _____ and supports higher transmission rates over longer distances than does UTP.

    interference

14. Twisted-pair cabling uses _____ telephone connectors to connect to a computer.

    RJ-45

15. The RJ-45 connection houses _____ cable connections, whereas the RJ-11 houses only _____.

    8, 4

16. Optical fibers carry _____ data signals in the form of light pulses.

    digital

17. Fiber-optic cable cannot be _____, and the data cannot be stolen.

    tapped

18. Fiber-optic cable is better for very high-speed, high-capacity data transmission than _____ cable because of the former's lack of attenuation and the purity of the signal it carries.

    copper

19. Fiber-optic cable transmissions are not subject to electrical _____.

    interference

20. Baseband systems use _____ signaling over a single frequency.

    digital

21. Each device on a _____ network can transmit and receive at the same time.

    baseband

22. Broadband systems use _____ signaling and a range of frequencies.

    analog

23. With _____ transmission, the signal flow is unidirectional.

    broadband

24. Wall-mounted _____ connected to the wired LAN maintain and manage radio contact between portable devices and the cabled LAN.

    transceivers

25. Broadband optical telepoint transmission is a type of _____ network capable of handling high-quality multimedia requirements.

    infrared

26. A component called a wireless _____ offers an easy way to link buildings without using cable.

    bridge

27. Spread-spectrum radio broadcasts signals over a range of
    _____.

    frequencies

28. Point-to-point transmission involves wireless _____ data transfer.

    serial

29. In LANs, a transceiver—sometimes called an _____
    _____ —broadcasts and receives signals to and from the
    surrounding computers.

    access point

30. Wireless _____ LANs use telephone carriers and public services to
    transmit and receive signals.

    mobile

31. CDPD uses the same technology and some of the same systems as
    _____ telephones.

    cellular

32. Currently, the most widely used long-distance transmission method in the
    United States is _____.

    microwave

33. The network interface card converts serial data from the computer into parallel
    data for transmission over the network cable.   True   False

    False. The reverse is true. The card converts parallel data to serial data.

34. The 16-bit and 32-bit widths are currently the two most popular bus widths.
    True   False

    True

35. To help move data onto the network cable, the computer assigns all of its
    memory to the NIC.   True   False

    **False. The computer can assign some of its memory to the card, but not
    all of it.**

36. Data is temporarily held in the NIC's transceiver, which acts as a buffer.
    True   False

    **False. Only RAM acts as a buffer. The transceiver transmits and receives
    data.**

37. Both sending and receiving NICs must agree on transmission speeds.
    True   False

    True

38. In an 80386 computer, COM1 typically uses IRQ _____ and LPT1 typically uses IRQ _____.

    4, 7

39. IRQ lines are assigned different levels of _____ so that the CPU can determine how important the request is.

    priority

40. The recommended setting for a NIC is IRQ _____.

    5

41. Every device on the computer must use a _____ IRQ line.

    different or separate

42. Each hardware device needs a default _____ ___/___ _____ number.

    base I/O port

43. Choosing the appropriate transceiver on a NIC that can use either an external or an on-board transceiver is usually done with _____.

    jumpers

44. ISA was the standard bus until Compaq and other manufacturers developed the _____ bus.

    EISA

45. The _____ _____ bus functions as either a 16-bit or a 32-bit bus and can be driven independently by multiple bus master processors.

    Micro Channel

46. Telephone wire uses an _____ connector.

    RJ 11

47. Plug and Play refers to both a design philosophy and a set of personal-computer _____ specifications.

    architecture

Chapter 3: Understanding Network Architecture

Lesson 5: AppleTalk and ArcNet

Exercise 3.1: Case Study Problem

Page 160

1. What kind of network should they install?

   Server-based _____

   Peer-to-peer _____

Tip This case study can be solved with several different combinations of components and cable.

A server-based network is suggested because the number of workstations (34), when combined, exceeds the recommended limit of 10 for a peer-to-peer network. Also, because this company uses a variety of computers (PCs and Macintoshes), it will be easier to implement the server-based network. By getting all the computers standardized and networked, this company is moving toward a more centralized administration. Installing the server-based network now will put them well on their way to a more centralized system and open to future expansion. A peer-to-peer network at this time would limit future expansion. Because the company needs a server-based operating system that serves both Macintoshes and personal computers, you could choose Microsoft Windows NT Server, although there are several other server-based operating systems, such as Netware, that could complete the same functions.

2. What type of network should the company implement within the offices?

   Fiber-optic Ethernet _____

   Fiber-optic Token Ring _____

   Fiber-optic ArcNet _____

   Ethernet 10BaseT _____

   Ethernet 10Base2 _____

   Token Ring _____

   LocalTalk _____

   ArcNet _____

Within the offices, Ethernet 10BaseT is the suggested solution because it is supported on all platforms and is easy to troubleshoot and install. Token Ring and ArcNet solutions would also work, but LocalTalk would not meet the requirements because:

- It is slow.
- It is difficult to find LocalTalk cards for personal computers.

3. What type of network should the company install between the two buildings?

Fiber-optic Ethernet _____

Fiber-optic Token Ring _____

Fiber-optic ArcNet _____

Ethernet 10BaseT _____

Ethernet 10Base2 _____

Token Ring _____

LocalTalk _____

ArcNet _____

A fiber-optic Ethernet solution called 10BaseF is suggested between the two buildings, for two reasons:

- Only fiber-optic cable can offer the distance capabilities necessary to cover 600 meters (2000 feet).
- A repeater can be used to connect the fiber-optic cable from one building to the 10BaseT cable in the other.

Exercise 3.2: Troubleshooting Problem

Page 161

1. List at least two things that could cause those nodes to fail to function.

Note This list contains the most common errors that could be causing the problem, but these are not the only correct possibilities.

The cables to the computers that are having problems might not be of the correct category. Category 5 wire, which can handle the 100 Mbps network, is fairly new and might have been too expensive when the older cable runs were installed.

The cables to the computers that are having problems might be of the correct category, but might not have been installed to Category 5 specifications. The cable might work fine for 10BaseT, but fail for 100BaseX.

The patch cables used to connect each of the problem computers to the wall jack might not be Category 5 patch cables and might work for 10BaseT, but not for 100BaseX.

Rough handling during the installation of the new computers might have damaged the existing network cabling.

2. What could you do to resolve each of the possible causes you listed above?

Upgrade to Category 5, and test the cable runs with appropriate test equipment (test equipment is discussed in Chapter 8, "Designing and Installing a Network") to determine if it will support 100-Mbps networking. Replace all cables that will not support your new network.

Test the patch cables with appropriate test equipment to determine if the cable will support 100-Mbps networking. Replace all cables that will not support your new network.

Visually inspect all the cables for damage and replace any that have obvious problems; then test the rest to determine if there are any hidden problems. And of course, replace all cables that will not support your new network.

Chapter Review

Page 170

1. Access methods prevent _____ access to the cable.

   simultaneous

2. With CSMA/CD, if there is data on the cable, no other computer may _____ until the data has reached its destination and the cable is clear again.

   transmit

3. CSMA/CD is known as a _____ access method because computers on the network compete for an opportunity to send data.

   contention

4. With more traffic on a CSMA/CD network, _____ tend to increase, slowing the network down.

   collisions

5. With the token-passing access method, only one computer at a time can use the token; therefore, there are no _____ or
   _____.

   collisions, contention

6. With the demand-priority access method, the _____ manage network access by doing round-robin searches for requests to send from all nodes.

   repeaters

7. In the demand-priority access method, transmissions are not _____ to all other computers on the network.

   broadcast

8. A token is a special type of _____ that circulates around a cable ring.

   packet

9. With data masses divided into _____, individual transmissions occur more frequently so that every computer on the network has more opportunities to transmit and receive data.

   packets

10. Packets may contain session-control codes, such as error correction, that indicate the need for a _____.

    retransmission

11. A packet's components are grouped into three sections: _____, data, and trailer.

    header

12. In a packet, the header usually contains an error-checking component called a CRC.   True   False

    False. The trailer contains this component.

13. The structure of the packets is defined by the communication method, known as a protocol, used by the two computers.   True   False

    True

14. Every network interface card sees all packets sent on its segment, but it interrupts the computer only if the packet's address matches its individual address. True   False

    True

15. The trailer of a packet contains the destination address.   True   False

    False. The header contains the destination address.

16. Typically, Ethernet is a baseband architecture that uses a _____ topology.

    bus

17. Ethernet relies on the _____ access method to regulate traffic on the main cable segment.

    CSMA/CD

18. The maximum length of a 10BaseT segment is _____ meters.

    100

19. The 10BaseT topology is an Ethernet network that uses _____ cable to connect stations.

    unshielded twisted-pair (UTP)

20. Typically, the hub of a 10BaseT network serves as a

    _____   _____.

    multiport repeater

21. A thinnet network can combine as many as _____ cable segments connected by four repeaters, but only three segments can have stations attached.

    five

22. Because single-segment 10Base2 Ethernet limits would be too confining for a large business, _____ can be used to join Ethernet segments and extend the network to a total length of 925 meters (about 3035 feet).

    repeaters

23. A 10Base5 topology is also referred to as _____.

    thicknet (or standard Ethernet)

24. Fast Ethernet is another name for the _____ topology.

    100BaseX

25. Ethernet can use several communication _____ including TCP/IP.

    protocols

26. The 100BaseTX topology runs on UTP Category _____ data-grade cable.

    5

27. A 100BaseVG network is built on a _____ topology with all computers attached to a hub.

    star

28. A Token Ring network is an implementation of IEEE standard

    _____.

    802.5

29. In the IBM implementation of Token Ring, a star-wired ring, the actual physical ring of cable is in the _____.

    hub

30. In a Token Ring frame the Access Control field indicates whether the frame is a _____ frame or a _____ frame.

    token, data

31. When a frame reaches the destination computer, that computer copies the frame into its _____ _____.

    receive buffer

32. Token passing is _____ , meaning that a computer cannot force its way onto the network as it can in a CSMA/CD environment.

    deterministic

33. When a frame returns to its sending computer, that computer _____ the frame and puts a new token back on the ring.

    removes

34. Cables attach the individual clients and servers to the MSAU that works like other _____ hubs.

    passive

35. When an IBM Token Ring network is full, adding another _____ can enlarge the network.

    MSAU

36. MSAUs were designed to sense when a _____ _____ _____ fails and to disconnect from it.

    network interface card

37. Each single Token Ring can accommodate _____ computers using STP cable.

    260

38. Most Token Ring networks use IBM Cabling System Type ____ UTP cabling.

    3

39. LocalTalk uses _____ as an access method in a bus or tree topology.

    CSMA/CA

40. When a device attached to an AppleTalk network comes online, the device broadcasts an _____ to determine if any other device is using it.

    address

41. A single LocalTalk network supports a maximum of _____ devices.

    32

42. Single LocalTalk networks can be joined together into one larger network through the use of _____.

    zones

43. ArcNet uses a token-passing access method in a _____-_____ topology.

    star-bus

44. An ArcNet token moves from one computer to the next according to the order in which it is connected to the _____, regardless of how they are placed on the network environment.

    hub

45. Each computer in an ArcNet network is connected by cable to a _____.

    hub

Chapter 4: Survey of Network Operating Systems

Lesson 1: Introduction to Network Operating Systems

Lesson Checkup

Page 182

1. In a networking environment, _____ provide resources to the network, and client network software makes these resources available to the client computer.

   servers

2. In _____ multitasking, the operating system can take control of the processor without the task's cooperation. In _____ multitasking, the task itself decides when to give up the processor.

   preemptive, nonpreemptive

3. A request to use a remote resource is forwarded out onto the network by the

   _____ .

   redirector

4. Most NOSs allow different users to gain different levels of access to

   _____ _____ .

   network resources

5. All group members have the same _____ as have been assigned to the group as a whole.

   privileges

6. It is not uncommon to find, in a single network, both a network interoperability _____ on the server and network _____ applications at each computer.

   service, client

Lesson 2: Novell Operating Systems

Lesson Checkup

Page 186

1. A NetWare network consists of _____ and _____ applications.

   client, server

2. NetWare is often the NOS of choice in _____ computer operating system environments.

   mixed

3. With NetWare client software installed, computers can view NetWare resources as if they were _____ to the client.

   native

4. NetWare _____ _____ can support up to 256 printers.

   print services

5. NetWare servers provide services to computers on a Windows NT network through the Windows NT server's _____ service.

   gateway

Lesson 3: Microsoft Network Operating Systems

Lesson Checkup

Page 190

1. In Windows NT networking, a _____ is a collection of computers that share a common database and security policy.

   domain

2. Each Windows NT domain has one _____ _____ _____.

   primary domain controller

3. Windows NT can provide directory- and file-level sharing on an _____ disk partition, but only directory-level sharing on a 16-bit _____ disk partition.

   NTFS, FAT

4. To set sharing on a Windows NT computer you must have _____ privileges.

   administrator

5. NWLink is a network protocol that helps Windows NT and NetWare
   _____.

   interoperate

6. On a Windows NT network, any client or server can function as a print
   _____.

   server

Lesson 4: Other Network Operating Systems

Lesson Checkup

Page 194

1. AppleTalk zones are _____ _____ of networks and
   network resources.

   logical groups

2. In a UNIX network, personal computers can be used as _____ terminals.

   dumb

3. Banyan Vines can communicate with Windows NT using the _____
   protocol.

   TCP/IP

4. Windows for Workgroups, Windows 95 and 98, MacOS, and OS/2 Warp
   incorporate _____ - _____ - _____ network operating systems.

   peer-to-peer

Lesson 5: Network Operating Systems in Multivendor Environments

Lesson Checkup

Page 201

1. In a multivendor environment, it is necessary to find a _____
   _____ in which all computers can communicate.

   common language

2. A redirector will _____ your request to the appropriate destination.

   forward

3. Each redirector handles only the _____ sent in the language or protocol that it can understand.

packets

4. Apple computers are brought into a Windows NT environment by means of communication _____ that are installed on the server.

services

Exercise 4.1: Case Study Problem

Page 202

The owner wants everyone on this network to be able to exchange files, use both printers, and have access to company e-mail through an Internet service provider. She has made it clear that she does not want a network that requires high administrative overhead.

There might not be a completely satisfactory solution in this situation, in which case it is important to satisfy the most important criteria. Because the owner is unwilling to consider a network that requires significant administrative overhead, a peer-to-peer network seems appropriate.

By enabling the peer-to-peer networking that resides in the company's existing computers and by connecting the computers and resources with 100Mb UTP cabling and TCP/IP, an adequate degree of interoperability is achieved. Using TCP/IP also allows both printers to be connected to the network itself, using network port hardware, rather than to individual computers.

Enabling sharing on all computers makes their resources available to the others. Enabling Apple services on the Windows NT computer creates a path between the graphic designer, who uses the Apple NOS, and the others, who use two of the Windows network operating systems.

Chapter Review

Page 205

1. A multitasking operating system can run as many tasks simultaneously as there are _____.

processors

2. The network operating system can take control of the processor without the task's cooperation in a multitasking operating system that uses _____ multitasking.

preemptive

3. The process of forwarding requests is carried out by a _____,
which is also commonly referred to as a "shell" or a "requester."

   redirector

4. Redirector activity originates in the _____ computer when the user
issues a request for a network resource or service.

   client

5. Redirectors can send requests to either computers or _____.

   peripherals

6. In the past, network operating systems were _____ that
were loaded on top of a stand-alone operating system.

   applications

7. Novell's NetWare operating system is a _____-based network.

   server

8. An advantage of using NetWare is that it works well in a _____
environment.

   multivendor

9. A Windows NT computer will not communicate with a NetWare network.
True   False

   False

10. Banyan Vines is an NOS that runs on top of another operating system.
True   False

    True

11. Your client is a small business, planning to install a small network for the
office, which includes five computers, running Windows 95, and two printers.
Security is not an issue because all employees work on the same projects.
Would you recommend upgrading to Windows NT?

    No

12. Will a Windows 95 or 98 workstation always work on a NetWare network?

    No

Chapter 5: Introducing Network Standards

Lesson 1: Open Systems Interconnection (OSI) Reference Model

Exercise 5.1: Reviewing the OSI Model Layers

Page 219

This two-part exercise will give you the opportunity to memorize and review the layers of the OSI model.

The left column is a listing of a memorization tool: "All People Seem To Need Data Processing." Next to each word in that column, enter the appropriate name of the applicable OSI layer in the center column and a brief description of that layer's function in the right column.

Memorization Tool	OSI Layer	Function
All	**Application**	**Interaction at the user or application level**
People	**Presentation**	**Translation of data**
Seem	**Session**	**Maintains a session between nodes on a network**
To	**Transport**	**Makes sure that transmissions are received**
Need	**Network**	**Manages addressing and routing of the packets**
Data	**Data-link**	**Physical addressing of packets and error correction**
Processing	**Physical**	**Manages the connection to the media**

In the second part of Exercise 1 that follows, a device or standard is listed in the left column. In the space provided in the right column, write in the applicable OSI layer(s) for each device or standard.

Device	OSI layer
Gateway	**Application–transport layer**
NIC	**Physical layer**
Hub	**Physical layer**
Router	**Network layer**
IEEE 802.x	**Physical and data-link layers**

Lesson 2: The IEEE 802.x Standard

Exercise 5.2: Describing IEEE 802.x Standards Categories

Page 224

In this exercise, IEEE 802 standards categories are listed in the left column. In the right column, enter a description of what each category represents.

802.x Standard	Basis for standard
802.1	Internetworking
802.2	Logical Link Control (LLC) sublayer
802.3	CSMA/CD Ethernet
802.4	Token bus LAN
802.5	Token Ring LAN
802.6	Metropolitan area networks (MAN)
802.7	Broadband technologies
802.8	Fiber-optic technologies
802.9	Hybrid voice/data networks
802.10	Network security
802.11	Wireless networks
802.12	High-speed LANs
802.13	Unused.
802.14	Defines cable modem standards.
802.15	Defines wireless personal area networks (WPAN).
802.16	Defines broadband wireless standards.

Lesson 3: Device Drivers and OSI

Lesson Checkup

Page 228

1. Define ODI and describe the role it plays in Novell and Apple NOSs.

   The Open Data-Link Interface (ODI) is a specification, developed for Novell and Apple network operating systems (NOSs). It has simplified driver development by allowing multiple protocols, such as IPX/SPX and TCP/IP, working at the data-link layer of the OSI reference model, to share the same NIC or driver. NIC manufacturers can make their boards work with Apple and Novell NOSs by supplying ODI-compliant software drivers.

2. Printer manufacturers are responsible for writing _____ for their printer products.

drivers

3. Drivers described in an operating system manufacturer's _____ have been tested and included with their operating system.

HCL

4. NIC drivers reside on the computer's _____ _____.

hard disk

5. Protocol drivers use an _____ interface to communicate with the NICs.

NDIS

6. Translation software is required to _____ _____ NDIS and ODI.

bridge between

Chapter Review

Page 230

1. The OSI model divides network activity into _____ layers.

seven

2. The purpose of each layer is to provide services to the next _____ layer and shield the upper layer from the details of how the services are actually implemented.

higher

3. At each layer, the software adds some additional formatting or _____ to the packet.

addressing

4. Each layer on one computer appears to communicate directly with the _____ layer on another computer.

same

5. The top, or _____, layer handles general network access, flow control, and error recovery.

application

6. At the sending computer, the _____ layer translates data from a format sent down from the application layer.

   presentation

7. The _____ layer determines the route from the source to the destination computer.

   network

8. The data-link layer is responsible for sending _____ _____ from the network layer to the physical layer.

   data frames

9. The _____ information in a data frame is used for frame type, routing, and segmentation information.

   control

10. The _____ layer defines how the cable is attached to the NIC.

    physical

11. Windows NT groups the seven OSI layers into three. The three NT layers are

    _____ _____ _____, _____ _____,

    and _____ _____.

    file system drivers, transport protocols, NIC drivers

12. An _____ provides the interface between the Windows NT applications and file system drivers layer.

    API

13. A _____ provides the interface between the Windows NT file system drivers layer and the transport protocols.

    TDI

14. An _____ provides the interface between the Windows NT, the transport protocols layer, and the NIC drivers.

    NDIS

15. The Project 802 specifications define the way _____ access and transfer data over physical media.

    NICs

16. The 802 project divided the _____ - _____ layer of the OSI model into two sublayers, the Logical Link Control (LLC) layer and the Media Access Control (MAC) layer.

    data-link

17. The _____ sublayer communicates directly with the NIC and is responsible for delivering error-free data between two computers on the network.

    MAC

18. The IEEE category _____ covers LAN standards for Ethernet.

    802.3

19. The IEEE category _____ covers LAN standards for Token Ring.

    802.5

20. A driver is _____ that enables a computer to work with a device.

    software

21. NICs work in the _____ sublayer of the _____ -_____ layer of the OSI model.

    MAC, data-link

22. NDIS defines an interface for communication between the _____ sublayer and the protocol drivers.

    MAC

23. NDIS was jointly developed by _____ and _____.

    Microsoft, 3Com

24. ODI works just like NDIS but was developed by _____ and _____ for interfacing hardware to their protocols.

    Apple, Novell

Chapter 6: Defining Network Protocols

Lesson 1: Introduction to Protocols

Exercise 6.1 (a): Matching the OSI Model Rules to Layers

Page 243

This exercise is designed to help you reinforce your understanding of network protocol stacks. The following table contains two columns. In the left column are listed the seven layers of the OSI reference model. In the right column, enter the rule that applies to the layer on the left.

OSI Reference Model Rules

OSI Layers	Rules
Application layer	Initiates a request or accepts a request to send a packet
Presentation layer	Adds formatting, display, and encryption information to the packet
Session layer	Adds traffic-flow information to the packet that determines when the packet gets sent
Transport layer	Adds error-handling information to the packet
Network layer	Adds sequencing and address information to the packet
Data-link layer	Adds error-checking information and prepares packet for sending out over the physical connection
Physical layer	Sends packet as a bit stream

Exercise 6.1 (b): Matching the OSI Model Layers with Communication Tasks

Page 244

Because many protocols were written before the OSI reference model was developed, some protocol stacks developed earlier don't match the OSI model; in those stacks, tasks are often grouped together.

Communication tasks can be classified into three groups. In this part of the exercise, the seven layers of the OSI model are again listed in the left column. In the right column, write in the name of one of the three groups in the following list. Your task is to identify which of these three groups maps to each of the OSI layers in the left column.

The three groups are:

- Transport services.
- Network services.
- Application-level network service users.

Matching OSI Reference Model with Communication Tasks

OSI Layers	Communication Task
Application layer	**Application-level network service users**
Presentation layer	**Application-level network service users**
Session layer	**Application-level network service users**
Transport layer	**Transport services**
Network layer	**Network services**
Data-link layer	**Network services**
Physical layer	**Network services**

Lesson 2: TCP/IP

Exercise 6.2: Comparing OSI and TCP/IP Layers

Page 251

Exercise 6.2 is designed to help you understand the relationship between the OSI model and Transmission Control Protocol/Internet Protocol (TCP/IP). Because TCP/IP was developed before the OSI reference model was developed, it does not exactly match the seven OSI model layers. In this exercise, you will be mapping the four layers of TCP/IP to the seven layers of the OSI model. The four layers of TCP/IP are the:

- Network interface layer.
- Internet layer.
- Transport layer.
- Application layer.

The left column lists the seven layers of the OSI model. In the right column, fill in the name of the corresponding TCP/IP layer.

Comparison of OSI and TCP/IP Layers

OSI Layers	TCP/IP Layers
Application layer	**Application layer**
Presentation layer	**Application layer**
Session layer	**Application layer**
Transport layer	**Transport layer**
Network layer	**Internet layer**
Data-link layer	**Network interface layer**
Physical layer	**Network interface layer**

Lesson 3: NetWare Protocols

Exercise 6.3: Comparing the OSI Model with NetWare Protocols

Page 255

This exercise is designed to help you understand the relationship between the OSI reference model and NetWare protocols. NetWare was developed earlier than the OSI model and, therefore, does not precisely match the seven layers. In this exercise, you will be mapping the various components of NetWare protocols to the seven layers of the OSI reference model.

In the table that follows, the column on the left lists the seven layers of the OSI model. The blank columns on the right represent various components of the NetWare protocol. In the blank columns, map the following NetWare protocol components to the OSI model.

- IPX/SPX
- Media Access Protocol
- NetWare Core Protocol
- Routing Information Protocol
- Service Advertising Protocol

Comparison of OSI Model with NetWare Protocols

OSI Layers	NetWare Protocols		
Application layer	**NetWare Core Protocol**	**Service Advertising Protocol**	**Routing Information Protocol**
Presentation layer			
Session layer			
Transport layer			
Network layer	**IPX/SPX**		
Data-link layer	**Media Access Protocols**		
Physical layer			

Lesson 4: Other Common Protocols

Exercise 6.4: Protocol Matching Problem

Page 262

Along with the better-known protocols, many other lesser, but still common, protocols exist. Five such protocols are listed below. In this exercise, you will be matching each of the protocols in the list that follows with the feature that describes what it does.

Five common protocols

A. AppleTalk

B. DECnet

C. NetBEUI

D. NetBIOS

E. X.25

In each blank space on the left, fill in the letter of the protocol that uses the feature listed on the right. Note that more than one protocol can be matched to a particular feature.

_____**C, D**_____ A protocol that is commonly used for Microsoft-based, peer-to-peer networks

_____**E**_____ A protocol used for packet switching

_____**A**_____ A protocol that is commonly used for Macintosh networks

_____**B**_____ A protocol designed by Digital Equipment Corporation (DEC)

_____D_____ A protocol originally offered by IBM

_____C_____ A small, fast, transport-layer protocol

_____C, D_____ A protocol that is nonroutable

Chapter Review

Page 265

1. A sending computer breaks the data into smaller sections, called
   _____, that the protocol can handle.

   packets

2. Several protocols can work together in what is known as a protocol
   _____.

   stack

3. A receiving computer copies the data from the packets to a _____
   for reassembly.

   buffer

4. Protocols that support multipath LAN-to-LAN communications are known as
   _____ protocols.

   routable

5. The receiving computer passes the reassembled data to the
   _____ in a usable form.

   application

6. To avoid conflicts or incomplete operations, protocols are _____
   in an orderly manner.

   layered

7. The _____ order indicates where the protocol sits in the protocol
   stack.

   binding

8. Three protocol types that map roughly to the OSI model are application,
   _____, and network.

   transport

9. Application protocols work at the upper layer of the OSI model and provide
   _____ _____ between applications.

   data exchange

10. A NIC-driver protocol resides in the _____ _____
_____ (_____) sublayer of the OSI model.

Media Access Control (MAC)

11. Rules for communicating in a particular LAN environment such as Ethernet
or Token Ring are called _____ protocols.

network

12. To help the network administrator install a protocol after the initial system
installation, a _____ is included with the operating system.

utility

13. TCP/IP supports routing and is commonly used as an
_____ protocol.

internetworking

14. NetBIOS is an IBM session-layer LAN interface that acts as an
_____ interface to the network.

application

15. APPC (advanced program-to-program communication) is IBM's
_____ protocol.

transport

16. NetBEUI is not a good choice for large networks because it is not
_____.

routable

17. X.25 is a protocol used for a _____ - _____ network.

packet switching

18. X.25 works in the _____, _____ - _____, and
_____ layers of the OSI model.

physical, **data-link**, and **network**

19. AppleTalk is a proprietary protocol stack designed for _____
computers.

Macintosh

20. EtherTalk allows a Macintosh computer to communicate on an
_____ network.

Ethernet

Chapter 7: Elements of Network Connectivity

Lesson 1: Connectivity Devices

Exercise 7.1: Troubleshooting Problem

Page 322

What can you do to start the troubleshooting process?

The first step is to carry out a simple test on your hardware. Much complex equipment is microprocessor-driven hardware with built-in software. Simply by following the shut-down and restart procedure for these devices (sometimes this is a simple on-off switch) you can restart the equipment and restore it to proper functioning again.

If shutting down and restarting the entire system does not get the system running, call the service provider and ask it to test the T1 line and verify that it is correctly configured.

If neither of those two options solve the problem, you will need to contact your vendor and ask for help in troubleshooting the WAN equipment you have. Very few experienced systems engineers have the expertise needed to successfully troubleshoot this kind of scenario.

Lesson 2: Connection Services

Exercise 7.2: Case Study Problem

Page 323

1. Identify at least two network items in each branch-office network site that need upgrading.

   Each site could upgrade to include the following:
   - **New cabling: from 10 Mbps Ethernet to 100Mbp Category 5.**
   - **New cards: from 10 Mbps Ethernet to 100Base.**
   - **New architecture: from linear bus to star bus (100BaseT) with hubs.**

2. The separate branch offices need to maintain voice and data communications with each other. Which type of WAN connection (link) might you use to connect the three sites to each other?

Use a T1 link, because it can carry voice and data simultaneously. (T1 is available through a carrier such as AT&T, MCI, Sprint, and others.) Note that E1 is a rough equivalent of T1 and is used outside the U.S.

3. Which type of device could be used to collect the multiple signals from voice and data and put them on the same WAN link?

A multiplexer mixes both types of signals and places them on the same WAN link.

4. Which type of connectivity device should be used to connect the LAN to the multiple paths in the WAN illustrated in the diagram above?

A router is the ideal device to connect the LAN to the multiple WAN paths. Routers can use multiple paths and can use best-path algorithms to determine the best path for each transmission.

Chapter Review

Page 332

1. An external modem is a small box that is connected to the computer by a _____ cable running from the computer's port to the modem's computer-cable connection.

serial

2. The modem at the _____ end converts digital signals into analog signals.

sending

3. Baud rate refers to the speed of oscillation of the _____ _____ on which a bit of data is carried.

sound wave

4. The bps can be greater than the _____ rate.

baud

5. Asynchronous transmission occurs over _____ _____.

telephone lines

6. The Microcom Network Protocol (MNP) is a standard for asynchronous
   _____ - _____ control.

   data-error

7. In asynchronous communication, it is possible to double throughput by using
   _____ without having to pay for a faster channel speed.

   compression

8. Synchronous communication relics on a _____ scheme coordinated
   between two devices.

   timing

9. More advanced, complex repeaters can act as multiport _____ to connect
   different types of media.

   hubs

10. Repeaters do not have a _____ function and so will pass
    along all data from one segment to the next.

    filtering

11. A repeater takes a weak signal and _____ it.

    regenerates

12. A repeater functions at the ___ _____ layer of the OSI model.

    physical

13. If the volume of traffic from one or two computers or a single department
    is flooding the network with data and slowing down the entire operation,
    a _____ could isolate those computers or that department.

    bridge

14. The bridge builds a routing table based on the _____ addresses
    of computers that have sent traffic through the bridge.

    source

15. Bridges work at the OSI _____ - _____ layer and, specifically, the
    _____ _____ _____ sublayer.

    data-link, Media Access Control

16. Bridges are often used in large networks that have widely dispersed segments joined by _____ _____.

telephone lines

17. Under spanning tree algorithm (STA), software can sense the existence of more than one _____, determine which would be the most efficient, and then configure the bridge to use that one.

route

18. Bridges connect two segments and regenerate the signal at the _____ level.

packet

19. Routers work at the _____ layer of the OSI model.

network

20. Because they must perform complex functions on each packet, routers are _____ than most bridges.

slower

21. Routers do not look at the destination node address; they look only at the _____ address.

network

22. Unlike bridges, routers can accommodate multiple active _____ between LAN segments and choose among them.

paths

23. The two major types of routers are _____ and _____.

static, dynamic

24. A brouter will _____ nonroutable protocols.

bridge

25. Most often, gateways are dedicated _____ on a network.

servers

26. The gateway takes the data from one environment, strips it, and repackages it in the _____ _____ from the destination system.

    protocol stack

27. Gateways are _____ specific, which means that they are dedicated to a particular type of transfer.

    task

28. With the exception of ADSL, public telephone lines require users to _____ make a connection for each communication session.

    manually

29. The three factors an administrator must take into account when considering how best to implement communication between two modems are _____, _____, and _____.

    throughput, distance, cost

30. Leased lines provide _____ connections that do not use a series of switches to complete the connection.

    dedicated

31. A good remote-access option that offers stable lines for companies that are constantly communicating between networks is to use _____ lines.

    leased (dedicated)

32. The _____ - _____ - _____ _____ _____ allows a remote client to establish a secure connection to the corporate LAN over the Internet and RAS.

    Point-to-Point Tunneling Protocol

33. Because the PSTN was designed primarily for voice, _____ - _____ lines do not have the consistent quality required for secure data communications.

    dial-up

34. A dedicated line is _____ and more _____ than a dial-up connection.

    faster, reliable

35. One advantage that dedicated lines offer over dial-up lines is that the service company implements _____ _____ to improve communication, thereby ensuring line quality.

line conditioning

36. Digital lines provide _____ - ___ - _____ synchronous communication.

point-to-point

37. Because DDS uses _____ communication, it does not require modems.

digital

38. T1 uses a technology called _____ in which several signals from different sources are collected into a component and fed into one cable for transmission.

multiplexing

39. T1 can accommodate 24 _____ data transmissions over each two-wire pair.

simultaneous

40. Subscribers who do not need or cannot afford the bandwidth of an entire T1 line can subscribe to one or more T1 _____.

channels

41. With packet switching, the data is broken down into packets, and each packet is tagged with a _____ _____ and other information.

destination address

42. At the destination, the packets are _____ into the original message.

reassembled

43. Two packets from the original data package can arrive out of sequence because thcy followed different _____ to reach the same destination.

paths

44. Virtual circuits are composed of a series of _____ connections between the sending computer and the receiving computer.

    logical

45. Because of its extensive _____ _____, X.25 can appear to be slow.

    error checking

46. X.25 was originally developed for the _____ environment.

    mainframe

47. Frame-relay data travels from a network over a _____ _____ line to a data switch and into the frame-relay network.

    digital leased

48. Frame-relay networks can also provide subscribers with _____ as needed, which lets the customer make nearly any type of transmission.

    bandwidth

49. Frame-relay networks are faster at performing basic _____ - _____ operations than are X.25 networks.

    packet-switching

50. ATM is an advanced implementation of _____ _____ that provides high-speed data transmission rates.

    packet switching

51. ATM transmits data in 53-byte _____ rather than variable-length frames.

    cells

52. ATM switches are multiport devices that can act as either _____ to forward data from one computer to another within a network or _____ to forward data at high speeds to remote networks.

    hubs, routers

53. ATM uses switches as _____ to permit several computers to put data on a network simultaneously.

multiplexers

54. ATM can be used with existing _____ designed for other communications systems.

media

55. Basic Rate ISDN divides its available _____ into three data channels.

bandwidth

56. FDDI is a specification that describes a high-speed (100 Mbps) token-ring LAN that uses _____ - _____ media.

fiber-optic

57. FDDI can be used for _____ networks to which other, low-capacity LANs can connect.

backbone

58. A computer on an FDDI network can transmit as many frames as it can produce within a predetermined time before letting the _____ go.

token

59. Traffic in an FDDI network consists of two similar streams flowing in opposite directions around two counter-rotating _____.

rings

60. An advantage of the dual-ring topology is _____.

redundancy

61. To isolate serious failures in the ring, FDDI uses a system called _____ in which a computer that detects a fault sends a signal onto the network.

beaconing

Chapter 8: Designing and Installing a Network

Lesson 1: Choosing a Network Design

Exercise 8.1: Creating a Peer-to-Peer Network/Part 1: Design a Topology

Page 351

Because peer-to-peer Ethernet can be implemented in the form of either a physical bus or a physical star, you will need to look at these two different topologies in planning for this network. On separate paper, draw:

1. A logical bus with a physical bus.
2. A logical bus with a physical star.

Though your drawings might not be as complex as these, you should have illustrated the following, at a minimum:

Physical bus—All computers should be connected individually to a point on the bus. Each peripheral should be connected to the appropriate computer.

Physical star—Each computer should be connected to a central hub with an individual cable. Each peripheral should be connected to the appropriate computer, and there should be no terminators.

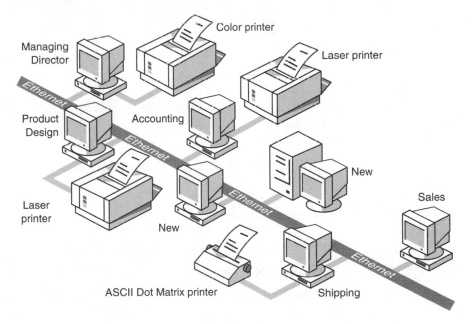

Figure 1   Sample network as a physical bus

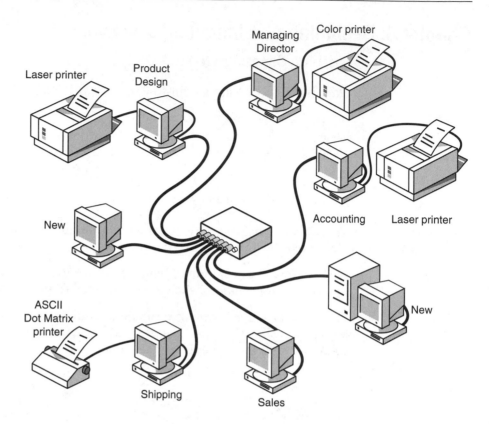

Figure 2   Sample network as a physical star

While there is no one-size-fits-all correct form for this design, there are a few things you must take into consideration when you design the network. Check to see if you considered these factors.

For the logical bus with physical bus, did you:

- **Use thinnet coaxial cable to connect each computer in a series?**
- **Terminate both ends of the bus?**

For the logical bus with physical star, did you:

- **Use CAT 5 UTP?**
- **Identify an appropriate location for the concentrator or hub?**

Exercise 8.1: Creating a Peer-to-Peer Network/Part 2: Select Your Materials

Page 352

Make a materials list for each of the topologies. Using the facility drawing provided earlier in Figure 8.1, identify the location of each workstation and estimate all the materials you will need to complete the job. Use the following table to help determine which materials are required.

Material Requirements

	Logical bus; physical bus	Logical bus; physical star
Type of Cable		
Length of Cable		
Connectors (type and count)		
Terminators		
Patch cables		
Patch Panel		
Hub		

Once again, there is no one-size-fits-all approach to selecting materials for networking. What is important is the process: thinking through the design and building the network on paper before you begin to spend money and time on the installation. You should take into account differences, such as cost, between the two types of network topology. For example, a small thinnet physical bus design is less material-intensive than a physical star.

Lesson 2: Establishing a Client/Server Environment

Exercise 8.2: Adding a Network Server

Page 362

In Exercise 8.1, we designed a peer-to-peer network and looked at two different topologies. While these designs meet the immediate needs of our client, the custom bicycle manufacturer, they are likely to fall short if the manufacturer decides to expand the business in the future. In this exercise, you will be modifying the design you carried out in Exercise 1 to include a network server.

In planning your new design, consider the following issues:

- Where should the server be located?
- What additional materials are required?
- What compatibility issues might arise?

From the standpoint of networking requirements, the server can be placed in any location provided it is connected correctly to the media. Thus, while it is necessary to locate the server where it can be accessed physically, it need not be centrally located. The logical choice would be to place it in a room by itself. However, in our client's office, no such room exists. The Accounting Department or the Product Design Group offer two possible locations. The server will be more physically secure in the Accounting Department office, where there is likely to be less traffic and where the door will probably be locked when the office is unattended. The office of the Product Design Group is another location in which the server could be somewhat isolated. The advantage of this site is that staff members in this department, who are likely to be computer-literate, will be on hand and can watch over the server's welfare.

When a network server is added to an existing peer-to-peer network, at least one computer must be added to the existing number. With a small network, such as that we are creating for our bicycle company, a single server can supply all the expected resources, including files, printers, and applications. Making the physical connection is the same as for a workstation: if the server computer is in the same location as the hub, simply connect it with a patch cable. Otherwise connect the server with an available cable in one of the vacant work areas.

Compatibility is another issue to consider. Each workstation needs to communicate with the server. Depending on which network operating system is installed, some of the computers on the network might need to be upgraded to meet the minimum requirements of the server.

Lesson 3: Working with Device Drivers and NICs

Exercise 8.3: Connecting a New Computer

Page 370

What steps do you need to take in order to successfully connect the new computer to the existing company network?

First, set up the computer and verify that it is in good working order. If the operating system allows it, check for available interrupts in case this information is needed when you configure the network interface card. Make a note of the computer's installed RAM and disk capacity; these might be inadequate for network use or for resource-intensive applications.

Once you have determined that the computer runs correctly and have taken notes on its configuration, close any applications and shut down the operating system. Disconnect all cables and open the CPU. Examine the main board for available bus slots, noting the type of slot or slots available. If a PCI slot is available, it should be your preferred choice; if not, an Industry Standard Architecture (ISA) slot might be available. (ISA is discussed in Chapter 2, "Basic Network Media.")

Obtain a network interface card of the correct bus type—PCI or ISA—and cable connector type—BNC or UTP—for the bicycle company's existing network. Remember that if the existing network has 100Mhz UTP cabling, the card needs to be capable of operating at that speed.

Compatible drivers normally accompany a network interface card. These drivers are often loaded on floppy disks, but are sometimes placed on compact discs; if the new computer does not have a CD reader installed, you might have to copy the drivers onto floppy disks using a computer that has a CD reader installed.

Install the network interface card in the appropriate slot and reconnect the computer cables. Also connect the network cable to the network interface card's connection jack. Start the computer and install the latest drivers after the computer is fully operational.

Before you can communicate with the network, you will have to install the appropriate communication protocols. This software can normally be found on the operating system's installation disks.

Test the completed installation by checking for network resources in whichever way is appropriate for the network.

Lesson 4: Ensuring Hardware Compatibility

Exercise 8.4: Upgrading a Network

Page 373

1. Which resources do you anticipate are likely to present problems in the future and, therefore, should be upgraded or replaced?

2. What do you suggest as the minimum operational requirements for equipment to be acquired in the future?

    The two Pentium computers should cause no problems, provided they have enough memory. Suggest upgrading to at least 64 MB of RAM if they do not meet that requirement.

The two 486 machines can provide a few more years of service. Extra memory here might make up for some lack of speed. You should also check closely to see what expansion slots are available for these computers.

The 286 computer must go. You might want to move one of the 486 computers to the Shipping Department and replace the computer in the Accounting Department.

All printers can be shared to the network, eliminating the requirement for the switch box. Unless the current printers are overworked, they are probably worth keeping. You might consider replacing the dot matrix printer, but not if the Shipping Department is printing forms. It is not possible to print multisheet forms on laser or ink jet printers.

Future machines should at least meet the minimum requirements for Windows NT. Remember that minimums aren't good enough. You should opt for at least 300 MHz and 64 MB of RAM. Also check the number of expansion slots available to ensure that you can add the necessary interface cards. Keep in mind that many lower-cost machines sacrifice expandability to keep the price low.

Chapter Review

Page 376

1. Using a peer-to-peer network implies that all computers on the network are
   _____.

   equal

2. One drawback to using a peer-to-peer network is _____
   _____.

   limited performance

3. On a server-based network, resources are _____.

   centralized

4. Before beginning to design a new network, you must take an inventory to determine what _____ and _____ you already have, as well as what you need to acquire.

   hardware, software

5. Working with a drawing of the _____ is the place to start when creating a map of the new network.

   facility

Circle the letter of the best answer for each of the following sentences:

1. A driver is:
    a. hardware.
    b. a peripheral device.
    c. a NIC.
    d. software.

    d.

2. In the networking environment, a NIC driver is needed to:
    a. communicate with other NICs on a network.
    b. communicate between the NIC and the computer's operating system.
    c. communicate between the file server and the other computers on the network.
    d. communicate between different types of computers on a network.

    b.

3. Select the correct statement about printer drivers.
    a. There is no universal printer driver that will ensure full functionality of all printers.
    b. Printers made by a specific printer manufacturer can always use the same printer driver and have full functionality.
    c. There is a specific printer driver designed for every model of printer that can ensure the full functionality of that model of printer on all operating systems.
    d. A laser-printer driver from one manufacturer will provide full functionality for all laser printers, regardless of the manufacturer.

    a.

Chapter 9: Establishing Network Shares and Accounts

Lesson 1: Creating Network Shares

Exercise 9.1: Case Study Problem

Page 387

Your task in this exercise is to designate shares in a peer-to-peer network configuration.

For this configuration, assume that the company to be networked is small, numbering 20 employees, only 10 of which have computers. These computers are running compatible operating systems. Employees include the managing director, three people in the Sales Department, two in the Accounting Department, two in the Product Design Department, and two in the Shipping Department. There are two laser printers available; one is connected directly to the managing director's computer, and the other is connected directly to the lead accountant's computer.

In this exercise you will:

- Designate which resources will be shared.
- Enable sharing on the appropriate computers.
- Share printers, disks, folders, and, if appropriate, files.

Configure all computers to share folders.

Configure the managing director's computer and the lead accountant's computer to share their printers with names MANAGE and ACCOUNT respectively.

Configure all computers except the managing director's to print to the ACCOUNT printer. The MANAGE printer will be used by the managing director, but will be available to others should the ACCOUNT printer fail.

Create one folder in each of the computers for exchanging files. Share each folder as PUBLIC. Set sharing for the PUBLIC folder so that all users have full rights within the folder.

Users will be able to make files in their PUBLIC folders available to others, and will have the option of copying files to the other PUBLIC folders if that is more convenient.

Lesson 2: Establishing and Managing Network Accounts

Exercise 9.2: Case Study Problem

Page 401

For this exercise we will return to the same 20-employee company that was the subject of Exercise 9.1 in Lesson 1. Your job is to design user and group accounts for the 10-computer server-based network. To do this, you should determine what kinds of groups are appropriate to the company and its work. You will also need to establish a password policy and a personnel policy that takes into account what will happen when an employee departs from the company.

After you have established the account policies, create the appropriate user and group accounts and set whatever restrictions will be necessary for each of the groups. These should include the days and hours during which groups can log on to the network. Assign printing rights to the groups as needed and, finally, add the users to the appropriate groups.

Account policies—Create groups that correspond to the working methods of the company. Set each user's account so that passwords must be changed every 30 days. Allow users to change their own passwords. If an employee leaves the company, all users should change their passwords, and the departed employee's account should be disabled or, better, deleted.

Accounts—Create an account for each user on the server. Create a group account on the server for the Managing Director, and one group each for the sales, accounting, design and shipping employees. Add the Managing Director to the DIRECTOR group. Add the three sales employees to the SALES group. Add the two accounting employees to the ACCOUNT group. Add the two product designers to the DESIGN group. Add the two shipping department employees to the SHIPPING group.

Account restrictions—Restrictions must follow the working methods of the company. The Managing Director and the accountant may need access during the evening or very early morning, or weekends. Restrict their accounts accordingly. The other employees are likely to work regular hours. Their accounts can be restricted to whatever their workgroup agrees upon.

Printing—Configure all computers except the Managing Director's to print to the ACCOUNT printer. The MANAGE printer will be used by the Managing Director, but will be available to others should the ACCOUNT printer fail.

Chapter Review

Page 404

1. Two computers running the MS-DOS operating system can be connected and information can be shared. (Yes or No).

   Yes

2. Connecting two computers with a communications cable is called

   _____ - _____ _____.

   Direct-cable connection

3. Sharing on a peer-to-peer network takes place at the _____ level.

   folder

4. The first person to log on to a Windows NT network uses the _____ account.

   administrator

5. The user account contains information that defines a user to the network's _____ system.

   security

6. Most network account-management utilities offer an account _____ feature with which an administrator can create a template user with certain characteristics and parameters that are common among multiple users.

   copying

7. A Windows NT administrator can use a _____ to configure and maintain a user's logon environment.

   profile

8. Two key pieces of information that should be entered when creating a user account are account name and _____.

   password

9. The _____ account is for people who do not have a valid user account but need temporary access to the network.

   Guest

10. An administrator can create a _____ account in order to simplify administrative tasks when dealing with a large numbers of users.

    group

11. A global group is used across an entire _____.

    domain

12. Groups are used to give users _____ to perform system tasks such as backing up and restoring files.

    rights

13. The network administrator assigns _____ to groups to access resources, such as files, directories, and printers.

    permissions

14. After being deleted, a user can no longer use the network, because the network _____ database will contain record or description of the user.

    security

Chapter 10: Ensuring Network Security

Lesson 1: Making Networks Secure

Lesson Checkup

Page 419

1. Describe two common ways by which unauthorized users can gain access to a network; for each, describe how unauthorized access can be prevented.

   Unauthorized users can gain access to most peer-to-peer networks by typing in a unique username and password at any of the networked computers. The best preventative measures include making the networked computers physically inaccessible by locking the area that contains them, or to enable BIOS security which allows the user to set a computer access name and password.

   Unauthorized users can also access a server-based network by using someone else's name and password. The best way to prevent this is to have an enforced password policy in which passwords are not written down and are changed regularly.

2. Describe the differences between password-protected shares and access permissions.

   Password-protected shares require that a password be assigned to each shared resource. Access to the shared resource is granted when a user enters the correct password. Access-permission security involves assigning certain rights on a user-by-user basis. A user types a password when logging on to the network. The server validates this user name and password combination and uses it to grant or deny access to shared resources.

3. Define data encryption and DES.

   Data encryption is the scrambling of data to make it inaccessible to unauthorized persons. In a network environment, data can be encrypted before being sent onto the network. This makes the data unreadable, even by someone who taps the cable and attempts to read the data as it passes over the network. When the data arrives at the proper computer, the code for deciphering encrypted data decodes the bits, translating them into understandable information.

   The Data Encryption Standard (DES) was developed by IBM and adopted as a specification for encryption by the government of the United States. DES describes how data should be encrypted and provides the specifications for the key to decryption. Both the sender and the receiver need to have access to the decryption key. Because the only way to get the key from one location to another is to physically or electronically transmit it, DES is vulnerable to unauthorized interception.

4. Identify four common types of computer viruses and describe how they are transmitted; describe three ways to help protect computers in a network against viruses.

Four types of computer virus are called companion, macro, polymorphic and stealth. Each is a kind of file infector virus. They can be transmitted by any physical means such as CDs, floppy disks or a direct cable connection between computers, and by electronic means such as e-mail and internet downloads. Three means of protection against a computer virus are the installation of current anti-virus software, write-protection of disks, and disabling macro capabilities in vulnerable software.

Lesson 2: Maintaining a Healthy Network Environment

Lesson Checkup

Page 426

1. Describe the ways in which heat, humidity, dust, and smoke can each have an adverse effect on computer health. For each, describe preventive measures that can be taken to protect computers in such environments.

If the room temperature in which the equipment is located is too high, a computer's cooling fan and ventilation slots will be unable to maintain the correct operating temperature and components will begin to overheat and fail.

High humidity promotes corrosion. Corroded contacts on cable connections and expansion cards will cause intermittent failures. Corrosion can also increase the resistance of electrical components, leading to a temperature increase that can be followed by component failure or fire.

Dust is electrostatically attracted to electronic equipment. It acts as an insulator that affects the cooling of components, causing them to overheat. Excessive dust on electronic equipment can cause electrical shorts and catastrophic equipment failure.

Smoke coats the surfaces of electronic components, acting as both insulator and conductor. Smoke residue also enhances the accumulation of dust.

Because electronic equipment is designed to operate within the same range of temperature and humidity that feels comfortable to human beings, the best preventative measure is to provide the computers with just such an environment.

2. Identify some of the human factors that can unintentionally alter a computer's operating environment. Describe the consequences to a computer of these factors, and suggest some preventive measures for each.

Because few employees have any awareness of the ventilation requirements for computer equipment, they impede the natural flow of air in and around the equipment. Once this happens, maintaining the proper temperature is impossible and failures begin. The spilling of liquid refreshment takes a toll on keyboards and computers. When it gets cold outside, space heaters are used in under-heated offices and are usually placed under the desk, often in close proximity to computers. This can present two problems: the computer becomes overheated, and the space heaters can overload power outlets, tripping circuit breakers or even causing fires. Humans can spill liquids such as coffee on computers, impede the flow of the computer's cooling air, and overheat computers with space heaters. The liquids can destroy the computer's internal circuitry and make keyboards unusable. Blocked air flow can cause a computer to overheat and burn out electronic components. The best preventative measure is to make computer users aware of the consequences of such behaviors.

3. Identify the principal hidden and industrial factors that can affect a network's health. Include out-of-view network equipment in both an office, and a manufacturing environment. Discuss what precautions can be taken, or what changes might need to be made, for each of these hidden and industrial factors.

Hidden factors include network wiring that runs through an attic, within walls or is otherwise invisible can be damaged during repairs to other objects in those spaces. Insects and rodents can use network materials for construction purposes of their own.

Industrial factors include noise, electromagnetic interference (EMI), vibration, corrosive and explosive environments, and untrained and unskilled workers.

These factors can be addressed by installing the networking equipment in separate enclosures with outside ventilation by using fiber-optic cabling to reduce electrical interference and corrosion problems with the cable by making sure that all equipment is properly grounded and by providing proper training to all employees that need to use the equipment.

Exercise 10.1: Case Study Problem

Page 440

A small organization recently suffered security breaches in its peer-to-peer network. The intruder stole valuable business data. The organization's need for security became apparent, and now a modest-sized, but more secure, server-based network is in place.

The organization is located in a small California community that experiences frequent earthquakes and power outages. Your job is to plan how to avoid breaches of security and plan for disaster recovery at the same time. In this exercise, examine preventive measures the organization can take to avoid data loss due to human activities and natural disasters such as earthquakes.

List the categories of things that can put the organization's data at risk. Discuss the preventive measures and recovery plans appropriate for each kind of data loss.

An organization's data can be put at risk by:

- **component failure.**
- **computer viruses.**
- **data deletion and corruption.**
- **fire caused by arson or electrical mishaps.**
- **natural disasters, such as lightning, floods, tornadoes, and earthquakes.**
- **power-supply failure and power surges.**
- **theft and vandalism.**

An organization can take the following preventive measures to avoid data loss due to human activities and natural disasters:

- **Use of tape and optical storage backup systems to minimize the risk of losing data. By maintaining current backup copies of existing files, data can be recovered if harm comes to the original data.**

- **Installation of Uninterruptible Power Supply (UPS) will allow computers to keep servers or other devices running in the event of a power failure. The best UPS systems perform online. When the power source fails, the UPS batteries automatically take over. The process is invisible to users.**

- **Incorporation of fault-tolerant disk systems such as Redundant Array of Independent Disks (RAID), Sector Sparing and disk clustering will protect data by duplicating data or by placing data in different physical sources, such as different partitions or different disks. Data redundancy allows access to data even if part of the data system fails.**

Disaster-recovery success is only as good as the disaster prevention and preparedness measures taken beforehand.

The only protection from a data-loss disaster is to implement one or more of the methods described earlier to back up data. Store your backups in a secure place, such as a bank safe deposit box, away from the network site. To fully recover from any disaster you will need to:

- Make a disaster-recovery plan.
- Implement the plan.
- Test the plan.

Chapter Review

Page 443

1. The first consideration in keeping data safe is to ensure the security of the network _____.

   hardware

2. Another term for access permissions is _____ - _____

   _____.

   user-level security

3. Implementing password-protected shares involves assigning a password to each shared _____.

   resource

4. If a share is set up as _____ - _____, users can look at the documents or copy them to their machines, but they cannot change the original documents.

   read-only

5. Access permission security involves assigning certain _____ on a user-by-user basis.

   rights

6. The most efficient way to assign permissions is through the use of

   _____.

   groups

7. Through auditing, selected types of events are recorded in the _____ _____ of a server in order to track network activities by user accounts.

   security logs

8. A data- _____ utility scrambles data before it goes out onto the network.

   encryption

9. The Commercial COMSEC Endorsement Program (CCEP) authorizes manufacturers to incorporate classified _____ into the communication systems they sell.

   algorithms

10. Diskless computers communicate with the server and log on through the use of a special ROM boot chip installed on the computer _____

    _____ _____.

    network interface card

11. The two most important environmental conditions to monitor are _____ and _____.

    temperature, humidity

12. Proper _____ is required to prevent a computer from overheating.

    ventilation

13. The potential for ESD increases as the humidity _____.

    drops

14. True or False: If network cables are installed in the walls and in the ceilings, they will be safe from all damage.

    False

15. A _____ atmosphere with high _____ will most certainly destroy any computer equipment in a matter of days or months.

    corrosive, humidity

16. The first line of defense against loss of data is usually a _____ _____ system.

    tape backup

17. It is important to have a regular _____ for backing up data.

    schedule

18. Maintaining a _____ of all backups is important for later file recovery.

    log

19. When backing up across a network, network traffic can be reduced by placing the backup computer on an isolated _____.

    segment

20. Fault-tolerant systems protect data by duplicating data or placing data in different _____ sources.

    physical

21. RAID level 0, called _____ _____, divides data into 64K blocks and spreads it equally in a fixed rate and order among all disks in an array.

    disk striping

22. Level 0 disk striping does not offer data _____.

    protection

23. Disk _____ duplicates a partition and moves the duplication onto another physical disk so that there are always two copies of the data.

    mirroring

24. Duplexing is intended to protect against disk _____ failures, as well as media failures.

    controller

25. Writing complete blocks of data to each disk in the array is known as disk _____.

    striping

26. In Windows NT Server, the _____ _____ program is used to configure Windows NT Server fault tolerance.

    Disk Administrator

27. In RAID level 10, data that is contained on a physical drive in one array is _____ on a drive in the second array.

    mirrored

28. "Clustering" is the term applied to a group of _____ systems working together as a single system.

    independent

Chapter 11: Printing on a Network

Lesson 1: Network Printing

Exercise 11.1: Term Definition Review

Page 449

In this exercise, a list of terms is given in the left column. For each term listed, fill in the definition in the space given in the column to the right.

Term	Definition
Redirection	**The direction of a request for services from the local computer out onto the network.**
Print spooler	**Software that intercepts a print job and sends it to a print queue.**
Print queue	**A buffer in which the print job is held until the printer is ready to print it.**
Print-sharing utility	**A utility that helps the network administrator manage all the functions of a print server.**
Share name	**The network name of a shared resource.**
Printer driver	**Software that allows the printer to work with the print server.**
Print Manager	**A Windows NT print-sharing utility.**

Lesson 2: Managing a Shared Printer

Lesson Checkup

Page 453

1. Identify and describe four tasks required for routine printer maintenance.

   Printer maintenance includes supplying the printer with paper and toner, clearing the printer if there is a paper jam, and monitoring the printer's output to ensure that print jobs do not back up and overflow the printer's output bin. Other tasks are monitoring the printer's performance and notifying a technician if a serious problem develops, as well as routinely cleaning the printer in accordance with the manufacturer's instructions.

2. Describe how a network administrator can allocate a single printer's resources among several workstations.

The best means of allocating a single printer's resources is to share the printer on a network. Then give users network permission to use the shared printer.

3. Define PDLs and describe their function in printing.

PDLs are page-description languages that tell a printer how printed output should look. The printer uses the PDL to construct text and graphics to create the page image.

Lesson 3: Sharing Fax Modems

Lesson Checkup

Page 455

1. How does a fax server compare with a shared printer? What are the roles of each?

A shared fax server does for fax communication what a shared printer does for printing: it makes fax capabilities available to all users on the network. A shared fax server allows anyone on the network to send a fax; a shared printer allows anyone on the network to access that printer's resources.

2. Define the function of a fax server.

A fax server gives users the ability to send a fax without having to leave their desks. Some fax servers allow an administrator to monitor incoming faxes and to route them to the intended recipients, while discarding others, such as advertisements.

3. Describe three enhancements that can be added to a fax server.

Some fax-enhancement software allows users to send faxes from word-processing packages, databases, spreadsheets, and e-mail. Some even provide diagnostic utilities, error reporting, and accounting features to make fax servers easy to administer.

Chapter Review

Page 457

1. When network users want to print data on a shared network printer, the data is sent to a _____ that feeds the data to the printer.

   server

2. Each network print job must be _____ away from a computer's local printer port and onto the network cable.

   redirected

3. The memory buffer in the print server's RAM that holds the print job until the printer is ready is called a _____.

   spooler

4. In order for users to access a shared printer, they must have a way to _____ the printer.

   identify

5. The printer uses the _____ to construct text and graphics to create the page image.

   PDL

6. Managing users who access printing over a computer network includes assigning _____, as with any other shared network resource.

   permissions

7. One task an administrator can accomplish from a remote location is to _____ print jobs in the queue.

   reorder

8. Most current network operating systems allow an administrator to manage a network printer with a _____ - _____ _____.

   print-sharing utility

9. A good fax server service allows an administrator to _____ incoming faxes and to _____ the appropriate one to the proper person.

   monitor, route

10. Fax-server enhancements that allow users to send faxes from _____, _____, and _____ are available.

    databases, spreadsheets, e-mail

Chapter 12: Administering Change

Lesson 1: Documenting a Running Network

Lesson Checkup

Page 471

1. What is a baseline of network performance? Why should you have one? How can you use it to determine if changes should be made to the network?

   A baseline is simply documentation of the network's normal operating values. The baseline needs to be updated whenever users, hardware, or software are added to or subtracted from the system. Administrators should be able to refer to a network baseline in order to compare current network performance with previous performance. A significant decline in performance numbers can indicate a need to upgrade the network.

2. What are network monitors and protocol analyzers? What part do they play in documenting network performance? In what ways can they alert you to degradation of network performance?

   A network monitor is a tool that captures and filters data packets and analyzes network activity. A protocol analyzer is a tool that keeps track of network statistics. It can capture bad frames and isolate their source. Together, these two tools can alert you to network performance and help isolate the source of network degradation. The information they provide can help you solve network performance problems more quickly.

3. Should the documentation that makes up a network history include specific information about the network's hardware and software? If so, why?

   Yes. Network documentation should contain a map of hardware for the entire network, server information, and software information such as licensing and support details. This information will provide a good foundation upon which to identify future needs for network modification.

Lesson 2: Upgrading a Network

Exercise 12.1: Case Study Problem

Page 481

You have been assigned to upgrade a network for a small manufacturer. Its network has been in place since 1989. Only minor upgrades or same-model equipment replacements have occurred. The network is configured as peer-to-peer, and there is no file server. The media is coaxial thicknet cable (Standard Ethernet). The network computers are 386-33 PCs. The operating system is Windows for Workgroups 3.11. The company uses shareware word-processing applications and spreadsheets as its office software.

The company would like to upgrade to a server-based network. It is adding office space to the building and would like to rewire the network with flexible, inexpensive media. The company is about to begin using new, powerful design software in its manufacturing process.

What do you recommend for the upgrade?

Add a mid-sized file server, and install server network software. Rewire with unshielded twisted-pair cabling. Upgrade the workstations to Pentium-class computers, and install workstation network software. Upgrade to an "Office Suite" software product for daily office operations. Install the new design software and test. Confirm the installation and train the end users as appropriate.

Lesson 3: Moving a Network

Exercise 12.2: Case Study Problem

Page 486

You have been assigned to move your company's file server, 10 workstations and two printers to a new office 500 miles away. The new office has been wired for the new network. Management has told you that the new network must be operational before the old one is turned off, because the business cannot afford any downtime. However, there will be no additional equipment purchased for the new office.

Can this network be moved without any downtime? If so, how? If not, what is your plan for relocating this network?

Because no equipment will be available to run a mirrored network during the relocation, this network must have some downtime. This move is best scheduled for a weekend. The move should include planning for coordination of staff during the discontinuation of the old network, packing, moving, and unpacking of equipment, installation of the workstation peripherals and server, testing each device for functionality and confirming the operation of the network as a whole.

Chapter Review

Page 489

1. Monitoring and documenting the network when it is in good working order provide a _____ against which unusual network performance can be compared.

   baseline

2. A network _____ is a tool that captures and filters data packets and analyzes network activity.

   monitor

3. _____ and _____ are utilities that are used to test the network connections by sending a packet to a remote host and monitoring its return.

   ping, tracert

4. During monitoring of network performance, _____ can indicate areas of poor performance that can benefit from upgrading.

   bottlenecks

5. Many network vendors provide a _____ _____ _____ software to aid in the monitoring and improvement of network performance.

   total system management

6. After creating a baseline for a network's performance, you will need to maintain a performance _____ to aid with future troubleshooting.

   history

7. To improve the performance of a network, an administrator can upgrade _____, _____, _____ and _____.

   servers, workstations, NICs, media

8. When working on electronic components, be careful to prevent _____ _____ _____ that will do damage to the components.

   static electrical charges

9. Installing a new NIC is the same as installing any _____ card.

   expansion

10. Upgrading routers, brouters, repeaters, and bridges is best carried out by a _____ _____.

    trained technician

11. The final step in any network upgrade is to _____ the upgrade.

    confirm

12. The best tool to use to confirm hardware changes to a network is the _____ utility.

    ping

13. How long the network can afford to be _____ is in important factor in organizing and timing a move.

    down

Chapter 13: Troubleshooting a Network

Lesson 1: Understanding the Problem

Exercise 13.1: Troubleshooting Problem

Page 498

Given the following scenario, describe how you would research, identify, prioritize, and resolve this network problem:

The network has been running well at the site of a small manufacturer. However, a user in the quality control division now calls to report that she is unable to get the daily status reports printed by the printer in the department. Meanwhile, the shipping department reports that a rerouted print job did not print in the quality control department. What is your strategy for solving this network problem?

The problem involves users in two different departments. They do not report any other problems with their system. Therefore, the problem probably lies with the printer. The priority of this problem is low to moderate.

Inspect the printer. Make sure that the power is attached and the network cable is attached to the printer. It is not uncommon for unusual signals on the network to cause a printer to stop printing. Before taking any disruptive steps, turn the printer off and then turn it on again. If this does not work, ask the users to reroute their print jobs to another printer, if possible, or make it possible for them to do so. Check the print queue for the presence of unprinted documents; corrupt print files can become stalled in the queue and prevent further printing. Conduct a self-test of the printer. Send a sample test page to the printer from a different computer than those experiencing the printing problem. Check the print queue for a reference to the sample page. After the cause has been determined, resolve the problem. If your research does not produce a cause, ask for assistance or consult the documentation that came with the device.

Lesson 2: Troubleshooting Tools

Lesson Checkup

Page 507

1. The _____ _____ is the primary all-purpose electronic measuring tool used by computer and electronic technicians.

   digital voltmeter

2. _____ - _____ _____ send sonar-like pulses along cables to locate breaks, shorts, or imperfections.

   Time-domain reflectometers

3. _____ are electronic instruments that measure the amount of signal voltage per unit of time and display the results on a monitor.

Oscilloscopes

4. In a crossover cable, the send wire from one computer is connected to the _____ port on the other computer.

receive

5. Protocol analyzers, also called "network analyzers," perform _____ - _____ network traffic analysis using packet capture, decoding, and transmission data.

real-time

6. A _____ _____ can help to establish a network's information baseline.

performance monitor

7. A network monitor allows the administrator to capture and analyze network _____ _____ to and from the server.

data streams

Lesson 3: Where to Find Help

Lesson Checkup

Page 519

1. Microsoft _____ provides information to support all aspects of networking with an emphasis on Microsoft products.

Technet

2. The Web, FTP, e-mail, news, and telnet are all services that are available on the _____.

Internet

3. An IP address consists of _____ sets of digits separated by dots.

four

4. The domain types for commercial organizations, educational institutions, government organizations, military organizations, network service providers, and organizations are _____, _____, _____, _____, _____, _____.

.com, .edu, .gov, .mil, .net, .org

5. Every Uniform Resource Locator (URL) consists of the _____, a colon (:), and the _____ of the resource.

protocol, address

6. The most common protocol used for sending files between computers is the

   _____ _____ _____.

   file transfer protocol

7. An e-mail address is composed of the user's _____, followed by the ___ sign, followed by the _____ of the recipient's computer.

   identification, @, location

8. The difference between Network News and e-mail is that with Network News, conversations take place in a _____ _____ called a newsgroup.

   public forum

9. The telnet protocol allows your computer to act as a _____ _____ to an Internet host.

   remote terminal

Chapter Review

Page 522

1. To isolate a network problem, the engineer can divide the network into

   _____.

   segments

2. A TDR sends _____ -like pulses along a cable looking for any kind of a break, short, or imperfection that might affect network performance.

   sonar

3. Protocol analyzers look inside the _____ to determine the cause of a problem.

   packet

4. Advanced cable testers will tell you if a particular cable or _____ is causing problems.

   NIC

5. One reason it is important to monitor network performance is to provide essential information for _____ detection.

   bottleneck

6. Windows NT Server Performance Monitor helps a network administrator view operations in both _____ time and _____ time.

   real, recorded

7. In an SNMP environment, programs called _____ monitor network traffic.

agents

8. A _____ monitor is a tool that is used to track network performance.

performance

9. Windows NT Performance Monitor has the ability to send an _____ to the network manager when there is a problem.

alert

10. Windows NT Server Network Monitor gives the administrator the ability to _____ and _____ network data streams to and from the server.

capture, analyze

11. The best source of information for Microsoft products is

_____.

TechNet

12. Other useful sources of information for network troubleshooting include _____, _____ _____, and _____.

BBSs, User Groups, periodicals

13. _____ is used to perform simple file transfers on the Internet.

FTP

14. _____ _____ _____ _____ is an Internet standard protocol defined for distribution, inquiry, retrieval, and posting of news articles.

Network News Transfer Protocol

15. You can use _____ to act as a remote terminal to an Internet host.

Telnet

16. In addition to URLs, every computer on the Internet has a unique _____ address.

IP

A P P E N D I X   B

Common Network Standards and Specifications

Standards have been responsible for the success and growth of both the computer and networking products industries. When a vendor subscribes to a set of standards, it means that the vendor is agreeing to make equipment that conforms to the specifications of the standard.

The Role of Standards in Networking

Most networks are a combination of hardware and software from a variety of vendors. This ability to combine the products manufactured by different vendors is made possible by the existence of industry standards.

Standards are guidelines that vendors adhere to voluntarily in order to make their products compatible with products from other vendors. In general those standards address:

- Size.
- Shape.
- Material.
- Function.
- Speed.
- Distance.

More specifically, the standards define physical and operational characteristics of:

- Personal computing equipment.
- Networking and communication equipment.
- Operating systems.
- Software.

For example, standards make it possible to buy a network interface card manufactured by one vendor for a computer manufactured by another vendor with reasonable assurance that the card will:

- Fit into the computer.
- Work with the network cabling.
- Translate signals from the computer and send them out onto the network.
- Receive data from the network and deliver it to the computer.

The Origin of Standards

Standards have grown primarily from two sources:

- Popular acceptance (customer driven)
- Organizational recommendations

Customer-driven standards emerge from popular acceptance. The best example of this is the term "PC-compatible," which means that a product will work with an IBM Personal Computer or clone. However, as the networking business grew through the mid- and late-1980s, it became apparent that customer-driven popularity was not adequate for creating and imposing standards.

The Influence of the Business Community

In the early years of networking, several large companies, including IBM, Honeywell, and Digital Equipment Corporation (DEC), used their own proprietary standards for how computers could be connected.

These standards described how to move data from one computer to another, but the standards applied only if all the computers were made by the same company. Getting equipment from one vendor to communicate with equipment from another vendor was problematic.

For example, networks adhering to IBM's complex networking architecture, called Systems Network Architecture (SNA), could not directly communicate with networks using DEC's Digital Network Architecture (DNA).

As networking technology matured, businesses began to trust crucial data to networking. But in the mid-1980s, the same communication problems existed between network vendors that had existed earlier among mainframe vendors. The increasing need for businesses to interact and share data was inescapable.

Computer manufacturers saw this as a business opportunity. They realized that networking technology which enabled communication by conforming to standards would be far more profitable in the long run than equipment that would work only in a single-vendor environment. As a result, standards gradually became a part of the computer and network environment.

The Influence of the Technical Community

Today, certain domestic and international organizations, rather than customers, create and define nearly all networking technical standards.

Some of these organizations have existed for many years, and some, such as the SQL Access Group, have evolved more recently as new applications have appeared. These, in turn, created new networking environments that required new guidelines.

Although there are probably dozens of organizations currently advocating standards of every description, only a few have gained the recognition required to enlist the support of major computing vendors. These associations and organizations have become the foundation upon which network acceptance is based. Therefore, network engineers need to be familiar with the names of the organizations and the networking areas they influence.

Standards Organizations

There is no single source for all networking standards. Usually, a standards organization coordinates the specifications for various pieces of equipment or sets the parameters for features or functions. However, sometimes a need for a new standard will set events in motion and eventually result in a standard through consensus or through the action of the marketplace.

Most local and international network standards have originated with a limited number of organizations. Each of these organizations defines standards for a different area of network activity. The organizations are:

- American National Standards Institute (ANSI).
- Comité Consultatif Internationale de Télégraphie et Téléphonie (CCITT).
- Electronics Industries Association (EIA).
- Institute of Electrical and Electronics Engineers (IEEE).
- International Organization for Standardization (ISO).
- Object Management Group (OMG).
- Open Software Foundation (OSF).
- SQL Access Group (SAG).

It is important to be aware of these organizations because their acronyms have become a common feature of the general networking vocabulary.

American National Standards Institute (ANSI)

ANSI is an organization of U.S. industry and business groups dedicated to the development of trade and communication standards. ANSI defines and publishes standards for:

- Codes.
- Alphabets.
- Signaling schemes.
- Communications protocols.

ANSI also represents the United States in the International Organization for Standardization (ISO) and the International Telecommunications Union (ITU).

ANSI in Microcomputers

In the microcomputer field, ANSI is commonly encountered in the areas of programming languages and the SCSI interface. Programming languages, such as C, conform to ANSI recommendations to eliminate problems in transporting a program from one type of computer system or environment to another.

ANSI Specifications

Major ANSI specifications and standards include:

- ANSI 802.1–1985/IEEE 802.5   Token Ring access, protocols, cabling, and interface.

- ANSI/IEEE 802.3   Coaxial-cable carrier-sense multiple-access with collision detection (CSMA/CD) for Ethernet networks.

- ANSI X3.135   Structured query language (SQL) database query methods for front-end clients and back-end database services.

- ANSI X3.92   A privacy and security encryption algorithm.

- ANSI X12   Electronic data interchange (EDI) defining the exchange of purchase orders, bills of lading, invoices, and other business forms.

- ANSI X3T9.5   Fiber Distributed Data Interface (FDDI) specification for voice and data transmission over fiber-optic cable at 100 Mbps.

- SONET   Synchronous Optical Network, a fiber-optic specification defining a global infrastructure for the transmission of synchronous and isochronous (time-sensitive data such as real-time video) information.

Comité Consultatif Internationale de Télégraphie et Téléphonie (CCITT)

The CCITT, which is also known as the International Telegraph and Telephone Consultative Committee, is based in Geneva, Switzerland. It was established as part of the United Nations International Telecommunications Union (ITU), and ITU remains its parent organization. The CCITT studies and recommends use of communications standards that are recognized throughout the world, and publishes its recommendations every four years. Each update is distinguished by the color of its cover.

CCITT Protocols

CCITT protocols apply to:

- Modems.
- Networks.
- Facsimile transmission (faxes).

The CCITT Study Groups

The CCITT has been divided into study groups for the 1997–2000 study period; each study group is preparing recommendations for standards in a different subject area. These subject areas include:

- SG 2   Network and service operation.
- SG 3   Tariff and accounting principles, including related telecommunications economic and policy issues.
- SG 4   TMN and network maintenance.
- SG 5   Protection against electromagnetic effects from the environment.
- SG 6   Outside plant.
- SG 7   Data networks and open system communications.
- SG 8   Characteristics of telematic systems.
- SG 9   Television and sound transmission.
- SG 10   Languages and general software aspects for telecommunication systems.
- SG 11   Signaling requirements and protocols.
- SG 12   End-to-end transmission performance of networks and terminals.
- SG 13   General network aspects.
- SG 15   Transport networks, systems, and equipment.
- SG 16   Multimedia services and systems.

The V Series

The recommendations for standardizing modem design and operations (transmission over telephone networks) are collectively called the V series. These include:

- V.22   1200 bps full-duplex modem standard.
- V.22bis   2400 bps full-duplex modem standard.
- V.28   Defines circuits in RS-232 interface.
- V.32   Asynchronous and synchronous 4800/9600 bps standard.
- V.32bis   Asynchronous and synchronous standard up to 14,400 bps.
- V.35   Defines high data-rates over combined circuits.
- V.42   Defines error-checking standards.
- V.90   Defines a standard for 56Kbps modem communication.

The X Series

The X series covers Open Systems Interconnection (OSI) standards including:

- X.200 (ISO 7498)   OSI reference model.
- X.25 (ISO 7776)   Packet-switching network interface.
- X.400 (ISO 10021)   Message handling (e-mail).
- X.500 (ISO 9594)   Directory services.
- X.700 (ISO 9595)   Common Management Information Protocol (CMIP).

Electronics Industries Association (EIA)

The EIA is an organization founded in 1924 by U.S. manufacturers of electronic parts and equipment. It develops industry standards for the interface between data processing and communications equipment and has published many standards associated with telecommunications and computer communications. The EIA works closely with other associations such as ANSI and ITU (CCITT).

EIA Serial Interface Standards

The EIA standards for the serial interface between modems and computers include:

- RS-232   A standard for serial connections using DB-9 or DB-25 connectors and maximum cable lengths of 50 feet. It defines the serial connections between DTE (Data Terminal Equipment—transmitting equipment) devices and DCE (Data Communications Equipment—receiving equipment) devices.
- RS-449   A serial interface with DB-37 connections that defines the RS-422 and RS-423 as subsets.
- RS-422   Defines a balanced multipoint interface.
- RS-423   Defines an unbalanced digital interface.

CCITT Equivalents

BIA standards often have CCITT equivalents. RS-232, for example, is also the CCITT V.24 standard.

Institute of Electrical and Electronics Engineers (IEEE)

The Institute of Electrical and Electronics Engineers (IEEE) is a U.S.-based society that publishes a variety of standards including those for data communications.

The 802 Committees

A subgroup of the IEEE, the 802 committees began developing network specifications in 1980 to ensure low-cost interfaces. These specifications are passed on to the ANSI for approval and standardization within the United States. They are also forwarded to the ISO.

Shortly after the 802 project began, the IEEE realized that a single network standard would be inadequate because it would not be able to account for the diverse hardware and emerging architectures. To adequately cover the wide range of subjects, the society established committees that were to be responsible for defining standards in different networking areas.

The 802 Committees

The 802 committees are:

- 802.1   Internetworking.
- 802.2   Logical Link Control (LLC).
- 802.3   CSMA/CD NETWORK (Ethernet).
- 802.4   Token Bus NETWORK.
- 802.5   Token Ring NETWORK.
- 802.6   Metropolitan Area Network (MAN).
- 802.7   Broadband Technical Advisory Group.
- 802.8   Fiber-Optic Technical Advisory Group.
- 802.9   Integrated Voice/Data Networks.
- 802.10   Network Security.
- 802.11   Wireless Network.
- 802.12   Demand Priority Access NETWORK (100VG-AnyLAN).
- 802.13   Cable TV Access Method and Physical Layer Specification.

International Organization for Standardization (ISO)

The International Organization for Standardization (ISO) is a Paris-based organization of member countries, each of which is represented by its leading standard-setting organization. For example, ANSI represents the United States, and the British Standards Institution (BSI) represents the United Kingdom. Other organizations represented at the ISO include:

- Governmental bodies such as the U.S. State Department.
- Businesses.
- Educational institutes.
- Research organizations.
- CCITT.

The ISO works to establish international standardization of all services and manufactured products.

ISO Computer Communication Goals

In the area of computing, the ISO's goal is to establish global standards for communications and information exchange. The standards will promote open networking environments that let multivendor computer systems communicate with one another using protocols that have been accepted internationally by the ISO membership.

The ISO Model

The ISO's major achievement in the area of networking and communications has been to define a set of standards, known as the OSI (Open Systems Interconnection) reference model which defines standards for the interaction of computers connected by communications networks.

Object Management Group (OMG)

The OMG consists of almost 300 organizations involved in developing a suite of languages, interfaces, and protocol standards that vendors can use to create applications that will operate in multivendor environments.

The OMG certifies products designed to meet the standards and specifications agreed upon by the OMG members.

In working toward its goals, the OMG developed the Object Management Architecture (OMA), a model for object-oriented applications and environments.

The OMG architecture has been adopted by the Open Software Foundation (OSF), which is developing portable software environments called the Distributed Computing Environment (DCE) and the Distributed Management Environment (DME).

The OMG standards are similar to elements in Microsoft object linking and embedding (OLE).

Open Software Foundation (OSF)

The OSF, part of the Open Group, creates computing environments by acquiring and combining technologies from other vendors and distributing the results to interested parties.

These vendor-neutral environments, referred to as the Open System Software Environment, can be used to create a collection of open systems technologies in which users can incorporate software and hardware from several sources.

The following components comprise the OSF software environment:

- Distributed Computing Environment (DCE)

  This platform simplifies the development of products in a mixed environment.

- Distributed Management Environment (DME)

  The DME makes tools available for managing systems in distributed and multivendor environments.

- The Open Software Foundation/1 (OSF/1)

  This is a UNIX operating system, based on the Mach kernel, that supports symmetric multiprocessing, enhanced security features, and dynamic configuration.

- OSF/Motif

  This is a graphical user interface that creates a common environment with links to IBM's Common User Access (CUA).

- OSF Architecture-Neutral Distribution Format (ANDF)

  Developers can use this environment to create a single version of an application that can be used on different hardware architectures.

SQL Access Group (SAG)

A part of the ANSI standards, SAG is a consortium of 39 companies that was founded in 1989 by Hewlett-Packard, Digital, Oracle Corporation, and Sun Microsystems. Its charter is to work with the ISO to create standards covering the interoperability of front- and back-end systems.

SAG's purpose is to promote interoperability among structured query language (SQL) standards so that several SQL-based relational databases and tools can work together in a multivendor database environment. This will make it possible for different database applications running on different platforms to share and exchange data.

SAG Technical Specifications

SAG has developed three technical specifications:

- Structured query language

  This is a specification that follows international specifications in implementing the SQL language.

- SQL Remote Database Access

  This specification defines communication between a remote database server and an SQL-based client.

- SQL Access Call-Level Interface (CLI)

  This group of APIs provides interfacing with SQL-based products.

Glossary

5-4-3 rule A rule that states that a thinnet network can combine as many as five cable segments connected by four repeaters. However, only three segments can have stations attached, which leaves two segments untapped.

10Base2 Ethernet topology that transmits at 10 Mbps over a baseband wire, and can carry a signal 185 meters. *See also* thinnet.

10Base5 *See* standard Ethernet.

10BaseFL An Ethernet network that typically uses fiber-optic cable to connect computers and repeaters.

10BaseT A 10 Mbps Ethernet network topology that typically uses unshielded twisted-pair (UTP) cable to connect computers. The maximum length of a 10BaseT segment is 100 meters (328 feet).

100BaseX Ethernet *See* Fast Ethernet.

100VG (Voice Grade) AnyLAN (100VGAnyLAN) An emerging networking technology that combines elements of both Ethernet and Token Ring.

A

access method The set of rules that defines how a computer puts data onto the network cable and takes data from the cable. When data is moving on the network, access methods help to regulate the flow of network traffic.

access permissions Features that control access to sharing in Windows NT Server. Permissions can be set for the following access levels:

No Access—Prevents access to the shared directory, its subdirectories, and its files.

Read—Allows viewing of file and subdirectory names, changing to a shared directory's subdirectory, viewing data in files, and running applications.

Change—Allows viewing of file and subdirectory names, changing to a shared directory's subdirectories, viewing data in files and running application files, adding files and subdirectories to a shared directory, changing data in files, and deleting subdirectories and files.

Full Control—Includes the same permissions as Change, plus changing permissions (taking ownership of the Windows NT file system [NTFS] files and directories only).

account *See* user account.

account policy Controls how passwords must be used by all user accounts in a domain or in an individual computer.

Address Resolution Protocol (ARP) Determines hardware addresses (MAC addresses) that correspond to an IP address.

ADSL *See* Asymmetric Digital Subscriber Line (ADSL).

advanced cable testers Cable testers that work beyond the physical layer of the OSI reference model up into layers 2, 3, and even 4. They can display information about the condition of the physical cable as well as message-frame counts, excess collisions, late collisions, error-frame counts, congestion errors, and beaconing. These testers can monitor overall network traffic, certain kinds of error situations, and traffic to and from a particular computer. They indicate if a particular cable or network interface card (NIC) is causing problems.

advanced program-to-program communication (APPC) A specification developed as part of IBM's SNA (Systems Network Architecture) model and designed to enable application programs running on different computers to communicate and exchange data directly. *See also* Systems Network Architecture.

AFP *See* AppleTalk filing protocol (AFP).

agent A program that performs a background task for a user and reports to the user when the task is done or when some expected event has taken place.

American National Standards Institute (ANSI) An organization of American industry and business groups dedicated to the development of trade and communications standards. ANSI is the American representative to the International Organization for Standardization (ISO). *See also* International Organization for Standardization (ISO).

amplifier A device, such as a repeater or bridge, that amplifies or increases the power of electrical signals, allowing them to travel on additional cable segments at their original strength. Amplifiers strengthen signals that have been weakened by attenuation.

analog Related to a continuously variable physical property, such as voltage, pressure, or rotation. An analog device can represent an infinite number of values within the range the device can handle. *See also* analog line, digital.

analog line A communications line, such as a telephone line, that carries information in analog (continuously variable) form. To minimize distortion and noise interference, an analog line uses amplifiers to strengthen the signal periodically during transmission.

ANSI *See* American National Standards Institute (ANSI).

APPC *See* advanced program-to-program communication (APPC).

AppleShare AppleShare is the Apple network operating system. Features include file sharing, client software that is included with every copy of the Apple operating system, and the AppleShare print server, a server-based print spooler.

AppleTalk The Apple network architecture that is included in the Macintosh operating system software. It is a collection of protocols that correspond to the OSI model. Thus network capabilities are built into every Macintosh. AppleTalk protocols support LocalTalk, Ethernet (EtherTalk), and Token Ring (TokenTalk).

AppleTalk filing protocol (AFP) Describes how files are stored and accessed on the network. AFP is responsible for the Apple hierarchical filing structure of volumes, folders, and files and provides for file sharing between Macintoshes and MS-DOS-based computers. It provides an interface for communication between AppleTalk and other network operating systems, allowing Macintoshes to be integrated into any network that uses an operating system that recognizes AFP.

application layer The top (seventh) layer of the OSI reference model. This layer serves as the window that application processes use to access network services. It represents the services that directly support user applications, such as software for file transfers, database access, and e-mail.

application programming interface (API) A set of routines that an application program uses to request and carry out lower-level services performed by the operating system.

application protocols Protocols that work at the higher end of the OSI reference model, providing application-to-application interaction and data exchange. Popular application protocols include:

FTAM (file transfer access and management)— A file access protocol.

SMTP (simple mail transfer protocol)—A TCP/IP protocol for transferring e-mail.

Telnet—A TCP/IP protocol for logging on to remote hosts and processing data locally.

NCP (NetWare core protocol)—The primary protocol used to transmit information between a NetWare server and its clients.

ArcNet (Attached Resource Computer Network) Developed by Datapoint Corporation in 1977, designed as a baseband, token-passing, bus architecture, transmitting at 2.5 Mbps. A successor to the original ArcNet, *ArcNetplus* supports data transmission rates of 20 Mbps. A simple, inexpensive, flexible network architecture designed for workgroup-sized LANs, ArcNet runs on coaxial, twisted-pair, and fiber-optic cable and supports up to 255 nodes. ArcNet technology predates IEEE Project 802 standards but loosely maps to the 802.4 document. *See also* Project 802.

ARP *See* Address Resolution Protocol (ARP).

ARPANET (Advanced Research Projects Agency Network) Acronym for the Department of Defense Advanced Research Projects Agency. A pioneering wide area network (WAN), ARPANET was designed to facilitate the exchange of information between universities and other research organizations. ARPANET, which became operational in the 1960s, is the network from which the Internet evolved.

ASCII (American Standard Code for Information Interchange) A coding scheme that assigns numeric values to letters, numbers, punctuation marks, and certain other characters. By standardizing the values used for these characters, ASCII enables computers and computer programs to exchange information.

Asymmetric Digital Subscriber Line (ADSL) A recent modem technology that converts existing twisted-pair telephone lines into access paths for multimedia and high-speed data communications. These new connections can transmit more than 8 Mbps to the subscriber and up to 1 Mbps from the subscriber. ADSL is recognized as a physical layer transmission protocol for unshielded twisted-pair media.

asynchronous transfer mode (ATM) An advanced implementation of packet switching that provides high-speed data transmission rates to send fixed-size cells over broadband LANs or WANs. Cells are 53 bytes—48 bytes of data with five additional bytes of address. ATM accommodates voice, data, fax, real-time video, CD-quality audio, imaging, and multimegabit data transmission. ATM uses switches as multiplexers to permit several computers to put data on a network simultaneously. Most commercial ATM boards transmit data at about 155 Mbps, but theoretically a rate of 1.2 gigabits per second is possible.

asynchronous transmission A form of data transmission in which information is sent one character at a time, with variable time intervals between characters. Asynchronous transmission does not rely on a shared timer that allows the sending and receiving units to separate characters by specific time periods. Therefore, each transmitted character consists of a number of data bits (that compose the character itself), preceded by a start bit and ending in an optional parity bit followed by a 1-, 1.5-, or 2-stop bit.

ATM *See* asynchronous transfer mode (ATM).

attachment unit interface (AUI) The connector used with standard Ethernet that often includes a cable running off the main, or backbone, coaxial cable. Also known as a DIX connector.

attenuation The weakening or degrading (distorting) of a transmitted signal as it travels farther from its point of origin. This could be a digital signal on a cable or the reduction in amplitude of an electrical signal, without the appreciable modification of the waveform. Attenuation is usually measured in decibels. Attenuation of a signal transmitted over a long cable is corrected by a repeater, which amplifies and cleans up an incoming signal before sending it farther along the cable.

auditing A process that tracks network activities by user accounts and a routine element of network security. Auditing can produce records of list users who have accessed—or attempted to access—specific resources; help administrators identify unauthorized activity; and track activities such as logon attempts, connection and disconnection from designated resources, changes made to files and directories, server events and modifications, password changes, and logon parameter changes.

AUI *See* attachment unit interface (AUI).

authentication Verification based on user name, passwords, and time and account restrictions.

AWG (American Wire Gauge) A standard that determines wire diameter. The diameter varies inversely to the gauge number.

B

backbone The main cable, also known as the trunk segment, from which transceiver cables connect to computers, repeaters, and bridges.

back end In a client/server application, the part of the program that runs on the server.

backup A duplicate copy of a program, a disk, or data, made to secure valuable files from loss.

backup domain controller (BDC) In a Windows NT Server domain, a computer that receives a copy of the domain's security policy and domain database and authenticates network logons. It provides a backup if the primary domain controller (PDC) becomes unavailable. A domain is not required to have a BDC, but it is recommended to have a BDC to back up the PDC. *See also* domain, domain controller, primary domain controller.

bandwidth In communications, the difference between the highest and lowest frequencies in a given range. For example, a telephone accommodates a bandwidth of 3000 Hz, or the difference between the lowest (300 Hz) and highest (3300 Hz) frequencies it can carry. In computer networks, greater bandwidth indicates faster or greater data-transfer capability.

barrel connector A component that can connect two pieces of cable to make a longer piece of cable.

baseband A system used to transmit the encoded signals over cable. Baseband uses digital signaling over a single frequency. Signals flow in the form of discrete pulses of electricity or light. With baseband transmission, the entire communication-channel capacity is used to transmit a single data signal.

base I/O port Specifies a channel through which information is transferred between a computer's hardware, such as the network interface card (NIC), and its CPU.

base memory address Defines the address of the location in a computer's memory (RAM) that is used by the NIC. This setting is sometimes called the RAM start address.

baud A measure of data-transmission speed named after the French engineer and telegrapher Jean-Maurice-Emile Baudot. It is a measure of the speed of oscillation of the sound wave on which a bit of data is carried over telephone lines. Because baud was originally used to measure the transmission speed of telegraph equipment, the term sometimes refers to the data-transmission speed of a modem. However, current modems can send at a speed higher than one bit per oscillation, so baud is being replaced by the more accurate bps (bits per second) as a measure of modem speed.

baud rate Refers to the speed at which a modem can transmit data. Often confused with bps (the number of bits per second transmitted), baud rate actually measures the number of events, or signal changes, that occur in one second. Because one event can actually encode more than one bit in high-speed digital communication, baud rate and bps are not always synonymous, and the latter is the more accurate term to apply to modems. For example, the 9600-baud modem that encodes four-bits per event actually operates at 2400 baud, but transmits at 9600 bps (2400 events times 4 bits per event), and thus should be called a 9600-bps modem.

BBS *See* bulletin board system (BBS).

BDC *See* Backup Domain Controller (BDC).

beaconing The process of signaling computers on a ring system that token passing has been interrupted by a serious error. All computers in an FDDI or Token Ring network are responsible for monitoring the token-passing process. To isolate serious failures in the ring, FDDI and Token Ring use beaconing in which a computer that detects a fault sends a signal, called a beacon, onto the network. The computer continues to send the beacon until it notices a beacon from its upstream neighbor. This process continues until the only computer sending a beacon is the one directly downstream of the failure. When the beaconing computer finally receives its own beacon, it assumes the problem has been fixed and regenerates a token.

bind To associate two pieces of information with one another.

binding A process that establishes the communication channel between a protocol driver and a NIC driver.

BISDN *See* broadband Integrated Services Digital Network (BISDN).

bisync (binary synchronous communications protocol) A communications protocol developed by IBM. Bisync transmissions are encoded in either ASCII or EBCDIC. Messages can be of any length and are sent in units called frames, optionally preceded by a message header. Because bisync uses synchronous transmission, in which message elements are separated by a specific time interval, each frame is preceded and followed by special characters that enable the sending and receiving machines to synchronize their clocks.

bit Short for binary digit: either 1 or 0 in the binary number system. In processing and storage, a bit is the smallest unit of information handled by a computer. It is represented physically by an element such as a single pulse sent through a circuit or small spot on a magnetic disk capable of storing either a 1 or 0. Eight bits make a byte.

bits per second (bps) A measure of the speed at which a device can transfer data. *See also* baud rate.

bit time The time it takes for each station to receive and store a bit.

BNC cable connector A connector for coaxial cable that locks when one connector is inserted into another and is rotated 90 degrees.

BNC components A family of components that include the BNC cable connector, BNC T connector, BNC barrel connector, and the BNC terminator. The origin of the acronym "BNC" is unclear; names ascribed to these letters range from "British Naval Connector" to "Bayonet Neill-Councelman."

boot-sector virus A type of virus that resides in the first sector of a floppy disk or hard drive. When the computer is booted, the virus executes. In this common method of transmitting viruses from one floppy disk to another, the virus replicates itself onto the new drive each time a new disk is inserted and accessed.

bottleneck A device or program that significantly degrades network performance. Poor network performance results when a device uses noticeably more CPU time than it should, consumes too much of a resource, or lacks the capacity to handle the load. Potential bottlenecks can be found in the CPU, memory, NIC, and other components.

bounce *See* signal bounce.

bps *See* bits per second (bps).

bridge A device used to join two LANs. It allows stations on either network to access resources on the other. Bridges can be used to increase the length or number of nodes for a network. The bridge makes connections at the data-link layer of the OSI reference model.

bridged network A network that is connected by bridges.

broadband Integrated Services Digital Network (BISDN) A consultative committee for the CCITT that recommends definitions for voice, data, and video in the megabit-gigabit range. BISDN is also a single ISDN network that can handle voice, data, and video services. BISDN works with an optical cable transport network called Synchronous Optical Network (SONET) and an asynchronous transfer mode (ATM) switching service. SMDS (Switched Multimegabit Data Services) is a BISDN service that offers high bandwidth to WANs. *See also* Synchronous Optical Network (SONET), asynchronous transfer mode (ATM), Switched Multimegabit Data Services (SMDS).

broadband network A type of LAN on which transmissions travel as analog (radio-frequency) signals over separate inbound and outbound channels. Devices on a broadband network are connected by coaxial or fiber-optic cable, and signals flow across the physical medium in the form of electromagnetic or optical waves. A broadband system uses a large portion of the electromagnetic spectrum with a range of frequencies from 50 Mbps to 600 Mbps. These networks can simultaneously accommodate television, voice, data, and other services over multiple transmission channels.

broadcast A transmission sent simultaneously to more than one recipient. In communication and on networks, a broadcast message is one distributed to all stations or computers on the network.

broadcast storm An event that occurs when there are so many broadcast messages on the network that they approach or surpass the capacity of the network bandwidth. This can happen when one computer on the network transmits a flood of frames saturating the network with traffic so it can no longer carry messages from any other computer. Such a broadcast storm can shut down a network.

brouter A network component that combines the best qualities of a bridge and a router. A brouter can act as a router for one protocol and as a bridge for all the others. Brouters can route selected routable protocols, bridge nonroutable protocols, and deliver more cost-effective and manageable internetworking than separate bridges and routers. A brouter is a good choice in an environment that mixes several homogeneous LAN segments with two different segments.

buffer A reserved portion of RAM in which data is held temporarily, pending an opportunity to complete its transfer to or from a storage device or another location in memory.

built-in groups One of four kinds of group accounts used by Microsoft Windows NT and Windows NT Server. Built-in groups, as the name implies, are included with the network operating system. Built-in groups have been granted useful collections of rights and built-in abilities. In most cases, a built-in group provides all the capabilities needed by a particular user. For example, if a domain user account belongs to the built-in Administrators group, logging on with that account gives a user administrative capabilities over the domain and the servers in the domain. *See also* user account.

bulletin board system (BBS) A computer system equipped with one or more modems or other means of network access that serves as an information and message-passing center for remote users. Many software and hardware companies run proprietary BBSs for customers that include sales information, technical support, and software upgrades and patches.

bus Parallel wires or cabling that connect components in a computer.

bus topology A topology that connects each computer, or station, to a single cable. At each end of the cable is a terminating resistor, or terminator. A transmission is passed back and forth along the cable, past the stations and between the two terminators, carrying a message from one end of the network to the other. As the message passes each station, the station checks the message's destination address. If the address in the message matches the station's address, the station receives the message. If the addresses do not match, the bus carries the message to the next station, and so on.

byte A unit of information consisting of 8 bits. In computer processing or storage, a byte is equivalent to a single character, such as a letter, numeral, or punctuation mark. Because a byte represents only a small amount of information, amounts of computer memory are usually given in kilobytes (1024 bytes or 2 raised to the 10th power), megabytes (1,048,576 bytes or 2 raised to the 20th power), gigabytes (1024 megabytes), terabytes (1024 gigabytes), petabytes (1024 terabytes), or exabytes (1024 petabytes).

C

cable categories The three major groups of cabling that connect the majority of networks: coaxial, twisted-pair (unshielded twisted-pair and shielded twisted-pair), and fiber-optic cabling.

cable testers *See* advanced cable testers.

cache A special memory subsystem or part of RAM in which frequently used data values are duplicated for quick access. A memory cache stores the contents of frequently accessed RAM locations and the addresses where these data items are stored. When the processor references an address in memory, the cache checks to see whether it holds that address. If it does hold the address, the data is returned to the processor; if it does not, regular memory access occurs. A cache is useful when RAM accesses are slow as compared to the microprocessor speed.

carrier-sense multiple access with collision avoidance (CSMA/CA) access method An access method by which each computer signals its intent to transmit before it actually transmits data, thus avoiding possible transmission collisions. *See also* access method.

carrier-sense multiple access with collision detection (CSMA/CD) access method An access method generally used with bus topologies. Using CSMA/CD, a station "listens" to the physical medium to determine whether another station is currently transmitting a data frame. If no other station is transmitting, the station sends its data. A station "listens" to the medium by testing the medium for the presence of a carrier, a specific level of voltage or light—thus the term carrier-sense. The multiple access indicates that there are multiple stations attempting to access or put data on the cable at the same time. The collision detection indicates that the stations are also listening for collisions. If two stations attempt to transmit at the same time and a collision occurs, the stations must wait a random period of time before attempting to transmit. *See also* access method.

CCEP *See* Commercial COMSEC Endorsement Program (CCEP).

CCITT (Comité Consultatif Internationale de Télégraphie et Téléphonie) An organization based in Geneva, Switzerland, and established as part of the United Nations International Telecommunications Union (ITU). The CCITT recommends use of communication standards that are recognized throughout the world. Protocols established by the CCITT are applied to modems, networks, and facsimile transmission.

Cellular Digital Packet Data (CDPD) A communication standard that uses very fast technology, similar to that of cellular telephones, to offer computer data transmissions over existing analog voice networks between voice calls, when the system is not occupied with voice communication.

central file server A network in which specific computers take on the role of server with other computers on the network sharing the resources. *See also* client/server.

central processing unit (CPU) The computational and control unit of a computer, the device that interprets and carries out instructions. Single-chip CPUs, called microprocessors, made personal computers possible. Examples include the 80286, 80386, 80486, and Pentium processors.

cladding The concentric layer of glass that surrounds the extremely thin, cylindrical glass core in fiber-optic cable.

client A computer that accesses shared network resources provided by another computer, called a server.

client/server A network architecture designed around the concept of distributed processing in which a task is divided between a back end (server), that stores and distributes data, and a front end (client) that requests specific data from the server. *See also* central file server.

coaxial cable (coax) A conductive center wire surrounded by an insulating layer, a layer of wire mesh (shielding), and a nonconductive outer layer. Coaxial cable is resistant to interference and signal weakening that other cabling, such as unshielded twisted-pair cable, can experience.

codec (compression/decompression) Compression/decompression technology for digital video and stereo audio.

Commercial COMSEC Endorsement Program (CCEP) A data-encryption standard introduced by the National Security Agency. Vendors who have the proper security clearance can join CCEP and be authorized to incorporate classified algorithms into communications systems. *See also* encryption.

companion virus A virus that uses the name of a real program, but has a different file extension from that of the program itself. The virus is activated when its companion program is opened. The companion virus uses a .COM file extension, which overrides the .EXE file extension and activates the virus.

concentrator A network physical-layer device that serves as a central connection for other network devices. *See also* hub.

contention Competition among stations on a network for the opportunity to use a communication line or network resource. Two or more computers attempt to transmit over the same cable at the same time, thus causing a collision on the cable. Such a system needs regulation to eliminate data collisions on the cable which can destroy data and bring network traffic to a halt. *See also* carrier-sense multiple access with collision detection (CSMA/CD) access method.

core In coaxial cable, the innermost part of the cable that carries the electronic signals which make up the data. It can be solid (usually copper) or stranded. In fiber-optic cable, digital data signals travel through an extremely thin cylindrical glass core surrounded by cladding.

CPU *See* central processing unit (CPU).

CRC *See* cyclical redundancy check (CRC).

crossover cable Used to connect two computers directly with a single patch cable, so that the send wire from one computer is connected to the receive port on the other computer. Crossover cables are useful in troubleshooting network connection problems.

crosstalk Signal overflow from an adjacent wire. When a second faint telephone conversation is heard in the background while one is making a phone call, crosstalk is occurring.

CSMA/CD *See* carrier-sense multiple access with collision detection (CSMA/CD) access method.

cyclical redundancy check (CRC) A form of error checking in transmitting data. The sending packet includes a number produced by a mathematical calculation made at the transmission source. When the packet arrives at its destination, the calculation is redone. If the two figures are the same, this indicates that the data in the packet has remained stable. If the calculation at the destination differs from the calculation at the source, this indicates that the data has changed during the transmission. In that case, the CRC routine signals the source computer to retransmit the data.

D

daisy chain A set of devices, such as Small Computer System Interfaces (SCSIs) and Universal Serial Buses (USBs), that are connected in a series. When devices are daisy-chained to a microcomputer, the first device is connected to the computer, the second device is connected to the first, and so on down the line. Signals are passed through the chain from one device to the next. *See also* Small Computer System Interface (SCSI) and Universal Serial Bus (USB).

database management system (DBMS) A layer of software between the physical database and the user. The DBMS manages all requests for database action from the user, including keeping track of the physical details of file locations and formats, indexing schemes, and so on. In addition, a DBMS permits centralized control of security and data integrity requirements.

Data Communications Equipment (DCE) One of two types of hardware connected by an RS-232 serial connection, the other being a DTE (data terminal equipment) device. A DCE device takes input from a DTE device and often acts as an intermediary device, transforming the input signal in some way before sending it to the actual recipient. For example, an external modem is a DCE device that accepts data from a microcomputer (DTE), modulates it, then sends the data along a telephone connection. In communication, an RS-232 DCE device receives data over line 2 and transmits over line 3. In contrast, a DTE device receives over line 3 and transmits over line 2. *See also* Data Terminal Equipment (DTE).

data encryption *See* encryption.

data encryption standard (DES) A commonly used, highly sophisticated algorithm developed by the U.S. National Bureau of Standards for encrypting and decoding data. *See also* encryption.

data frames Logical, structured packages in which data can be placed. Data being transmitted is segmented into small units and combined with control information such as message start and message end indicators. Each package of information is transmitted as a single unit, called a frame. The data-link layer packages raw bits from the physical layer into data frames. The exact format of the frame used by the network depends on the topology. *See also* frame.

data-link layer The second layer in the OSI reference model. This layer packages raw bits from the physical layer into data frames. *See also* Open Systems Interconnection (OSI) reference model.

data stream An undifferentiated, byte-by-byte flow of data.

Data Terminal Equipment (DTE) According to the RS-232 hardware standard, a device, such as a microcomputer or a terminal, that has the ability to transmit information in digital form over a cable or a communication line. A DTE is one of two types of hardware connected by an RS-232 serial connection, the other being a DCE (Data Communications Equipment) device, such as a modem, that normally connects the DTE to the communication line itself. In communication, an RS-232 DTE device transmits data over line 2 and receives it over line 3. A DCE receives over line 2 and transmits over line 3. *See also* Data Communications Equipment (DCE).

DB connector A connector that facilitates parallel input and output. The initials DB stand for *data bus*. The numbers which follow DB indicate the number of wires within the connector. For example, a DB-15 connector has 15 pins and supports up to 15 lines, each of which can connect to a pin on the connector; a DB-25 connector has 25 of each.

DBMS *See* database management system (DBMS).

DCE *See* Data Communications Equipment (DCE).

DECnet Digital Equipment Corporation hardware and software products that implement the Digital Network Architecture (DNA). DECnet defines communication networks over Ethernet LANs, Fiber Distributed Data Interface metropolitan area networks (FDDI MANs), and WANs that use private or public data transmission facilities. It can use TCP/IP and OSI protocols as well as Digital's DECnet protocols. *See also* Fiber Distributed Data Interface, metropolitan area network (MAN).

dedicated server A computer on a network that functions only as a server and is not also used as a client. *See also* server, server-based network.

DES *See* data encryption standard (DES).

device A generic term for a computer subsystem. Printers, serial ports, and disk drives are referred to as devices.

DHCP *See* Dynamic Host Configuration Protocol (DHCP).

digital A system that encodes information numerically, such as 0 and 1, in a binary context. Computers use digital encoding to process data. A digital signal is a discrete binary state, either on or off. *See also* analog.

digital line A communication line that carries information only in binary-encoded (digital) form. To minimize distortion and noise interference, a digital line uses repeaters to regenerate the signal periodically during transmission. *See also* analog line.

digital video disc (DVD) An optical storage medium with higher capacity and bandwidth than a compact disc. A DVD can hold a full-length film with up to 133 minutes of high-quality video, in MPEG-2 format, and audio. Also known as digital versatile disc.

digital voltmeter (DVM) A basic, all-purpose electronic measuring tool. In addition to indicating the amount of voltage passing through resistance, in network cable testing, voltmeters measure continuity to determine if a cable is able to carry current.

DIP (dual inline package) switch One or more small rocker or sliding switches that can be set to one of two states—closed or open—to control options on a circuit board.

direct memory access (DMA) Memory access that does not involve the microprocessor, frequently employed for data transfer directly between memory and an "intelligent" peripheral device such as a disk drive.

direct memory access (DMA) channel A channel for direct memory access that does not involve the microprocessor, providing data transfer directly between memory and a disk drive.

disk duplexing *See* disk mirroring, fault tolerance.

disk duplicating *See* disk mirroring.

diskless computers Computers that have neither a floppy disk nor a hard disk. Diskless computers depend on special ROM in order to provide users with an interface through which they can log on to the network.

disk mirroring A technique, also known as disk duplicating, in which all or part of a hard disk is duplicated onto one or more hard disks, each of which ideally is attached to its own controller. With disk mirroring, any change made to the original disk is simultaneously made to the other disk(s). Disk mirroring is used in situations in which a backup copy of current data must be maintained at all times. *See also* disk striping, fault tolerance.

disk striping Divides data into 64K blocks and spreads it equally in a fixed rate and order among all disks in an array. However, disk striping does not provide any fault tolerance because there is no data redundancy. If any partition in the set fails, all data is lost. *See also* disk mirroring, fault tolerance.

DIX (Digital, Intel, Xerox) connector The connector used with standard Ethernet that often includes a cable running off the main, or backbone, coaxial cable. This is also known as an AUI connector. *See also* attachment unit interface (AUI).

DMA *See* direct memory access (DMA).

DMA channel *See* direct memory access (DMA) channel.

DNS *See* Domain Name System (DNS).

domain For Microsoft networking, a collection of computers and users that share a common database and security policy that are stored on a Windows NT Server domain controller. Each domain has a unique name. *See also* workgroup.

domain controller For Microsoft networking, the Windows NT Server–based computer that authenticates domain logons and maintains the security policy and master database for a domain. *See also* Backup Domain Controller (BDC), Primary Domain Controller (PDC).

Domain Name System (DNS) A general-purpose distributed, replicated, data-query service used primarily on the Internet for translating host names into Internet addresses.

downtime The amount of time a computer system or associated hardware remains nonfunctioning. Although downtime can occur because hardware fails unexpectedly, it can also be a scheduled event, such as when a network is shut down to allow time for maintaining the system, changing hardware, or archiving files.

driver A software component that permits a computer system to communicate with a device. For example, a printer driver is a device driver that translates computer data into a form understood by the target printer. In most cases, the driver also manipulates the hardware in order to transmit the data to the device.

DTE *See* Data Terminal Equipment (DTE).

dual shielded cable Cable that contains one layer of foil and insulation and one layer of braided metal shielding.

dumb terminal A device used for obtaining or entering data on a network that does not contain any "intelligence" or processing power provided by a CPU.

duplex transmission Also called full-duplex transmission. Communication that takes place simultaneously, in both directions, between the sender and the receiver. Alternative methods of transmission are simplex, which is one-way only, and half-duplex, which is two-way communication that occurs in only one direction at a time.

DVD (digital video disc, also known as digital versatile disc) *See* digital video disc (DVD).

Dynamic Host Configuration Protocol (DHCP) A protocol for automatic TCP/IP configuration that provides static and dynamic address allocation and management. *See also* Transport Control Protocol/Internet Protocol (TCP/IP).

E

EBCDIC *See* Extended Binary Coded Decimal Interchange Code (EBCDIC).

EISA *See* Extended Industry Standard Architecture (EISA).

encryption The process of making information indecipherable to protect it from unauthorized viewing or use, especially during transmission or when the data is stored on a transportable magnetic medium. A key is required to decode the information. *See also* CCEP, data encryption standard (DES).

Enhanced Small Device Interface (ESDI) A standard that can be used with high-capacity hard disks and tape drives to enable high-speed communication with a computer. ESDI drivers typically transfer data at about 10 Mbps.

ESDI *See* Enhanced Small Device Interface (ESDI).

Ethernet A LAN developed by Xerox in 1976. Ethernet became a widely implemented network from which the IEEE 802.3 standard for contention networks was developed. It uses a bus topology and the original Ethernet relies on CSMA/CD to regulate traffic on the main communication line.

EtherTalk Allows the AppleTalk network protocols to run on Ethernet coaxial cable. The EtherTalk card allows a Macintosh computer to connect to an 802.3 Ethernet network. *See also* AppleTalk.

event An action or occurrence to which a program might respond. Examples of events are mouse clicks, key presses, and mouse movements. Also, any significant occurrence in the system or in a program that requires users to be notified or an entry to be added to a log.

exabyte *See* byte.

Extended Binary Coded Decimal Interchange Code (EBCDIC) A coding scheme developed by IBM for use with IBM mainframe and Personal Computers as a standard method of assigning binary (numeric) values to alphabetic, numeric, punctuation, and transmission-control characters.

Extended Industry Standard Architecture (EISA) A 32-bit bus design for *x*86-based computers introduced in 1988. EISA was specified by an industry consortium of nine computer-industry companies (AST Research, Compaq, Epson, Hewlett-Packard, NEC, Olivetti, Tandy, Wyse, and Zenith). An EISA device uses cards that are upwardly compatible from ISA. *See also* Industry Standard Architecture (ISA).

F

fast Ethernet Also called 100BaseX Ethernet. An extension to the existing Ethernet standard, it runs on UTP Category 5 data-grade cable and uses CSMA/CD in a star-wired bus topology, similar to 10BaseT in which all cables are attached to a hub.

fault tolerance The ability of a computer or an operating system to respond to an event such as a power outage or a hardware failure in such a way that no data is lost and any work in progress is not corrupted.

Fiber Distributed Data Interface (FDDI) A standard developed by the ANSI for high-speed, fiber-optic local area networks. FDDI provides specifications for transmission rates of 100 Mbps on networks based on the Token Ring standard.

fiber-optic cable Cable that uses optical fibers to carry digital data signals in the form of modulated pulses of light.

file infector A type of virus that attaches itself to a file or program and activates any time the file is used. Many subcategories of file infectors exist. *See also* companion virus, macro virus, polymorphic virus, stealth virus.

File Transfer Protocol (FTP) A process that provides file transfers between local and remote computers. FTP supports several commands that allow bidirectional transfer of binary and ASCII files between computers. The FTP client is installed with the TCP/IP connectivity utilities. *See also* ASCII (American Standard Code for Information Interchange), Transport Control Protocol/Internet Protocol (TCP/IP).

firewall A security system, usually a combination of hardware and software, intended to protect a network against external threats coming from another network, including the Internet. Firewalls prevent an organization's networked computers from communicating directly with computers that are external to the network, and vice versa. Instead, all incoming and outgoing communication is routed through a proxy server outside the organization's network. Firewalls also audit network activity, recording the volume of traffic and information about unauthorized attempts to gain access. *See also* proxy server.

firmware Software routines stored in ROM. Unlike RAM, ROM stays intact even in the absence of electrical power. Startup routines and low-level I/O instructions are stored in firmware.

flow control Regulating the flow of data through routers to ensure that no segment becomes overloaded with transmissions.

frame A package of information transmitted on a network as a single unit. Frame is a term most often used with Ethernet networks. A frame is similar to the packet used in other networks. *See also* data frame, packet.

frame preamble Header information, added to the beginning of a data frame in the physical layer of the OSI reference model.

frame relay An advanced, fast-packet, variable-length, digital, packet-switching technology. It is a point-to-point system that uses a private virtual circuit (PVC) to transmit variable-length frames at the data-link layer of the OSI reference model. Frame relay networks can also provide subscribers with bandwidth, as needed, that allows users to make nearly any type of transmission.

front end In a client/server application, front end refers to the part of the program carried out on the client computer.

FTP *See* File Transfer Protocol (FTP).

full-duplex transmission Also called duplex transmission. Communication that takes place simultaneously, in both directions. *See also* duplex transmission.

G

gateway A device used to connect networks using different protocols so that information can be passed from one system to the other. Gateways functions at the network layer of the OSI reference model.

Gb *See* gigabit.

GB *See* gigabyte.

gigabit 1,073,741,824 bits. Also referred to as 1 billion bits.

gigabyte Commonly, a thousand megabytes. However, the precise meaning often varies with the context. A gigabyte is 1 billion bytes. In the context of computing, bytes are often expressed in multiples of powers of two. Therefore, a gigabyte can also be either 1000 megabytes or 1024 megabytes, where a megabyte is considered to be 1,048,576 bytes (2 raised to the 20th power).

global group One of four kinds of group accounts used by Microsoft Windows NT and Windows NT Server. Used across an entire domain, global groups are created on a Primary Domain Controller (PDC) in the domain in which the user accounts reside. Global groups can contain only user accounts from the domain in which the global group is created. Members of global groups obtain resource permissions when the global group is added to a local group. *See also* group, Primary Domain Controller (PDC).

group In networking, an account containing other accounts that are called members. The permissions and rights granted to a group are also provided to its members; thus, groups offer a convenient way to grant common capabilities to collections of user accounts. For Windows NT, groups are managed with User Manager. For Windows NT Server, groups are managed with User Manager for Domains.

H

half-duplex transmission Two-way communication occurring in only one direction at a time.

handshaking A term applied to modem-to-modem communication. Refers to the process by which information is transmitted between the sending and receiving devices to maintain and coordinate data flow between them. Proper handshaking ensures that the receiving device will be ready to accept data before the sending device transmits.

hard disk One or more inflexible platters coated with material that allows the magnetic recording of computer data. A typical hard disk rotates at up to 7200 revolutions per minute (RPM), and the read/write heads ride over the surface of the disk on a cushion of air 10 to 25 millionths of an inch deep. A hard disk is sealed to prevent contaminants from interfering with the close head-to-disk tolerances. Hard disks provide faster access to data than floppy disks and are capable of storing much more information. Because platters are rigid, they can be stacked so that one hard-disk drive can access more than one platter. Most hard disks have between two and eight platters.

hardware The physical components of a computer system, including any peripheral equipment such as printers, modems, and mouse devices.

hardware compatibility list (HCL) A list of computers and peripherals that have been tested and have passed compatibility testing with the product for which the HCL is being developed. For example, the Windows NT 3.51 HCL lists the products which have been tested and found to be compatible with Window NT 3.51.

hardware loopback A connector on a computer that is useful for troubleshooting hardware problems, allowing data to be transmitted to a line, then returned as received data. If the transmitted data does not return, the hardware loopback detects a hardware malfunction.

HCL *See* hardware compatibility list (HCL).

HDLC *See* High-Level Data Link Control (HDLC).

header In network data transmission, one of the three sections of a packet component. It includes an alert signal to indicate that the packet is being transmitted, the source address, the destination address, and clock information to synchronize transmission.

hermaphroditic connector A connector that is neither male nor female, such as IBM cable connectors in which any two can be connected together, as opposed to BNC connectors that require both a male part and female part before a connection can be made.

hertz (Hz) The unit of frequency measurement. Frequency measures how often a periodic event occurs, such as the manner in which a wave's amplitude changes with time. One hertz equals one cycle per second. Frequency is often measured in kilohertz (KHz, 1000 Hz), megahertz (MHz), gigahertz (GHz, 1000 MHz), or terahertz (THz, 10,000 GHz).

High-Level Data Link Control (HDLC) HDLC is a widely accepted international protocol, developed by the International Organization for Standardization (ISO), that governs information transfer. HDLC is a bit-oriented, synchronous protocol that applies to the data-link (message packaging) layer of the OSI reference model. Under the HDLC protocol, data is transmitted in frames, each of which can contain a variable amount of data, but which must be organized in a particular way. *See also* data frames, frame.

hop In routing through a mesh environment, the transmission of a data packet through a router.

host *See* server.

hot fixing *See* sector sparing.

HTML *See* Hypertext Markup Language (HTML).

hub A connectivity component that provides a common connection among computers in a star-configured network. Active hubs require electrical power but are able to regenerate and retransmit network data. Passive hubs simply organize the wiring. *See also* Multistation Access Unit (MAU).

hybrid hub An advanced hub that can accommodate several different types of cables.

hybrid network A network made up of mixed components.

Hypertext Markup Language (HTML) A language developed for writing pages for the World Wide Web. HTML allows text to include codes that define fonts, layout, embedded graphics, and hypertext links. Hypertext provides a method for presenting text, images, sound, and videos that are linked together in a nonsequential web of associations.

Hypertext Transport Protocol (HTTP) The method by which World Wide Web pages are transferred over the network.

I

IAB *See* Internet Architecture Board (IAB).

IBM cabling system Used in a Token Ring environment. Introduced by IBM in 1984 to define cable connectors, face plates, distribution panels, and cable types. Many parameters are similar to non-IBM specifications. Uniquely shaped, the IBM connector is hermaphroditic. *See also* hermaphroditic connector.

ICMP *See* Internet Control Message Protocol (ICMP).

IDE *See* Integrated Device Electronics (IDE).

IEEE *See* Institute of Electrical and Electronics Engineers (IEEE).

IEEE Project 802 A networking model developed by the IEEE. Named for the year and month it began (February 1980), Project 802 defines LAN standards for the physical and data-link layers of the OSI reference model. Project 802 divides the data-link layer into two sublayers: Media Access Control (MAC) and Logical Link Control (LLC).

impedance Impedance has two aspects: the first is resistance, which impedes direct and alternating current. Resistance is always greater than zero. The second is reactance, which impedes alternating current only. Reactance varies with frequency and can be positive or negative.

Industry Standard Architecture (ISA) An unofficial designation for the bus design of the IBM Personal Computer (PC) PC/XT. It allows various adapters to be added to the system by inserting plug-in cards into expansion slots. Commonly, ISA refers to the expansion slots themselves; such slots are called 8-bit slots or 16-bit slots. *See also* Extended Industry Standard Architecture (EISA), Micro Channel Architecture.

infrared transmission Electromagnetic radiation with frequencies in the electromagnetic spectrum in the range just below that of visible red light. In network communications, infrared technology offers extremely high transmission rates and wide bandwidth in line-of-sight communications.

Institute of Electrical and Electronics Engineers (IEEE) An organization of engineering and electronics professionals; noted in networking for developing the IEEE 802.x standards for the physical and data-link layers of the OSI reference model, applied in a variety of network configurations.

Integrated Device Electronics (IDE) A type of disk-drive interface in which the controller electronics reside on the drive itself, eliminating the need for a separate network interface card. The IDE interface is compatible with the Western Digital ST-506 controller.

Integrated Services Digital Network (ISDN) A worldwide digital communication network that evolved from existing telephone services. The goal of the ISDN is to replace current telephone lines, which require digital-to-analog conversions, with completely digital switching and transmission facilities capable of carrying data ranging from voice to computer transmissions, music, and video. The ISDN is built on two main types of communications channels: B channels, that carry voice, data, or images at a rate of 64 Kbps (kilobits per second), and a D channel, that carries control information, signaling, and link-management data at 16 Kbps. Standard ISDN Basic Rate desktop service is called 2B+D. Computers and other devices connect to ISDN lines through simple, standardized interfaces.

interfaces Boundaries that separate the layers from each other. For example, in the OSI reference model, each layer provides some service or action that prepares the data for delivery over the network to another computer.

intermediate systems Equipment that provides a network communication link, such as bridges, routers, and gateways.

International Organization for Standardization (ISO) An organization made up of standards-setting groups from various countries. For example, the United States member is the American National Standards Institute (ANSI). The ISO works to establish global standards for communications and information exchange. Primary among its accomplishments is development of the widely accepted OSI reference model. Note that the ISO is often wrongly identified as the International Standards Organization, probably because of the abbreviation "ISO"; however, ISO is derived from "isos," which means "equal" in Greek, rather than an acronym.

International Telecommunications Union (ITU) The organization responsible for setting the standards for international telecommunications.

Internet Architecture Board (IAB) A body that develops and maintains Internet architectural standards as part of the Internet Society (ISOC). It also adjudicates disputes in the standards process.

Internet Control Message Protocol (ICMP) Used by IP and higher-level protocols to send and receive status reports about information being transmitted.

Internet Protocol (IP) The TCP/IP protocol for packet forwarding. *See also* Transport Control Protocol/Internet Protocol (TCP/IP).

Internetworking The intercommunication in a network that is made up of smaller networks.

Internetwork Packet Exchange/Sequenced Packet Exchange (IPX/SPX) A protocol stack that is used in Novell networks. IPX is the NetWare protocol for packet forwarding and routing. It is a relatively small and fast protocol on a LAN, is a derivative of Xerox Network System (XNS), and supports routing. SPX is a connection-oriented protocol used to guarantee the delivery of the data being sent. NWLink is the Microsoft implementation of the IPX/SPX protocol.

interoperability The ability of components in one system to work with components in other systems.

interrupt request (IRQ) An electronic signal sent to a computer's CPU to indicate that an event has taken place that requires the processor's attention.

IP *See* Internet Protocol (IP). *See also* Transport Control Protocol/Internet Protocol (TCP/IP).

ipconfig A diagnostic command that displays all current TCP/IP network configuration values. It is of particular use on systems running DHCP because it allows users to determine which TCP/IP configuration values have been configured by the DHCP server. *See also* winipcfg.

IPX/SPX *See* Internetwork Packet Exchange/ Sequenced Packet Exchange (IPX/SPX).

IRQ *See* interrupt request (IRQ).

ISA *See* Industry Standard Architecture (ISA).

ISDN *See* Integrated Services Digital Network (ISDN).

ISO *See* International Organization for Standardization (ISO).

ITU *See* International Telecommunications Union (ITU).

J

jitter Instability in a signal wave form over time that can be caused by signal interference or an unbalanced ring in FDDI or Token Ring environments.

jumper A small plastic-and-metal plug or wire for connecting different points in an electronic circuit. Jumpers are used to select a particular circuit or option from several possible configurations. Jumpers can be used on network interface cards to select the type of connection through which the card will transmit, either DIX or BNC.

K

Kevlar A brand name of the DuPont Corporation for the fibers in the reinforcing layer of plastic that surrounds each glass strand of a fiber-optic connector. The name is sometimes used generically.

key In database management, an identifier for a record or group of records in a data file. Most often, the key is defined as the contents of a single field, called the key field in some database management programs and the index field in others. Keys are maintained in tables and are indexed to speed record retrieval. Keys also refer to code that deciphers encrypted data.

kilo (K) Refers to 1000 in the metric system. In computing terminology, because computing is based on powers of 2, kilo is most often used to mean 1024 (2 raised to the 10th power). To distinguish between the two contexts, a lowercase k is often used to indicate 1000, an uppercase K for 1024. A kilobyte is 1024 bytes.

kilobit (Kbit) One thousand twenty-four bits. *See also* bit, kilo.

kilobyte (KB) Refers to 1024 bytes. *See also* byte, kilo.

L

LAN *See* local area network (LAN).

LAN requester *See* requester (LAN requester).

laser transmission Wireless network that uses a laser beam to carry data between devices.

LAT *See* local area transport (LAT).

layering The coordination of various protocols in a specific architecture that allows the protocols to work together to ensure that the data is prepared, transferred, received, and acted upon as intended.

link The communication system that connects two LANs. Equipment that provides the link, including bridges, routers, and gateways.

local area network (LAN) Computers connected in a geographically confined network, such as in the same building, campus, or office park.

local area transport (LAT) A nonroutable protocol from Digital Equipment Corporation.

local group One of four kinds of group accounts used by Microsoft Windows NT and Windows NT Server. Implemented in each local computer's account database, local groups contain user accounts and other global groups that need to have access, rights, and permissions assigned to a resource on a local computer. Local groups cannot contain other local groups.

LocalTalk Cabling components used in an AppleTalk network, including cables, connector modules, and cable extenders. These components are normally used in a bus or tree topology. A LocalTalk segment supports a maximum of 32 devices. Because of LocalTalk's limitations, clients often turn to vendors other than Apple for AppleTalk cabling. Farallon PhoneNet, for example, can accommodate 254 devices.

local user The user at the computer.

Logical Link Control (LLC) sublayer One of two sublayers created by the IEEE 802 project out of the data-link layer of the OSI reference model. The Logical Link Control (LLC) is the upper sublayer that manages data-link communication and defines the use of logical interface points, called service access points (SAPs), used by computers to transfer information from the LLC sublayer to the upper OSI layers. *See also* Media Access Control (MAC) sublayer, service access point (SAP).

lost token Refers to an error on a Token Ring network that causes an errant station to halt the token, leaving the ring without a token.

M

macro virus A file-infector virus named because it is written as a macro for a specific application. Macro viruses are difficult to detect and becoming more common, often infecting widely used applications, such as word-processing programs. When an infected file is opened, the virus attaches itself to the application, then infects any files accessed by that application. *See also* file infector.

magneto-optical (MO) disc A plastic or glass disc, coated with a compound containing special properties, that is read by bouncing a low-intensity laser beam off the disc.

MAN (metropolitan area network) *See* metropolitan area network (MAN).

MAU *See* Multistation Access Unit (MSAU or MAU).

Mb *See* megabit (Mb).

MB *See* megabyte (MB).

Mbps *See* millions of bits per second (Mbps).

media The vast majority of LANs today are connected by some sort of wire or cabling that acts as the LAN transmission medium, carrying data between computers. The cabling is often referred to as the media.

Media Access Control (MAC) driver The device driver located at the Media Access Control sublayer of the OSI reference model. This driver is also known as the NIC driver. It provides low-level access to NICs by providing data-transmission support and some basic NIC management functions. These drivers also pass data from the physical layer to transport protocols at the network and transport layers.

Media Access Control (MAC) sublayer One of two sublayers created by the IEEE 802 project out of the data-link layer of the OSI reference model. The Media Access Control (MAC) sublayer communicates directly with the network interface card and is responsible for delivering error-free data between two computers on the network. *See also* Logical Link Control (LLC) sublayer.

megabit (Mb) Usually, 1,048,576 bits; sometimes interpreted as 1 million bits. *See also* bit.

megabyte (MB) 1,048,576 bytes (2 raised to the 20th power); sometimes interpreted as 1 million bytes. *See also* byte.

mesh network topology Connects remote sites over telecommunication links. Common in wide area networks (WANs), meshes use routers to search among multiple active paths (the mesh) and determine the best path at that particular moment.

metropolitan area network (MAN) A data network designed for a town or city. In geographic breadth, MANs are larger than local area networks but smaller than wide area networks. MANs are usually characterized by very-high-speed connections using fiber-optic cable or other digital media.

Micro Channel Architecture The design of the bus in IBM PS/2 computers (except Models 25 and 30). The Micro Channel is electrically and physically incompatible with the IBM PC/AT bus. Unlike the PC/AT bus, the Micro Channel functions as either a 16-bit or 32-bit bus. The Micro Channel also can be driven independently by multiple bus master processors. *See also* Extended Industry Standard Architecture (EISA), Industry Standard Architecture (ISA).

Microcom Network Protocol (MNP) The standard for asynchronous data-error control developed by Microcom Systems. The method works so well that other companies have adopted not only the initial version of the protocol, but later versions as well. Currently, several modem vendors incorporate MNP Classes 2, 3, 4, and 5.

Microsoft Technical Information Network (TechNet) Provides informational support for all aspects of networking, with an emphasis on Microsoft products.

millions of bits per second (Mbps) The unit of measure of supported transmission rates on the following physical media: coaxial cable, twisted-pair cable, and fiber-optic cable. *See also* bit.

MNP *See* Microcom Network Protocol (MNP).

MO (magneto-optical) disc *See* magneto-optical (MO) disc.

mobile computing Incorporates wireless adapters using cellular telephone technology to connect portable computers with the cabled network.

modem A communication device that enables a computer to transmit information over a standard telephone line. Because a computer is digital, it works with discrete electrical signals representing binary 1 and binary 0. A telephone is analog and carries a signal that can have many variations. Modems are needed to convert digital signals to analog and back. When transmitting, modems impose (modulate) a computer's digital signals onto a continuous carrier frequency on the telephone line. When receiving, modems sift out (demodulate) the information from the carrier and transfer it in digital form to the computer.

MSAU See Multistation Access Unit (MAU).

multiplexer (mux) A device used to divide a transmission facility into two or more channels. It can be a program stored in a computer. Also, a device for connecting a number of communication lines to a computer.

Multistation Access Unit (MAU) The name for a Token Ring wiring concentrator. Also referred to as a hub. MAUs are sometimes referred to as MSAUs.

multitasking A mode of operation offered by an operating system in which a computer works on more than one task at a time. There are two primary types of multitasking: preemptive and nonpreemptive. In preemptive multitasking, the operating system can take control of the processor without the task's cooperation. In nonpreemptive multitasking, the processor is never taken from a task. The task itself decides when to give up the processor.

A true multitasking operating system can run as many tasks as it has processors. When there are more tasks than processors, the computer must "time slice" so that the available processors devote a certain amount of time to one task and then move on to the next task, alternating between tasks until all the tasks are completed.

mux See multiplexer (mux).

N

Name Binding Protocol (NBP) An Apple protocol responsible for keeping track of entities on the network and matching names with Internet addresses. It works at the transport layer of the OSI reference model.

narrowband (single-frequency) transmission High-frequency radio transmission similar to broadcasting. The user tunes both the transmitter and the receiver to a certain frequency to send and receive data.

NBP *See* Name Binding Protocol (NBP).

nbtstat A diagnostic command that displays protocol statistics and current TCP/IP connections using NBT (NetBIOS over TCP/IP). This command is available only if the TCP/IP protocol has been installed. *See also* netstat.

NDIS *See* Network Device Interface Specification (NDIS).

NetBEUI (NetBIOS extended user interface) A protocol supplied with all Microsoft network products. NetBEUI advantages include small stack size (important for MS-DOS-based computers), speed of data transfer on the network medium, and compatibility with all Microsoft-based networks. The major drawback of NetBEUI is that it is a LAN transport protocol and therefore does not support routing. It is also limited to Microsoft-based networks.

NetBIOS (network basic input/output system) An application programming interface (API) that can be used by application programs on a LAN consisting of IBM-compatible microcomputers running MS-DOS, OS/2, or some version of UNIX. Primarily of interest to programmers, NetBIOS provides application programs with a uniform set of commands for requesting the lower-level network services required to conduct sessions between nodes on a network and transmit information between them.

netstat A diagnostic command that displays protocol statistics and current TCP/IP network connections. This command is available only if the TCP/IP protocol has been installed. *See also* nbtstat.

NetWare Core Protocol (NCP) Defines the connection control and service-request encoding that make it possible for clients and servers to interact. This is the protocol that provides transport and session services. NetWare security is also provided within this protocol.

network In the context of computers, a system in which a number of independent computers are linked together to share data and peripherals, such as hard disks and printers.

network adapter card *See* network interface card (NIC).

network analyzers Network troubleshooting tools, sometimes called protocol analyzers. They perform a number of functions in real-time network traffic analysis and carry out packet capture, decoding, and transmission. They can also generate statistics based on the network traffic to help create a picture of the network's cabling, software, file server, clients, and NICs. Most analyzers have a built-in TDR. *See also* time-domain reflectometer (TDR).

Network Device Interface Specification (NDIS)
A standard that defines an interface for communication between the Media Access Control (MAC) sublayer and protocol drivers. NDIS allows for a flexible environment of data exchange. It defines the software interface, called the NDIS interface, which is used by protocol drivers to communicate with the network interface card. The advantage of NDIS is that it offers protocol multiplexing so that multiple protocol stacks can be used at the same time. *See also* Open Data-Link Interface (ODI).

network interface card (NIC) An expansion card installed in each computer and server on the network. The NIC acts as the physical interface or connection between the computer and the network cable.

network layer The third layer in the OSI reference model. This layer is responsible for addressing messages and translating logical addresses and names into physical addresses. This layer also determines the route from the source to the destination computer. It determines which path the data should take based on network conditions, priority of service, and other factors. It also manages traffic problems such as switching, routing, and controlling the congestion of data packets on the network. *See also* Open Systems Interconnection (OSI) reference model.

network monitors Monitors that track all or a selected part of network traffic. They examine frame-level packets and gather information about packet types, errors, and packet traffic to and from each computer.

Network News Transfer Protocol (NNTP) A protocol defined in RFC 977. It is a de facto protocol standard on the Internet used for the distribution, inquiry, retrieval, and posting of Usenet news articles over the Internet.

NIC *See* network interface card (NIC).

NNTP *See* Network News Transfer Protocol (NNTP).

node On a LAN, a device that is connected to the network and is capable of communicating with other network devices. For example, clients, servers, and repeaters are called nodes.

noise Random electrical signals that can get onto the cable and degrade or distort the data. Noise is generated by power lines, elevators, air conditioners, or any device with an electric motor, relays, and radio transmitters. *See also* shielding.

nonpreemptive multitasking A form of multitasking in which the processor is never taken from a task. The task itself decides when to give up the processor. Programs written for nonpreemptive multitasking systems must include provisions for yielding control of the processor. No other program can run until the non-preemptive program gives up control of the processor. *See also* multitasking, preemptive multitasking.

Novell NetWare One of the leading network architectures.

O

ODI *See* Open Data-Link Interface (ODI).

ohm The unit of measure for electrical resistance. A resistance of 1 ohm will pass 1 ampere of current when a voltage of 1 volt is applied. A 100-watt incandescent bulb has a resistance of approximately 130 ohms.

Open Data-Link Interface (ODI) A specification defined by Novell and Apple to simplify driver development and to provide support for multiple protocols on a single network interface card. Similar to NDIS in many respects, ODI allows Novell NetWare drivers to be written without concern for the protocol that will be used on top of them.

Open Shortest Path First (OSPF) A routing protocol for IP networks, such as the Internet, that allows a router to calculate the shortest path to each node for sending messages.

Open Systems Interconnection (OSI) reference model A seven-layer architecture that standardizes levels of service and types of interaction for computers exchanging information through a network. It is used to describe the flow of data between the physical connection to the network and the end-user application. This model is the best known and most widely used model for describing networking environments.

OSI layer	Focus
7. application layer	Program-to-program transfer of information
6. presentation layer	Text formatting and display code conversion
5. session layer	Establishing, maintaining, and coordinating communication
4. transport layer	Accurate delivery, service quality
3. network layer	Transport routes, message handling, and transfer
2. data-link layer	Coding, addressing, and transmitting information
1. physical layer	Hardware connections

optical drive A drive that accommodates optical discs.

optical fiber Medium that carries digital data signals in the form of modulated pulses of light. An optical fiber consists of an extremely thin cylinder of glass, called the core, surrounded by a concentric layer of glass, known as the cladding.

oscilloscope An electronic instrument that measures the amount of signal voltage per unit of time and displays the results on a monitor.

OSI *See* Open Systems Interconnection (OSI) reference model.

OSPF *See* Open Shortest Path First (OSPF).

P

packet A unit of information transmitted as a whole from one device to another on a network. In packet-switching networks, a packet is defined more specifically as a transmission unit of fixed maximum size that consists of binary digits representing data; a header containing an identification number, source, and destination addresses; and sometimes error-control data. *See also* frame.

packet assembler/disassembler (PAD) A device that breaks large chunks of data into packets, usually for transmission over an X.25 network, and reassembles them at the other end. *See also* packet switching.

Packet Internet Groper (ping) A simple utility that tests if a network connection is complete, from the server to the workstation, by sending a message to the remote computer. If the remote computer receives the message, it responds with a reply message. The reply consists of the remote workstation's IP address, the number of bytes in the message, how long it took to reply—given in milliseconds (ms)—and the length of time-to-live (TTL) in seconds. Ping works at the IP level and will often respond even when higher level TCP-based services cannot.

packet switching A message delivery technique in which small units of information (packets) are relayed through stations in a computer network along the best route available between the source and the destination. Data is broken into smaller units and then repacked in a process called packet assembly and disassembly (PAD). Although each packet can travel along a different path, and the packets composing a message can arrive at different times or out of sequence, the receiving computer reassembles the original message. Packet-switching networks are considered fast and efficient. Standards for packet switching on networks are documented in the CCITT recommendation X.25.

PAD *See* packet assembler/disassembler (PAD).

page-description language (PDL) A language that communicates to a printer how printed output should appear. The printer uses the PDL to construct text and graphics to create the page image. PDLs are like blueprints in that they set parameters and features such as type sizes and fonts, but leave the drawing to the printer.

parity An error-checking procedure in which the number of 1s must always be the same—either odd or even—for each group of bits transmitted without error. Parity is used for checking data transferred within a computer or between computers.

partition A portion of a physical disk that functions as if it were a physically separate unit.

password-protected share Access to a shared resource that is granted when a user enters the appropriate password.

PBX Private Branch Exchange (PABX Private Automated Branch Exchange) A switching telephone network that allows callers within an organization to place intraorganizational calls without going through the public telephone system.

PDA *See* Personal Digital Assistant (PDA).

PDC *See* Primary Domain Controller (PDC).

PDL *See* page-description language (PDL).

PDN *See* public data network (PDN).

peer-to-peer network A network in which there are no dedicated servers or hierarchy among the computers. All computers are equal and, therefore, known as peers. Generally, each computer functions as both client and server.

performance monitor A tool for monitoring network performance that can display statistics, such as the number of packets sent and received, server-processor utilization, and the amount of data going into and out of the server.

peripheral A term used for devices such as disk drives, printers, modems, mouse devices, and joysticks that are connected to a computer and controlled by its microprocessor.

Peripheral Component Interconnect (PCI) 32-bit local bus used in most Pentium computers and in the Apple Power Macintosh. Meets most of the requirements for providing Plug and Play functionality.

permanent virtual circuit (PVC) A permanent logical connection between two nodes on a packet-switching network; similar to leased lines that are permanent and virtual, except that with PVC the customer pays only for the time the line is used. This type of connection service is gaining importance because both frame relay and ATM use it. *See also* packet switching, virtual circuit.

permissions *See* access permissions.

Personal Digital Assistant (PDA) A type of hand-held computer that provides functions including personal organization features—like a calendar, note taking, database manipulation, calculator, and communications. For communication, a PDA uses cellular or wireless technology that is often built into the system, but that can be supplemented or enhanced by means of a PC Card.

petabyte *See* byte.

phase change rewritable (PCR) A type of rewritable optical technology in which the optical devices come from one manufacturer (Matsushita/Panasonic) and the media comes from two (Panasonic and Plasmon).

physical layer The first (bottommost) layer of the OSI reference model. This layer addresses the transmission of the unstructured raw bit stream over a physical medium (the networking cable). The physical layer relates the electrical/optical, mechanical, and functional interfaces to the cable and also carries the signals that transmit data generated by all of the higher OSI layers. *See also* Open Systems Interconnection (OSI) reference model.

piercing tap A connector for coaxial cable that pierces through the insulating layer and makes direct contact with the conducting core.

ping *See* Packet Internet Groper (ping).

plenum The space in many buildings between the false ceiling and the floor above, used to circulate warm and cold air throughout the building. The space is often used for cable runs. Local fire codes specify the types of wiring that can be routed through this area.

Plug and Play (PnP) Refers to the ability of a computer system to automatically configure a device added to it. Plug and play capability exists in Macintoshes based on the NuBus and, since Windows 95, on PC-compatible computers. Also, refers to specifications developed by Intel and Microsoft that allow a PC to configure itself automatically to work with peripherals such as monitors, modems, and printers.

point-to-point configuration Dedicated circuits that are also known as private, or leased, lines. They are the most popular WAN communication circuits in use today. The carrier guarantees full-duplex bandwidth by setting up a permanent link from each end point, using bridges and routers to connect LANs through the circuits. *See also* Point-to-Point Protocol (PPP), Point-to-Point Tunneling Protocol (PPTP), and duplex transmission.

Point-to-Point Protocol (PPP) A data-link protocol for transmitting TCP/IP packets over dial-up telephone connections, such as between a computer and the Internet. PPP was developed by the Internet Engineering Task Force in 1991.

Point-to-Point Tunneling Protocol (PPTP) PPTP is an extension of the Point-to-Point Protocol that is used for communications on the Internet. It was developed by Microsoft to support virtual private networks (VPNs), which allow individuals and organizations to use the Internet as a secure means of communication. PPTP supports encapsulation of encrypted packets in secure wrappers that can be transmitted over a TCP/IP connection. *See also* Virtual Private Networks (VPN).

polymorphic virus A variant of file-infector virus that is named for the fact that it changes its appearance each time it is replicated. This makes it difficult to detect, because no two versions of the virus are exactly the same. *See also* file infector.

preemptive multitasking A form of multitasking (the ability of a computer's operating system to work on more than one task at a time). With preemptive multitasking—as opposed to nonpreemptive multitasking—the operating system can take control of the processor without the task's cooperation. *See also* nonpreemptive multitasking.

presentation layer The sixth layer of the OSI reference model. This layer determines the form used to exchange data between networked computers. At the sending computer, this layer translates data from a format sent down from the application layer into a commonly recognized, intermediary format. At the receiving end, this layer translates the intermediary format into a format useful to that computer's application layer. The presentation layer manages network security issues by providing services such as data encryption, provides rules for data transfer, and performs data compression to reduce the number of bits that need to be transmitted. *See also* Open Systems Interconnection (OSI) reference model.

Primary Domain Controller (PDC) The server that maintains the master copy of the domain's user-accounts database and that validates logon requests. Every network domain is required to have one, and only one, PDC. *See also* domain, domain controller.

print queue A buffer in which a print job is held until the printer is ready to print it.

Project 802 A subgroup of the IEEE, originally formed in 1980, that defined network standards for the physical components of a network, the network interface card, and the cabling, which are accounted for in the physical and data-link layers of the OSI reference model.

protocol The system of rules and procedures that govern communication between two or more devices. Many varieties of protocols exist, and not all are compatible, but as long as two devices are using the same protocol, they can exchange data. Protocols exist within protocols as well, governing different aspects of communication. Some protocols, such as the RS-232 standard, affect hardware connections.

Other standards govern data transmission, including the parameters and handshaking signals such as XON/OFF used in asynchronous (typically, modem) communications, as well as such data-coding methods as bit- and byte-oriented protocols. Still other protocols, such as the widely used XMODEM, govern file transfer, and others, such as CSMA/CD, define the methods by which messages are passed around the stations on a LAN. Protocols represent attempts to ease the complex process of enabling computers of different makes and models to communicate. Additional examples of protocols include the OSI model, IBM's SNA, and the Internet suite, including TCP/IP. *See also* Systems Network Architecture (SNA), Transport Control Protocol/ Internet Protocol (TCP/IP).

protocol analyzers *See* network analyzers.

protocol driver The driver responsible for offering four or five basic services to other layers in the network, while "hiding" the details of how the services are actually implemented. Services performed include session management, datagram service, data segmentation and sequencing, acknowledgment, and possibly routing across a WAN.

protocol stack A layered set of protocols that work together to provide a set of network functions.

proxy server A firewall component that manages Internet traffic to and from a local area network (LAN). The proxy server decides whether it is safe to let a particular message or file pass through to the organization's network, providing access control to the network, and filters and discards requests as specified by the owner, including requests for unauthorized access to proprietary data. *See also* firewall.

public data network (PDN) A commercial packet-switching or circuit-switching WAN service provided by local and long-distance telephone carriers.

punchdown block A wiring terminal, or series of terminals, into which cable can be plugged or "punched down." It is designed for environments that require a centralized location for all cabling to facilitate making changes; wiring running to the jacks can be more easily organized and maintained.

punchdown tool A specialized tool used to "punch down" cable wires into a wiring terminal. Using this tool ensures a solid connection.

PVC (permanent virtual circuit) *See* permanent virtual circuit (PVC).

PVC (polyvinyl chloride) The material most commonly used for insulating and jacketing cable.

Q

quad shielding Cable that contains two layers of foil insulation and two layers of braided metal shielding.

R

RAID *See* redundant array of independent disks (RAID).

random access memory (RAM) Semiconductor-based memory that can be read and written to by the microprocessor or other hardware devices. The storage locations can be accessed in any order. Note that the various types of ROM memory are also capable of random access. However, the term RAM is generally understood to refer to volatile memory, which can be written as well as read. *See also* read-only memory (ROM).

read-only memory (ROM) Semiconductor-based memory that contains instructions or data which can be read but not modified. *See also* random access memory (RAM).

redirector Networking software that accepts I/O requests for remote files, named pipes, or mail slots and sends (redirects) the requests to a network service on another computer.

Reduced Instruction Set Computing (RISC) A type of microprocessor design that focuses on rapid and efficient processing of a relatively small set of instructions. RISC design is based on the premise that most of the instructions that a computer decodes and executes are simple. As a result, RISC architecture limits the number of instructions that are built into the microprocessor, but optimizes each so it can be carried out very rapidly, usually within a single clock cycle. RISC chips execute simple instructions faster than microprocessors designed to handle a much wider array of instructions. They are, however, slower than general-purpose CISC (complex instruction set computing) chips when executing complex instructions, which must be broken down into many machine instructions before they can be carried out by RISC microprocessors.

redundancy system A fault-tolerant system that protects data by duplicating it in different physical sources. Data redundancy allows access to data even if part of the data system fails. *See also* fault tolerance.

redundant array of independent disks (RAID) A standardization of fault-tolerant options in five levels. The levels offer various combinations of performance, reliability, and cost. Formerly known as redundant array of inexpensive disks (RAID).

redundant array of inexpensive disks (RAID) *See* redundant array of independent disks (RAID).

remote-boot PROM (programmable read-only memory) A special chip in the network interface card that contains the hardwired code that starts the computer and connects the user to the network, used in computers for which there are no hard-disk or floppy drives. *See also* diskless computers.

remote user A user who dials in to the server over modems and telephone lines from a remote location.

repeater A device that regenerates signals so that they can be transmitted on additional cable segments to extend the cable length or to accommodate additional computers on the segment. Repeaters operate at the physical layer of the OSI reference model and connect like networks, such as an Ethernet LAN to an Ethernet LAN. Repeaters do not translate or filter data. For a repeater to work, both segments that the repeater joins must have the same media-access scheme, protocol, and transmission technique.

requester (LAN requester) Software that resides in a computer and forwards requests for network services from the computer's application programs to the appropriate server. *See also* redirector.

resources Any part of a computer system. Users on a network can share computer resources, such as hard disks, printers, modems, CD-ROM drives, and even the processor.

rewritable optical disc An optical disc that can be written to more than once.

RG-58 A/U Stranded-core coaxial cable. The version of this cable used by the United States military is known as RG-58 C/U.

RG-58 /U Solid-core coaxial cable.

rights Authorization with which a user is entitled to perform certain actions on a computer network. Rights apply to the system as a whole, whereas permissions apply to specific objects. For example, a user might have the right to back up an entire computer system, including the files that the user does not have permission to access. *See also* access permissions.

ring topology A topology in which computers are placed on a circle of cable. There are no terminated ends. The data travels around the loop in one direction and passes through each computer. Each computer acts as a repeater to boost the signal and send it on. Because the signal passes through each computer, the failure of one computer can bring the entire network down. The ring can incorporate features that disconnect failed computers so that the network can continue to function despite the failure. *See also* token passing, Token Ring network.

RIP *See* Routing Information Protocol (RIP).

RISC *See* Reduced Instruction Set Computing (RISC).

RJ-11 A four-wire modular connector used to join a telephone line to a wall plate or a communications peripheral such as a modem.

RJ-45 An eight-wire modular connector used to join a telephone line to a wall plate or some other device. It is similar to an RJ-11 telephone connector but has twice the number of conductors.

ROM *See* read-only memory (ROM).

routable protocols The protocols that support multipath LAN-to-LAN communications. *See also* protocol.

router A device used to connect networks of different types, such as those using different architectures and protocols. Routers work at the network layer of the OSI reference model. This means they can switch and route packets across multiple networks, which they do by exchanging protocol-specific information between separate networks. Routers determine the best path for sending data and filter broadcast traffic to the local segment.

Routing Information Protocol (RIP) A protocol that uses distance-vector algorithms to determine routes. With RIP, routers transfer information among other routers to update their internal routing tables and use that information to determine the best routes based on hop counts between routers. TCP/IP and IPX support RIP.

RS-232 standard An industry standard for serial communication connections. Adopted by the Electrical Industries Association (EIA), this recommended standard defines the specific lines and signal characteristics used by serial communications controllers to standardize the transmission of serial data between devices.

S

SAP (service access point) *See* service access point (SAP).

SAP (Service Advertising Protocol) *See* Service Advertising Protocol (SAP).

SCSI *See* Small Computer System Interface (SCSI).

SDLC *See* Synchronous Data Link Control (SDLC).

sector A portion of the data-storage area on a disk. A disk is divided into sides (top and bottom), tracks (rings on each surface), and sectors (sections of each ring). Sectors are the smallest physical storage units on a disk and are of fixed size—typically capable of holding 512 bytes of information apiece.

sector sparing A fault-tolerant system also called hot fixing. It automatically adds sector-recovery capabilities to the file system during operation. If bad sectors are found during disk I/O, the fault-tolerant driver will attempt to move the data to a good sector and map out the bad sector. If the mapping is successful, the file system is not alerted. It is possible for SCSI devices to perform sector sparing, but AT devices (ESDI and IDE) cannot.

security Making computers and data stored on them safe from harm or unauthorized access.

segment The length of cable on a network between two terminators. A segment can also refer to messages that have been broken up into smaller units by the protocol driver.

Sequenced Packet Exchange (SPX) Part of Novell's IPX/SPX protocol suite for sequenced data. *See also* Internetwork Packet Exchange/Sequenced Packet Exchange (IPX/SPX).

Serial Line Internet Protocol (SLIP) Defined in RFC 1055. SLIP is normally used on Ethernet, over a serial line; for example, an RS-232 serial port connected to a modem.

serial transmission One-way data transfer. The data travels on a network cable with one bit following another.

server A computer that provides shared resources to network users. *See also* client.

server-based network A network in which resource security and most other network functions are provided by dedicated servers. Server-based networks have become the standard model for networks serving more than 10 users. *See also* peer-to-peer network.

server message block (SMB) The protocol developed by Microsoft, Intel, and IBM that defines a series of commands used to pass information between network computers. The redirector packages SMB requests into a network control block (NCB) structure that can be sent over the network to a remote device. The network provider listens for SMB messages destined for it and removes the data portion of the SMB request so that it can be processed by a local device.

service access point (SAP) The interface between each of the seven layers in the OSI protocol stack that has connection points, similar to addresses, used for communication between layers. Any protocol layer can have multiple SAPs active at one time.

Service Advertising Protocol (SAP) Allows service-providing nodes (including file, printer, gateway, and application servers) to advertise their services and addresses.

session A connection or link between stations on the network.

session layer The fifth layer of the OSI reference model. This layer allows two applications on different computers to establish, use, and end a connection called a session. This layer performs name recognition and functions, such as security, needed to allow two applications to communicate over the network. The session layer provides synchronization between user tasks. This layer also implements dialog control between communicating processes, regulating which side transmits, when, for how long, and so on. *See also* Open Systems Interconnection (OSI) reference model.

session management Establishing, maintaining, and terminating connections between stations on the network.

sharing Means by which files are publicly posted on a network for access by anyone on the network.

shell A piece of software, usually a separate program, that provides direct communication between the user and the operating system. This usually, but not always, takes the form of a command-line interface. Examples of shells are Macintosh Finder and the MS-DOS command interface program COMMAND.COM.

shielded twisted-pair (STP) cable An insulated cable with wires that are twisted around each other with a minimum number of twists per foot. The twists reduce signal interference between the wires, and the more twists per foot, the greater the reduction in interference (crosstalk).

shielding The woven or stranded metal mesh that surrounds some types of cabling. Shielding protects transmitted data by absorbing stray electronic signals, sometimes called noise (random electrical signals that can degrade or distort communications), so that they do not get onto the cable and distort the data.

short A disruption in an electrical circuit that occurs when any two conducting wires or a conducting wire and ground come in contact with each other.

signal bounce The process by which, on a bus network, the signal is broadcast to the entire network. The signal travels from one end of the cable to the other. If the signal were allowed to continue uninterrupted, it would keep bouncing back and forth along the cable and prevent other computers from sending signals. To stop the signal from bouncing, a component called a terminator is placed at each end of the cable to absorb free signals. Absorbing the signal clears the cable so that other computers can send data. *See also* terminator.

Simple Mail Transfer Protocol (SMTP) A TCP/IP protocol for transferring e-mail. *See also* application protocols, Transport Control Protocol/Internet Protocol (TCP/IP).

Simple Network Management Protocol (SNMP) A TCP/IP protocol for monitoring networks. SNMP uses a request and response process. In SNMP, short utility programs, called agents, monitor the network traffic and behavior in key network components in order to gather statistical data which they put into a management information base (MIB). To collect the information into a usable form, a special management console program regularly polls the agents and downloads the information in their MIBs. If any of the data falls either above or below parameters set by the manager, the management console program can present signals on the monitor locating the trouble and notify designated support staff by automatically dialing a pager number.

simplex transmission One-way transmission of data.

simultaneous peripheral operation on line (spool) Facilitates the process of moving a print job from the network into a printer.

SLIP *See* Serial Line Internet Protocol (SLIP).

Small Computer System Interface (SCSI) A standard, high-speed parallel interface defined by the ANSI. A SCSI interface is used for connecting microcomputers to peripheral devices, such as hard disks and printers, and to other computers and LANs. SCSI is pronounced "scuzzy."

SMB *See* server message block (SMB).

SMDS See Switched Multimegabit Data Services (SMDS).

SMP *See* symmetric multiprocessing (SMP).

SMTP *See* Simple Mail Transfer Protocol (SMTP).

SNA *See* Systems Network Architecture (SNA).

SNMP *See* Simple Network Management Protocol (SNMP).

software Computer programs or sets of instructions that allow the hardware to work. Software can be grouped into four categories: system software, such as operating systems, that control the workings of the computer; application software, such as word-processing programs, spreadsheets, and databases, which perform the tasks for which people use computers; network software, which enables groups of computers to communicate; and language software, which provides programmers with the tools they need to write programs.

SONET *See* Synchronous Optical Network (SONET).

spanning tree algorithm (STA) An algorithm (mathematical procedure) implemented to eliminate redundant routes and avoid situations in which multiple LANs are joined by more than one path by the IEEE 802.1 Network Management Committee. Under STA, bridges exchange certain control information in an attempt to find redundant routes. The bridges determine which would be the most efficient route, then use that one and disable the others. Any of the disabled routes can be reactivated if the primary route becomes unavailable.

spread-spectrum radio technology A technology that provides for a truly wireless network. Spread-spectrum radio broadcasts signals over a range of frequencies, avoiding the communication problems of narrowband radio transmission.

SPX *See* Sequenced Packet Exchange (SPX).

SQL *See* structured query language (SQL).

STA *See* spanning tree algorithm (STA).

stand-alone computer A computer that is not connected to any other computers and is not part of a network.

stand-alone environment A work environment in which each user has a personal computer but works independently, unable to share files and other important information that would be readily available through server access in a networking environment.

standard Ethernet A network topology that transmits at 10 Mbps over a baseband wire and can carry a signal 500 meters (five 100-meter segments). *See also* thicknet.

star topology A topology in which each computer is connected by cable segments to a centralized component called a hub. Signals transmitted by a computer on the star pass through the hub to all computers on the network. This topology originated in the early days of computing with terminals connected to a centralized mainframe. The star topology offers centralized resources and management. However, because each computer is connected to a central point, much cable is required in a large installation, and if the central point fails, the entire network goes down. *See also* hub.

stealth virus A variant of file-infector virus. This virus is so named because it attempts to hide from detection. When an antivirus program attempts to find it, the stealth virus tries to intercept the probe and return false information indicating that it does not exist.

STP *See* shielded twisted-pair (STP).

stripe set A form of fault tolerance that combines multiple areas of unformatted free space into one large logical drive, distributing data storage across all drives simultaneously. In Windows NT, a stripe set requires at least two physical drives and can use up to 32 physical drives. Stripe sets can combine areas on different types of drives, such as Small Computer System Interface (SCSI), Enhanced Small Device Interface (ESDI), and Integrated Device Electronics (IDE) drives.

structured query language (SQL) A database sublanguage used to query, update, and manage relational databases. Although not a programming language in the same sense as C or Pascal, SQL can be used either in formulating interactive queries or embedded in an application as instructions for handling data. The SQL standard also contains components for defining, altering, controlling, and securing data.

SVC *See* switched virtual circuit (SVC).

Switched Multimegabit Data Services (SMDS) A high-speed, switched-packet service that can provide speeds of up to 34 Mbps.

switched virtual circuit (SVC) A logical connection between end computers that uses a specific route across the network. Network resources are dedicated to the circuit, and the route is maintained until the connection is terminated. These are also known as point-to-multipoint connections. *See also* virtual circuit.

switching *See* packet switching.

symmetric multiprocessing (SMP) SMP systems, such as Windows NT Server, use any available processor on an as-needed basis. With this approach, the system load and application needs can be distributed evenly across all available processors.

synchronous A form of communication that relies on a timing scheme coordinated between two devices to separate groups of bits and transmit them in blocks called frames. Special characters are used to begin the synchronization and check its accuracy periodically. Because the bits are sent and received in a timed, controlled (synchronized) fashion, start and stop bits are not required. Transmission stops at the end of one transmission and starts again with a new one. It is a start/stop approach, and more efficient than asynchronous transmission. If an error occurs, the synchronous error detection and correction scheme implements a retransmission. However, because more sophisticated technology and equipment is required to transmit synchronously, it is more expensive than asynchronous transmission.

Synchronous Data Link Control (SDLC) The data link (data transmission) protocol most widely used in networks conforming to IBM's SNA. SDLC is a communications guideline that defines the format in which information is transmitted. As its name implies, SDLC applies to synchronous transmissions. SDLC is also a bit-oriented protocol and organizes information in structured units called frames.

Synchronous Optical Network (SONET) A fiber-optic technology that can transmit data at more than one gigabit per second. Networks based on this technology are capable of delivering voice, data, and video. SONET is a standard for optical transport formulated by the Exchange Carriers Standards Association (ECSA) for the ANSI.

Systems Network Architecture (SNA) A widely used communication framework developed by IBM to define network functions and establish standards for enabling its different models of computers to exchange and process data. SNA is a design philosophy that separates network communication into five layers. Each layer, like those in the similar ISO/OSI model, represents a graduated level of function moving upward from physical connections to applications software.

T

T1 line A high-speed communications line that can handle digital communication and Internet access at a rate of 1.544 Mbps (megabits per second).

T1 service The standard digital line service. It provides transmission rates of 1.544 Mbps and can carry both voice and data.

tap A connection to a network. This usually refers specifically to a connection to a cable.

T connector A T-shaped coaxial connector that connects two thinnet Ethernet cables while supplying an additional connector for a network interface card.

TCP *See* Transmission Control Protocol (TCP).

TCP/IP *See* Transport Control Protocol/Internet Protocol (TCP/IP).

TDI *See* transport driver interface (TDI).

TDR *See* time-domain reflectometer (TDR).

Technet *See* Microsoft Technical Information Network (TechNet).

Telnet The command and program used to log in from one Internet site to another. The Telnet command and program brings the user to the login prompt of another host.

terabyte *See* byte.

terminator A resistor used at each end of an Ethernet cable to ensure that signals do not reflect back and cause errors. It is usually attached to an electrical ground at one end. *See also* signal bounce.

terminator resistance The level of resistance in a terminator, measured in ohms. It must match the network architecture specification. For example, Ethernet using RG-58 A/U thinnet cable requires a 50-ohm resistor in the terminator. Terminating resistance that does not match the specifications can cause the network to fail. *See also* ohm.

thicknet (standard Ethernet) A relatively rigid coaxial cable about 0.5-inch in diameter. Typically, thicknet is used as a backbone to connect several smaller thinnet-based networks because of its ability to support data transfer over longer distances. Thicknet can carry a signal for 500 meters (about 1640 feet) before needing a repeater.

thinnet (ThinWire Ethernet) A flexible coaxial cable about 0.25-inch thick. It is used for relatively short-distance communication and is fairly flexible to facilitate routing between computers. Thinnet coaxial cable can carry a signal up to approximately 185 meters (about 607 feet) before needing a repeater.

throughput A measure of the data transfer rate through a component, connection, or system. In networking, throughput is a good indicator of the system's total performance because it defines how well the components work together to transfer data from one computer to another. In this case, the throughput would indicate how many bytes or packets the network could process per second.

time-domain reflectometer (TDR) A troubleshooting tool that sends sonar-like pulses along a cable looking for any kind of a break, short, or imperfection that might affect performance. If the pulse finds a problem, the TDR analyzes it and displays the result. A good TDR can locate a break to within a few feet of the actual separation in the cable.

token A predetermined formation of bits that permits a network device to communicate with the cable. A computer cannot transmit unless it has possession of the token. Only one token at a time can be active on the network, and the token can travel in only one direction around the ring. *See also* token passing, Token Ring network.

token passing A media access control method in a Token Ring network in which a data frame, called a token, is passed from one station to the next around the ring. *See also* token, Token Ring network.

Token Ring network A network in which computers are situated on a continuous network loop through which a token is passed from one computer to the next. Computers are centrally connected to a hub called a Multistation Access Unit (MAU) and are wired in a star configuration. Computers use a token to transmit data and must wait for a free token in order to transfer data. *See also* token, token passing.

TokenTalk An expansion card that allows a Macintosh II to connect to an 802.5 Token Ring network.

tone generator and tone locator Standard wiring tools used for troubleshooting. The tone generator is used to apply an alternating or continuous tone signal to a cable or conductor and is attached to one end of the cable. A matching tone locator is used to detect the correct cable at the other end of the run. These tools are also referred to as a "fox and hound."

tone locator *See* tone generator and tone locator.

topology The arrangement or layout of computers, cables, and other components on a network. Topology is the standard term that most network professionals use when referring to the network's basic design.

tracert A Trace Route command-line utility that shows every router interface through which a TCP/IP packet passes on its way to a destination.

trailer One of the three sections of a packet component. The exact content of the trailer varies depending on the protocol, but it usually includes an error-checking component (CRC).

transceiver A device that connects a computer to the network. The term is derived from transmitter/receiver; thus, a transceiver is a device that receives and transmits signals. It switches the parallel data stream used on the computer's bus into a serial data stream used in the cables connecting the computers.

Transmission Control Protocol (TCP) The TCP/IP protocol for sequenced data. *See also* Transport Control Protocol/Internet Protocol (TCP/IP).

Transport Control Protocol/Internet Protocol (TCP/IP) An industry standard suite of protocols providing communications in a heterogeneous environment. In addition, TCP/IP provides a routable, enterprise networking protocol and access to the Internet and its resources. It is a transport layer protocol that actually consists of several other protocols in a stack that operates at the session layer. Most networks support TCP/IP as a protocol.

transport driver interface (TDI) An interface that works between the file-system driver and the transport protocols, allowing any protocol written to TDI to communicate with the file-system drivers.

transport layer The fourth layer of the OSI reference model. It ensures that messages are delivered error free, in sequence, and without losses or duplications. This layer repackages messages for efficient transmission over the network. At the receiving end, the transport layer unpacks the messages, reassembles the original messages, and sends an acknowledgment of receipt. *See also* Open Systems Interconnection (OSI) reference model.

transport protocols Protocols that provide for communication sessions between computers and ensure that data is able to move reliably between computers.

"Trojan horse" virus A type of virus that appears to be a legitimate program that might be found on any system. The Trojan horse virus can destroy files and cause physical damage to disks.

trunk A single cable, also called a backbone, or segment.

trust relationship Trust relationships are links between domains that enable pass-through authentication, in which a user has only one user account in one domain, yet can access the entire network. User accounts and global groups defined in a trusted domain can be given rights and resource permissions in a trusting domain even though those accounts do not exist in the trusting domain's database. A trusting domain honors the logon authentication of a trusted domain.

twisted-pair cable A cable that consists of two insulated strands of copper wire twisted together. A number of twisted-wire pairs are often grouped together and enclosed in a protective sheath to form a cable. Twisted-pair cable can be shielded or unshielded. Unshielded twisted-pair cable is commonly used for telephone systems. *See also* shielded twisted-pair (STP) cable, unshielded twisted-pair (UTP) cable.

U

UART *See* universal asynchronous receiver transmitter (UART).

UDP *See* User Datagram Protocol (UDP).

Uniform Resource Locator (URL) Provides the hypertext links between documents on the World Wide Web (WWW). Every resource on the Internet has its own location identifier, or URL, that specifies the server to access as well as the access method and the location. URLs can use various protocols including FTP and HTTP.

uninterruptible power supply (UPS) A device connected between a computer or another piece of electronic equipment and a power source, such as an electrical outlet. The UPS ensures that the electrical flow to the computer is not interrupted because of a blackout and, in most cases, protects the computer against potentially damaging events such as power surges and brownouts. Different UPS models offer different levels of protection. All UPS units are equipped with a battery and loss-of-power sensor. If the sensor detects a loss of power, it immediately switches over to the battery so that users have time to save their work and shut off the computer. Most higher-end models have features such as power filtering, sophisticated surge protection, and a serial port so that an operating system capable of communicating with a UPS (such as Windows NT) can work with the UPS to facilitate automatic system shutdown.

universal asynchronous receiver transmitter (UART) A module, usually composed of a single integrated circuit, that contains both the receiving and transmitting circuits required for asynchronous serial communication. Two computers, each equipped with a UART, can communicate over a simple wire connection. The operation of the sending and receiving units are not synchronized by a common clock signal, so the data stream itself must contain information about when packets of information (usually bytes) begin and end. This information about the beginning and ending of a packet is provided by the start and stop bits in the data stream. A UART is the most common type of circuit used in personal-computer modems.

Universal Serial Bus (USB) A serial bus with a data transfer rate of 12 megabits per second (Mbps) for connecting peripherals to a micro-computer. USB can connect up to 127 peripheral devices to the system through a single, general-purpose port. This is accomplished by daisy chaining peripherals together. USB is designed to support the ability to automatically add and configure new devices and the ability to add such devices without having to shut down and restart the system.

unshielded twisted-pair (UTP) cable A cable with wires that are twisted around each other with a minimum number of twists per foot. The twists reduce signal interference between the wires. The more twists per foot, the greater the reduction in interference (crosstalk). This cable is similar to shielded twisted-pair (STP) cable, but lacks the insulation or shielding found in STP cable.

UPS *See* uninterruptible power supply (UPS).

URL *See* Uniform Resource Locator (URL).

USB *See* Universal Serial Bus (USB).

user account Consists of all of the information that defines a user on a network. This includes the user name and password required for the user to log on, the groups in which the user account has membership, and the rights and permissions the user has for using the system and accessing its resources.

User Datagram Protocol (UDP) A connectionless protocol, responsible for end-to-end data transmission.

user groups Groups of users who meet online or in person to discuss installation, administration, and other network challenges for the purpose of sharing and drawing on each other's expertise in developing ideas and solutions.

UTP *See* unshielded twisted-pair (UTP) cable.

V

vampire tap (piercing tap transceiver) An Ethernet transceiver housed in a clamp-like device with sharp metal prongs that "bite" through thicknet cable insulation and make contact with the copper core. The transceiver's DIX (DB15) connector provides an attachment for an AUI cable that runs from the transceiver to either the computer or a hub or repeater. Along thick coaxial cable that includes bands spaced 2.5 meters (8 feet) apart, a vampire tap is inserted into each band; an AUI, DIX, or DB15 connector then attaches a cable from the tap to the computer or other device to be added to the Ethernet network.

virtual circuit A series of logical connections between a sending computer and receiving computer. The connection is made after both computers exchange information and agree on communication parameters that establish and maintain the connection, including maxi-mum message size and path. Virtual circuits incorporate communication parameters such as acknowledgments, flow control, and error control to ensure reliability. They can be either temporary, lasting only as long as the conversa-tion, or permanent, lasting as long as the users keep the communication channel open.

Virtual Private Network (VPN) A set of computers on a public network such as the Internet that communicate among themselves using encryption technology. In this way their messages are safe from being intercepted and understood by unauthorized users. VPNs operate as if the computers were connected by private lines.

virus Computer programming, or code, that hides in computer programs or on the boot sector of storage devices such as hard-disk drives and floppy-disk drives. The primary purpose of a virus is to reproduce itself as often as possible; a secondary purpose is to disrupt the operation of the computer or the program.

voltmeter *See* digital voltmeter (DVM).

volume set A collection of hard-disk partitions that are treated as a single partition, thus increasing the disk space available in a single drive letter. Volume sets are created by combining between 2 and 32 areas of unformatted free space on one or more physical drives. These spaces form one large logical volume set which is treated like a single partition.

W

wide area network (WAN) A computer network that uses long-range telecommunication links to connect networked computers across long distances.

winipcfg A diagnostic command specific to Microsoft Windows 95 and 98. Although this graphical user interface utility (GUI) duplicates the functionality of ipconfig, its GUI makes it easier to use. *See also* ipconfig.

wireless bridge A component that offers an easy way to link buildings without using cable.

wireless concentrator A component that acts as a transceiver to send and receive signals while communicating with network interface cards.

wireless network An emerging networking option consisting of wireless components that communicate with a network that uses cables in a mixed-component network called a hybrid.

workgroup A collection of computers grouped for sharing resources such as data and peripherals over a LAN. Each workgroup is identified by a unique name. *See also* domain, peer-to-peer network.

World Wide Web (the Web, or WWW) The Internet multimedia service that contains a vast storehouse of hypertext documents written in HTML. *See also* Hypertext Markup Language (HTML).

WORM *See* Write-Once Read-Many (WORM).

Write-Once Read-Many (WORM) Any type of storage medium to which data can be written only once, but can be read any number of times. Typically, this is an optical disc whose surface is permanently etched using a laser, in order to record information.

X

X.25 A recommendation published by the CCITT that defines the connection between a terminal and a packet-switching network. A packet-switching network routes packets whose contents and format are controlled standards such as those defined in the X.25 recommendation. X.25 incorporates three definitions: the electrical connection between the terminal and the network, the transmission or link-access protocol, and the implementation of virtual circuits between network users. Taken together, these definitions specify a synchronous, full-duplex, terminal-to-network connection. Packets transmitted in such a network can contain either data or control commands. Packet format, error control, and other features are equivalent to portions of the HDLC protocol defined by the ISO. X.25 standards are related to the lowest three levels of the OSI reference model.

X.400 A CCITT protocol for international e-mail transmissions.

X.500 A CCITT protocol for file and directory maintenance across several systems.

XNS (Xerox Network System) Protocol developed by Xerox for its Ethernet LANs.

Z

Zones Logical groupings of users and resources in an AppleTalk network.

Index

System Requirements

The following indicates the minimum hardware and software requirements necessary to view the demonstration video files included on the companion CD-ROM.

Hardware Requirements

Each computer must have the following minimum configuration. All hardware should be on the Microsoft Windows Hardware Compatibility List.

- Pentium 90 MHz processor (Pentium 120 MHz or better recommended)
- 16 MB RAM (32 MB or more of RAM recommended)
- 16-color display card (256-color display card or better recommended)
- 16-bit sound card
- VGA or better monitor (SVGA monitor or better recommended)
- CD-ROM drive
- Mouse or other pointing device (recommended)

Software Requirements

The following software is required to view the demonstration videos in this course.

- Microsoft Windows 95, or later, or Microsoft Windows NT 4.0, Service Pack 3, or later
- Standard multimedia player, such as Microsoft Windows Media Player (Windows Media Player 6.4 is included on the companion CD)
- Microsoft Internet Explorer 4.01 or later (required for Windows Media Player to install correctly; Internet Explorer 5 is included on the companion CD)

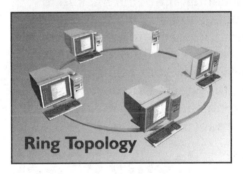
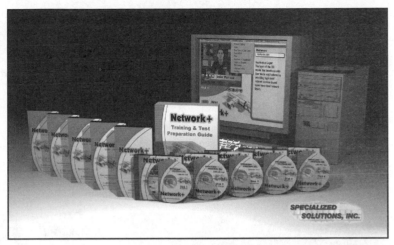

MCSE
Most Comprehensive Set Ever

Order Specialized Solutions Self Study Technology Based Training & Certification Programs and Receive 25% Off.

Course Title/Contents	Part #	Retail Price	Discount Price
Microsoft - MCSE Complete Package	97261	$1895.00	$1421.00
Microsoft Windows NT Workstation Package (70-073)	97221	$395.00	$296.00
Microsoft Windows NT Server Package (70-067)	97225	$459.00	$344.00
Microsoft Networking Essentials Package (70-058)	97219	$295.00	$221.00
Microsoft TCP/IP for NT Package (70-059)	82119	$395.00	$296.00
Microsoft NT SVR in the Enterprise Package (70-068)	97215	$395.00	$296.00
Microsoft Internet Information Server 4.0 (70-087)	92250	$199.00	$149.00

Please see our web site for detailed course descriptions - www.specializedsolutions.com

Our comprehensive program prepares you for the MCSE 4.0 track. We include training materials for the core exams and two of the most popular electives required to become a MCSE (Microsoft Certified Systems Engineer). With this course you will receive your choice of 21 video tapes or CD-ROMs (over 40 hours of instruction) featuring industry experts, Kim During and Kathy Dellinger. Together they provide the technical training you need to support NT and prepare for the Microsoft exams. You also receive 6 MCSE Training Guides plus 2400 QuickCert practice exams and 1 year of FREE educational support. We have proven over the years that by combining Videos, Computer Based Training and Technical Reference Books, our customers have a much higher retention rate than programs using only one study method. Call now and get MCSE certified!
• CD-ROMS meet the new Adaptive Training needed for the new MCSE exams!! •

Other titles available: CDIA, Windows 2000, Office Training & Certification and many more. Call Now!

SPECIALIZED SOLUTIONS, INC.

338 E. Lemon St.
Tarpon Springs, FL 34689

U.S. & Canada
1-800-942-1660 Ext. 2500

International
1-727-942-1660 Ext. 2500

www.specializedsolutions.com

MICROSOFT LICENSE AGREEMENT

Book Companion CD

IMPORTANT—READ CAREFULLY: This Microsoft End-User License Agreement ("EULA") is a legal agreement between you (either an individual or an entity) and Microsoft Corporation for the Microsoft product identified above, which includes computer software and may include associated media, printed materials, and "on-line" or electronic documentation ("SOFTWARE PRODUCT"). Any component included within the SOFTWARE PRODUCT that is accompanied by a separate End-User License Agreement shall be governed by such agreement and not the terms set forth below. By installing, copying, or otherwise using the SOFTWARE PRODUCT, you agree to be bound by the terms of this EULA. If you do not agree to the terms of this EULA, you are not authorized to install, copy, or otherwise use the SOFTWARE PRODUCT; you may, however, return the SOFTWARE PRODUCT, along with all printed materials and other items that form a part of the Microsoft product that includes the SOFTWARE PRODUCT, to the place you obtained them for a full refund.

SOFTWARE PRODUCT LICENSE

The SOFTWARE PRODUCT is protected by United States copyright laws and international copyright treaties, as well as other intellectual property laws and treaties. The SOFTWARE PRODUCT is licensed, not sold.

1. GRANT OF LICENSE. This EULA grants you the following rights:

   a. **Software Product.** You may install and use one copy of the SOFTWARE PRODUCT on a single computer. The primary user of the computer on which the SOFTWARE PRODUCT is installed may make a second copy for his or her exclusive use on a portable computer.

   b. **Storage/Network Use.** You may also store or install a copy of the SOFTWARE PRODUCT on a storage device, such as a network server, used only to install or run the SOFTWARE PRODUCT on your other computers over an internal network; however, you must acquire and dedicate a license for each separate computer on which the SOFTWARE PRODUCT is installed or run from the storage device. A license for the SOFTWARE PRODUCT may not be shared or used concurrently on different computers.

   c. **License Pak.** If you have acquired this EULA in a Microsoft License Pak, you may make the number of additional copies of the computer software portion of the SOFTWARE PRODUCT authorized on the printed copy of this EULA, and you may use each copy in the manner specified above. You are also entitled to make a corresponding number of secondary copies for portable computer use as specified above.

   d. **Sample Code.** Solely with respect to portions, if any, of the SOFTWARE PRODUCT that are identified within the SOFTWARE PRODUCT as sample code (the "SAMPLE CODE"):

   i. **Use and Modification.** Microsoft grants you the right to use and modify the source code version of the SAMPLE CODE, *provided* you comply with subsection (d)(iii) below. You may not distribute the SAMPLE CODE, or any modified version of the SAMPLE CODE, in source code form.

   ii. **Redistributable Files.** Provided you comply with subsection (d)(iii) below, Microsoft grants you a nonexclusive, royalty-free right to reproduce and distribute the object code version of the SAMPLE CODE and of any modified SAMPLE CODE, other than SAMPLE CODE (or any modified version thereof) designated as not redistributable in the Readme file that forms a part of the SOFTWARE PRODUCT (the "Non-Redistributable Sample Code"). All SAMPLE CODE other than the Non-Redistributable Sample Code is collectively referred to as the "REDISTRIBUTABLES."

   iii. **Redistribution Requirements.** If you redistribute the REDISTRIBUTABLES, you agree to: (i) distribute the REDISTRIBUTABLES in object code form only in conjunction with and as a part of your software application product; (ii) not use Microsoft's name, logo, or trademarks to market your software application product; (iii) include a valid copyright notice on your software application product; (iv) indemnify, hold harmless, and defend Microsoft from and against any claims or lawsuits, including attorney's fees, that arise or result from the use or distribution of your software application product; and (v) not permit further distribution of the REDISTRIBUTABLES by your end user. Contact Microsoft for the applicable royalties due and other licensing terms for all other uses and/or distribution of the REDISTRIBUTABLES.

2. DESCRIPTION OF OTHER RIGHTS AND LIMITATIONS.

   • **Limitations on Reverse Engineering, Decompilation, and Disassembly.** You may not reverse engineer, decompile, or disassemble the SOFTWARE PRODUCT, except and only to the extent that such activity is expressly permitted by applicable law notwithstanding this limitation.

   • **Separation of Components.** The SOFTWARE PRODUCT is licensed as a single product. Its component parts may not be separated for use on more than one computer.

   • **Rental.** You may not rent, lease, or lend the SOFTWARE PRODUCT.

   • **Support Services.** Microsoft may, but is not obligated to, provide you with support services related to the SOFTWARE PRODUCT ("Support Services"). Use of Support Services is governed by the Microsoft policies and programs described in the user manual, in "on-line" documentation, and/or in other Microsoft-provided materials. Any supplemental software code provided to you as part of the Support Services shall be considered part of the SOFTWARE PRODUCT and subject to the terms and conditions of this EULA. With respect to technical information you provide to Microsoft as part of the Support Services, Microsoft may use such information for its business purposes, including for product support and development. Microsoft will not utilize such technical information in a form that personally identifies you.

   • **Software Transfer.** You may permanently transfer all of your rights under this EULA, provided you retain no copies, you transfer all of the SOFTWARE PRODUCT (including all component parts, the media and printed materials, any upgrades, this EULA, and, if applicable, the Certificate of Authenticity), **and** the recipient agrees to the terms of this EULA.

- **Termination.** Without prejudice to any other rights, Microsoft may terminate this EULA if you fail to comply with the terms and conditions of this EULA. In such event, you must destroy all copies of the SOFTWARE PRODUCT and all of its component parts.

3. **COPYRIGHT.** All title and copyrights in and to the SOFTWARE PRODUCT (including but not limited to any images, photographs, animations, video, audio, music, text, SAMPLE CODE, REDISTRIBUTABLES, and "applets" incorporated into the SOFTWARE PRODUCT) and any copies of the SOFTWARE PRODUCT are owned by Microsoft or its suppliers. The SOFTWARE PRODUCT is protected by copyright laws and international treaty provisions. Therefore, you must treat the SOFTWARE PRODUCT like any other copyrighted material **except** that you may install the SOFTWARE PRODUCT on a single computer provided you keep the original solely for backup or archival purposes. You may not copy the printed materials accompanying the SOFTWARE PRODUCT.

4. **U.S. GOVERNMENT RESTRICTED RIGHTS.** The SOFTWARE PRODUCT and documentation are provided with RE-STRICTED RIGHTS. Use, duplication, or disclosure by the Government is subject to restrictions as set forth in subparagraph (c)(1)(ii) of the Rights in Technical Data and Computer Software clause at DFARS 252.227-7013 or subparagraphs (c)(1) and (2) of the Commercial Computer Software—Restricted Rights at 48 CFR 52.227-19, as applicable. Manufacturer is Microsoft Corporation/One Microsoft Way/Redmond, WA 98052-6399.

5. **EXPORT RESTRICTIONS.** You agree that you will not export or re-export the SOFTWARE PRODUCT, any part thereof, or any process or service that is the direct product of the SOFTWARE PRODUCT (the foregoing collectively referred to as the "Restricted Components"), to any country, person, entity, or end user subject to U.S. export restrictions. You specifically agree not to export or re-export any of the Restricted Components (i) to any country to which the U.S. has embargoed or restricted the export of goods or services, which currently include, but are not necessarily limited to, Cuba, Iran, Iraq, Libya, North Korea, Sudan, and Syria, or to any national of any such country, wherever located, who intends to transmit or transport the Restricted Components back to such country; (ii) to any end user who you know or have reason to know will utilize the Restricted Components in the design, development, or production of nuclear, chemical, or biological weapons; or (iii) to any end user who has been prohibited from participating in U.S. export transactions by any federal agency of the U.S. government. You warrant and represent that neither the BXA nor any other U.S. federal agency has suspended, revoked, or denied your export privileges.

6. **NOTE ON JAVA SUPPORT.** THE SOFTWARE PRODUCT MAY CONTAIN SUPPORT FOR PROGRAMS WRITTEN IN JAVA. JAVA TECHNOLOGY IS NOT FAULT TOLERANT AND IS NOT DESIGNED, MANUFACTURED, OR INTENDED FOR USE OR RESALE AS ON-LINE CONTROL EQUIPMENT IN HAZARDOUS ENVIRONMENTS REQUIRING FAIL-SAFE PERFOR-MANCE, SUCH AS IN THE OPERATION OF NUCLEAR FACILITIES, AIRCRAFT NAVIGATION OR COMMUNICATION SYSTEMS, AIR TRAFFIC CONTROL, DIRECT LIFE SUPPORT MACHINES, OR WEAPONS SYSTEMS, IN WHICH THE FAILURE OF JAVA TECHNOLOGY COULD LEAD DIRECTLY TO DEATH, PERSONAL INJURY, OR SEVERE PHYSICAL OR ENVIRONMENTAL DAMAGE. SUN MICROSYSTEMS, INC. HAS CONTRACTUALLY OBLIGATED MICROSOFT TO MAKE THIS DISCLAIMER.

DISCLAIMER OF WARRANTY

NO WARRANTIES OR CONDITIONS. MICROSOFT EXPRESSLY DISCLAIMS ANY WARRANTY OR CONDITION FOR THE SOFTWARE PRODUCT. THE SOFTWARE PRODUCT AND ANY RELATED DOCUMENTATION ARE PROVIDED "AS IS" WITHOUT WARRANTY OR CONDITION OF ANY KIND, EITHER EXPRESS OR IMPLIED, INCLUDING, WITHOUT LIMITATION, THE IMPLIED WARRANTIES OF MERCHANTABILITY, FITNESS FOR A PARTICULAR PURPOSE, OR NONINFRINGEMENT. THE ENTIRE RISK ARISING OUT OF USE OR PERFORMANCE OF THE SOFTWARE PRODUCT REMAINS WITH YOU.

LIMITATION OF LIABILITY. TO THE MAXIMUM EXTENT PERMITTED BY APPLICABLE LAW, IN NO EVENT SHALL MICROSOFT OR ITS SUPPLIERS BE LIABLE FOR ANY SPECIAL, INCIDENTAL, INDIRECT, OR CONSEQUENTIAL DAMAGES WHATSOEVER (INCLUDING, WITHOUT LIMITATION, DAMAGES FOR LOSS OF BUSINESS PROFITS, BUSINESS INTERRUP-TION, LOSS OF BUSINESS INFORMATION, OR ANY OTHER PECUNIARY LOSS) ARISING OUT OF THE USE OF OR INABILITY TO USE THE SOFTWARE PRODUCT OR THE PROVISION OF OR FAILURE TO PROVIDE SUPPORT SERVICES, EVEN IF MICROSOFT HAS BEEN ADVISED OF THE POSSIBILITY OF SUCH DAMAGES. IN ANY CASE, MICROSOFT'S ENTIRE LIABIL-ITY UNDER ANY PROVISION OF THIS EULA SHALL BE LIMITED TO THE GREATER OF THE AMOUNT ACTUALLY PAID BY YOU FOR THE SOFTWARE PRODUCT OR US$5.00; PROVIDED, HOWEVER, IF YOU HAVE ENTERED INTO A MICROSOFT SUPPORT SERVICES AGREEMENT, MICROSOFT'S ENTIRE LIABILITY REGARDING SUPPORT SERVICES SHALL BE GOV-ERNED BY THE TERMS OF THAT AGREEMENT. BECAUSE SOME STATES AND JURISDICTIONS DO NOT ALLOW THE EXCLUSION OR LIMITATION OF LIABILITY, THE ABOVE LIMITATION MAY NOT APPLY TO YOU.

MISCELLANEOUS

This EULA is governed by the laws of the State of Washington USA, except and only to the extent that applicable law mandates governing law of a different jurisdiction.

Should you have any questions concerning this EULA, or if you desire to contact Microsoft for any reason, please contact the Microsoft subsidiary serving your country, or write: Microsoft Sales Information Center/One Microsoft Way/Redmond, WA 98052-6399.

OWNER REGISTRATION CARD   *Register Today!*   0-7356-0912-8

Return the bottom portion of this card to register today.

ALS Networking Essentials Plus, Third Edition

FIRST NAME   MIDDLE INITIAL   LAST NAME

INSTITUTION OR COMPANY NAME

ADDRESS

CITY   STATE   ZIP

(   )

E-MAIL ADDRESS   PHONE NUMBER

U.S. and Canada addresses only. Fill in information above and mail postage-free.
Please mail only the bottom half of this page.

For information about Microsoft Press®
products, visit our Web site at
mspress.microsoft.com

Microsoft®